1986

DEVELOPMENTAL PSYCHOLOGY
Fourth Edition

Robert M. Liebert
State University of New York at Stony Brook

Rita Wicks-Nelson
West Virginia Institute of Technology

Robert V. Kail
Purdue University

Prentice-Hall, Englewood Cliffs, New Jersey 07632

Library of Congress Cataloging-in-Publication Data

Liebert, Robert M., 1942–
    Developmental psychology.

    Bibliography: p.
    Includes index.
    1. Developmental psychology. I. Wicks-Nelson,
Rita, 1933–   .   II. Kail, Robert V.   III. Title.
BF713.L53   1986   155   85-28144
ISBN 0-13-208109-1

DEVELOPMENTAL PSYCHOLOGY fourth edition
Robert M. Liebert / Rita Wicks-Nelson / Robert V. Kail

© 1986, 1981, 1977, 1974 by Prentice-Hall,
A Division of Simon & Schuster, Inc.,
Englewood Cliffs, N.J. 07632

Editorial/production supervision: Sylvia Moore
Cover and interior design: Suzanne Behnke and A Good Thing
Cover photo: John Kelly/Image Bank
Photo research: Charlotte Greene
Manufacturing buyer: Barbara Kelly Kittle

Printed in the United States of America
10 9 8 7 6 5 4 3 2

ISBN 0-13-208109-1   01

Prentice-Hall International (UK) Limited, London
Prentice-Hall of Australia Pty. Limited, Sydney
Prentice-Hall Canada Inc., Toronto
Prentice-Hall Hispanoamericana, S.A., Mexico
Prentice-Hall of India Private Limited, New Delhi
Prentice-Hall of Japan, Inc., Tokyo
Prentice-Hall of Southeast Asia Pte. Ltd., Singapore
Editora Prentice-Hall do Brasil, Ltda., Rio de Janeiro
Whitehall Books Limited, Wellington, New Zealand

CONTENTS

PREFACE

As in the preceding editions, our aim in this fourth edition is to present a broad but selective introduction to developmental psychology as a branch of science that is at once basic and applied. We continue to believe that there is a fundamental continuity among all developmental processes, and that the many practical applications of the field are best appreciated in the light of the theory and research that spawned them.

In accord with this belief, Chapter 1 begins with a brief overview of the history of our field as a science and includes an introduction to the theories and research methods that have guided its development. In Chapter 2 we turn to the building blocks of human development, beginning with evolutionary and genetic processes. Chapter 3 brings us to the individual's physical development, from infancy through adolescence, and includes consideration of the wide array of factors that influence and are influenced by physical growth and change. Chapter 4 continues this discussion by turning to early experience and behavior, including basic perceptual and learning processes and an extensive discussion of the roots of social and emotional development. Chapter 5 turns to language, which is presented as a cornerstone for all social interaction. Chapters 6 and 7 extend our discussion to theory and research in cognitive development, beginning with a broad discussion of both Piaget's theory and various neo-Piagetian work and then going on to newer information-processing approaches. Chapter 8 takes us to intelligence, including both traditional measurement issues and a discussion of how intelligence develops and changes over the entire lifespan. In this chapter we also introduce newer perspectives on intelligence, most notably Gardner's theory of multiple intelligences.

The next four chapters are devoted to social development, beginning in Chapter 9 with a discussion of processes and factors which influence socialization. Chapter 10 discusses self-control, achievement, and moral values, and Chapter 11 discusses altruism, aggression, and friendship. Chapter 12 is devoted entirely to sex typing, emphasizing the manner in which it influences all aspects of cognitive and social development

Chapter 13 deals with how development can go awry; it considers the full range of behavioral difficulties that can arise in childhood. Chapter 14 provides an overview of adolescence and adulthood, culminating in a discussion of the end of life.

This sequence of chapters is generally similar to that of the previous editions in considering biological, cognitive, and social factors. However, we have no longer drawn a hard distinction among these three closely related aspects of development. Instead, we have given increasing attention to their interplay throughout the text. This change of approach has led to a certain amount of reorganization. For example, early experience, previously not discussed until Chapter 11, now appears in Chapter 4, where it is presented as one of the essential building blocks for later development. Similarly, our discussion of evolutionary and genetic processes, previously discussed in Chapter 5, has been moved forward to Chapter 2. Finally, our discussion of learning processes, previously treated in relative isolation, has now been distributed throughout the text to show how learning is involved in various aspects of development as they are discussed.

Another major change in the book, in keeping with changes in the field, is an increased emphasis on cognitive processes. Thus, we now devote two chapters to cognitive development and also emphasize the role of cognition in all aspects of social development.

Those familiar with previous editions will also note that our Road to Maturity section has been consolidated into a single chapter, while discussion of many aspects of adolescent and adult development have been added to the various topical chapters as natural extensions of how the relevant processes and changes occur in children. This reorganization is in keeping with the increased trend within the field to view development as an integrated, lifelong process.

As in previous editions, we have continually tried to stress the importance of solid research in advancing our knowledge and understanding. Much of the research we discuss is theory-guided, and thus we have emphasized the interplay of theory and research. At the same time, we have taken every occasion to present the practical side of developmental psychology, both in the text itself and in the various Close-ups which are scattered throughout the book.

We owe a debt of thanks to many people for helping make this edition become a reality. John Isley and Sylvia Moore of Prentice-Hall patiently dealt with us as we moved slowly from draft to draft, and Jeanine Ciliotta provided enormous help in shaping the writing style and tone which we hoped to achieve in this edition. Valuable input on various matters was also provided by Rita Baker-Walker, Thomas J. Berndt, Laurence B. Leonard, and Molly Moore. Finally we thank the staff of the Vining Library, West Virginia Institute of Technology, for considerable assistance.

Robert M. Liebert   Rita Wicks-Nelson   Robert V. Kail

ACKNOWLEDGMENTS

We are greatly indebted to those who reviewed the manuscript during its preparation; without their thoughtful input this book would be less complete, less accurate, and less interesting.

Kenneth Beauchamp, *University of the Pacific*
Robert C. Coon, *Louisiana State University*
Mary Courage, *Memorial University of Newfoundland*
Emily S. Davidson, *Texas A & M University*
Mark T. Greenberg, *University of Washington*
G. Marilyn Hadad, *University of Toronto*
Melvyn B. King, *State University of New York College at Cortland*
Louise C. Perry, *Florida Atlantic University*
Carol Sigelman, *Eastern Kentucky University*
Deborah G. Ventis, *College of William and Mary*

WHAT IS DEVELOPMENTAL PSYCHOLOGY?

At conception we begin as a tiny cell, too small to be seen except with a microscope. Gradually each of us is transformed into a baby, a child, an adolescent, and finally a mature adult. This astonishing development proceeds along several parallel tracks. One is physical and involves the growth of bone, muscle, nervous system, and bodily organs. At the same time there is continuing mental growth, shown by an increasing ability to solve problems and deal with ideas. Social growth also occurs continuously, as we become better able to deal with others and adjust to the needs and demands of the world around us. Because physical, mental, and social development proceed side by side, we recognize categories of development (infant, toddler, child, adolescent, adult). From toddlerhood through childhood, adolescence, and adulthood, this remarkable pattern of growth and change goes on continually.

Developmental psychology is the branch of psychology concerned with when and how we change over time. Developmental psychologists study people of all ages in an attempt to understand when and how physical, mental, and social functions change and interact throughout the entire life span. Simply put, it is a very broad field.

Surprisingly, recognition of the fact that we all develop continually is quite recent. The idea of childhood as a separate and distinct period did not really emerge until the last century, and it is only in the past 20 years or so that psychologists have looked beyond adolescence to study development as a set of interrelated processes and events occurring over the entire life span.

CHANGING PORTRAITS OF CHILDHOOD

In medieval times, children were viewed as "ill formed adults at the edges of society" (Kessen, 1965), a notion reflected in the art of the time (see Figure 1–1). The seventeenth and eighteenth centuries brought the idea of childhood as a special period in which youngsters had unique psychological, educational, and physical needs. But how to understand these needs and cope with them remained a controversial subject.

The clash is captured in the differing views of philosophers John Locke (1632–1704) and Jean Jacques Rousseau (1712–1778). Locke asserted that at birth the human infant is a *tabula rasa*, or "blank slate," and that experience, transmitted through the senses, molds each human into a unique individual. Locke burdened parents with the responsibility of teaching their children self-control and rationality, and of planning their environment and experiences from the moment of birth. Rousseau saw the newborn human as a "noble savage," endowed with an innate sense of justice and morality. He believed that all virtues are inborn and develop naturally. For Rousseau, human nobility was imperiled by an interfering society.

By the middle of the nineteenth century there was a new approach to understanding childhood: Speculation about the child's "nature" was replaced by efforts to record and to study actual behavior and development. This was the dawn of contemporary developmental psychology.

The impetus for the new science came from many sources. Evolutionary biology and its founder, Charles Darwin (1809–1892), played an important role in generating the nineteenth century's interest in development of all sorts, but developmental psychology had a founder of its own. G. Stanley Hall focused Darwin's general viewpoint in a particular way. Hall administered questionnaires to large groups of children of different ages in order to discover age trends in children's beliefs, knowledge, and feelings as they grew older. Hall, who was founder and first president of the American Psychological Association (APA), also turned to children for the study of such topics as perception, memory, and learning. Meanwhile, Alfred Binet had begun to distinguish between intellectually normal and subnormal children in France. Sigmund Freud had startled the world with his suggestion that the experiences of early childhood seemed to account for patterns of behavior in adulthood. There was clearly much to be learned.

By the 1920s developmental psychology had become the source of solutions to practical problems. John Watson, the founder of behaviorism, had begun to write and lecture on child-rearing practices. Clinics were established for the purpose of assessing children and advising parents. This interest led to an enormous research investment in child development. Short-term studies were set up in numerous university-based nursery schools, and long-range (or longitudinal) projects were established at such places as Berkeley and Yale in the United States and in several European cities.

Childhood was now seen as the psychological as well as the physical precursor of adulthood. But many years passed before psychologists realized that development is a continuous process which covers the entire human life span.

RECURRING ISSUES IN DEVELOPMENTAL PSYCHOLOGY

In their search for underlying causes and explanations, modern developmental psychologists face two issues that seem to arise regardless of the aspect of development being studied. They are heredity versus environment, and continuity versus discontinuity.

Biological versus Environmental Determination

We all know that people differ in striking and important ways. Some individuals are very outgoing, others are more reserved, and a few are timid. Likewise, some people are highly creative; others are less imaginative and may prefer more conventional ways of thinking and acting. These examples illustrate the enormous range of individual differences we see in the people around us. And they raise the question of whether each of us is born with our particular characteristics or whether we are more a product of the environments in which we were brought up. The problem has been called the *heredity-environment* issue, the *nature-nurture* controversy, and many other names as well. For developmental psychologists, it has also been a constant and far from simple question. How

(a)

(b)

(c)

FIGURE 1–1

Portraits of childhood: (a) Erasmus Quellin's "Portrait of a Boy with a Dog," painted in the seventeenth century, shows that little distinction was made between childhood and adulthood, for the child is depicted simply as a miniature adult. (b) "Ralph Izard," by Jeremiah Theuss (1753), gives a first hint of childhood. The trend sharpens in "The Wilson Children" (c), by an unknown artist circa 1860, and "A Sunflower for Teacher" (d), by Winslow Homer (1875). (e) Robert Henri's "Forces of

(d)

(f)

(e)

Peace" is definitely a little girl in the modern sense. But only in this Norman Rockwell painting (f) of two boys do we see the mood of childhood as it has recently emerged.   (a) From the Museum of Fine Arts, Antwerp, SCALA New York/Florence; (b) Private collection, photograph by Jerome Drown; (d) The Georgia Museum of Art, The University of Georgia; (e) © Sotheby Parke-Bernet, Agent; Editorial Photocolor Archives; (f) Rockwell illustration reproduced by permission of Editorial Archives, Inc.

much of the individual's behavior is contributed by his or her biological and genetic makeup? How much by social and environmental influences?

As Anastasi (1958) noted in a classic analysis, these questions overlook the fact that heredity and environment must *interact* in order to produce behavior. Because both make an absolutely necessary contribution to behavior, the idea that these factors simply differ in quantity or importance, like two bank accounts, is not likely to get us very far. Instead, we ultimately must ask *how* biological and environmental influences combine to result in various kinds of behavior. Much of this book is devoted to explaining how these two forces interact.

Continuity versus Discontinuity in Development

Two types of behavioral change are often identified in the study of human development: those that are gradual or *continuous* and those that are sudden or *discontinuous*.

To understand this distinction, consider the following example suggested by the work of Jean Piaget (whose theory of cognitive development is discussed in Chapter 6). An experimenter begins by showing to a 4-year-old child two short, wide glass beakers, each containing the same quantity of milk. The youngster is asked whether both beakers have an equal amount of fluid, and agrees that they do. Then, while the child watches, the experimenter pours the entire contents of one of these beakers into a third beaker—a tall, thin one. When the child is asked to compare the two beakers that now contain milk, he or she often will say that the tall, thin beaker has more milk in it than the original short, wide one. Older children, like adults, will immediately point out that the two beakers in question must have the same amount of milk, for the volume of the two original beakers was equal at the beginning and no liquid was lost or gained by pouring the contents of one of them into a container of a different shape.

How and why does this transition in handling the problem occur? Is there a qualitative change or *discontinuity* from one mode of thinking to another as the child grows older? Or would the change, if we were able to watch it more closely, appear to be a gradual, *continuous* process of growing sophistication? The former viewpoint leads to the suggestion that development proceeds in a series of relatively discrete *stages* that should be identified and described. As we shall see, this is the conclusion that, with some qualifications, Piaget reached in examining the child's intellectual development. Some stage theorists have also argued that many aspects of human emotional and social development proceed in the same discontinuous fashion.

Other theorists have emphasized the possibility that development may only seem discontinuous. Observers who compare children of different ages may be unable to detect gradual changes as they occur, and thus may take large or dramatic shifts as evidence of discontinuity. Even if the same children are observed over time, the frequency and nature of the observations can play an important role in determining whether developmental changes seem gradual or relatively abrupt.

The continuity-discontinuity issue involves much more than measurement or timing. Major questions revolve around the processes through which change occurs. Stage theorists often insist that universal, biologically based factors play a prominent role in development. Relatively uniform structural changes, they argue, occur in the psychological processes of almost all children and give rise to relatively discontinuous changes in behavior. In contrast, theorists who emphasize continuities stress that social and experiential factors underlie many changes. Children, they point out, must *learn* to behave as they do. The learning is likely to be a gradual, continuous process that will vary from one child to another depending on individual differences in socioeconomic, ethnic, and cultural background, as well as other factors.

THE ROLE OF THEORY

Even in our brief discussion thus far, it has been impossible to avoid the word "theory." What functions do theories serve in developmental psychology? Let's see.

Theories always serve an explanatory-descriptive role. They provide a basis for organizing and condensing known facts. They also should enable us to predict future events. To do so, a theory must be *testable* and thus potentially *capable of being proved wrong*. It must lead to the derivation of specific hypotheses or predictions that can be confirmed or disconfirmed. Theories also guide research into areas that might not otherwise attract interest or that might seem too complicated. Like a prospector's map of secret treasure, they lead us to expect substantial yields in areas that would otherwise seem to have little promise.

Modern developmental research has for the most part been guided by four broad formal theories, and each merits a brief introduction here.

Maturational Theory

A scholarly analysis of the impact of theories of child development (Caldwell and Richmond, 1962) labels "maturational theory" as one of the major theories in developmental psychology. The idea behind this theory is that most of the changes that take place in children over time occur because of a specific and prearranged scheme or plan within the body. Maturation, according to this view, reveals the natural unfolding of the plan, and patterns of growth charted over time are like the trail of a skywriting plane, which shows us only that part of the mission that is already completed.

The view that all development, from infant nursing patterns to the emergence of moral values, is largely self-regulated by the unfolding of natural processes and biological plans was popularized by Arnold Gesell (1940, 1956). Gesell himself studied primarily children's physical and motor development. His work generated major interest but only minor controversy. Almost everyone was willing to agree that body growth is heavily influenced by physical maturation. But the maturational view of

intellectual and personality development—that is, of complex social behavior—continues to be vigorously attacked and defended. We will have
many occasions to mention it in later chapters.

Psychoanalytic
Theory

Freud's psychoanalytic theory ranks among the most far-reaching
and influential views in modern history. Freud too was convinced that
people mature psychologically according to principles that apply universally. But he was also convinced that each individual personality is
shaped by experience in a social context.

Freud's great message to developmentalists was his insistence on the
importance of early experience for establishing patterns that endure
through the entire life span. Developmentalists who have revised classical psychoanalytic theory, among them Erik Erikson, have provided a
bridge from which we can view the psychological characteristics of adolescence, middle age, and old age in social terms.

Freud's most important insight is that humans are not always conscious of their own motives. He attributed great strength, durability, and
enormous motivational properties to unconscious impulses and warned
that the rational and the rationalizing person are not easy to tell apart.

FIGURE 1–3
Sigmund Freud in London in June 1938, after being rescued from Nazi-occupied Vienna. Wide World Photos.

The influence of Freud's views will be evident in several chapters of this book.

Social Learning Theory

John Watson was among the first psychologists to champion Locke's view that the infant's mind is a blank slate on which experience writes. Watson held that the child *learns to be* what he or she becomes, usually in a social context. He assumed that with the correct techniques, anything could be learned, by almost anyone. B. F. Skinner explained learning on the basis of external reward and punishment, as another learning-oriented psychologist, E. L. Thorndike, had begun to do years before.

Modern social learning theory was developed by Albert Bandura. He accepted the idea that conditioning, reward, and punishment all contribute to social development. But he questioned whether all (or even most) of what actually goes on during childhood learning can be explained in these terms. Children learn by observation, he argued, and this type of learning can take place without any direct reward or punishment at all. This approach speaks directly to the issue of *processes* of social development. It has inspired a large body of research, as we will see.

FIGURE 1-4
Albert Bandura recognized that socialization involves learning from positive and negative consequences, but his social learning theory emphasizes the role of observation of others (social models). Courtesy of Albert Bandura, Stanford University.

Cognitive-Developmental Theory

Still another way to approach psychological development is to focus on thought processes and knowledge. Jean Piaget took just such an approach in his cognitive-developmental theory. Piaget postulated four basic periods in cognitive development (see Chapter 6), each characterized by unique and more sophisticated types of reasoning.

Piaget was primarily interested in the interaction of biological maturation and environmental experience; he emphasized that it is these two forces working together that cause most developmental change. For example, a preschool boy who believes that the amount of milk in a short, wide beaker increases merely by pouring it into a tall, thin one will overcome his misconception only when he is sufficiently mature to appreciate the underlying principle of conservation *and* has had an opportunity to explore the effects of pouring for himself.

Another important aspect of Piaget's theory is that it is *holistic*, meaning that cognitive and social development are assumed to be closely linked. For example, children cannot take another's point of view into account in social situations until they understand the basic principle that objects in the physical environment look different from different perspectives.

Because Piaget's theory attempts to tie together maturation and ex-

FIGURE 1–5
Jean Piaget focused on the development of thought processes and knowledge in his approach to cognitive-developmental theory. The Bettmann Archive, Inc.

perience on the one hand and cognitive and social development on the other, it has inspired developmentalists with a wide variety of interests.

At one time developmental psychologists believed that a single theory would prevail over the others, but it has become plain that agreement at this level is impossible. The four theories discussed here are so all-encompassing that today we think of them more as viewpoints than as scientific formulations. Psychologists do not usually follow one or another; instead, they often select aspects of various theories to form new combinations as they investigate specific topics. The theories, too, continuously interact, combine, and change.

RESEARCH IN DEVELOPMENTAL PSYCHOLOGY

All research in developmental psychology shares a commitment to the *scientific method*. This method distinguishes the studies we have drawn upon in this book from casual observation and other informal methods of studying people. At the general level, the scientific method specifies appropriate ways of studying people, provides a language for thinking about and reporting evidence, and gives guidelines for evaluating the evidence that has been accumulated.

The central requirement of the scientific method is *objectivity*: The evidence put forth must be derived from procedures that can be repeated and results that can be verified by others. Even when we are interested in theoretical ideas that have no specific concrete form, we must define them in terms of procedures and responses that *can* be observed. Intelligence, for example, is a theoretical construct that is often operationalized as scores on IQ tests. Similarly, mother-child attachment is often operationally defined by the child's clinging to the mother.

Developmental research is chiefly concerned with two goals: demonstrating that certain changes occur with age (that is, so-called *developmental trends*) and demonstrating cause and effect relationships. Central to both goals is the requirement that observations and descriptions be objective and reliable.

Observation and Description

All scientific research begins with observation and description. Which individuals or behaviors to observe and how to observe and describe them are therefore always central questions. For example, suppose a researcher wished to describe the spoken language of 12-month-old infants. It would first be necessary to decide on the number of infants to be observed and on how to go about doing the observing. These decisions would be made partly on practical grounds and partly on the basis of the specific goals of the study. But there are some general principles.

Representative Sampling. The question of which individuals to observe revolves around the problem of *sampling*. Rarely does an investigator's interest end with the particular individuals observed in a study. Rather, the actual subjects are chosen to represent some larger group. In studying the language of 12-month-old infants, for example, twenty infants might be observed. But the purpose of the investigation would probably be not simply to learn about these particular infants, but about the language of 12-month-olds in general. The twenty infants would be a *representative sample*, from which the investigator draws inferences about the language of some larger *population* (e.g., infants in general). Researchers in such situations must satisfy their critics that the sample is really representative of the population of interest.

Measurement Procedures. Our hypothetical investigator would also face the related questions of how and when to measure the infants' language. This would involve finding or creating a method for recording infant language. The method would have to be one that could be applied consistently from one infant to another and from one observer to another. In turn, this would mean that the relevant class of behaviors would have to be defined (perhaps all the infants' vocalizations), a means of recording them would have to be selected (such as a tape recorder in the home), and appropriate times for making the recordings (such as certain fixed time periods every day) would have to be chosen and justified.

Equally important would be the choice of a scoring or coding procedure for classifying the recorded vocalizations. The procedure would then be taught to judges, and the investigator would have to demonstrate that the procedure is clear and precise enough to be *reliable*. Two judges independently listening to the same recording should agree quite closely on their scoring of it.

Correlation: Describing Relationships. In the example we have been using, the investigator was trying to describe a single aspect of the behavior of infants of a particular age. However, research in developmental psychology is often aimed at describing the relationship between two or more variables. This involves observing and measuring each of the variables and then determining the degree to which they are related. For example, we might ask questions such as: Is a child's performance in school related to his or her socioeconomic status? Is there a relationship between late toilet training and compulsiveness in adulthood? Is frequency of dating behavior during adolescence related to later marital success and happiness?

Researchers often compute a correlation coefficient to describe the relationship between variables. Correlation coefficients indicate both the direction and the magnitude of the relationship and may range from $+1.00$ to -1.00.

The *direction* of the relationship is shown by the sign of the coefficient. A positive sign means that high scores on one variable, X, tend to be associated with high scores on another variable, Y, and low scores on X tend to go with low scores on Y. For example, a positive correlation is found between children's age and height; older children are likely to be taller. A negative sign means that high scores on X tend to be associated with low scores on Y and low scores on X with high scores on Y. Age and quickness of reflexes are usually found to be negatively correlated in adults; as people grow older, their reflexes become slower.

The *magnitude* or strength of a correlation is indicated by the absolute value of the coefficient (disregarding the sign). Correlation coefficients of $+.60$ and $-.60$ are equivalent with respect to how strongly the variables under consideration are related. The strongest relationship is indicated when the correlation is either $+1.00$ or -1.00; in both cases the two variables are perfectly correlated so that either can be determined from the other with perfect accuracy. As the coefficient decreases in absolute value, the magnitude of the relationship becomes weaker, and the ability to estimate one variable from the other decreases. A coefficient of 0.00 indicates that the variables are unrelated: Knowledge of one does not tell us anything at all about the other.

A word of caution: Because correlation coefficients range in absolute value from 0.00 to 1.00, it is tempting to view them as percentages (to assume that a correlation of .60 means a "60 percent" correlation). We may be tempted to conclude that a correlation of .50 is twice as large as one of .25. Not so. The appropriate rule of thumb is to compare squared correlation coefficients to get an idea of the relative strengths of each. Thus, in a sense, a correlation of .80 is approximately *four* times as large as a correlation of .40 (i.e., $.80^2 = .64$ and $.40^2 = .16$; .64 is four times .16).

The Role of Case Studies. Studying groups of children is one technique; case studies are another. Systematic biographies of individual children from birth or early childhood were the earliest source of data for developmental psychology and are still useful today for some purposes. Case studies are very flexible because simple observation can be done in various ways and in nearly any situation. But this flexibility has a price. Because one or two children hardly make up a representative sample, we cannot be sure that what is true for them is also true for a larger group of children. Most contemporary developmental psychologists view case studies as, at best, a preliminary or adjunct research method that cannot replace or rival broader and more systematic studies with representative samples.

But case studies are often useful when we want to provide a typical example of some form of behavior or development. To illustrate both the remarkable verbal ability of children of very high intelligence and the continuity and growth of this ability over time, Munn (1946) presented the following poem, written by a 7-year-old girl with an IQ of 188:*

> *Oh, Master of fire! Oh, Lord of air,*
> *Oh, God of waters, hear my prayer!*
> *Oh, Lord of ground and of stirring trees,*
> *Oh, God of man and of pleasant breeze,*
> *Dear Father, let me happy be—*
> *As happy as a growing tree!* [p. 418]

Noting that "follow-up studies of children whose IQs were high when first determined have shown that, in most instances, the promise of early childhood has been fulfilled," Munn then examined the writings of the child at 12 years of age and eventually reported that she grew up to become a writer of poetry and fiction.

Piaget introduced a variant of the case study, which he called the *clinical case study*, and used it extensively in his own research. (Here the word "clinical" is used in the sense of deeply probing and does not refer to clinical-level problems or abnormalities.) In his early work Piaget observed the development of his own three children at home. He recorded his observations and later published them. His research was "child-guided" in that his aim was to follow the child's natural way of thinking. For example, Piaget observed, milestone by milestone, the development of his infant daughter's ability to guide her hand with her eyes. He

*Copyright © 1946 by Houghton Mifflin Company. Reprinted by permission of the Publishers.

watched and recorded each faltering step and permitted the child's natural development to form the basis for his observations.

At the same time, however, Piaget intervened occasionally, as we would expect a skilled clinician to do, in order to clarify for himself the structure and content of the child's thoughts. When Piaget's daughter Lucienne was 2 years old, he noted her success at removing a watch chain from a partly open matchbox. To probe the child's understanding of how the matchbox opened, Piaget altered the situation by concealing the chain in the box so that Lucienne had to slide the box open systematically—or fail in her mission. With older children the clinical probe took a verbal form. Piaget interviewed not only his own but other children, asking them question after question: "Why do boats float?" "Where does the sun come from?" "What causes the tide?" From material gathered in this way, Piaget fashioned one of the most important psychological theories of the century.

Demonstrating Developmental Trends

Many investigations in developmental psychology are aimed at identifying changes that occur with increasing age. There are two ways of approaching such questions: the longitudinal method and the cross-sectional method.

In a *longitudinal study*, the same individuals are observed or tested repeatedly at different points in their lives, and stability or change in characteristics or behavior is noted over time. In a *cross-sectional study*, each individual is observed only once, but developmental changes are identified by including persons of different ages in the study. Development is charted not by observing the change in the same individuals over time, but by noting the differences between individuals of different ages at the same point in calendar time.

The Logic of Longitudinal Research. As the name implies, the longitudinal approach involves a lengthwise account of development, and it has long been recognized as the most obvious and direct way to "see" actual growth occurring. In one of the earliest longitudinal studies on record, Buffon measured the change in height of a single child over the seventeen years between 1759 and 1776. Much later, changes in height as related to age were charted in a large sample of children who participated in the first and second Harvard Growth Studies. It was inevitable that the longitudinal method would be applied next to the development of truly psychological characteristics—the emergence of emotional and social behavior, along with intellectual functioning. One such study, begun by Lewis Terman in 1921, focused on children with IQ test scores so high that many would consider them geniuses. Terman's aim was to follow the development of these gifted children to determine what kind of adults they would become and whether their lives would be extraordinary (we discuss some of Terman's findings in Chapter 8).

The longitudinal approach is well suited to studying almost any aspect of the course of development. More important, it is the *only* way to answer certain questions about the stability (or instability) of behavior: Will characteristics (such as aggression, dependency, or mistrust) observed in infancy or early childhood persist into adulthood? Will a traumatic event such as being abandoned by one's parents influence later social and intellectual development? How long will the beneficial effects of special academic training in the preschool years last? Such questions can be explored only by using the repeated measurement technique of the longitudinal approach.

The approach, however, has disadvantages that may frequently offset its strengths. An obvious one is cost: The expense of merely keeping up with a large sample of individuals can be staggering. Then, there is the related problem of sample constancy over time. Experience has shown how difficult it is to maintain contact with people over several years (as long as 30 years in some longitudinal studies!) in a highly mobile society. And even among those who do not move away, some lose interest and choose not to continue. These "dropouts" are often significantly different from their more research-minded peers, and this fact may also distort the outcome. For example, a group of individuals may *seem* to show intellectual growth between the seventeenth and twenty-fifth year of life. What has actually happened, however, is that those who found earlier testing most difficult are the very ones who have quit the study and thereby raised the group average on the next round. Fortunately, statistical techniques can partly correct these problems (Labouvie, Bartsch, Nesselroade, and Baltes, 1974).

Even if the sample remains constant, though, the fact that children are given the same test many times may make them "test-wise." Improvement over time may be attributed to development when it actually stems from practice with a particular test. Changing the test from year to year would solve the practice problem but raise the question of how to compare responses to different tests.

The Logic of the Cross-Sectional Approach.   The cross-sectional approach, with its focus on the behavior of individuals of different ages at the same point in time, avoids almost all the problems associated with repeated testing; it avoids costly recordkeeping and sample loss as well.

This approach, however, is not without problems of its own. The most serious logical tangle is the problem of *cohort effects*, meaning that differences between age groups (cohorts) may result as easily from chance environmental events as from significant developmental processes. Suppose, for example, that a researcher devises a way to measure how imaginative children are and then tests a group of 5-year-olds and a group of 10-year-olds as a first step in studying the development of imagination. Let us say that the 5-year-olds were found to be more imaginative than the 10-year-olds. Can we then conclude that imagination declines within this period? Not without raising serious objections. If testing were carried out in, say, 1977, a critic might point out that our 10-

year-olds were born in 1967 and our 5-year-olds in 1972, which means that they differ in "generation" as well as age. Our society may have changed enough between 1967 and 1972 to make the experiences that influence the growth of imagination very different for different generations of children. A new curriculum adopted to nourish the imagination may have been too late for the children born in 1967, but may have benefited the younger children. Alternatively, the country may have been recovering from an economic depression that more severely affected the lives of the older children. Since social conditions change, they can be expected to affect different generations differently, making differences between age groups difficult to interpret.

The Cross-Sequential Approach. Because the longitudinal and cross-sectional approaches have complementary strengths and weaknesses, some researchers have suggested combining the two approaches into *cross-sequential designs*. The basic idea is simultaneously to study individuals of different ages (as in the cross-sectional approach), but to follow the individuals and retest them after some period of time has elapsed (as in the longitudinal approach). The advantage of this arrangement is that it provides direct information about the presence of cohort differences, while allowing a shorter and more economical study.

Suppose, for example, that a team of investigators was interested in determining how mathematical reasoning increases between the ages of 6 and 12. They might give 6-, 8-, and 10-year-olds a test of mathematical reasoning and then retest each youngster two years later, when the cohorts were 8, 10, and 12. The design would provide information on mathematical reasoning at four different ages (6, 8, 10, and 12) using only three cross-sectional groups. At the same time, longitudinal changes could be estimated over a six-year period even though the investigation would take only two years to complete. Using appropriate (and somewhat complex) statistical procedures, the relative contributions of cohort differences and rate of change over time can also be estimated reasonably well.

Determining
Cause and Effect

In the examples mentioned so far, we have emphasized producing adequate descriptions of behavior and behavior change. Many investigations in developmental psychology are designed to go beyond description to *explain* what has been observed. Suppose that in our earlier example of the language of 12-month-olds some of the infants were regularly using several identifiable words, while others were still babbling unintelligibly. Such a result might raise the question of why some infants appeared more advanced than others.

"Why" questions arise frequently in developmental research, and answering them is at the heart of what we usually mean by explanation. There are two broad ways of trying to answer questions about cause and effect. One is to propose hypotheses about what factors influence the behavior of interest and then to manipulate these factors and observe the effects. The other way is to examine factors associated with the behavior of interest and try to construct a useful causal model without manipulation. The first are usually referred to as *experimental methods*; the second are called *nonexperimental* (or correlational) *methods*.

Experimental Methods. The classic "true experiment" in science is designed to lead to unambiguous inferences about cause and effect. In developmental psychology, the true experiment requires that the investigator begin with one or more treatments, circumstances, or events (*independent variables*) that are hypothesized to produce some effect on behavior. Subjects are then assigned randomly to conditions that differ in the treatment they are given; then an appropriate measure (the *dependent variable*) is taken for all subjects to see if the treatment or treatments had the expected effect. Because subjects are assigned so that each has an equal chance of being assigned to each treatment condition (the definition of *random assignment*), it can be assumed that in the long run the groups will not differ except in the treatment they have received. Any observed differences can be attributed to the differential treatment the subjects received in the experiment, rather than to other factors. There are, in fact, many different versions of the true experiment, but they all derive from the same underlying logic.

Suppose, for example, that an investigator believed adolescents can learn more from a short story in a quiet room than in a room in which loud music is playing. A test of this hypothesis might be done in a high school. The investigator would first seek the cooperation of appropriate school authorities and families. The research participants would be told about the general nature of the experiment and the role they would be expected to play (reading a short story and then taking a test on the material), but would not be told the specific hypothesis until they were "debriefed" at the end of the experiment. A suitable short story would be identified or written especially for the experiment, and subjects would be brought to a location (perhaps an available room in the school) where they would read the story and then take a test on its contents. Based on random assignment, individual subjects would read the story either while the room was quiet or while loud music was being played. The loud music would be the same music, played at the same volume, for all subjects in the loud-music condition. All subjects would read the identical story under circumstances held as constant as possible except for the presence or absence of the music. They would all get the same amount of time to read the story, and they would all be given the same test afterward. If scores on the test were, on the average, better in the quiet condition than in the loud-music condition (as determined by an appropriate statistical test), the investigator could say with confidence that the music had an unfavorable effect on learning the story. Causal inference is possible in this example because there was a direct manipulation under controlled conditions.

Nonexperimental (Correlational) Methods. Many investigators have attempted to draw causal inferences using what is called *passive correlation* rather than manipulation. Instead of creating different experiences for subjects (as in the experimental method), researchers study differences in experience that have occurred naturally. For example, to determine the relationship between viewing violent TV shows and aggressive behavior, investigators have obtained self-reports of youngsters' TV viewing preferences and correlated these with various measures of aggressive behavior (such as school records or teachers' reports). When appropriate statistical techniques are used, a pattern of simple correlations allows the researcher to demonstrate the presence and magnitude of relationships between variables. But unlike the true experiment, this often leaves the question of cause and effect ambiguous. For example, TV viewing of violence and aggressive behavior are positively correlated (the more TV violence a youngster watches, the more aggressive he or she is likely to be). But this does not necessarily imply that viewing violence on TV causes aggressive behavior. There are two other plausible ways of interpreting the relationship. One possibility, reflecting the *directionality problem* in nonexperimental research, is that a preoccupation with aggression may cause a youngster to watch more than the average amount of TV violence. That is, instead of TV violence viewing causing aggressiveness, aggressiveness may cause TV violence viewing. Another possibility is that the relationship may be caused by some *third variable*. For example, youngsters who receive little supervision from their parents may be the ones most likely to watch violent shows *and* the ones most likely to be aggressive.

Both the third-variable and directionality problems can be avoided to some extent by using more complex nonexperimental designs, such as looking at patterns of correlation over time and showing that they fit one causal model far better than another. However, even these methods do not provide the certainty of a true experiment. Nevertheless, nonexperimental data often suggest certain causal relationships, and many developmental psychologists draw on them, especially in situations where true experimentation is impossible because of practical or ethical problems.

The Importance of Converging Evidence

Even from our relatively brief discussion it can be seen that each of the research methods used by developmentalists has both strengths and weaknesses. There is no one best method, and the selection of a specific method usually depends as much on practical considerations as on suitability. For these reasons, no single investigation can definitely settle a question. Developmental psychologists rarely rely on one study (or even one method) to reach conclusions. They prefer to find converging evidence from as many sources as possible.

A good example of this approach is the investigation mentioned previously of the influence of television violence on the young. The earliest

Ethical Responsibilities of Developmental Researchers

Until the end of World War II, individual investigators were expected to establish ethical standards and safeguards for their subjects. In the past few decades, however, professional organizations, government agencies, and scientists themselves have moved away from allowing the ethics of research to be determined solely by individual researchers. Instead, a number of formal codes of research ethics have been developed. Such codes have been established by the U.S. National Commisssion for Protection of Human Subjects of Biomedical and Behavioral Research. This commission conducts hearings and recommends guidelines for safeguarding the rights and safety of research participants.

In the early 1970s, the American Psychological Association (APA) appointed a committee on ethical standards in psychological research to revise the APA's code of ethics. The committee first solicited information from APA members concerning research that posed ethical questions. Five thousand research descriptions were generated, and after reviewing these the committee wrote the first draft of a new set of ethical principles. This first draft was distributed throughout the profession and was published in the *APA Monitor*, a newspaper distributed to all members of the APA. Reactions to the first draft were then considered, and in 1973 a set of ten principles was adopted. The principles were revised in 1982 to take into account issues and ambiguities raised by the 1973 version. The current principles are listed here, along with the preamble:

The decision to undertake research rests upon a considered judgment by the individual psychologist about how best to contribute to psychological science and human welfare. Having made the decision to conduct re-search, the psychologist considers alternative directions in which research energies and resources might be invested. On the basis of this consideration, the psychologist carries out the investigation with respect and concern for the dignity and welfare of the people who participate and with cognizance of federal and state regulations and professional standards governing the conduct of research with human participants.

A. In planning a study, the investigator has the responsibility to make a careful evaluation of its ethical acceptability. To the extent that the weighing of scientific and human values suggests a compromise of any principle, the investigator incurs a correspondingly serious obligation to seek ethical advice and to observe stringent safeguards to protect the rights of human participants.

B. Considering whether a participant in a planned study will be a "subject at risk" or a "subject at minimal risk," according to recognized standards, is of primary ethical concern to the investigator.

C. The investigator always retains the responsibility for ensuring ethical practice in research. The investigator is also responsible for the ethical treatment of research participants by collaborators, assistants, students, and employees, all of whom, however, incur similar obligations.

D. Except in minimal-risk research, the investigator establishes a clear and fair agreement with research participants, prior to their participation, that clarifies the obligations and responsibilities of each. The investigator has the obligation to honor all promises and commitments included in that agreement. The investigator informs the participants of all aspects of the research that might reasonably be expected to influence willingness to participate and explains all other aspects of the research about which the participants inquire. Failure to make full disclosure prior to obtaining informed consent requires additional safeguards to protect the welfare and dignity of the research participants. Research with children or with participants who have impairments that would limit understanding and/or communication requires special safeguarding procedures.

E. Methodological requirements of a study may make the use of concealment or deception necessary. Before conducting such a study, the investigator has a special responsibility to (1) determine whether the use of such techniques is justified by the study's prospective scientific, educational, or applied value; (2) determine whether alternative procedures are available that do not use concealment or deception; and (3) ensure that the participants are provided with sufficient explanation as soon as possible.

F. The investigator respects the individual's freedom to decline to participate in or to withdraw from the research at any time. The obligation to protect this freedom requires careful thought and consideration when the investigator is in a position of authority or influence over the participant. Such positions of authority include, but are not limited to, situations in which research participation is required as part of employment or in which the participant is a student, client, or employee of the investigator.

G. The investigator protects the participant from physical and mental discomfort, harm, and danger that may arise from research procedures. If risks of such consequences exist, the inves-

tigator informs the participant of that fact. Research procedures likely to cause serious or lasting harm to a participant are not used unless the failure to use these procedures might expose the participant to risk of greater harm or unless the research has great potential benefit and fully informed and voluntary consent is obtained from each participant. The participant should be informed of procedures for contacting the investigator within a reasonable time period following participation should stress, potential harm, or related questions or concerns arise.

H. After the data are collected, the investigator provides the participant with information about the nature of the study and attempts to remove any misconceptions that may have arisen. Where scientific or humane values justify delaying or withholding this information, the investigator incurs a special responsibility to monitor the research and to ensure that there are no damaging consequences for the participant.

I. Where research procedures result in undesirable consequences for the individual participant, the investigator has the responsibility to detect and remove or correct these consequences, including long-term effects.

J. Information obtained about a research participant during the course of an investigation is confidential unless otherwise agreed upon in advance. When the possibility exists that others may obtain access to such information, this possibility, together with the plans for protecting confidentiality, is explained to the participant as part of the procedure for obtaining informed consent.

Principles A, B, and C focus on the researcher's responsibility before an investigation is carried out. Principle D requires a fair and explicit agreement between researcher and participant concerning the responsibilities of each. The participant must get something from the study commensurate with the demands made on him or her. Increased self-knowledge, awareness of having contributed to scientific knowledge, and monetary rewards are all possible compensations.

Principle D also deals with what is called *informed consent.* Ideally, prospective subjects should be given all the details of the research so they can make an informed decision about whether to participate. But some potential subjects are infants, young children, or hospitalized mental patients who may not be competent to participate in the informed consent procedure. In these cases, consent must also be obtained from parents or legal guardians.

Principle E deals with a difficult problem: Some social science research requires that subjects *not* be fully informed about all the details of the study until after the critical observations have been made. The need for such deception is often claimed in studies examining honesty, sharing, and aggression, to name just a few. In these cases, providing complete information about the study in advance might easily bias or distort the way the subjects respond.

Deception has been a thorny problem in psychological research. For example, during the 1950s and 1960s hundreds of experimental studies were done on the effects of test anxiety. Typically this research involved selecting participants who had indicated that they were very anxious in test-taking situations. These individuals would be given tests, often labeled IQ tests, and then deceived concerning their performances. Very often the "false feedback" would indicate that a participant had failed badly. The effects of this failure experience would then be evaluated by giving the subject a second test. The critical question in such studies is whether the value of the research can in some way justify the creation of anxiety, lowered self-esteem, and other negative effects in these participants. Principle E does, however, require that subjects be given complete information as soon as possible.

Thus, subjects in a test anxiety study must be told that they have not really failed. The reasons for the deception must also be provided. The entire postexperimental explanation is referred to as *debriefing.*

Principle F deals with a participant's right to decline or discontinue participation, particularly in situations in which the participant may feel obliged to go along because of the (presumed) power of the investigator. For example, there is a particular ethical concern when prisoners or mental patients are asked to participate in a study being conducted by someone on the staff of the institution in which they are confined. Participants may feel that failing to "volunteer" will bring some penalty or loss of favor. The researcher must therefore stress the right of prospective participants to decline freely. He or she must assure them that they will not be penalized in any way if they decline.

Another potential problem is raised by the "research requirement" associated with many undergraduate social science courses. This requirement generates a subject pool for faculty and graduate student research. Sometimes the courses require students to participate in a fixed number of hours of research; sometimes students may participate in research for extra credit toward course grades. In either case, one can question whether the system is truly voluntary. Nowadays, most undergraduate courses provide alternative ways of meeting the research requirement or earning extra credit, such as reading and reporting on a fixed number of articles in professional journals instead of participating in the subject pool.

Principles G, H, and I all emphasize the obligation to protect subjects from harm, to inform them of possible risks, and to minimize any stress that may be produced. The investigator must be able to detect and remove any negative aftereffects. It may be necessary to follow up participants to be sure that the debriefing was effective. But researchers should also ask whether there are alternative means of answering a research question that would not induce stress in the participants. For example, test anxiety can be studied by observing students as they take actual, scheduled course examinations as part of their usual life experiences.

Principle J concerns confidentiality. Although assurances of confidentiality are routinely offered by social science researchers, the law does not recognize the contract between subject and researcher, nor does it consider the information provided by subjects as "privileged communication." The courts can, in fact, subpoena an investigator's data and records.

studies were simply case reports in which individual youngsters had apparently learned or copied violent or antisocial acts from a television show. Soon correlational studies disclosed a general positive relationship between the amount of aggressive behavior exhibited by children and adolescents and the amount of television violence viewed at home. Finally, experimental studies began to demonstrate that the introduction of violent television programming in laboratory or even school settings directly caused an increase in young viewers' willingness to aggress against others. No single study or method could have made a strong case for the contribution of television violence to aggressive behavior, but the combined body of evidence is highly persuasive (Liebert, Sprafkin, and Davidson, 1982).

SUMMARY	1. Developmental psychology studies all the changes in physical, mental, and social functioning that occur throughout the life span.
	2. *Development* refers to a process of growth and change in capability over time, as a function of both maturation and interaction with the environment.
	3. The idea of childhood as a special period did not become scientifically important until the middle of the nineteenth century. Thereafter there was much interest in children's physical, cognitive, and social development. But it is only in the past two decades that investigators have extended their interest beyond childhood and adolescence toward a view of development encompassing continuing change throughout the lifespan.
	4. Two issues pervade theory and research in developmental psychology: the relative contributions of biological and environmental factors to development, and the degree to which development proceeds in a continuous or discontinuous way. It is widely acknowledged that both nature and nurture interact to influence development and that some aspects of development are relatively continuous, whereas others are relatively discontinuous.
	5. Four important theories have guided developmental psychology: maturational theory, psychoanalytic theory, social learning

theory, and cognitive-developmental theory. Theories offer predictions that must be scientifically tested by research.

6. All research in developmental psychology shares a commitment to the *scientific method*, which means that research procedures and results must be subject to verification by others. Data obtained from samples must be representative of the populations in which the researcher is interested. The measurement procedures used must be *reliable*, or clear and consistent from one sample to another and from one observer to another.

7. *Correlation* refers to the joint relation between two or more factors and allows us to answer questions of the form: "Do variable X and variable Y go together or vary together in some way?" A *correlation coefficient* indicates the degree of relation between two sets of data by showing both the direction (positive or negative) and the magnitude (high or low) of the relation. The correlation may range from + 1.00 (perfect positive relation) to − 1.00 (perfect negative relation), with .00 indicating no relation. The higher the numerical value of the correlation coefficient, regardless of whether it is in a positive or a negative direction, the stronger and more certain is the relation.

8. Case studies involve single individuals rather than groups. Although they cannot ordinarily provide information about the general population, case studies are sometimes useful to illustrate a phenomenon or to provide the groundwork for theoretical development.

9. Developmental studies aimed at identifying changes that occur with increasing age (*developmental trends*) may take either a *longitudinal* or a *cross-sectional* approach. In a longitudinal study, the same individuals are observed and tested at different ages. In a cross-sectional study there is usually only one observation for each individual, and developmental trends are identified by studying individuals of different ages. The *cross-sequential* approach combines both longitudinal and cross-sectional techniques and overcomes some of the difficulties of each.

10. Two major classes of methods are used in developmental research to explain what has been observed and why. *Experimental methods* involve direct manipulation of treatments and subsequent measurement of their effects. They can lead to unambiguous inferences about cause and effect. *Nonexperimental (correlational) methods* attempt to determine causal relationships from events that have occurred without interference, such as examining the naturally occurring relationship between viewing violent TV and aggressive behavior. Nonexperimental methods are limited in their ability to determine cause and effect by the *directionality problem* and the *third variable problem.* Correlational studies are important for studying conditions that cannot be manipulated and for measuring characteristics in a natural environment rather than in an artificial situation in a laboratory.

2 BIOLOGICAL FOUNDATIONS OF DEVELOPMENT

119, 483

We are all alike—we have two arms, two legs, two eyes; we crawl and then walk; we communicate verbally; we express joy, anger, and elation; we form social attachments; we suffer accidents, illnesses, and the infirmities of old age. We are also different: in hair color and body size; artistic and intellectual abilities; maturity; and tendencies to be excitable or placid, outgoing or introverted, selfish or altruistic. How can this be?

Understanding these similarities and differences leads us to the study of the basic structures of life—the chromosomes and genes that make up every body cell. These structures direct our early physical development, and continue to regulate physical changes throughout life. They constantly interact with our environment in transactions that shape our intellectual, social, and personal functioning.

This century has brought an enormous increase in knowledge about the genetic basis of development and behavior. Some of the early models of genetic processes and influence have been verified, and new ones have been discovered. This chapter provides an overview of the genetic foundations of development, including basic biological structures and genetic mechanisms. We begin with the theory of evolution, which recognizes the similarities among individuals of a species, and also the individual differences.

THE THEORY OF EVOLUTION

Evolution was proposed almost simultaneously by two Englishmen, Charles Darwin and Alfred Russel Wallace (1858, in Appleman, 1970), but it is Darwin who won public acclaim for *Origin of Species,* published in 1859. Fascinated from childhood by nature (as a boy he collected minerals and insects), Darwin had been struck by the enormous variability he had observed in plants and animals during a five-year voyage. The question for many scholars of the day was: What caused the formation of new species of life? Darwin proposed an answer using two key concepts, the *struggle for existence* and *the survival of the fittest:*

1. Animals and plants have excessive numbers of offspring, all of which *vary* somewhat as individuals, due at least in part to inheritance. These offspring *struggle for existence* in the environment in which they find themselves.
2. Depending on the specific environment and the characteristics of the offspring, only the *fittest* will survive.
3. Those that survive will pass on their adaptive characteristics. The attributes of the nonsurvivors will not be passed on. Over long periods of time, then, species will change or evolve, or become extinct. This is a process of *natural selection.*

In *The Descent of Man and Selection in Relation to Sex* (1871) Darwin applied his theory to humans: He proposed that behavioral traits are selected over time in the same way as physical traits (Plomin, DeFries, and McClearn, 1980). When Darwin proposed it, the theory of evolution

FIGURE 2–1
Charles Darwin. The
Bettmann Archives,
Inc.

caused an uproar. It seemed to contradict the idea of divine creation and
the special place of humans in nature and the world. Despite the controversy, however, the theory has endured because it brings order to our
observations of life. As details of inheritance have been discovered,
many have proved to be consistent with the theory.

Darwin's theory had, and still has, a broad influence on the study of
development. It encouraged interest in the ideas of instinct and maturation, explanations of development that emphasize the role of biological
factors. By accenting the relationship between humans and other species, the theory led to comparisons of one species with another. It also
encouraged the view that behavior in a species reflects the species' adjustment to its environment.

Finally, Darwin's interest in heredity and individual differences stimulated investigation in these areas. In observing variability in living
forms, Darwin noted that both large and small differences in individuals
seemed to be passed on from generation to generation (Ashton, 1967).
Little was known, though, about the structures and processes that could
account for individual differences and their inheritance.

We are becoming so sophisticated about nature that it is difficult to grasp how recent our knowledge is. The egg cell was not discovered in the ovary of a mammal until 1831 (Grinder, 1967). And despite long speculation, it was only in this century that the fundamentals of heredity began to be well understood.

Today it is known that all the cells of the body—whether bone, muscle, or nerve cells—have a nucleus that contains *chromosomes*. Segments of chromosomes that are functional units are called *genes*. The exact form and number of chromosomes is distinct for each species. All human cells except the reproductive cells (the gametes, or ova and sperm) contain twenty-three pairs of chromosomes. Twenty-two pairs of these, called the *autosomes*, are alike for both sexes; but one pair, the *sex chromosomes*, differs in females and males. Figure 2–2 shows the chromosome complement for both sexes. Note that the sex chromosomes in females are alike; they are called X chromosomes. Males, in contrast, have one X and one Y chromosome.

Ova and sperm differ from other cells in the number of chromosomes they contain. Most body cells multiply by *mitosis*, in which the chromosome set first doubles, the cell divides into two cells, and then each new cell receives a complete chromosome set. In contrast, the gametes undergo *meiosis*, a specialized cell division during maturation that results in their carrying only twenty-three single chromosomes (one from each

FIGURE 2–2
The chromosome complement in all human cells except the reproductive cells. On the left is the male complement, with an X and Y chromosome; on the right is the female complement, with two X chromosomes. Courtesy M. M. Grumbach, University of California, San Francisco.

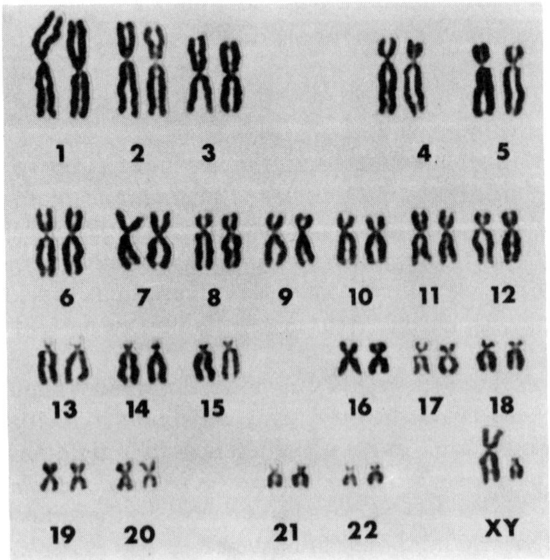

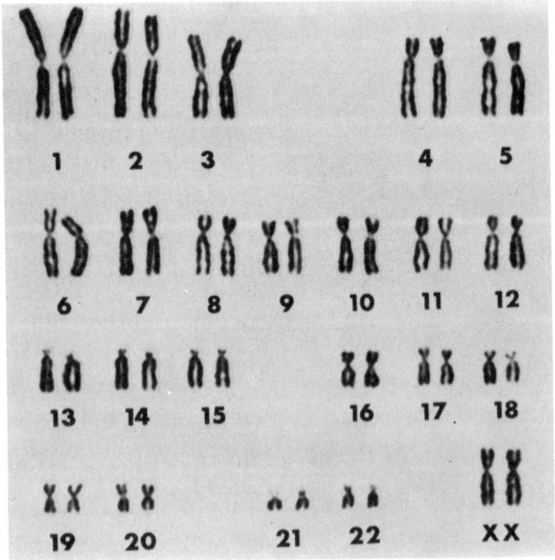

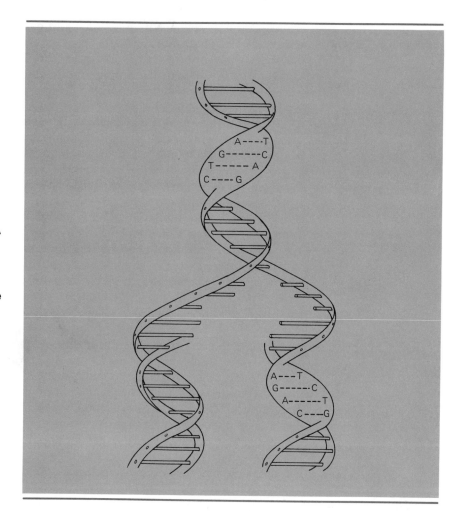

FIGURE 2–3
Diagram of the DNA molecule. When DNA replicates, the strands uncoil and the base pairs separate. The single units then combine with other single units, with the bases always pairing in specific ways. The molecules vary, however, because the base pairs can line up on the strands in various orders. Genetic information is carried by the ordering of the bases.

of the original twenty-three pairs). When the gametes unite sexually, ova and sperm each provide half of the chromosomes of the newly forming organism.

The basic genetic stuff of life resides in the genes, in the form of deoxyribonucleic acid (DNA). One of the most dramatic scientific breakthroughs of this century was the description of the structure and function of DNA. In 1962 Francis Crick, James Watson, and Maurice Wilkins received the Nobel Prize for their work on a model of DNA.* They proposed that the DNA molecule consists of two strands of phosphate and sugar groups connected by nitrogen-carrying bases. The bases always occur in specific pairs. The molecule is shaped like a double helix, resembling a spiral staircase, with the steps being the paired bases, which can be arranged in any order along the molecule (Figure 2–3).

*Rosalind Franklin and DNA, a book by Anne Sayre, tells the story of Wilkins' colleague, who undoubtedly would have shared this prize except for her untimely death at age 37.

As simple as it appears, this structure gives DNA remarkable characteristics. For one, DNA duplicates ingeniously. The DNA strands uncoil themselves and the base pairs separate, leaving single strands with single bases. These units then combine with other single DNA units produced by the cell—with the bases being properly paired. The new DNA is thus identical to the original.

DNA is also well suited to manage biochemical functioning in the cells. Human beings have perhaps as many as 100,000 genes, each of which consists of spirals of DNA that average many hundreds of base pairs. The arrangement of the bases on the outer strands is critical. This arrangement is conveyed to messenger RNA (ribonucleic acid), a chemical that resembles DNA. RNA carries its message from the nucleus out into the cell, where the information is used to direct the production of proteins (Scarr and Kidd, 1983). Proteins are complex substances that comprise many parts of the body, such as nails and hemoglobin. They also make up *enzymes*, the chemical catalysts critical in controlling the biochemical reactions necessary for life. Genes that are directly involved in protein production are sometimes called *structural genes*. Structural genes are turned on and off by other genes according to the needs of the organism. These "on-off" genes are known as *regulator genes*.

This regulation helps account for the general functioning of the organism—and for the timing of development. Through complex processes the genes regulate protein production, and changes in protein production are basic to developmental change throughout the life span (Scarr-Salapatek, 1975). Prenatal development and biological changes at puberty are perhaps the most dramatic examples of such genetic timing.

The system in which the basic genetic apparatus operates is still more elaborate and dynamic. For example, during meiosis one member of a chromosome pair may exchange genes with the other member (crossing over). Genes are known to move from one position to another within a chromosome ("jumping genes") and to modify the effects of other genes. They also undergo spontaneous changes, or *mutations*, that are passed on from generation to generation.

But genes cannot act in a void; they are in continuous interaction with the environment. The nature of this interaction is at the heart of much debate about development.

NATURE AND NURTURE

Investigators first asked whether heredity or the environment was responsible for individual development. As we saw in Chapter 1, the French philosopher Rousseau argued the extreme heredity view; the British philosopher Locke, the extreme environmentalist position. When neither extreme view proved accurate, investigators became more interested in studying *how much* nature and nurture separately contribute to development. This question receives considerable attention today. For example, researchers continue to ask how much of the variation in intelligence in a population can be attributed to genes and how much to experience. As it turns out, this question has contributed to discovering *how* the environment and genes work together.

Biologists have long recognized that the relationship between the genes carried, the *genotype,* and the characteristics displayed, the *phenotype,* is complex. A particular gene typically affects more than one characteristic. And how genes are expressed depends partly on interaction with the environment. For example, in individuals who have the genotype for "very tall" height, height may vary depending on individual diet. The broadest possible expression of a genotype is the *reaction range.* "Very tall" individuals might vary from six-feet-five inches to six-feet-nine inches, but not go outside this range. A set of genes does not *fix* a corresponding characteristic. Rather, genes contribute to determining a range of potential, and interactions with the environment determine the phenotype.

However, genetic and environmental factors do not contribute equally to all characteristics. Genetic effects seem to be more powerful for some characteristics than for others. These characteristics are said to be strongly *canalized* (Waddington, Wilson, 1978). Behaviors that are critical to survival may be the most strongly canalized—as if nature had decided not to be overly trusting of nurture. For example, most infants babble by the time they are 3 to 6 months old and walk by 15 months. Only drastic environmental events prevent these characteristics from developing. Even so, experience helps shape the frequency of babbling and the confidence with which the toddler first attempts to maneuver around a room.

Innumerable environmental factors can interact with the gene complement. Social experiences—such as opportunity for social attachment and how individuals are accepted or rejected, encouraged or discouraged, attended to or ignored—are likely to be important. So is the quality and amount of intellectual, perceptual, and motor stimulation. Physical attributes of the environment, such as diet and exposure to chemicals and disease, must also be considered. We would not expect all these factors to affect all aspects of development at all times in the same way. A central task for developmental psychology, in fact, is to describe gene-environment interactions for specific aspects of development at specific ages (Wachs, 1983).

PKU: An Example of Nature-Nurture Interaction

Phenylketonuria (PKU) is a clear example of how heredity interacts with the environment. The biological basis for PKU is the absence or inactivity of an important liver enzyme. Ordinarily this enzyme converts phenylalanine—found in dairy products, bread, and fish—into tyrosine. Without this enzyme, phenylalanine accumulates and results in the production of substances that are injurious to the nervous system. The defect occurs only when both parents pass on the defective gene. PKU occurs in one case per 20,000 live babies. Infants born with this defect tend to have blue eyes, fair hair, and light-colored skin: They generally are irritable, hyperactive, and short-tempered. Many have seizures and abnormal brainwaves, impaired communication, bizarre movements, and perceptual problems (Cytryn and Lourie, 1980).

It is possible to detect PKU within the first two weeks of life with urine

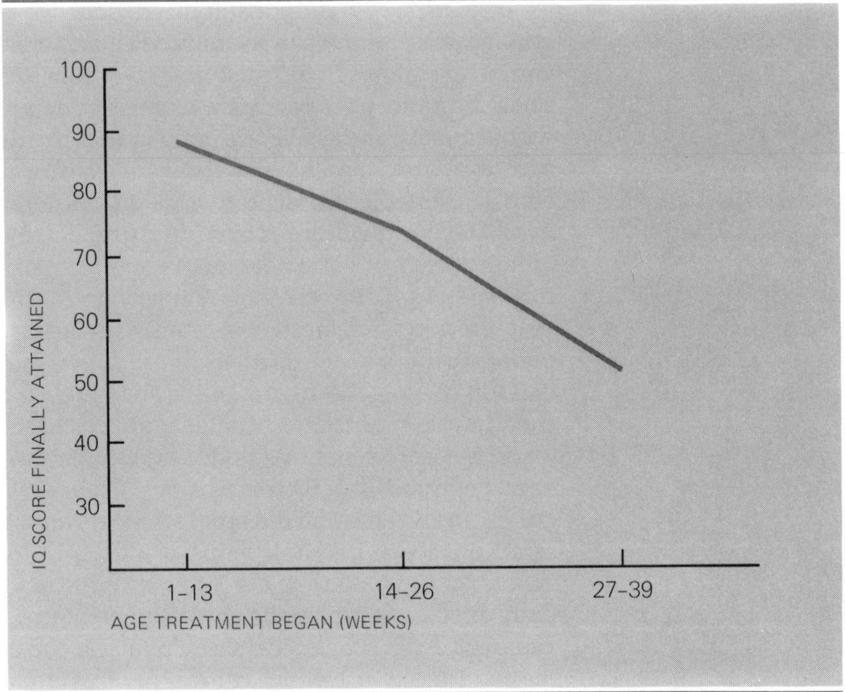

FIGURE 2-4
The effect of diet restriction on the intellectual development of children who inherit PKU. The later diet treatment begins, the less effective it is. Data from Baumeister. Copyright 1967, the American Association on Mental Deficiency.

or blood tests, and screening programs are prevalent throughout the United States. Early detection is extremely important because it has been found that children placed on diets that limit intake of phenylalanine within the first few weeks of life show only minimal impairment. But if diet is not corrected early, there will be substantial and permanent intellectual impairment. The pattern is shown in Figure 2-4.

The PKU syndrome is an interesting example of how heredity and the environment interact to determine behavior. Noticeable retardation does not appear in children who carry the genetic component if they are given a special diet early enough. Children with the defective genetic endowment *and* an uncontrolled diet frequently are retarded.

Nature and Nurture in Development

PKU is a specific example of gene-environment interaction. Now we turn to the broader question of how genetic endowment and the environment are related over the life span.

G-E Relationships. Three kinds of genotype-environment (G-E) relationships that shape development have been identified and labeled: *passive*, *evocative*, and *active* (Scarr and McCartney, 1983).

Passive   Children are given genotypes by their parents and early environments related to these genotypes.

Evocative   Children are reacted to according to their genotypes.

Active   Children seek environments according to their genotypes.

In passive G-E relationships, no action by the child is involved. Parents pass on genotypes to their children. In addition, they provide an early environment that results, in part, from their own genetic makeups. To take an example, parents who excel intellectually may transmit genes that influence their children in this direction, and they also are likely to provide books, museum visits, and stimulating discussions that have similar influence. In evocative G-E relationships, different genotypes evoke different responses from the environment. Thus children with certain genotypes may pay attention to their teachers and ask relevant questions and, in turn, receive more positive attention in school than children who show little interest. In active G-E relationships, individuals actively seek environments related to their genetic makeup. Intellectually able children may actively seek peers, adults, and activities that strengthen their intellectual development.

These are all positive relationships. Genetic tendencies are encouraged and maintained by experience. But negative relationships also occur. A negative passive relationship exists, for example, when parents who are socially outgoing have a child whose genetic disposition is to be quiet and withdrawn, and expose this child to group activities. Here, the environment set up by the parents works against the child's genetic disposition. An example of a negative evocative relationship occurs when teachers and friends react to this quiet child by encouraging participation in group games. And if at some point the child deliberately seeks social participation, then a negative active G-E relationship is operating. Negative or positive, the existence of G-E relationships points to the fact that genotypes and environments occur together by more than chance.

Active Niche Building. Drawing on these relationships, Scarr and McCartney have proposed a theory to describe the usual course of behavioral development. They speculate that the importance of G-E relationships changes with development. The influence of the passive kind decreases from infancy to adolescence, and the importance of the active kind increases. Individuals increasingly select aspects of the environment to which they respond, learn about, or ignore. The selections are related to motivational, personality, and intellectual aspects of their genotypes. According to Scarr and McCartney, this active niche building is the most powerful connection between people and their environments. It is the most direct expression of the genotype in experience.

Central to this theory is the argument that although genetic and environmental influences are both necessary for development, the genotype comes first. It influences both the child's phenotype and the rearing environment. It plays a critical role in determining which environments are actually experienced by the child and what effects they have on the child. In short, *the genotype guides and drives experience.* Scarr and McCartney propose that when the environment is rich, most differences among people arise from genetically determined differences in the experiences to which they are attracted and which they evoke from their environments.

FIGURE 2–5
Active niche building is a powerful influence on the development of individual differences. Charles Gatewood.

This theory suggests how heredity and the environment may interact to shape development over the life span. It assumes some genetic influence on intellectual and social behaviors and interests, an assumption that seems reasonable. But the theory goes beyond this to draw parents and other people and the individuals themselves into the developmental process. Will it stand the test of time? Scarr and McCartney suggest several ways in which it can be tested, and they point to prior supportive findings from human genetic research. Later in this chapter we will examine some of these findings. First, though, we look at basic genetic mechanisms and methods used in genetic research.

GENETIC MECHANISMS

Our understanding of genetic mechanisms had its modern beginning in the work of Johann Gregor Mendel (1828–1884), an Austrian monk who conducted his experiments in the garden of his monastery. Mendel first published his studies in 1865, but they received little attention. At the turn of the century, however, Mendel's work was rediscovered almost simultaneously by several others.

Using common garden peas, Mendel first identified characteristics in which the plants differed and then mated dissimilar ones. For example, he carefully cross-fertilized smooth-seeded and wrinkle-seeded plants to see what would happen in the next generation. All the offspring displayed smooth seeds. When these second-generation plants were allowed to self-fertilize, however, the third generation had both smooth and wrinkled seeds, in the ratio of 3:1. A similar pattern was found for several other characteristics (see Table 2–1). Mendel wanted to explain why some characteristics disappeared in the second generation and then reappeared in one-fourth of the third generation.

Mendel assumed that the parent plants each contained two hereditary factors that were forms for the particular characteristic. These factors were later called genes, and each form of the gene pair, an *allele*. Mendel proposed that each parent passed on only one allele to the offspring. (Today we know that the gametes carry only one allele of each pair.) If the offspring received the same form of allele from each parent, it was *homozygous* for the characteristic. If it received different forms from each parent, it was *heterozygous*. Mendel also proposed that one form was *dominant* over the other, always displaying itself. The other allele, the *recessive* form, displayed itself only in the absence of the dominant form. A form not showing itself may still be present, to be passed on to future generations. Mendel therefore made the distinction between genotype and phenotype.

By applying these assumptions, Mendel was able to explain his curious findings. The first generation parents each carried two genes for a particular characteristic, but one parent carried only genes for the dominant form (e.g., smooth seeds) and the other parent carried only genes for the recessive form (e.g., wrinkled seeds). The second generation plants thus each inherited a gene for the dominant form and a gene for the recessive form, and they displayed the dominant form (e.g., smooth seeds). When these plants were self-fertilized, however, 25 percent of their offspring inherited two genes for the recessive form and thus displayed the recessive form (e.g., wrinkled seeds).

Today we know that Mendel's assumptions, along with other suggestions he made, help account for particular patterns of inheritance found not only in plants, but in other species as well. These Mendelian

TABLE 2–1
Mendel's Experiment with the Pea Plant

Parent Plants, First Generation	All Second-Generation Plants	Third-Generation Plants*
Smooth vs. wrinkled seeds	Smooth	2.96:1
Yellow vs. green seeds	Yellow	3.01:1
Violet vs. white flowers	Violet	3.15:1
Inflated vs. constricted pods	Inflated	2.95:1
Green vs. yellow pods	Green	2.82:1
Axial vs. terminal flower position	Axial	3.14:1
Tall vs. dwarf stem length	Tall	2.84:1

*Ratio of dormant to recessive characteristic.
Source: The Royal Horticultural Society, London.

patterns of inheritance involve the transmission of attributes that are influenced by only one or a few gene pairs. In some cases, human studies support Mendel's ideas, and his assumptions account for the results. In other instances, research findings have needed a variety of further explanations. For example, dominant and recessive genes do not always express themselves fully, depending on other genes and the environment. And several alleles (forms) exist for some genes. Also, genes located on the sex chromosomes are expressed in unique patterns. Moreover many characteristics appear to be influenced not just by a single gene pair, but by many genes (*polygene inheritance*).

Single Gene Pair,
Recessive
Inheritance

Many human traits that are influenced by a single gene pair are displayed only when both parents transmit the recessive form, as in Mendel's original experiments. As Table 2–2 shows, these include straight hair and eye color, as well as the abnormalities of albinism, forms of cystic fibrosis, and phenylketonuria.

Figure 2–6 shows the genetic mechanism involved in the transmission of phenylketonuria when the parents are heterozygous for the characteristic. Each parent has an equal chance of passing on the recessive gene for the trait (r) and the normal dominant gene (N). The result is a 25% chance that any one of their offspring will inherit the recessive gene from both parents. This individual will have the disorder and transmit it to another generation. A 50 percent chance exists for an offspring to inherit one recessive and one dominant gene. In this case the child does not display phenylketonuria, but carries the recessive as well as the dominant gene. A 25 percent chance exists that an offspring will inherit two dominant genes, not display the disorder, and transmit only the dominant gene.

TABLE 2–2
Human Conditions Transmitted by Known Genetic Mechanisms

Single Pair, Recessive Genes	Single Dominant Genes	Sex-linked Genes
Eye color (blue vs. brown)	Eye color (brown vs. blue)	Red-green color blindness
Straight hair	Curly hair	Hemophilia (defect in blood clotting)
Attached ear lobes	Extra fingers and toes	Pattern baldness
Dry ear wax	Free ear lobes	Some forms of deafness
Albinism (lack of pigment for color)	Piebald trait (white forelock of hair)	Some forms of muscular dystrophy (muscle deterioration)
Cystic fibrosis (malfunctioning of glands)	Ability to curl tongue back	
Phenylketonuria (abnormal metabolism)	Ability to curl tongue toward center	
Tay-Sachs disease (nervous system disorder)	Huntington's chorea (nervous system disorder)	
Cretinism (thyroid gland dysfunction)		

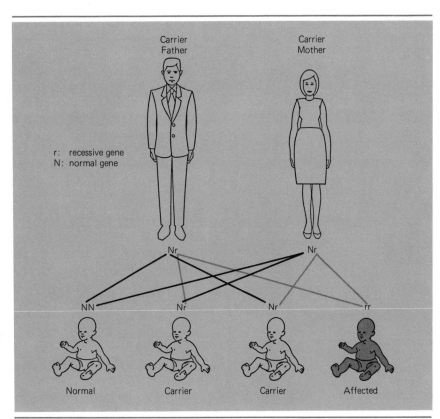

FIGURE 2–6
Inheritance of
phenylketonuria
when both parents
are heterozygous for
the condition. On the
average, 25 percent
of the children will
display the
condition, even
though their parents
do not.

This single gene pair, recessive inheritance pattern underlies many disorders in humans. It is one reason for prohibiting closely related individuals from having offspring. All families carry harmful recessive genes, and marriage within families increases the chance that both parents will carry the same recessive genes, setting up the situation described in Figure 2–6.

Single Gene, Dominant Inheritance

A characteristic carried by a dominant gene will always display itself when passed on to offspring. One pattern occurs when the dominant gene is carried heterozygously by one parent and not at all by the other. In this case there is a 50 percent chance of the gene's being transmitted and displayed in the children. Table 2–2 shows examples of human attributes inherited in this way.

One example is Huntington's chorea, a fatal disease characterized by progressive degeneration of the nervous system. Limb spasms, mental deterioration, and psychotic behavior develop. This is a genetic disease that is not present at birth; in fact, the average age at which it develops is 40 to 45 (Stern, 1973). By this age most adults have already produced

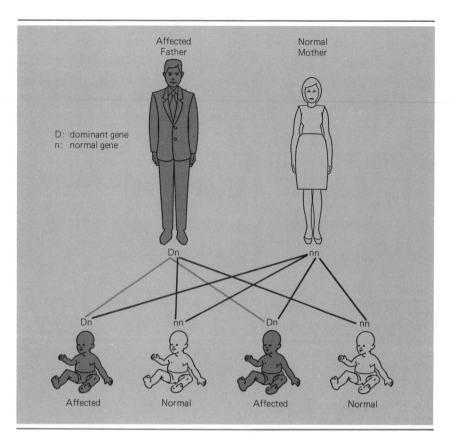

FIGURE 2–7
Inheritance of Huntington's chorea when one parent carries the dominant gene and the other does not. On the average, 50 percent of the children will display the disease and perhaps pass it to the next generation.

offspring, many of whom will later display the disease themselves (Figure 2–7). Woody Guthrie, a well-known folksinger, succumbed to this disease (Yurcheno, 1970).

Sex-Linked Inheritance

Certain characteristics are said to be sex-linked because they are influenced by genes on the sex chromosomes. The Y chromosome does not have many genes, whereas the X chromosome has almost 100 (McKusick, 1975). In some cases of sex-linked inheritance, the relevant allele is recessive and located on the X chromosome. One is hemophilia, in which the blood does not clot normally; another is red-green color blindness. The frequency of the sex-linked characteristic is higher in males than in females; red-green color blindness, for example, is eight times more frequent in males (McClearn, 1970). Why is this so? Suppose a female receives from her mother the recessive gene that may produce color blindness. The daughter will probably *not* be color blind because the X chromosome she received from her father will most likely contain the dominant gene for normal color vision. When a son receives the recessive color blindness gene from his mother, its influence cannot be offset by a dominant normal-vision gene from his father because the Y chromosome

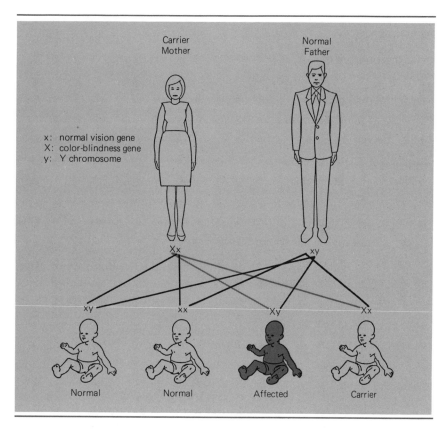

FIGURE 2–8
Inheritance of red-green color blindness when the father carries the gene for normal vision and the mother carries one gene for normal vision and one for color blindness. Daughters have a 50 percent chance of being carriers; sons have a 50 percent chance of being color blind and a 50 percent chance of having normal vision and not carrying the color-blindness gene.

Carrier Mother

Normal Father

x: normal vision gene
X: color-blindness gene
y: Y chromosome

Xx

xy

xy

xx

Xy

xx

Normal

Normal

Affected

Carrier

he received from his father has no gene for this type of color vision (see Figure 2–8). The same reasoning can be used to demonstrate that all color-blind women must have had fathers who were also color blind. Can you see why?*

Polygene Inheritance

So far we have discussed only relatively simple Mendelian patterns that involve one gene pair and often result in either-or categories. Mendel's pea plants displayed seeds that were either smooth or wrinkled; in humans albinism is present or absent. Over 2,000 such characteristics are known or suspected in humans. (Plomin, DeFries, and McClearn, 1980). Well over 150 abnormalities produce mental retardation.

Countless other attributes are influenced by several genes. These traits do not fall into an either-or category; rather, they are displayed along a continuum. In the case of intelligence, for example, individuals are not just extremely bright or very dull; instead, they fall into the entire range between those extremes. The same is true for height, weight, skin

*A color-blind woman must have received the recessive color-blind gene from both her mother and her father. If her father carried color blindness on his X chromosome he must have been color blind, because his Y chromosome does not have a color-vision gene.

FIGURE 2–9
As the number of genes increases, so does the number of resulting phenotypes. Involvement of many genes results in the characteristic's being displayed along a continuum. Adapted from I. H. Herskowitz, *Genetics* (Boston: Little, Brown and Co., 1965).

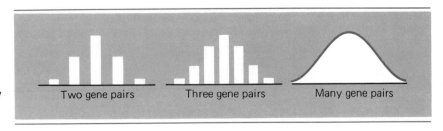

color, and temperament. Each of the many genes involved contributes only a small influence. As the number of genes increases, so does the number of phenotypes, until separate phenotypes cannot be distinguished; Figure 2–9 shows this relationship.

In studying polygene inheritance, we cannot trace the effects of each gene. Instead, we examine the distributions of traits in populations with complex statistical methods. It is assumed that population traits are due to both genetic and environmental effects. So researchers try to separate these components by comparing groups of people who are either unrelated or related in certain ways.

HEREDITARY INFLUENCE ON HUMANS

Behavior genetics is the branch of science that deals with the influence of an organism's genotype on its behavior. Part of behavior genetics is concerned with explaining differences among species. Many behaviors involved in mating, aggression, and territoriality have been shown to be affected by species-wide genetic endowments resulting from evolutionary pressures (Gottlieb, 1983). Another part of behavior genetics is the search for explanations of individual differences within a species and how these differences develop and change over the life span.

A research strategy in which either heredity or environment is varied while the other is held constant is ideal to sort out genetic and environmental influences on behavior. This kind of experiment is not possible with humans, so researchers depend on experiments with animals and correlational studies of humans.

Animal Studies

Genetic experimentation with animals has become very sophisticated, but here we need consider only the relatively simple methods of inbreeding of strains and selective breeding.

Inbreeding experiments involve the mating of related animals, such as brothers and sisters. After a number of generations of family matings, often as many as twenty, this process will produce a "pure" strain in which the animals are genetically alike. Many pure strains can be produced, each of which will be genetically different from the others. Throughout the entire process, the animals experience identical environments. Any behavioral differences between the strains can therefore be attributed to genetic factors. This method has demonstrated a genetic component in such behaviors as learning, sexual behavior, alcohol preference, aggression, taste perception, activity level, and seizure susceptibility (DeFries and Plomin, 1978).

Selective breeding is the mating, over several generations, of animals who are extreme on some characteristic; for example, fast-running rats can be mated with each other and slow-running rats can be mated with each other. Genetic effects are demonstrated when the groups become more and more dissimilar over generations in running time, despite identical environments. In investigations of learning, for example, experimenters saw that some rats learned much more quickly than others to find their way through a complex of unfamiliar corridors to the feeder of a maze. One investigator (Thompson, 1954) then interbred maze "bright" rats and maze "dull" ones for six succeeding generations. The difference in learning ability between the two groups steadily increased with each new generation. Selective breeding studies have also demonstrated the genetic selection of emotionality (Broadhurst, 1958), aggressiveness (Lagerspetz, 1961), and sex drive (Wood-Gush, 1960).

The results of animal experiments such as these clearly demonstrate the possibility of genetic influence on a wide range of behaviors. But animals are not humans; for more direct information about humans, we rely on family studies, twin studies, and adoption studies.

Family Studies

Families are studied in various ways to determine whether, and possibly how, characteristics are passed on from generation to generation.

One type of family study is *pedigree analysis*. It consists of tracing a characteristic through the family to try to discover some known genetic pattern. A pattern not only serves as evidence for genetic transmission, but also indicates the specific mechanism involved. For the most part, this method applies to characteristics that are clearly identifiable—that is, influenced by only a few genes and transmitted according to Mendelian principles.

Figure 2–10 shows a hypothetical pedigree for an X-linked recessive trait. The pedigree traces four generations, beginning with the mating of a normal male and a carrier female that produced a normal male, an affected male, and a carrier female. It was assumed that each subsequent mating was with a normal individual. When the normal male of the second generation mated, the trait did not appear in the family. However, in the other families it continued to be transmitted by affected males who passed it to their carrier daughters, or by carrier females who passed it to their affected sons or carrier daughters. From this family tree, we can see sex-linked inheritance.

Closely related people have more genes in common than people not as closely related. For example, a parent and a child share one-half of their genes, as do siblings, on the average. First cousins, however, share only one-eighth. If a trait is influenced by genes, parents and their children should be more alike than first cousins. Furthermore, cousins would be more alike than unrelated people. The *consanguinity* study is

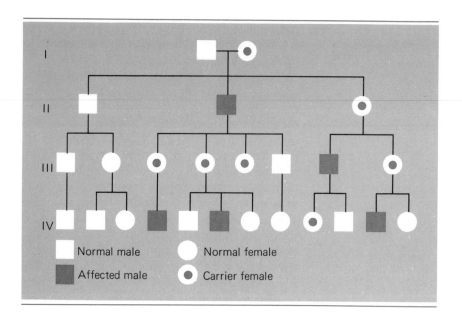

FIGURE 2–10
A hypothetical pedigree for an X-linked recessive trait. Adapted from A. E. H. Emery, *Elements of Medical Genetics*, 5th ed. (Edinburgh: Churchill Livingstone, 1979).

□ Normal male   ○ Normal female

■ Affected male   ◉ Carrier female

based on this reasoning: as the degree of relationship among individuals increases, so should the frequency of the characteristic. (Consanguinity means "of the same blood.") The problem with this method is that close relatives might be similar because they shared more similar environments as well as more genes. This *confound*, or confusion, always exists in consanguinity studies unless relatives have been reared in different homes. Thus the method can be a helpful first step in research, but the results must be interpreted cautiously and followed up with other kinds of research.

Twin Studies

Twins are especially appealing to most people, the more so when they strongly resemble each other. As it turns out, identical twins are more alike than are fraternal twins on many physical and psychological characteristics, including weight, height, and behavioral habits (Figure 2–11, 2–12). The *twin-study method* is based on the important difference between identical (monozygotic) and fraternal (dizygotic) twins. Identical twins develop from a single union of egg and sperm, so they have identical genotypes. Fraternal twins develop from two separate unions so, like nontwin siblings, they share 50 percent of their genes, on the average. The degree to which identical twins are more alike on a characteristic than are fraternal twins suggests the influence of genetic endowment.

Farber (1981), for example, studied identical twins who had been separated and reared in different homes for various periods of time, some not knowing of the existence of the other twin until adulthood. Many of the twin pairs had similar voices, laughed and walked in the same way, had a similar number of tooth cavities, and showed similar interests, such as in the arts or carpentry.

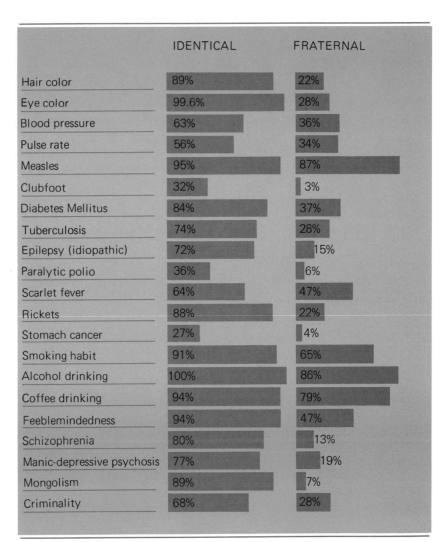

	IDENTICAL	FRATERNAL
Hair color	89%	22%
Eye color	99.6%	28%
Blood pressure	63%	36%
Pulse rate	56%	34%
Measles	95%	87%
Clubfoot	32%	3%
Diabetes Mellitus	84%	37%
Tuberculosis	74%	28%
Epilepsy (idiopathic)	72%	15%
Paralytic polio	36%	6%
Scarlet fever	64%	47%
Rickets	88%	22%
Stomach cancer	27%	4%
Smoking habit	91%	65%
Alcohol drinking	100%	86%
Coffee drinking	94%	79%
Feeblemindedness	94%	47%
Schizophrenia	80%	13%
Manic-depressive psychosis	77%	19%
Mongolism	89%	7%
Criminality	68%	28%

FIGURE 2–11
Percentage of identical and fraternal twins showing similarity to each other on a variety of characteristics and diseases. Reprinted with permission of Macmillan Publishing Co. Inc., from *Genetics* by M. W. Strickberger. Copyright © Monroe W. Strickberger, 1968.

These likenesses might easily lead to the conclusion that heredity certainly plays a role in the development of many traits. But the issue is not settled so quickly. For example, the twin study method has been faulted on the ground that the procedures used to distinguish the kind of twins have not been reliable. In the past, twins were labeled fraternal when they were born with two separate sets of amnions, chorions, and placentas (tissues that support the organisms when they are developing in the uterus). However, identical twins sometimes also develop in this way instead of sharing one set of these tissues (Scheinfeld, 1973). And although twins are often labeled identical when they strongly resemble each other, fraternal twins may be strikingly alike. Recent twin studies have relied on more sophisticated methods of identification, particularly on blood

FIGURE 2–12
Photographs of a pair of identical twins taken at ages 5, 20, 55, and 86. From F. J. Kallman and L. F. Jarvik, Individual differences in constitution and genetic background. In J. E. Birren, ed., *Handbook of Aging and the Individual*, p. 241. Copyright © 1959 The University of Chicago Press. Courtesy Dr. John Rainer.

typing and on carefully constructed ratings of physical traits that agree well with blood typing.

Another criticism of the twin method is that it assumes the environments shared by identical twins are no more alike than the environments shared by fraternal twins. But research tells us that identical twins share more activities, have more friends in common, dress more alike, and, of course, are always of the same sex (Loehlin and Nichols, 1976). It is also likely that others perceive them as more alike and treat them more alike than they do fraternal twins. Could greater similarity of environment underlie the greater similarity of identical twins? Perhaps. But there is evidence that neither physical nor environmental similarity is related to personality or intellectual similarity in twins (Matheny, Wilson, and Dolan, 1976).

Adoption Studies

When parents bring up their biological children, the source of any parent-child similarity observed later is uncertain. Parents transmit genes that may be responsible for similarities, but social transmission of abilities, attitudes, and personality is also involved. On the other hand, parents who bring up adopted children influence them only by social transmission. This reasoning is at the heart of *adoption studies*—comparisons of adopted children with their biological and their adoptive families. Resemblances between adopted children and their biological families suggest genetic effects; resemblances between adopted children and their adoptive families suggest environmental influences.

The logic of these studies requires that the children cease to have contact with their biological families soon after birth. Furthermore, they should be randomly placed in adoptive homes. However, adoption agencies often try to place youngsters in homes similar to those of their biological parents. This can bias the results of adoption studies. The biological and adoptive parents may be genetically similar—which means that the adoptive parents may be genetically similar to their adopted children. In this case, similarities between children and adopted parents would reflect a genetic as well as an environmental component. We might expect too that the adoptive parents may provide an environment similar to the environment that would have been provided by the biological parents. Such an outcome would add an environmental component to similarities between children and their biological parents (Horn, 1983).

Another suspected weakness of this method is that adoptive homes may be special in many ways, so that the environment may not be typical. Adoptive children may indeed have special benefits that other children do not have. At the same time, adoptive families do represent a wide range of social and economic levels (Plomin and DeFries, 1983; Scarr and Weinberg, 1983).

But despite weaknesses, the adoption method can tell us much about hereditary and environmental effects, especially when children are immediately adopted and selective placement is small or controlled by statistical analyses. What is particularly compelling, is the simultaneous use of well-designed and well-controlled adoption and twin methods. We look now at some aspects of behavior and development that have been studied with a combination of research techniques.

INTELLIGENCE

There is no totally satisfactory definition of intelligence. Whether the concept should mean ability to learn, rate of learning, the limit on what can be learned, or some other human capacity is still undecided. Chapter 8 discusses this topic in detail; for our purposes here, *intelligence* means performance on a variety of tasks or tests that presumably tap mental ability.

The notion that human intelligence is at least in part genetically determined may be distasteful to a society which cherishes the belief that all people are created equal. But animal studies and a great deal of research with humans suggest that intellectual variations within the normal range of functioning seem to involve both polygene inheritance and environmental effects.

Twin Studies

The performance of identical twins is more alike than that of fraternal twins (Scarr and Kidd, 1983). Table 2–3 shows this result; it also shows that similarity on specific intellectual tasks is higher for identical than for fraternal twins. Overall, similarity between fraternal twins is about the same as similarity between nontwin siblings. Some of this similarity may be accounted for by identical twins having more similar environments than fraternal twins, especially when the fraternal twins are of the opposite sex. However, research on intelligence with identical twins reared in different environments suggests that even when these twins are separated, they tend to be similar (Bouchard, 1983; Newman, Freeman, and Holzinger, 1937).

One important goal of behavior genetics is to examine the relative influences of genes and environment over time. Genes may turn on and

---

TABLE 2–3
Correlations For Fraternal and Identical Twins on Intellectual Tasks

	Fraternal Twins	Identical Twins
General intelligence (IQ)	.59	.82
Verbal comprehension	.59	.78
Number and mathematical ability	.59	.78
Spatial visualization	.41	.65
Memory	.36	.52
Reasoning	.50	.74
Verbal fluency	.52	.67

From Nichols, 1978.

off, and environments may change as individuals' social worlds vary with age (Plomin, DeFries, and McClearn, 1980). The Louisville Twin Study traced similarity in twins and their siblings from 3 months of age to 15 years (Wilson, 1983). The results indicate that children's mental development shows distinctive patterns of spurts and lags, and that intelligence stabilizes by school age. Furthermore, patterns of development, reflected in mental test scores (IQ), are more alike for identical twins than for fraternal twins. In Figure 2–13, graphs A through D show that scores can vary substantially across age in young children. Graphs A and B, compared to C and D, also demonstrate that identical twins develop with

FIGURE 2–13
Trends in mental development in early childhood for two pairs of identical and two pairs of fraternal twins. Adapted from Wilson, 1983. The Society for Research in Child Development, Inc.

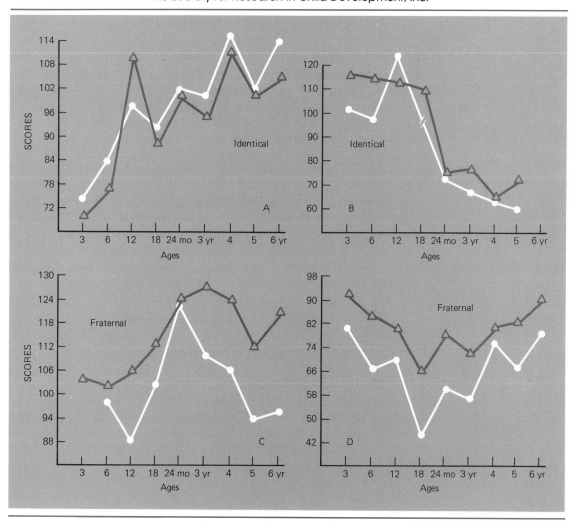

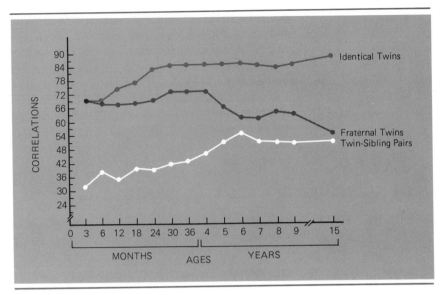

FIGURE 2–14
Mental-development correlations for identical twins, fraternal twins, and twin-sibling pairs. Adapted from Wilson, 1983. The Society for Research in Child Development, Inc.

more *synchrony* than do fraternal twins. Identical twins are not only more alike in IQ, but in developmental paths as well.

And there is more to the story. In examining similarity across time for twins and other family members, the researchers in Louisville showed that identical twins become more like each other with age. In contrast, fraternal twins become less similar over time (even when of the same sex). By age 15 they are no more like each other than they are like their nontwin siblings. As Figure 2–14 shows, the correlations for fraternal twins and for the twins and their siblings are about .50 at age 15. This is about the degree of similarity that has been found between parents and offspring. Fraternal twins, twin-sibling pairs, and parent-child pairs all share half of their genes, on the average, whereas identical twins, who become increasingly alike, have identical genes. This suggests that gene effects increase over time during the age range examined in this study.

Adoption Studies

Although investigations involving adopted children can be traced back several decades, recent studies are more sophisticated and have better controls. One of these is the Texas Adoption Project (Horn, 1983; Horn, Loehlin, and Willerman, 1979). This study examined 300 families whose children had been adopted when their unwed biological mothers had permanently given them up soon after birth. Selective placement was practiced by the adoption agency, which also gave the biological mothers intelligence tests as part of counseling services. Intelligence tests were also given to the adoptive families and the children, and all the data were compared in various ways.

One finding concerns correlations involving children's test score performance. Children's test scores were more highly correlated with the scores of their biological parents than with the scores of their adopted parents. In other words, children with high test scores tended to have biological parents with high test scores but not necessarily adoptive parents with high test scores. Such a finding is evidence for inheritance.

Another interesting result emerged from the Texas project. The average score of the children as a group was more similar to the average score of the adoptive parents than to the average score of the biological mothers. That is, the biological mothers scored the lowest, adoptive parents scored the highest, and the children scored in between, but more like the adoptive parents. So although the children were influenced by genes transmitted to them from their mothers, they also were influenced by the environmental advantage provided by the adoptive parents.

Although many complex adoption studies are in the early stages of investigation, the pattern of results described above has been found. Overall, adoptees tend to be more like their biological parents than like their adoptive parents, but their intelligence falls somewhere between that of their two sets of parents (Scarr and Weinber, 1983). Adoptees of biological parents with relatively high intellectual ability, compared to those of biological parents with lower intellectual ability, seem to benefit more from advantaged adoptive homes. So intelligence can be shaped by the environment, but genetic influence seems to set some limit on that shaping.

Adoption studies often also report that intelligence test scores of adopted children and their adoptive siblings are related (Plomin, De-Fries, and McClearn, 1980). Family environment thus seems to make children in a family alike compared to children in other families. However, biologically unrelated siblings are less alike than related siblings and seem to become less similar over time, perhaps as they approach adolescence (Scarr and McCartney, 1983). Shared family influences may be quite strong for young children, but with maturity unique individual experiences may result in their becoming increasingly different from each other.

Some Conclusions

What can we conclude from the extensive research into the origins and maintenance of intellectual functioning (as defined on tests of mental ability)? The following statements appear to reflect what we know at this point about genetic and environmental influences:

1. Both heredity and environment contribute to individual differences in intelligence.
2. Intellectual functioning varies over time for individuals, and the patterning of the variations seems to be influenced by both genetic and environmental factors.
3. There is some evidence that genetic effects may increase over time throughout childhood.
4. The level of functioning can be raised by an advantaged environment, but individuals may respond according to potential that has been largely determined by genetic factors.

5. The effects of the environment are not well understood. Emphasis is often given to shared family factors—that is, to influences that affect all the children in a family, making them like each other but unlike children in other families. However, unshared family factors are also important. They operate differentially on siblings, making them different from each other. Such experiences might include parents' treating offspring differently, birth order, illness, individual reactions to death or divorce, sibling interaction, and interactions with friends and teachers. Children in the same family have many different experiences, and these have not been adequately examined.

Finally, there is Scarr and McCartney's (1983) developmental model, which holds that the gene-environment relationship becomes less passive and more active over time. Scarr and McCartney consider the evidence that fraternal twins and adopted siblings, in contrast to identical twins, become less alike over time. They ask: How can it be that the longer you live with someone, the less like them you are? They suggest that fraternal twins and adopted siblings increasingly select different niches, based on different genetic dispositions. Identical twins select similar niches, based on genetic similarity. This argument is also applied to the finding that identical twins reared apart show considerable similarity. Given reasonable opportunity, they would be inclined to build similar niches based on genetic similarity—as well as experience similar reactions from others.

SOCIAL BEHAVIOR AND PERSONALITY

Interesting research has also been conducted on variations in social behavior and personality. Many different kinds of behaviors and attributes have been examined, including introversion-extroversion, activity level, social responsiveness, and temperament. Parents and their offspring are somewhat similar on measures of personality, but the relationship appears to be modest. The same is true for siblings, even though siblings probably share more of the same environment than parent-children pairs.

Several twin studies suggest that genes play a part in determining introversion or extroversion. An extreme *introvert* is shy and anxious in novel social situations; an extreme *extrovert* is friendly and at ease among people. Differences on the introversion-extroversion dimension are observed during the first years of life and do not change much over time. Friendly infants tend to become friendly adolescents; unfriendly infants tend to become unfriendly teenagers (Schaefer and Bayley, 1963).

Scarr (1969) gave psychological tests to twenty pairs of female identical and fraternal twins who had been identified by blood groupings and found identical twins more similar on measures of introversion-extrov-

FIGURE 2–15
Individual children differ considerably in overall activity level, a characteristic that is believed to be influenced, in part, by genetic factors. Photos by Rocky Weldon, Laimute E. Druskis (for boy with Rubik's cube).

ersion. In another investigation each member of the twin pairs was filmed individually in many situations over an eight-month period (Freedman and Keller, 1963). Then the films of one twin in each pair were shown to judges, while the films of the other twin were presented to a comparable group of judges. The judges rated each child, and once again there was greater similarity in social behavior for identical twins.

In yet another study hundreds of pairs of twins were selected from a sample of high school students who had taken a national scholarship examination. The adolescents completed personality and attitude scales that assessed many dimensions of behavior, including self-control, tolerance, flexibility, responsibility, and dominance (Loehlin and Nichols, 1976). The overall correlation for identical twins was .50; for the fraternal twins, it was .32. Nearly all of the comparisons showed higher identical-twin correlations. Thus, on numerous measures of social behavior, identical twins appear more alike than fraternal twins.

The picture that emerges from twin and adoption studies is an interesting one. Genetic effects, as suggested in twin studies, are responsible for a moderate amount of variation in personality. Common experiences in the family also have a small effect. However, what seems to be more powerful in shaping social behavior and personality are unshared family factors that make children in the same family different from each other. This effect is stronger for personality than for intellectual functioning. As Scarr and Kidd (1983) note: "Although we often think that parents want 'chips off the old block,' in fact parents are probably quite respectful of individual differences in offspring" (p. 419).

DISORDERED BEHAVIOR: SCHIZOPHRENIA

A considerable amount of genetic research is directed toward increasing our understanding of a variety of behavior disorders, such as schizophrenia, depressions, learning disabilities, and antisocial behavior. *Schizophrenia*, which has probably received the most attention, is a serious disorder that involves emotional, behavioral, and intellectual deficits. Schizophrenics may experience delusions and hallucinations, communicate in disorganized ways, and display inappropriate emotions.

Theories that propose a genetic basis for schizophrenia predict that the closer the genetic relationship between two individuals, one of whom is schizophrenic, the higher the risk that the other will also display schizophrenic behaviors. When both individuals are schizophrenic, they are said to be *concordant* for the disorder.

The risk of anyone in the general population becoming schizophrenic is about 1 percent. Risk increases as the degree of the relationship with a schizophrenic person becomes stronger. Parents and siblings of schizophrenics have a greater risk of schizophrenia than the general population. Furthermore, these first-degree relatives have a greater risk than second-degree relatives, while the risk for third-degree relatives is only slightly greater than that for the population at large (Rosenthal, 1970). Another interesting finding is that children who have two affected parents have a risk in the range of 40 to 68 percent. It appears that schizophrenia "runs in families."

Nevertheless, the risk associated with family membership does not match the level that would be expected on the basis of shared genes. For example, although first-degree relatives share about 50 percent of their genes with the affected relative, their risk for schizophrenia is only about 5 to 16 percent (Davison and Neale, 1982).

Investigations with twins provide further clues about the causes of schizophrenia. Concordance is consistently higher for identical than for fraternal twins. Figure 2–16 shows this pattern from five twin studies.

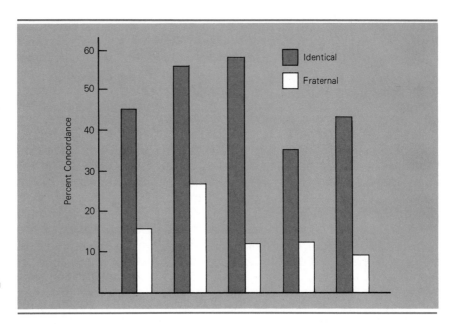

FIGURE 2–16
Results from five studies of concordance for schizophrenia in identical and fraternal twins. Adapted from Gottesman and Shields, 1973.

Discrepancies in the exact figures among these studies can probably be explained by differences in how schizophrenia was defined and in its severity (Gottesman and Shields, 1972). But the consistency of the overall pattern is impressive.

The twins in these studies had been reared together. However, concordance has also been examined in sixteen cases of identical twins reared apart. One of each pair was known to be schizophrenic; evaluation of the co-twins revealed that ten of them were also schizophrenics (Rosenthal, 1970). Even this quite high concordance makes it clear that an identical genotype does not always result in an identical phenotype.

Heston (1966) investigated forty-seven adoptees who had been born to schizophrenic mothers while the mothers were being treated in state psychiatric hospitals. The infants were taken from their mothers shortly after birth and were placed in foundling homes or with family members who were unrelated to the mothers. Fifty other infants, also separated from their mothers at birth but for nonpsychiatric reasons, were identified as controls.

Heston performed extensive follow-up assessments on both groups at the average age of 36 years. The results showed that 16.6 percent of the offspring of schizophrenic mothers were themselves diagnosed as schizophrenic, whereas none of the offspring of control mothers were so diagnosed. The offspring of schizophrenic mothers were also more likely than the controls to be diagnosed as neurotic and, on the average, had been involved more frequently in criminal activity. Similar results, including a tendency to display psychological disorders other than schizophrenia, were found in a large-scale study of adopted children in Denmark (Kety, Rosenthal, Wender, and Schulsinger, 1976).

Genetic Screening and Counseling

Thousands of genetic disorders have been identified; they account wholly or in part for about 25 percent of all diseases (Brown, 1978; Karp, 1976). The first genetic counseling clinic was opened in England in 1946, and the first book on the subject was published in the United States in 1955 (Berry, 1982). Hundreds of genetic counseling centers now exist in this country alone. In fact, most states have a genetic screening and counseling program of some sort. The counseling centers aid in screening, provide information about the risk of genetic disorders, and assist individuals in making decisions about having children.

Screening includes identifying those who are carrying recessive or dominant genes associated with known genetic disorders, as well as prenatal diagnosis. One widely used method of prenatal diagnosis is *amniocentesis*. This procedure is simple: A long needle is inserted into the amnion sac that surrounds the developing child and a sample of fluid is drawn. The fluid and the cells floating in it can then be examined for biochemical and chromosome abnormalities. In an even newer procedure, *chorionic villus biopsy*, embryonic tissue is extracted and examined. Abnormal growth can also be identified by *ultrasound* "pictures." All these methods are particularly recommended when a genetic disorder is suspected in the family or the prospective mother is over 35, because these factors increase the risk of genetic problems.

The advantages of genetic screening are obvious. Carriers of PKU, sickle cell anemia, and countless other diseases can be identified. Down's syndrome and other chromosome abnormalities can be diagnosed prenatally, providing couples with the alternative of deciding whether or not to continue a pregnancy.

A dramatic example of genetic counseling involving an entire family came to light some years ago (*The New York Times*, September 30, 1975). The family began to notice a definite pattern of illness and death, but was unsure of what it meant. One member finally sought help from the National Genetics Foundation. After gathering information from as many family members as possible, geneticists were able to determine that a rare disorder was being transmitted by a dominant gene. The disease is now called Joseph's disease, after the ancestor to whom it has been traced. Joseph's disease, which is fatal, does not display itself until early adulthood. By then, many of the sufferers have had children. An unusual meeting of the eighty-five family members was held to diagnose them individually and to educate them about the risk of the disease.

Despite such benefits, there is considerable concern about the implications of our new knowledge. For example, prospective parents are put into the position of making difficult ethical choices about parenthood and medical abortions. When screening identifies the carrier of the genetic disorder already passed to a child, the carrier often suffers guilt.

Another concern is the potential misuse of information (Lappé and Morison, 1976). *Eugenics*, the attempt to improve the human species through inheritance, can be dangerous. The word "eugenics," which means well born, was coined by Francis Galton in 1883. Galton was interested in the fact that intelligence seemed to run in families. He suggested that the human species could be improved by encouraging talented people to mate (Karp, 1976). The idea was not new, but it became particularly popular in the United States during the 1920s. The result was restriction of "inferior" immigrants and compulsory sterilization laws for mentally retarded, criminal, and other "socially inadequate" individuals. Even though sterilization laws are now unconstitutional, our constantly expanding knowledge of genetics and more and more sophisticated technology open up new and perhaps dangerous possibilities. We need to apply our knowledge and skills wisely if we are to protect individuals as well as society and our species as a whole.

CHROMOSOME ABNORMALITIES

So far in this chapter we have discussed evidence for genetic influence on a variety of human behaviors or attributes. Such effects are hereditary because they involve transmission from one generation to the next. But one type of genetic effect, chromosome abnormalities, usually is *not* inherited. Chromosome aberrations fall into two categories: abnormal number and abnormal structure. Abnormalities in number probably occur during meiosis, when ova and sperm are developing, but they may also occur early in the development of the fertilized egg. In either case, the chromosome pair does not separate as it should, causing either an extra chromosome or the loss of a chromosome in cells. Abnormalities in structure involve chromosome breakage and reunion in various deviant arrangements. Radiation, chemicals, viruses, mutations, and age of parents are all implicated as possible causes of chromosome abnormalities.

In humans, chromosome aberrations account for about 50 percent of spontaneous abortions, and about 6 percent of deaths occurring around birth. Approximately .6 percent of live newborns carry chromosome defects, although not all of these infants show deficits (Alberman, 1982; Hamerton, 1982; Jagiello, 1982). Fortunately, genetic screening and counseling can help prevent and manage these and other genetic abnormalities.

Down's Syndrome

For many years, both genetic and environmental factors were suspect in Down's syndrome. The fact that concordance was almost perfect for identical twins and low for fraternal twins strongly suggested a genetic basis (Carter, 1964). In 1959 it was discovered that most cases of Down's syndrome are caused by an extra #21 chromosome and that this condition is not inherited. The risk that a woman will bear a child with Down's syndrome increases markedly with the mother's age; this is one reason why women over 35 are routinely screened by amniocentesis. Nevertheless, in about one-quarter of the cases the extra chromosome has been traced to fathers (Holmes, 1978).

Individuals with Down's syndrome show from moderate to severe retardation and are strikingly alike in physical appearance. They frequently have small skulls, chins, and ears; short, broad necks, hands, and feet; flat nasal bridges; sparse hair, a fissured tongue; and, perhaps most recognizable, a fold over the eyelid, which appears oriental to Westerners and suggested the name *Mongolism*. There is substantial risk of heart defects, intestinal malfunctioning, and leukemia (Robinson and Robinson,

FIGURE 2–17
The progress in the average child and the Down's syndrome child reared at home. The widest point of each diamond shows the average age of development for each group. The length of the diamonds shows the age range for each developmental task for each group.   From Smith and Wilson, 1973.

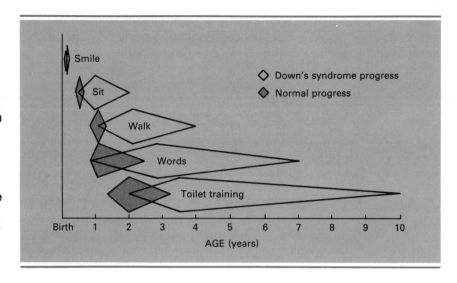

1976). Aside from the usual physical attributes and poor muscle tone, Down's syndrome babies may not at first appear mentally deficient. During the first two years, however, deficits begin to emerge. Development in many areas then lags behind that of the average child, and continues over a much longer time period (Figure 2–17).

Sex-Chromosome Abnormalities

Several known disorders involve abnormalities of the sex chromosomes.

Turner's Syndrome.   This disorder occurs only in females. Turner's syndrome girls lack normal ovarian tissue and do not develop sexually. They are short in stature and thick in body build; they often have webbed necks, prominent earlobes, and abnormalities of the elbows, knees, kidneys, and aortas. Mild levels of mental retardation may exist, but more typical are problems in space-form perception (Rovet and Netley, 1982). Map reading and making one's way in a complex spatial environment may be difficult. Turner's syndrome victims have only one instead of two X chromosomes. Treatment with female sex hormones can bring about sexual development, and adjustment can be quite satisfactory.

Klinefelter's Syndrome.   Klinefelter's syndrome is the most common sex-chromosome abnormality; it occurs in one per 500 male newborns. Most individuals suffering from this defect have an additional X chromosome (XXY). As in Down's syndrome, the mothers of Klinefelter males tend to be older than those in the general population. About 25 percent of these males exhibit below-normal intelligence and suffer from atypical sexual development: They often have small genitals, a lack of sperm, low levels of male sex hormones, and female development of the breasts. They tend to be introverted, passive, timid, lacking in self-confidence, and impaired in sexual interest (Bancroft, Axworthy, and Ratcliffe, 1982). They are also very tall. Treatment with male sex hormones can be helpful to varying degrees; it can facilitate penis enlargement, hair growth, and deep-voice development.

XYY Complement. This abnormality, which occurs in about one in 1,000 male births, has attracted enormous attention since it was first revealed in a report associating it with both mental retardation and aggressive behavior (Jacobs, Brunton, and Melville, 1965). XYY males were unusually tall and appeared with high frequency among institutionalized criminals. Follow-up data disclosed that the XYY male tended to show behavioral disorders at an early age and were less likely to have violent siblings than normal control males (Price and Whatmore, 1967). Several case studies appeared to confirm the relationship between the XYY configuration and mental deficiency and aggression. Forssman (1967), for example, described an atypically tall XYY male who had an IQ of 69 at age 16 and who had become extremely aggressive during adolescence.

What was the most intriguing was the association of the Y chromosomes and violence. Later research cast doubt on this interpretation. A study by Witkin and his colleagues (1976) of over 4,000 men in Denmark substantiated the atypical height, low intelligence scores, and high frequency of XYY men in penal institutions. The criminal XYY men had not, however, been involved in violent acts; if anything, their crimes appeared rather mild. These investigators concluded that low intelligence, not extreme aggression, could underlie the quite mild criminal behavior and lead to imprisonment. Other research with XYY boys, however, revealed no predisposition to violence and antisocial behavior, but suggested instead a depressive reaction to stress (Ratcliffe and Field, 1982).

"Fragile" X. Relatively recently attention has been called to "fragile" X chromosomes, so-called because of their tendency to break (Brown, Mezzacappa, and Jenkins, 1981). The abnormality may be the second most common cause of mental retardation, and 10 to 20 percent of retarded males may be undiagnosed for the condition. Although all levels of retardation have been found, retardation in females appears mild (Daker and Mutton, 1982). In fact, the defect is transmitted in a sex-linked pattern. With two X chromosomes, females are protected, whereas males suffer the full consequence. Males with the condition also frequently have large ears and, after puberty, oversized testicles and long faces. Treatment for the fragile X syndrome is currently being sought.

Our discussion of chromosome abnormalities makes it obvious that individual development sometimes can be dramatically affected by genetic programming. In these instances, the range of possibilities for development falls below average for at least some areas. Nevertheless, development still varies with environmental factors such as medical care, educational opportunities, and diet. If there is one critical lesson that has emerged from explorations of biological influences on human development, it is that genetic and environmental variables work hand in hand throughout the life cycle.

SUMMARY

1. The theory of evolution, proposed by Darwin in *Origin of Species* in 1859, attempted to explain the formation of new species of life and the enormous variability found in living forms on the basis of two key concepts: the struggle for existence, and the survival of the fittest.

2. All human cells except the reproductive cells contain twenty-three pairs of *chromosomes,* whose functional units are called *genes.* Due to the specialized cell-division process of *meiosis,* the ova and sperm contain only twenty-three single chromosomes, one from each of the original pairs. At fertilization each parent thus contributes half of the chromosome complement to the new organism.

3. The basic genetic material resides in the genes, in the form of deoxyribonucleic acid (DNA). DNA has the ability to replicate itself and to direct biochemical functioning and development.

4. The genes are in continuous interaction with the environment, so there is no one-to-one relationship between the gene complement (*genotype*) and the overt characteristics (*phenotype*) of the organism. A genotype may be expressed in various ways under various environmental conditions; the broadest possible expression is called the *range of reaction.*

5. Genetic effects are probably more powerful for some characteristics than for others. Characteristics strongly influenced by genes are said to be strongly *canalized* and are those critical to survival.

6. All characteristics are influenced by gene-environment interactions. An example is *phenylketonuria (PKU),* an abnormal condition that is inherited when both parents transmit the defective gene. The mental retardation that commonly results from PKU is reduced or eliminated when children are put on special diets early in life.

7. One theory of how genetic and environmental effects operate over the life span to shape development proposes three genotype-environment (G-E) relationships: passive, evocative, and active.

8. Our understanding of genetic mechanisms began with Mendel's experiments with pea plants. Mendel suggested that each parent passes on one form (*allele*) of each gene, and that some forms are *recessive* and some *dominant.* When a characteristic is determined by one gene pair, the dominant form always displays itself. The recessive form displays itself only in the absence of the dominant form.

9.   Some human characteristics are inherited from recessive, dominant, and sex-linked genes. Other characteristics, such as intelligence, are influenced by a combination of many genes (polygene inheritance).

10. Behavior genetics is the study of genetic influences on behavior. Experiments with animals using *inbreeding* and *selective breeding* demonstrate a genetic component in such characteristics as learning ability, sex drive, aggressiveness, and emotionality. The major methods used to study genetic determinants in humans are *family studies, twin studies,* and *adoption studies.*

11. Much research supports the view that there is some hereditary component in mental ability. Overall, it appears that both heredity and the environment contribute to individual differences in intelligence.

12. Some genetic research has focused on variations in social behavior. The results suggest a moderate influence from genes, some small role for environmental factors shared by family members, and a larger effect for unshared environmental factors that make children in the same family different.

13. Family, twin, and adoption studies all provide some evidence for genetic influence on schizophrenia, but there is also evidence of environmental effects. For example, although first-degree relatives of schizophrenics are at greater risk for the disorder than the population at large, the risk is not as high as would be expected on the basis of shared genes.

14. Genetic screening, prenatal diagnosis, and counseling are helpful in determining the risk of defects, in identifying carriers, and in identifying disorders. Amniocentesis, chorionic villus biopsy, and ultrasound examinations are 3 methods used for prenatal diagnosis.

15. Genetic processes are implicated in many defects and diseases. Examples of hereditary diseases are PKU and Huntington's chorea. Some disorders caused by noninherited chromosome abnormalities are Down's, Klinefelter's, Turner's, the XYY, and "fragile" X syndromes.

3 PHYSICAL AND MOTOR DEVELOPMENT

Humans have always been curious about their origins and early development. One idea popular in the late seventeenth and early eighteenth centuries was that the reproductive cells contained a completely preformed human, who simply grew larger in the uterus (Simpson, Pittendrigh, and Tiffany, 1957). We now look at such ideas with amusement, but the facts of conception and prenatal development are just as amazing.

In this chapter we turn to current knowledge about conception, prenatal development, birth, and later physical and motor growth. We focus on what usually happens, and we also look at what can happen in unusual cases.

CONCEPTION

Conception takes place when an ovum is released by an ovary and joins with a sperm in the Fallopian tube leading from the ovary. When an ovum and sperm cell unite, the sex of the new organism is immediately determined. Gametes carry twenty-three single chromosomes, including one sex chromosome. An X-chromosome sperm united with the X-chromosome ovum produces a female zygote. A Y-chromosome sperm produces a male zygote. Theoretically, there should be an equal chance of the zygote's being male or female, but in fact, more males are conceived, for the ratio of male to female births is approximately 106:100.

Sometimes a zygote divides very early and develops into identical twins. In other cases, two conceptions occur simultaneously, resulting in fraternal twins. Twin births occur in about one in every eighty-three deliveries in the United States, and two-thirds of these are fraternal pairs (Plomin, DeFries, and McClearn, 1980). The rate of twinning increases with a woman's age until the late 30s. Black women have a greater chance of having twins than white women, who in turn have a greater chance than Oriental women. There may also be some inherited tendency to produce twins. A woman who has a sister with twins or is a twin herself has a higher than average chance of bearing twin children (Scheinfeld, 1973).

Whether the developing organism is male or female, single, or even a twin, it is bound to be unique. Because the chromosome pairs sort out by chance in meiosis, there are 2^{23}, or 8,388,608, possible combinations of chromosomes for each possible ovum and sperm combination. This means that for each new zygote, billions of chromosome combinations are possible, because the particular ovum and sperm that form a zygote also unite by chance. So what you may inherit from parents or pass on to offspring depends very much on the luck of the draw.

PRENATAL DEVELOPMENT

Ovum, Embryo, Fetus

Development before birth takes place in three stages or periods: ovum, embryo, and fetus. Within a few days after conception, the fertilized ovum journeys down the Fallopian tube toward the uterus (Figure

FIGURE 3–1
Diagram of
conception and
early development.
The ovum leaves the
ovary and is
fertilized by a sperm
in the Fallopian
tube. The resulting
zygote immediately
begins to develop
and travels to the
uterus within a few
days. Adapted from
K. L. Moore, *Before We
Are Born*
(Philadelphia: W. B.
Saunders, 1974), p. 25.

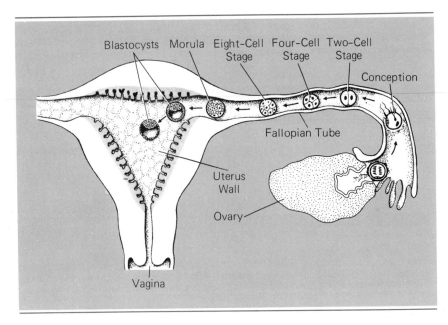

3–1). The zygote has already begun to multiply by mitosis, at first slowly and then more rapidly (Figure 3–2). A hollow ball of perhaps 100 cells burrows into the uterine wall. The inner part is destined to be a new individual and the outer layer develops into the life-support system: the chorion (outer sac), amnion (inner sac), umbilical cord, and placenta. The umbilical cord (Figure 3–3) is a lifeline: its arteries and veins serve as a transport system between the developing child and the mother. The vessels in the umbilical cord make indirect contact with the adult's system at the placenta. Nutrients, oxygen, some vitamins, drugs, hormones, and some disease-producing organisms pass to the developing child; waste materials pass in the opposite direction.

The embryonic period begins during the second week after implantation in the uterus and lasts until about the eighth week. It is a dramatic time of rapid growth in which cell and organ differentiation occur. By two months the embryo is slightly more than one inch long and roughly resembles a human being. The body appears top heavy and the head is bent over. The ears, eyes, mouth, and jaws are clearly recognizable. The limbs, beginning as broad buds, lengthen and begin to form fingers and toes. The spinal cord and other parts of the nervous system take shape. Most organs exist at least in some rudimentary form. The heart, at first disproportionately large, begins to beat.

From about the eighth week until birth, the developing organism is called the fetus. The rate of growth reaches its peak during the early fetal period and then declines. Development involves further growth of existing structures, changes in body proportion, and refinement in functions. Only a few parts make their first appearance—the hair, nails, and external sex organs. Bones harden, and the lower body region grows so that the head is no longer quite so dominant (Figure 3–4).

The beginning of the fetal period is when the prospective mother becomes especially aware of the developing child (Rugh and Shettles, 1971). Spontaneous movement can be felt at about sixteen weeks. Some fetuses are quiet; others kick and squirm a great deal. The arms bend at the wrist and elbow; the hands can form a fist; the fetus can frown, squint, and open its mouth. Reaction to stimulation is global at first but soon becomes specific. For example, if the eyelids are touched at the end of the third month, squinting occurs instead of a previous jerking of the entire body. Many *reflexes*, which are automatic and unlearned responses to specific stimuli, appear: swallowing, coughing, and sucking.

Changes during the last trimester prepare the fetus for living independently. For example, respiration movements are practiced even though oxygen is being provided through the placenta. Vital functions for swallowing, urinating, and moving the gastrointestinal tract become refined. Weight gain is noticeable. A fetus born after about twenty-six weeks stands a good chance of survival, although a full term of thirty-eight weeks is normal and optimal.

Few of us believe today that an evil eye cast upon a pregnant woman brings a deformed child, or that the amount of reading a mother does during pregnancy influences intelligence. Nevertheless, the mother's

FIGURE 3–2
Photographs of the fertilized ovum and early multiplication into two, eight, and several cells. The first multiplication takes about thirty-six hours, but then the rate quickens. From L. Nilsson, *A Child Is Born* (New York: Delacorte Press, 1974).

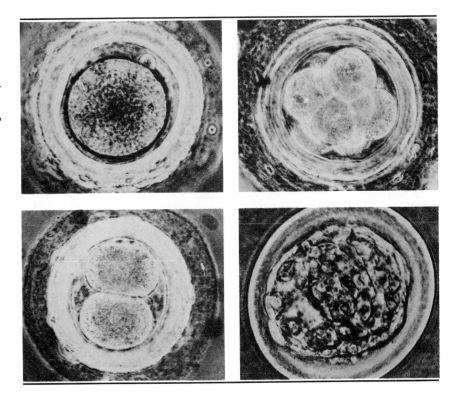

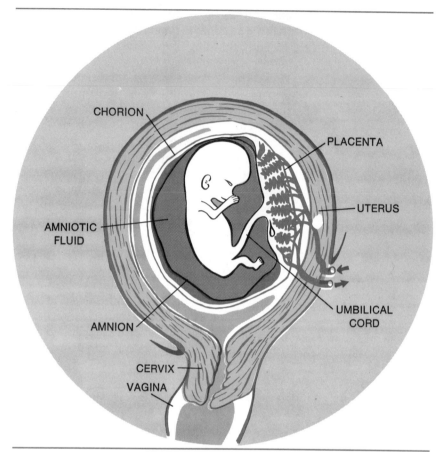

FIGURE 3–3
The developing child floats freely within the amnion, except for where it is attached to the placenta by the umbilical cord. From W. A. Kennedy, *Child Psychology*, 2nd ed. (Englewood Cliffs, N.J.: Prentice-Hall, Inc., 1975). © 1975, p. 49. Reprinted by permission of Prentice-Hall, Inc.

CHORION

PLACENTA

UTERUS

AMNIOTIC
FLUID

UMBILICAL
CORD

AMNION

CERVIX

VAGINA

body, through its interaction with the fetus by way of the placenta, provides the entire fetal environment. This fact has two implications for prenatal care. First, adequate diet, rest, exercise, and medical checkups are important. Second, efforts should be made to avoid agents or circumstances that could cause abnormal or less than optimal development for the child.

The study of malformations and other deviations from normal prenatal development is called *teratology*. A basic principle of prenatal growth is that structures emerge in a fixed order, and that rapid differentiation and growth occur during the so-called *critical period*. The embryonic period and the beginning of the fetal period are critical for most body systems, and exposure to teratogens during these weeks can cause major structural damage. As Figure 3–5 shows, the critical time is somewhat different for the different body parts. Still, the amount of exposure affects the outcome, and individuals probably vary in susceptibility to certain teratogens.

We now know about many possible influences on the developing

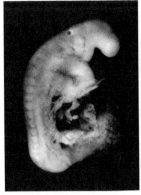

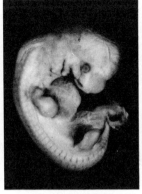

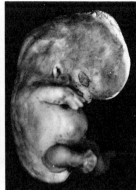

Three and one-half
weeks

Five and one-half
weeks

Seven
weeks

FIGURE 3–4
Prenatal
development during
the first three months
after conception.
Courtesy of Carnegie
Laboratories of
Embryology, University
of California, Davis.

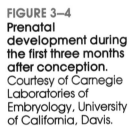

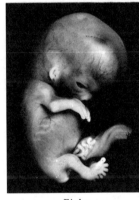

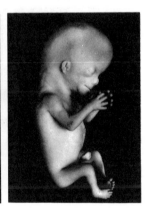

Eight
weeks

Twelve
weeks

child. But we cannot usually trace a specific abnormality to a specific teratogen—there are just too many variables.

Some General Risk Factors

Maternal Age. Women over 35 and under 18 years of age have a higher risk for infant defect, prematurity, and infant death (Jensen, Benson, and Bobak, 1981; Vital and Health Statistics, 1972). In older women the ova, which have been present in an immature state from birth, may have been affected by aging or exposure to chemicals, drugs, and other harmful agents. In young women the reproductive system may not be fully developed. Pregnant teenagers may also have generally poor prenatal care.

Maternal Nutrition. Because the mother is the sole source of nutrition for the unborn child, a diet providing the proper balance of proteins, fats, carbohydrates, minerals, and vitamins is vital. Many correlational studies of humans indicate a relationship between maternal diet deficiencies and prematurity, low birthweight, stillbirth, growth retardation, and

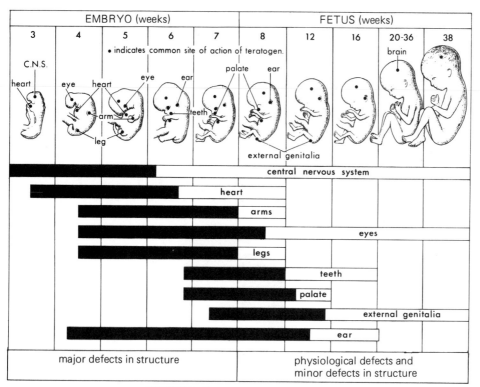

EMBRYO (weeks)					FETUS (weeks)				
3	4	5	6	7	8	12	16	20-36	38

• indicates common site of action of teratogen.

FIGURE 3–5

The early months of prenatal development are critical, although the period of maximal sensitivity varies somewhat for the different body parts. The black shaded areas indicate maximal sensitivity; the white areas indicate less sensitivity. Adapted from K. L. Moore, *Before We Are Born* (Philadelphia: W. B. Saunders, 1974), p. 96.

poor mental functioning (Knobloch and Pasamanick, 1974). Diet deficiencies during the first trimester of pregnancy are especially harmful, but deficiencies during the last trimester may also be important because of rapid brain growth during that time (Lester, 1975). Animal studies show that inadequate maternal diet may actually result in fewer nerve cells (Dickerson, 1981). Despite these findings, we still have much to learn about the effects of maternal nutrition. Poor nutrition may simply not meet the diet needs of the fetus; it may also act indirectly by increasing the mother's vulnerability to pregnancy complications and disease.

Maternal stress. The effects of maternal stress are even less understood than the effects of maternal nutrition. Much of the research on stress involves animals; in general, anxiety and stress in pregnant animals can alter offspring behavior, such as increasing emotionality (Thompson and Grusec, 1970). It seems reasonable that maternal emotions could influence the growing child. The emotions act through the autonomic nervous system that activates the endocrine glands, which, in turn, regulate the secretion of hormones such as adrenalin. Because hormones can pass through the placenta, they may affect the fetus. An early study by Sontag (1944) showed that babies who were active *in utero*, presumably as the result of maternal stress, later had high levels of crying, squirming, diarrhea, and eating problems. Other investigations demonstrated a relationship between maternal anxiety and infant fussiness, vomiting, crying, and sensitivity to sound (Copans, 1974). In a more recent study, motor depression in newborns was associated with anxiety rated in prospective mothers during the last month of pregnancy, but also with the use of medication during childbirth (Standley, Soule, and Copans, 1979). So there is no way to know if the infants were affected by anxiety, by medication, or by both. The most that can be said is that maternal stress may affect fetuses (Stechler and Halton, 1982). In general, we do not expect serious effects from mild stress, but risk may increase with severe, prolonged stress.

Rh Incompatibility.   The Rh factor, named after the rhesus monkey in which it was first discovered, is an inherited protein found in the blood of 85 percent of the general population. Difficulty arises only when the father carries the factor (Rh positive), the mother does not (Rh negative), and the child develops as Rh positive. If the offspring's blood comes into contact with the mother's, the mother's system may manufacture antibodies to ward off the foreign Rh protein. The antibodies destroy the child's oxygen-carrying red blood cells, a condition known as *erythroblastosis* and death or mental retardation can occur.

These effects do not usually show up during the first pregnancy because the Rh factor cannot cross the placenta. However, the mother may receive the Rh factor when the placenta separates at birth, and she may then begin to manufacture antibodies. Should she become pregnant again, the antibodies, which can cross the placenta, are available to damage the fetus. This process can be prevented by administering a substance that deters antibody formation, rhoGAM, to the mother at the birth of her first child.

Some Specific
Risks

Maternal Diseases.   Table 3–1 lists some maternal diseases implicated in fetal defect and death and their possible effects. Rubella (German measles) and cytomegalovirus disease are among the most potentially dangerous of the infectious diseases.

In 1942 Australian physicians noted that women who contracted Rubella early in pregnancy had a high incidence of defective babies. If it crosses the placenta, the Rubella virus can result in miscarriage; stillbirth; prematurity; deafness; blindness; heart, liver, and pancreas defects; and mental retardation. Estimates of defect caused during the first month of pregnancy are as high as 50 percent, but exposure during the last two trimesters is not considered harmful. Women can thus be most dangerously exposed before they realize they are pregnant. During the 1964

| TABLE 3–1 |
| Maternal Diseases That Can Cause Prenatal Damage |

Anemia (iron deficiency)	Death; brain impairment
Cytomegalovirus	Death; stillbirth; mental retardation; liver, spleen, and blood disorders; microcephaly
Diabetes mellitus	Death; stillbirth; respiratory difficulties; metabolic disturbances
Influenza A	Malformations
Mumps	Death; malformations; heart disease
Pneumonia	Early death
Rubella	Death; prematurity; deafness; blindness; heart, liver, pancreas defects; mental retardation
Scarlet fever	Early death
Syphilis	Death; blindness; deafness; mental retardation
Toxoplasmosis	Mental retardation; heart defects; brain defects; death
Tuberculosis	Death; lowered resistance to tuberculosis

worldwide epidemic of Rubella, an estimated 20,000 to 30,000 defective babies were born in the United States (Chess, 1974). Fortunately, pregnant women who have already had Rubella or taken the vaccine are unlikely to contract the disease.

The strain of virus causing cytomegalovirus disease (CMV) is widespread in human adults, especially among those in the lower social classes (Jensen, Benson, and Bobak, 1981). Transmitted by way of the respiratory and reproductive systems, the virus rarely causes any symptoms in adults. However, it can result in miscarriages and stillbirths, as well as undersized and damaged neonates. The infants commonly suffer from nervous system abnormalities such as *microcephaly* (an excessively small head), oversized livers and spleens, anemia, and other blood abnormalities. No prevention or treatment exists for CMV.

A noninfectious maternal disease that can be extremely hazardous is diabetes mellitus. Along with the possibility of inheriting diabetes, the unborn child is subjected to a generally unhealthy uterine environment. If the mother is not treated, the probability of fetal death and stillbirth is 50 percent. And many of the surviving babies show some abnormalities: enlarged pancreases, excessive weight, a puffy appearance, respiratory difficulty, and metabolic disorders such as low blood sugar. With medical care, risk is greatly reduced (Moore, 1983).

Drugs, Chemicals, and Hormones.   The best policy for the prospective mother is to avoid all drugs unless they are professionally recommended and monitored. In a culture as drug dependent as ours, however, this is not always easy. Table 3–2 gives a general summary of the possible effects of some drugs and chemicals. We look here at some specific cases.

One particularly tragic example involved the drug *thalidomide*, a chemical that was synthesized in 1953 and at first appeared to be a harmless sleep-inducing agent. Late in 1959, however, reports describing the malformed infants of mothers who had taken thalidomide during pregnancy began to mount, especially in Germany (Jensen, Benson, and Bobak, 1981). In many cases, the drug caused the stunting or complete absence of the arms, legs, and fingers. Abnormalities of the internal organs also occurred.

Although having an occasional drink may not cause damage, greater consumption of alcohol is known to harm the developing embryo and fetus (Abel, 1980; Stechler and Halton, 1982). Maternal consumption of three or more drinks per day during pregnancy is associated with a distinct pattern of malformation called *fetal alcohol syndrome*. The children show permanent growth retardation; microcephaly and brain-cell abnormalities; eye, ear, and other facial disfigurations; joint and limb abnormalities; heart defects; mental retardation; and attentional deficits (Figure 3–6). Even smaller daily consumption of alcohol by pregnant women may result in poor attention and reaction time in their children at preschool age (Streissguth et al., 1984).

The potential damage of cigarette smoking during pregnancy had been suspected for several years before a large-scale study by Simpson in 1957 found that smokers had a high risk of delivering prematurely (Ferreira, 1969). Many later studies confirmed that smoking is associated with prematurity and low birthweight, possibly due to the effects of nicotine and the by-products of carbon monoxide. Whether these children suffer later growth and cognitive deficiencies is debated (Lefkowitz, 1981; Streissguth et al., 1984).

Maternal use of narcotics is associated with prematurity, low birthweight, and fetal death. Many children of addicted mothers are addicted themselves, and they show withdrawal symptoms within one to three days after birth. They may display irritability, shrill crying, tremors, inability to sleep, hyperactivity, respiratory problems, huge appetites, diarrhea, and vomiting (Householder et. al, 1982). These disturbances may last for two to three months. Long-term effects are not well established, but there is some evidence of hyperactivity and poor attention span.

Miller (1974) noted two striking examples of general environmental conditions in Japan that adversely affected infants through maternal ex-

---

TABLE 3–2
Possible Prenatal Effects of Some Drugs and Chemicals

Alcohol	Growth retardation; microcephaly; disfigurations; cardiac anomalies; behavioral and cognitive deficits
Antihistamines	Fetal death; malformations, especially of the limbs
Aspirin (in excess)	Bleeding in the newborn; possible circulatory anomalies
Barbituates	Depressed breathing; drowsiness during the first week of life
Heroin, morphine	Convulsions; tremors; death; withdrawal symptoms
Lead	Anemia; hemorrhage; miscarriage
Quinine	Deafness
Thalidomide	Malformations, especially of the limbs
Tobacco	Low birthweight; prematurity; high heart rate; convulsions

FIGURE 3–6
This child and her deceased mother were diagnosed as suffering from fetal alcohol syndrome. Several typical features are evident: narrow eye openings, a thin upper lip, and possible drooping of the upper eyelids. Courtesy of March of Dimes Birth Defects Foundation.

posure. In one case, congenital cerebral palsy was associated with expectant mothers who had eaten fish contaminated with methyl mercury from industrial wastes. In the other, the birth of undersized infants exhibiting skin discolorations was attributed to maternal intake of cooking oil that had been contaminated with biphenyls (PCBs). In the United States pregnant women's consumption of Lake Michigan fish contaminated with PCB was also associated with later poor motor functioning and depressed responsiveness in their infants (Jacobson, Jacobson, Fein, Schwartz, and Dowler, 1984).

Diethylstilbestrol (DES) is a synthetic female hormone that was given to pregnant women in the 1950s and 1960s to prevent miscarriages. Tragedy came to light years later when abnormalities and cancer of the reproductive organs were found in daughters of the treated women, now young women themselves. Abnormalities of the sex organs and sperm have been discovered in sons of these women as well (Jensen, Benson, and Bobak, 1981).

Radiation. Radiation may be responsible for leukemia, microcephaly, cataracts, stunted growth, miscarriages, and stillbirths (Rugh and Shettles, 1971). Today, x-rays are seldom taken during pregnancy except in emergencies.

Paternal Influences.   There is evidence that birth defects may be higher than usual for the children of males who are exposed to certain substances before their offspring are conceived.

Most of the research to date has been done with animals. The first demonstration involved the administration of thalidomide to male rabbits. During the past fifteen years, administering lead, narcotics, alcohol, caffeine, and methadone to male animals has produced offspring with birth defects. Joffe and Soyka (cited in Kolata, 1978) gave methadone to male rats. The litters produced by mating these males were smaller than average; they were also more likely to die before weaning, have low birthweights, and perform abnormally on a behavioral test. As evidence of the effects in humans, Kolata cited a study of males who, as operating-room personnel, were exposed to anesthetic gases. Wives of these men had significantly higher rates of miscarriages and their offspring were more likely to be born with defects.

How can these effects be explained? Joffe and Soyka offer a few possibilities. The sperm cells might be damaged, perhaps during maturation, or the detrimental substances might act through the semen. Some substances (e.g., thalidomide and narcotics) are in fact excreted in the semen and enter the female circulation through the vaginal walls. During pregnancy they might contaminate the fetus through the placenta.

From our discussion of risk factors it might appear as if the developing child has little chance of escaping harm. But most babies are born in good health. Nevertheless, care and cautiousness on the part of pregnant women can help optimize prenatal development and even prevent tragedy.

BIRTH

Biological preparation for birth begins with *lightening*. The head of the fetus turns down so that birth occurs with the head first. The fetus's movement into this position relieves ("lightens") the pressure against the mother's diaphragm so that she can breathe more freely. *Labor*, the process by which the fetus is expelled from its mother's uterus, occurs within a few hours to a few weeks after lightening. Labor is divided into three stages (Figure 3–7). In stage one the cervix of the uterus dilates and frequently the amnion ruptures, allowing the escape of fluids. The first stage generally takes from seven to twelve hours, but varies greatly among individual women. The fetus emerges during the second stage, which usually lasts from one-half to two hours. Stage three involves the expulsion of the placental membranes, the *afterbirth*. The average length of labor in the United States is fourteen hours for the first child, and less for subsequent births.

In the United States, many couples now seek to make childbirth more "natural" (Jensen, Benson, and Bobak, 1981). They believe that parents should have greater control over the birth experience than traditional hospitals permit. They prefer greater participation by the father and other family members, avoidance of what they consider unnecessary

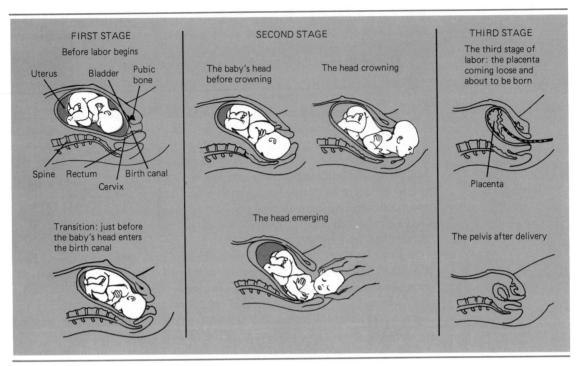

FIGURE 3–7
The three stages of childbirth.

medical procedures, and minimization of anesthesia (Figure 3–8). Many enroll in Lamaze programs, which emphasize relaxation and breathing techniques for the women and encourage the men to help throughout labor and delivery (Lamaze, 1970). Also popular with these couples are birth centers, which are clinics staffed by medical personnel committed to natural childbirth, and birthing rooms, which are homelike hospital rooms where couples participate fully in decisions but receive some medical assistance. Home delivery has grown in popularity; this often involves a midwife or nurse practitioner who consults with a physician. Some professionals fear that inadequate medical service in these settings might endanger infants and mothers. Such settings can be dangerous when the mother has health problems and a history of birthing difficulties, particularly when full medical services cannot be easily reached in emergencies. Otherwise, alternative settings for childbirth appear safe and seem to provide great satisfaction to most couples who select them.

Birth Complications

Birth is not usually a complicated business; in fact, it generally proceeds according to expectation. Among the difficulties that can arise is the abnormal positioning of the infant. The normal fetal position for birth is head first, face down. If the buttocks emerge first, the full breech position, or the fetus is in a face-up position, delivery is more difficult and

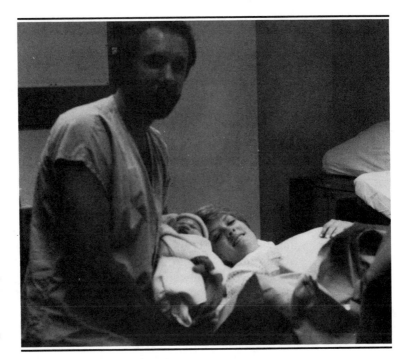

FIGURE 3–8
Many of today's
fathers are
participating in
childbirth. This father
shared in the birth of
both his son and his
daughter. Courtesy
S. and C. Weidemann
and R. Molla.

dangerous. Surgical instruments are used more cautiously now than in the past, because they can cause brain damage when they are applied to the baby's head. For a variety of reasons (e.g., the fetus is too large for the mother or the fetus must be delivered early to ward off the threat of disease), fetuses are sometimes delivered by *Caesarean section*, a surgical opening of the uterus and abdominal walls.

Anoxia, or lack of oxygen, may occur at birth if the umbilical cord fails in any way to provide oxygen until the newborn begins to use its lungs. This may happen if the cord is damaged, knotted, squeezed shut, or detached too soon, or if the respiratory system does not react properly. The nervous system is especially sensitive to oxygen loss, and severe anoxia may result in retardation and cerebral palsy.

The purpose of medication during childbirth is to reduce the mother's pain and stress. Many of the drugs reach the child through the placenta. Short-term effects from these drugs have been shown on sucking, nursing, visual attentiveness, motor performance, and sleep (Aleksandrowicz and Aleksandrowicz, 1974; Brazelton, 1970; Stechler and Halton, 1982; Yang, Zweig, Douthitt, and Federman, 1976). The effects vary with the specific drug, the dosage, and the point during delivery when it is administered.

The evidence for long-term effects is not clear. A report by Brackbill and Broman (Kolata, 1978), on data for 3,500 children who were healthy and had experienced uncomplicated in utero development and births showed that medication was related to their behavior through at least the first seven years of life. Babies of highly medicated mothers lagged in sitting, standing, moving about, and in the capacity to inhibit crying and reactions to distracting stimuli.

But it is also possible that women who take medication are different from those who do not. Yang and his colleagues (1976) found that the number of drugs received by women during delivery was correlated positively with irritability, tension, depression, and fears for themselves during pregnancy. If such behaviors are at all enduring, they might affect children's later development through mother-child interaction.

Prematurity and Low Birthweight

The length of pregnancy is forty weeks because gestation is calculated from the last menstrual period, about two weeks prior to conception. Infants may be born before or after the usual term. When born before thirty-eight weeks the neonate is *preterm* or *premature;* when born forty-two or more weeks into gestation, it is *postterm.* When infants are in the tenth percentile of weight for their gestational age they are labeled *small-for-dates.* When they are in the ninetieth percentile they are labeled *large-for-dates.* Such infants are considered to be at risk during or after the birth process. Birth can be hazardous for oversized babies, especially when they are born in an unusual position that makes them vulnerable to tears, broken bones, lack of oxygen, and nervous system damage.

Premature and small babies have a higher risk of death than normal-term infants, and risk increases with the degree of prematurity and smallness. Low birthweight babies are vulnerable to numerous physical defects and impairments such as visual problems, hearing deficits, muscle spasms, and abnormal brain waves (DeHirsch, Jansky, and Langford, 1966). Premature babies do less well than full-term infants on measures of visual behavior, language development, and general development (Crnic, Razogin, Greenberg, Robinson, and Bashan, 1983; Rose, 1983). There is some evidence, too, for long-term effects. For example, a Johns Hopkins study followed small preterm infants until they were 12 to 13 years of age; the children showed deficits in intellectual and perceptual-motor functioning as they developed (Weiner, 1968). A relationship has also been established between poor social adjustment and low birthweight (Caputo and Mandell, 1970). Child-parent interaction shows early disturbance, and such infants are also more likely to be abused later in life.

Despite these findings, however, there is much variation in the developmental level eventually reached by low birthweight infants and those who experience other birth complications. Longitudinal investigations of thousands of these children indicate that eventually only a small proportion of them are different from full-term children (Kopp and Krakow, 1983). So the important question is: What determines the eventual outcome?

One factor is the extent of the birth and pregnancy complications. Nervous-system damage, physical handicaps, and illness appear related to poor outcome (Holmes et al., 1982). Knobloch and Pasamanick (1972)

Parents and At-Risk Infants

The parent-child relationship is one important aspect of the quality of infant care. In normal circumstances parents hold their newborn infants, touch them a great deal, try to make eye contact, and talk to them. These behaviors help parents feel emotionally attached to their infants. In fact, some developmentalists believe that such early interaction is necessary for the formation of emotional attachments (Klaus and Kennell, 1978). According to this line of reasoning, any interference with the establishment of the very early emotional bond may lead to damage.

Today, vastly improved medical care for premature or small-for-dates infants may be causing just such interference. When difficulties are suspected prior to birth, infants may be monitored in various ways. At birth they are placed in environmentally controlled incubators (Figure 3–9). The incubators may contain moving water beds and rhythmic sounds, because these are soothing to newborns (Burns, Deddish, Burns, and Hatcher, 1983).

The medical benefit of these procedures is beyond question: the death rate is drastically reduced, and even infants weighing under two pounds are surviving under highly specialized care (Liederman, 1983). But these newborns are also deprived of normal human contact and sensory stimulation. Is such deprivation an important cause of poor developmental outcome in low birthweight or premature infants?

Attempts have been made to answer this question by providing at-risk infants with environments that are rich in stimulation and human contact. In one case, preterm infants who received special hospital care were compared to preterm babies who in addition to special care were rocked by, handled by, and talked to by their mothers and nurses (Scarr-Salapatek and Williams, 1973). When the infants went home, the mothers were trained to interact with them to foster development. These babies gained more weight and obtained higher scores on a test of infant

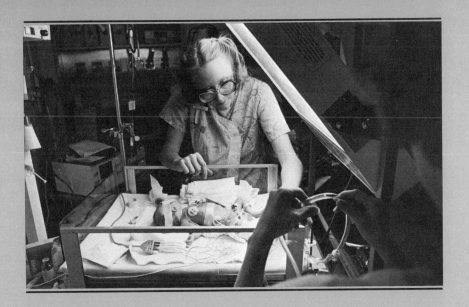

FIGURE 3–9
Premature infants receive extraordinary care. Will McIntyre, Photo Researchers.

development than infants who had received the special hospital treatment.

In general, such efforts have some positive results. Babies' motor development can benefit, and mothers who handle their infants seem to feel closer to their babies and more self-confident. But these effects wear off, sometimes do not occur at all, and sometimes occur without interventions. So although early intervention may be helpful in some cases, the first hours or days of life are not critical in the formation of a healthy parent-child relationship.

Research is beginning to tell us more about parents' involvement with their low birthweight or premature infants. Adults generally respond negatively to the physical appearance of the small, preterm baby and are less sympathetic to its cries (Frodi, Lamb, Leavitt, and Donovan, 1981). Perhaps parents must overcome similar, unfavorable reactions. To add to this, the infants require much care but are less active, alert, and responsive than full-term babies, so that the usual rewards of parenting are diminished (Crnic et al., 1983). Parents, in turn, seem less actively involved at first, but within a few months become overstimulating and obtrusive (Field, 1980). Obtrusiveness may serve an appropriate purpose (e.g., to increase food intake), but it is not always beneficial. Finally, parental expectations that the child will have problems can be a self-fulfilling prophecy. And unrealistic expectations for rapid development can result in disappointment and stress (Stern and Hildebrandt, 1984). All these factors may operate in any family caring for an at-risk infant. They are more likely to be overwhelming in families that suffer from economic strain, inadequate parenting skills, and lack of social support.

recognize what they call the *continuum of reproductive casualty*. These researchers studied children whose disorders ranged from cerebral palsy, epilepsy, and mental retardation to hyperactivity, learning disabilities, and mild behavioral disorders. They point out that more birth and pregnancy complications were involved in the more severe disorders.

Children from poor socioeconomic environments have less chance to overcome complications than those from middle-class environments. A striking example of the interplay of birth factors and environment emerged from a longitudinal investigation of 1,000 children living on the island of Kauai, Hawaii (Werner, 1980). These children were studied from the beginning of pregnancy to 18 years of age. Observations of sixty variables were recorded during pregnancy, birth, and the early period of life. Records were also kept of any problems the children displayed. In addition, information was obtained about the environments in which the children were reared, including economic status, parental intelligence, and family stability.

No association was found at birth between birth complications and social class, perhaps because all the mothers had received good medical care. (Other studies *do* show this relationship.) However, follow-up studies when the children were 2, 10, and 18 years old showed an effect of social class. A relationship between birth complications and developmental outcome became obvious, and it was due primarily to poor environments. For example, at 2 years of age the most developmentally retarded children (physically, intellectually, and socially) had experienced both the most severe birth complications *and* the poorest environments. Children growing up in middle-class homes who had suffered the most severe birth complications were almost comparable in intelligence to children with *no* birth complications who lived in low social-class homes. Except for a small group of children with moderate or severe complications, the influence of social-class factors was stronger than the effects of birth complications (Werner, 1980).

Recognizing the strong impact of the environment, Sameroff and Chandler (1975) note that a *continuum of caretaking casualty* influences the eventual results of birth and pregnancy complications more than biological factors. This refers to the range of the quality of care infants receive, which is related to economic strain, medical attention, parenting skills, and social support systems.

THE NEWBORN

At birth the newborn child is approximately twenty inches long and weighs about seven and one-half pounds. Its skin is smooth; it has a relatively large head, flat nose, high forehead, and receding jaws. These standard features soon give away to more individual characteristics.

It is often said that newborns are not very interesting; they seem to do little but eat, sleep, and cry. To some degree this is certainly true. However, the more we are able to evaluate newborns, the more we appreciate how much is actually happening. One researcher put it in these words:

> I am impressed by the great repertoire of newborns, but you must give them the chance to show it. If you put a newborn baby in a supine position in its cot and cover it with a blanket up to its neck, of course it gives the impression of being a kind of vegetable which just cries and sucks from time to time and that's all. But if, for example, you watch a baby on the skin of its mother, without clothes but at a warm temperature, it shows a lot of things. . . . (Prechtl, cited in Stone, Smith, and Murphy, 1973, p. 240)

What, in fact, can the neonate do? And how do we find out?

One of the most useful and popular measures of the condition of the infant at birth is the Apgar instrument, devised by Virginia Apgar in 1953. The measure is simply a rating of heart rate, respiration, reflex irritability, muscle tone, and color that is made one minute after birth (and sometimes repeated three, five, and ten minutes later). Each of the five dimensions is scored as 0, 1, or 2, with the larger numbers indicating the more superior condition. Table 3–3 illustrates this measuring system. The Apgar rating is particularly helpful in alerting medical staff to life-threatening conditions at birth. The Brazelton Neonatal Behavioral Assessment Scale is widely used to evaluate a variety of behaviors and abilities (Brazelton, 1973). Twenty-six items tap motor skill, response to stimuli such

TABLE 3–3
The Apgar Scoring Method

Dimension	Score		
	0	1	2
Heart rate	Absent	Slow, below 100 beats per minute	100–140 beats per minute
Respiration	Absent	Slow, irregular	Good, accompanied by crying
Reflex irritability	Absent	Grimace or cry	Cough, sneeze, vigorous cry
Muscle tone	Limpness	Some flexion	Active motion
Color	Pale or blue	Pinkish body, blue extremities	Pinkish

Source: Adapted from "Proposal for a New Method of Evaluating the Newborn Infant" by V. Apgar, *Anesthesia and Analgesia*, 1953, 32, 260–267.

as noise and a pin prick, general alertness and cuddliness. This scale discriminates neonates from different cultures as well as those born prematurely, drug addicted, and developmentally disabled (Lester and Brazelton, 1980).

Reflexive Motor
Behavior

Newborns cannot support their heads, voluntarily grasp objects, or hold up their feet. However, neonatal behavior is rich in reflexes: close to 100 have been described at one time or another. (See Table 3–4 and Figure 3–10.)

Some reflexes are directly related to vital functions: breathing, blink-

TABLE 3–4
Some Neonatal Reflexes

Babinski	Stroking the sole of the foot results in the spreading out of the toes and the upward extension of the big toe.
Babkin	Pressing the neonate's palm causes the mouth to open, the head to turn sideward, and the eyes to close.
Galant	Stroking the neonate's back along the spine results in the trunk's arching toward the side.
Moro	Withdrawing physical support (dropping, allowing the head to drop, changing position) or presenting a sharp noise results in the arms's extending outward and returning to midline.
Palmar grasp	Touching the palm causes the fingers to grasp the object.
Placing	Stroking the top of the foot with an edge, such as a table edge, results in raising the foot and placing it on the edge.
Plantar grasp	Touching the balls of the foot results in inward flexion of the toes.
Rooting	Stroking the cheek or corner of the mouth causes the head to turn toward the object and to move in a way that looks as if the neonate is searching for something to suck.
Stepping	Holding the infant upright with the feet touching a surface results in stepping movements.
Sucking	Placing an object in the mouth results in sucking.

Moro reflex

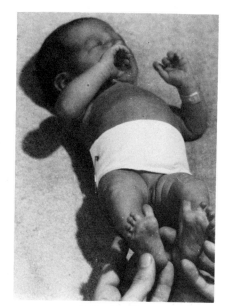

Babinski reflex

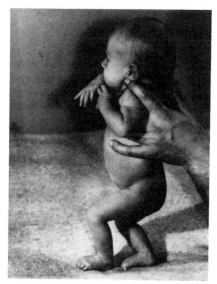

Stepping reflex

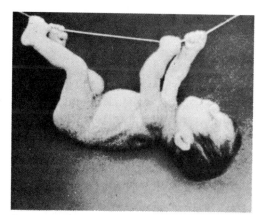

Grasping reflex

FIGURE 3–10
Four reflexes present at birth. Photos from Prechtl (1977) except lower right from Peiper (1967).

ing, sneezing, sucking, swallowing, and rooting. Postural reflexes help maintain the orientation of the body in space (Capute, Accardo, Vining, Rubenstein, and Harryman, 1978). Primitive reflexes such as the Moro, Babinski, and grasp reflexes seem to have little purpose, although researchers speculate that they may be leftovers of evolution.

A good number of the neonatal reflexes persist into adulthood, but many of the postural and primitive reflexes seem to disappear during the first year of life. Their appearance, strength, and disappearance at specific times are taken as signs of nervous system functioning.

Sensory and Learning Capacity

In order to behave at all, the neonate must be able to sense the environment. It has been difficult to discover the quality of early sensory abilities because neonates obviously cannot tell us about their experiences. However, newer research methods confirm that all the basic senses are operating at some level at birth. The world outside the uterus is immediately seen, heard, smelled, tasted, and felt. And soon after birth infants show some capacity to *learn*—that is, to change due to experience. Within a few months their behavioral repertoire increases remarkably in size and complexity. (In Chapter 4 we look at these early sensory and learning processes in detail.)

States of Consciousness

Neonatal behavior has been classified according to levels of consciousness; they include sleep states, drowsiness, alert activity, waking activity and crying (Brazelton, 1973). Such states of consciousness, which are described in Table 3–5, depend heavily on biological variables such as hunger and the sleep-awake cycle. The amount of time spent in each state varies with individuals and changes with age.

One of the most obvious characteristics of newborns is that they sleep a great deal but for relatively short periods of time. This gradually changes: for example, newborns sleep for about seventeen hours a day, but 3- to 5-year-olds sleep about eleven hours a day. (Amount of daily sleep continues to decline throughout the life span.) Periods of sleep become fewer and longer, with the longest period at night, much to everyone's delight. From birth to 3 to 5 years of age the proportion of REM (rapid-eye-movement) sleep to nonREM sleep decreases from about 50 percent to 20 percent, which is the proportion found in adults (Anders, Carskadon and Dement, 1980). In REM sleep in adults, brainwaves register fast activity, the eyes move rapidly, heart and lung function in-

---

TABLE 3–5
Levels of Consciousness in Infancy

Deep sleep	Eyes closed, no body movement except occasional startles, even breathing
Light sleep (REM)	Eyes closed but rapid eye movements evident, random body and facial movements, irregular breathing
Drowsiness	Eyes open or closed but when open they are glazed, variable activity, breathing irregular
Quiet alert	Eyes open and brightly fixating external stimuli, little movement, breathing somewhat variable
Active alert	Eyes open, very active motor movements with some fussiness, irregular breathing
Crying	Crying with eyes open or closed, motor activity, irregular breathing, little attention to external environment

Adapted from Brazelton, 1973.

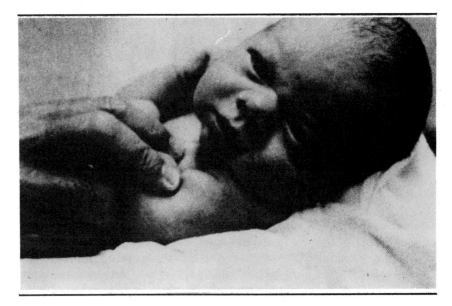

FIGURE 3–11
A newborn in the alert, inactive state. This infant appears to be focusing intently on a source of stimulation. From T. B. Brazelton, *Neonatal Behavioral Assessment Scale* (London: SIMP/Heinemann Medical; Philadelphia: Lippincott, 1973).

creases, and dreaming occurs. Although the function of REM sleep is not well understood, lack of REM sleep has been associated with behavioral disturbances ranging from irritability to hallucinations.

As the amount of sleep decreases in young babies, alertness and wakefulness increase. The alert inactive state has been singled out as especially important in the development of attention. It is then that infants appear deliberately to inspect the environment, thereby taking in information about the world (Figure 3–11). Alertness and activity increasingly become tied to the social environment.

Individual Differences

At first glance one newborn may seem just like the next, but in fact neonates show individuality from the moment of birth. In one study babies between 2 to 5 days were presented with a soft tone, a loud tone, a cold disk applied to the thigh, and a pacifier (Birns, 1965). The infants were tested four times, and the intensity of their reactions was observed. Some of the babies tended to react vigorously to all the stimuli; others responded quite consistently in a mild way.

In another investigation, six infants were observed on a daily basis during the first week of life, about an hour after feeding (Brown, 1964). They showed considerable individuality and consistency in their behavior. One child, Dorothy, slept quite a bit (37 percent of the time), cried a lot (39 percent), and was rarely alert (4 percent). She hardly reacted to the stimulation used by the experimenter to test sensitivity. Ted slept a great deal (56 percent of the time) and cried very little (17 percent). Most of his activity seemed directed at decreasing tension and returning to sleep. Charles was alert, quiet, and receptive (37 percent of the time). He slept a good deal, but was able to remain quietly awake for long periods of time.

Although we do not usually think of newborns as having "person-ality" or displaying much social behavior, these studies indicate that very early in life babies show individual differences that do indeed give them "personality." Such differences, sometimes called temperamental differences, were examined in a landmark study by Thomas, Chess, and Birch (1970). These investigators defined *temperament* as sensitivity to stimuli, extent of motor activity, response to new objects, and the like. They followed the development of 141 children for over a decade by interviewing the parents periodically—every three months during the first year, every six months during years 1 to 5, and annually after age 5. The interviews were structured so that parental statements, such as that their baby "couldn't stand" a new food, had to be restated by the parent in terms of specific descriptions. In addition, some home observations were conducted by individuals unfamiliar with the child's behavioral history. The researchers concluded that children show distinct individuality in temperament in the first weeks of life. Many of the children could be classified as "easy," "difficult," or "slow-to-warm-up" based on general mood, intensity of reactions, and adaptability to new situations (Chess and Thomas, 1977). For some children, temperamental style persisted over several years. However, the researchers did not suggest that temperament is fixed; instead, they described how it is strengthened or transformed by interactions with the environment.

POSTNATAL GROWTH

Physical growth and change have been a constant research topic for developmentalists. Does growth follow any particular pattern? How does growth differ in males and females? What causes adolescents to "shoot up" in height? In addition to answers to these questions, developmentalists are also interested in understanding how these physical developments influence the psychological characteristics of individuals.

Patterns of Growth

Physical growth in humans follows standard, orderly patterns. It proceeds in two directions: from the top down, and from the center outward As Figure 3–12 shows, the young child is top heavy, and not until adolescence do the proportions of adulthood appear. Function generally follows physical growth. Infants are able to lift their heads within the first weeks of life, but they cannot stand until the end of the first year. The refined motion of the fingers requires a longer time to develop than do the movements of the arm.

Growth occurs through approximately the first twenty years of life in humans. This period is generally divided into three major times: infancy and early childhood (to about the fifth year of life), middle and late childhood (to about age 12), and adolescence (to about age 20). Growth is more rapid and more likely to show spurts during both the infant-early childhood period and the adolescent period than during middle childhood.

However, different parts of the body show different growth patterns

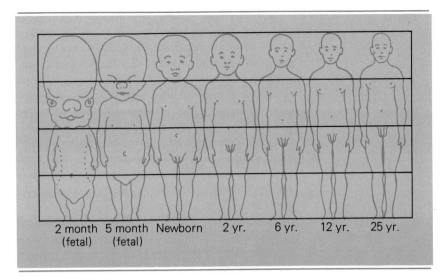

2 month 5 month Newborn 2 yr. 6 yr. 12 yr. 25 yr.
(fetal) (fetal)

relative to age. Figure 3–13 depicts the growth curves of three body systems. The nervous system is almost fully developed by the age of 6. Body size, which includes the skeleton, muscles, and internal organs, shows moderate early growth but then slows down until adolescence, when it increases again. The reproductive system grows very slowly until adolescence, and then undergoes rapid development. These differential patterns have implications for social and psychological development.

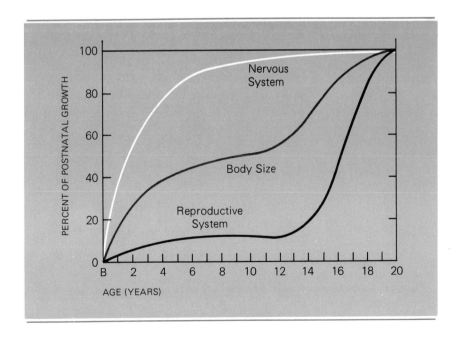

The nervous system consists of the brain, the spinal cord, and nerves that transmit impulses to and from the body. This complex system is composed of neurons and neuroglia. Each neuron consists of a cell body, treelike branches called dendrites, and an axon that is often covered with a fatty sheath, the myelin. Neurons are responsible for the transmission of nerve impulses, although they are not in direct contact with each other. The nerve impulses are carried across the small spaces between the neurons (the synapses) by neurotransmitters. Neuroglia are not involved in nerve transmission; they are probably concerned with nourishment and support of the neurons.

The nervous system originates in the outer layer of the embryo when a group of cells, the neural plate, thickens very soon after conception. The plate folds, and its edges meet to form the neural tube. The entire nervous system arises from this structure (see Figure 3–14). At birth the brain is about 25 percent of its adult weight, which is a greater proportion than for most of the organs of the body (Tanner, 1978). The brain attains 50 percent of its eventual weight by 6 months of age, 75 percent by 2 years, 90 percent by 5 years, and 95 percent by 10 years. This size increase

FIGURE 3–14
Prenatal development of the brain, a side view. The brain originates at the head end of the neural tube. From Cowan, 1979.

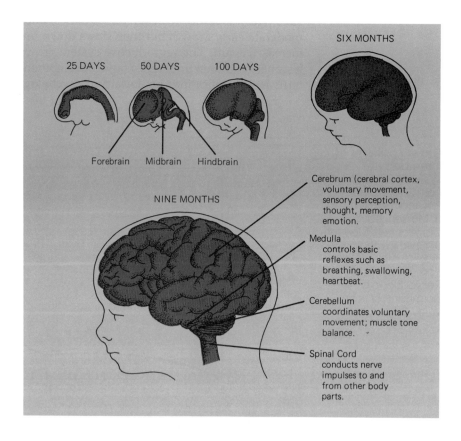

reflects, in part, the following changes (Brooksbank and Balazs, 1981; Prechtl, 1981; Wolff, 1981).

First, the number of neurons and neuroglia increase. The axons and dendrites also grow in number and size, so that connections among the neurons are increased. Neuron connections depend in part on the individual's experience and behavior, which indicates some role for the environment in nervous system maturation. Myelination, growth of the fatty nerve sheath, accompanies growth of the axons and dendrites; it is thought to increase the rate of nerve transmission and to be related to behavioral development.

Second, the nervous system grows in spurts, and it does so at a faster rate in structures that are necessary for vital functions. For example, nerves that control the reflexes are already myelinated at birth, but those involved in vision, complex motor coordination, and voluntary action are myelinated during the first year of life. The cerebellum, which is centrally involved in voluntary movement, is not well developed at birth; it rapidly grows during the first nine months, although the nerve fibers that link it to the cerebrum are not completely myelinated until about age 4. The cerebrum shows considerable growth after birth, first in the primary motor area, which initiates most movements. The primary sensory areas for vision, touch, and hearing develop next. Then growth occurs in the association areas, which integrate impulses from various areas and are responsible for the higher mental processes.

Body Size

The rate of growth in body size is faster during the first six months after birth than it is in any other period of life. Birth weight doubles in about three months and triples before the first birthday.

Figure 3–15 shows the average weight and height for 2- to 18-year-olds in the United States. The curves depict well-known sex differences. Boys are generally taller and heavier than girls. However, between approximately 10 and 13 years of age, girls are larger on both these measures. Overall, increases in height taper off during childhood, but they accelerate dramatically at about 11 to 13 years in girls and 13 to 15 years in boys (Figure 3–16). This adolescent growth spurt levels off, and growth largely ceases at age 17 in girls and 19 in boys. By this time only 2 percent of total height is still to be reached. From about 30 to 45 years of age height remains constant; then it begins to decline very slowly (Tanner, 1970).

The adolescent growth spurt is accompanied by growth in most organs: the heart, lungs, pancreas, stomach, intestines, and reproductive system. From infancy to adolescence boys have somewhat larger muscles. Then, due to their earlier growth spurt, girls actually have larger muscles for about one year. Boys' muscles subsequently catch up and surpass girls'. On the other hand, girls have slightly more fat tissue at birth, and after some variations eventually surpass boys.

These and other tissue adjustments bring about changes in body pro-

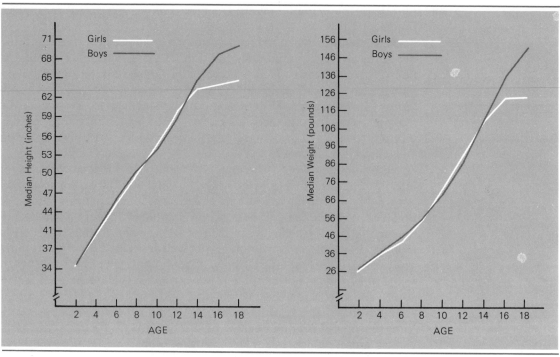

FIGURE 3–15
Changes in height and weight for both sexes during the major growth period. From *The World Almanac & Book of Facts.* (New York: Newspaper Enterprise Association, 1984), p. 911. Source: National Center for Health Statistics.

portion, some of which are not considered attractive for a period of time. For example, the arms and legs become relatively long and the lower jaw may become noticeably large compared to the rest of the face. Adult bodily proportion is achieved gradually. Changes in hormones also bring on secondary sexual characteristics such as the growth of underarm and pubic hair, the onset of menstruation and the development of breasts in girls, and in boys, the lowering of voice pitch and the ability to ejaculate.

Individual Rates of Growth. Physical growth differs in several ways for males and females. Within each sex, however, individual variations occur and are sometimes quite striking (Figure 3–17). Each individual's size and timing of growth probably have relatively strong biological determinants (Tanner, 1970). The correlation between adult weight and height during the first year of life is greater than .70 (Plomin, 1984). It also appears that when children's rate of growth slows down due to some adverse event, growth may "catch up" when circumstances change. Whether such catching up always occurs is not clear. In any event, the strong relationship between early and later size does not mean that biology is destiny; environment also plays a role in the eventual outcome.

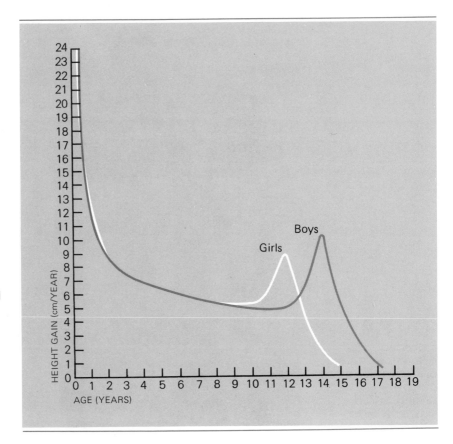

FIGURE 3–16
Increase in height for typical boys and girls, showing the adolescent growth spurt. From J. M. Tanner, Physical Growth, in P. H. Mussen, ed., *Carmichael's Manual of Child Psychology,* 3rd ed. Vol. 1 (New York: Wiley, 1970).

Psychosocial
Effects

Physical attributes influence psychosocial functioning. This is true for both the quality of characteristics and the rate at which they develop.

Is Beauty only Skin Deep?   Research tells us that people generally prefer physical attractiveness in adults and associate it with likability, goodness, and competence (Dion and Stein, 1978). Does this relationship hold when it comes to children? It seems so. In one investigation, undergraduate students evaluated photographs of infants less than 1 year old; the attractive babies were seen as more likable, good, and smart (Stephan and Langlois, 1984). Given the strong tendency for adults to act as if beauty is more than skin deep, it is not surprising to find that children also perceive attractive children as friendlier, smarter, more likable, more altruistic, and less mean than unattractive children (Langlois and Stephan, 1977).

The significance of these findings is that from early in life children may be treated quite differently on the basis of physical beauty. In fact, there is research to support this view. For example, when adult females delivered penalties to children for making errors on a task, they treated the attractive boys with more tolerance than the attractive girls and the

FIGURE 3–17
Individual differences in size and timing of growth can be **striking.** Alice Kandell, Photo Researchers.

unattractive children of both sexes (Dion, 1974). To the extent that differential treatment occurs, children can be expected to behave differently and to feel differently about themselves (Stephan and Langlois, 1984).

The Timing of Maturation. Individuals mature at varying rates, due to heredity, diet, health, and other factors. Early maturation appears to be advantageous for boys (Jones, 1965). Early maturers are more likely to be elected class officers, have their names in the school newspaper, be rated as attractive, excel in athletics, and be less impulsive. Late maturers seem to be restless, talkative, tense, and attention seeking. These adolescents are less popular, less dominant, more dependent, and more rebellious. They seem to feel inadequate and rejected. Superior size and the physical strength that goes with it are in accord with male sex-role expectations. Early maturers may also be given tasks, privileges, and responsibilities typically assigned to older persons—and thus special opportunities for personal satisfaction and rewards (Eichorn, 1963).

Differences between early and late maturing males gradually diminish as size contrast lessens. Moreover, the overall picture begins to change (Siegel, 1982). As adults early maturers are poised, responsible, and achieving in a conventional way. But they are also somewhat un-flexible and emotionally restricted. Those who mature later are relatively more active, exploring, insightful, perceptive, independent, impulsive, and flexible. It seems that in coping with being behind their peers, late maturers develop many valuable behaviors.

The effects of timing on females are less clear-cut. Early data indicated that late maturers played more prominent roles in school and were rated higher on poise, sociability, cheerfulness, leadership, and expressiveness (Weatherley, 1964). When these adolescents were older (17 years of age), however, they showed few differences on projective tests, though the early maturers seemed to have a slight advantage (Jones and Mussen, 1958). The picture that emerges is complex. Early-maturing girls may initially suffer some disadvantage because they are not only larger than their male peers, but also tend to be stocky. They may date older males while lacking the adequate emotional and social sophistication necessary to deal with such relationships. They may be looked on with jealousy by their female peers. Even if this is so, however, the disadvantages appear to vanish rapidly, or perhaps to reverse themselves. The most consistent result is that the timing of maturation is simply not as powerful for females as it is for males.

The Secular Trend: Growing Bigger and Faster.   The differences we have just considered are *individual* differences. There is, however, a general growth trend that also affects children and adolescents. People in general are both taller and heavier than they were in the past (Muuss, 1972), probably due to better diet and health care. The armor of medieval knights seems to fit the 10- to 12-year-old American boy today; seats constructed in the La Scala opera house in Milan about 1788 were 13 inches wide; the average height of American sailors in the War of 1812 was 5 feet 2 inches.

Children now grow faster earlier and attain adult size earlier than they did in the past. Today the average girl reaches her adult height two years earlier than did females at the turn of the century; a similar comparison in boys is even more striking. Given the relationship between general body growth and maturation of the reproductive system, it is not surprising to find a lowering of the age of puberty. Figure 3–18 illustrates this pattern by indicating the age of *menarche*—or onset of menstruation—of girls in many countries.

What does the trend mean? Muuss (1972) suggests that we might expect several changes in the interests, attitudes, and social sophistication of today's adolescents compared to those of the past. Studies indicate earlier interest in sex, love, and marriage; greater tolerance of others; and increased seriousness and social awareness. Perhaps earlier maturation is related to increases in premarital sex, venereal disease, and illegitimate births (Dreyer, 1982). The social calendar of youth seems to have moved ahead, much to the dismay of many parents. It is not possible, of course, to draw a cause-and-effect relationship between these facts and trends in physical development. Still, the overall picture is one of a consistent downward extension of adolescence into the years we previously might

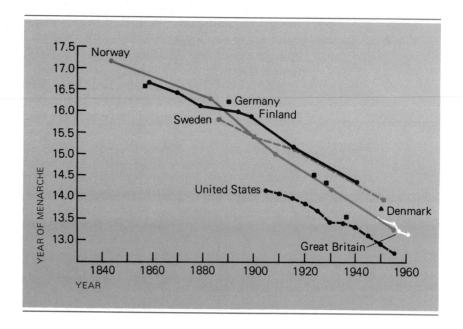

FIGURE 3–18

Secular trend in average age of menarche. From J. M. Tanner, *Growth at Adolescence* (Oxford: Blackwell Scientific Publications, 1962), p. 153.

have considered childhood. It is unclear whether adolescent psychosocial development has kept pace with this change.

MOTOR DEVELOPMENT

As children mature physically, their ability to move about and manipulate the environment also develops rapidly. Well before adolescence is reached, they can thread a needle, operate a jig saw, and throw a basketball through a hoop. We call the process of mastering these skills perceptual-motor development, because it involves complex perceptual and cognitive processes that gradually build on themselves.

Basic Principles

Motor development relies on changes in the neuromuscular system. First, motor functions follow a predictable pattern. Babies cannot walk before they sit, or write before they grasp voluntarily. Second, gross motor control involving large areas of the body is achieved more easily than fine motor control involving smaller muscle groups. Children can hold their bottles during the latter part of their first year of life, but lack the ability to play a flute. In other words, over time mass movement becomes specific or *differentiated*. Third, complex motor skills develop progressively through differentiation and *hierarchic integration* (Werner, 1948). Once specific control (differentiation) is achieved, the individual actions can be put together or integrated into larger, complex, and more coherent whole units. After gaining greater and greater control over arm, leg, and neck movements (differentiation), the infant will begin to put these relatively simple actions together and perform the more complex and integrated act of sitting up without support.

The principles just described are reflected in descriptions of average growth of posture and movement. But norms should not be applied uncritically to any one individual. Williams (1946) likened the issue to determining the amount of shoe leather needed to outfit an army. The problem could be approached by establishing average foot size. But we could not order the average size shoe for everyone. So it is with developmental norms: We do not expect each person to fit the average rate of development.

Posture and Locomotion.   Within a little over one year's time, changes in posture and locomotion transform the child from a relatively immobile bit of humanity to an upright organism that moves through space by crawling, climbing, and walking. The nature of these changes and the approximate times at which they are achieved are shown in Figure 3–19. The figure cannot show, however, the practice, the waverings, and the failures that are the foundations for progress. Shirley, who followed the growth of upright locomotion, suggested that it occurs in five fundamental stages (cited by Eckert, 1973). In the first the infant achieves control of the upper body, and in the second, of the entire trunk. During the third stage the infant makes an active effort toward locomotion. In the fourth stage the baby is able to crawl. In the fifth stage the infant can control posture and coordination for walking. Throughout the entire sequence the infant must first be able to control his or her new body posture in a static position, and then movement concerned with that posture. For example, the posture of standing with good control is required before walking can be accomplished. By about 2 years of age children can jump. Soon afterward they are able to walk up and down stairs with both feet on each step, and then to hop and eventually skip. With each achievement, the world widens and becomes a more exciting place.

Manual Skills.   Another development that enlarges the child's environment is the ability to manipulate objects, which brings information to the child about the shapes, textures, and movements in the environment. The newborn has virtually no control over the arms, much less the hands and fingers. Then, flailing of the arms begins, and gradually it comes under some control. By 4 months of age babies are interested in observing the movement of their hands and in touching and manipulating objects. During the latter half of the first year they actively manipulate and explore, guiding their hands visually. They are particularly drawn to objects that are novel and complex in texture and movement (Ruff, 1984). Coordination of the hands and fingers increases; by 1 year of age most babies are able to produce the precise pincer movement (Figure 3–20 and Figure 3–21).

Dramatic change continues. By 18 months children can scribble spontaneously, fill a cup with cubes, and build a tower with a few blocks. Before they go to kindergarten, most youngsters can reasonably copy a circle and square, draw some semblance of the human figure, and use

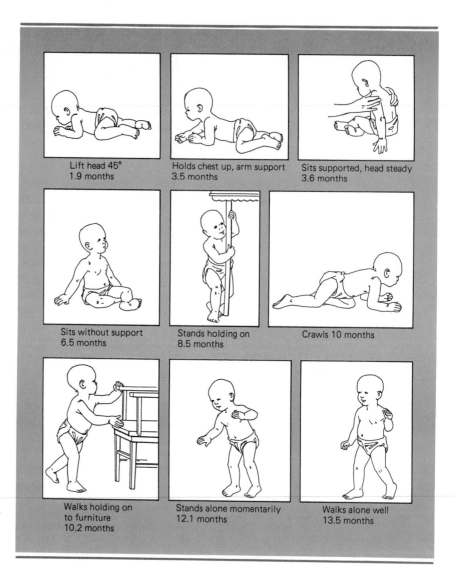

FIGURE 3–19
Age at which 75 percent of babies achieve specific motor milestones for posture and locomotion. Primary source: Frankenburg, W. K., and Dodds, J. B. (1969). *Manual, Denver Developmental Screening Test.* Mead Johnson Laboratories.

Lift head 45°
1.9 months

Holds chest up, arm support
3.5 months

Sits supported, head steady
3.6 months

Sits without support
6.5 months

Stands holding on
8.5 months

Crawls 10 months

Walks holding on
to furniture
10.2 months

Stands alone momentarily
12.1 months

Walks alone well
13.5 months

crayons with confidence (Frankenburg and Dobbs, 1969). Chances are that a preference for one hand over the other has already been firmly established.

Determinants of
Motor
Development

To what extent is development a function of physical maturation, and to what extent does it rely on experience? This question has continually woven itself into inquiries concerning motor behavior. Maturation refers to an unfolding of the capacities of the organism that is relatively independent of training or experience. The fact that development occurs in such an orderly fashion in all cultures argues for the importance of maturation. Moreover, many examples illustrate that practice may not be necessary for the basic growth of some motor behaviors.

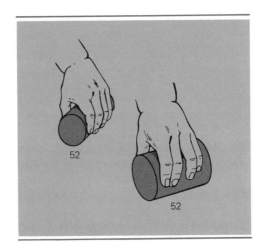

FIGURE 3–20
The pincer movement allows humans to manipulate objects with great precision.

A classical animal experiment demonstrating maturational processes in motor development was conducted by Carmichael in the late 1920s. Carmichael divided salamanders into a control group and an experimental group. The latter were placed in water containing an anesthetic; the control animals were allowed to develop in fresh water. In time, the control salamanders began to show vigorous movement, whereas those in the anesthetic were immobile. But when the drugged animals were placed in fresh water, they immediately began to swim. Within half an hour they were indistinguishable from the controls, who had been swimming for five days (Carmichael, 1970). Although similar experiments

FIGURE 3–21
Young infants are interested in movement of their hands. Teri Stratford.

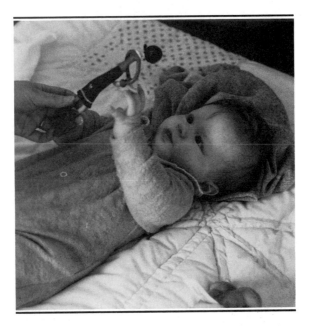

Is One Hand Better than the Other?

With rare exceptions, adults prefer use of one hand over the other. *Handedness* (also called *laterality*) is not absolutely consistent across activities; that is, some people may write with their left hands and eat with their right. Approximately 90 percent of the adult human population all over the world shows a preference for the right hand. Still, developmental norms and patterns are not well established. Six-month-old babies make contact with objects with their left hands as much as with their right hands. By 7 months most begin to use their right hands more than their left (Lewkowicz and Turkewitz, 1982).

Theories of handedness range from the social psychological (children simply acquire the habit) to the genetic. Heredity may indeed be involved (Blau, 1977), but preference can be affected by specific brain damage, educational practices, and family and cultural values. The influence of cultural tolerance for left-handedness is difficult to assess, but the frequency of left-handedness has been estimated at 10.4 percent, 5.9 percent, and 1.8 percent in cultures that were extremely permissive, permissive, and harsh/restrictive, respectively (Dawson, cited in Hardyck and Petrinovich, 1977).

Being left-handed is a disadvantage because virtually all environments are set up for right-handed people. There is another disadvantage: Left-handedness has long been associated with evil, corruption, dishonesty, and deficiency. The French word *gauche* means left and awkward, and the English word *sinister* means toward the left and evil. One analysis of the Bible revealed eighty positive references to right-handedness and only negative references to left-handedness (Hardyck and Petrinovich, 1977). Left-handed children are thought to exhibit more than average problems in social behavior, reading, bladder control, schizophrenia, and motor perceptual performance (e.g., Blau, 1977). A subset of left-handed individuals may have specific deficits, but it appears that many do not (Gillberg, Waldenström, and Rasmussen, 1984). When deficits do exist, they have multiple causes—probably biological in some cases and the result of attitudes regarding left-handedness in other cases.

have not shown such clear effects, this study served to strengthen the belief that built-in processes operate independently of experience.

A few early investigations of the maturation-experience issue involved human infants. Dennis and Dennis (1940) collected information about Hopi Indian children on the development of walking. Traditionally reared Hopi infants were secured to cradle boards in such a way that they were unable to move their hands, roll over, or raise their bodies. The babies were removed from the cradle boards only once or twice a day to have their clothes changed. Other Hopi infants, whose parents were influenced by European ways, were not restricted in this manner. Dennis and Dennis found that infants in *both* groups walked at about 15 months.

Although it is widely recognized that basic patterns of movement are strongly canalized, this does not mean that experience plays no role. For example, in both monkeys and mice physical exercise results in changes in the cerebellum, which is involved with movement (Thelen and Fisher, 1982). There are also many reports of exceptionally early motor growth in African children, due perhaps to the way in which the children are handled by adults (Zelazo, 1976). And experience and practice cannot easily be ruled out when it comes to complex movement: Most people are biologically capable of skiing but without practice cannot ski. The task for developmentalists, then, is to understand the interplay of maturation and experience.

Motor behavior is initially controlled by the lower centers of the brain, notably the cerebellum. As the cerebellum and the cortex continue to develop during the first year of life, the cortex takes on the job of controlling voluntary movement. It seems likely that growth of the motor cortex is directly related to increases in voluntary behavior. However, the exact nature of this reorganization of the brain is not well understood. Nor is the relationship between reflexive and voluntary behavior. Some reflexes seem to simply disappear. For example, the grasp reflex is actually quite different from voluntary grasp. The reflex and voluntary grasp exist side by side for a while, but then the reflex gradually disappears (Prechtl, 1981). The story is quite different for the stepping reflex. When newborns are held upright, they make stepping movements, but this reflex disappears in about two months. It is not until many months later that voluntary stepping is observed.

Thelen and Fisher's (1982, 1983) extensive studies suggest a connection between reflexive and voluntary stepping. When infants lie on their backs they often make spontaneous kicking movements. Thelen and Fisher showed that kicking and the stepping reflex involve the same muscle functioning. They believe that the reflex disappears because muscle growth does not keep up with leg growth. That is, in the upright position the muscle is not strong enough to lift the leg. The lying-down position lessens the pull of gravity, and so kicking can occur. This suggests that the stepping reflex is actually connected to later walking through spontaneous kicking.

Can practice facilitate the development of walking? Perhaps. Zelazo, Zelazo, and Kolb (1972) investigated whether exercise of the stepping reflex would affect later walking. One group of male infants received daily active exercise during the second to eight weeks of life. These infants were held upright with their feet touching a flat surface. They were moved forward when they made stepping motions. A second group of infants received passive exercise: Their mothers moved their legs and arms while they lay in cribs or sat in infant seats. A no-exercise group was tested weekly along with the other groups. A fourth group was tested only once at the end of the study. The results showed that active exercise increased walking responses over time during the experiment. Moreover, later parental reports indicated that walking had occurred earlier for the infants who had actively exercised.

Environmental influences involve practice, and other processes as well (Adams, 1984). Motor development probably relies strongly on ob-

FIGURE 3–22
The ability to perform complex motor acts depends on several factors. © Barbara Young 1971, Photo Researchers, Inc.

servations of others and attempts to imitate them. In learning to play tennis, for example, beginners watch others and then try the movements themselves. Feedback from others and from our own bodies helps shape our behavior (Figure 3–22). In complex motor sequences, such as tennis playing, a series of known motor acts must also be connected in proper order and time. Individuals can learn what acts follow the preceding one, and so can construct the sequence. It is likely that a "motor program"— a mental representation of the sequence—is learned. The opportunity for such learning begins early; for example, during the latter part of the infant's first year, play is characterized by games such as pat-a-cake, peek-a-boo, and clapping (Crawley et al., 1978). Infants playing any of these games with an adult receive a good deal of feedback. So it seems that, in general, motor learning depends on physical maturation, the task being learned, and the match between feedback and capacity to process information (e.g., Newell and Kennedy, 1978).

SUMMARY

1. The joining of an ovum and a sperm cell results at conception in the formation of the *zygote*, which differentiates into all body parts during the prenatal period.

2. When the sperm cell contains an X chromosome, a female organism results. When the sperm contains a Y chromosome, the new organism is male. On occasion the zygote divides early and

develops into identical twins. In other instances, two conceptions occur almost simultaneously, resulting in fraternal twins.

3. Three periods of prenatal development are identified: ovum, embryo, and fetus. The *period of the ovum* begins at conception and ends during the second week, after implantation in the uterus. The second to eighth weeks constitute the *period of the embryo;* most body parts begin to develop during this time. The *fetal period* is from the eighth week to birth; it is characterized primarily by refinement and growth of existing structures.

4. Influences on prenatal development include maternal age, diet, stress, the Rh factor and specific *teratogens*, agents or conditions that result in abnormalities of the child.

5. Birth typically occurs at about thirty-eight weeks after conception (forty weeks gestation). Lightening is soon followed by the three stages of labor. Birth is usually predictable and uncomplicated, but abnormal positioning of the fetus, anoxia, and excessive use of anesthesia for the mother can cause complications.

6. Infants born preterm, postterm, undersized, or oversized are at risk for a variety of problems. Prematurity and low birthweight are particularly threatening.

7. The greater the degree of birth and pregnancy complications, the more likely that eventual outcome will be poor. This relationship between developmental outcome and degree of birth and pregnancy complications is referred to as the *continuum of reproductive casualty*. The quality of the rearing environment of the child also influences developmental outcome; this is referred to as the *continuum of caretaking casualty*. Children of lower social classes are less able to overcome birth and pregnancy problems.

8. The medical condition and capacities of the neonate can be evaluated with the Apgar and Brazelton scales. Neonates display diverse reflexes, basic sensory and learning abilities, various states of consciousness, and temperamental differences.

9. Postnatal physical growth usually follows an orderly pattern. The body grows from head to tail, and from the center to the extremities. Different body systems develop at different rates during infancy, childhood, and adolescence. The nervous system is quite well developed at birth and continues to develop rapidly during the first few years of life. Overall body size increases rapidly during the first months of life, then slows down until a dramatic acceleration at puberty. From about 10 to 13 years of age girls are both taller and heavier than boys because they experience the growth spurt at an earlier age. The reproductive system matures slowly until puberty, when it rapidly advances.

10. In addition to variations of the growth of different body systems, individual differences occur in both the rate of maturation and the degree of physical attractiveness. Early maturation in males

appears to benefit boys initially; rate of development has less impact on girls. Attractiveness is valued by society.

11. Children today are growing larger at younger ages than did children in past generations.

12. As a child grows, motor abilities develop in a predictable pattern; they become more proficient, refined, and complex. *Differentiation* is the increased control and specificity exhibited by an individual. Individually learned actions are then combined, forming more sophisticated behavior. This process is referred to as *hierarchic integration*.

13. Motor milestones mark the approximate periods when an infant masters certain skills—postural control, stages of locomotion, and various manual skills.

14. Motor development may be strongly canalized, but it depends on both maturation and experience. The learning of movement involves several processes: practice, observation and imitation of others, feedback from others and from the body itself, and capacity to understand the feedback.

4 EARLY BEHAVIOR AND EXPERIENCE

The events of early life are currently the focus of an extraordinary surge of research. This may seem surprising: After all, most of us cannot recall our first year of life and have only vague memories of our first few years. But this is in fact the time when a great many later patterns are set on their course. No major theory of development looks at the early months and years of life as a waste of time (Lipsitt, 1983).

In this chapter, we examine the infant's capacity to learn from experience, and basic perceptual abilities and processes. Learning and perception take place within a social context. For the very young child, parents (or some other primary caretakers) are the center of the social world, and so we examine infants' attachments to their caretakers. Finally, we consider a question that haunts all students of development: What happens to the child who, instead of having the usual experiences, suffers deprivation or separation?

THE ABILITY TO BENEFIT FROM EXPERIENCE

Innate biological mechanisms permit humans to learn from experience from the very first week of life. Learning undoubtedly causes some change in the nervous system, but it is known primarily by changes in behavior. The ability to learn increases throughout childhood as a result of maturation and previous learning.

Habituation

When presented with a strong or interesting stimulus, an individual displays a reflexive startle and orienting response. That is, he or she moves rapidly, fixates the eyes on the object, and shows physiological changes in heart rate and brain-wave patterns. After repeated presentation of the stimulus, these responses diminish and eventually disappear. This process of "getting used to" a stimulus is called *habituation*. It is considered a type of learning, because responses are changed by experience with environmental stimulation.

Habituation has been shown in newborn infants (Schaffer, 1973). For example, an infant automatically startles in response to a loud noise. Consider the infant whose family lives near an airport. When the newborn first arrives home from the hospital, it may startle and begin to cry when an airplane flies over the house. But as time passes, the infant gets used to the loud noise of the airplane, and eventually seems not to notice it.

Classical Conditioning

Like habituation, *classical conditioning* involves a change in the situations in which a particular reflexive or innate response will occur. The difference is that in habituation the individual stops responding to situations that had previously elicited the response; in classical conditioning, the individual begins to respond to situations that had *not* previously elicited the response. Thus, in a fundamental way, classical conditioning is a more active learning process than is habituation.

Pavlov's demonstration of classical conditioning in dogs first focused attention on this process. He placed meat powder into the mouths of his dog subjects and then measured the flow of digestive juices. During the course of his work, Pavlov ran into what at first seemed to him to be an irritating problem. The dogs often appeared to anticipate the food, so that salivary flow began even before any meat powder had been introduced. Pavlov reasoned that since untrained dogs salivated when meat powder was placed on their tongues, salivation was a natural or *unconditioned response* (UCR). But salivation that came to be elicited by the sight of the food had to be acquired by some form of experience and was thus a learned or *conditioned response* (CR).

This reasoning led Pavlov to investigate how conditioned responses are formed. He presented the dogs with the sound of a tone (*conditioned stimulus*, or CS), followed in a few seconds by food (*unconditional stimulus*, or UCS). After a number of presentations, saliva was secreted before the meat powder was presented, apparently in response to the CS. This salivation was the learned or the conditioned response (CR). Once the conditioned response was learned, the sounding of a similar tone would cause the conditioned response. But the more dissimilar the second tone was to the original tone, the weaker the CR would be. This process was called *generalization*. In addition, the dogs could also be taught to salivate to a particular tone but not to others, depending on the UCS being paired with the particular tone but not with others. The animals thus learned *discrimination*. Finally, the newly conditioned response could be eliminated by repeated presentation of the tone without the meat powder; this was called *extinction*.

The importance of classical conditioning in human development is that this form of learning operates over a wide variety of stimuli and responses. It may have particular significance in shaping emotional responses. Consider, for example, how a father may come to elicit positive emotions in his infant son through classical conditioning (Figure 4–1). The father's feeding of the child (UCS) presumably elicits feelings of satisfaction (UCR) in the hungry infant. If the father then smiles at and talks to his son (CS) immediately before presenting food, these social behaviors will gradually come to elicit feelings of satisfaction (CR) in the absence of the food.

FIGURE 4–1
Schema of classical conditioning of positive emotions.

Preconditioning	Father feeds child (UCS) ⟶ Child feels satisfied (UCR)
	Father smiles and talks ⟶ Child feels neutral
Conditioning trials	Father smiles and talks (CS) ⟶ Child feels satisfied (UCR) followed by feeding (UCS)
Postconditioning	Father smiles and talks (CS) ⟶ Child feels satisfied (CR)

Psychologists have been interested in demonstrating classical conditioning in infancy to determine whether such learning operates as a developmental process early in life. Most investigators now agree that during the first few weeks of life, a variety of responses can be classically conditioned (Sameroff and Cavanaugh, 1979). These responses include sucking, head turning, eye blinking, crying, and heart rate. But human conditioning is influenced by certain factors. The state of the infant—that is, drowsiness and alertness—plays a role; so does the length of time between the presentation of the CS and the UCS, with younger infants requiring a longer time interval than older infants.

A growing body of research also suggests that certain stimuli and responses may be conditioned or associated more easily than others. For example, sucking can be conditioned to sound and visual stimulation more readily than dilation of the pupils of the eye or heart rate. This illustrates the general finding that members of different species learn some associations more easily than others. Such *preparedness* is considered a biologically determined species difference that is important to adaptation to the environment (Garcia and Koelling, 1966). So sucking and head turning in the human infant, both of which are likely to be adaptive, are relatively easily conditioned.

Operant Conditioning

Operant conditioning (or instrumental learning) focuses on the consequences that follow behavior. The pioneer investigator in this area was E. L. Thorndike. In a typical experiment, Thorndike (1898) placed a cat in a slatted cage with food located outside; escape led to food reward. The cat had to perform a particular response, such as pulling a cord or pressing a lever, to open the door. Sooner or later, it "accidentally" performed the act and succeeded in escaping. On subsequent trials the act that led to escape was more likely to occur than it had previously. From his observations, Thorndike formulated a general law, the *law of effect*, applicable to the behavior of all organisms: "Any act which in a given situation produces satisfaction becomes associated with that situation, so that when the situation recurs the act is more likely than before to recur also" [Thorndike, 1905, p. 203]. Later B. F. Skinner and many others continued and extended the work Thorndike had begun.

Behaviors performed by the organism are referred to as *operants*. A consequence that strengthens an operant is a *reinforcer*. A consequence that weakens an operant is a *punisher*. Examples of operants are doing homework, playing chess, driving a car, and dressing oneself. Completion of any one of these acts results in some consequences. For example, driving a car may result in viewing the beautiful countryside, avoiding unpleasant work at home, or getting a speeding ticket. Future behavior, in turn, is influenced by these consequences. Individuals are more likely to take a drive again if previous driving resulted in a beautiful view rather than a speeding ticket.

Research has shown generalization, discrimination, and extinction of operant learning. Suppose, for example, upon completion of an arithmetic assignment, a young boy is told by his teacher, "You did a good job!" This positive feedback is likely to strengthen the tendency to complete arithmetic in the future. Furthermore, the boy might *generalize* this tendency to spelling assignments. If the teacher withholds praise for the spelling, soon the child will probably withdraw his efforts in spelling. He has *discriminated* the situation in which he receives reward from the situation in which he does not. Moreover, should the teacher forget to comment positively on the arithmetic performance, effort in that subject may eventually decrease. In this case, behavior has been *extinguished* because the previously given reinforcement no longer occurs.

Operant learning occurs in many species across a wide variety of circumstances. It has been responsible for pigeons learning to peck on keys, chimpanzees learning human sign language, and children acquiring academic, physical, and social skills. It would seem that such a prominent process would start early. Does it begin at birth? Until the 1960s it had been impossible to demonstrate operant conditioning in newborns or very young infants, primarily due to the infants' limited range of responses. Eventually this problem was overcome. In one example the rooting reflex was used as the basis for conditioning (Siqueland and Lipsitt, 1966). When newborns were touched on the cheeks, they turned their heads in the direction of the touch in about 25 percent of the trials. Each time they did so, they were allowed to suck on a bottle of sweetened water for a few seconds. Head turning in the direction of the touch increased within a short time to 75 percent of the trials.

Observational Learning

Observational learning involves learning about the world from observing the actions of others. It plays a role in all aspects of development—from learning motor skills to accomplishing intellectual tasks to participating in social interactions (Bandura, 1977). In its most obvious form, observational learning involves imitating another's behavior. It is well established that imitation occurs within a few months after birth. Some researchers argue that it occurs from the first days of life; they present evidence that very young infants are able to imitate a variety of facial gestures and expressions.

Meltzoff and Moore (1977, 1983) exposed 2- to 3-week-olds to a human model who made specific facial gestures, such as sticking out the tongue and opening and closing the mouth. They concluded that the infants did indeed imitate these gestures. Field (1982) and her colleagues presented evidence that neonates (with an average age of 36 hours) discriminated and imitated three facial expressions. As Figure 4–2 shows, the expressions were happy, sad, and surprised. These demonstrations are important because they seem to indicate an unexpectedly high degree of competence in infancy.

The findings have been challenged, however, by investigations that failed to demonstrate such early imitation. In a study conducted by Abravanel and Sigafoos (1984), infants between 4 and 21 weeks of age were presented with three facial and two bodily gestures (e.g., hand opening,

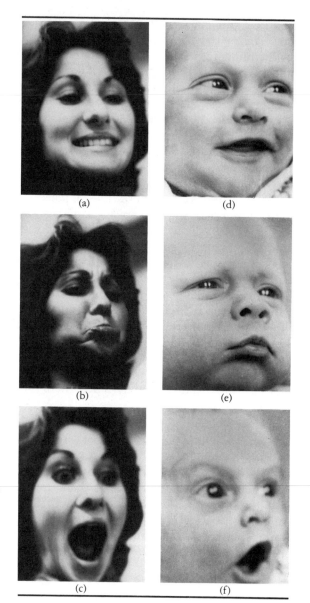

FIGURE 4–2
Photographs of a
model's happy, sad,
and surprised
expressions and a
newborn's
corresponding
expressions.
Courtesy T.M. Field,
University of Miami
Medical School.

(a)

(b)

(c)

(d)

(e)

(f)

eye blinking, tongue protruding). Little evidence for imitation was found overall: only in some instances did 4- to 6-week-olds partly protrude their tongues after observing the model engage in this behavior.

The conflicts in the research findings touch on a theoretical issue: Major theories of learning and cognitive development predict that imitating an act like tongue protrusion does not occur very early in life. Such imitation requires that infants match their own bodily movements with stimuli that they perceive only through vision. This kind of matching, it is widely thought, can occur only after greater experience and perhaps biological maturation of the mental apparatus. If imitation does occur, how can it be explained? Abravanel and Sigafoos suggest that it is simply a social reflex elicited by specific stimuli. Meltzoff and Moore (1983) argue that the imitative behaviors shown by infants are much more flexible than reflex acts. For example, infants often produce approximations of the modeled behavior before they gradually come to match the model's actions. Although this issue is still unsettled, other evidence exists that infants are able to take in information in one mode of functioning and transfer it to another. Before we look at this evidence, however, we examine the infant's capacities to process information received by the sensory systems.

PERCEPTUAL DEVELOPMENT

Stimulation from the environment bombards us from the moment of birth. Two related processes, sensation and perception, enable us to receive stimulation and organize it. These terms are often confusing because they overlap in meaning. *Sensation* involves stimulation of the sensory receptors by physical energy from the internal and external environment. The retina of the eye, for example, reacts to light rays and translates information into nerve impulses. The nerve impulses are transmitted to the brain, which reacts to the stimulation in various ways. It is at this point that *perception* is said to occur. The brain may select, organize, and modify sensory input. It integrates the impulses from the different sense organs and compares the impulses with previous input. In a way, then, sensation and perception are actually names for different points in a complex process of *information gathering* that ultimately leads to "knowing."

The study of perception in children and adults typically involves presenting the individuals with stimuli and asking them to respond in some way—for example, by pressing a button or answering questions. Because these methods obviously cannot be used with infants, researchers have had to devise other ways to collect data. Some of these methods rely on physiological responses, such as heart rate and dilation of the pupils of the eyes. Others rely on the simple motor behaviors that infants can perform, such as head turning, sucking, and fixating the eyes on objects. For example, an investigator wishing to determine whether an infant can see an object might prop the infant in a special chair or crib and present the object within the infant's visual field. If the object is visually fixated the child is able to see the stimulus to at least some extent.

Another method, *preferential looking*, allows a researcher to determine whether an infant "prefers" one stimulus over another. The infant is presented with two visual stimuli. If one is visually fixated for a longer time than the other, it is "preferred." Because such a finding requires that the infant visually discriminate the stimuli, preferential looking is also evidence that the stimuli can be seen. Another method used in perceptual research takes advantage of habituation. As we have already noted, when a stimulus is first presented to an infant, the child will respond in a variety of ways, perhaps with a change in heart rate or with visual fixation or sucking. After repeated presentations, these responses gradually drop to some stable level or disappear completely—that is, habituation occurs. If a second stimulus is then introduced, and if the infant responds with renewed vigor, *dishabituation* has occurred. When dishabituation takes place, it can be inferred that the new stimulus is being perceived.

Let us now look at some of the research findings that describe the sensory and perceptual abilities of infants.

Smell and Taste

The sense of smell, or *olfaction*, appears to be one of the most highly developed senses in the newborn (Rovee, Cohen, and Shlapack, 1975). In fact, premature babies as young as 28 weeks of age may be able to detect odors (Sarnat, 1978). Infant discrimination of odors was tested in a series of investigations in which the babies were placed in a special apparatus, a stabilimeter, which measures activity level and breathing (Figure 4–3). A cotton swab saturated with an odorant was then placed beneath their nostrils, and changes in activity and breathing were taken as measures of ability to detect the substances. Neonates of about 1 to 3 days of age discriminated the four odors employed. They also habituated—that is, they responded more weakly to repeated presentations (Engen, Lipsitt, and Kaye, 1963; Lipsitt, Engen, and Kaye, 1963). By about a week after birth, infants may be able to detect their mothers by the sense of smell (MacFarland, 1975). They also seem able to localize odors in space, because they turn away from aversive odors (Bower, 1974).

Displeasure and pleasure can be seen in another way—by facial expression (Steiner, 1979). Newborns were tested with food-related

FIGURE 4–3
This neonate is being tested in a stabilimeter, which is sensitive to activity level. The apparatus around the abdomen is a pneumograph, which measures breathing. Courtesy Dr. Lewis P. Lipsitt.

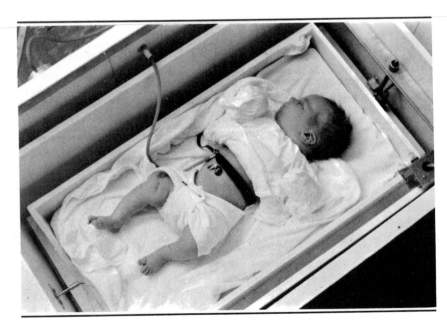

odors that had been rated as pleasant or unpleasant by adults. Although the infants had had no contact with food, they reacted to the odors rated as pleasant with a relaxed retraction of the lips, sucking, and licking. Their reactions to the unpleasant odors included depression of the corners of the mouth, arching of the lips, and spitting and salivation. Smell perception undergoes some further development, but by 6 years of age sensitivity to odors is well developed and remains relatively stable for much of the life span (McCartney, 1968; Rovee, Cohen, and Shlapack, 1975).

Like the sense of smell, taste perception exists at birth or prior to birth. The receptors for taste, found primarily on the tongue but also in other parts of the mouth and in the throat, are present early in prenatal development. Quite possibly the fetus is sensitive to the taste of amniotic fluid (Acredolo and Hake, 1982). There is no doubt that the neonate is able to distinguish salty, sour, bitter, and sweet, and that the level of sensitivity is quite high. Furthermore, a distinct preference for sweet has been demonstrated. Even when presented with a substance that is more nutritious but less sweet, neonates prefer the sweeter substance (Bower, 1977). They react to sweetness by eager sucking, licking the upper lip, and an expression that resembles a smile (Steiner, 1979). Newborns appear to perceive saltiness somewhat neutrally or with displeasure, and they display definite displeasure at bitter and sour substances. In general there is a decreased preference for sweets by adulthood and increased preference for saltiness, perhaps for bitter and sour as well. Sensitivity itself remains stable, although some of the elderly may show a decrease in ability to taste.

Touch and Pain

Humans are able to respond to tactile stimulation early in life. Prematures respond to touch with fanning of the toes, slight motor responses, and waking from half-sleep (Saint-Anne Dargassies, 1966). Touching various areas of the neonate's body produces many of the reflexes discussed in Chapter 3, including the Babinski, the grasp, and the rooting reflex.

Perception of pain is probably not well developed at birth, but it rapidly improves. Fewer pinpricks and less electric shock are required to arouse a 5-day-old infant than a neonate (Lipsitt and Levy, 1957; Spears and Hohle, 1967). Babies only a few days old also appear to experience pain from circumcision (Acredolo and Hake, 1982). When a painful stimulus is applied, the newborn cries and tries to withdraw. If unable to do so, the child might attempt to push away the stimulus with a hand or foot.

Tactual stimulation becomes increasingly important as young children develop sufficient motor ability to handle objects and navigate within their surroundings. As they feel the hard floor and soft carpet, the rough stones and the smooth sidewalk, or the round ball and the square block, they begin to collect information about the world. Under usual circumstances, such perception is the result of the combination of touch and vision. But it is possible to examine the effects of touch alone by asking children to perform various tasks as they handle objects they cannot see. The ability to recognize objects by touch increases with age as exploration of the objects becomes more systematic (Gliner, 1967).

Hearing

The unborn fetus displays both physiological and behavioral responses to auditory stimulation (Areodolo and Hake, 1982). Very young infants respond to sound with a variety of reactions—sudden startles, muscle changes, breathing disruptions, eye blinking, and changes in heart rate and activity level. They are also able to locate sounds. They have been observed at birth to turn their eyes in the direction of a source of sound (Butterworth and Castillo, 1976), although they seem unable to locate the exact position (Bower, 1974).

Early auditory perception is quite remarkable, too, in its sensitivity to the characteristics of sound that are related to speech (Acredolo and Hake, 1982). Newborns are able to discriminate different pitches, and they seem to have clear pitch preferences. Low pitches have a calming effect; high pitches tend to elicit stress reactions (Eisenberg, 1976). Neonates can also discriminate sounds of different duration, which is critical to processing spoken language. Constant sound, such as a bland tone, often results in widening of the eyes, gross motor movements, and increased heart rate. Speechlike sounds elicit such fine motor movements as facial grimacing, pupil dilation, and searching with the eyes. And the story does not end there: Freedman (1971) reported that newborns respond more to a female human voice than to an inanimate object (a bell). Condon and Sander (1974) found that involuntary bodily movements in very young infants match the fluctuations in male or female speech, but not in disconnected vowel sounds or tapping sounds. These researchers suggest that infants have a special sensitivity to human language, a topic we return to in Chapter 5.

Seeing the World

In many ways, vision may be considered our most important sense. Adults report that they value their eyesight more than any of their other senses. They relate vision to comprehension by saying "I see what you mean." Visual stimulation is an extremely important source of contact between infants and the environment. Indeed, whenever they are awake, infants seem to be preoccupied with looking at the broad environment or examining particular parts of it. No reinforcement is needed for this activity other than sufficiently interesting sights (Fantz, 1969). Perhaps for these reasons, more research has been devoted to vision than to any other perceptual process.

Until a few decades ago, the newborn infant was believed to be incapable of processing visual information meaningfully. Today we know that the visual system is relatively well developed at birth and that the neonate demonstrates considerable visual ability. Every structure in the visual system undergoes some early postnatal change, however (Banks and Salapatek, 1983). Cells in the retina shift their location, the optic nerve completes myelination, and connections between neurons in the visual cortex grow dramatically in number. It would be surprising *not* to see parallel growth in visual capacities.

What Does the World Look Like to the Young Infant?   Although we have no definitive answer to this question, we can make some reasonable guesses. For example, we know that infants respond to brightness immediately after birth. The newborn is also sensitive to movement. A few days after birth babies are able to track some moving objects, although this response is uneven and focus is easily lost. By about 2 months of age smooth, accurate tracking is evident, due to coordination of the eye muscles and perhaps to development of the brain centers that control vision (Bronson, 1974).

If newborns are sensitive to brightness and movement, can they also distinguish color? It appears that they can (Banks and Salapatek, 1983), and that their color perception may closely resemble that of mature individuals. Color perception is related to the wavelength of light. But color vision is not simply a response to wavelength gradations; humans naturally tend to see categories of color. For example, if a yellow light's wavelength is gradually increased, it will suddenly be perceived as a shade of red rather than a shade of yellow. Bornstein and his associates (1975), using the habituation technique, asked whether this kind of perception exists early in life. They presented 4-month-olds with wavelengths that correspond to what adults see as blue, green, yellow, and red. Infants repeatedly presented with one wavelength habituate to that wavelength. When a change in wavelength produces renewed attention, it can be concluded that a different color is being perceived. The infants' reactions indicated that they were viewing the stimuli much as adults would—that is, in categories of color. This finding is important because it suggests that human color categorization is not the result of language or naming systems. Rather, an innate tendency to perceive color categories may give rise to language categories for color.

Another basic visual ability that has been studied is *visual acuity,* the capacity to detect both small stimuli and small details of large visual patterns. Visual acuity is evaluated by physicians when they ask individuals to identify letters on Snellen charts. Infants' acuity is tested by various means. One method takes advantage of the involuntary sideward movements of the eyes in response to moving stimuli. When infants are presented with a striped pattern, for example, sideward movements of the eyes occur only when the babies detect the stripes. The width of the spaces between the stripes can then be taken as a measure of visual acuity. Such measurements show that young infants see at 20 feet what adults normally see at 150 to 400 feet (Fantz, Ordy, and Udelf, 1962; Marg, Freeman, Peltzman, and Goldstein, 1976). Between 6 months and 1 year of age, acuity approaches that of the adult with normal vision.

Pattern Perception. Extensive research has been conducted to determine exactly the kinds of patterns or forms infants can discriminate, and what their preferences are. The work of Robert Fantz (1958, 1961) is important because it proved wrong the earlier assumption that infants cannot distinguish pattern and form. Fantz used preferential looking to show that infants could recognize particular patterns. He began by building a special crib that was partially enclosed. Above the infants' head was a plain gray ceiling, on which various pairs of target stimuli were placed. An identical pair of figures, such as two triangles, was hung from the ceiling one foot apart and one foot above the infant's head. By means of a peephole in the top of the apparatus, Fantz could tell how much time the infant looked at each of the triangles. Not surprisingly, looking time was equivalent for identical figures. But when a "bull's-eye" and horizontal stripes were introduced together, infants over 8 weeks of age preferred the bull's-eye to the stripes. Such a finding indicated that infants were able to discriminate one pattern from another. To reduce the likelihood that differences in looking time were due to very early visual experience and learning, Fantz later tested infants under 5 days of age. Various stimulus configurations were also used, including a drawing of

FIGURE 4–4
Fixation time
(preference) of very
young children to
patterned and plain
disks. Black bars
show the results for 2
to 3 months olds,
gray bars for those
more than 3 months
old. Adapted from
Origin of form
perception, by Robert
Fantz. Copyright ©
1961 by *Scientific
American,* Inc. All rights
reserved.

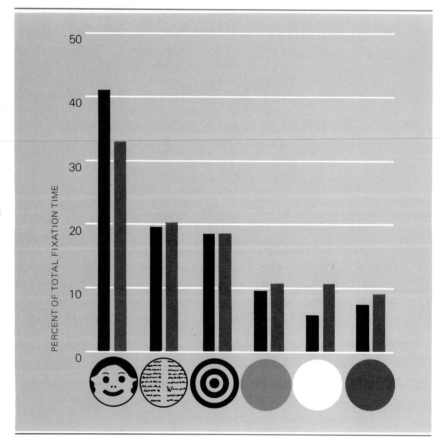

the human face. Some of the results of this later work appear in Figure 4–4, which shows a definite preference by the very young for patterned stimuli.

Fantz also suggested that infants prefer the more complex of two patterns, and numerous later studies confirmed this (Acredolo and Hake, 1982). Complexity is defined in different ways: as number of elements, number of turns, amount of randomness, and the like. Complexity is also related to contour—outline, border, edge, or black-and-white contrast. The amount of contour in a stimulus is a critical component of early visual preference (Fantz, Fagan, and Miranda, 1975).

Developmental Progression. From the enormous amount of research on vision, a developmental progression has been revealed. During the first 2 months of life, infants process lines, angles, and high contrast. From 2 months to 4 or 5, such simple dimensions as color and form can be processed as categories and units. Abstract relationships are perceived. For example, 3-month-olds are able to discriminate three dots arranged in a straight line from three dots arranged in a triangle (Milewski, 1979). At approximately 5 months, more complex patterns, such as the human face, are perceived as whole units (Cohen, 1979).

Changes in the way in which infants visually explore stimuli accompany this general progression. At first infants are captivated with particular features of objects or patterns. In one demonstration of this, newborns were placed in a special crib; a visual display—a black triangle on a white field—appeared above their eyes, and a camera recorded the scanning of their eyes (Salapatek and Kessen, 1966). The infants tended to look at the corners of the figure, where contrast (that is, contour) is the highest. Perhaps because of an attraction to contour, 1-month-olds tend to scan the outside of a stimulus. However, this gradually changes, so that 2- and 4-month-olds begin to scan the interior as well (Milewski, 1979). From infancy through early and middle adulthood, the child becomes less dependent on the stimulus itself and comes to select, attend, and more systematically and extensively explore the stimulus based on previous experience and the growing capacity to think and process information (Maurer and Salapatek, 1976).

Depth Perception. Many years ago it was determined that perception of depth is almost as accurate in 4-year-olds as in adults (Updegraff, 1930). Recent work has explored the question of whether the ability to perceive depth is present at birth or soon thereafter. Gibson and Walk provide the following overview of the problem:

> Human infants at the creeping and toddling stage are notoriously prone to falls from more or less high places. They must be kept from going over the brink by side panels on their cribs, gates on their stairways and the vigilance of adults. As their muscular coordination matures they begin to avoid such accidents on their own. Common sense might suggest that the child learns

Faces as Sources of Social and Emotional Information

The infant's ability to perceive the human face has received much attention from researchers. Fantz' discovery that infants can distinguish pattern and prefer facial configurations over other patterns pointed to a fascinating connection between perceptual and social-emotional development. Today we know that perception of the face follows the general course of perceptual growth. Newborns readily look at faces, presumably because they are attracted to stimuli that move (the eyes and mouth) and have dark and light contrast. At first infants scan the outer edges of the face and fixate the eyes and points of contrast. By 2 months of age they focus more on the interior parts of the face while attending to the eyes as well (Figure 4–5). Later they perceive the face as a whole unit and distinguish one face from another.

This sequence has broad implications. Because the face is a source of social and emotional information, it is important in the development of various environmental interactions. How do infants come to use the information carried by the facial expressions of others? Klinnert, Campos, Sorce, Emde, and Svejda (1983) propose that they do this through a gradual process consisting of four levels. During level 1, from birth to about 6 weeks, infants primarily scan the periphery of the face, and therefore miss most information related to emotional expression. Young infants do not consistently discriminate among facial emotions, much less use the information. During level 2, which lasts until about 4 to 5 months of age, infants come to better discriminate emotional expression as they pick up information from the interior of faces. However, they probably have little appreciation of the meaning of the different expressions they perceive. Such appreciation develops during level 3, which lasts until about 9 months

FIGURE 4–5
At first infants tend to scan the periphery of faces and points of contrast. They soon shift their interest more to the interior of the face. From Maurer and Salapatek (1975).

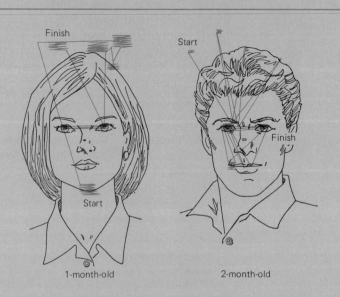

of age. Infants at this age are able to perceive faces as whole units and to react with positive or negative expressions, depending on the configurations they see. This emotional communication between infants and other people becomes extended to aspects of the environment at the final level, reached at about 9 months of age. Now children come to appreciate what others are reacting to in the environment, and deliberately search others' faces for information about ambiguous environmental events. This deliberate use of such information, called *social referencing*, provides the child with a powerful tool for benefitting from experience.

to recognize falling-off places by experience—that is, by falling and hurting himself. But is experience really the teacher? Or is the ability to perceive and avoid a brink part of the child's original endowment? (1960, p. 64)

To investigate the question, Gibson and Walk developed a special experimental setup, which they called the visual cliff. The "cliff," shown in Figure 4–6, is constructed from a heavy sheet of glass with a platform in the center that is raised slightly above the surface of the glass. The center platform, covered with a patterned material, is wide enough to hold the baby when it is creeping. The "shallow" side of the cliff is created by fastening the same patterned material directly beneath the glass on one side of the platform. The illusion of depth is created on the other side of the platform by placing the material several feet below the glass. The infant's mother stands at either the deep or the shallow side and beckons to the child to come to her (Gibson and Walk, 1960; Walk and Gibson, 1961).

Gibson and Walk began by testing thirty-six infants between 6½ and 14 months of age. The results were quite clear: Twenty-seven of the infants were willing to crawl off the center onto the shallow side, but only three ventured into the deep area. A number of infants actually crawled *away* from their mothers when called from the cliff side; others cried, presumably because it appeared to them that it was not possible to reach their mothers without crossing the brink. Clearly, infants old enough to crawl display perception of depth.

Are younger infants capable of perceiving depth? Campos, Langer, and Krowitz (1970) devised a measure that did not require locomotive abilities and thus could be used with younger infants. The investigators simply placed 44- to 115-day-old infants on either the shallow or the deep side of the visual-cliff apparatus and measured changes in heart rates. The study showed that infants as young as 2 months of age reacted differently to the sides of the cliff.

But do infants in visual-cliff studies actually perceive depth, or are they responding to other visual stimulation, such as differences in contour (Banks and Salapatek, 1983)? To help answer this question, attempts have been made to determine when functioning begins for certain visual processes that are known to be involved in depth perception. These pro-

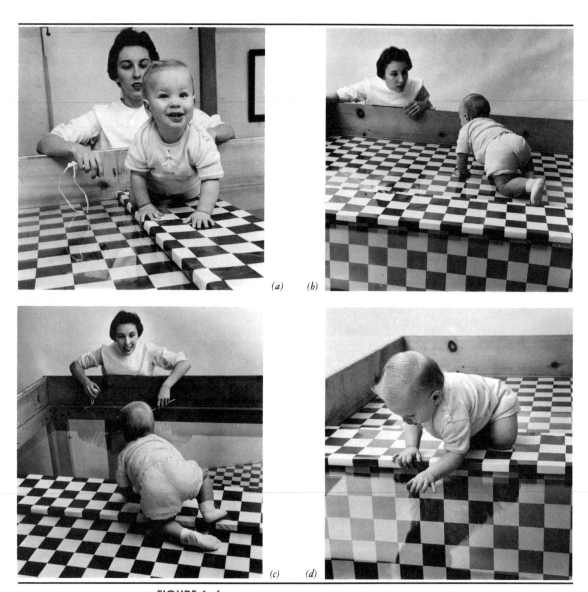

(a) *(b)*

(c) *(d)*

FIGURE 4–6
An infant on the visual cliff crawls to his mother across the shallow side but refuses to do so on the deep side, even though he has tactual evidence that the cliff is solid. From E. J. Gibson and R. D. Walk, "The visual cliff," *Scientific American,* April 1960, 65. Photos by William Vandivert. Reproduced by permission.

cesses sometimes require the use of both eyes (binocular cues); for example, when we look at an object each eye receives slightly different information depending on the distance of the object. Other visual cues for depth require only the use of one eye (monocular cues); for example, when we look down a long hallway the walls seem to approach each other with distance. Some of these cues for depth perception are developed by 2 months of age, and all are developed by 7 months. We thus have good reason to suspect that very young infants perceive depth, but exactly when and how is not firmly established.

Interaction of the Perceptual Systems

So far we have discussed the perceptual systems as independent. But perception frequently involves the simultaneous use of more than one system. Eye-hand coordination requires interaction of vision and touch; learning to read aloud requires vision and hearing.

Vision and Touch. These two perceptual systems appear to be integrated in young infants. The relationship has been suggested by showing a small and large ball to infants 2 to 4 months old. At this age, children are unable to reach and grasp objects voluntarily. The infants nevertheless reacted differently depending on the size of the balls. The small ball elicited movement of clenched hands to a center line; the large ball elicited a swiping motion (Bruner and Koslowski, 1972). In other words, seeing the objects seemed to affect movement related to grasping the objects.

Vision-touch interaction can be investigated more directly by having

FIGURE 4–7
Intersensory perception involves translating information from one sense modality into another. Left, © Louis Goldman, Rapho/Photo Researchers. ; right, © Alan Caruba, Photo Researchers.

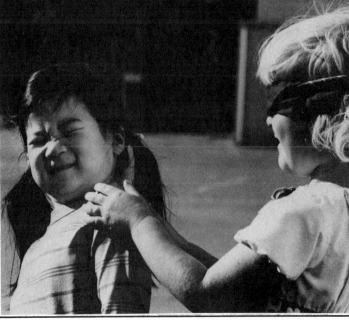

children explore objects with one perceptual system and then determining whether the information acquired can be transferred to the other perceptual system. For example, in one study babies who were allowed to explore objects tactually later chose those objects when allowed visually to explore several objects without touching them (Bryant, Jones, Claxton, and Perkins, 1972). This kind of transfer occurs by at least 6 months of age, depending on the characteristics of the objects and the time permitted for exploration (Acredolo and Hake, 1982; Ruff, 1980). In another study, 1-month-olds were allowed to explore either soft or hard plastic objects with their mouths, without seeing the objects (Gibson and Walker, 1984). They were then shown objects that looked identical to the original ones; one of the objects could be squeezed (it thus "looked" soft), but the other could not be. The amount of time the infants looked at the objects indicated that they related what they had mouthed (soft or hard) to what they saw.

Both visual and tactual exploration of objects becomes more systematic with age. It might thus be expected that as children age, they take in more information, which in turn leads to better recognition and transfer. In fact, intersensory recognition does improve throughout the first seven years of life (Abravanel, 1967; Birch and Lefford, 1963, 1967).

Vision and Hearing. Vision and hearing too seem to be integrated at birth; when infants hear sounds they orient their eyes in the direction from which they come. Aronson and Rosenbloom (1971) examined the reactions of 3-week-old babies to a situation in which their usual expectations for sound were not met. Mothers and their infants were positioned on opposite sides of a window, and the mothers spoke to the infants through microphones. Their voices were then displaced so that the sounds seemed to come from a few feet to the right or left of the mothers. The infants were definitely disturbed by the situation. Later it was shown that young infants oriented their eyes midway between the location of the mouth and the sounds, whereas older infants looked at their mothers but turned their heads to better pick up the sounds (Aronson and Dunkel, cited in Bower, 1974). The older babies appeared able to deal with the two perceptual systems as independent of each other.

Young babies can also link sound and vision according to synchrony. Spelke (1979) showed 4-month-olds a film of a toy monkey and simultaneously showed another film of a toy donkey. Each animal bounced up and down, but at a different rate. A sound track that matched the rhythm of one of the animals was also played. The infants showed greater visual fixation to the film to which the sound was synchronized. They apparently were able to identify the way in which the visual information matched the auditory information.

The results of the studies just described can be explained in terms of learning, since the infants could have learned to associate the human voice with the human face and rhythmic movement with rhythmic sound. It is more difficult to employ a learning explanation to the findings reported by Wagner, Winner, Cicchetti and Gardner (1981). The infants in this research, most of whom were 9 to 13 months old, were presented with pairs of visual and auditory stimuli that matched each other along abstract dimensions. For example, a broken line/continuous line (the visual pair) was matched with a pulsing tone/continuous tone (the auditory pair). Or an arrow pointing up/arrow pointing down (the visual stimuli) was matched with an ascending tone/descending tone. Using a complex experimental design, the researchers were able to determine whether the infants perceived similarity between the matching visual and auditory stimuli. For three of the eight stimuli sets, the infants were able to do so. The ability is quite remarkable, because infants typically do not experience the events to which they were experimentally exposed.

Although no one doubts that learning plays a role in the development of integration, and it appears that some coordination may be built into the organism of the perceptual systems, it has become increasingly clear that the perceptual and learning abilities of young infants are geared for rapid and active interaction with the environment. As illustrated by the progression of perception of faces, much of this interaction is tied to the growth of social and emotional processes. We turn now to this aspect of human functioning.

SOCIAL-EMOTIONAL DEVELOPMENT

The development of social and emotional behavior in early life rivals the dramatic rate of growth in the perceptual, learning, and motor systems. Social relationships do not appear suddenly, of course; they are shaped gradually by the interplay of the maturing child with its primary caretakers. Various theories have attempted to explain social-emotional development; some specifically emphasize the importance of early life.

Freud's View

Freud was among the first to stress that certain experiences in infancy establish behavioral and personality patterns that endure throughout the entire life span. Few developmentalists today subscribe to all of Freud's views, but psychoanalytic thinking has had an enormous impact on contemporary ideas and research.

Freud's theory is a comprehensive description of development that focuses on internal, or intrapsychic, events. Freud believed that personality consists of three components or structures: id, ego, and superego. The id, characterized as a reservoir of primitive instincts and drives, is present at birth; it is the force that presses for immediate gratification of bodily needs and wants. The ego is the practical, rational component of personality. The ego begins to emerge during the first year of life, in response to the fact that the infant cannot always have what it wants. An example of the emerging ego is the child's learning other strategies for coaxing adults into action when crying does not produce immediate results. Between the third and fourth years of life the superego or "moral agent" of personality develops as the child identifies with its same-sexed parent and begins to incorporate adult standards of right and wrong.

Freud also proposed that development occurs in universal stages that do not vary in sequence. These stages are largely determined by an innate tendency to reduce tension and achieve a pleasurable experience. Each stage is given its unique character by the development of sensitivity in a particular part of the body or *erogenous zone*—that is, an area that is particularly sensitive to erotic stimulation—at a particular time in the developmental sequence. Freud described these stages as "psychosexual" to indicate that development is the outcome of the successive focusing on and reduction of tension in various erogenous zones that predominate at different times in life. Each stage is associated with a particular conflict that must be resolved before the child can move psychologically to the next stage.

There are two reasons why difficulty may be experienced in leaving one stage and going on to the next. One is that the child may not be able to satisfy the demands others make; in this case the child's own needs will also not be satisfied and the resulting conflict, according to Freud, can leave permanent frustration in the individual's psychological makeup. Alternatively, needs may be so well satisfied that the child is unwilling to leave the stage and, as a result, the behaviors that characterize that stage may continue. Thus, either frustration or overindulgence or a combination of the two is presumed to result in some *fixation* at a particular stage of development, although chronologically the individual has already passed through it.

Freud drew an analogy between this situation and military troops on the march. As they advance, they are met by opposition or conflict. If they are successful in winning the first battle (resolving the conflict), then most of the troops (psychological energy, or *libido*) will be available to move on to the next battle (stage). However, the greater the difficulty in winning the battle, the more troops will be left behind on the battlefield (fixation) and the fewer will be available to go on to the next confrontation. Presumably all individuals have some psychological energy remaining at each of the stages through which they pass, but when the amount is substantial, personality is adversely affected.

Oral Stage.   From birth through approximately the first year of life the infant's mouth is presumed to be the prevailing source of pleasurable sensations—for example, the pleasurable sensations associated with sucking.

At the same time, children of this age are quite physically and psychologically immature, so that they must be cared for by others. They may, therefore, be characterized psychologically in terms of *dependence* (upon the mother or other caretakers) and behavior involving acts of incorporation (taking things in). According to psychoanalytic theory, these behaviors represent durable or potentially durable styles of interaction with the world. The focus of personality organization at this period is not the mouth itself but dependency, the wish to be mothered, and the enjoyment of human closeness and warmth (Strupp, 1967).

Freud believed that individuals who become fixated at the oral stage are likely to develop an optimistic view of the world, to have relationships in adulthood that are primarily dependent in character, to be friendly and generous, but to expect, in turn, that the world will "mother them." We can readily see how this type of theorizing, which is central to psychoanalytic theory, attempts to explain patterns of later behavior in terms of earlier experiences.

The oral stage is said to end when the child is weaned, and with weaning comes the conflict that is presumed to be crucial during this period. That is, the more difficult it is for the child to leave the mother's breast or the bottle and its accompanying pleasures, the greater will be the proportion of libido left at this stage.

Anal Stage   From about one to three years of age, the focus shifts to the anal zone, with its functions of elimination and retention. Until this time, the infant has experienced few demands from others; now parents begin to interfere with the pleasure obtained from the excretory functions. The conflict of this stage is between parental demands and the sensations of pleasure associated with the anus.

Various aspects of the anal period may be related to later behavior. If children view their feces as a possession, toilet-training experiences may be the foundation for a host of attitudes about possessions and valuables (Baldwin, 1967). If the bowel movement is viewed as a gift to parents, love may become associated with material possessions or bestowing gifts. Excessive cleanliness or being pedantic also are viewed as stemming from the demands of toilet training. Still other psychological features of this stage involve the development of shame, shyness (a reaction to being looked at), and impulsivity.

Toilet training is the major focus of resolving the conflicts of the anal stage. According to psychoanalytic theory if parental demands are met with relative ease, then the basis for self-control is established. If there is difficulty, children may "fight back" by, for instance, deliberately defecating when and where they please—or, more precisely, when and where it displeases parents. Such aggressiveness and hostility, it is reasoned, may be carried into adulthood, where they take the form of excess stubbornness, willfulness, and related behavior. On the other hand, the child may react by retaining feces, thus setting the stage for the later characteristics of stinginess and stubbornness.

Phallic Stage.   At about 3½ years of age, the genital region becomes the focus of libidinal pleasure, as reflected in the young child's masturbation, curiosity, and inspection of the sexual organs. The conflict of this stage, according to Freud's theory, is the desire of the child to possess the opposite-sexed parent and fear of retaliation from the same-sexed parent. The male child, desirous of his mother as a love-sex object, fears castration at the hands of his father. He solves this *Oedipal conflict* by identifying with his father, thereby vicariously possessing his mother.

Identification involves the young boy "introjecting" the attitudes, ideals, and behaviors of his father—that is, becoming like his father. The female child experiences a parallel situation, the *Electra conflict*, brought about when she notes her lack of a penis and blames her mother for the deficiency. At the same time she becomes desirous of her father because he possesses a penis. Although the girl cannot fear castration, she does fear the loss of her mother's love. To allay her anxiety and prevent such a loss, the daughter identifies with her mother in a manner similar to the identification of a son with his father.

According to psychoanalytic theory, identification influences social, moral, and sex-role behaviors of both boys and girls. Should the Oedipal and Electra conflicts not be resolved satisfactorily, a wide array of behaviors can be affected.

Latency and the Genital Stage. The final two stages proposed by Freud, latency and the genital stage, are of less importance to understanding the early foundations of social and emotional behavior. Not only do they occur after the age of five or six years, but Freud himself considered them insignificant to the development of the basic structure of personality (Baldwin, 1967). Latency includes the years from the resolution of phallic conflicts to puberty and, by definition, is a time during which the libido lies dormant. The latency years are described as a relatively stable and serene period during which the child acquires many cultural skills. During the last psychosexual stage, the genital stage, the libido is seen as being reactivated and directed toward heterosexual involvements. Providing that strong fixations at earlier stages have not taken place, the individual is well on the way to establishing fruitful relationships with others and otherwise leading a "normal," satisfying life.

Erikson's View

Many theorists followed in Freud's footsteps, but fashioned psychoanalytic views in their own directions. Erik Erikson is one of these theorists.

Erikson accepts the idea that the libido exists at birth and is at the core of human functioning. He also assumes that there are stages of development, several of which coincide with Freudian ones (Table 4–1). Nevertheless, he has made some distinct deviations from Freudian theory (Maier, 1969).

First, Erikson places much greater emphasis on the role of the *ego*, or rational part of the personality, whereas Freud concentrated largely on the nonrational, instinctual components of the personality, the *id*. Because society and the changes that occur in it are important to the developing child, the psychosexual stages postulated by Freud are transformed by Erikson into psycho*social* stages. Second, the growing individual is placed within the larger social setting of the family and its cultural heritage rather than in the more restricted triangle of mother-child-father. Third, Erikson stresses the opportunity each individual has for resolving developmental crises, whereas Freud focused on the pathological outcomes of failure to resolve them adequately. "There is little," Er-

TABLE 4-1

Comparison of Erikson's Psychosocial and Freud's Psychosexual Stages of Development

Chronological Stages	Erikson's Stages	Freudian Stages
infancy	basic trust vs. mistrust	oral
1½-3 years (approximately)	autonomy vs. shame, doubt	anal
3-5½ years (approximately)	initiative vs. guilt	phallic
5½-12 years (approximately)	industry vs. inferiority	latency
adolescence	identity vs. role confusion	genital
young adulthood	intimacy vs. isolation	
adulthood	generativity vs. stagnation	
maturity	ego integrity vs. despair	

ikson writes, "that cannot be remedied later, there is much that can be prevented from happening at all" (Erikson, 1963, p. 104).

Because of Erikson's emphasis on social context, his theory frequently appears more relevant than Freud's to the kinds of encounters that children have with their everyday world. Additionally, despite his agreement with Freud on the importance of the early years, Erikson's recognition that humans continue to develop throughout the entire life span resulted in a developmental scheme involving eight stages extending from infancy to old age. Thus he provided a valuable extension to psychological theory. For our present purposes, however, discussion will focus on Erikson's interpretation of the four earlier stages of life.

Basic Trust vs. Mistrust. The foundation of development, according to Erikson, is woven around the theme of trust and hope. Newborns are seen as coming into the world experiencing a change from the warmth and regularity of the uterus. Yet they are not defenseless. Parents, particularly the mother, generally respond to their bodily needs, and the handling of the child largely determines the establishment of attitudes of trust or mistrust. During the early months contact with the world is not only through the mouth but also through the manner in which parents embrace, talk to, or smile at the infant. If a consistent and regular satisfaction of needs is received, certain expectancies about the world are established. The child comes to trust the environment and, in doing so, becomes open to new experiences.

Autonomy vs. Shame and Doubt. The major theme that next evolves, from about 1½ to 3 years of age, is the conflict of whether to assert or not assert one's will. During this time, children rapidly acquire the physical skill to explore the world and begin to see themselves as capable of manipulating some parts of it. The young child attempts to establish autonomy, which sometimes requires disruption of the previously established dependency upon others. But shame and doubt exist alternatively with the thrust for autonomy. They are based on the child's remaining dependency and on fear of going beyond one's capabilities. Toilet training reflects the essence of the conflicts of this stage; shame and doubt result from failure to meet parental expectations and an inability to be assertive, whereas autonomy is the outcome of self-control and assertion.

Initiative vs. Guilt.   Coinciding with Freud's phallic stage, Erikson postulates a conflict between initiative and guilt. The environment of three- to five-year-olds now invites—or even demands—that they assume some responsibility and master certain tasks. The child must initiate action in many spheres—action that sometimes conflicts with and intrudes upon the autonomy of others, and thus results in feelings of guilt. Like Freud, Erikson recognizes the increased interest in sex displayed by both girls and boys at this stage. But he sees the child's attraction for the opposite-sexed parent as less sexual and more the result of a reaching out to the one available representative of the opposite sex who has proven herself or himself. The sense of rivalry that naturally occurs with the same-sexed parent leads to a gradual replacement of the desired parent by other love objects. At the same time a more realistic view of the inequality between child and the same-sexed parent results in stronger relations with peers. The rival parent becomes the ideal toward which to strive (Maier, 1969). During this time, then, the child gradually comes to understand the roles and opportunities presented by society and must overcome feelings of failure and guilt with a sense of accomplishment.

Industry vs. Inferiority.   Given the above outcome, the youngster is ready to wrestle with the challenges that arise with entrance into the competitive world of formal schooling. This is the time of latency of sexual striving. With the Oedipal and Electra conflicts settled, peers become increasingly important. The child identifies with peers and regards them as a standard of behavior. The theme of this stage is the mastery of tasks in face of feelings of inferiority. As children achieve such mastery they become capable of facing the turbulent adolescent years that lie directly ahead. Erikson has much to say about this period, as we will see in chapter 14. For now, though, we will move on to the third major theoretical approach to early experience.

The Ethological View

Ethology has its basis in the study of animals. A fundamental thesis is that all animals, including humans, possess species-wide characteristics, which are the foundations for the development of at least some social behaviors. As Freedman (1968) has noted, ". . . [this] emphasis . . . is not meant to deny that familial and cultural institutions do indeed differentially influence behavior and personality. We . . . emphasize that such institutions only support or shape man's behavior and do not create it, as it were, out of the blue" (p.2). From this point of view, behavioral dispositions are considered to have evolved as the result of a Darwinian process of natural selection. Pressures from the environment exerted over long periods of time ensure that members of a species with the most adaptive behavior are most likely to survive and, thus, pass these characteristics on to their offspring. It is argued, then, that behavioral patterns shared by all members of a species are, or were, necessary for survival.

The manner in which ethologists have employed the evolutionary perspective to account for human behavior can be illustrated by considering the grasp reflex of the human infant. As we saw in chapter 3, the infant will respond to a light touch on the palm by closing the fingers firmly around the object. Ethologists believe that this reflex served the evolutionary ancestors of humans by permitting the young to hold onto the fur of their mothers. The reflex obviously has lost this specific function, but infants still grasp.

Grasping, clinging, and several other behaviors are viewed by ethologists as being biologically "wired-in" to ensure that infants become psychologically attached to their mothers. Attachment increases the chances of survival in a potentially hostile environment. As we see in the next section, the concept of attachment has become crucial in discussions of early experience.

ATTACHMENT: THE FIRST SOCIAL RELATIONSHIP

Attachment is the formation of an enduring social-emotional relationship between an infant and another person, usually a parent or primary caretaker. Almost all infants in all cultures form attachments, and only extreme departures in childrearing practices prevent their formation (Ainsworth, 1977).

Early Infant-Parent Communication

The simple physical appearance of infants elicits adult caretaking (Alley, 1983). Adults seem disposed to protect and display affection to infants based on the children's sizes and their body proportions. Other infantile characteristics such as roundness, softness, skin smoothness, helplessness, and perhaps even lack of coordination may also be especially appealing to adults.

Crying, among the most noticeable of the neonate's behaviors that serve to attract attention, can be caused by hunger, sudden sounds, and visual stimulation (Wolff, 1969). Crying is unappealing to most adults; mothers in particular may react with quickened heart rates and annoyance. Thus, a desire to end the crying, as well as a desire to meet the child's needs, probably account for much early caretaking. On the other hand, parents are frequently afraid to attend to crying, because they do not want to "spoil" their infants. But crying in very young children probably reflects real physical discomfort that needs to be alleviated.

When parents observe their infants smile, they appear amused and delighted. The smile is considered "cute" and perhaps an intimate communication of happiness and contentment. Newborns may imitate a smiling adult, but smiling is more likely to occur when a child is sleeping lightly (Konner, 1982). Such smiles appear to be related to the internal state of the child. The true *social* smile does not occur until the second month of life, when the infant responds to external stimuli with satisfaction and pleasure. Soon smiling occurs to a variety of environmental events—the presence of toys, a sleeping cat, a playful father. Most important, smiling rapidly becomes part of the communication between child and caretakers. Parents and infants reward each other with smiles for certain kinds of behavior, shaping each other in the process (Brackbill 1958; Gewirtz and Etzel, 1967).

This is not to say that parent-child interaction is always, or even mostly, conscious manipulation. On the contrary: Parents and children seem to have a remarkable intuitive ability to "tune in" to each other. Papousek and Papousek (1983) studied this interaction by filming parents and their offspring. They found that many parents intuitively set up intereaction. (See Figure 4–8.) For example, parents will test muscle tone to determine level of wakefulness before presenting stimulation. They may touch the child's hands to check whether the fist is open or closed or if grasping occurs. Parents also maximize visual contact, which is an important aspect of early communication. When holding the child, they adjust the distance between their eyes and the eyes of the child, to maximize the infant's ability to focus visually. They also try to center themselves in the baby's visual field at a specific distance from the child. Mothers in particular carry out a "greeting response"; they bend their heads, raise their eyebrows, and open their eyes widely. Observations of nursing infants provide further examples of coordination between child and mother. Sucking occurs in bursts of activity with pauses in between (Alberts, Kalverboer, and Hopkins, 1983): While the baby is sucking, the mother is quiet. When the infant pauses, the mother becomes active—touching the child and speaking to him or her. Nursing becomes an opportunity for establishing a social-emotional relationship.

Through such continual, mutual stimulation and responding infants and caretakers become especially important to each other. Within a relatively short period of time, a relationship develops that is considered crucial to the child's growth.

Theoretical Views

Early studies of attachment were guided by Freud's theory of psychosexual development. Freud proposed that attachment occurs during the oral stage of development. The mother (or the mother substitute) becomes the child's first object of attachment, due to her role in satisfying the infant's need for nourishment and the libidinal drives associated with the oral stage. It is not surprising, then, that experiences related to feeding and weaning were considered crucial to the development of personality and adjustment. Research did not support the specific connection between early feeding and weaning practices and later personality de-

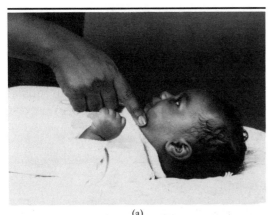

(a)

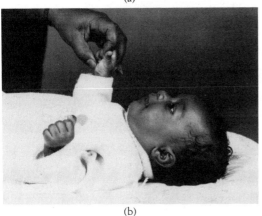

(b)

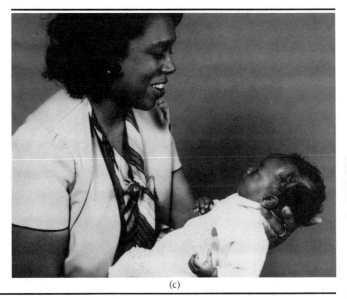

(c)

FIGURE 4–8
Many parents are intuitively competent. (a) and (b) demonstrate how mothers physically touch their infants to test the infants' condition. The mother in (c) demonstrates that parents distance infants to maximize visual fixation.   After Papousek and Papousek (1983). Courtesy A. Russell and R. Molla.

velopment (Caldwell, 1964). It did suggest, however, that the absence of the mother during infancy led to poor developmental outcomes (Campos, Barrett, Lamb, Goldsmith, and Stenberg, 1983). This finding fostered research into the effects of mother absence.

One of the ways in which ethology contributed to knowledge of attachment is through Konrad Lorenz's work on the "following" response. Lorenz was interested in the fact that certain kinds of animals seemed to have an innate tendency to follow the first moving objects that crossed their visual fields during some period of time soon after birth. Lorenz demonstrated the response by making himself the first object baby ducks saw after birth. He published a most convincing film showing ducklings following him as he walked and swam (Figure 4–9). Lorenz called the phenomenon *imprinting* and described it as inborn behavior that occurs during a *critical period* early in the animal's life. Imprinting is adaptive:

FIGURE 4–9
Konrad Lorenz and ducklings demonstrating the imprinting phenomenon. From "An Adopted Mother Goose," *Life,* August 22, 1955, 74. Copyright Thomas McEvoy, *Life* Magazine, © 1955 Time Inc. Reproduced by permission.

following the mother ensures protection and care. It was later hypothesized that human neonates may become attached to their mothers through a similar process. During a short time early in life, it was proposed, infants form a permanent attachment to another person, usually the mother. Should attachment not form at this critical time, development would not proceed optimally. The hypothesis encouraged much research on infant-parent attachment.

Among those who applied the ethological view to human development was John Bowlby. Bowlby suggested that infant behaviors such as crying, smiling, clinging, and sucking elicit parental caretaking and protection. This reciprocal system is the basis for attachment. Bowlby also claimed that evolutionary pressures would favor the child who stayed close to the mother (for food and protection) and yet explored the environment. Bowlby's ideas have been extremely influential and helpful in interpreting parent-child interaction. Babies do visually fixate their mothers, touch them, cry for attention, smile, and move close to them. During and following separation from their mothers, they cry and look in the direction where they last saw their mothers. Moreover, the process is a reciprocal one: Mothers respond to their infants' smiling, looking, and crying. This pattern of attachment is reasonably similar in very different societies (Ainsworth, 1967) and may be a species-wide characteristic that is biologically programmed.

Learning theorists look at attachment in a different way. One learning approach analyzes attachment in terms of the principles of operant conditioning (Gewirtz, 1968, 1972). This view suggests that the interaction between infant and caretaker is mutually reinforcing, so that each comes to exert control over the other's behavior. The mother (or mother substitute) satisfies the basic needs of the child, providing positive reinforcement and removing aversive stimuli. In providing food, a primary reinforcer, the mother and her behavior become secondary reinforcers. The child responds positively by smiling, cooing, or ceasing to cry, which in turn reinforces the parent's behavior. This reciprocal interaction results in mutual attachment. Differences among infants in attachment behavior may result from differences in the kinds of reinforcements with which they are provided. For example, a mother who enjoys talking to her infant during feeding may be shaping verbal responses, whereas a mother who likes to cuddle her infant may be shaping hugging behavior.

The Attachment Process

Although most infants form attachments to specific people at about 6 to 8 months of age (Figure 4–11), attachment is a gradual process that requires certain social-emotional skills (Ainsworth, 1973; Yarrow, 1972; Yarrow and Pedersen, 1972). These skills appear in the formation of all human attachments, but our discussion here focuses on attachment to the mother.

To begin with, infants must establish boundaries between themselves and the external environment, and they must discriminate between people and objects. Maturation is probably involved in these processes, but so is learning. Infants learn, for example, that crying brings an adult into view. Success in operating on the environment helps the infant to distinguish him- or herself from the rest of the world. It also aids in the discrimination between people and objects. Most infants give sustained

FIGURE 4–10
Patterns of attachment between infants and caretakers are quite similar across societies. Left, Victor Englebert © 1979; right, Kenneth Murray, Photo Researchers.

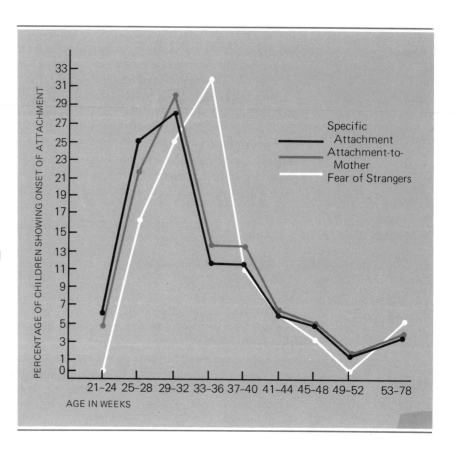

FIGURE 4-11
For most infants attachment occurs between 6 to 8 months of age. Adapted from H. R. Schaffer and P. E. Emerson, The development of social attachments in infancy, *Monographs of the Society for Research in Child Development* (1964), 29, no. 3. Copyright 1964 by the Society of Research in Child Development, Inc. Reproduced by permission. Kenneth Murray, Photo Researchers.

attention to another person by about 4 weeks of age and begin to show clearly differentiated responses to persons and objects shortly thereafter.

The next requirement is that the infant be able to discriminate familiar and unfamiliar people. Recognition of the mother may have already begun. The simplest way to assess this is to present the mother and a stranger (or their pictures) to the child. If the infant looks at the mother more than at the stranger, then at least passive discrimination must be taking place. We can also look for active discrimination—for example, if the baby smiles differently toward the mother or actively reaches out for her. Such behaviors are observed in most babies by the time they are 6 months old. Nevertheless, smiles, cries, looks, vocalizations, and approaches are directed toward an array of persons; infants typically go quite readily to most others.

At about 6 months, selective orientation to the mother occurs. Crying, smiling, clinging, looking, and approaching are now directed much more to the mother. In the mother's presence, the baby might explore the environment but also intermittently return to the mother or look in her direction, as if to check on her whereabouts. The attached child protests by crying or otherwise showing distress when the mother leaves the room. When the mother reappears, the child may cry intensely or stop crying, either of which suggests that the baby expects attention.

These behaviors require certain abilities on the part of the young child: perceptual discrimination, rudimentary memory, understanding that objects exist even though they are out of sight, and some idea that people cause events to happen (Hodapp and Mueller, 1982). Attachment indicates that the child has established trust and confidence in the mother. This is shown by the child's greater willingness to explore the environment in her presence than in the presence of a stranger or when alone. Such trust probably arises from earlier interaction in which the mother promptly and consistently responded to the infant's needs (Lamb, 1982). Indeed, children may construct a working mental model of their caretakers and of themselves that affects their behavior (Bretherton, 1985).

Another phenomenon that is often observed soon after the child shows attachment is fear or anxiety of strangers. Babies may refuse to go to strangers, cry when left with strangers, or cling to their mothers in the presence of strangers. Stranger anxiety is relatively common during the second half-year of life (Konner, 1982). This behavior does not occur in all infants in all situations, and like attachment, it probably arises gradually (Waters, Matas, and Sroufe, 1975).

To Whom Are Infants Attached? Although the infant's first attachment is often to the mother, attachments to others occur quite early. Schaffer and Emerson (1964) were among the first to investigate the formation of attachments to other family members. As a measure of attachment they used reports of infant crying or protesting brief everyday separations from specific individuals. Schaffer and Emerson found that a very high percentage of babies did indeed form first attachments to their mothers. But shortly afterward, or sometimes simultaneously, attachments were formed with familiar persons, such as fathers, grandparents, and siblings. By 6 months of age, over 50 percent of the infants were attached to their fathers as well as to their mothers, and by 18 months of age, over 70 percent were attached to both parents.

Subsequent research confirmed these basic results. Kotelchuck and his colleagues found that infants almost invariably become attached to both parents (Kotelchuck, Zelazo, Kagan, and Spelke, 1975; Ross, Kagan, Zelazo, and Kotelchuck, 1975). Moreover, fathers are eager to interact with their babies and can do so competently and sensitively (Parke and Sawin, 1980).

However, the basis for attachments with mothers and fathers may be different, because parents interact with their offspring differently depending on their own sex (Figure 4–12). Fathers most frequently pick up their infants for the purposes of play, while mothers are far more likely to pick up infants for caretaking or to move them away from undesirable activities. It is unclear whether this difference is due to females being trained for the traditional caretaking role, biologically based gender differences between mothers and fathers, or a combination of these factors (Lamb, Frodi, Hwang, Frodi, and Steinberg, 1982).

Parents also seem to prefer to interact with offspring of their own sex.

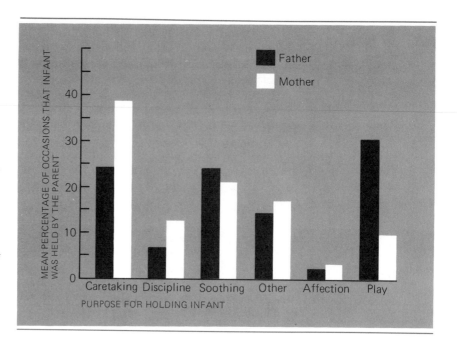

FIGURE 4–12
Reasons why mothers and fathers picked up their infants at seven and eight months of age. Note especially the dramatic differences in caretaking and play. Reprinted with permission from M. E. Lamb, ed., *The Role of the Father in Child Development.* Copyright © John Wiley & Sons, New York, 1976.

Fathers have been found to provide perceptual stimulation for infant sons more than for infant daughters, and to vocalize more with their young sons (Campos et al., 1983). Mothers also seem to prefer interaction with their same-sex babies. Infants, too, may have a preference for parents based on sex. Lamb (1977) found that all but one of the boys in a sample of infants in their second year of life preferred their fathers over their mothers.

How Do Parents Become Attached?

Pregnancy usually brings an anticipatory bonding, unless the pregnancy is unwanted (Hunt, 1979). Acceptance of the mothering role has been shown to be directly related to observed maternal responsiveness to an infant. For example, Moss (1967) interviewed mothers before the birth of their child and then observed mother-infant interaction when the infants were 3 weeks old. The attitudes of the mothers were clearly related to the way that they responded to their children. Ratings of the animation in the mother's voice during pregnancy have been shown to correlate positively with the amount of stimulation the mother provided the infant at 1 and 3 months of age (Moss, Robson, and Pedersen, 1969). And a prenatal measure of interest in affectionate contact related positively to the frequency with which mother and infant gazed at each other when the child was 1 month of age (Robson, Pedersen, and Moss, 1969).

Another variable thought to influence attachment is the opportunity for contact between parents and their children during the first hours or days following birth (Klaus and Kennell, 1978). The health of infants and mother-child relationships sometimes are improved by early contact following birth. And fathers have been found markedly to increase caregiving after being asked to undress their infants twice and to establish eye-to-eye contact with the children for 1 hour during the first 3 days of life. Nevertheless other investigations have found no or few effects from special early contact on immediate or long-term parent behaviors (Goldberg, 1983; Lamb and Hwang, 1982; Svejda, Pannabecker, and Emde, 1982). As we saw in Chapter 3, the weight of the evidence suggests that early parent-child contact is not critical for the development of healthy socioemotional bonds between parents and their infants. But early contact can serve as a stepping stone to parental attachment, which occurs gradually over several months.

The growth of attachment in mothers has been studied more than the growth of attachment in fathers. Immediately after the birth of their infants, at least some mothers perceive their infants as anonymous asocial objects and report only impersonal feelings of affection (Robson and Moss, 1971). When their infants begin to show smiling responses and make eye contact (in the second month), mothers begin to view the infants as real people with unique characteristics. Thus, it appears that as an infant begins to recognize the mother, the mother responds with an intensification of maternal feelings.

Quality of Attachment

So far we have discussed attachment as if it is an all-or-nothing relationship. In fact, attachments vary qualitatively.

The most common method used to evaluate the quality of attachment is the Strange Situation, developed by Ainsworth and Wittig (1969). The Strange Situation is a brief procedure conducted in a room with toys. Over a series of eight episodes an infant is observed alone, with the mother, with the mother and a stranger, and with only the stranger. The procedure involves separating the child involuntarily from the mother in an unfamiliar environment that includes an unfamiliar adult. A variety of behaviors are recorded to assess attachment and exploration under this stressful situation. The results of several studies demonstrate individual differences that divide children into three major categories.

Infants classified as *securely attached* behave in a way predicted by Bowlby's ethological theory. After involuntary separation from their mothers they attempt to reestablish interaction and proximity and act positively toward their parents. When in the presence of their mothers they actively explore the environment, using the mothers as a secure base. Other infants are classified as *insecurely attached*. Some of them, the *avoidant* group, actively avoid their returning mothers by looking away, turning away, or ignoring them. Other insecurely attached children, labeled *resistant*, act ambivalently: they seek interaction and contact but angrily or subtly reject it as well.

Ainsworth and her colleagues suggested that sensitive interaction between infants and caretakers is crucial in determining quality of attachment. Sensitivity involves responding to the child in a predictable and appropriate way. Emotional intensity may come into play, as well as the

Attachment In Rhesus Monkeys

Research with animals has been helpful in providing a general context within which to interpret the development of human attachment. Among the best is the work of Harry Harlow and his colleagues, who explored the basis of attachment in a series of studies of rhesus monkeys.

In one investigation Harlow and Zimmerman (1959) separated infant monkeys from their mothers and placed them individually in a cubicle with both a wire and a terry cloth "surrogate" mother. Half of the infants received milk from the wire surrogates; the cloth mothers "nursed" the remaining newborn monkeys. The monkeys spent more time in contact with the cloth mothers, regardless of the source of nourishment. Those who received milk from the wire surrogates went to them for that purpose, but otherwise they remained with the cuddly terry cloth mothers much of the time. Moreover, when the infants were exposed to fear-eliciting objects, they sought out and clung to the soft mothers. Harlow and Zimmerman demonstrated that physical contact, tactile stimulation, and the clinging response—which they labeled *contact comfort*—were especially important in these situations.

An initial period of mother-infant reciprocal interaction, which includes the clinging response, is important to the mother monkeys as they gradually become attached to their

FIGURE 4–13

Left, the wire and cloth "surrogate" mothers used by Harlow and his associates. Right, the infant's typical response was to run to the cloth mother when frightened, even if he or she had been fed by the wire one. From H. F. Harlow and R. R. Zimmerman, Affectional responses in the infant monkey. *Science,* 130 (August 21, 1959), 431–432. Reproduced by permission of the publisher and Harry F. Harlow, University of Wisconsin Primate Laboratory.

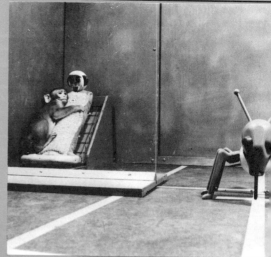

infants. When mother monkeys are separated from their infants they are upset by the separation; however, if the offspring are only a week to 10 days old, maternal upset can be relieved by the sight of *any* monkey infant. After this time, separation can be relieved only by the sight of the mothers' own infants. The mothers thus become attached to their infants after they have interacted with them for a period of time (Jensen, 1965). Furthermore, reciprocity is important, particularly in regard to contact comfort.

In several experiments, mother monkeys who had been separated from their infants were given substitute infants who would not cling to them (Harlow, 1971). In one case, the mother monkey was given a kitten. She made every effort to mother the kitten, and even attempted to nurse it! However, when the kitten failed to return the mother's clinging efforts, the monkey's maternal instincts waned and she totally abandoned the kitten. Similar rejection occurred when a mother monkey was given a 1-month-old monkey who had developed an "autistic pattern" of behavior, clutching itself and refusing contact with the mother monkey.

The Harlow studies imply that contact comfort may be quite important in human attachment. They also suggest that attachment of mothers develops gradually. Finally, they indicate that reciprocal interaction is extremely important in the growth of attachment. Human attachment may, of course, differ somewhat from attachment in monkeys, but the processes appear remarkably similar.

mutual delight mother and child receive from their interactions (Ainsworth and Bell, 1974). Quality of attachment has also been related to various patterns of child care during the first year (Joffe and Vaughn, 1982). Based on parental consistency and response appropriateness, infants develop expectations that determine their behavior in the Strange Situation.

Researchers have asked whether babies consistently display secure or insecure attachment over time as measured in the Strange Situation. Some have found remarkable consistency, others have not (Thompson, Lamb, and Estes, 1982). In many of these studies children changed from secure to insecure, or vice versa, within six months' time. Some of the findings might be attributable to methodological problems (Campos et al., 1983). However, several investigators noted that change was associated with family stress and change in child-care arrangements. Behavior in the Strange Situation seems to be related to current circumstances and will be stable over time to the extent that circumstances remain stable (Lamb, 1982).

Predicting Later Behavior.   Another question concerns the relationship between quality of attachment and other behaviors. This is an extremely important issue, especially when it involves the prediction of later behavior. Sroufe (1979) and his colleagues assume that development is best viewed in terms of an early foundation that is elaborated and transformed throughout life. Sroufe, Fox, and Pancake (1983) did research with 4- and 5-year-olds. These investigators argue that secure attachment—which involves trust in the caretaker—should be related to later confidence and skill in dealing with peers and in performing other tasks of the preschool period. They requested teachers to complete several ratings of dependency in the classroom. Some classroom observation was also conducted. The children had all been classified as securely attached, avoidant, or resistant in the Strange Situation at age 12 and 18 months. Most of them had shown consistency of classification across this time period. The clear finding was that children who had been securely attached as toddlers were less dependent and more self-reliant than their preschool peers. They sought help when their resources were insufficient, or when they were ill, injured, or distressed. They actively greeted the teachers and carried on frequent positive social exchanges. They were well liked by their teachers, involved with friends, and popular with peers.

Behavior in the Strange Situation has also been shown to predict various other later behaviors, such as compliance, cooperativeness, a game-like spirit, positive affect, sociability, resiliency, self-esteem, and social competence (Campos et al., 1983). Toddlers classified as securely attached appear to show more of these behaviors at later times than do toddlers classified as insecurely attached.

But a direct link between secure attachment and later behavior cannot be assumed from these findings. It is quite possible that the circumstances and the particular caretakers that encourage secure attachment also continue to support the child in a desirable way (Sroufe et al., 1983). This possibility presents a challenge to understand the process. For example, parents who sensitively meet the needs of their toddlers may continue the same sensitive interactions as their children grow older. If so, studies of these parents would be valuable.

SOCIAL DEPRIVATION AND SEPARATION

So far we have described early development that occurs in more or less typical circumstances. Neonates rapidly show advances in learning and perceptual abilities. They immediately enter into social relationships and by the end of the first year are socially and emotionally attached to the major figures in their lives, primarily the parents. It is reasonable to assume that certain basic experiences are necessary for such growth to occur. Most developmentalists also believe that early experiences set the stage for later growth (Lipsitt, 1983).

As we have already seen, Freud postulated that particular events during particular stages of early development would result in the thwarting of optimal growth. He regarded the infant's love for the mother as the model for all later love relationships, and early parent-child interaction as crucial to personality development (Freud, 1949). Following Freud and the ethological viewpoint, Bowlby (1969) argued that early defective mothering of orphans resulted in socially, intellectually, and physically impaired individuals. Watson and other behaviorists recognized that early learning, because of its being *first* and thus having no interference from previous experience, could be especially powerful in shaping the child's future (Lamb, 1978; Lipsitt, 1983).

Over the years, concern about the possible influence of adverse experience during the first few years of life has translated into research. Most investigators have focused on the effects of a disturbed mother-child relationship, due either to separation from the mother or to abusive mothering. Much of what is known is based on three types of investigations: experimental work with animals, research with children who lived in institutions or otherwise suffered maternal separation, and case studies of children exposed to extreme deprivation in their own homes.

Social Isolation in Animals

Innumerable studies show adverse effects of social deprivation on development in a variety of animals. Among the most important work is that of Harlow and his colleagues with young rhesus monkeys.

Harlow and Harlow (1970) isolated individual monkeys at birth in a stainless steel chamber in which all light was diffused, the temperature controlled, the air flow regulated, and all environmental sounds filtered. Food and water were provided automatically and the cage was cleaned by remote control. All physical needs were met, but animals saw no other living creature. After being raised in this manner for either three, six, or twelve months, each monkey was taken from the special chamber and placed in its own individual cage. Thereafter, the Harlows exposed each subject to a peer (another monkey who had also been reared in isolation) and to two other monkeys who had been reared in open cages with others. All four individuals were then put in a special playroom, typically for half an hour a day, five days a week, for six months. The playroom was equipped with a variety of toys. The Harlows report:

> *Fear is the overwhelming response in all monkeys raised in isolation.* Although the animals are physically healthy, they crouch and appear terror-stricken by their new environment . . . . When the other animals become aggressive, the isolates accept their abuse without making any effort to defend themselves. (1970, p. 95, italics added)

In later studies, efforts were made to correct this outcome. The first attempts were largely unsuccessful, suggesting that the lack of appropriate contact during the first months of life may leave permanent and irreversible scars (Suomi and Harlow, 1972). Repeated exposure to competent agemates similarly was unsuccessful and actually exaggerated the disturbed behavior. Finally, however, another method met with success.

Socially competent monkeys of 3 months of age were allowed to interact with 6-month-old previously isolated disturbed monkeys. The young monkey "therapists" were deliberately chosen because they could be depended upon, due to their age, to exhibit certain kinds of behavior. As predicted, they initiated social contact with the isolates, clinging to them. The isolates responded to the clinging and their self-directed behaviors, such as self-huddling and rocking, abated. When the "therapists" directed play behavior to the isolates, the older monkeys gradually began to reciprocate. Within two months virtually all behavioral disturbance was eliminated.

In interpreting this research, we must note that the infants initially experienced severe social deprivation, not just separation from the mother. However, the potential for adequate social development had not been destroyed (Suomi and Harlow, 1972). The researchers discussed the results in terms of the critical-period hypothesis. That is, it had previously been proposed that social contact during the early months of life is a critical experience for the growth of normal social responses in monkeys. According to this proposal, lack of social contact at that time would result in *irreversible* deficits. Because this did not occur, Suomi and Harlow suggested that early life, at least with regard to socialization in the rhesus monkey, be considered a *sensitive* but not a critical period. As it turns out, this suggestion may apply equally well to humans.

Institutionalization and Separation

Emotional, physical, and intellectual problems are known to occur with some frequency among children who have been separated from their primary caretakers and placed in institutions. Spitz (1965), for example, reported that institutionalized children who were adequately cared for in every bodily respect were retarded in physical and emotional development. They often withdrew and became depressed, and some died.

Although children living in institutions are frequently said to be deprived, the nature of the deprivation is not always clear (Figure 4–14). Nor has it always been agreed upon. An outgrowth of Freud's theory is the belief that the infant needs a primary love object to develop in a healthy manner, that this object should be a single adult figure, and that multiple mothers or dilution of the primary attachment is detrimental

FIGURE 4–14
Foundling-home children, at least in the past, were often deprived of social attachment and stimulation as well as perceptual and intellectual stimulation. The New York Public Library Picture Collection.

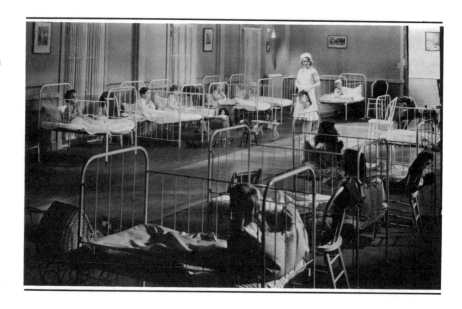

(Jersild, 1968). This position further maintains that such love is an essential element not only for the child's emotional development, but also for intellectual growth and physical well-being. Separating a child from his or her mother once an attachment is formed is said to be traumatic and may lead to retarded, impaired development or even death due to "emotional starvation."

Other theorists have emphasized various caretaker functions as crucial for the child's well-being (e.g., Yarrow, Goodwin, Manheimer, and Milowe, 1971). One of these is to provide perceptual stimulation; another is to stimulate the child intellectually, especially by the use of language. Adequate caretakers also interact with the child and shape appropriate social behaviors. Researchers have been interested in describing the consequences of deprivation, particularly long-term effects. One question has been of paramount concern: Does deprivation inevitably result in poor developmental outcome? We will look at the work of Tizard and her colleagues as an example of efforts to address this question.

These researchers followed a group of children who had been placed in residential nurseries in England as healthy, full-term infants less than 4 months of age (Tizard and Hodges, 1978; Tizard and Rees, 1974). The institutions were of high quality: staff-child ratio was favorable, and toys and books were readily available. However, personal relationships between the children and the caretakers were discouraged, and each child had many caretakers. All the children lived continuously in the institutions until at least 2 years of age. Then most were gradually adopted or restored to their natural parents.

An assessment conducted when the children were 4.5 years of age revealed that those still in the institutions and the restored children had no more behavior problems than a comparison group of home-reared youngsters. The adopted children were reported to have even fewer problems, and to have formed close attachments to their adoptive parents. Nevertheless, a minority of the institutional and ex-institutional children were said to be overly friendly, indiscriminately affectionate, and attention-seeking. Those who remained in the institutions and those who were restored to their mothers scored in the average range on standardized intelligence tests, whereas the adopted children scored somewhat higher than average.

When the children were 8, another evaluation was conducted. By this time only a few of the youngsters remained in the institution, so the main comparisons were between the adopted and the restored children. Overall, those adopted early scored higher than average on tests of intelligence, whereas the other children scored about average. The higher social class of the families of the early adopted was related to this difference. The adopted children were also reported by their adoptive parents to have fewer behavioral problems and to be more attached emotionally to their adoptive mothers. This finding reflected a difference in attitudes between the mothers of these groups of children: More of the adoptive mothers felt positively toward their children. Both sets of parents agreed, however, that the youngsters tended to be overfriendly and attention-

Effects of Day Care

Approximately 48 percent of all mothers of preschool children in the United States today work outside the home. Forty-five percent of these children are cared for by nonrelatives—32 percent in private homes and 13 percent in day care or nursery school programs (Clarke-Stewart and Fein, 1983). Millions of young children are thus experiencing maternal separation and multiple caretakers in the normal course of events. The impact of day care and nursery school has become a vital focus of research.

According to most research, day care programs are not necessarily detrimental to children and may even result in positive gains. Kagan, Kearsley, and Zelazo (1975) compared Chinese and Caucasian infants who attended day care centers from age 3½ months to 30 months with home-reared children of the same age. The groups were matched according to socioeconomic status of their families, ethnicity, and sex. The investigators found no differences in separation protest in the groups and an overwhelming preference for mother over other adults, including the caretaker at the center. The only significant difference found between the groups was that the Chinese infants, both day care and home-reared, exhibited more proximity behaviors and touching of the mother than the Caucasian group. The researchers interpreted these results as showing that the child's attachment to his or her mother is influenced more by the home experience than by whether or not the child has attended day care centers. Kagan and his colleagues concluded that it is the quality of the home experience that is critical to the development of the mother-infant bond, and that day care does not dilute the bond that is formed.

Other studies support the conclusion reached by the Kagan group. Maccoby and Feldman (1972) compared *kibbutz*-reared Israeli children who are separated from their mothers much of the time and American children of the same age. The investigators found that both groups of children exhibited similar attachment behaviors toward their mothers despite very different rearing conditions. Another study found no differences among day care children and those reared with mothers at home, particularly in relationships with their mothers or in their affiliation, nurturance, hostility, happiness, or emotionality (Caldwell, Wright, Honig, and Tannenbaum, 1970).

Clarke-Stewart and Fein's (1983) extensive review of the research agrees with these findings. Children in early childhood programs form affectionate bonds with other caretakers, and these bonds provide security and comfort. The children still prefer their mothers, however. Clarke-Stewart and Fein report that the quality of attachment may be affected for some children, in the direction of greater distance, avoidance, and independence from the mother. This pattern may be more extreme when day care begins before a secure attachment has been formed. For most children, the pattern may be an adaptive response to the situation rather than a pathological disturbance.

Clarke-Stewart and Fein address other questions about the effects of day care. The most consistent finding concerning social development is that children who attend early childhood programs are more socially competent and mature. They are more self-confident, assertive, outgoing, self-sufficient, and knowledgeable about the world. Some displays of social behavior are negative: The children may be less agreeable, less polite, less compliant to directives, and less respectful of others' rights, as well as more irritable, rebellious, and hostile. Because these kinds of negative behaviors typically increase during the preschool period, they may actually reflect maturation. In addition, youngsters in programs advance more rapidly intellectually. Effects on physical health are more mixed. Children from poor families show increases in height and weight and decreases in pediatric problems. Independent of social class, program children have more—but not more serious—infectious diseases, such as colds, flu, and rashes.

Factors that are likely to influence the success of day care for any one child include the developmental level of the child and characteristics of child and mother. For example, babies of 2 years and younger need loving, stimulating adult contact more than they need peer interactions (Scarr, 1984). Day care in private homes, which usually provides a consistent adult relationship, might thus be optimal for such children. In contrast, 3 year olds are ready for and can benefit more from the variety of peer interactions and educational activities typically offered by large day care centers. Moreover, the better programs have received the most research attention, and programs could be expected to vary in quality. Thus, the term "day care" is meaningless without a description of the goals and quality of the particular program in question (McCrae and Herbert-Jackson, 1976). Positive outcome is likely to be associated with continuity and stability of the program, well-trained personnel, clear goals, a favorable child-staff ratio, and availability of toys, books, and other appropriate materials.

seeking. Teachers rated both the adopted and the restored groups as having peer problems and as being restless, attention-seeking, and difficult to discipline.

In summarizing this research, Tizard and Hodges' (1978) primary conclusion is that the subsequent development of early institutionalized children strongly depends on the environment to which they are moved. This applies to social and emotional behavior as well as to cognitive growth. Children who went into adoptive homes went to parents who wanted them and were willing to spend much time with them. These parents gave favorable reports of their children, and the children were doing well intellectually. In contrast, parents of the restored children, who had left their offspring in institutions for several years, were at least ambivalent about having their children back. Moreover, many of the restored youngsters returned to homes in which they had to compete for time and affection with siblings and stepfathers. The later the child was restored, the less chance there was for mutual attachment, as if the mother had little room in her life for the child. In several ways these children were not doing as well as the adopted children.

Nevertheless, adopted and restored children did resemble each other; that is, they were rated by teachers as having problems and were considered by their parents as overfriendly to strangers and attention-seeking. It appears that early institutionalization might have adversely affected a certain portion of the youngsters—about half of the adopted and two-thirds of the restored. As with all studies of institutionalization, it is difficult to establish causes. For example, the family backgrounds of the youngsters or their environments at age 8 might account for their difficulties. Thus, the investigators are cautious in their interpretations.

What does seem clear is that children reared in institutions during the preschool years are at risk for later social difficulties, but the lack of early stable parenting can be overcome by later positive experiences (Rutter and Garmezy, 1983).

Extreme Deprivation In Humans

Another way in which deprivation in early childhood has been studied is through case studies of individual children who experienced deprivation in their own homes or in the homes of their primary caretakers. In many of these instances the children were exposed to severe impoverishment. Skuse (1984a, 1984b) reviewed several recent cases involving nine children. Following is a description of male identical twins whose mother had died shortly after giving birth. For the first eleven months the twins lived in a children's home. They then spent six months with a maternal aunt, and subsequently resided with their father and stepmother.

> For 5½ yr, until their discovery at the age of 7, the twins lived under most abnormal conditions, in a quiet street of family houses in Czechoslovakia. Because of the actions of their stepmother, who had her own children whom she actively preferred, the boys grew up in almost total isolation, never being allowed out of the house but living in a small unheated closet. They were often locked up for long periods in the cellar, sleeping on the floor on a plastic sheet, and they were cruelly chastised. When discovered at the age of 7 they could barely walk. They showed reactions of surprise and horror to objects and activities normally very familiar to children of that age, such as moving mechanical toys, a TV set or traffic in the street. Their spontaneous speech was very poor, as was their play. (Koluchova, 1972, 1976, cited by Skuse, 1984, p. 546)

The twins had only a handful of building blocks for play. They received minimal language stimulation. Their father beat them regularly with a rubber hose until they were unable to move. They suffered malnutrition.

Although the environment of the Koluchova twins would certainly be considered impoverished by most standards, some cases reviewed by Skuse were even more extreme. Almost half of the children suffered severe malnutrition, communication was limited for all, half had been physically restrained, and all experienced lack of stimulation. These children had some contact with primary caretakers, but the relationships were characterized by neglect and/or punishment and pain.

When discovered or brought for help (at ages 2.5 to 13.7 years) most of the youngsters displayed certain behaviors: motor retardation, absent or rudimentary language, grossly retarded perceptual-motor skills, lack of emotional expression, lack of attachment behavior, and social withdrawal. Deficits this severe are typically seen only in children who are mentally retarded or seriously disturbed (Skuse, 1984a). Variations were observed among the children, however. For example, the Koluchova twins were timid and mistrustful; others were variously affectionate, eager for social contact, profoundly withdrawn, or hostile toward strangers.

Most of the children were then placed in foster homes and nursery groups. Follow-up evaluations showed considerable differences concerning their progress. (At follow-up they ranged in age from 13 to 20 years. One child had died a natural death.) Three of the children showed relatively poor outcomes; the others had made remarkable and quite rapid improvement. The Koluchova twins, who had been placed with a foster family, were among those who had improved immensely. They had good motor and self-help skills. Intelligence was described as above average, and by age 20 the twins had completed a demanding training program in office machinery maintenance. Social-emotional development appeared very satisfactory, with the twins having emotional bonds to their foster mother and sisters. The twins also reportedly have normal relationships with other females.

Although Skuse's review is obviously limited to a handful of children, the author attempted to draw some useful conclusions:

1. Congenital abnormalities (that is, microcephaly, which is generally related to mental retardation) and malnutrition appeared to be associated with poor outcome. So did the lack of expressive and comprehensive speech at the time the children were rescued. The social behavior of the children when they were examined was not strongly related to eventual outcome. However, children who seemed attached to one specific adult at that time appeared to easily form relationships with subsequent caretakers and peers.

2. Some areas of functioning were less affected by deprivation than others. Perceptual-motor and gross motor skills were relatively resilient. Expressive speech was seriously affected and improved more slowly than comprehension in the adequate environment.

3. When improvement occurred, it did so quite rapidly. This was notable in visual perception and language skills.

4. Intensity of intervention (such as language training) did not appear crucial in bringing about improvement. Rather, stimulation in the new environment, coupled with the opportunity to form social-emotional bonds with a caring adult, formed the backbone of developmental progress.

Does Early Deprivation Lead To Trouble Later?

Evidence that has so far accumulated from both animal and human studies indicate that both "yes" and "no" are appropriate answers to this important question. Severe isolation and moderate to severe deprivation of stimulation and social-emotional bonds do indeed often result in deficits. It is not inevitable, however, that the lack of a positive mother figure leads to permanent problems. Children are clearly capable of showing dramatic reversals in the course of development. Given a biological system that is free of abnormalities, the way to adequate development is not easily and permanently lost.

But it would be a mistake to assume that every child recovers from impoverishment. Because continuity potentially exists between early deprivation and later development (Lipsitt, 1983), the quality of the later environment is important to the eventual outcome. Adequate social-emotional relationships, intellectual stimulation, and diet seem to be central. Peer interaction and opportunity for formal learning also undoubtedly play a role.

SUMMARY

1. The very young infant is able to benefit from experience due to the ability to learn. *Habituation,* the decrement in responding to repeated presentations of a stimulus, occurs, as do *classical* and *operant conditioning.* The infant is thus able to learn new associations and to act on the world with consequences. *Observational learning* also has an early foundation.

2. *Sensation* involves stimulation of the sensory receptors by physical energies from the internal and external environment. *Perception* is the selection, organization, and modification of sensory input. Visual fixation and preferential looking, dishabituation, changes in movement and breathing in the stabilimeter, and changes in facial expressions are examples of the responses used to indicate perception. The sensory systems appear to operate before birth and the infant thus comes into the world with the ability to receive stimulation. Perceptual ability is somewhat limited, but develops rapidly.

3. Neonates discriminate odors, find some more pleasant than others, and have limited ability to localize odors in space. They distinguish sweet, bitter, salty, and sour tastes, and show a definite preference for sweetness. Neonates respond to touch, sometimes with reflexes; in a short period of time they have a well-established sensitivity to pain. Auditory perception is remarkably sensitive in discriminating sounds in ways that are helpful for later language development.

4. Visual perception, often considered our most important perceptual system, has been extensively studied in babies. Early in life infants respond to brightness and movement. Acuity, the ability to detect small stimuli and small details, approaches normal levels by the time the infant is 6 to 12 months of age. Babies perceive pattern and form, and prefer complex stimuli.

5. The infant's ability to perceive human faces follows the general developmental course of visual perception. The child first scans the outline of the face and then the internal parts. Because humans use the facial expressions of others to gain information about ambiguous situations, a process known as *social referencing,* the capacity of the infant to "read" facial expression is being studied. Babies appear to use social referencing by about 9 months of age.

6. Another area of study concerns the interaction of the perceptual systems. It appears that the systems are coordinated to some extent at birth. Much is yet to be discovered about the growth of the interaction of the perceptual systems, but it is obvious that perception is intricately linked to social-emotional development.

7. Freud's stage theory of psychosexual development puts much emphasis on early experience. Erikson's psychosocial stages extend theory into later life, but rely heavily on Freud's ideas. Ethological theory emphasizes a biological basis for social behaviors.

8. Social relationships are, of course, shaped gradually, but infants and parents are primed to enter into an interaction. Adults react to an infant's size, body shape, helplessness, crying, and smiling by initiating interaction and caring for the child. Crying in the neonate signals the need for care. The true social smile occurs during the second month, and quickly becomes part of parent-child interaction. Parents are often very sensitive in dealing with their babies.

9. The concept of *attachment*, the formation of an enduring bond with the available and sensitive caretaker, is central. Freud and the *ethological* approach taken by Lorenz and Bowlby both emphasize the importance of attachment, and suggest that it is a critical event with implications for later development. Learning theorists attribute attachment to different causes, but nevertheless consider it important. Attachment develops by the time the child is 6 to 8 months of age, in a series of social-emotional accomplishments. At the same time, infants often show discomfort or fear of strangers.

10. Parental interaction is partly determined by sex: Fathers are playful, whereas mothers are more concerned with childcare. There is also some evidence that parents prefer to interact with their same-sex children. Parents are not automatically attached to their infants; attitudes about the pregnancy and the child's social behavior help determine parental attachment.

11. Although attachment occurs in most situations, its quality depends on parental consistency and sensitivity. Babies show secure or avoidant and resistant attachment in the Strange Situation. Quality of attachment may change with changing environmental circumstances. Secure attachment has been shown to be related to later adaptive behaviors, perhaps because parents who support secure attachment continue to provide positive support.

12. The hypothesis that adverse early experience causes irreversible damage to children has been explored in animal and human research of infants who experienced lack of stimulation, poor mothering, and abusive mothering. There is no doubt that early adverse experiences put the child at developmental risk. Eventual outcomes depend on many factors, however.

5 LANGUAGE AND COMMUNICATION

A child's first spoken word is a momentous occasion: The beginning of the ability to communicate with others through speech. We are always speaking to others—at school, at home, and in business. Through written language, we are able to preserve our ideas and to benefit from the accomplishments of the past. Language is also necessary in social situations. If we cannot understand and communicate with others, we can have difficulty coping with even simple problems.

Sophisticated communication is more than linguistic ability: it involves knowing what to say as well as how and when to say it. The speaker must be sensitive to the person(s) to whom he or she is communicating as well as to the context. The picture that has begun to emerge from recent studies is that linguistic competence is achieved fairly early. The broader ability to communicate effectively continues to develop well into adolescence and perhaps throughout the life span.

This chapter begins with a description of language development from the earliest babbling in the crib. We then focus on how words are learned, and the processes through which words are arranged into grammatical and understandable sentences. Finally, we examine language as it is actually used by children and adults in social contexts.

PREVERBAL BEHAVIOR

Children usually say their first words sometime around their first birthdays. However, until then infants are not quiet—they laugh, cry, and make speechlike sounds. In addition, from very early in life they are able to hear subtle but essential distinctions among speech sounds.

Perceiving Speech

To hear speech and other sounds accurately, the ears must function properly, as must the nervous system. Many of the structures of the ear reach their mature sizes by birth. For example, the bones of the middle ear, which link the eardrum to receptors in the inner ear, reach adult proportions by approximately eight months after conception. The nerve pathways leading from the ear to the brain develop in the fetal period; at birth, many of these pathways are even myelinated (Hecox, 1975). All these facts suggest that the infant is well prepared to hear very early in life. In fact, as we saw in chapter 4, infants do hear remarkably well from birth; indeed, they hear almost as well as adults (Aslin, Pisoni, and Jusczyk, 1983).

Perception of Speech Material. To understand how infants understand and produce language, we need to know more about what speech is. The raw materials of language are *phonemes*, which are distinctive sounds that can be combined to form words. Consider, for example, the sound represented by the *p* in *pin, pat,* and *pet,* as well as the sound associated with the *b* in *bin, bat,* or *bed.* Each is a phoneme, an elemental sound that can be combined with other elemental sounds to form words. These two particular phonemes are closely related because both are produced by first closing the lips to stop the flow of air from the lungs, then opening the lips to release the trapped air. The differences between them are subtle, but infants can perceive these very subtle differences in adult speech. If a 1-month-old infant is presented with the sound *pa* and then with successive versions of *pa* that sound more like *ba,* the infant will respond as if the sound had suddenly shifted from *pa* to *ba* rather than behave as if the shift had been gradual. Moreover, the shift seems to occur at the same boundary as it does when adult listeners discriminate the two sounds in normal conversation (Jusczyk, 1981).

Infants do not need to experience speech sounds in their environments to be able to discriminate them. An example would be the distinction between nasal and nonnasal vowels. The nonnasal form is illustrated by the *o* in *cod;* the nasal form is demonstrated by saying *cod* while holding your nose. Some languages, like French and Polish, distinguish nasal and nonnasal vowels. English does not. Infants with English-speaking parents have no experience with the contrast between nasal and nonnasal vowels, but they can hear the differences between them when tested in the laboratory (Trehub, 1976). This finding is characteristic of many other speech contrasts as well: Infants are able to distinguish speech sounds that are not differentiated in their native languages (Eilers, Gavin, and Oller, 1982).

Word Comprehension.   As children near their first birthdays, they often seem to be able to understand what others say even though they are not yet speaking themselves. If a parent asks, "Where is the ball?" children often look for it. They seem to understand the question, even though they have never spoken the words *where* or *ball.*

The lag between understanding and producing speech has been clearly demonstrated by Oviatt (1980, 1982). Young children were shown an unfamiliar but highly interesting object, such as a hamster in a cage. The object was named many times in each child's presence. Later the experimenter distracted the child's attention from the object and asked about its location, e.g., "Where's the hamster?" Oviatt defined a correct answer to this question as looking at the object for five seconds immediately after the question. Only one of ten 10-month-olds answered correctly, compared to half of the 13-month-olds and most of the 16-month-olds. Furthermore, only one child ever said the name of the object spontaneously. This lag continues after children begin to speak: There is a brief period when children will respond to most words correctly but not produce them spontaneously; this is followed by a period of successful comprehension and production.

Producing Speech

Many animal species are able to communicate with members of their own kind in various ways. The songs of birds appear to function as signals, as do the unique flying patterns or "dances" displayed by some types of bees. But their methods are almost completely innate and cannot be varied (McNeill, 1970). Primates such as chimpanzees have been taught to communicate using hand symbols taken from sign language

(Gardner and Gardner, 1969), or with distinctively designed plastic chips used as "words" (Premack, 1976). But it has proved impossible to teach apes to use speech in even its simplest form (Hayes, 1951). Humans remain alone as true speakers, probably because of our unusual control of the vocal tract and an innate capacity to handle complex symbols linguistically.

Children normally do not begin to speak meaningfully until after the first year of life. But "real" speech is preceded by various forms of vocalization and reaction to vocalization in others. For the first two or three months, cries and grunts predominate; then, at about 3 months of age, cooing begins. These early sounds have been studied with a sophisticated device called the sound spectrograph, which provides a visual record of both the physical aspects and the acoustic qualities of sound. Spectrograms show crying to be little more than the blowing of air along the vocal tract. Cooing produces a sound spectrogram that is quite different. The coo lasts about one-half second in duration—much shorter than the cry—and the articulatory organs, mainly the tongue, move during cooing. Infant cooing sometimes sounds "vowel-like," but it is not like adult vowel production. The difference between the sound production of an adult speaker and that of a prelanguage child is illustrated in Figure 5–1. Note that even when the mother tries to imitate her own child, she makes very different sounds than does the infant.

Babbling. Social babbling, which develops after cooing, often sounds like an effort to communicate in a foreign language. One early investigator's report of infant babbling included pronouncements such as "uggle-uggle," "erdah-erdah," "oddle-oddle," "a-bah-bah," and "bup-bup-bup" (Shirley, 1933).

As the infant develops, babbling becomes more and more like human speech. It shifts from odd single sounds to sequences of sounds that are like syllables. A 4- or 5-month-old's babbling often consists of a single consonant and vowel, like *da*. By 7 or 8 months of age, this sound will be repeated to form a string, such as *dadada*. Only later will an infant produce a string of different syllables, as in *dabamaga* (Ferguson and Macken, 1983).

Another early developmental change is an increase in the number of distinct sounds, which emerge in a predictable sequence. For example, babbling usually contains *stop consonants (p, t, k)* before it contains *fricatives (f, sh, z)*. These and other changes in the specific sounds of babbling are probably best explained in terms of growing control over the vocal tract. Fricatives require greater control over the lips, tongue, and teeth, which probably explains why they are not produced until after the stop consonants (Stark, 1980).

A further change in babbling between 4 and 12 months of age is the appearance of *intonation,* the pattern of rising or falling pitch. For adults, intonation is often the basis for interpreting a sentence. This is the difference between "You're hungry?" and "You're hungry." Pitch varia-

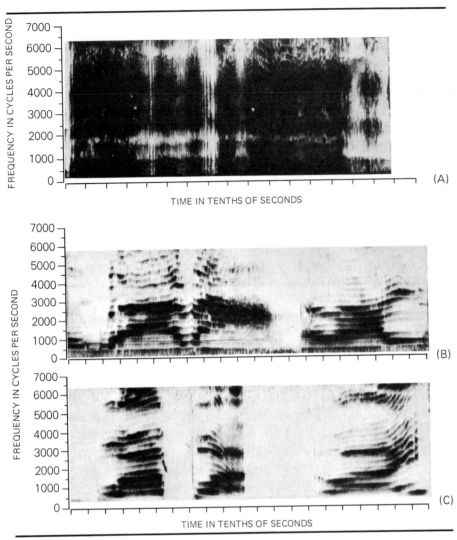

FIGURE 5-1
Some sample spectrograms of infants' and mother's speech.
Spectrograms of (a) a 2-week-old boy crying vigorously; (b) a 3-month-old boy cooing; (c) a mother imitating her child after listening to a tape on which the baby's noises are recorded. From E. H. Lenneberg, *Biological Foundations of Language.* Copyright 1967. Reproduced by permission of John Wiley & Sons, Inc.

tions in babbling are first noticed at approximately 4 to 6 months of age. Around the first birthday children sometimes use intonation to indicate commands and later to indicate questions (Greenfield and Smith, 1976).

Some children continue to babble for several months after they begin to produce real speech; others precede the onset of talking with a short period of relative quiet (Ferguson and Macken, 1983). Children who continue to babble seem to be actively experimenting with their newly acquired speech sounds. Labov and Labov (1978) describe one child, J, who frequently babbled this way. During one week, for example, J babbled a number of different sequences that included the syllable *da* as in *dat*. After several days J said *daddy* for the first time, and within a few weeks the word was part of her vocabulary.

This gradual movement toward correct production of speech sounds in one's native tongue is thought to reflect a type of learning based on hypothesis testing (Macken and Ferguson, 1983). This view assumes that children are motivated to produce the "correct" sounds required by their language and that they try out various versions in an effort to produce the right one. A child may first say *dodi* and then shift to *goggie* before finally learning to produce a recognizable version of the adult *doggie*. According to the hypothesis-testing view, children "have a clearly defined goal from the very start; they are trying to learn how to say recognizable words. They have to learn not only how to produce a sound close to the adult target, but also just how close they have to be before others can identify the segment they are aiming at" (Clark and Clark, 1977, p. 397).

First Words and After. The ability to produce speech sounds improves gradually throughout the preschool years (Ingram, Christensen, Veach, and Webster, 1980). At first, many children simply avoid using words containing sounds they cannot say easily. To verify this, Schwartz and Leonard (1982) taught children two types of nonsense words. Some words consisted of sounds a particular child had already mastered; other words consisted of sounds the child had never attempted to produce. For example, one child had produced the consonant sound *m* but not *sh*. For this child, a nonsense word using familiar sounds was *moemoe*; a word using sounds not yet mastered was *oashoash* (as in *ocean*). Each nonsense word was paired randomly with an action or object whose real name the child did not know. Thus, several times during each training session, the experimenter might have said, "Here's an oashoash" while holding a baster. Once in each session, the child was shown the action or object and was asked "What's this?"

Children were more likely to learn words consisting of sounds they had already mastered. Furthermore, children's learning of words with new sounds occurred more slowly than their learning of words with familiar sounds.

Because speech is mastered gradually, certain mispronunciations are quite common in young children's speech. As a result, children may pronounce *fish* as *pish* and *suit* as *toot*. Children seem to be aware of their own mispronunciations and are often able to distinguish correct and incorrect pronunciations in the speech of adults that they are not yet capable of producing themselves. This ability leads to some amusing interchanges. In a recent demonstration, Kuczaj (1983) presented his 3-year-old son Ben with two talking puppets. One of the puppets pronounced ten target words in the way Ben did (*kunk* for *skunk*, *kate* for *skate, tick* for *stick, pider* for *spider,* and *neeze* for *sneeze).* The other puppet used the correct adult pronunciations. Kuczaj simply asked Ben which of the puppets talked like his father and which talked like him. Ben unerringly recognized the difference between his father's pronunciations and his own. Ben also spontaneously offered his father an explanation of the difference:

> You talk like him. You say " 'neeze." I can't say " 'neeze" like you. I say "neeze." I'll say " 'neeze" (sneeze) like you when I get big. (Kuczaj, 1983, p. 74)

LEARNING WORDS AND THEIR MEANINGS

The first word that most children produce sounds very much like *mama.* It is believed that this happens because *mama* is derived from the natural murmur that infants make when sucking ("mmmh-ah"). As a bit of meaningful speech, *mama* is most often used to demand that a need be filled (Jakobson, 1962), but the specific age at which it is first said may precede its meaningful use. Other meaningful words do not usually appear until around children's first birthdays (McCarthy, 1954). The three categories most common in children's first ten words are animals, food, and toys (Nelson, 1973). Action words (such as *go*) also appear quite early, and are used to describe a child's own actions before describing the actions of others (Huttenlocher, Smiley, and Charney, 1983).

By the age of 24 months vocabulary has multiplied 200 to 300 times. The number of words used continues to increase thereafter at a rapid rate (see Figure 5–2).

Language-Learning Styles

For many years it was thought that the early phases of language acquisition were much the same for all children. Although the specific words learned would vary from child to child, as would the exact age at which they were acquired, the same *processes* were at work. Beginning in the 1970s, it became clear that this view was not entirely accurate. Katherine Nelson (1973) was the first investigator to reveal systematic differences among children in acquisition of language. Nelson studied a group of eighteen children for about a year, starting at approximately their first birthdays, a period during which the children's vocabularies increased from fewer than 10 words to nearly 200. Each child was visited monthly for about an hour. The experimenter tape-recorded a large sample of spontaneous speech in addition to giving various tests of language development.

By the time children had 50-word vocabularies—typically at about 1½ years of age—two distinct groups had emerged. Some children, whom Nelson called the Referential group, had vocabularies dominated by words that were the names of objects, persons, or actions. The remaining children, the Expressive group, also learned some names but knew a much higher percentage of words that were used in social interactions

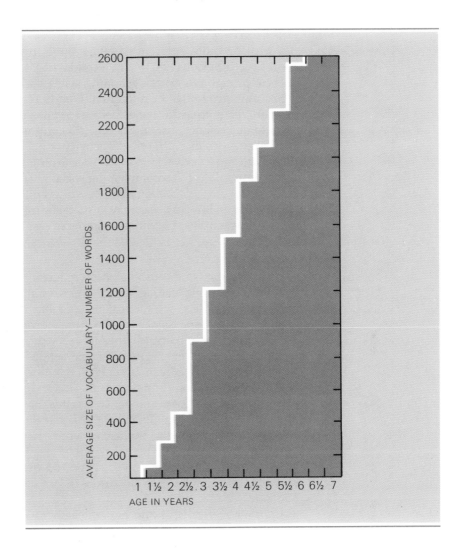

FIGURE 5–2
Size of average vocabulary of children at various ages. Data from Smith (1926).

(*go away, I want it*) and question words *(what, where)*. For example, Rachel, a referential child, had forty-one name words in her fifty-word vocabulary but only two words in the categories of social interaction or questions; Elizabeth, an expressive child, had a more balanced vocabulary: twenty-four name words and fourteen in the social-interaction and question categories.

These two groups of children also differ in later language development. Expressive children typically have smaller vocabularies than referential children, and are more likely to use pronouns than nouns (Nelson, 1975). In addition, expressive children often use "dummy" terms—words that have no apparent meanings but instead simply fill places in sentences—perhaps to substitute for words they do not know. For example, one child used the dummy term *uh uh* and said things like *uh uh down* (Nelson, 1981).

Nelson believes that the parents of expressive and referential children may provide quite different language environments for their children. According to Nelson (1981), ". . . a child who is exposed to a mother who teaches through relevant questioning is likely to conclude that language is basically a cognitive or referential medium" (p. 181). These children are more likely to learn names because names can be used to refer precisely to objects, actions, and people. In contrast, a child whose mother uses language to direct the child's activity (e.g., "Put the doll in the bed." "Play with the truck." "Stop that.") is learning that groups of words are useful "formulas" for accomplishing social goals. Hence, for expressive children ". . . the vocabulary can be quite limited, and the learner can concentrate on how to use common syntactic forms—questions and negatives, for example, in addition to imperatives" (Nelson, 1981, p. 184).

The Role of Cognitive Development

A child's first words are an obvious milestone. They are also evidence of a number of intellectual changes that occur near the first birthday. Since the mid-1970s, Elizabeth Bates and her colleagues have demonstrated that the emergence of the first words is linked to cognitive changes, notably growing abilities to use symbols. For example, late in the first year children begin to *imitate* actions they have seen before (McCall, Parke, and Kavanaugh, 1977). Children are capable of making mental representations of past events—that is, they are capable of using their first symbols. Bates and her colleagues (Bates, Benigni, Bretherton, Camaioni, and Volterra, 1979) believed that the use of symbols in imitation is closely related to the use of words to symbolize objects. They examined the relationship between imitation and language acquisition in 9- to 12-month-olds and found the expected significant positive correlation: Infants who were more advanced in language were also more likely to imitate.

In other work, Bates and her colleagues have been particularly intrigued by one specific type of symbol: the gesture. When friends or relatives leave, even very young children often wave and say "bye-bye." The gesture and the word convey a message equally effectively. For Bates and other theorists (Piaget, 1962; Werner and Kaplan, 1963), both reflect the child's developing ability to use symbols to represent actions and objects.

A good deal of evidence supports this link between vocal and gestural symbols. First, there are parallel changes in words and gestures between 9 and 13 months of age. The early stages in both involve the use of the gesture or the word to label an object: A child will label a toothbrush by saying the word or by making gestures that resemble toothbrushing. In later stages, children use gestures and words in pretend play: A child might pick up a toy screwdriver and label it a toothbrush, either vocally or through gesture (Volterra, Bates, Benigni, Bretherton, and Camaioni, 1979). And at 20 months of age there are striking similarities between vocal and gestural communication: An utterance averages 1.1 words and

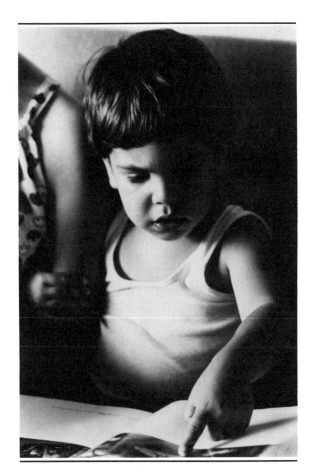

FIGURE 5–3
Pointing is an early and highly effective form of communicating.
© 1979 Jan Lukas, Photo Researchers.

1.3 gestures; the longest utterance averages 2.4 words and 2.6 gestures (Shore, O'Connell, and Bates, 1984).

Accordingly, Bates and her colleagues argue that for 1-year-olds:

> vocal and gestural symbols are cognitively equivalent. . . . Indeed, we see no evidence to suggest that a 13-month-old is in any way biased toward the development of vocal language as opposed to gestural language. (Volterra et al., 1979, p. 177)

Early Semantic Development: Understanding Words

Semantics is the study of the relationship of language to meaning. Developmental psychologists interested in semantics have asked when and how meaning is acquired. The growth of a child's vocabulary proceeds in an orderly way that provides some important hints. First of all, certain words appear very early in the working vocabularies of most children. The outstanding characteristics of these few words is that they refer to things that move or change by themselves or that can be acted on by the children. As Nelson (1974) points out:

> "Dog," "cat," "car," and "ball" are the most common "thing" words produced by young children. . . . Of the clothing items found in early vocabularies, two thirds are shoes and other footwear that the child acts on. It is furthermore noteworthy that early vocabularies do not include items that are just "there," that the child sees but does not interact with and that do not themselves move, for example, furniture. (p. 279)

This finding suggests that semantic development may be based on a child's forming functional concepts out of his or her own experience and then identifying words that seem to fit the concept. This view is supported by the finding that when young children cannot find words to express particular meanings, they often invent them (Werner and Kaplan, 1963).

Obviously, an important part of semantic development involves learning the usual or commonly understood meanings of words. The process involves some sort of concept formation, but the first efforts to tie together concepts and words are somewhat imprecise. One common example is the tendency to *overextend* meanings. For example, young children often call all four-legged animals "dogs" or all adult males "Daddy" (Bowerman, 1976).

Semantic feature theory (Clark, 1973) was one of the first attempts to explain what happens. According to this theory, a child's first attempts at grasping word-thing relationships involves attaching only one or two features of a thing to the word that names it. As a result of exposure to adult correction and usage, new and more discriminating features may be added to a word's meaning until it includes all the features recognized as essential by adults. Thus, a child may at first refer to all four-legged animals as "dogs" because four-leggedness is the only feature associated

FIGURE 5—4
Words that refer to objects that engage children actively, such as articles of clothing they must put on, are among the first to enter their vocabularies.
Christelow/Jeroboam.

FIGURE 5—5
Young children often overgeneralize the meaning of words—for example, by calling all four-legged animals "dogs." Shumsky, ICON.

with the word. Over time, however, other features will be added (fur, paws, the ability or tendency to bark, and so on) until the child's meaning of "dog" corresponds to the usual adult meaning.

Semantic feature theory has been criticized in recent years. One problem stems from children's tendency to *underextend*. Underextension is illustrated in a report by Bloom (1973) about a 9-month-old girl who used the word *car* to refer only to cars that she watched through the window, but not to cars she rode in herself. Underextensions are a problem for semantic feature theory, because if children are gradually acquiring additional features, their meanings should be more general than adult meanings, not more specific.

A second problem with the original version of semantic feature theory is that all features were assumed to contribute equally to a word's meaning. To see the drawback with this approach, consider the list of features associated with a thief: (1) steals; (2) carries a weapon; (3) is nasty; (4) wears a mask; and (5) goes to prison. Although features (2)–(5) might apply to many thieves, only (1) *defines* a thief. Theorists such as Keil and Batterman (1984) distinguish between features that define a concept and those that are merely characteristic of it.

Young children seem to treat all features as characteristic. This can be seen in the types of overextensions children make. Eva, a 14-month-old studied by Bowerman (1978), said *gee* (as in *giddiup*) in a number of situations: (1) bouncing on a spring horse; (2) riding on a tricycle; (3) watching horses on television; and (4) bouncing on her mother's leg. The examples suggest that Eva apparently associates three characteristics with *gee:* horse, as in examples 1 and 3, bouncing as in 1 and 4, and sitting astride an object as in 1, 2, and 4. No single feature that appears in all examples would define *gee;* instead, its meaning varies, emphasizing one or more features in a particular situation.

Through the elementary school years children gradually recognize the importance of defining features. Keil and Batterman (1984), for example, created stories like those in Table 5–1 in which they varied the features used to describe a particular concept. Some stories included only defining features, other stories included only characteristic features. Each story ended with a question asking children if the story could be referring to a particular concept.

Keil and Batterman found that even 4- and 5-year-olds typically relied on characteristic features in defining concepts. For example, the following interchange took place after one 5-year-old heard the description of the museum in Table 5–1 that contained the defining features:

Experimenter: Could that be a museum?

Child: No . . . a museum is something with dinosaur bones.

Experimenter: Well suppose (repeats story). Could that be a museum . . . can they have dirty shirts?

Child: No, that's a laundromat! (Keil and Batterman, 1984, p. 229)

TABLE 5–1
Stories from the Study by Keil and Batterman (1984)

Characteristic Features, No Defining Features
There is this beautiful building with columns. Mr. Johnson lives there, but he has a big problem. There are all these cracks in his floors and his walls. So he covers them with paintings and statues, and he never lets anyone inside to see them. Could that be a museum?

Defining Features, No Characteristic Features
There is this small, wooden shack in the countryside. People come from all over and pay 50 cents to get inside and see the interesting display of dirty shirts with rings around the collar and spots and stains. Could that be a museum?

From: F. C. Keil and N. Batterman. (1984). A characteristic-to-defining shift in the development of word meaning. *Journal of Verbal Learning and Verbal Behavior, 23,* 227.

Not until children are 8 or 9 are defining features central to understanding a word's meaning (Landau, 1982).

One question raised by this theory is how children identify features. Many theorists (e.g., Greenberg and Kuczaj, 1982) believe that children's first word meanings are associated with the first examples of particular concepts they experienced. *Car,* for example, might first refer to the family station wagon or a particular toy car. As children hear words associated with other examples (a neighbor's car, a car on television), they compare these different experiences and begin to determine some of the characteristic features of cars. Later they learn which features are defining instead of simply typical.

If this theory is correct, then examples of a category that are not typical should be more difficult to learn. Children, for example, are likely to first hear *bird* in connection with robin and sparrow, which means that their prototype is likely to be *songbird.* So children should readily learn that a *canary* is a bird. But they should have some difficulty learning that *owl* and *eagle* are *birds.* By the same logic, children should have even more difficulty learning that *penguins* and *turkeys* are birds. In fact, Mervis and Pani (1980) demonstrated exactly this pattern of results with 5-year-olds using artificial categories (so that children would have no prior knowledge of the names to be learned).

Toddlers frequently give objects unconventional names. For example, a child may refer to a streak of skywriting as a "scar on the sky" or call a yellow baseball bat a "stick of corn." These labels are not simply errors; rather, they appear to be intentional violations chosen to underscore the similarity between familiar and new visual experiences. In this sense, the young child is something of a poet (Mendelsohn, Robinson, Gardner and Winner, 1984).

Within a few months after uttering the first meaningful one-word sentence, a child will begin to produce pairs of words that make some type of statement. The transition from two one-word sentences to a functional two-word sentence is gradual. After beginning to use a few single words, the child will string them together, pausing between each. Then the location of the pause will gradually change. For example, the child will begin by saying "baby" and "chair" together, but will soon combine them to form "baby chair" (Bloom, 1973). Such constructions may be statements of fact or various requests (see Table 5–2).

The Two-Word Sentence

Once the child begins to produce two-word sentences, he or she expands their use at a very rapid rate. It is as if the child suddenly discovers the power to express an almost unlimited set of ideas and cannot resist doing so. One early case study showed that more than 1,000 new and distinct two-word utterances per month appear during this phase of development (Braine, 1963). And Brown (1965) has pointed out that "by the age of thirty-six months some children are so advanced in the construction process as to produce all of the major varieties of English simple sentences up to a length of ten or eleven words" (p. 286).

What rules do children follow when they construct sentences? An early suggestion was that children begin with a *pivot-open* grammar (Braine, 1963). Consider the usual two-word sentences of the young child. Sequences such as "my shoe," "a hand," and "see papa" are extremely common; verbalizations such as "shoe my," "hand a," and "papa see" occur infrequently—if at all. According to the pivot-open theory, young children divide their word "lists" into two classes. The smaller of the classes is called the "pivot" class, and the other is called the "open" class. In the sequences "see papa," "see hand," and "see

---

TABLE 5–2
Assertions and Requests at the Two-Word Stage

SPEECH ACT	UTTERANCES
Assertions	
Presence of object	See boy. See sock. That car.
Denial of presence	Allgone shoe. No wet. Byebye hot.
Location of object	Bill here. There doggie. Penny innere.
Possession of object	My milk. Mamma dress.
Quality of object	Pretty boat. Big bus.
Ongoing event	Mommy sleep. Hit ball. Block fall.
Requests	
For action	More taxi. Want gum. Where ball?
For information	Where doggie? Sit water?
Refusal	No more.

Source: Adapted from Clark and Clark (1977); based on data from Slobin (1970), Bowerman (1973), and Brown (1973).

shoe," *see* is a "pivot" word, and all the other words fall into the "open" category. Any particular pivot word occurs in the same position in every sentence. Some pivot words appear in the first position only; others appear in the second position only.

This idea has its limitations. One problem is that pivot-open grammar does not seem to be related to the grammar that develops later. Some research has indicated quite contradictory results. Bloom's (1970) study of two young children reports that the overwhelming majority of their sentences were *not* of the pivot-open form. Perhaps the most important criticism is that pivot-open grammar ignores the meaning children try to convey. For example, Bloom (1970) reported that one child said "Mommy sock" twice: Once was when the mother was putting on the child's socks; a second time, when the child found her mother's stocking. These would appear to be two very different uses of the same phrase.

Bloom (1970) also suggested that young children use a grammar in which the *function* of a word plays a role. The two-word sentence *that book* serves a nominative function (it names something), whereas *mommy lunch* serves a possessive function, and *Eve read* serves to link an agent and its action.

Once it had been agreed that psycholinguists needed to consider the meaning of children's utterances, a question that was studied throughout much of the 1970s emerged: How many distinct functions or meanings can children express in two-word speech, and how general are these functions? Brown (1973) proposed eight different semantic relationships during the two-word phase. Included were the nomination, possession, and agent-action functions, as well as action-object *(push car)* and action-location *(walk home)*. Other investigators (e.g., Leonard, 1976) identified similar categories in their analyses of children's two-word speech.

Braine (1976) then argued that many of these categories were too general. He suggested that children develop formulas for generating two-word sentences based on past experiences and current needs. Not every child invents the same formulas, so we would expect children to differ in the general forms they give to their two-word utterances. This appears to be what happens. For example, although many of the two-word utterances made by one of the children studied by Braine fell in the general category of agent-action, they were quite specific; in fact, many of the actions concerned a particular person's movement: "Andrew walk," "Daddy sit."

Grammatical Morphemes

Although children move rapidly beyond two-word speech, their early speech still contains very few sentences that are well formed by adult standards (see Table 5–3). Note the absence of most articles and auxiliary verbs, particularly in phrases such as "put suitcase . . . for?" "Where birdie go?" "What inere?" and "Yep, it fit."

Because of the similarity between the telegram and the pared-down verbal communications of young children, many writers have described

TABLE 5–3

Typical Conversation between Adult and a Young Child

Child (28 Months)	Adult
What dat . . . somebody pencil	Whose pencils are they?
Floor	Floor?
Where birdie go?	
Birdie	
Birdie up dere	
Birdie	
Read dat?	
Read dat?	Will you read it to me?
What inere?	Is that a hammer, Adam?
Hammer	
Hit hammer, mommy	
No Cromer _____, mommy?	
Hurt	Poor Adam, Did you hurt yourself?
	What happened, Adam?
Screw (did) happen	Screw happened? You didn't even have a screw.
have screw	
_____no down there . . .	
table . . . get broom	Does that one fit?
Yep, it fit	
Yep, it fit	Does it fit?
No . . . fit	
Put suitcase . . . for?	What did you put it in the suitcase for?
What dat?	That's tape. We'll use that one tomorrow.
All right 'morrow	Shall we use it tomorrow?
Yep	
Use morrow, yep	
Sure, use morrow	

Source: R. Brown and U. Bellugi, "Three Processes in the Child's Acquisition of Syntax," Harvard Educational Review, 1964, 34, 133–151. Copyright 1964 by the President and Fellows of Harvard College.

their speech as *telegraphic*. The essentials always come first; refinements and frills appear later.

In the preschool years, *grammatical morphemes* like prepositions, articles, and auxiliary verbs emerge (Brown, 1973). Another type of grammatical morpheme emerging during this period is the *inflection,* a change in a word—often a suffix—that alters sense without altering fundamental meaning (adding *-ed* to *walk* marks the past tense, as does converting *swim* to *swam*).

Children's use of grammatical morphemes is based on rules, not just memory. In a classic study, Berko (1958) presented children with totally unfamiliar words that required inflection. The children could not rely on direct past experience. More specifically, Berko showed children some pictures of nonsense objects, such as the one in Figure 5–6, and said "This is a *wug.*" She then showed each child a picture of two such objects and said, "These are two——," providing the child with an opportunity to supply the plural form of *wug.* Her subjects, preschool children, were

FIGURE 5–6
An example of the pictures used by Berko to show that children know and use morphological rules even by preschool age. Although the child has never heard the word *wug* before, he or she will "correctly" pluralize it into *wugs.*
Adapted from Berko (1958).

This is a wug.

Now there is another one.
There are two of them.
There are two

able to perform remarkably well (by application of the rule, the plural of *wug* ought to be *wugs*).

We can see patterns of rule-regulated language of the type identified by Berko even in casual observation of young children's language. For example, Bowerman (1982) described how two preschoolers learned the grammatical morpheme *un-*. When these children first used *un*, they appeared to be imitating specific verbs they had heard (*untangle, unbuckle, uncover*). Later, the children apparently learned a rule that "*un* + verb" means to reverse or stop the action of a verb, for they created a number of novel verbs (see Table 5–4).

TABLE 5–4
Christy's Novel Use of the Prefix *un-*

Age (in years, months)	Utterance
4, 5	[Christy has asked her mother why pliers are on the table.] Mother: I've been using them for straightening the wire. Christy: And *unstraightening* it?
4, 7	Christy: I hate you! And I'll never *unhate* you or nothing! Mother: You'll never unhate me? Christy: I'll never like you.
5, 1	Mother [working on strap of Christy's backpack]: Seems like one of these has been shortened, somehow. Christy: Then *unshorten* it.
6, 0	Christy [watching a freshly poured, foamy Coke]: Wait until that *unfizzes.*
7, 11	Christy [taking a stocking down from the fireplace]: I'm gonna *unhang* it.

Adapted from Table 11.1 of (1982). Reorganizational processes in lexical and syntactic development. In M. Bowerman, E. Wanner, and L. R. Gleitman (Eds.), *Language acquisition: The state of the art.* Cambridge, Eng.: Cambridge University Press.

Order of Acquisition. Different grammatical morphemes are acquired gradually, in a reasonably consistent order. Among the first to be acquired are the addition of *-ing* to verbs to indicate ongoing action, the addition of *-s* to nouns to indicate plural, and the use of the prepositions *in* and *on* (deVilliers and deVilliers, in press). Articles (*a, the*) appear late, as do possessives (*-'s*). Among the last to be acquired are verb contractions (*-m* as in *I'm* or *-re* as in *they're*). This order seems to reflect the complexity of the grammatical morpheme; children first master the least complex forms (Block and Kessell, 1980). According to this explanation, *-ing* is acquired early because it is *always* added to a verb to refer to an ongoing event. Correct use of *a* and *the* is more complicated. The correct article is *the* if a specific experience or object is referred to, but it is *a* if the referent is unspecified and general. For example, a child would say, "I saw a new girl in school today," if simply reporting an event for the first time. If the topic had been discussed before, "*the* new girl" would be correct.

Mastery of each grammatical morpheme also occurs in a predictable sequence. Children's acquisition of the past tense, which has been studied extensively, is typical. You would probably guess that the first tendency is to regularize irregular words, and that the error is corrected later by overhearing adult speech. In fact, this is not the sequence at all. Children usually begin by using the correct form of irregular verbs, such as *came* and *broke*, probably because they are imitating frequently heard adult forms. Then, perhaps weeks or even months later, the child will shift from correct to incorrect usage by regularizing all verbs. The child who begins by saying *I broke it* will "advance" to the stage of saying *I breaked it*, rather than the other way around. By the time they start school, of course, most children will have returned permanently to common irregular forms (Ervin, 1964).

It was once thought that this process involved distinct stages (Cazden, 1968), but we now know that children use both incorrect and correct verb forms at the same age. For instance, children sometimes use *goed*, *went*, and *wented* at the same time (Kuczaj, 1981). In addition, children first learn to use the past tense with verbs that refer to actions with well-defined endpoints (Bloom, Lifter, and Hafitz, 1980).

Questions

Anyone spending even a few minutes with children will discover that they constantly and persistently ask questions. But the questions differ in both structure and content as children mature. The child's first questions are marked by intonation alone. Soon after a child can declare *My ball*, he or she can also ask *My ball?* Then comes experimentation with the *wh* words (*who, what, when, where, why*). However, although the use of *wh* words as part of questions appears quite early, it does not follow adult form. The young child merely attaches the needed word to the beginning of a sentence (*Why him go? What her eat?*), without altering the base sentence at all. Even when the base sentence already has a negative form, the first questions are produced by simply adding *why not* and the questioning intonation while leaving the base sentence intact, as in *Why not Susie can't walk?* (deVilliers and deVilliers, in press).

Children begin to use *wh* questions in a distinct order: *what* and *where* emerge early, followed by *why* and *how* (Wootten, Merkin, Hood, and Bloom, 1979). This sequence, like the sequence for grammatical morphemes, reflects the complexity of the questions. Forms that are mastered early—*what* and *where*—ask information about an individual component of a sentence; the later forms ask information about relationships among several components.

In addition, the verb of a sentence may determine the ease with which children ask and answer questions. For example, some verbs often take direct objects (*The child is eating ice cream*). With these verbs, children often answer questions that concern this direct object (*What is the child eating?*) before questions that deal with components not routinely associated with the verb (*Where is the child eating?*).

Experience and the Acquisition of Grammar

At one time we thought that children learned to speak grammatically by listening to and then copying adult sentences. It is now clear that this is not the case. Children produce many more sentences than they have ever heard. More important, even when children imitate adult sentences, they do not imitate adult grammar. Even in simply trying to repeat *I am drawing a picture*, young children will say *I draw picture*. And, finally, children who cannot speak at all and thus never imitate language may come to understand it perfectly (Lenneberg, 1967).

But experience, in some form, must play a major role in the acquisition of grammar. Children all over the world come to speak the language and use the grammar of those around them, and this is as true of children adopted from one culture to another as it is of those who never leave their native group. Children must learn a major part of language from exposure to native speakers. The question is: What processes are involved in the learning? One approach has emphasized the role of children's ability to abstract the underlying rules that govern a model's behavior in language and in other areas as well. Once such rules have been formulated, the observer can generate an endless number of responses that are consistent with them (Zimmerman and Rosenthal, 1974). Both the formation of sentences (syntax) and the formation of words (morphology) appear to be governed by rules.

Applying this type of reasoning to the study of syntactic development, Leonard (1975) studied 2- and 3-year-old children who used two- and three-word utterances ("More milk," "That kitty"), but did not produce true subject-verb sentences ("Man read," "Boy go," "I drink"). Training consisted of exposure to an adult model who was rewarded for describing various pictures and situations in two-word, subject-verb sentences. When he compared these children with a group of controls who had received no special training, Leonard found that the modeling groups showed significant gains in the production of novel, grammatical two-word sentences. The test he used, which avoided the problem of having to give special verbal hints or instructions, was to ask children to describe pictures that invited the subject-verb construction, such as a picture of a man walking.

Controlled laboratory experimentation of this sort demonstrates that the acquisition of grammar may be determined, to a large extent, by experiences. To demonstrate this in the natural environment involves two matters. First, if children learn language from adult speech, then we need evidence that adults are good models, that they in fact adjust their speech to help children to learn. Second, there should be significant correlations between the parental speech that serves as input and children's language acquisition (output).

Adults Talking to Children.   That adults modify their speech to children is well documented. One problem in talking with a young child is simply getting the child's attention. We use various devices, such as saying the child's name at the beginning of a sentence ("Bobbie, look at the horse"), using exclamations (such as "Hey!"), repeating portions of what they have said in order to capture and hold the child's attention ("Yes, horsie!"), or looking and pointing at the objects about which they are talking (Collis, 1977). Adults also monitor children carefully to be sure that attention is sustained. Sachs, Brown, and Salerno (1976) found that adults raise the pitch of their voices at the end of sentences when they are telling a story to young children. This is the same device adults generally use when asking questions; it presumably signals to children that adults want some type of feedback (Clark and Clark, 1977).

Adults also often simplify their speech in various ways when talking to young children (Maratsos, 1983). Articles and possessives are omitted so that these words occur least frequently when adults talk to 2-year-olds, more frequently when they talk to 10-year-olds, and most frequently when talking to other adults. Adults also avoid pronouns when talking to young children, repeating the relevant noun instead. Furthermore, parents are sensitive to their children's communication skills, and adjust vocabulary and grammar and the amount of interaction they give to the ages and perceived language facilities of their children (Rogoff, Ellis, and Gardner, 1984).

Do children profit from the special models of speech that adults provide for them? The answer seems to be "sometimes." In recent years researchers have tried to identify the situations in which parental speech is most likely to affect children's language acquisition. Newport, Gleitman, and Gleitman (1977) computed correlations between the frequency of various constructions in mothers' speech (e.g., *wh* questions) and language development of children between 12 and 27 months of age. They measured two general components of children's language. Some, like the use of nouns and verbs, were considered to be language universals (found in all known languages). Other components, such as auxiliary verbs and noun inflections, were not universal. The researchers found that maternal speech was not related to the acquisition of the universals but that it was related to the growth of the language-specific components. One interpretation of these findings is that experience is important only for the language-specific components.

Not all investigators have found this same pattern. Furrow, Nelson, and Benedict (1979) found that a number of characteristics of maternal speech were related to the growth of both universal and language-specific components. The two studies are difficult to compare directly because they differ along many dimensions, including the types of maternal speech that were measured, the methods of statistical analysis, and the age of the children (Hoff-Ginsberg and Shatz, 1982). But the underlying message is clear: Simple exposure to a particular class of parental speech does not automatically lead to increases in the child's use of that same class.

Imitation with Modification. Adults frequently rephrase or expand something a child has said, often to transform an ungrammatical structure into one that is grammatical (see Table 5–5). For example, the child's question "Read da?" may be recast by the adult into "Will you read it to me?" and "Put suitcase . . . for?" may be expanded into "What did you put it in the suitcase for?" In imitative expansion the adult adds to the child's message, making the utterance clearer as well as more grammatically correct.

Several investigators have shown that use of these *recasts* is associated with more rapid language acquisition. For example, in a study by Nelson

TABLE 5–5
Imitation with Reduction (by the Child) and Imitation with Expansion (by the Mother)

Imitation with Reduction	
Mother	**Child**
Daddy's brief case.	Daddy brief case.
Fraser will be unhappy.	Fraser unhappy.
He's going out.	He go out.
No, you can't write on Mr. Cromer's shoe.	Write Cromer shoe.

Imitation with Expansion	
Child	**Mother**
Baby highchair.	Baby is in the highchair.
Mommy sandwich.	Mommy'll have a sandwich.
Pick glove.	Pick the glove up.

Adapted with permission of The Free Press, a division of Macmillan, Inc., from *Social Psychology* by Roger Brown. Copyright © 1965 by The Free Press.

(1974), 2-year-olds received five one-hour training sessions in which an experimenter conversed informally with each child. The method was simple: In one condition the experimenter often responded to the child's statements by reworking them into questions:

> Child: You can't get in!
> Experimenter: No, I can't get in, can I?

In another condition the experimenter recast many of the child's statements to represent more advanced verb forms:

> Child: Where it go?
> Experimenter: It will go there.

By the end of training, all children had made significant gains: They were more likely to use the constructions that had been recast by the experimenter.

Naturalistic studies also point to beneficial effects of parental expansions on language acquisition. Newport et al. (1977) found that the frequency with which mothers expanded their children's utterances was positively related to children's use of auxiliary verbs. But only simple recasts are beneficial; complex recasts, in which more than a single element in a sentence is changed, actually impede language acquisition (Nelson, 1982). This finding emphasizes an important general point: "Input cannot *solve* the problem of acquisition for the child. The problem is to induce general patterns from specific examples" (Maratsos, 1983, p. 736). Linguistic experience is most likely to be beneficial when it provides a few specific examples that allow children to discover particular language rules.

COMMUNICA-TION SKILLS

Early Skills

We all need to communicate. Spoken and written language are unique to humans, but humans also display, recognize, and use nonverbal signs and signals. Communications specialists have increasingly come to view communication as involving an implicit contract between communicator and communicatee. Mastering the art of communication involves refining and complying with this contract, which in turn requires understanding its rules. Adult conversations, for example, are guided by a number of implicit rules: People should take turns speaking, what they say should relate to the previous speaker's remarks, they should be understandable, and so on.

Children master many of these rules at a surprisingly early age. As soon as children begin to talk at all, parents seem to promote the idea of taking turns and alternating the roles of speaker and listener. In fact,

SES and Language

Experiences outside the home can influence language acquisition. Preschool children who receive day care in someone's home show more advanced language development than those who attend day-care centers (Cochran, 1977). In addition, the more language stimulation a day-care center provides, the more rapidly the children advance in language skills (McCartney, 1984).

For children, communication competence is especially important for interactions with teachers in school. Most of these interactions take the form of direct questions posed by the teacher, to which the child must reply. The ability to respond adequately in such situations is crucial to success in school. In this regard, it is important to note that children from poor backgrounds are less able to respond to such questions than are middle-class children (Blank, Rose, and Berlin, 1978). In turn, these findings raise the question of whether the language competence of poor children in school can be increased by an appropriate early-intervention program. A recent report by Gordon (1984) suggests that the answer is yes, provided that the intervention is intensive and begins early in life.

Gordon's report is based on the Abcedarian Project, a longitudinal study of children born at risk of sociocultural retardation because of their poor backgrounds. The children in the project were identified at birth and matched into pairs on a number of risk factors. Then, one member of each pair was randomly assigned to a day-care intervention program while the other member of the pair was assigned to a nonintervention control group and simply followed over time.

The intervention program involved attending the day-care program eight hours a day, five days a week, fifty weeks a year until the child entered public kindergarten. The curriculum was designed to focus on language development and communication skills, especially the use of language as a tool to stimulate thought. Among the other components of the curriculum, teachers read and discussed a story daily with each child on a one-to-one basis or in very small groups.

To determine the effects of the intervention, Gordon tested children from the intervention and control groups during their first year in kindergarten (when they were about 5 years and 9 months old), and also tested a group of middle-class children of the same age as a further basis for comparison. The test consisted of asking each child to converse individually with an adult for about twenty minutes, and recording the entire conversation for subsequent analysis. The adult led the conversation in an informal, friendly manner, but actually brought up a set of thirteen predetermined topics. These raised questions that obliged the child to respond. "How do you play hide-and-seek?" "What would you do if you found a lost puppy?" and "What would happen if animals could talk just like people?" were some questions. The questions were selected to have no obvious right answers and to elicit a maximum amount of speech from the child. Trained raters then listened to the recordings and coded each of the child's responses for adequacy on a five-point scale from 1 to 5. The results were impressive. Whereas the at-risk children in the control group produced many responses that were less than adequate, the poor children in the intervention group rarely gave less than adequate answers and gave almost as many more than adequate responses as the middle-class children. Thus, intensive, long-term intervention can eliminate differences in language skill that often distinguish disadvantaged children from those who are not disadvantaged.

However, although disadvantaged children's language may be poorly suited for some settings, notably schools, it may be perfectly adequate for many purposes. That is, many disadvantaged children may have learned a perfectly adequate variant of the language that is used by most members of their culture (Labov, 1970).

many parents begin to teach their children the idea of taking turns long before the children are producing any words of their own (Field and Widmayer, 1982):

> . . . the adult asks, "Do you want to tell me a story?"; the infant coos, and the adult responds, "Oh, yeah? And then what happened?"; the infant coos again, and the adult replies, "Oh, that's funny!" (Field and Widmayer, 1982, p. 689)

As soon as an infant is able to produce words, he or she is *required* to use words (rather than gestures alone) to keep a conversation going. To assist in this form of training, parents often model both sides of conversation so that their children can learn how the game should be played (Ervin-Tripp, 1970). For example, in an effort to teach turn taking, parents may model the child's role as well as their own by creating dialogues like this one:

> Parent: [initiating conversation in role of parent] What's the doggie doing?
> Parent: [modeling appropriate reply for child] The doggie is eating!

Between 2 and 3 years of age children become much better conversational partners, and they are more likely to respond to an adult's utterance with a pertinent remark. Bloom, Rocissano, and Hood (1976) found that 2-year-olds were just as likely to follow an adult's statement with an irrelevant comment as with one that was relevant. For example, when an adult asked Eric, a 25-month-old, to "put the light on," he responded "cookie." Even 3-year-olds made some of these irrelevant remarks, but at this age relevant remarks far outnumbered irrelevant ones.

Somewhat older preschoolers can be quite sophisticated in their understanding of the conventions governing conversations. When preschoolers talk to one another, more often than not they will follow a speaker's comment with a relevant remark or action (Garvey and Hogan, 1973). They typically do so promptly—in less than two seconds. If a listener does not respond promptly, preschoolers use a number of tactics to encourage a response. Sometimes they repeat their remarks or paraphrase them to make explicit the need for a response (Garvey and Berninger, 1981).

167

By the time children reach the age of 5 or so, their literal face-to-face conversations are impressively like communications among adults. Most major grammatical forms have appeared, and youngsters have adequate vocabularies. However, any particular word can be used to refer to many different things, and any particular thing can be referred to by many different words. Therefore, children must learn not only a vocabulary, but how to select words from that vocabulary. In addition, constructing an effective message means that speakers must consider characteristics of the setting, characteristics of the listener, and the aim of the message (Schmidt and Paris, 1984). In fact, with increasing age and experience, children develop the ability to edit their communications more effectively.

Adaptation to Different Visual Perspectives. Glucksberg, Krauss, and their associates (Glucksberg and Krauss, 1967; Glucksberg, Krauss, and Weisberg, 1966; Krauss and Weinheimer, 1964) pioneered the systematic study of referential communication in young children. In their experimental situation children are seated out of sight of each other, as in Figure 5–7, and asked to play a game called "stack the blocks." One child is the speaker and has the job of encoding a message to relay to another child. The second youngster, the listener, must decode the speaker's message and act on the information. In front of each player is an array of six blocks and a peg on which the blocks can be stacked. The speaker receives blocks one by one from a dispenser and must put them on the peg in the order they are received. The listener's blocks, however, appear in a random array on the table. The object of the game is to form two identical stacks of blocks. To accomplish this goal, the speaker must instruct the listener verbally. Each block carries a design (see Figure 5–8) by which it can be identified, but the designs have been carefully chosen and do not have readily available English names.

In the first in a series of experiments, 4- and 5-year-old children tended to use reference phrases that were private and idiosyncratic. One youngster, referred to form 5 in Figure 5–8 as "a pipe, a yellow part of a pipe," a phrase that communicates much less well than such labels as a "boot," a "horse's head," or an "ax head"—which represent average adult responses. (Incidentally, the adjective "yellow" conveyed no useful information, since the forms were stamped with black ink on natural redwood blocks.) Another young speaker referred to form 6 as "Mommy's hat." Apparently it resembled a particular hat belonging to that child's mother. Adults, in contrast, tended to refer to it as "An upside down cup. It's got two triangles, one on top of the other." It is not surprising that not one of the seven pairs of children was able to complete a single game without error.

Subsequent studies indicate that Glucksberg and Krauss' task probably *underestimates* children's ability to tailor messages to the needs of listeners. Notice that to perform well on this task, children need to (1) recognize the need to adapt their messsage for a listener; and (2) provide

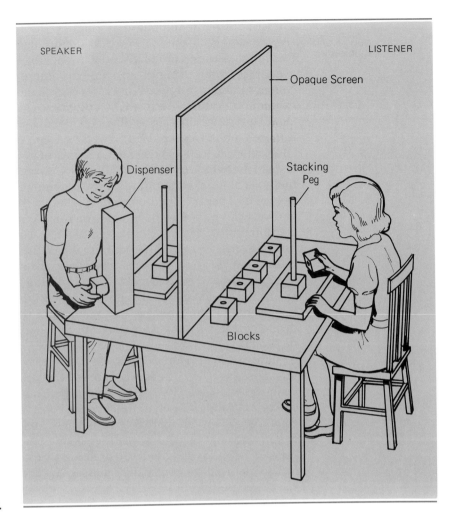

FIGURE 5–7
The experimental task used by Glucksberg, Krauss, and their associates.

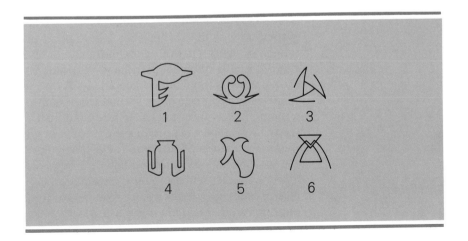

FIGURE 5–8
The six novel forms used in the Glucksberg and Krauss experiments.

a description of the stimulus that will allow the listener to distinguish that stimulus from all others. Much evidence suggests that the second of these processes is particularly troublesome for 5- and 6-year-olds. However, even brief training can markedly improve children's referential communications. To succeed, it is necessary to present appropriate rules for communicating effectively, to encourage children to apply the rules, and to give them specific feedback about how well they are doing (Pratt, McLaren, and Wickens, 1984).

Pratt et al. (1984) presented a series of referential communication tasks to first-grade children and then taught some of the children to apply the rules of good communication by reminding themselves of the rules as each task began. Children were first taught to say both a general comparison rule and a specific comparison rule aloud: "First I'll figure out all the different things my clues could mean to you. . . . Then I'll tell you how the one I mean is different from the rest." After practice saying the rules aloud, children practiced whispering the rules to themselves at the beginning of each task. Finally, they practiced saying each rule silently to themselves. Feedback was given after each task. Compared to a control group that practiced the task without rules or feedback, children in the training group showed marked improvement in their referential communication.

Other work also indicates that 5- and 6-year-olds are capable of adapting messages when listeners cannot see the topic of conversation. Pratt, Scribner, and Cole (1977) asked individual nursery school, first-grade, and third-grade children to describe the rules of a new game to another child. As shown in Figure 5–9, at all ages children gave more elaborate descriptions of the game when the playing board was not visible to the peer. This work, along with the training studies, suggests that children realize the need to modify their messages when listeners have different visual perspectives.

Adjustments for the Listener's Age and Knowledge.   Even preschoolers converse differently with younger children than they do with peers or adults. When 4-year-olds talk to 2-year-olds they use more attention-getting devices than when they talk to peers or adults. In addition, preschoolers' speech to younger children includes shorter and less complex sentences, and avoids topics that 4-year-olds believe are too complicated for 2-year-olds (Shatz and Gelman, 1977).

Sensitivity to a listener's knowledge is also shown in the *given-new contract*. Given information is information the listener presumably already knows, and it provides the context in which to transmit information not previously known to the listener. For example, in the sentence "It was psychology that Bob failed," the given information is that Bob failed a course, while the new information is that the course Bob failed was psychology. Speakers are responsible for "marking" their communications so that listeners can distinguish which information is new and which information is given.

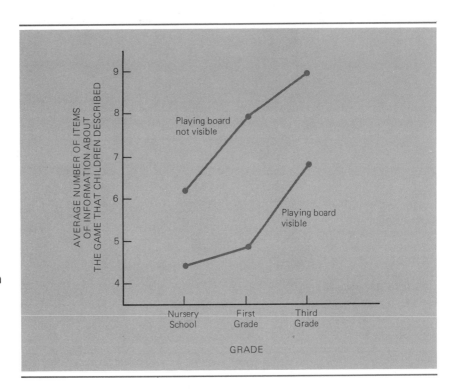

FIGURE 5–9
Average length of description of a game as a function of grade level, when the playing board was visible and when it was not. From Pratt et al. (1977). © The Society for Research in Child Development, Inc.

Young children tend to indicate new information in a two-word sentence by giving it greater stress. For example, a girl who has recently discovered the color name for her favorite ball is much more likely to say "RED ball" than "Red BALL." As soon as the child's sentences become more complex than two words, a further device is needed. Adults frequently use the definite article, *the,* to indicate given information and the indefinite article, *a,* to indicate new information. For example, an adult may say, "I found *a key* yesterday, and it turned out to be *the key* to my old suitcase." In one study 3-year-old children who told stories to peers used the indefinite article on the first mention of a new piece of information slightly less than half the time, meaning that they used definite and indefinite articles almost indiscriminantly (Warden, 1976). Five- and 7-year-olds were somewhat more likely to use the indefinite article on the first mention of a piece of information, and 9-year-olds used the indefinite article when first mentioning a piece of information most of the time. (The problem is not one of familiarity with the two words, for most children begin to use both *the* and *a* by the time they are 3.)

Adjustments to a Listener's Emotional Needs. Children also learn what not to say. For example, Weiner and Handel (in press) presented 5- to 12-year-old children with scenarios in which a child faced social rejection. The subjects' tasks were to decide whether they would reveal the reason for rejection to the other child and to indicate the likelihood that

revealing the reason would cause the child in the story to feel hurt or angry. Older children were more likely than younger ones to say they would withhold the reason for rejection from the child in the story. This age difference in "prudent silence" was greatest when revealing the reasons for rejection were likely to cause anger.

Children also learn how to comfort others by saying things that are soothing, supportive, or reassuring. The ability to comfort with words presumably depends on a wide range of skills, including the ability to grasp what would and would not be comforting in a situation. We would expect that facility with comforting communication increases with age, and a recent study shows that indeed it does.

Burleson (1982) presented boys and girls from grades one through twelve with hypothetical situations in which a friend was distressed or upset (for example, the friend was upset because he or she had not been invited to a particular party). The subjects were to indicate what they would say that would make the friend feel better. Subjects' replies were recorded and later scored for the number and quality of comforting statements offered. The number, quality, and variety of comforting strategies suggested all increased with age. In addition, at all ages, girls showed a greater ability to produce such communications.

Pragmatic Skill. Speakers sometimes convey their messages directly ("I want ice cream."), and sometimes indirectly ("Your ice cream looks delicious."). These *pragmatic* components are an important part of communication.

In making requests and in understanding the requests of others, we

FIGURE 5–11
As children grow older, they become better able to use language to comfort others. Alice Kendall, Photo Researchers.

need to master many subtleties. For example, Grimm (1975) reported a dramatic difference between the way in which 5- and 7-year-olds grant permission to peers. Whereas the permissions issued by 5-year-olds sounded much like commands (such as "You can swing"), 7-year-olds were more likely to say something softer such as, "I don't mind your swinging." Likewise, 5-year-olds would forbid the action by saying "You mustn't swing!" whereas 7-year-olds were more likely to say something such as, "I'd rather you didn't swing." The older children were also more likely to add *please* when making requests.

Wilkinson, Wilkinson, Spinelli, and Chiang (1984) have shown that older children are more indirect in their requests for help on schoolwork. Eight-year-olds typically said: "Please help me spell this word." or "Can you help me spell this word?" They rarely simply said: "Help me spell this word." Most 6- and 7-year-olds also used indirect methods, but a sizable minority relied upon direct methods.

Even 2½-year-olds occasionally use indirect methods of communication. Newcombe and Zaslow (1981) studied the way in which 2½-year-olds requested an adult to do something. Typically they used imperatives (simply saying "juice" to request juice). Occasionally, however, children's requests were more subtle. In a few instances children hinted to adults:

Samantha (holding a can of Playdough): What's in this?
Adult: Hm?
Samantha: What's in this? (Adult does not respond.)
Samantha: Open it.

In addition, when adults did not respond, children sometimes repeated their requests but more politely, by adding "please" or "okay?"
or changing the intonation from a statement to that of a question.

Effective Listening

Messages are sometimes vague or confusing, and in these situations
a listener needs to ask the speaker to clarify the message. Frequently,
young children have difficulty recognizing when a message is ambiguous
(Ironsmith and Whitehurst, 1978), and they may therefore not realize
that they are responding incorrectly. In one study, unseen speakers told
kindergarten children to "put the red block on the tray." In fact, the children had two red blocks of different shapes in front of them. Though the
children were at first puzzled by this communication, most arbitrarily selected one of the red blocks to put on the tray. Moreover, when questioned after making their decisions, the children maintained that: (1) they
had correctly identified the specific block to which the speaker was referring; and (2) the speaker had done a good job of communicating to
them. Older children and adults would, of course, recognize the problem
in the message and realize that the communication itself was faulty
(Singer and Flavell, 1981).

Preschool children can be taught to be better listeners. Sonnenschein
(1984) had 5-year-old children watch a speaker doll and a listener doll
play a game in which the speaker was to identify which of two common
objects had a hidden star on it that could be seen by the speaker but not
by the listener. The two objects presented on any trial were always of the
same class (clowns, chairs, triangles), but differed on one dimension
(such as color or size). The speaker always gave ambiguous messages.
Depending on the group to which they had been randomly assigned, the
children heard the listener respond correctly (pick the object with the
hidden star), respond incorrectly, or note the ambiguity explicitly without responding by saying "They're both _____. Do you mean the
_____ or the _____?" (p. 289). One week later, the children themselves interacted as both speaker and listener. Those who had heard the
ambiguity pointed out to them the week before now performed significantly better than those in the other groups. So even at this age appropriate training can lead children to monitor their own communications
more closely.

SUMMARY

1. Language is recognized as central to human social behavior and
   communication. The course of language development is best
   thought of as a number of emerging competencies in distinct
   aspects of language.

2. In many ways, the infant is well prepared to learn language: The
   auditory system functions well at birth. Perception of the acoustic
   characteristics of consonants and vowels, the "raw materials" of
   speech, is well established in young infants.

3. Toward their first birthdays, infants are able to understand adults' speech, even though they cannot talk themselves. This lag between comprehension and production of words is typical throughout development.

4. For the first two months of life cries and grunts are common. Cooing begins at about 3 months of age. Babbling emerges at approximately 4 months, and progressively becomes more like human speech: The number of distinct sounds increases and intonation emerges. These changes are thought to reflect infants' testing of hypotheses about correct sounds in their language.

5. After children learn to talk, there is additional improvement in their production of speech sounds. Children are more likely to imitate words with sounds they already know. Also, certain difficult sounds are consistently mispronounced.

6. Children typically say their first words near their first birthdays. In the year that follows, the size of their vocabularies increases dramatically. For children with referential language-learning styles, names dominate the early vocabulary. For those with expressive learning styles, a number of different types of words are represented.

7. Children's first words represent an intellectual accomplishment that is not specific to language. Instead, the onset of language is due to a child's ability to interpret and use symbols. Consistent with this view, there are parallel developments in the use of gestures and words in sentences.

8. Young children often overextend or underextend the meaning of a word, until they have developed an exact idea of what the word really means. For preschoolers a word's meaning is likely to be determined by its characteristic features; only school-age children know the importance of defining features.

9. Not long after the first birthday, children produce two-word sentences that seem to be formulas for expressing ideas or needs. As children gradually learn rules that govern the use of grammatical morphemes like prepositions, articles, and auxiliary verbs, their sentences become longer and more sophisticated. They first learn simple grammatical morphemes and later master more complex forms.

10. Young children often ask questions by changing intonation, but soon they begin to learn to use different *wh* questions. The ease with which children learn questions depends, in part, on the verbs used in the questions.

11. Laboratory research indicates that experience can be an important factor in language learning. Adults speak to children in ways that should help children to learn language. However, direct relationships between children's language experiences and their language development are often difficult to find. One exception is

parents' use of imitation with modification, which does aid language growth. In addition, intense language experience may aid language development for children disadvantaged by poverty.

12. Mastering the art of communication involves recognizing and understanding the implicit contract between speaker and listener. Children first learn about this contract during infancy. By the preschool years, children have mastered many of the conventions concerning turn taking, including ways to get responses from listeners.

13. Beginning in the preschool years, children gradually become much more skilled at constructing efficient messages. They are better able to consider the needs of listeners. They become skilled in the use of indirect methods of communicating. They become able to determine if a message is vague or ambiguous.

6 PIAGET'S APPROACH TO COGNITIVE DEVELOPMENT

"I think, therefore I am." This saying, attributed to the French philosopher René Descartes, captures an assumption that has been ingrained in Western societies for over 2,000 years. Most of us consider the abilities to reason and to acquire knowledge to be unique to our species, and to be the essence of human existence.

Because the intellect is prized, psychologists and lay people have long been interested in what encourages intellectual growth. One step toward understanding these conditions is to describe the usual course of intellectual growth. In fact, as children grow, their intellectual or *cognitive* skills rapidly expand. Many school-age children, for example, walk from home to school and back, even though the route is often long and not marked. Rarely would preschool children be permitted to make these trips, because they have limited *way-finding* skills compared to their older siblings.

This age difference is typical because in most intellectual domains there are systematic developmental changes in children's abilities. Adults' thinking is more sophisticated than that of adolescents, whose thought is more advanced than that of children. Of course, this is hardly the entire story. The challenging problem for developmental psychology is to explain the underlying forces that orchestrate psychological development. What mechanisms are responsible for this steady progression toward mature intellectual skill?

For many years our best answer to this question was provided in a theory formulated by Jean Piaget (1896–1980). Piaget began to study intellectual development in the 1920s and spent nearly sixty years revising and elaborating his theory. As we see in the first half of this chapter, Piaget's theory draws heavily on concepts from biology and formal logic.

Beginning in the late 1960s, many developmental psychologists proposed variations on Piaget's theory of intellectual development. These extensions and refinements are now so numerous that they are often collectively referred to as neo-Piagetian approaches to cognitive development. We discuss them in the last section of this chapter.

PIAGET'S THEORY

Piaget was a biologist by training but he had a keen interest in *epistemology*, the branch of philosophy dealing with the origin and nature of knowledge. Piaget's scientific training meant he did not think these issues could be decided by debate. Instead, he sought answers in evidence from scientific research, by studying how humans acquire knowledge.

To gain experience with psychological research, Piaget traveled to various psychological laboratories in Europe, including that of Theophile Simon, a collaborator on the first intelligence tests (a topic we discuss more in Chapter 8). Piaget was asked to administer some new reasoning tests developed in England. He was impressed by the parallels between children's reasoning on these tests and the principles of formal logic. In addition, Piaget saw parallels between biological adaptation and intellectual development: Intellectual growth seemed to involve interplay between children and their environment, just as biological adaptation involves adjustments between organisms and their environments.

A central concept in Piaget's theory is the *scheme*, which he described as the mental structure underlying a sequence of behaviors, such as grasping. Schemes differ in complexity, but even simple grasping organizes the actions of reaching, finger curling, and drawing in. As an infant gains experience, he or she will learn to grasp in different ways—for example,"for something far away," "for something nearby," "for something small," "for something large," and so on. The grasping scheme then becomes a kind of category that includes a collection of distinct but similar action sequences.

The infant's first schemes are almost entirely reflexive and inborn. For instance, the neonate exhibits a sucking scheme when almost anything comes into its mouth. All schemes gives rise to organized behavior patterns and all schemes (even those that are innate) are modified through the interaction of individual and environment.

Schemes apply throughout cognitive development. Adolescents, for example, often acquire a *proportionality scheme*, which refers to understanding the relationships that can exist between two ratios. Suppose one child has three crayons, two red and one blue, and another has six crayons, four red and two blue. Proportionally, they have the same quantity of red crayons relative to blue ones—twice as many. This scheme, like grasping, refers to an organized set of actions (in this case, mental actions) that can be applied to diverse objects.

The most important property of schemes for cognitive development is that they can be combined to form larger units. The initial schemes of looking, listening, and grasping become woven together over the course of early cognitive development until the infant is able, for example, to execute an intelligent search procedure for a missing person or object. Schemes formed during early infancy gradually become sophisticated models of the world, which emerge in later life and define the most advanced forms of human thought.

Contents, Functions, and Structures

Piaget (1952) distinguished three aspects of intellect: contents, functions, and structures. The *contents* of intelligence refer to the behavioral products that result when a scheme is applied. Because schemes change as children develop, ordinarily the contents of intelligence change considerably with age.

Functions are constant throughout development, so Piaget called them *functional invariants*. One functional invariant is *adaptation*. In biology, adaptation refers to changes in structures or forms that result in better fit (greater likelihood of survival) of an animal or plant to its environment. To maintain a favorable balance with their environments, all animals must adjust to ecological change. Herds instinctively seek new grazing in a drought, and chameleons change color to conceal themselves from predators.

Humans also have unique methods of adaptation. For Piaget, intellectual adaptation always involves two complementary processes, *assimilation* and *accommodation*. To understand these processes, imagine a toddler in a garden with his father. Seeing a rose, violet, and tulip, the youngster names each a flower. The child's word *flower* represents assimilation. The child's schemes are used to interpret and organize incoming information.

Now suppose the child called a dandelion a flower. Apparently the child's scheme for flower refers simply to small, colorful plants. If the father corrected him, the child might then refer to dandelions as weeds. This would represent accommodation. What was once one scheme is now two, as the original scheme is modified to incorporate this new information.

Another functional invariant, *organization*, concerns relationships among different schemes and leads to Piaget's conceptualization of *structures*. Imagine that a 10-month-old has several schemes, including grasping, sucking, and waving. Piaget held that these schemes are always organized to form integrated mental structures. The types of mental structures change as children develop. But the presence of an organized mental structure of some sort is a constant.

Because schemes are linked together, changing one scheme influences others as well. Development will be marked by reorganization of these overarching mental structures. Piaget believed that an organism periodically "outgrows" the existing mental structure, which is replaced by a qualitatively different, more sophisticated structure. That is, accommodation and assimilation are usually in balance, creating a state of cognitive equilibrium. There are critical times, however, when so many schemes are forced to accommodate to new information that the result is a state of disequilibrium. Resolving the problem and restoring equilibrium leads to more advanced mental structures.

FiGURE 6–1
**Jean Piaget, the
Swiss psychologist
whose stage theory
of cognitive
development
focuses on the
interaction of nature
and nurture.**
Courtesy of Wayne
Behling.

Piaget proposed four distinct periods of cognitive development:

1. Sensorimotor period (0 to 2 years);
2. Preoperational period (2 to 7 years);
3. Concrete operational period (7 to 11 years);
4. Formal operational period (11 through adulthood).

The ages are only averages and vary considerably with the environment and background of each child. However, the sequence of the stages is constant. Intellectual development *always* consists of the sequence sensorimotor, preoperational, concrete operational, and formal operational periods, regardless of environment or ability. Children cannot "skip" a stage and move directly from preoperational to formal operational, any more than a caterpillar can become a butterfly without first going through the pupa stage.

Though without experience, the newborn infant is not completely helpless because he or she is born with inherited reflexes and a number of innate perceptual abilities. During the first two years of life these inborn abilities evolve so that the child is able to engage in increasingly flexible and purposeful actions.

Piaget divides the sensorimotor period into six substages. Like the larger periods described in Piagetian theory, the chronological ages associated with each substage are approximations.

The First Month of Life (Stage 1).   During this stage the infant displays increasingly smooth and systematic use of its natural reflexes, engaging in what Piaget calls "reflex exercise." For example, subtle but noticeable advances in the coordination of the sucking scheme occur during the first month of life (Flavell, 1963).

Modification of a reflex is the first evidence of accommodation; there is also evidence of assimiliation during this stage. First infants suck only the nipple, but soon they suck toys and blankets as well. By sucking a range of objects, infants begin their initial assimilations with the environment. They learn that some objects yield nourishment but others do not.

The Second to the Fourth Months (Stage 2).   During the first stage of sensorimotor thought reflexes become more finely tuned; in the next few months they change through experience. The chief means for change is the *primary circular reaction*, in which some event triggers a reflex by chance. Infants, for example, may accidentally touch their lips with their thumbs, initiating sucking and the pleasant sensations that accompany sucking. Later, they try to repeat the event to re-create those pleasant sensations.

The Fourth to the Eighth Months (Stage 3). Between the fourth and eighth months of life *secondary circular reactions* appear. Circular reactions at this stage are aimed at maintaining environmental events originally brought about by chance. For example, suppose the infant accidentally shakes a rattle and hears a noise. The infant will repeatedly shake the rattle, trying to produce the noise again. This secondary circular reaction has many of the properties of the primary circular reaction: It first occurs by chance, the outcome is pleasing, and the infant strives to repeat the event. The critical difference is that primary circular reactions result in direct sensory stimulation and so often involve the infant's body. Secondary circular reactions produce indirect sensory input and so are usually oriented toward objects and activities beyond the infant's body. Thumb sucking, for example, is a primary circular reaction; shaking a rattle is a secondary circular reaction.

The Eighth to the Twelfth Months (Stage 4). Examples such as those above suggest at least the threshold of intelligent behavior. However, Piaget theorizes that it is not until stage 4 that truly purposeful behavior appears. The reason is that in stage 3, different secondary circular reactions are not coordinated. In stage 4, one circular reaction is a means to achieve a second:

> . . . [at six months] I present Laurent with a matchbox, extending my hand laterally to make an obstacle to his prehension. Laurent tries to pass over my hand, or to the side, but he does not attempt to displace it. . . . [At seven months, ten days,] Laurent tries to grasp a new box in front of which I place my hand. . . . He sets the obstacle aside, but not intentionally; he simply tries to reach the box by sliding next to my hand and when he touches it, tries to take no notice of it. . . . Finally [at age seven months, thirteen days,] Laurent reacts quite differently almost from the beginning of the experiment. I present a box of matches above my hand, but behind it, so that he cannot reach it without setting the obstacle aside. But Laurent, after trying to take no notice of it, suddenly tries to hit my hand as though to remove or lower it; I let him do it to me and he grasps the box. (Piaget, 1952, p. 217)

Pushing the obstacle aside is not an accident; rather, it is a way to reach the object. Secondary circular reactions combine to launch new behavior that is intentionally goal-directed, as the first glimmer of real intelligence appears.

The Twelfth to the Eighteenth Months (Stage 5). Variation is first systematically introduced into circular reactions with the *tertiary circular reaction*. As in the case of primary and secondary circular reactions, the tertiary reactions begin with chance events that infants try to repeat. The critical difference is that infants now systematically vary the reactions as they are repeated, as if trying to understand why different objects yield different outcomes. For example, at 10 months of age, Laurent acciden-

FIGURE 6–2
During the sensorimotor period, infants begin to construct reality by integrating sensory and motor experience. Censer, Monkmeyer.

tally dropped an object from his crib. Soon thereafter he began to drop different toys and objects and intently studied each as it fell (Piaget, 1952). This and other tertiary circular reactions clearly look intentional: Tertiary circular reactions represent active efforts to adapt to new situations, rather than to simply repeat old behaviors.

The Eighteenth to the Twenty-fourth Months (Stage 6).   This is the climax of the sensorimotor period, for infants are now capable of *mental* representations. The child is now able to use symbols, such as words, to refer to objects not present. For Piaget, several events signal children's use of mental symbols beginning at approximately 18 months of age. One is that children are capable of *deferred imitation.* Younger children will imitate the actions of other children and adults, but only when the actions happen. Deferred imitation occurs long after the children see the others' acts.

Perhaps the most impressive feat of stage 6 is that the active experimentation characteristic of stage 5 is now carried out *mentally* rather than *behaviorally.* No longer must children literally try out all possible events to determine their consequences; they can *anticipate* some of these consequences mentally:

. . . Jacqueline, at [age 20 months] arrives at a closed door—with a blade of grass in each hand. She stretches out her right hand toward the knob but sees that she cannot turn it without letting go of the grass. She puts the grass on the floor, opens the door, picks up the grass again and enters. But when she wants to leave the room things become complicated. She puts the grass on the floor and grasps the doorknob. But then she perceives that in pulling the door toward her she will simultaneously chase away the grass which she placed between the door and the threshold. She therefore picks it up in order to put it outside the door's zone of movement. (Piaget, 1952, p. 338–339)

This capacity to use mental symbols signals the end of the sensorimotor period. The child has progressed in two years from using reflexive acts to using mental symbols. Of course, 2-year-olds' use of symbols is not at all the same as that of adults; in fact, their mental representations differ systematically from those of older children and adolescents.

The Preoperational Period (2 to 7 Years)

The end of the sensorimotor period is also the beginning of the preoperational period. Henceforth the child will begin to deal with increasingly complex problems and will gradually come to rely on mental representations to solve them. During the preoperational period, the child begins to develop a perspective of the world and displays an increased ability to accommodate to new information and experience. Preschool children's thought seems to have a logic all its own, a logic differing considerably from adults'. Four characteristics of preoperational thought show its limitations:

Action-Based. Preoperational children's thinking often seems to be the mental equivalent of the infant's sensorimotor actions. Rather than actively experimenting with objects, like a 15-month-old does, a 3-year-old performs exactly the same sequence of actions, only mentally.

Irreversible. Preoperational thinking is unidirectional and irreversible; young children cannot reverse their thinking. This property was demonstrated in one of Piaget's best-known experiments: conservation of liquid quantity. Children are shown two identical beakers, both filled with the same amount of liquid (see Figure 6–3). Water from one of the beakers is poured into a third beaker, which differs in shape from the first two. Concrete operational children would say that the two beakers still contain the same amount of liquid, and they would justify their answers by saying that the water could be poured back into the original beaker. They realize that the pouring can be reversed. Preoperational children typically believe that the quantities are no longer the same when poured into different beakers.

Centered. Conservation problems reveal another characteristic of preschooler's thinking. When asked why they believe the taller of the beakers contains more water, preoperational children characteristically refer to the level of the water. In doing so, they ignore the change in the diameter of the beaker that compensates perfectly for the change in height.

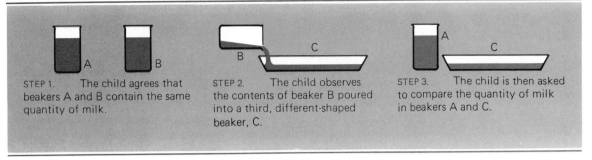

STEP 1. The child agrees that beakers A and B contain the same quantity of milk.

STEP 2. The child observes the contents of beaker B poured into a third, different-shaped beaker, C.

STEP 3. The child is then asked to compare the quantity of milk in beakers A and C.

FIGURE 6–3
A typical sequence for studying conservation of liquid quantity.

This tendency for thinking to be *centered* on a particular aspect of a problem, to the exclusion of others, is a common characteristic of preschool thought.

Egocentric. Young children have difficulty grasping the fact that their view of the world—both literally and figuratively—may be but one of many. *Egocentrism* refers to this inability to see the world from another's perspective. The preoperational child is an unknowing prisoner of his or her own egocentric point of view.

In the classic demonstration of egocentrism (Piaget and Inhelder, 1956, chapter 8), children were seated on one side of a display consisting of three toy mountains and were asked to show how the display looked to a doll seated elsewhere (see Figure 6–4). Children under the age of 7 or 8 generally indicated that the doll saw what they themselves saw. Egocentrism lessens during the preoperational period through contact with

FIGURE 6–4
The three-mountains problem devised by Piaget to study perspective taking. The child's task is to judge how the mountains would appear to the doll. From R. Kail and J. W. Pellegrino, (1985). *Human Intelligence, Perspectives and Prospects.* New York: W. H. Freeman.

friends, siblings, and classmates who have their own perspectives (Flavell, 1974; Piaget and Inhelder, 1969).

The Concrete
Operational
Period (7 to 11
Years)
According to Piaget, the concrete operational period is characterized by orderly thinking that gives rise to the ability to decenter and recognize transformations, an awareness that some transformations are reversible, and a grasp of the concept of conservation. A clue to the underlying difference between peroperational and concrete operational thought is provided in the terms themselves: Preschoolers' thinking is somehow *pre*operational, but older children's thinking is operational. For Piaget, the key to successful performance now is the *mental operation*. In mathematics, operations denote actions like addition or subtraction that yield some outcome. Piaget proposed that psychological operations are much the same; they are actions that can be performed on objects or ideas and that yield a result.

To illustrate what Piaget means, we can examine children's understanding of classes and relationships that exist among classes, which Piaget studied with the *class-inclusion problem*. Children are shown objects from two categories—pictures of five boys and four girls, two dogs and three cats, or seven roses and four tulips. Each problem consists of two subsets, one larger than the other. After children are shown the sets they might be asked, for example, "Are there more roses or flowers?" Preoperational children typically respond, "Roses." They apparently believe that roses cannot be a distinct subset and simultaneously a member of the larger set of flowers. Not until approximately 8 or 9 years of age do children routinely answer such problems correctly.

Piaget proposed that the mental structures of the concrete operational period are described by nine different sets of mental operations, which he called *groupings*. Grouping I, for example, specifies several operations for combining classes. The operations of this grouping are essential for success on class-inclusion problems. When asked if there are more roses or flowers, concrete operational children can use the principle of reversibility to realize that roses = flowers − tulips. That is, roses are included in the class of flowers; the class of flowers therefore is larger than the class of roses.

Groupings like this one give flexibility and coherence to thought. But, concrete operational children are still bound up with the world as it is, and they cannot get any further until they begin to delineate all possible explanations at the outset of considering a problem. This ability to appreciate the possible as well as the real characterizes the transition to formal operational thought. It is not that the concrete operational child is unintelligent; by middle childhood youngsters have at their command an impressive array of cognitive tools. However, in Flavell's colorful words, the concrete operational child takes "an earthbound, concrete, practical-minded sort of problem-solving approach, one that persistently fixates on the perceptible and inferable reality right there in front of him . . . A theorist the elementary-school child is not." (Flavell, 1985, p. 98).

Children's Humor

Piaget's developmental periods are not limited to logical, scientific, and mathematical reasoning. To the contrary—Piaget believed that the mental structures associated with each stage of intellectual development are the means by which children interpret all experiences, including, for example, interpersonal experiences (Barenboim, 1977).

Piaget's stages have even been used as the basis for understanding children's humor. Many theories of humor claim that children's

> comprehension and appreciation of ludicrous situations will depend to a great extent ... on the match between the individual's existing developmental level and the cognitive demands placed upon him by the humorous event. All things being equal, the individual's appreciation of humor is expected to increase as cognitive demands ... [of] the humor increase, up to the point where the stimulus becomes too difficult, complex, or novel to be assimilated by the individual's cognitive structures. (Brodzinsky and Rightmyer, 1980, pp. 187–188)

One prominent theory, proposed by Paul McGhee (1979, 1983), takes these general ideas and links them explicitly to Piaget's developmental stages. According to McGhee, children's understanding and appreciation of humor is determined, in large part, by their level of cognitive development. For example, a child who has just entered concrete operations should particularly enjoy humor that taps these newly acquired mental structures. This child would find preoperational jokes silly and would be puzzled by formal operational humor.

In one study McGhee (1976) examined the relationship between children's understanding of conservation and their appreciation of

jokes that presume understanding of conservation. An example would be:

> Mr. Jones went into a restaurant and ordered a whole pizza for dinner. When the waiter asked if he wanted it cut into six or eight pieces, Mr. Jones said: "Oh, you'd better make it six! I could never eat eight!" (McGhee, 1976, p. 422)

As predicted by McGhee's theory, the children most likely to enjoy such jokes were in the transition from preoperational to concrete operational thought, when the humor was challenging for their newly acquired mental structures. Children enjoyed these jokes significantly less prior to the onset of concrete operational thinking and after such thinking was well established.

Subsequently, McGhee (1976) demonstrated this same sort of relationship with humor that is based on understanding of class-inclusion relationships:

> "Please stay out of the house today," Susie's mother said. "I have too much work to do." "OK," said Susie, as she walked to the stairs. "Where do you think you're going?" her mother asked. "Well," said Susie, "If I can't stay in the house, I'll just play in my room instead." (McGhee, 1976, p. 424)

This joke requires that a child understand the set-subset relationship that exists between a house and the rooms within it. As in the other study, children in the transition to concrete operations thought jokes like this one were funnier than did either preoperational children or children whose concrete operational skills were well established.

These results indicate that understanding some forms of humor is really nothing more than a distinctive, particularly pleasant form of solving problems. "Typically, some incongruous or otherwise puzzling event is presented as a key component of the intended humor. We must figure out the puzzle or resolve the incongruity before we can appreciate the humor" (McGhee, 1979, pp. 152–153). People are most likely to appreciate humor when their levels of cognitive development make resolving the incongruity neither so transparent that there is no challenge nor so complex that it becomes tedious.

The Formal Operational Period (11 through Adulthood)	Beginning with preadolescence, people begin to display the ability to engage in formal reasoning on an abstract level. They can draw hypotheses from their observations, imagine hypothetical as well as real events, and deduce or induce principles regarding the world around them. They begin to consider all possible explanations for a problem, and only then do they try to discover, systematically, which explanation really applies.

According to Piaget, adolescents' more sophisticated thinking represents significant advances on two fronts. The first concerns *hypothetico-deductive reasoning,* which is any type of reasoning that starts with a fact, premise, or hypothesis, and then draws conclusions. For example, consider the following:

> Premise 1: If an animal has gills, it is a fish.
> Premise 2: A trout has gills.

From these premises, an adolescent will reach the logical conclusion "A trout is a fish."

Sometimes concrete operational children will reach this conclusion as well, but not via deductive reasoning. To see why, suppose we replace the second premise in our example with the following:

> Premise 2A: A giraffe has gills.

The conclusion "A giraffe is a fish" follows from the premises just as necessarily as the first conclusion about trout, and formal operational adolescents would draw these conclusions in both cases. For concrete operational children, conclusions are derived from experience. They would draw the first conclusion but not the second.

The example we have used here illustrates a type of reasoning that logicians call *inference,* represented by "if P then Q." Actually, this is only one of sixteen forms of deductive reasoning that Piaget identifies with formal operations. For example, *equivalence* is defined as "if and only if P, then Q." These sixteen operations form an integrated system that affords flexibility of thought that is not possible with the nine distinct groupings of the preoperational period. In addition, the Ps and Qs of propositional logic can denote concrete entities such as objects or people, but they can just as easily refer to abstractions such as ideas, values, or even thinking itself.

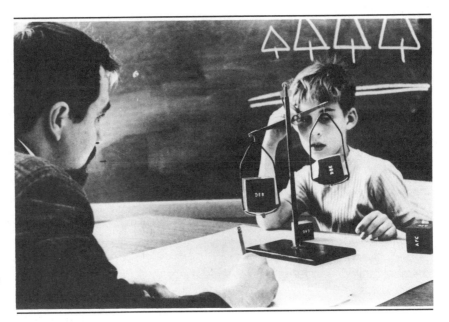

Another important component of reasoning, determining the validity of premises, is known as *inductive reasoning*. Inhelder and Piaget (1958) proposed that several schemes emerge during formal operations that allow adolescents to induce correct generalizations across different problems that are similar in structure. One of these general-purpose schemes is *separation of variables*, which is useful for understanding causal relationships. Piaget's research on the pendulum problem demonstrates the use of this scheme. The subject is presented with a pendulum consisting of an object hanging from a string. He or she is permitted to vary the length of the string, change the weight of the suspended object, alter the height from which the pendulum is released, and push the pendulum with varying degrees of force. The problem that must be solved is a classical one in physics: to discover and state which of these factors alone or in combination will influence how quickly the pendulum swings back. (In fact, length of the string is the critical variable. The shorter it is, the faster the pendulum swings.)

Concrete operational children approach the problem unsystematically and soon give up because their chaotic approach leaves them without any real clue to the answer. Formal operational children, in contrast, handle the problem quite systematically. First, the adolescent envisions all the possible factors and combinations of factors that could influence the speed of the pendulum: string length, weight, height of release, force, length and height, length and weight and height, and so on. The formal operational child can cast the possibilities into the form of propositions, which function as hypotheses. Finally, these hypotheses are tested empirically. To construct a valid test of each hypothesis the child varies one dimension, such as length of string, while holding all other

Educational Implications of Piaget's Theory

Educators have traditionally sought clues from developmental psychology concerning conditions that improve children's learning. Not surprisingly, many have found Piaget's theory useful in formulating general principles. One illustrative principle concerns the *timing* of instruction. According to Piaget's theory, children are most likely to profit from instruction when they are in transition from one stage of cognitive development to the next. For example, instruction designed to teach concepts associated with concrete operations should be most effective when children have already become aware of some of the shortcomings of preoperational thought, and thus are ready for new ways of organizing their experiences (Brainerd, 1978; Zimmerman, 1982).

A second implication of Piaget's theory concerns the settings in which learning is most likely to occur and the role of the teacher in those settings. Recall that cognitive changes are brought about by disequilibrium. So the optimal setting for learning is one that will induce states of disequilibrium. One approach would be "discovery learning": Children are given materials that allow them to explore and try to understand, on their own, the basis for some unexpected event (Zimmerman, 1982). Another approach is to form groups consisting of children at different intellectual levels. They are asked to solve problems together, and in resolving their conflicting opinions, the cognitively less mature children often advance to the level of the cognitively more mature (Murray, 1982). In either of these approaches, the teacher's role is indirect: establishing the setting in which children can learn "spontaneously."

Some educators have outlined detailed programs for children that are based on Piaget's theory. (Actually, these programs are best described as Piaget-inspired, for Piaget believed his theory did not have immediate, practical implications for education.) One of the best-known programs is that of Kamii and DeVries (1977, 1978). A description of part of their program shows the influence of Piagetian theory:

in contrast with the child-development curriculum in which group games are not considered particularly "educational," our curriculum gives a central place to group games as an important means for children to develop social cooperation and overcome their egocentrism. . . . In Hide and Seek, the teacher attempts to promote decentering (thinking about what the other player thinks and sees and coordinating one's own point of view with that of the other) and spatial reasoning (thinking about possible spaces to hide or seek). [Kamii and DeVries, 1977, p. 409]

This is just one instance of an entire preschool curriculum in which many of the activities were motivated by Piaget's theory. Whether educational programs derived from Piaget's theory are more effective than traditional approaches remains an unanswered and controversial question (Johnson and Hooper, 1982).

dimensions constant. For example, a 100-gram weight with a long string will be compared with a 100-gram weight with a short string. Formal operational thinkers realize that an experiment would yield inconclusive results if both weight and string length were varied together because they would be unable to deduce which factor produced the difference in speed.

These schemas allow adolescents systematically to explore and discover relationships that exist in the world. It is important to keep in mind, though, that formal operational reasoning is something most older adolescents and adults are capable of, but not necessarily something they do all, or even most, of the time. Adolescents and adults may often fail to think logically, even when they are capable of doing so and when such thinking would be highly beneficial.

CRITICISMS OF PIAGET'S THEORY

In the 1960s and the 1970s, literally hundreds of studies were published in which the aim was to probe various facets of Piaget's theory. This research provided support for many of Piaget's claims but also revealed some important shortcomings in the theory. One problem concerned the logical structures Piaget used to characterize thinking at different ages (the groupings of concrete operations). Linking these structures to performance on particular tasks proved to be extremely difficult, which made it hard to know exactly what sort of performance was predicted from the theory.

We can illustrate this difficulty with the class-inclusion problem described earlier, in which children might be shown three roses and two daffodils and asked, "Are there more flowers or roses?" Stated symbolically, the problem is, given the sets A and B where $A > B$ and $C = A + B$, which is larger A or C? This analysis implies that all class-inclusions problems that conform to the underlying logical relationships of $A > B$ and $C = A + B$ should be equally difficult. They are not; perceptual and linguistic variables influence children's performance markedly (Brainerd, 1978; Trabasso, Isen, Dolecki, McLanahan, Riley, and Tucker, 1978).

A study by Wilkinson (1976) illustrates this point. Children were shown the pictures in Figure 6–7. The pictures in the top row of this figure represent the standard procedure in which children are asked, "Are there more boys or more children?" The bottom row depicts a problem in which the question would be, "Are there more houses that have a door or more houses that have a window?" Both problems correspond to the logical structure described by Piaget. No preschoolers answered the top problem correctly, but nearly two-thirds were correct on the bottom problem.

Wilkinson (1976) explains these differences in terms of children's rules for counting. Children learning to count are taught the rule to count each object once and only once. This rule is essential for most situations in which children count. However, in class-inclusion problems this means that having determined that there are two boys, preschoolers may be reluctant to count those boys again to determine the number of children. The problem in the bottom row of Figure 6–7 may be easier for preschoolers because the windows and doors can be counted separately, with no need to double count.

In a similar way, the difficulty of the traditional conservation of liquid quantity problem (shown in Figure 6–3) varies with subtle changes in procedures. For example, in the standard procedure, children are asked twice about the similarity of the two quantities, once before and once after the liquid is poured. When situations like this occur in everyday

FIGURE 6–7
Problems used in Wilkinson's study of class inclusion. The problem in the bottom was substantially easier, which Wilkinson attributed to the fact that it eliminated the need to "double count." Reprinted with permission from A. Wilkinson (1976). Counting strategies and semantic analysis as applied to class inclusion. *Cognitive Psychology*, *8*, 64–85. Copyright by Academic Press.

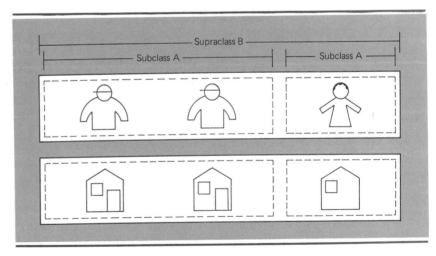

conversation, they usually mean one of two things: Either the first answer was wrong (as when a parent questions a child a second time about some misdeed because the parent suspects the first answer may have been less than the full truth) or something has happened in the interim that should change the child's response (as when a parent asks a child about his or her hunger before and after a meal). Thus, children may interpret the repeated question in the standard conservation procedure as an implicit request that they should change their answers. If this argument is correct, asking children about the quantities once—after they have been poured—should increase the likelihood that children conserve. And usually, it does (Silverman and Rose, 1979).

Thus, in class inclusion as well as in perspective taking (e.g., Liben and Belknap, 1981), predictions from Piaget's theory are not always supported. Furthermore, researchers have explained children's performance via processes quite unlike Piaget's groupings, using instead rules for counting and language.

Consistency of Thought within Stages

For Piaget, each period of intellectual development consists of a unified set of mental operations that is implicated in all aspects of a child's thinking. This view leads to obvious experimental tests. According to Piaget, preschool children should perform at the preoperational level across all cognitive tasks. If they do not, this would be inconsistent with Piaget's view that the children's thinking is unified at each stage.

In fact, children's performances on Piaget's tasks are often *not* consistent in the way suggested by the theory. Research by Siegler (1981) illustrates this inconsistency on the three Piagetian tasks shown in Figure 6–8. In the *balance scale* task, individuals are shown a balance scale in which weights have been placed at various distances to either side of a fulcrum. Individuals must decide which side of the balance scale will go down, if either, when the supporting blocks are removed. On the *projection of shadows* task, the T-shaped bars are placed at various distances from the light source, and the horizontal part of the T varies in length. Subjects judge which of the two bars will cast a longer horizontal shadow. In the *probability* task, subjects are shown two piles of marbles, each containing red and blue marbles. They decide which pile would be more likely to produce a red marble if they must choose with their eyes closed.

Despite apparent differences in the nature of the tasks, the underlying structure is the same for each: It involves a comparison of ratios. The scale will balance when the ratio of weight to distance is the same on the two sides of the fulcrum. The shadows will be the same size when the ratio of the length of the horizontal part of the T-bar to the distance of the bar from the light is the same for both bars. The probability of selecting a red marble will be the same when the ratio of the number of red marbles to the total number of marbles is the same for both piles.

Because the underlying structure of the tasks is fundamentally the same, we would expect consistency in performances across the three

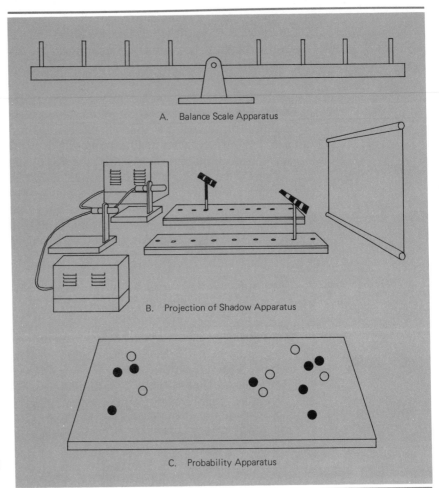

FIGURE 6—8
Apparatus for balance scale, projection of shadows, and probability tasks used by Siegler (1981). From R.S. Siegler (1981). Developmental sequences within and between concepts. *Monographs of the Society for Research in Child Development*, 46, Serial #189. Reprinted by permission of the Society for Research in Child Development, Inc.

A. Balance Scale Apparatus

B. Projection of Shadow Apparatus

C. Probability Apparatus

tasks. In fact, Siegler (1981) found that only one-third of the subjects performed at the same level on all three tasks. The remainder differed in performance, sometimes considerably. For example, all eleven subjects whose level of performance on the balance scale task corresponded to formal operational thought were only at the level of concrete operations on the shadows task. Such variability across tasks is far from what one would expect from the homogeneous mind that is described in Piaget's theory.

Training Piagetian Concepts

Another implication of Piaget's view of the mind is that efforts to teach children advanced concepts should be unsuccessful. For example, it should be impossible to teach concrete operational concepts to preschoolers because they lack the necessary mental apparatus to profit from the experience.

Beilin (1965) was the first to try teaching children the conservation rule itself. In teaching conservation of length, for example, Beilin's experimenters would respond to an error by a child with a clear statement of the rule: "Whenever we start with a length like this one (pointing) and we don't add any sticks to it or take away any sticks . . . it stays the same length even though it looks different. See, I can put them back the way they were, so they haven't really changed" (p. 326). While reciting the rule, the experimenter made the appropriate changes in the object so that the child would have a physical as well as a verbal representation of it. Beilin was quite successful in inducing specific conservation on the training task. But his simple procedures failed to produce significant generalization to related tasks. Later investigators have been much more successful (Siegler and Liebert, 1972a, 1972b) because they have taken additional steps to bolster the rule training. Siegler and Liebert (1972a, 1972b), for example, found that children were most likely to master conservation problems when the experimenter provided *both* the relevant rule and feedback. These experiments conclusively answer the original question of whether 4- and 5-year-olds can be taught conservation skills. The numerous unsuccessful and partially successful earlier studies, however, show the difficulty of inducing conservation in these children.

Training has not been restricted to conservation; investigators have also asked whether children below the age of formal operations can learn to master formal operational problems. A series of studies by Siegler and his colleagues (Siegler, 1975; Siegler and Atlas, 1976; Siegler, D. E. Liebert, and R. M. Liebert, 1973; Siegler and R. M. Liebert, 1975) indicates that they can. In one of these studies, Siegler, Liebert, and Liebert attempted to teach the pendulum problem to 10- and 11-year-olds. The procedure included definitions of key scientific concepts, application of these concepts to particular problems, and demonstration of the use of precise measuring instruments. Roughly 70 percent of the children who were given instruction mastered the pendulum problem, compared to less than 10 percent of the uninstructed children. The other studies in the series also testify to the ability of concrete-operations-aged children to learn formal operational concepts—although, in line with Inhelder and Piaget's findings, these children rarely solve the problems without instruction.

Simply finding that Piaget's concepts can be trained does not make Piaget's theory wrong. After all, many of the children in these studies were near the age when they would acquire the concepts anyway. Training may have simply induced a cognitive change sooner. This interpretation does have a testable implication—that "children at more advanced stages should derive greater benefit from training than should children at less advanced stages—or more simply, the higher the stage, the greater the learning" (Brainerd, 1977, p. 921). For example, suppose we tested a large number of 5- and 6-year-olds on conservation tasks and divided the children into those who never conserve versus those who are "transitional"—they sometimes conserve but more often do not. If previous training studies have simply facilitated a cognitive change, then transitional children should profit more from training than nonconservers. In fact, both groups are equally likely to learn to conserve from training (Brainerd, 1977). This is an outcome that does not follow from Piaget's theory.

In the face of these criticisms, many theorists have tried to modify Piaget's theory.

Use of Rules and Strategies

One specific approach has been to retain Piaget's claim of general qualitative change at approximately 2, 7, and 11 years of age. However, the changes are described in terms of the specific rules or strategies that people use to solve particular tasks. In this view, as individuals develop they use more sophisticated rules and strategies in their thinking (Gholson & Beilin, 1979). Research on the concepts of probability and balance illustrate this approach.

Concepts of Probability and Chance. Piaget believed that understanding of probability and chance is intimately linked to children's understanding of causality. When some event, A, causes another, B, to occur, this is called a cause-effect relationship. In contrast, when the occurrence of B does not depend on any known A, B is said to occur randomly—by chance or by luck. Piaget believed mature understanding of chance required that the child understand that particular phenomena are not attributable to cause-effect relationships.

Piaget and his colleague Barbel Inhelder (Inhelder and Piaget, 1958) believed that children's understanding of the concepts of probability and chance progresses through three stages. According to their theory, preschoolers do not understand cause and effect relationships and cannot understand probabilities. During the elementary school years children distinguish causal from chance events. They can sometimes even calculate probabilities of various outcomes, as long as the tasks are not too complex. Not until adolescence, however, do children learn the formal characteristics of permutations and combinations that allow them to deal with a wide range of probabilities.

The methods used in Piaget's original research, as well as in subsequent studies, are straightforward. Children are shown the contents of two containers, each having two distinct categories of objects, such as red and blue marbles. Children are then asked to select the container from which they would be most likely to draw a marble of a particular color. Usually there are several problems in which the numbers of marbles are varied, as are the proportions of the colors of the marbles. For example, one container might have four red and two blue marbles; the other container, three red and two blue marbles.

Several investigators have shown that selection of the correct container increases with age. For example, Chapman (1975) found that 6-year-olds chose the appropriate container approximately 60 percent of the time, compared to approximately 90 percent for 10-year-olds and 99 percent for adults.

Thus, as Piaget and Inhelder suggested, as children develop they are better able to reason proportionally. In another way, however, these percentages are perplexing. Children who lack these reasoning skills could presumably only guess on each trial, which means they should be correct on exactly 50 percent of the trials. In fact, 5- and 6-year-olds are usually slightly but significantly more accurate than would be expected if they were only guessing (Brainerd, 1981). In addition, 10- and 11-year-olds often err on 10 percent of their choices. Both findings suggest that there may be several intermediate stages in the acquisition of these reasoning skills.

Let us return to our earlier example: Asked to select the container that maximizes obtaining a red marble, children might select the container with four red and two blue marbles because the probability of selecting a red marble is .67 compared to .6 in the container with three red and two blue marbles. However, children might have selected the first container simply because it contained more red marbles. In fact, children perform poorly on problems in which the more likely container contains fewer of the specified color. For example, given five red and four blue marbles in one container but three red and two blue in the other, most 5- and 6-year-olds routinely select the first container as the better source of a red marble (Siegler, 1981). This comparison of the number of the specific marbles (instead of the probabilities) is common until at least 8 or 9 years of age (Offenbach, Gruen, and Caskey, 1984).

Somewhat older children apparently realize that it is wrong to compare the numbers of desired marbles in the two containers, but they do not yet know just what to compare. Frequently they *subtract* the number of objects in the unspecified category from those in the specified category, and then select the container in which this difference is larger. Given a container with five red and two blue marbles and another with three red and one blue, these children select the former container because red marbles exceed blue ones by three compared to a difference of only two in the other container. This approach is most frequent among adolescents, although some children and even some young adults reason in this manner (Siegler, 1981).

Mature forms of probabilistic reasoning, then, do not seem to emerge until mid to late adolescence. A similar pattern emerges in understanding the related concept that events sometimes occur by chance or luck. Outcomes in many children's games are determined entirely by chance, as in rolling dice or turning a spinner. Yet young children sometimes believe they can influence these outcomes by trying harder or by practicing.

Weisz (1980) used a gamelike setting to test 5- and 9-year-olds' understanding of chance. Children played a game in which they first counted out five cards with blue spots and five with yellow spots. The experimenter shuffled these cards and allowed each child to select a card. Children were told that they would receive a chip for each blue card drawn (yellow for half the children) and that if they won enough chips they would get a prize.

Later children were asked to predict the number of chips that would be won by (1) a child who practiced a lot versus a child who never practiced; (2) a child who picked cards very carefully versus one who chose quickly; and (3) a very smart child versus a child who was not so smart. Shown in Figure 6–9 is the percentage of children at each age who predicted that children who practiced, were careful, or were smart would win more chips compared to children who did not practice or were not careful or smart. A slight developmental trend emerges: Older children are less likely to believe that variables like practice and intelligence can influence random events. Even among the older children, however, the vast majority do not understand the truly random nature of the outcomes of this game.

This experiment was devised to make the random nature of the outcome as obvious as possible to subjects. Of course, many chance events outside the laboratory are not so obvious, and here we might expect even older individuals to believe that random outcomes are at least partially predictable. Weisz (1981) examined this by interviewing children at a

FIGURE 6–9

Percentage of children who believed that practice, intelligence, and effort could influence the outcome of a random event. Data from Weisz (1980, 1981). Copyright © 1981 by the American Psychological Association. Reprinted by permission of the author.

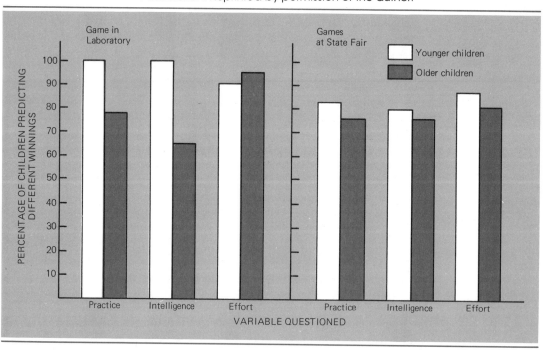

state fair after they had participated in four games in which the outcomes were dependent on chance. As part of the interview, children were asked questions from the earlier study about the roles of intelligence, effort, and practice on success. As Figure 6–9 shows, even though the children were older, the findings resemble those from the study with the laboratory game. Both 8- and 11-year-olds have limited understanding of chance. They believe instead that outcomes *can* be influenced by practice, intelligence, and effort. Thus, just as adolescence marks the onset of mature reasoning about probability, it also marks the emergence of a mature concept of chance.

The Concept of Balance. Like probabilistic reasoning, understanding of the concept of balance develops gradually. Even preschoolers have some correct intuitions about the concept of balance, but mature reasoning does not emerge until young adulthood.

Inhelder and Piaget (1958) described three distinct stages of reasoning about balance. In their research, individuals were shown a balance scale in which identical weights had been placed at various distances to either side of a fulcrum. Individuals simply decided which side of the balance scale would go down, if either, when the supporting blocks were removed. In stage I, children do not follow any rule systematically, though by the end of this stage, they have "intuitions" that the number of weights is important. In stage II, people know that the number of weights is important, as is their distance from the fulcrum; by the end of this stage, they know that weight and distance are related in some manner. Not until stage III, however, do individuals discover the precise form of this relationship: the number of weights on one side of the fulcrum multiplied by their distance from the fulcrum must equal the number of weights on the other side multiplied by their distance from the fulcrum.

Siegler (1976) reconceptualized Piaget's stages as a set of developmentally ordered rules. Typically, 5 and 6 year olds use rule I, in which only the number of weights is considered. If the weights on the two sides are equal, the child predicts that the scale will balance; otherwise, the child predicts that the side with the greater number of weights will go down.

For 9- and 10-year-olds, two rules are common. Rule II is just a variation of rule I: As before, when the number of weights on the two sides is unequal, children always predict that the side with more weights will go down. When the weights are equal, children no longer automatically predict the scale to balance. Instead, they consider the distance of the weights from the fulcrum, then predict. The other rule used frequently by 9- and 10-year-olds (rule III) involves consideration of both weight and distance on every problem. However, when weight and distance lead to different predictions regarding which side is heavier, rule III provides no method of reducing the conflict.

Rules II and III are both used by 13- and 14-year-olds, but rule III is more frequent. Finally, some 16- and 17-year-olds use rule II, most use rule III, and some use rule IV, in which the number of weights is multiplied by their distance.

Mechanisms of Development

Research on probability and balance illustrates an effort to provide a more precise description of how thinking changes as individuals develop. But *why* do these changes occur? Accommodation and assimilation are the fundamental mechanisms in Piaget's account of cognitive change, but these terms have been criticized as being too vague (Klahr, 1982). An alternative view has been proposed by Pascual-Leone (1970, 1980), Case (1978), and their colleagues. It is that cognitive development could be explained in terms of ". . . the size of central computing space M which increases in a lawful manner during normal development" (p. 304). M space was defined as $e + k$. The first quantity, e, is the processing capacity needed to store general information about how to perform the task. The k refers to the capacity necessary for storing information from the task and specific procedures for solving the task. The value of e is thought to be constant. That is, at different ages the instructions and general task information occupy the same amount of M space. However, k increases in steps that are linked to a child's chronological age. As Table 6-1 shows, Pascual-Leone suggested that k increases by one unit every other year between 3 and 16 years of age.

In this theory, children who fail Piagetian tasks do so because the information required exceeds the available M space. Consider, for example, conservation of liquid quantity. Pascual-Leone (cited in Case, 1978) argued that success hinges on storing three units of information: (1) keeping in M space the initial equality of the two beakers; (2) storing the nature of the transformation (pouring); and (3) storing the rule that pouring liquid from one container to another does not affect its quantity. The

TABLE 6–1
M **Values at Different Developmental Levels**

Age	Piagetian Substage	*M* Value (e + k)*
3–4	Early preoperational	$e + 1$
5–6	Late preoperational	$e + 2$
7–8	Early concrete operational	$e + 3$
9–10	Late concrete operational	$e + 4$
11–12	Early formal operational	$e + 5$
13–14	Middle formal operational	$e + 6$
15–16	Late formal operational	$e + 7$

*The value of e is constant across ages and refers to the capacity needed to store information about task instructions.
Table derived from Case, 1972.

three units exceed the two available *M* units for 5- and 6-year-olds, so they fail the task. By 7 or 8 years of age, *M* has increased to *e* + 3, and children perform the task successfully.

Another example of a neo-Piagetian theory is Fischer's (1980) skill theory. According to Fischer, cognitive development involves the acquisition of complex skills. However, the complexity of skill that children can master is determined by their *optimal level*, "the upper limit of a person's general information processing capacity" (Fischer and Pipp, 1984, p. 47). Fischer proposes ten levels that he groups into three *tiers*. The *sensorimotor tier* corresponds directly to Piaget's sensorimotor period. In this tier, skills are limited to actions; not until the *representational tier*, which includes both the preoperational and concrete operational periods, are children able to understand and reflect on their skills.

The final tier is the *abstract tier*, corresponding to Piaget's formal operational period. In this tier, individuals can understand relationships between two sets of facts. For example, at this tier individuals could formulate a general understanding of conservation by abstracting from two specific facts: (1) The amount of water is unchanged by pouring it from one container to another, and (2) the amount of clay is unchanged by molding it in different shapes.

One important contribution of skill theory concerns cognitive development in adolescence. In Piaget's theory, adolescence is effectively the end point of cognitive development, since children are thought to enter the formal operational period at approximately 11 or 12 years of age. Many theorists (e.g., Arlin, 1975) have criticized this aspect of Piaget's theory and proposed ways that cognitive development might continue during adolescence and adulthood.

In skill theory, individuals enter the abstract tier at approximately 10 to 12 years of age. However, this tier consists of four distinct levels, marked by greater and greater degrees of abstraction. Individuals do not reach the last two tiers until early adulthood. For example, at the second level in this tier, adolescents are capable of "abstract mappings," which means they can relate abstract concepts to one another. A teenage girl, for example, could notice that she wants a job with an excellent salary and pressure to succeed, while her mother was happy with a modest salary but little pressure. In the final level of the abstract tier, what Fischer calls "systems of abstract systems," people are able to coordinate several abstract systems of thought. The same teenage girl, as an adult, might compare changes over the years in her occupational identity and aspirations.

Fischer's skill theory, like the theories by Pascual-Leone and Case, illustrates the important characteristics of neo-Piagetian theories of cognitive development. These theories share Piaget's effort to provide a general account of cognitive development, one that has at its core the claim that thinking changes qualitatively with development. However, the stages have been replaced by M-power units in Pascual-Leone's theory and by tiers in Fischer's theory.

SUMMARY

1. Piaget distinguishes the contents, functions, and structures of the intellect. *Contents* refer to behavioral acts, which are products of applying a *scheme*. The contents change considerably with age. The *functions* of intelligence are constant throughout development and include *organization* and *adaptation*. Adaptation, in turn, consists of *assimilation*, the use of schemes to interpret and organize information, and *accommodation*, the modification of schemes to reflect the acquisition of new knowledge.

2. Piaget identified four distinct intellectual *structures* that form an invariant developmental sequence: the sensorimotor, preoperational, concrete operational, and formal operational periods.

3. The *sensorimotor period* lasts from approximately birth to 2 years of age. A key component is the *circular reaction*, which refers to an event that first happens by chance and produces pleasant consequences for the infant, who then tries to repeat the event.

4. The *preoperational period* lasts from approximately 2 to 7 years of age. Thinking during this period has four important characteristics. It is (1) action-based: thinking seems to be the mental analog of behavior; (2) irreversible: children are incapable of mentally reversing an operation to return to the original values; (3) centered: children attend to one facet of a problem and ignore other relevant aspects; (4) egocentric: children are unaware that others view the world differently than they do.

5. The *concrete operational period* lasts from 7 to 11 years of age. Children's thinking is no longer action-based, and it is reversible, decentered, and nonegocentric. The basis for these achievements is nine sets of mental operations that Piaget called groupings.

6. The *formal operational period* begins at approximately 11 years of age and continues into adulthood. At this stage individuals are able to think abstractly, hypothetically. These advances reflect the ability to reason deductively, which involves starting with premises and drawing appropriate conclusions. They also reflect inductive reasoning, the ability to make valid generalizations from experience.

7. Piaget's theory has been criticized on a number of grounds. First, deriving specific predictions from the theory is difficult. Second, the theory predicts that thinking within a particular stage should be relatively similar on all tasks, but researchers often find that a child will show considerable diversity in thinking across tasks. Third, children can learn individual Piagetian concepts with relatively brief training; according to the theory, such changes occur spontaneously following states of disequilibrium.

8. Neo-Piagetian theorists adhere to many of the basic claims of Piaget's theory but differ in the specifics of cognitive

development. One approach has been to view qualitative change as the acquisition of more sophisticated rules or strategies.

9. Neo-Piagetian theorists have also proposed that cognitive-developmental change may reflect changes in general information-processing capacity. Pascual-Leone (1970, 1980) proposed that M-space, a measure of processing capacity, increases regularly with age. Fischer (1980), in his skill theory, described three distinct tiers of cognitive development, each consisting of several different cognitive levels. An attractive feature of Fischer's theory is that it suggests ways in which cognitive skills continue to develop during adolescence and adulthood.

7 PROCESS APPROACHES TO COGNITIVE DEVELOPMENT

Suppose we asked two people to describe a computer. One might say, "Well, it's an enormously complex system of electronic hardware, including memories, processing units, and peripheral devices, like printers and terminals. There's also software of all kinds, which consists of incredibly long lists of very specific instructions that actually get the hardware to do something." A second person might say, "Computers are fundamentally quite simple—They're really just electronic circuits that can be turned on or off and that get linked together in many different ways."

Both are correct, but their answers illustrate different approaches to describing a computer. The first individual approaches the computer as a system and describes it in terms of the organization of the components. The second individual emphasizes the fundamental element of the computer, the building block that forms the basis for all the complex actions and operations computers can perform.

These two approaches are also seen in efforts by developmental psychologists to understand human thought and its development. As we saw in Chapter 6, a cornerstone of Piaget's theory is that, at any age, thinking is organized and forms a cohesive system of mental operations. Some developmental psychologists have taken the other approach, of trying to identify and understand the elementary operations, the building blocks of human cognition. For much of the 20th century, psychologists believed that conditioned responses might provide the elementary unit for learning and thinking. Few developmental psychologists today believe that conditioning alone can account for all human thinking; other, more complex, forms of learning are involved.

In the 1970s and 1980s, some developmental psychologists became disillusioned with efforts to view cognitive development as simply an accumulation or piling up of responses. They argued that cognitive processes are similar to computer operations which interpret and transform data. This *information-processing approach* has become an increasingly important view of cognitive development, and we explore it in detail in this chapter. But first we look at the concept of learning.

LEARNING

What Is Learning?

Definitions of learning have changed over the years. For a long time, learning was defined as a change in behavior that was the result of experience (Stevenson, 1972). This definition worked as long as research on learning was limited to studies of conditioning. However, starting in the 1960s, psychologists began to study other phenomena under the heading of learning. The definition was revised: Learning now refers to changes in behavior or to changes in the state of an individual's knowledge that are due to experience (Greeno, 1980). The first section of this chapter focuses on conditioning in children. The next sections concern relatively more complex forms of learning, observational learning and mediated learning.

Conditioning

Classical conditioning involves changes in the situations in which reflexive responses will occur. Operant conditioning focuses on the consequences that follow behavior. Not until the 1940s and 1950s was there any systematic effort by developmental psychologists to study conditioning. Much of the work since that time has been on conditioning of infants. Learning theorists have believed that behavior is "the product of a multitude of conditioned responses built up during the course of the individual's life" (Stevenson, 1972, p. 11).

For this account to make sense, it is essential to demonstrate that even very young infants can be conditioned. In fact, as we described in Chapter 4, conditioning can be demonstrated during the first few months of life. However, in classical conditioning associations differ in conditionability. Infants are biologically prepared to learn some things quickly but other things only with difficulty or not at all (Seligman, 1970). Visual stimuli are more readily conditioned to pain, whereas stimuli associated with smell and taste are much more readily conditioned to nausea and "sickness" (Whitehurst and Vasta, 1977). If a person—child or adult—is shown a light and then receives a shock, after a number of pairings the light alone will produce a startle response. But if a person is given something to taste and is then shocked, the taste alone will probably not come to produce the response, even after many pairings.

Readiness is a requirement for the development of operant responses. If an operant response entails perceptual, motor, or intellectual skills, it is locked into biological development. For example, a majority of newborns are biologically incapable of executing the sequence of reaching and grasping as two separate responses (Bower, 1974). Very young infants may thus be unable to learn to reach and grasp effectively, even when the environment is arranged appropriately.

Observational Learning

Observational learning refers to learning that occurs through exposure to the behavior of others; these others can be presented either live or symbolically in literature, films, television, and the like. The importance of observational learning was recognized more than 2,000 years ago when Aristotle wrote: "Man is the most imitative of living creatures, and through imitation learns his earliest lessons."

Observational learning includes a surprisingly large range of phenomena. Early forms of observational learning are represented by the infant's vocal and gestural imitations that we described in Chapter 4. Observational learning was also described by innumerable studies showing that older children learn about many behaviors—aggression, sharing, social interaction, delay of gratification, cooperation—by watching others perform them.

In one well-known experiment dealing with aggression, Albert Bandura (1965) presented a view of observational learning in which the learning or *acquisition* of the modeled acts is distinguished from the *performance* of the modeled acts. The study also demonstrated the importance of the outcomes to the model. In Bandura's experiment, modeling and outcomes were provided by showing nursery school children a remarkable five-minute film on the screen of a television console:

The film began with a scene in which a model walked up to an adult-sized plastic Bobo doll and ordered him to clear the way. After glaring for a moment . . . the model laid the Bobo doll on its side, sat on it, and punched it in the nose while remarking, ''Pow, right in the nose, boom, boom.'' The model then raised the doll and pommeled it on the head with a mallet. Each response was accompanied by the verbalization, ''Sockeroo . . . stay down.'' Following the mallet aggression, the model kicked the doll about the room, and these responses were interspersed with the comment, ''Fly away.'' Finally, the model threw rubber balls at the Bobo doll, each strike punctuated with ''Bang.'' (Bandura, 1965, p. 590–591)

One group of children saw, in addition to the film segment, a final scene in which the model was rewarded generously for assaults on the doll. A second group of children watched the film end with a final scene in which the model received punishment for aggressive behavior. A third group that served as a control also saw the film, but without any final scene.

Thereafter, all children were brought individually into an experimental room that contained a plastic Bobo doll, three balls, a mallet, a peg board, plastic farm animals, and a dollhouse equipped with furniture and a miniature doll family. This wide array of toys was provided so that each child would be able to engage in imitative aggressive responses—that is, the model's responses—or in nonaggressive and nonimitative forms of behavior. Each child was left alone with this assortment of toys for ten minutes while his or her behavior was periodically recorded by judges who watched from behind a one-way vision screen.

Children who saw the model punished exhibited far fewer imitative aggressive responses than did those in either of the other two groups. But—and this is the major point of Bandura's analysis—we cannot conclude that because the children in this group did not imitate, they had learned nothing. Later, the experimenter reentered the room well supplied with incentives (color sticker pictures, sweet fruit juices in an attractive dispenser, and so on) and told each child that, for each act of imitative aggression he or she could reproduce, an additional juice treat and sticker would be given. When incentives were specifically offered for imitation of the model's acts, the effects of punishment were wiped out. All groups showed the same very high level of learning.

Thus, observational learning apparently involves at least three steps: *exposure* to the responses of others, *acquisition* of what one has seen, and *acceptance* of the modeled acts as a guide for one's own behavior (Liebert and Poulos, 1975). This view of observational learning is very different from that of traditional learning theorists. Traditional learning theorists view the child as a more or less passive responder. The cognitive social learning formulation emphasizes cognitive processes—attention, memory, and problem solving—all of which are at least partially instigated by the observer.

Recent social learning theory would add *interpretation* to the list of cognitive processes that are important for observational learning. After children imitate the actions of others, they try to understand *why* they behaved as they did. Sometimes children view their behavior as a reflection of their own interests and intentions, referred to as *internal causes*. On other occasions, they see their behavior as caused by an adult's presence, strict penalties, or other *external forces* (Perry and Perry, 1983). For example, children often share after seeing others share. Sometimes they explain their behavior in terms of internal causes, such as saying they share because they like to help people. Or they may say they share because they thought the experimenter wanted them to. Not surprisingly, the impact of observational learning is greater when children attribute learning to internal causes rather than to external forces, and older children are more likely to explain their behavior in terms of internal causes (Perry and Perry, 1983).

Mediated Learning

Mediation theorists place a similar emphasis on the child's role in learning. A *mediator* is some internal event intervening between a stimulus and an overt response. The initial stimulus results in a mediator that, in turn, acts as a stimulus for the final response. Tracy and Howard Kendler, among the first to focus on the role of *verbal mediation* in learning, held that the intervening response involves the use of covert language (H. H. Kendler and T. S. Kendler, 1975; T. S. Kendler, 1963, 1979). To demonstrate this approach, the Kendlers tested children in a discrimination-learning task. First, pairs of stimuli that differed on two dimensions were presented. Rewarded each time they responded to one attribute of one of the dimensions, children learned the solution to the problem. For example, a child was shown two cups. One was black and the other white (color dimension); one—sometimes the black cup, sometimes the white—was large and the other small (size dimension). Each time the large cup was selected, regardless of whether it was black or white, a reward was received; selecting the small cup never led to reward. The child learned that size was the relevant dimension, and large, the correct attribute.

Then the rules for reward were changed, without telling the children. For some children the correct dimension remained the same, but the attribute was changed. In our example, such a *reversal shift* (see Figure 7–1) would mean that now "small" leads to reward instead of "large." For other children the dimension changed (and so, by definition, did the correct attribute). Thus, a *nonreversal shift* would mean that one of the colors—"black" or "white"—would be the correct choice.

According to traditional explanations of learning in this task, reward alone determines the difficulty of these two new problems. The nonreversal shift should be easier than the reversal shift. The reason is that the correct answer following a reversal shift has never been rewarded previously; but the correct answer following a nonreversal shift has been rewarded on 50 percent of the trials during original learning.

Mediation theory leads to different predictions. Here, children are be-

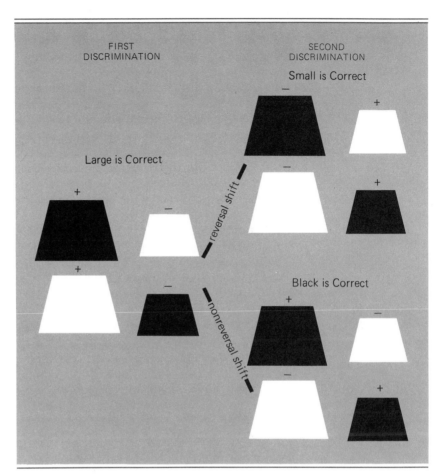

FIGURE 7–1 **Examples of a reversal and a nonreversal shift where (+) indicates the rewarded and (−) the nonrewarded stimuli.** Adapted from H. H. Kendler and T. S. Kendler (1962). Vertical and horizontal processes in problem-solving. *Psychological Review*, 69 1–16. Copyright 1962 by the American Psychological Association. Reproduced by permission.

Within the figure:

FIRST DISCRIMINATION

SECOND DISCRIMINATION

Small is Correct

Large is Correct

reversal shift

nonreversal shift

Black is Correct

lieved to learn the initial discrimination by using a verbal mediator. Presentation of the two squares elicits an internal response something like "Size is important—it's the large one" that leads to the response. Modifying this mediator on reversal shifts is straightforward, as children only have to replace "large" in the mediator with "small." Nonreversal shifts are more difficult because the entire mediator must be replaced.

The Kendlers believed that mediated learning was more likely as children developed. They predicted that reversal shifts would become progressively easier with age, an outcome they obtained in a number of studies (Kendler and Kendler, 1975). Tracy Kendler has elaborated her account of mediated learning to propose that mediators are hypotheses, rules, or strategies, and that as children develop they become more likely to use these rules and strategies during the course of learning (Kendler, 1979). This view of learning and thinking is also central to information-processing approaches to cognitive development.

The term *information processing* is derived from computer science. To understand the behavior of a cognitive system—whether computer or human—we must examine the processes that intervene between input and output. In a computer system, these processes are specified in a program that provides instructions for the computer.

In effect, the information-processing perspective leads us to ask questions about human problem solvers that are like those we would ask about the computer. We would attempt to discover the steps—the cognitive processes—required to solve the problem and to identify the strategy or plan that integrates specific processes into a functional package that produces the desired results. We would also ask what type of information is needed to solve the task, how this knowledge is represented in memory, and how new information from the environment is incorporated into this system (Kail and Bisanz, 1982). According to one information-processing view (Ornstein, 1977), the mind is like a mental computer system consisting of structural features, the "hardware" of the system, and techniques or programs for using and operating the system, the "software." Figure 7–2 shows a diagram of the components of the mind in this model.

The hardware consists of three components. *Sensory memory* is where information is held in raw sensory form for no more than 1 to 2 seconds. Information is then categorized and passed on to the short-term store or forgotten altogether. *Short-term store* is a temporary working memory of limited capacity. This limited capacity can be demonstrated with a memory span task, in which individuals are asked to recall stimuli in the order they were presented. Adults' span for digits is nearly 8; for letters, 6; and for words, 5. Control processes such as rehearsal are used to transfer information from short-term to *long-term store*—a limitless, permanent storehouse of knowledge of the world. Once information reaches long-term store, very little is lost. Failure to remember at this stage is due to the inability to retrieve information rather than an actual loss of the information (Tulving and Pearlstone, 1966).

**FIGURE 7–2
Movement of
information within
the memory
system.** From "The
Control of Short-Term
Memory" by Richard
C. Atkinson and
Richard M. Shiffrin.
Copyright © August
1971 by Scientific
American, Inc. All
rights reserved.

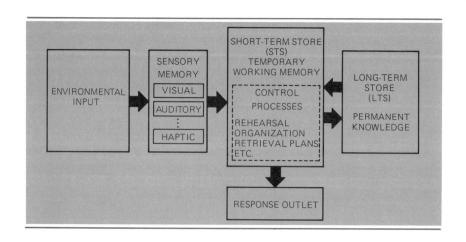

Sensory memory seems to function in much the same manner in children as in adults (Kail and Siegel, 1977). However, in short- and long-term storage there are developmental changes which we discuss in the next section.

MEMORY STRATEGIES

The Edmonton *Journal* carried the following story on January 13, 1981:

> A nine-year-old boy memorized the licence plate number on a getaway car following an armed robbery, a court was told Monday. . . . The boy and his friend . . . looked in the [drug] store window and saw a man grab a 14-year-old cashier's neck. . . . After the robbery, *the boys mentally repeated the licence number until they gave it to police.* (emphasis added)

This mental repetition is called *verbal rehearsal*, a strategy of repetitively naming stimuli that are to be remembered. Rehearsal is only one of many memory strategies or *mnemonics* that can be used to transfer information from short- to long-term store, or to retrieve information from long-term store. Children begin to rehearse on many memory tasks at approximately 7 or 8 years of age, and they rehearse an increasingly large number of words as they grow older (Flavell, Beach, and Chinsky, 1966).

Adolescents become increasingly flexible in their rehearsal, and modify it to meet the demands of particular problems. In a study by Ornstein,

FIGURE 7-3
As children grow older, the ability to "operate" their own memory increases dramatically. Paul Conklin, Monkmeyer.

Naus, and Liberty (1975), words from familiar categories, presented in a random order, were to be recalled. For example, a list might include the words, *dog, table, blue, lamp, cat, red*. A useful strategy for remembering lists of this type is to rehearse same-category members together: *dog, cat, table, lamp, red, blue*. Children's rehearsal consisted of rote repetition of the words in a list. Only adolescents modified their rehearsal to fit the structure of the material to be remembered.

Much the same pattern occurs in children's efforts to retrieve information from long-term store. For example, suppose children were trying to remember the birthday when they received a particular present. One strategy would be to think back to the gifts received for the most recent birthday, and if the gift was not among them, to go back to the previous birthday. This process could be repeated until the child found the appropriate birthday. Another strategy might be to remember distinctive facts associated with the present—the names of children who attended the party, its location, and the like—and use this information to determine the birthday. In fact, 10- and 11-year-old children are likely to use elaborate strategies such as these to retrieve information from long-term memory, but 5- and 6-year-old children are not (Kreutzer, Leonard, and Flavell, 1975).

Study Strategies

The research described thus far involves recall of specific words, pictures, or events. In learning more complex "stimuli," like information in textbooks, literal recall of individual sentences or individual words is generally not the objective; the aim is to recall the main points. An effective study strategy must distinguish the key ideas in the text. Also, it must organize these key ideas in some concise format.

Research by Ann Brown and her colleagues has examined developmental change in the use of these complex study strategies. In one study by Brown and Smiley (1978), subjects from grades five to twelve were asked to learn passages approximately 400 words long. Each passage was read to the subjects twice, and they were then asked to recall the main ideas. After recall was completed, each subject was given a printed copy of the passage along with a pen and a note pad. The subjects were told they had five minutes in which to study the passage and that they could "undertake any activity they wished in order to improve their recall" (Brown and Smiley, 1978, p. 1080).

Only 6 percent of the fifth graders took notes spontaneously, compared to 12 percent and 50 percent of the junior and senior high school students. Another strategy was underlining. Older subjects underlined more often than younger ones. More important, the oldest individuals were the most selective in what they underlined. They typically underlined only key passages.

Underlining and taking notes are both strategies for remembering large bodies of information, just as rehearsal and use of categories are strategies for remembering sets of pictures or words. At all ages some individuals were capable of some means of learning a text—they all used some sort of strategy. However, only the older adolescents showed the subtle and sophisticated skills necessary to break down a large volume of infomation into the key components that should receive priority in learning (Kail, 1984).

Young Children's Use of Strategies: Another Look

Young children do not rehearse, do not group material according to semantic similarity, and do not suggest many solutions for real-world memory problems. Does that mean they have no idea of how to remember? Parents of preschoolers often report that their children remember exceptionally well. And, in fact, preschoolers perform exceptionally well on recognition memory tasks in which they must identify pictures they have seen many days before (Brown and Scott, 1971). In addition, parents sometimes mention behaviors that imply use of strategies by young children (Perlmutter, 1980).

Why, then, is there a discrepancy between how young children performed on the memory tasks we have described and what we feel they are capable of doing? Answering this question has been the aim of a series of studies by Wellman and his colleagues. Wellman, Ritter, and Flavell (1975) discovered that even preschool children sometimes use simple mnemonic strategies to store information. Three-year-olds were told a story about a dog. Four identical cups were used as props to tell the story. Midway through the story, a toy dog was placed under one of the cups ("in the doghouse," according to the story). At this point, the experimenter told each child that additional props were needed to finish the story and asked the child to remember the location of the dog while he left to get the props. During the experimenter's absence, the individual children looked at and touched the cup where the dog was hidden more frequently than they looked at or touched any of the other identical cups. Furthermore, frequency and duration of looking and touching were associated with more accurate retention of the dog's location.

This and other research by Wellman suggests that young children can act strategically when the appropriate behaviors are "simple" ones, and that improved recall is the result (DeLoache, 1984). Of course, the preschooler's strategies are quite limited compared to those of adolescents and adults.

Metamemory

The specific strategies examined thus far really represent only the "tip of the iceberg" in terms of important memory skills. To see why, consider a physician treating a patient. First the physician attempts to understand the patient's symptoms in order to form a *diagnosis*. Based on the diagnosis, some form of *treatment* is selected. The physician then *monitors* the patient's recovery, and modifies treatment if necessary.

The sequence of diagnosis-treatment-monitoring holds equally well for memory skills. A person's use of a specific strategy is based on an analysis of the task to determine its goals and how those goals might best be achieved. Once an appropriate strategy is selected, people should periodically evaluate their progress.

These diagnostic and monitoring skills are often collectively called *metamemory* (Flavell and Wellman, 1977).

Diagnosis.   Children as young as age 6 know that a familiar item is easier to remember (Kreutzer et al., 1975). In addition, preschoolers believe that a larger set of pictures will be more difficult to remember than a smaller set (Yussen and Bird, 1979). However, young children apparently do not realize that, given certain relationships among stimuli, memorizing even a lengthy list may be easy.

This point is illustrated by a finding from Kreutzer et al.'s (1975) study. Children first practiced learning to associate pairs of words in a list (*car* and *shirt, boat* and *apple*). Next, they were shown two lists and asked to predict which would be easier to learn and remember. One list consisted of names and actions paired randomly (*Mary* and *walk, Anne* and *sit*); the second list consisted of highly associated antonyms (*cry* and *laugh, black* and *white*). Although 9- and 11-year-olds were confident that the second list would be much easier, 6- and 7-year-olds believed that the two lists would be equally difficult.

Another factor that contributes to the difficulty of memory problems is the type of memory test. Consider, for example, the difference between recognition and recall tasks. In recognition tasks, children are shown numerous stimuli and simply discriminate those that were presented previously from those that were not. In recall tasks, the instruction is simply, "Tell me the names of all the stimuli that I just showed you." Recall tasks are generally more difficult, a fact known by many 6- and 7-year-olds (Speer and Flavell, 1979).

Many 6-year-olds also know that verbatim recall is more difficult than paraphrased recall, and by age 10 or 11 nearly all children understand the difference (Myers and Paris, 1978).

Choosing a Strategy.   After children evaluate the difficulty of a memory problem, they must select a memory strategy to achieve the goal. This choice is presumably based on their understanding of different strategies and the fit between a given strategy and a particular memory problem.

Several investigators have examined children's ability to select strategies appropriate to the task (Lodico, Ghatala, Levin, Pressley, and Bell, 1983; Moynahan, 1978; Pressley, Levin, and Ghatala, 1984). In these studies, the task was to learn to associate ten pairs of stimuli. Included were pairs such as *airplane* and *couch* and *lion* and *mirror*. Upon presentation of *airplane*, children were to respond with *couch*. On one trial, children were told that a good way to remember the items in a pair would be to say their names together aloud, repeatedly (a simple rehearsal strategy). On another trial, with ten different pairs, children were taught to use an elaboration strategy in which they should make the items "do something together or put them together in some way" (Moynahan, 1978, p. 259). The repetition and elaboration strategies were chosen because the first should be a much less effective mnemonic in this task than the second. This was true: Children recalled approximately twice as many pairs when using the elaboration strategy than when using the repetition strategy.

Given that one strategy is more effective for this task than the other, the key issue in remembering seems to be what children will do when asked to remember a third set of ten pairs and when told, "This time you can use any way you want to remember which things go together" (Moynahan, 1978, p. 260). Many 7-year-olds use the less effective repetition strategy, but most 10-year-old children use the more efficient interaction stategy (Lodico et al., 1983). These data indicate a gradual but steady rise in the percentage of children using the more efficient strategy.

Monitoring. Skilled learners periodically judge the status of information to be learned. That is, individuals try to decide (1) which information is well learned; (2) which will be well learned with just a bit more effort; and (3) which will require substantial additional study. If most information is in category 1, then the problem is solved and the learner can stop. If most information is in category 2, then the rational choice would be to keep going, using the same strategy until the problem is solved. If category 3 applies, learners may reevaluate what they are doing, with the possible outcomes including returning to the diagnostic phase to find a better strategy, continuing the current effort, or quitting altogether.

How accurately can children monitor the extent to which they have learned something? Consider individual items first. How accurately can children distinguish information that has been learned, from that which is partially known, from that which is completely unknown? Studies designed to answer this question first test children's retention of stimuli. At some later point, subjects are shown each stimulus and asked if they recalled it or forgot it on the previous test trial. Even preschool children are able to make these judgments, but accuracy improves considerably between 6 and 9 years of age (Cultice, Somerville, and Wellman, 1983).

Presumably, by evaluating progress on each item in a set, children can judge how well they are doing on the set as a whole. That is, children somehow "average" their progress on individual items to derive an estimate of overall progress. Because there are developmental differences in the accuracy with which children judge their learning of individual items, we would expect developmental differences in ability to evaluate the extent to which the entire set has been learned. Flavell, Friedrichs, and Hoyt (1970) determined the memory spans of nursery school, kindergarten, grade two and grade four children. The children were then told to try to remember many pictures. The exact number for each child was equal to his or her individual memory span. The children could take as much time as necessary to study the pictures. The experimenter emphasized to the children that they should study until they could remember all the pictures, not just some of them. When a child was ready to recall the pictures, he or she rang a bell to signal the experimenter to return.

Memory in the Elderly

Elderly persons often claim that forgetting is a frequent and frustrating problem. They report increased forgetting of names, appointments, addresses, and telephone numbers. And, in fact, on many laboratory measures of memory, elderly persons remember less accurately than middle-aged and young adults (Poon, 1985).

What causes this decline in memory skill among the elderly? A number of theorists have used the information-processing model shown in Figure 7–2 to determine the locus of memory problems in the aged. For example, neither the capacity nor decay rates of sensory memory change much from childhood onward. However, the time required to clear information out of sensory memory appears to increase during the later years (Poon, 1985). This means that the elderly are more likely to lose information before it can be transferred to short-term store.

The capacity of short-term store remains relatively constant throughout life. For example, on digit span tasks in which subjects recall sequences of digits in order, elderly persons are often as accurate as young adults (Fozard, 1980).

In contrast to the findings for sensory memory and short-term store, elderly persons often perform poorly on memory tasks that involve transfer of information between short- and long-term stores. For example, older adults are less able to recall the details of stories about common activities, such as writing a letter to a friend (Light and Anderson, 1983). Despite the fact that both younger and older adults know the activities equally well, older adults are less able to use that knowledge during recall. This seems to be due to difficulties associated with both entering information in and retrieving information from long-term store (Poon, 1985).

Some well-educated elderly individuals often show relatively small deficits on memory tasks (Till, 1985). However, for the many elderly who do suffer from memory problems, retraining does provide some help. For example, elderly persons are less likely to forget names and faces if they learn to associate them with mental imagery (Yesavage, Rose, and Bower, 1983).

Despite the improvement that results from this and other procedures, we are far from full-fledged memory retraining programs for the aged. One nagging problem is that not all elderly people benefit from memory retraining. Some improve a great deal, and some show little change. Furthermore, even when individuals improve following memory training, they often fail to use memory strategies when it would be appropriate (Poon, Walsh-Sweeney, and Fozard, 1980). Thus, although research leads us to be optimistic concerning the future prospects for reducing or even eliminating memory problems in the elderly, a good deal of work remains in creating truly effective retraining programs.

Because the number of pictures to be recalled was equal to the individual's memory span, the recall task was comparably difficult for children from the different grades. Still, a real developmental increase was found in the number of children who recalled the pictures perfectly. Second and fourth graders were quite proficient; the majority of children in these grades recalled the pictures perfectly on each of three trials. Most nursery school children were correct on only one of the three trials. Thus, the ability to monitor learning improves during childhood, as does the ability to diagnose memory problems. These developmental changes in metamemory skill make it more likely that older children will be able to store information in long-term store and retrieve it when necessary.

LONG-TERM STORE: PERMANENT KNOWLEDGE

Adults know an enormous amount of information. For example, most college students have vocabularies of 150,000–250,000 words (McCarthy, 1954). And within their fields of expertise, adults probably know more than 50,000 facts (Simon, 1981). Obviously, then, we cannot hope to trace the acquisition of all knowledge. Instead, we will consider knowledge in two essential but distinct cognitive domains: *quantitative knowlege* and spatial knowledge—or, as it is sometimes called, *way-finding ability*.

Quantitative Knowledge

Quantitative skills range from simple counting to calculus and beyond. Few individuals progress to the most advanced levels, but knowledge of numbers and simple mathematical operations is widespread in most cultures (Gardner, 1983). For example, the Oksapmin people living in remote New Guinea developed a complex system of counting that relies on different parts of the body (see Figure 7–4).

Origins of Number Skills. Preschoolers can count. Can we consider this the first step in the development of quantitative skills? No; in fact, counting is the crowning achievement in a developmental sequence that begins soon after birth:

> Infants lie in cribs with a certain number of bars. The walls in their rooms display repetitions of bricks or wooden boards or regularity in the pattern of wallpaper. Their parents go into the room and out of it over and over again. Some of their toys are bigger than others; some are identical and others are equivalent in size. If they push a toy it moves; and the harder they push, the harder it moves. Infants thus have ample opportunity to learn about number, repetition, regularity, differences in magnitude, equivalence, causality and correlation (Ginsburg, 1977, p. 30).

For many years psychologists could only speculate about what infants might learn about number from experiences such as these. Beginning in the early 1980s several investigators used habituation (see Chapter 4) to study infant knowledge of numbers. For example, an infant will stare at a red triangle for several seconds when it first appears; after several presentations, the infant will glance briefly at the triangle, then look away. Several investigators have used this phenomenon to demonstrate that infants can discriminate between sets of objects that differ only in quantity. Starkey and Cooper (1980) were the first to do so. In their experiment, 4-month-olds were shown a predetermined number of dots, in

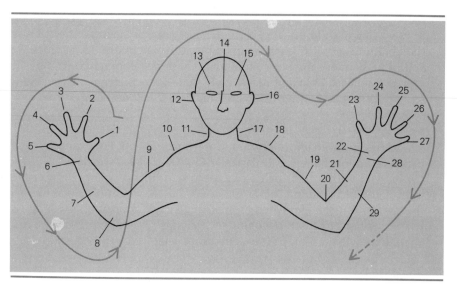

FIGURE 7-4
The conventional sequence of body parts used by the Oksapmin. In order of occurrence: (1) tip∧na, (2) tipnarip, (3) bumrip, (4) h∧tdip, (5) h∧th∧ta, (6) dopa, (7) besa, (8) kir, (9) tow∧t, (10) kata, (11) gwer, (12) nata, (13) kina, (14) aruma, (15) tan-kina (16) tan-nata, (17) tan-gwer, (18) tan-kata, (19) tan-tow∧t, (20) tan-kir, (21) tan-besa, (22) tan-dopa, (23) tan-tip∧na, (24) tan-tipnarip, (25) tan-bumrip, (26) tan-h∧tdip, (27) tan-h∧th∧ta. From G.B. Saxe (1982). Culture and the development of numerical cognition: studies among the Oksapmin of Papua, New Guinea. In C.J. Brainerd (Ed.), *Children's Logical and Mathematical Cognition*. (New York: Springer-Verlag) Copyright 1982 by Springer Verlag. Reprinted by permission.

patterns that varied from trial to trial. For example, some infants saw two patterns, each depicting two dots (see Figure 7–5). When infants looked at these patterns half as long as they had initially, they were shown an array of three dots. Their looking time increased substantially, indicating that they discriminated the novel three-dot pattern from the now familiar two-dot patterns.

The result was the same when infants first looked at different three-dot patterns and then two-dot patterns. However, when infants were shown four-dot patterns until they habituated, looking time did not increase to a pattern of six dots.

Apparently infants discriminated the change in quantity in the smaller patterns but not in the larger ones. But before concluding that infants know the difference betwen "twoness" and "threeness," we need to rule out any characteristics associated with particular patterns that might have caused infants to look longer at the novel arrays. Perhaps infants attended to the top two-dot pattern in Figure 7–5 but not the bottom pattern. Then they looked longer at the three-dot pattern because the dot in the middle was novel or because of differences in brightness (the ratio of white to black) between two- and three-dot patterns.

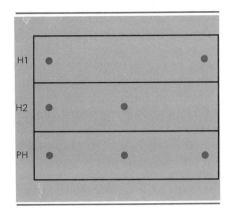

Curtis and Strauss (1983) demonstrated that number was the key variable by using habituation stimuli that varied in terms of the specific objects presented, their size and color, and how they were arranged. For example, an infant might see a picture of two small dogs aligned horizontally, followed by two large butterflies presented along a diagonal, and so on. Once infants had habituated, they were shown a pattern consisting of either one more or one fewer element than they had seen previously. These procedures meant that infants could discriminate stimuli only on the basis of number. In fact, as in Starkey and Cooper's (1980) study, 5-month-olds distinguished twoness from threeness but not larger quantities. However, 11-month-olds tested with these procedures successfully discriminated twoness from threeness and threeness from fourness (Strauss and Curtis, 1981).

How do infants do this? Older children and adults might do so by counting, but of course infants have not yet learned number names. Instead, the process is probably more perceptual in nature. As we noted in Chapter 4, we know that the infant's perceptual system is designed to be sensitive to certain characteristics of stimuli such as color (Bornstein, 1981). Quantity may well be another of these sensitive characteristics. (Strauss and Curtis, 1984).

Strictly speaking, the research we have just described indicates that infants are sensitive to the *cardinal* properties of number. Knowing that . . . . . contains exactly five dots demonstrates cardinality. *Ordinality* refers to the knowledge that one quantity is greater or less than another. Ordinality seems to be acquired during the second year of life. Suppose we show pairs of pictures of circles in which one member of each pair always contains exactly one more circle than the other. As in the earlier experiments, the sizes and positions of the circles vary from trial to trial. Choosing the correct picture—the picture with more circles for some children, the picture with fewer circles for others—produces reward in the form of a moving toy. In such a task, 16-month-olds can learn to pick the greater or lesser of two quantities, especially if the quantities are small (Strauss and Curtis, 1984).

Counting. Not long after children have learned to talk, they begin to learn number words. Some of these number names are learned in isolation, but many are probably learned in the context of counting. Parents and teachers sing counting songs and television programs like *Sesame Street* emphasize counting.

Rochel Gelman and her colleagues have traced the acquisition of counting from its origins in 2-year-olds to its near-mature form in 5- and 6-year-olds (Gelman, 1980, 1982; Gelman and Gallistel, 1978). Gelman believes that successful counting involves mastering three principles:

1. *The one-to-one principle:* There must be one and only one number name for each object in a set to be counted.
2. *The stable-order principle:* Names for numbers must be used in the same order every time a person counts.
3. *The cardinality principle:* The last number name is distinctive in denoting the number of objects in a set.

Gelman has shown that children begin to acquire these principles as 2- and 3-year-olds. In her research, she placed plates with varying numbers of objects in front of each child, who was simply asked: "How many?" A child was credited with following the one-to-one principle if there were as many number words as items. Thus, counting four objects as "1, 2, 3, 4" or "1, 2, 2, 3" or even "1, 2, A, B" would each be consistent with the one-to-one principle. The stable-order principle required that the child use number names—whether correct names or idiosyncratic ones like letters of the alphabet—in a consistent order on each counting trial. That is, children might be asked to count six different sets of five objects. They would receive credit for the stable-order principle only if they used the same order of names in counting four of the six sets.

Finally, there were several ways that children could demonstrate the cardinality principle. One way—most frequent among the older children—was that they simply responded immediately with the proper cardinal value without counting aloud. Other criteria for exhibiting the cardinality principle were stressing the last number word or repeating the last number word. For example, counting five objects as "one, two, three, four, five—five!!" illustrates both stress and repetition.

Figure 7–6 shows the percentages of 3-, 4-, and 5-year-olds who followed all three principles. Most 3-year-olds followed all three when counting a small number of objects. As children grow older, they apply the principles when counting ever larger numbers of objects.

Gelman considers the how-to-count principles the "nuts and bolts" of counting. She has also studied preschoolers' understanding of two more conceptual properties of counting. The *abstraction* principle refers to the fact that any set of distinct objects can be counted regardless of their relationship (or lack of relationship) to one another. The set "giraffe, zebra, cat, dog" is counted just as readily as the set "transistor, Corvette, Democrat, eraser." In fact, preschoolers are equally likely to count heterogeneous sets of objects as homogeneous ones, indicating they appar-

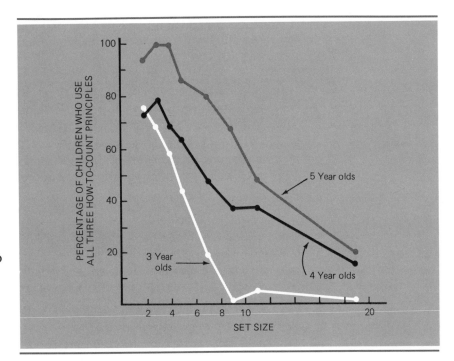

FIGURE 7–6
Percentage of 3-, 4-, and 5-year-olds who adhered to all three "how-to-count" principles, as a function of set size. Data from Gelman and Gallistel (1978).

ently understand that "counting can be applied to any collection of real and imagined objects" (Gelman, 1982, p. 183).

A second conceptual principle is *order irrelevance*, the fact that as long as one obeys the how-to-count principles, the order in which items in a set are counted does not matter. Gelman tested preschoolers' understanding of this concept by asking them to count the same set of objects repeatedly. Only rarely did children count the objects in exactly the same order each time; usually they counted them in different orders. Another procedure was to ask children to recount a set making a particular object the first, second, or third item. The most frequent response among 3-year-olds was to ignore the experimenter's request! However, many 4-year-olds and most 5-year-olds were capable of altering their counting so that an item would be counted at the requested point in the sequence. In other words, by the time most children enter school, they have mastered the abstraction and order-irrelevance principles, as well as the how-to-count principles.

Counting from 1 to 19 is particularly difficult because the number names form a sequence of words that is largely arbitrary. However, beginning with 20, learning must no longer be purely rote, because of the repetitive structure of number names. For example, if 4- and 5-year-olds are simply asked to count as high as they can, most will count past 20 but stop before 100 (Fuson, Richards, and Briars, 1982). They almost always stop at a number ending in 9. Furthermore, a common error is to skip decades, as in counting 37, 38, 39, 70 (Siegler and Robinson, 1982).

Both features show how preschool children learn number names past 20 by relying on the repetitive structure of those names.

Addition and Subtraction. Counting is the starting point for children as they learn to add. In fact, most preschoolers first add by counting. Suppose children were told to imagine that they have four oranges and they then get two more. Asked to determine the total number of oranges, many children first count out four fingers—1, 2, 3, 4—then two more—5, 6 (Siegler and Shrager, 1984). To subtract, they reverse these acts.

Young children often abandon this approach for a more efficient method. Instead of counting out the fingers on the first hand, they simultaneously extend the number of fingers on one hand corresponding to the larger of the two numbers to be added, then they count out the smaller number, using fingers on the other hand (Groen and Resnick, 1977). Ginsburg (1975) describes how one second grader would use this approach to add nine and six imaginary dots:

> Kathy: I would draw a box and put the dots in and count them.
> Interviewer: Know any other ways?
> Kathy: Well, I could count by my fingers, like 9, 10, 11, 12, 13, 14, 15.
> Interviewer: And you think that will give you the total number of dots in the boxes?

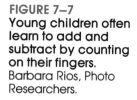

FIGURE 7–7
Young children often learn to add and subtract by counting on their fingers.
Barbara Rios, Photo Researchers.

Kathy: Yes. 'Cause I used the biggest number first so I don't have to count as much. (pp. 15–16)

In first grade, children start to receive formal instruction in arithmetic. Addition problems are solved less and less by counting aloud or by counting one's fingers. Instead, children add and subtract by counting *mentally*. However, early mental addition is still closely linked to counting aloud. Children behave as if they are counting silently, beginning with the largest number and adding on. By 8 or 9 years of age, children typically have learned the addition tables so well that sums of the single-digit integers (0 to 9) are facts that are simply retrieved from memory (Ashcraft, 1982).

Of course, arithmetic skills continue to improve after age 8. Children gain greater proficiency in addition and subtraction, learn multiplication and division, and extend these skills to quantities other than integers. What is most impressive is how early in life children master the essentials of quantitative knowledge. As we shall see in the next section, much the same can be said for way-finding abilities.

Way-Finding Skills

Most mornings children get from home to school and back without getting lost, although the routes they take are often indirect. In contrast, 3- and 4-year-olds are rarely permitted to make such journeys, despite various protections such as stop lights and street-crossing guards. Very young children, unlike their slightly older siblings, have limited way-finding skills. They cannot travel betwen two points unless the end can be seen from the starting point.

Siegel and his colleagues (Anooshian and Siegel, 1985; Siegel and White, 1975) have described a three-stage sequence in the development of spatial representations that provide the basis for way-finding. First, *landmarks* are noticed and remembered. Second, a child uses landmarks to form *routes*, sequences of action that lead from one landmark to another. Third, landmarks and routes are formed into clusters, or *configurations*. These ultimately form a *cognitive map*—a unified mental configuration of an environment that integrates many landmarks and routes.

Landmark Knowledge. The basic elements of cognitive maps are landmarks—salient objects or points of decision in the environment that are noticed and remembered and around which the child's action and decisions are coordinated. Children's and adults' descriptions of environments typically begin with the mention of landmarks (Downs and Stea, 1973). For children, landmarks might be the candy store, the playground, and the school crossing. These landmarks are the points to and from which a person moves or travels and are used to maintain course during travel.

Learning about landmarks begins very early in life. Before children can walk, they move through environments in parents' arms, in strollers, and in automobiles. Even when they are still, infants see people and ob-

FIGURE 7–8
Young children successfully walk to and from school, even though their destination cannot be seen at the start of the journey.
Will McIntyre, Photo Researchers.

jects move in their environments. According to Piaget (Piaget and Inhelder, 1967), a child first thinks of the positions of an object in space exclusively in terms of the object's position relative to the child's body—what Piaget called an *egocentric frame of reference*. Only later do children acquire an *objective frame of reference* in which an object's location is thought of relative to the positions of other objects in space.

One research technique has been particularly useful in tracing the development of these two ways of locating objects in the environment. Subjects are seated in a room in which there are two identical objects, one to the subject's left and one to the right. On each of several trials, a particular event *always* occurs at either the left or right object (see Figure 7–9). For example, the objects might be identical windows on the left and right walls of a room. When the infant is looking straight ahead, an experimenter sounds a buzzer. Shortly thereafter a person always appears in the left window, saying the infant's name and showing toys (Acredolo, 1978, 1979). As we would expect based on the research described in Chapter 4, infants quickly learn to anticipate the appearance of the person in the window when they hear the buzzer.

Once infants have learned to anticipate the face, they are turned 180 degrees, so that they are facing exactly the opposite direction. Once again the buzzer sounds. The crucial question is, "Which way will the infant look?" Consider first infants whose understanding of objects in the environment is still egocentric. What they have learned in the initial phase of the experiment is that the face appears to their left. Turned 180 degrees, this means that they will look in the wrong direction. Infants whose understanding of locations is objective realize that even though

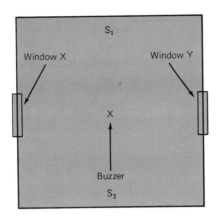

FIGURE 7–9
Experimental situation used by Acredolo to distinguish objective and egocentric frames of references. S_1 refers to the position of the infant on the learning trials; S_2, the infant's position after being rotated 180°. From L.P. Acredolo (1978). Development of spatial orientation in infancy. *Developmental Psychology,* 14, 224–34.

they have moved, the object has not. So, they will look to the same window as before, even though this means turning in a different direction.

In fact, for much of the first year of life, infants respond egocentrically. At the first birthday, egocentric and objective responses are equally likely; during the second year, objective responses become more frequent (Wishart and Bower, 1982). Acredolo (1978) found that approximately 90 percent of the 6-month-olds in her study responded egocentrically, compared to 67 percent of 11-month-olds and 25 percent of 16-month-olds.

Once objects in an environment are located in terms of an objective frame of reference, they can become associated with particular routes through that environment. By age 7 children are quite accurate at selecting landmarks associated with particular routes. Cousins, Siegel, and Maxwell (1983) asked children to imagine they were walking between two locations at their school. They were then given pictures of many school landmarks and asked to select those that they would see on their imaginary walks. The 7-year-olds accurately selected 89 percent of the landmarks that they would see.

Even preschool children know the prominent landmarks on routes they have learned. Hazen, Lockman, and Pick (1978) taught 3- to 6-year-olds a route through a series of rooms, each of which contained a distinct toy as a landmark. After the children had learned the route, the experimenter walked them through the route backwards. Before entering each room, the children were asked to name the toy inside. Older children were more likely to name the toy than younger children, but even 3-year-olds were accurate more than 70 percent of the time.

Young children can identify landmarks that are associated with a route and can anticipate the landmark they should see next. A related skill that is essential to way finding involves the *selection* of landmarks. In traveling in unfamiliar environments, one key is finding distinctive landmarks that will be recognized when one travels the route again. For example, suppose a child were walking down the street shown in Figure 7–10 and wanted to remember to turn right at the intersection, which is

one of many on this street. The stoplight would be of little value as a landmark, because many intersections have stoplights. The parked car would be equally poor as a landmark, because it will not always be in this location. However, the store on the corner would be an excellent choice: It is a distinctive storefront that children would probably notice whenever they walked along this street.

Allen, Kirasic, Siegel, and Herman (1979) examined developmental change in choices of landmarks. They took photographs of the walk shown in Figure 7–11, depicting what people would see if they walked along the sidewalk always looking straight ahead. Some of the photographs (those in locations that are solid black in Figure 7–11) showed no intersections where subjects might turn. Other photographs (those in locations with diagonal lines in Figure 7–11) included intersections that represent a potential change in heading. These photographs were shown to 7-year-olds, 10-year-olds, and adults in succession, to give them the impression of taking a walk through an unfamiliar neighborhood. Then all fifty-two photographs were presented at once, and subjects were asked to select "the nine scenes that would most help them to remember where they were along the walk" (Allen et al., p. 1064).

Virtually all the photographs that adults chose—94 percent—included intersections at which one would need to know whether to continue or to turn. The 10-year-olds were less likely to choose these key photographs, but they still selected a substantial number of them. The 7-year-olds selected even fewer of these photographs—62 percent—but this figure is greater than would be expected if these children were simply guessing. In other words, by 7 years of age children apparently know some of the fundamental characteristics of useful landmarks.

Route Learning.   Although landmarks are essential to way finding in large environments, they are not enough for constructing a cognitive map unless they are embedded in a method for getting from landmark to landmark. We have a route if we expect a particular landmark at the beginning and know that a succession of landmarks in a particular order will follow if a particular direction is taken. The last landmark in the succession is the destination. If the sequence of landmarks does not conform to expectations, we quite quickly have the feeling of ''being lost.'' Routes can then be considered a kind of spatial glue that links environmental landmarks.

The ability to learn routes improves consistently throughout the preschool years. For example, Hazen et al. (1978) found that 3-year-olds needed 50 percent more trials than 5-year-olds to learn a route through four rooms. By school age, children have acquired considerable skill in route learning (Cornell and Hay, 1984). In one study (Cohen and Schuepfer, 1980), subjects saw a sequence of photographs depicting a walk through hallways. Each photograph contained an intersecting hallway, and the subject's task was to learn the sequence of left and right turns that would lead to the end of the corridor. Seven-year-olds and adults

FIGURE 7–11
Schematic diagram illustrating the walk used by Allen et al.; diagonal lines indicate standpoints from which critical areas were visible in the slide presentation.   From G. L. Allen et al., (1979). Developmental issues in cognitive mapping: the selection and utilization of environmental landmarks. *Child Development,* 50, 1062–70. Copyright 1979 by the Society for Research in Child Development. Reprinted by permission.

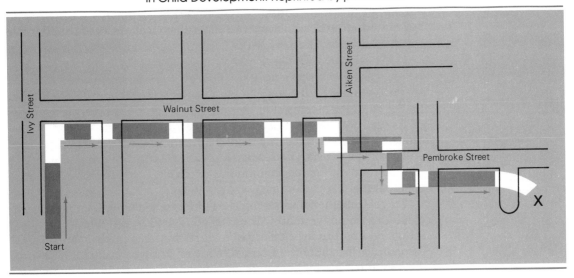

learned this sequence at approximately the same rate. In addition, school-age children and adolescents are very good at arranging photographs of landmarks in the order in which they were encountered along a route (Cousins et al., 1983).

However, this similarity in learning does not mean that children and adults have equal knowledge about the routes. Both groups know the sequence of turns. Adults and older children may have more than this minimal knowledge of the route. One example of such knowledge would be the distance between landmarks. Distances between landmarks are important because they allow people to estimate the time needed to travel between two points. In addition, we feel "lost" when a landmark that is expected after a certain distance fails to appear.

Adults sometimes judge distances between landmarks more accurately than children (Cohen and Weatherford, 1980). However, a number of factors seem to influence the accuracy with which both children and adults judge distances. For instance, both tend to overestimate a distance that is covered slowly and underestimate one that is covered rapidly (Herman, Roth and Norton, 1984).

Children's estimates of distances are also distorted if the landmarks are segregated in clusters. When a barrier separates two landmarks so that one is not visible from the other, children and adults usually overestimate the distance between them (Cohen and Weatherford, 1980). Even landmarks that can be seen are subject to this distortion if they are part of different subdivisions of a route. Consider the neighborhood represented in Figure 7–12. Suppose children were asked to judge the distance between houses A and B as well as the distance between houses C and D. The distance between the pairs of houses is exactly the same in the two routes. However, the top route in Figure 7–12 is entirely in a residential neighborhood, with relatively similar landmarks. The bottom route begins in a neighborhood, passes through a small commercial section, and ends in another residential area. Children and adults would agree that this route consists of three distinct segments. Furthermore, both children and adults overestimate distances on these subdivided routes (Allen, 1981).

Cognitive Maps.   One way to know an environment is as a set of potential landmarks connected by potential routes. However, learning 10 or 100 or 1,000 different separate routes through an environment is tedious. A *cognitive map* is the mental structure by which humans apparently store all the way-finding information about an environment (where routes cross, landmarks common to two routes, which routes are adjacent, parallel).

Piaget, Inhelder, and Szeminska (1960) were among the first to study children's cognitive maps. They asked 4- to 12-year-olds to draw the school building and the principal features in the immediate area, and to reconstruct the route from school to a well-known landmark. The landmarks named by children up to 6 or 7 years old were uncoordinated. For

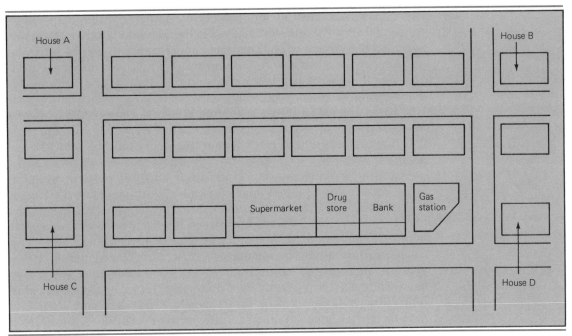

FIGURE 7–12
The route from house C to house D is the same distance as the route from house A to house B. However, because the former route consists of "clusters," it would be judged as longer.

example, younger children made no attempt to link the endpoint of a route with its starting point. At a more advanced level, children reconstructed routes and used subsystems of reference. But the various routes and subsystems were not coordinated as a whole. "Their plan of the district is made up of several portions which are correct in themselves but do not agree with one another" (Piaget et al., 1960, p. 8). At the next level, children reproduced a coordinated whole in sketching their journeys. "What began as a sketch-plan of a route finishes as a general map of the district" (Piaget et al., 1960, p. 20).

Having children draw maps often underestimates their knowledge of landmarks because children know more than they can accurately draw (Siegel, Kirasic, and Kail, 1978). Investigators after Piaget have used a number of ingenious approaches to probe configurational knowledge. Consider the two routes shown in Figure 7–12. Children's knowledge of that neighborhood would be called configurational if, as children are traveling along either route, they know the location of all four houses. If, for example, children are walking past the bank, their knowledge is configurational if they know that (1) house D is straight ahead; (2) house C is directly behind; (3) house B is ahead, off to the left; and (4) house A is behind, off to the left.

Anooshian and Young (1981) used procedures devised by Hardwick, McIntyre, and Pick (1976) to test configurational knowledge in 7-, 10-, and 13-year-olds. The four landmarks were scattered throughout a large residential area. All subjects had lived in this neighborhood for about two years, so the groups of children had similar opportunities to learn the environment. In addition, Anooshian and Young (1981) devised a questionnaire to measure familiarity with and preferences for different landmarks in the neighborhood. Subjects were walked to each of the four landmarks and asked to use a sighting tube that resembled a telescope to locate the remaining three landmarks. The 7-year-olds' average error of 27 degrees was substantially higher than that of the 10- and 13-year-olds.

Knowing the direction of a landmark is only one part of configurational knowledge. Children must also know the approximate distance of that landmark. Children could well know that a landmark is in a particular direction and at the same time have a relatively poor idea of how far to travel in that direction. In judging distances between landmarks along a familiar route, adults are sometimes more accurate than children. However, we are concerned with children's estimates of distance when they have *not* traveled between the two landmarks. As we might expect, children estimate distances along routes they have traveled more accurately than those they have not, and estimates of these latter distances become increasingly accurate with age (Cousins et al., 1983).

The research we have described thus far indicates that configurational knowledge is present by 6 or 7 years of age and that it becomes increasingly more precise thereafter. Are younger children capable of configurational knowledge? There is only a relatively small amount of research on this question, but most of it suggests that preschoolers *are* capable of at least limited forms of configurational knowledge. Lockman and Pick (1984), for example, used the sighting technique with preschoolers in their own homes. Asked to locate landmarks that were out of sight but on the same floor of the house, preschoolers were just as accurate as their parents.

Some of the limits of configurational knowledge in young children are revealed in the study by Hazen et al. (1978) in which children learned to walk a route through several unfamiliar rooms. Even though preschool children were able to anticipate landmarks and to walk the route in reverse, they did poorly on two tests of configurational knowledge. On one test, each child was asked to indicate what room was adjacent to the room in which the child was currently standing. The 3- to 5-year-olds answered correctly only about 50 percent of the time. On a second test, children were given four small blocks that corresponded to the different rooms and asked to put them "in the same shape as the big house" (Hazen et al., 1978, p. 627). Only one of twenty-four 3-year-olds built a model that had all four rooms in the correct location. Half of the 4-year-olds and two-thirds of the 5-year-olds did so. This performance is much poorer than in the Lockman and Pick study (1984). One interpretation of this difference is that the first environments children know as configurations may be their homes (Anooshian and Siegel, 1985).

Way-Finding in Blind Children

In discussing the different components of spatial knowledge, we have implied that many of the underlying processes are *visual*. Recognition of landmarks was always *visual* recognition. A good landmark was defined as one that was distinctive *visually*. However, none of this research has demonstrated that vision is necessary to know landmarks, routes, or configurations. Many blind individuals are quite mobile in large-scale environments. Blind individuals might recognize landmarks by their sounds, odors, or textures. Effective landmarks would again be distinctive locations, but distinctive in terms of sounds or odors.

Research by Landau, Gleitman, and Spelke (1981) shows that a very young blind child can acquire impressive spatial knowledge. The subject in their study, Kelli, was a 2½-year-old who had been blinded shortly after birth due to retrolentile fibroplasia, a syndrome in which blood vessels in the retina are destroyed. Landau et al. tested Kelli on a task that has much of the same logic as the "sighting studies" of configurational knowledge

(e.g., Hardwick et al., 1976). Kelli and her mother were seated in an unfamiliar room. The experimenter walked with Kelli from her mother to a landmark and then walked with Kelli back to her mother. They repeated this procedure for two additional landmarks. Then Kelli was taken to each of the three landmarks and was coaxed to walk to one of the other two, a route she had not traveled previously. She did this successfully on two-thirds of the trials, which was also the success rate of sighted 3 year olds and sighted adults performing the task blindfolded. As Landau et al. (1981) wrote:

> In order to accomplish this, the child must have access to information about the lengths of the two connecting routes travelled during training and the angular separation of those routes. From this information, the child can derive new angular relationships: the angular direction of one object from the other. . . . [These results] indicate that vision plays no essential role in the early development of knowledge of such properties. (p. 1277)

Sequence of Acquisition. Throughout this section, we have seen that knowledge of landmarks, routes, and configurations increases with age. However, Siegel and White's (1975) analysis of spatial knowledge predicts a very specific order in which knowledge is acquired. Individuals first learn landmarks, then they connect those landmarks to form routes, and finally they configure an entire environment to form what has been called a cognitive map.

A very general prediction of this theory is that age differences should be smallest for knowledge of landmarks, as this is the first component of spatial knowledge that children master. Age differences should be larger for measures of route knowledge, and larger still for measures of configurational knowledge. In fact, much of the research described here *is* generally consistent with these predictions. However, there is a stronger test of the theory. For any given environment, we can test individual children's knowledge of landmarks, routes, and configurations. If Siegel and White are correct, only certain combinations of knowledge are possible. For example, a child could know the landmarks and routes of the environment. However, a child who knew routes but not landmarks would be a contradiction.

Cousins et al. (1983) used exactly this approach to evaluate Siegel and White's theory. Children—7-, 10-, and 13-year-olds—were tested on measures of landmark, route, and configurational knowledge. The environment was their school and its grounds. Of the forty children, thirty-seven performed consistently with the theory. Only three children's knowledge was inconsistent with the theory: All had some form of route knowledge yet failed the landmark task.

The predicted sequence also holds in the earliest stages of spatial knowledge acquisition. Anooshian, Pascal, and McCreath (1984) tested 3- to 6-year-olds on measures of landmark and route knowledge similar to those used by Cousins et al. (1983). Of the forty-eight children tested, forty-two had combinations of landmark and route knowledge consistent with Siegel and White's theory. Thus, at least from the preschool years through early adolescence, most individuals acquire spatial knowledge in a consistent sequence: They first learn to recognize landmarks, then their order along a route, then distances between those landmarks, and finally the configuration of those landmarks in the entire space.

SUMMARY

1. Some developmental psychologists have tried to understand cognitive development by identifying the "building blocks" of cognition and charting their development.

2. Both classical and operant conditioning can be demonstrated in newborns, but are subject to biological constraints. Observational and mediated learning are considered to be more complex forms of learning that do not conform to a strict stimulus-response explanation. These varieties of learning are thought to be more akin to problem solving, in that children formulate strategies to perform learning tasks.

3. A more recent approach to cognitive development likens the mind to a computer consisting of mental hardware and software. The hardware consists of *sensory memory*, *short-term store*, and *long-term store*; the software consists of strategies used to transfer information between the hardware components. Developmental changes occur in children's use of strategies such as verbal rehearsal, use of categories, and taking notes.

4. *Metamemory* refers to the fact that intelligent use of memory strategies includes diagnosing the memory problem and monitoring one's progress toward the solution of the problem. Preschoolers know that in diagnosing memory problems, the familiarity and amount of information to be remembered contribute

to the difficulty of the problems. Many other memory variables, such as the impact of semantic relationships or the difference between verbatim and paraphrased recall, are not well understood until the middle elementary years. In addition, effective diagnosis does not guarantee success for young children, because they do not always select a strategy that fits the problem.

5. Monitoring performance on memory problems involves determining how well one knows separate parts of the information to be learned, plus integrating this information to judge how well one is progressing on the material as a whole.

6. Long-term store is the storehouse of permanent knowledge. *Quantitative skill* emerges in the first year of life. Infants are able to distinguish sets of different sizes and apparently have rudimentary understanding of *ordinality*, the knowledge that one quantity is greater or less than another.

7. Counting involves a number of distinct procedures, including the *one-to-one principle*, the *stable-order principle*, and the *cardinality principle*. Even 3-year-olds can apply many of these principles as long as the sets to be counted are fairly small. Two other principles—the *abstraction* and *order-irrelevance principles*—are also mastered by school age.

8. Counting is the starting point for addition and subtraction. Children quickly resort to more efficient modes of counting, ultimately doing all counting mentally. Finally, by 8 or 9 years of age, children no longer achieve sums and differences by counting, but instead by simply retrieving them from memory.

9. *Way-finding skill* is another important form of permanent knowledge. A theory proposed by Siegel and White (1975) distinguishes landmarks, routes, and configurations. *Landmarks* are salient objects in the environment that form the basis of the child's spatial knowledge. By the preschool years, children are quite capable of recognizing landmarks and anticipating their appearances on *routes*. Ultimately children form landmarks and routes into clusters, or *configurations*, which in turn form cognitive maps—mental configurations of an environment that integrate many landmarks and routes.

8 INTELLIGENCE

In previous chapters we described the basic processes through which the child comes to know and to adapt to the world. Learning, perception, memory, and the construction of a vision of reality in the ways described by Piaget and others are fundamental aspects of the overall process of intellectual development. In this chapter we examine intelligence from another point of view. We look at individual differences in intelligence, including their measurement and origin. We begin with the practical side of intelligence testing, asking how tests are developed and what intelligence scores mean. Next we consider intelligence test scores as a rich source of information about intellectual development. We also consider the truly exceptional—those who do not achieve the typical standards of intelligence or who go far beyond them. Finally, we discuss several theories of intelligence that propose different explanations of what intelligence is and how it develops.

WHAT IS INTELLIGENCE?

Although everyone has some notion of what is meant by intelligence, the idea is difficult to define. There is some agreement that intelligence refers to a person's ability to adapt to the environment successfully and to benefit from experience (Sternberg and Powell, 1983). This is hardly a definition, however, because the skills required for adaptation will depend on the environment one happens to be in. Adapting to the crib and nursery as an infant may involve quite different abilities from adapting to the demands of school as a student. Adapting to country life involves very different skills from adapting to the fast-paced business world of New York City. In fact, there is no one satisfactory definition of intelligence, because intelligence is not a "thing" but an idea. Intelligence is not something concrete that you possess a specific amount of, such as money. Intelligence is an abstraction and is not real in the tangible sense at all (Gould, 1981).

MEASURING INTELLIGENCE

For much of the twentieth century, intelligence tests have been part of instruction, beginning in the earliest school grades. These tests are designed to determine the intellectual tasks individuals can perform. With this information, educators have tried to match instruction with ability. Poor test performance, sometimes combined with other information, has often been used as a reason for placing a child in a special class. Intelligence tests are used in the armed services, in admission of students to college, in evaluation of the success of educational institutions, and in selection of employees. To understand and evaluate this so-called mental testing movement, we must first know how the tests are constructed.

Test Construction Principles

Initial Item Selection. The first step in constructing any kind of psychological test is to select appropriate items—that is, the test questions. The choice will obviously depend on the purpose of the test and the theoretical approach of the people constructing it. However, the general principle is that the items should be a representative sample of the behaviors or skills of interest.

> In this respect, the psychologist proceeds in much the same way as the biochemist who tests a patient's blood or a community's water by analyzing one or more samples of it. If the psychologist wishes to test the extent of a child's vocabulary, a clerk's ability to perform arithmetic computations, or a pilot's eye-hand coordination, he or she examines their performance with a representative set of words, arithmetic problems, or motor tests. (Anastasi, 1982, pp. 22–23).

Norms and Standardization.   Next, the test items must be administered to a representative group of individuals in order to establish *normative* performance. This group, the *standardization* sample, must be chosen carefully because its scores will be used as a standard against which later scores will be compared. For example, if the test is being designed for children of varying ages and socioeconomic backgrounds, the standardization group should include appropriate proportions of individuals reflecting these characteristics.

Still another part of standardization procedures concerns the context within which the test is administered. When classroom tests are given in school—for example, in spelling or arithmetic—individual teachers may differ widely in their selection of content, allotment of time for taking the test, policy on using notes, and so forth. Such tests do not permit direct comparisons from one classroom to another. A child who correctly answered 80 percent of the questions on Mr. Jones's arithmetic test might very well have learned less—or more—than one who earned the same score on Ms. Smith's test. If we are to compare many children from different parts of the country, or even from different classrooms, successfully, this problem must be overcome. *Standardization of test procedures* is used for this purpose. A *standardized test* is one in which the apparatus, procedure, and scoring have been fixed so that exactly the same test is given at different times and places.

Some people feel that one of the weaknesses of psychological tests is this standardization, which does not allow the examiner to provide the best conditions for any one individual. But if we want to use the test for comparison with others, it must be conducted in a standard way for all who take it.

Reliability.   After a test has been standardized, efforts must be made to check its reliability. *Reliability* means how closely sets of scores are related or how consistent they are over various time intervals. One common method of determining reliability is to administer a test to the same individuals on two different occasions. Another consists of administering equivalent forms of the test or items from the same form on separate occasions. In either case the two sets of scores are then correlated. The higher the correlation coefficient, the higher the reliability.

Validity. According to many psychologists, questions of validity are the most important that can be asked about any psychological test. Simply, the *validity* of a test is the degree to which it actually measures what it purports to measure.

How does one determine validity? Usually, one or more independent *criterion measures* are obtained and correlated with scores from the test in question. Criterion measures are chosen on the basis of what the test is designed to measure. Anxiety exhibited in a public-speaking situation, for example, might be a criterion measure for a test to evaluate self-consciousness. If anxiety test scores rise and fall like other measures of anxiety, evidence exists that the test enjoys some validity.

The validity of intelligence tests is usually determined by using as criterion tasks measures of academic achievement, such as school grades, teacher ratings, or scores on achievement tests. The reported correlations for the more widely used intelligence tests and these criterion tasks are reasonably high. For example, they fall between .40 and .75 for the Stanford-Binet intelligence test. Furthermore, children who have been accelerated or "skipped" one or more grades do considerably better on the Stanford-Binet than those who have shown normal progress. Youngsters who were held back one or more grades exhibit considerably lower than average scores (McNemar, 1942). Low scores on the Stanford-Binet also predict poor performance in school, and this is true regardless of race or socioeconomic background (Cleary, Humphreys, Kendrick, and Wesman, 1975). So the Standford-Binet is a reasonable test of intelligence, at least insofar as intelligence is reflected in school performance, and is relatively successful in predicting school achievement. This *predictive* validity is the major reason for the wide use of tests of intelligence.

Types of
Intelligence Tests

All the widely used tests discussed here are administered individually rather than in groups. Individual testing optimizes the motivation and attention of the examinee and provides an opportunity for a sensitive examiner to assess factors that may influence test performance. The examiner may notice that the examinee is relaxed and that therefore test performance is a reasonable sample of the individual's talents. Or the examiner may observe that intense anxiety is interfering with performance. Such clinical judgments are not possible with group tests. On the other hand, group tests have the advantage of providing information about many individuals quickly and inexpensively, often without the need of highly trained psychologists. For this reason group tests have been widely used for general placement in schools—not, however, without controversy, as we see later in the chapter.

Tests for Children
and Adults

The Binet Scales. In 1905 Alfred Binet and Theophile Simon, commissioned by the minister of public education in Paris, devised the first successful test of intellectual ability. It was called the Metrical Scale of Intelligence, and was made up of thirty problems in ascending order of difficulty. The goal was to identify children who were likely to fail in school so that they could be transferred to special classes. It was the first systematic comparison between normal and mentally retarded children. Revisions of the test, in 1908 and 1911, were based on the classroom observations of characteristics that teachers called "bright" and "dull," as well as on trial-and-error adjustment. Test scores agreed strongly with teacher ratings of intellectual ability.

Beginning with the 1908 revision, the Binet-Simon test was arranged into age levels. For example, the investigators placed all tests that normal 3-year-olds could pass in the three-year level, all tests that normal 4-year-olds could pass in the four-year level, and so on up to age 13. This arrangement gave rise to the concept of *mental age (MA)*. A child's mental age is equivalent to the *chronological age (CA)* of children whose performance he or she equals. A 6-year-old child who passed tests that the average 7-year-old passed would be said to have an MA of 7. This simple procedure did much to popularize the mental testing movement generally.

The Stanford-Binet Tests. The Binet-Simon tests attracted much interest, and translations soon appeared in many languages. In the United States, Lewis Terman at Stanford University revised the test into the first Stanford-Binet in 1916. The Stanford-Binet was a new test in many ways. Items had been changed, and it had been standardized on a relatively large American population including about 1,000 children and 400 adults. Furthermore, Terman and his associates used the notion of the *intelligence quotient* or *IQ*—the ratio of an individual's mental age to his or her chronological age, multiplied by 100 to avoid decimals. Thus:

$$IQ = \frac{MA}{CA} \times 100$$

This quotient was a really clever idea at the time. If a child's mental age and chronological age were equivalent, the child's IQ, regardless of actual chronological age, would be 100—reflecting average performance. The procedure also made it possible to compare the intellectual development of children of different chronological ages. If a 4-year-old boy has a mental age of 3, his IQ will be 75 ($3/4 \times 100$), as will that of an equally retarded 12-year-old with a mental age of 9 ($9/12 \times 100 = 75$).

The Stanford-Binet was revised in 1937, 1960, and 1972, and restandardized in 1937 and 1972. Since the 1960 revision, an individual's IQ is calculated by comparing test results with the average score earned by those of the same age in the standardization group. Statistical procedures allow the average score for each age group to be set at 100, with approximately the same number of scores falling below 100 as falling above it. An IQ score thus reflects how near and how far, and in what direction, the individual is from the average score of the age group. Moreover, it is possible to calculate the percentage of individuals who perform higher and lower than any particular IQ score. This kind of comparison is now used in many intelligence tests.

Like the earlier versions, the Stanford-Binet today consists of many cognitive and motor tasks, ranging from the extremely easy to the extremely difficult. The test may be administered to individuals ranging in age from approximately 2 years to adulthood, but not every individual is given every question. For example, young children (or older retarded children) may be asked to recognize pictures of familiar objects, string beads, answer questions about everyday relationships, or fold paper into shapes. Older individuals may be asked to define vocabulary words, reason through to the solution of an abstract problem, or decipher an unfamiliar code. Some of the materials used in the Stanford-Binet children's scales are shown in Figure 8–1. The examiner determines, according to specific guidelines, the appropriate starting place on the test and administers progressively more difficult questions until the child fails all the questions at a particular level. An IQ score is assigned on the basis of how many questions the child passed compared with the average number passed by children of the same age.

The Wechsler Scales. A second set of intelligence scales widely used in assessment and research with children is based on the work of David

FIGURE 8–1
Some of the test materials used in administering the Stanford-Binet to children. From N. L. Munn, L. D. Fernald, Jr., and P. S. Fernald, *Introduction to Psychology.* (Houghton Mifflin, 1972.) By permission of the publishers.

Wechsler. The original Wechsler scale, the Wechsler-Bellevue, was published in 1939 and was geared specifically to the measurement of adult intelligence for clinical use. Later revisions resulted in instruments for adults (Wechsler Adult Intelligence Scale, or WAIS), for schoolchildren (Wechsler Intelligence Scale for Children, or WISC), and for children 4 to 6 years of age (Wechsler Preschool and Primary Scale of Intelligence, or WPPSI). All these tests follow a similar format.

The WISC, unlike the Stanford-Binet, includes subtests that are categorized into verbal or performance subscales; the latter taps nonverbal symbolic skills. Children thus are assessed on verbal IQ, performance IQ, and a combination of the two, the full-scale IQ. A second major difference between the WISC and the Stanford-Binet is that each child receives the same subtests, with some adjustment for either age level or competence or both. The subtests include vocabulary, knowledge of the social environment, puzzles, and memory tasks.

Infant Tests

Neither the WISC nor the Stanford-Binet can be used to test intelligence in infants. For this purpose, several individual tests have been developed during the last fifty years: the Gesell Developmental Schedules, the Cattell Intelligence Tests for Infants and Young Children, and the Bayley Scales of Infant Development. Performance on these tests is labeled DQ, for developmental quotient, rather than IQ.

Gesell's test was the first specifically designed to measure mental ability in early infancy (Bayley, 1970). It evaluates behavior in four basic areas: motor, adaptive, language, and personal-social (Figure 8–2). The first three scales are based on the examiner's observations of the infant; the last scale is scored mainly from a parental interview. The child's performance is compared with norms derived from a relatively small group of middle-class children who were followed longitudinally.

The Bayley Scales of Infant Development (Bayley, 1970) are designed for infants 2 to 30 months old. They consist of motor and mental scales and an Infant Behavior Record. The motor scale includes such items as holding the head up, walking, and throwing a ball. The mental scale, designed to assess development of adaptive behavior, includes such behaviors as attending to visual and auditory stimuli, following directions, looking for a fallen toy, and imitating. The Infant Behavior Record is a rating of the child on such responses as fearfulness, happiness, endurance, responsiveness, and goal directedness.

Early Test Performance and Later IQ Scores

Infant Tests. How well do early tests predict scores on tests given at later times? A strong positive relationship would indicate that assessment early in life does provide information about later performance. In one classic study, correlations were calculated between tests given at 3, 6, 9, 12, 18, and 24 months with Stanford-Binet scores obtained at 5 years (Anderson, 1939). As shown in Table 8–1, the relationships were low and tended to decrease as the time between assessments increased. The low

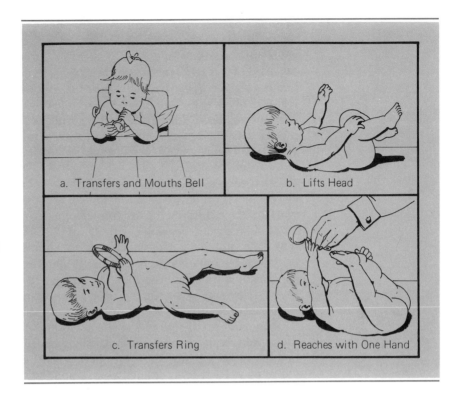

FIGURE 8–2
Illustrations from the Gesell Developmental Schedules of behaviors typical at 28 weeks of age. Adapted from A. Gesell and C. S. Amatruda, *Developmental Diagnosis.* (New York: Paul B. Hoeber, Inc.) Copyright 1941, 1947 by Arnold Gesell. By permission.

a. Transfers and Mouths Bell

b. Lifts Head

c. Transfers Ring

d. Reaches with One Hand

correlation between early and later tests has also been shown in subsequent studies (Pease, Wolins, and Stockdale, 1973; Rubin and Balow, 1979).

Predictability is sometimes higher when more global categories, rather than specific IQ scores, are considered and when clinical judgment is used along with test scores. MacRae (1955) asked examiners to assign

TABLE 8–1
Correlation Coefficients between Infant Intelligence Tests Given at Various Ages and Stanford-Binet IQ at 5 Years

Ages	Correlation Coefficient
3 months–5 years	.01
6 months–5 years	−.06
9 months–5 years	.00
12 months–5 years	.06
18 months–5 years	.23
24 months–5 years	.45

Source: Adapted from Anderson, 1939.

infants to one of five categories on the basis of their subjective assessments of test performance: superior, above average, average, below average to borderline, mentally defective. Correlations with test scores obtained at 9 years, 2 months were .56, .55, and .82 when the infant tests had been given at 0 to 11 months, 12 to 23 months, and 24 to 35 months, respectively. Illingworth (1961) has argued that general mental inferiority can be diagnosed during the first year of life. In one study employing modified Gesell tests, histories, and clinical judgment, Illingworth predicted deficiency with 75 percent accuracy as it was measured independently at school age.

Such success speaks well for the practical benefits of early diagnosis of problems, primarily because it makes it possible to design treatment plans or place children into adoptive homes (Knobloch and Pasamanick, 1974). A study of 4-year-olds with IQs of 140 or higher, however, showed that their superior performance was not predictable from scores on the Bayley scales obtained at 8 months (Willerman and Fiedler, 1974). The consensus is that children must be at least 18 to 24 months old before their Bayley scores, or similar scales, can predict later IQ scores on the Wechsler or Stanford-Binet scales (Kopp and McCall, 1982).

Why isn't predictive power greater? One reason is that there is relatively little room for the display of individual differences during the early months of life (Ames, 1967), so infants can be differentiated only in a global way. Early temperamental variations (activity level or reactivity to stimulation) may influence performance in a different way from that in which they affect later performance. Another explanation, perhaps the most important, is that infant tests tap abilities other than those evaluated on later tests: They place more emphasis on sensorimotor items and less on tasks involving language and abstract problem solving.

You might expect that early precociousness or retardation on sensorimotor tasks would foretell later intelligence. Bayley suggests that there is little reason to anticipate a strong relation between early simple functions and the more complex processes that develop later:

> The neonate who is precocious in the development of the simpler abilities, such as auditory acuity or pupillary reflexes, has an advantage in the slightly more complex behaviors, such as (say) turning toward a sound, or fixating an object held before his eyes. But these more complex acts also involve other functions, such as neuro-muscular coordinations, in which he may not be precocious. The bright one-month-old may be sufficiently slow in developing these later more complex functions so as to lose some or all of his earlier advantages. (Bayley, 1955, pp. 807–808)

A recent study suggests that there may be some exceptions to this general rule. O'Connor, Cohen, and Parmelee (1984) assessed twenty-eight infants' responsiveness to novel auditory stimuli at age 4 months. These researchers followed the children longitudinally, and obtained IQ scores for them when they were 5 years old. A statistically significant (and, in fact, impressively high) correlation of +.60 was found between early responsiveness and later IQ scores, which suggests the possibility that certain aspects of very early perceptual-memory development, in the authors' words, "may reflect early cognitive processes necessary for later intellectual performance" (p. 159).

Tests Given in Childhood and Beyond. What happens when test scores obtained by older children are correlated with yet later performance? Generally the correlations (1) are substantially higher than those for infant tests and (2) progressively increase as the time interval between tests decreases. Figure 8–3 shows the correlations from several studies of scores obtained at maturity with those obtained earlier. These studies clearly show that although the relationship increased progressively as time of testing approached maturity, even tests obtained during childhood substantially predict later performance when data for groups of people are examined.

FIGURE 8–3
Correlations between intelligence (test scores) obtained at each age and intelligence at maturity. The graph lines represent data from different investigations, and they illustrate the substantial power of tests obtained during early childhood to predict later performance. Adapted from B. S. Bloom, *Stability and Change in Human Characteristics.* Copyright 1964. Reproduced by permission of John Wiley & Sons, Inc.

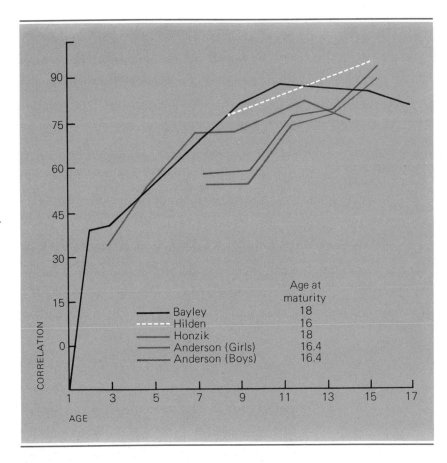

These results at first appear to support the old concept of intelligence as being relatively fixed (and some may assume from this that intelligence must therefore be predetermined by biological factors). However, when *individual* performance over time is examined, we see that constancy is *not* a hard-and-fast rule. Honzik, MacFarland, and Allen (1948), for example, found that almost 60 percent of 252 children in the Child Guidance Study, tested several times between the ages of 6 and 18 years, changed by fifteen or more points. As part of the Fels Study, Sontag, Baker, and Nelson (1958) administered the Stanford-Binet several times to children between 3 and 12 years of age. The large majority did not obtain the same IQ scores, and there was considerable change for some children. Figure 8–4 shows the average gains for the thirty-five children exhibiting the greatest increase and the average loss for the thirty-five children displaying the greatest decline.

In summarizing their own work and that of others, McCall, Appelbaum, and Hogarty (1973) noted that:

1. IQ changes of thirty and forty points are found fairly often.
2. Boys are somewhat more likely to show increases in IQ than girls, and girls oriented toward masculine roles tend to show more increases than girls not so oriented.
3. Children of low-income families tend to show no change or a decrease in IQ scores.
4. Differences in personality have been found between those who show increases and those who show decreases in IQ. Preschool

FIGURE 8–4
Mean IQ points gained or lost by children who demonstrated the greatest increases or greatest declines. Adapted from Sontag, Baker, and Nelson (1958). Copyright 1958 by the Society for Research in Child Development, Inc. Reproduced by permission.

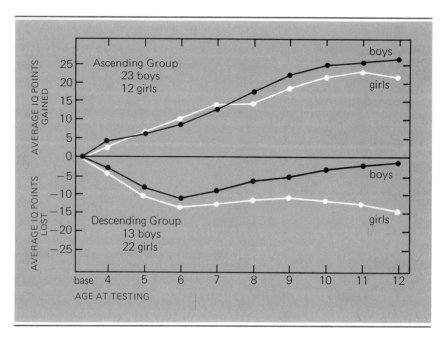

children who gain are independent and competitive; the same is true for elementary school children who gain. These children are also self-initiating and enjoy problem solving.

Intelligence Scores and Aging

For a long time, we thought that mental functioning increases with age until adulthood and then declines, perhaps after reaching a plateau at a certain age. Early data collected from cross-sectional studies supported this view: They showed a performance peak at 18 to 25 years, a gradual decline until approximately 50 years of age, and then more rapid decline after 50 (Botwinick, 1973). However, the people measured at different ages were different people, and thus the decline might have been due to age-related differences in diet, opportunity for learning, test-taking sophistication, motivation, and the like. Consider, for example, the hypothetical case of a group of 60-year-olds who obtained an average IQ of 95 and a group of 25-year-olds who obtained an average IQ of 105. Can we conclude that aging itself is responsible for this apparent change over time? No, because the two age groups may have had different experiences. The 25-year-olds undoubtedly had more formal education and may have experienced greater encouragement to achieve, better nutrition, and more practice in taking standardized tests. Perhaps these cohort differences, rather than age itself, underlie the higher IQ scores obtained by the 25-year-olds.

Green (1969) conducted a cross-sectional study among Puerto Ricans between ages 25 and 64 and noted the same pattern that had led other investigators to conclude that from early adulthood on, there is a steady decrease in intelligence (Bromley, 1966). However, Green also observed that the older subjects, on the average, had received fewer years of education. When he adjusted the analysis so that educational level was equated for all age groups, full-scale IQ scores increased until age 40 and then remained constant. When verbal and nonverbal sections were examined separately, verbal intelligence steadily increased from ages 25 to 64. Nonverbal intelligence was constant from 25 to 40, after which it showed some decline.

Using a longitudinal design, Blum, Jarvik, and Clark (1970) reported a small decline in intelligence test scores between 65 and 73 and a much steeper decline between 73 and 85. Like Green, they also observed that the rate of change for different parts of the intelligence test was not constant. On tests of pure information, such as vocabulary, no decline was observed through age 85. On tests requiring speed or perceptual-spatial reasoning, there was a sharp decline between ages 65 and 73. Many other longitudinal studies lead to the conclusion that intelligence test scores obtained from the *same* subjects over time are maintained and may even increase through early and middle adulthood (Horn, 1970).

The distinction between abilities that decline more rapidly and those that do not has been conceptualized along the dimensions of fluid and crystallized intelligence (Horn, 1970). *Fluid* intelligence refers to abilities to solve problems that are relatively uninfluenced by experience. *Crys-*

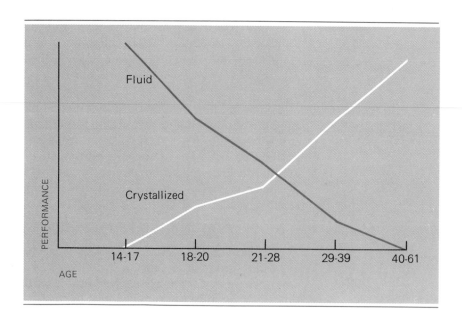

FIGURE 8–5
Performance on
tasks utilizing fluid
and crystallized
intelligence. From
Horn (1970), p. 463.

tallized intelligence involves knowledge of the information and skills of the culture. Figure 8–5 demonstrates the Horn and Cattell findings that fluid intelligence is high during adolescence, but drops throughout the life span. Crystallized intelligence follows a reverse trend. These investigators have also suggested a life span pattern. Early in life both abilities would be expected to grow at a rapid and approximately even rate. Fluid intelligence then would begin a downward swing due to biological wear and tear in the central nervous system. Crystallized intelligence would tend to continue to develop with cultural experience, and it would decline only when environmental restriction occurs or when biological wear and tear is overpowering.

Such results are gladly accepted by those of us who want to believe that all intellectual ability does not decline rapidly in adulthood. But we must realize that the picture is far more complicated. First, the problem of losing subjects (called *differential attrition*) inevitably causes trouble. Regardless of the research design, with increasing age there is increasing loss of people due to poor motivation, and perhaps more important, to illness and death. The sample of the older people thus does not include many who, on the average, would obtain the lower scores. Riegel and Riegel (1972), for example, traced the subjects who had dropped out of their study and found that as a group these individuals had obtained lower scores on the previous testing. On the other hand, the Riegels also emphasized that test performance drops when a person is relatively close to death. Because groups of older subjects include a greater number of people close to death, average performance may indicate a greater decline than is actually the case for most healthy older people.

These considerations make it extremely difficult to interpret the age patterns on tests. It is understandable that investigators disagree on the findings, even when sophisticated research designs have been used (Baltes and Schaie, 1974, 1976; Denney, 1982; Horn and Donaldson, 1976). The most widely agreed upon pattern appears to be that performance peaks sometime in the 20s, is at a plateau during the 30s and 40s, and perseveres well into adulthood. But all abilities cannot be lumped together; some follow a different pattern than others and to the extent that individuals biologically age at different rates and accumulate different experiences, their performances will certainly vary.

FACTORS INFLUENCING INTELLIGENCE TEST PERFORMANCE

Investigations have often focused on the factors to which intelligence is related. Such studies help us to understand what intelligence scores measure. They also help to reveal how intellectual development may be enhanced or restrained by environmental factors. Our discussion begins with correlations that have been observed between the kind of interactions children have with their parents and their IQ test scores. We then turn to the relationship between sociocultural factors and intelligence, and explain efforts to disentangle social class from race and ethnic background. As we will see, the fact that the data are almost all correlational leaves us unsure of the nature of the cause and effect relationship between all these factors and the development of intelligence.

Parental Interaction

The number of parental behaviors and attitudes affecting children's intellectual performance is presumably very large. Our discussion will provide only a sample of the kinds of variables being studied and some of what is known about them (Wachs and Gruen, 1982).

Using a specially designed inventory to assess the home environment, Caldwell and her associates (Caldwell, Bradley, and Elardo, 1975) found that increases in intellectual functioning from 6 to 36 months were related to maternal involvement with the children and availability of play material. Bayley and Schaefer (1964) reported that hostility in mothers was related to high IQ scores in boys during infancy; for girls, loving, controlling maternal behavior was related to high IQ scores during infancy.

Similarly, Honzik (1967) found a positive relation between IQ scores, particularly for boys, and mothers' worrisomeness, tenseness, concern, and energy. The author suggested that such mothers are probably more responsive to the wants and needs of their children and do more for them.

There is some evidence that mothers' intellectual levels are more closely associated than fathers' with children's functioning (Willerman and Stafford, 1972). However, fathers may have greater influence on their sons' cognitive development than on their daughters'. Radin's (1972, 1973) work with boys from lower- and middle-class families showed a positive correlation between paternal nurturance and IQ. Fear of the father did not enhance growth, and in the lower-class families, a negative correlation was found between restrictiveness of the father and IQ. Radin suggested that nurturant paternal behavior allows the child to identify with the father and internalize the father's ideas and behaviors. Also, in accordance with social learning theory, the father's attitude toward the son may assure the child that exploratory behavior will be rewarded and thus increase such behavior, which leads to cognitive growth. The influence of the father's availability on intelligence was demonstrated by Reis and Gold (1977), who studied 4-year-old boys with available fathers (average time with child, nineteen hours per week) and those with less available fathers (eleven hours per week with child). Reis and Gold found a positive correlation between availability and three measures of problem solving.

Paternal influence on a daughter may operate indirectly through the mother. Honzik (1967) reported an association between paternal friendliness toward the mother and intellectual development in the daughter. Radin (1976) suggested that the father's warmth toward the mother may increase the mother's warmth toward the child. Such positive parental interaction may create an atmosphere that supports cognitive growth in daughters. However, it is not clear why this effect does not appear in a son's development.

Socioeconomic Status, Race, and Ethnicity

There is a positive relationship between socioeconomic status (SES) and IQ (Bradley and Tedesco, 1982). The pattern has shown up continuously on tests such as the Stanford-Binet and the Wechsler. For example, children whose fathers were classified as professionals obtained an average Stanford-Binet score of 115, whereas children whose fathers held slightly skilled occupations obtained an average score of 97 (McNemar, 1942). Table 8–2 indicates a similar relation for the WISC. In general, a

TABLE 8–2
Mean IQ Scores for the Normative Sample on the Wechsler Intelligence Scale for Children Categorized on the Basis of Father's Occupation

Occupational Category	Verbal	Mean IQ Performance	Full Scale
Professional and semiprofessional workers	111	108	110
Proprietors, managers, and officials	106	106	106
Clerical, sales, and kindred workers	105	104	105
Craftspeople, supervisors, and kindred workers	101	102	101
Operatives and kindred workers	99	100	99
Domestic, protective, and other service workers	98	97	97
Farmers and farm managers	97	99	97
Manual laborers	95	94	94

Source: Adapted from Seashore, Wesman, and Doppelt, 1950.

fifteen- to twenty-five-point difference exists between the scores of children of professionals and laborers.

Race is also related to IQ. Blacks do less well on standard IQ tests than whites (Vernon, 1979). The difference is in the range of fifteen to twenty points—that is, the average score for blacks is about 80 to 85, compared with the average score for whites of 100. One group of investigators (Kennedy, van de Riet, and White, 1963) established norms for 1,800 black children in grades one to six in the southeastern United States. The mean IQ on the Stanford-Binet was 80.7. Children from metropolitan schools performed better than those from urban and rural communities, and those of higher social class had the higher scores. Figure 8–6 shows the distribution of scores, compared with the distribution of the original standardization sample for this test. Note that there is considerable overlap between the two distributions. This means that a large percentage of black and white children score within the same range. But remember that in many studies race and SES interact to confuse the results, because a larger proportion of blacks than whites are living under poverty conditions.

In addition, ethnic and racial groups show distinct patterns of performance on intelligence tests. One study tested first-grade children from middle- and lower-class families with Chinese, Jewish, black, and Puerto Rican cultural backgrounds (Lesser, Fifer, and Clark, 1965). Tests measured verbal ability, reasoning, number facility, and space conceptualization. Although middle-class children obtained higher scores on all the scales, the pattern of performance within ethnic groups differed. For example, Jewish children performed best on the verbal tasks and least well

FIGURE 8–6
IQ distribution on the Stanford-Binet for the normative white sample and 1,800 black elementary school children in the Southeast.
Adapted from W. A. Kennedy, V. van de Riet, and J. C. White, Jr. (1963). Copyright 1963 by the Society for Research in Child Development Inc. Reproduced by permission.

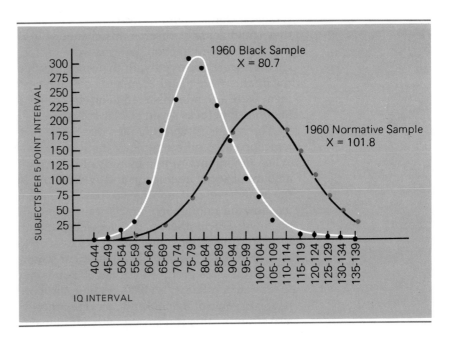

on reasoning and spatial tasks. Puerto Rican children performed best on spatial tasks and least well on verbal ones.

Differences associated with SES and race often increase with age. Bayley and Schaefer (1964), among others, found that starting at about 2 years of age, measures of SES correlated more and more positively with IQ. Before that age, there was either no relationship or a negative one. Similarly, differences among blacks and whites generally do not show up until the preschool years; black infants do as well as whites on the kinds of skills required by infant tests.

How do we interpret the growing correlations with age? It could reflect the accumulative influence of the environment, the late appearance of genetically based abilities, or a combination of these factors.

SES Differences in Mothers' Interactions with Toddlers. SES itself cannot cause differences in intellectual performance. Rather, one or more factors associated with SES must be responsible. In an important longitudinal study, Farran and Ramey (1980) examined the hypothesis that SES differences in IQ test scores result, in part, from differences in the amount of social interaction (talking, reading to the child, and the like) lower- and middle-class mothers offer their children.

Prior to the Farran and Ramey study two facts had already been established. One is that no difference exists in the amount of interaction that lower- and middle-class mothers have with their infants—that is, those less than 1 year of age (Lewis and Wilson, 1972). The other is that significant differences exist in the amount of interaction between lower- and middle-class mothers and their toddlers. Poverty-stricken mothers interact less with their 3- to 5-year-olds than do middle-class mothers (Walters, Connor, and Zunich, 1964). Farran and Ramey set out to see if they could actually observe this change and to determine whether SES differences in interaction patterns were related to later IQ. Thirty-seven children were observed with their mothers in a small living room when the infants were 6 and 20 months old. Bayley Scales of Infant Development were also administered to all children at 6 and 18 months, and the Stanford-Binet was given at 48 months.

The results fit with the idea that SES differences in mother-child interactions account for some of the IQ differences between SES groups. When the infants were 6 months old, the mothers did not differ in the amount of social interaction and stimulation they provided. By the time the infants were 20 months old, however, the middle-class mothers had *increased* the amount of interaction and stimulation they offered, whereas the lower-SES mothers had *decreased* the amount they provided (see Figure 8–7). In addition, whereas the Bayley scores of the lower- and middle-class children were virtually identical at 6 months, the average score of the middle-class group was about 30 points higher at 48 months.

Farran and Ramey's (1980) findings support an environmental explanation of some of the SES and race differences in IQ tests. Other research also supports this conclusion with additional correlational data. Still, as

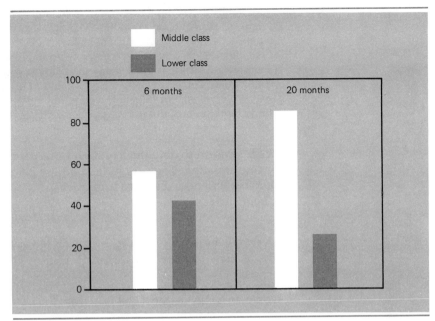

FIGURE 8–7
Proportion of lower-and middle-class mothers showing high stimulation of their children at 6 and 20 months. Adapted from Farran and Ramey (1980). Copyright 1980 by the Society for Research in Child Development, Inc. Reproduced by permission.

we noted in Chapter 2, hereditary factors also appear to make a measurable contribution to IQ. The relative contributions of the two factors, as well as the exact way in which they interact, continue to be topics of heavy research interest and much debate (Wachs and Gruen, 1982).

The Cultural Bias of Intelligence Tests.   Psychological testing has come under increasing criticism since the 1950s. One criticism is a response to the consistent finding that individuals from cultural backgrounds other than the middle or upper class perform less well than those from the general population. Critics assert that conclusions about the intelligence of various minority groups are based on tests that are biased against them. Consider the following informal description of cultural bias as it was suggested by Kenneth Eells (1953):*

> Let us suppose for a moment that you have a friend in Australia and that you have gone to visit him in his home country. He has told you that he is to take an intelligence test that afternoon and suggests that you take it too, just for the fun of it. . . . When you first open the test booklet you say to yourself, "Well, I'm in a foreign country, but since they speak English, I shouldn't have any special difficulty with this." But soon you are in trouble. . . . You realize that because of the mutton and the kangaroo, the strange words, the local information, and the variations in word connotations your friend had an advantage over you. If he thinks this is a good measure of your intelligence you are glad that he cannot compare your score with his. . . . As a measure of

your ability to get along in a certain portion of the Australian culture the test might be excellent and you might willingly accept your low score as an accurate reflection of your "current ability." It is the labeling of the test as an "intelligence" test, with its accompanying implication that this is somehow a measure of some basic ability or potentiality of yours, that disturbs you. . . . You wouldn't object to being told you couldn't understand Australian newspapers very well; but to be told you're not very "intelligent" implies something more serious, doesn't it? (pp. 284–285)

Eells goes on to note that children from poor areas in America are in the same situation. They are judged on the basis of test items requiring cultural experiences different from their own. Consider, for example, a test item such as:

A symphony is to a composer as a book is to what?
    paper   author   musician   man

It would surprise no one if children from the upper classes chose the correct answer, simply on the basis of experience, more often than those from the lower classes. And yet, this outcome is frequently used to argue that individuals in the lower classes lack some inherent ability called intelligence.

A dramatic example of the limitations of standard IQ testing for children from other than white middle-class backgrounds was offered by Mercer (1971). Mercer developed a system of assessment that included direct measures of children's ability to adapt to their environments (ranging from relatively simple tasks such as dressing oneself to complex tasks such as shopping), as well as a standard Wechsler IQ test. She administered both tests to over 600 Chicano, black, and white children in California. As might have been predicted, white children with standard IQ scores below 70 invariably failed her adaptive behavior scale. The surprise, however, was that the same was *not* true of black and Chicano children with IQ scores below 70. In fact, a clear majority of these children passed the skills test despite their supposedly low IQs. These results suggest that for minority children, low IQ scores should not be considered a measure of adaptive skill or potential, although for middle-class white children they may be interpreted that way.

There have been attempts to construct tests that eliminate some cultural differences, such as in content, language, and speed (Anastasi, 1968). Today several culture-fair tests are relatively good predictors of academic success. Raven's Progressive Matrices, for example, consist of designs, each of which has a missing section (Figure 8–8). Examinees are required to select the missing part from several alternatives. There is no time limit and instructions are simple. The Goodenough-Harris Drawing Test requires subjects to draw a picture of a man, a woman, and themselves. It is reasonably reliable and correlates with other intelligence tests. But both tests are more culture-laden than originally expected.

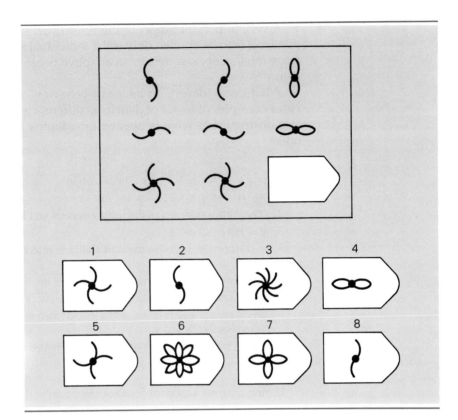

FIGURE 8–8
Materials similar to those used in Raven's Progressive Matrices Test.

Results from Raven's Progressive Matrices reflect amount of education (Anastasi, 1968), and those from the Goodenough-Harris Drawing Test are related to the degree to which representational art exists in particular cultures (Dennis, 1966). A study of the Drawing Test showed that aboriginal Australian boys, but not girls, outperform the average U.S. child (Money and Nurcombe, 1974). The aborigines have a strong cultural heritage of painting totemic designs with which boys are involved. It does not seem possible, at this point in time, to construct tests that are *completely* free of cultural content.

MENTAL RETARDATION

Mental retardation has been mentioned a number of times in this chapter. Intelligence as it is defined by standard tests has been crucial to the definition of mental retardation. The American Association on Mental Deficiency (AAMD) defines *mental retardation* as "significantly subaverage functioning existing concurrently with deficits in adaptive behavior and manifested during the developmental period [that is, before the age of 19]" (Grossman, 1977, p. 5). By "significantly subaverage" the AAMD means at least two standard deviations below the mean on a widely accepted general intelligence test (67 or below on the Stanford-Binet and 69 or below on the Wechsler scales).

A very important aspect of the AAMD definition is that the retardation label is to be applied only if the individual shows significant subaverage intelligence *and* deficits in adaptive behavior. This is illustrated in Figure 8–9.

What does "deficits in adaptive behavior" mean? The AAMD provides examples of levels of deficits at different ages (Grossman, 1983). It also distinguishes what is needed for adaptive functioning in each age range:

During INFANCY AND EARLY CHILDHOOD in:

1. SENSORY-MOTOR SKILLS DEVELOPMENT

2. COMMUNICATION SKILLS (including speech and language)

3. SELF-HELP SKILLS

4. SOCIALIZATION (development of ability to interact with others)

During CHILDHOOD AND EARLY ADOLESCENCE in:

5. APPLICATION OF BASIC ACADEMIC SKILLS IN DAILY LIFE ACTIVITIES

6. APPLICATION OF APPROPRIATE REASONING AND JUDGMENT IN MASTERY OF THE ENVIRONMENT

7. SOCIAL SKILLS (participation in group activities and interpersonal relationships)

and

During LATE ADOLESCENCE AND ADULT LIFE in:

8. VOCATIONAL AND SOCIAL RESPONSIBILITIES AND PERFORMANCES

(Grossman, 1977, p. 13)

Causes

Although the causes of mental retardation vary considerably, two distinct categories have been identified and can help us understand the range of characteristics and abilities displayed by retarded individuals.

Familial mental retardation is said to account for roughly 80 percent of all mental deficiency. A familially retarded child may be viewed as having an IQ within the lower range of the normal IQ distribution. As we would expect from this distribution, most children in this category are only mildly retarded. They are physically normal and have no history of brain damage or neurological defect.

FIGURE 8–9
The relationship between intellectual functioning, adaptive behavior, and mental retardation.

		INTELLECTUAL FUNCTIONING	
		Retarded	Not Retarded
ADAPTIVE BEHAVIOR	Retarded	Mentally Retarded	Not Mentally Retarded
	Not Retarded	Not Mentally Retarded	Not Mentally Retarded

Biologically caused mental retardation stems from some particular damage or defect. These include chromosomal anomalies such as Down's syndrome and gene defects such as phenylketonuria, both of which were discussed in Chapter 2, as well as brain damage caused by infectious disease, oxygen deprivation, or physical trauma. Most, though not all, individuals with IQs below 50 appear to be in this category.

Levels and Measurement

Historically, retardation has been classified according to severity. Over the years three or four categories have generally been recognized, although the labels associated with them have varied with the time and the setting. The terms *moron, imbecile,* and *idiot,* for example, were once standard designations for retarded individuals. Today the AAMD uses the terms *mild, moderate, severe,* and *profound.* Current labels used by educators in the United States reflect the school capabilities of each group: *educable (EMR), trainable (TMR),* and *custodial* levels. Table 8–3 shows the parallel between these classification schemes, as well as the accepted IQ range from each category. Variations in the labels are not due simply to current fashion. They reflect a specific orientation toward retardation.

Changes in labels have also served the beneficial purpose of helping to overcome prejudices and stereotypes. Today most of us would be horrified to hear a mentally retarded person referred to as an imbecile or idiot. And children labeled slow learners are judged more favorably than those labeled mentally retarded (Hollinger and Jones, 1970).

Identifying levels of retardation on the basis of adaptive functioning is nowhere near as precise as is using intelligence test scores. Ideally, such identification would involve numerous observations of the individual in various settings. In practice, it is based on interviews and rating scales. The Vineland Social Maturity Scale consists of 117 items arranged hierarchically into several categories: self-help general, self-help eating, self-help dressing, self-help direction, occupation, communication, locomotion, and socialization. The AAMD Adaptive Behavior Scale is com-

---

TABLE 8–3
Categories of Mental Retardation and the Associated IQ Ranges

	IQ			
System	100 95 90 85 80 75 70 65 60 55 50 45 40 35 30 25 20 15 10 5 0			
American Association on Mental Deficiency	Mild	Moderate	Severe	Profound
American Educators	Educable		Trainable	Custodial

Source: From D. P. Hallahan and J. M. Kauffman, *Exceptional Children,* © 1978, p. 68. Reprinted by permission of Prentice-Hall, Inc., Englewood Cliffs, New Jersey.

TABLE 8–4

Behavioral and Personality Domains Evaluated by the AAMD Adaptive Behavior Scale

Part I	Part II
Independent functioning	Violent and destructive behavior
Physical development	Antisocial behavior
Economic activity	Rebellious behavior
Language development	Untrustworthy behavior
Numbers and terms	Withdrawal
Domestic activity	Stereotype behavior and odd mannerisms
Vocational activities	Inappropriate interpersonal manners
Self-direction	Unacceptable vocal habits
Responsibility	Unacceptable or eccentric habits
Socialization	Self-abusive behavior
	Hyperactive tendencies
	Sexually aberrant behavior
	Psychological disturbances
	Use of medications

Source: Adapted from J. M. Kauffman and J. S. Payne, eds. Mental retardation: Introduction and personal perspectives (Columbus, Ohio: Charles E. Merrill, 1975), pp. 99–101.

posed of two major sections and subdivisions, shown in Table 8–4. These two scales are among the most frequently used to evaluate adaptive behavior, but they are used only as general measures of functioning.

As a group, mentally retarded children are slow to walk, talk, and feed themselves. They also take unusually long periods of time before they are toilet trained. In the more severe cases, retardation extends to almost all areas of anatomical, motor, and verbal development. Because intellectually normal children also may display one or more of these indicators, it is usually not assumed that a young child is retarded unless a pattern of deficits is present.

By far the largest group of retarded individuals are classified as mildly or educably mentally retarded; these people are rarely institutionalized. Of course, even with a mild level of retardation a child will have a difficult time in school and is likely to lag behind average children of the same age. An educably retarded youngster can acquire many of the academic skills mastered by elementary school children, but reaches this level of achievement at a later age. There are many jobs the mildly retarded are quite capable of filling; they have become welders, miners, painters, and tailors. Because success depends more on social skills than on occupational ones (Telford and Sawrey, 1972), parents of these children must avoid the temptation to keep such children dependent, or to "excuse" them because of intellectual deficit.

The moderately or trainably retarded are usually unable to hold jobs except within sheltered workshops; they rarely marry and often are institutionalized. For the profoundly retarded—with IQs below 25—institutionalization is almost inevitable. Among these individuals, interpersonal communication is minimal or lacking. Learning even the simplest kind of self-care often proves extremely difficult or downright impossible.

Cognitive Deficits

Retardation literally means slowness in development. In fact, mentally retarded individuals often perform like younger nonretarded children who are their intellectual peers. For example, on memory tasks, retarded adolescents whose *mental* age is 6 years perform like nonretarded 6-year-olds (Kail, 1984). Retarded adolescents and younger nonretarded children also perform similarly on Piaget's conservation tasks: Individuals in both groups with a mental age of 5 years typically fail the conservation tasks, but those with a mental age of 9 years pass them (Gruen and Vore, 1972).

These similarities in performance are so widespread that Piaget's associate, Bärbel Inhelder (1968), has described levels of retardation in terms of Piaget's stages. The mildly retarded are viewed as functioning no higher than the concrete operational stage; the moderately retarded as not surpassing the preoperational stage; and the severely and profoundly retarded as functioning at the sensorimotor stage (Robinson and Robinson, 1976). Retardation can thus be considered a failure to progress beyond certain stages. The retarded child passes through the usual stages of cognitive development more slowly than the nonretarded child and reaches a lower limit (Weisz and Zigler, 1979).

One implication of this developmental viewpoint is that efforts to train cognitive skills in the mentally retarded can be based on training studies with young nonretarded children. The Close-Up illustrates this for the case of memory deficits in mentally retarded persons.

The developmental model of mental retardation has had an enormous impact on educational practices for the mentally retarded in recent years. The model provides three basic ideas to guide education of the retarded: (1) The growth of intellectual skills follows a developmental hierarchy that is largely the same for all children. (2) The development of these skills always proceeds from the simpler to the more complex. (3) The more complex skills are created or "built" from combining and coordinating the simpler ones (Haring and Bricker, 1976). Nevertheless, educators must remember that the developmental model itself is a theoretical concept and that even intellectually normal children do not follow the same lock-step pattern of intellectual growth. Thus, the model is not a cookbook; it should be just a guide, not a rule (Switzky, Rotatori, Miller, and Freagon, 1979).

Social and Emotional Factors

If we think of mental retardation as simply an intellectual disadvantage, then we will pay little attention to the way in which it may be intertwined with social and emotional factors. Yet it is clear that these other factors are important (Cytryn and Lourie, 1980). Regardless of the depth or cause of a child's intellectual disability, the home environment and the incentives provided to learn important skills can do much to relieve the problem—or make it worse.

Teaching Retarded Individuals to Use Memory Strategies

Educable mentally retarded individuals typically perform poorly on memory tasks. One reason is that mentally retarded persons are not likely to use memory strategies like those described in Chapter 7 (Kail, 1984). That is, the mentally retarded child, like the preschool and young school-age child, does not routinely use strategies when confronted with a memory problem. For example, retarded individuals are unlikely to rehearse information to be remembered and they are equally unlikely to organize information into categories.

Having identified a memory limitation in retarded people, a logical next step is to determine if we can improve retention through training. Ideally, such training would result in long-lasting improvements that can be generalized to other situations. Such long-lasting training *can* be achieved. Brown, Campione, and Murphy (1974) taught retarded children to rehearse as an aid to memory. Six months later, the subjects were retested without further instruction or reference to the training. They rehearsed just as effectively as they had immediately following instruction.

Amount of training is one key to success. Brief training can improve use of strategies, but the improvement is short. Apparently, training must continue until the individuals use the strategy nearly perfectly (Borkowski and Cavanaugh, 1979).

Generalization of a trained strategy has been more difficult to achieve (Campione and Brown, 1977). The fragility of training was also illustrated by Brown, Campione, and Murphy (1977). The same retarded individuals who had demonstrated long-lasting training effects (Brown et al., 1974) were later tested on a slightly different memory task for which rehearsal was again appropriate. Their performance resembled that of a control group of retarded subjects who had received no

training. Rehearsal training seemed to be linked specifically to a particular context.

One idea for improved training stems from the diagnosis-treatment-monitoring sequence described in Chapter 7. Memory training programs typically involve the treatment phase of this sequence; diagnosis and monitoring are neglected. The consequences of such training become evident if we continue the medical analogy. Suppose physicians were well trained in the treatment of heart disease, but were taught to recognize only one symptom. They would not recognize other symptoms, and, like the retarded adolescent, would not "generalize" (prescribe appropriate treatment). The training given to retarded persons in previous studies may result in similar tunnel vision: The trained strategy may be associated only with a specific task and goal.

This analogy suggests a way to improve training programs. Medical students learn that multiple symptoms can point to a common diagnosis and treatment. Perhaps retarded individuals should be taught the same way. A study by Belmont, Butterfield, and Borkowski (1978) illustrates this type of training and its impact on memory. These investigators began by teaching retarded adolescents to rehearse. Some retarded subjects were taught the essentials of verbal rehearsal. Then they were encouraged to use this strategy on a number of different memory problems. Other individuals were also taught to rehearse but they were shown how rehearsal could be modified to fit different tasks. That is, these subjects learned how careful diagnosis of a problem dictates the best form for a memory strategy.

Subsequently, there was a test of generalization involving a memory task that was new to all subjects. Subjects who had received only the original rehearsal training did not rehearse on the generalization task. Their recall was very poor. Individuals given diagnostic training rehearsed skillfully, and their recall on the generalization task was essentially as accurate as on tasks used during training. Thus, a retarded person appears to be most likely to generalize a newly learned strategy if he or she understands some of the reasons why the strategy works.

Home Environment. A child's home environment plays a primary role in all aspects of social and emotional development. So it is not surprising to discover that distinct patterns of home and family environment accompany retardation. The President's Task Force on Manpower Conservation (1964) found that the families of draftees rejected for intellectual deficits were characterized by poverty and poor education. Benda, Squires, Ogonik, and Wise (1963) indicated that among 205 retarded persons with IQs greater than 50, the majority had another retarded person in the immediate family. Three-quarters of the families were separated or not able to provide even bare necessities. Other family factors include low achievement motivation of parents, father's absence, low emphasis on education, and lack of sensory stimulation (Bradley and Tedesco, 1982; Robinson and Robinson, 1970).

A rather specific effect of early home experiences on retardation has to do with motivation. Retarded children may have been neglected more frequently by adults and may therefore crave attention and praise to a greater degree than their mental age alone would predict. To test this, Zigler and Balla (1972) compared the influence of social praise on the behavior of normal and retarded children of mental ages 7, 9, and 12. They predicted that younger and retarded children, if given praise, would continue to perform a boring task for a longer time than older and normal individuals. The results confirmed their expectation; younger children performed the boring task longer than older ones and retarded children persisted more than normals. Especially striking was the finding that even the oldest retarded individuals performed the boring task for a greater period of time than the youngest normal children.

Finally, the home environment may influence the most important decision of all: whether to institutionalize the child. For brighter retarded persons, institutionalization is much more likely when the home environment has been inadequate than when parents have been able to provide the attention and care their children need (Zigler, 1968).

Educational Environment. All education is based on incentives of one sort or another, but retarded children may be motivated by different incentives than typical middle-class youngsters. And it is middle-class children's needs and tastes that determine many educational practices.

Talkington (1971) trained educable mentally retarded adolescents to perform a rather complex motor task under four incentive conditions. In the *reward only* condition, students simply received a token reward (later

exchangeable for money) for each correct response; in the *response cost* condition, participants received twenty tokens as a sort of legacy at the beginning of each training session but lost one token for each error. Youngsters in the *reward and cost* condition received ten tokens at the beginning of each session and then received a token for each correct response but lost one for each error. Finally, subjects in the *no reward, no cost* condition served as a control group and received no incentives.

Talkington's results were very clear. The *response cost* condition was by far the most effective way to teach these youngsters, and it resulted in fewer errors than reward alone, regardless of whether it was used by itself or combined with reward. What is more, performance was at essentially the same level for both *response cost* and *reward and cost* groups, indicating that the reward provided no additional motivation. Talkington interprets the token removal procedure as a failure experience and suggests that the *response cost* technique was effective for these retarded youngsters just because it elicited their strong motivation to avoid failure.

Talkington's study meshes with a considerable body of earlier evidence showing that retarded persons are generally more motivated to avoid failure than to achieve success (Zigler, 1968). The underlying process appears to arise from the fact that retarded individuals have backgrounds of many failures. As a result, the desire to avoid failure is particularly important for them when faced with new problems. Retarded children are therefore more likely than normal children of the same *mental* age to "settle for" poor performance even when they can do better (Balla and Zigler, 1979). Building positive self-concepts should be a high-priority goal for anyone teaching retarded children.

Does intellectual retardation prevent the development of appropriate social skills? There is a clear correlation between mental age and social competence (Goulet and Barclay, 1963). It has been argued, though, that the relationship may not be a direct result of mental retardation. Perhaps it is not mental retardation itself but the lack of training in more advanced social skills that gives rise to the correlation (Gunzburg, 1965).

Severy and Davis (1971) have provided evidence for this view. They studied helping behavior of normal and retarded children under conditions in which the retarded children were "in a milieu containing models of and rewards for helping behavior" (p. 1019). There was no evidence of a lack in helping behavior among retarded children in this situation; in fact, the older retarded individuals actually attempted to give help more often than the groups of intellectually normal children.

Even among severely retarded children, careful and systematic use of modeling and reinforcement can be used to teach positive social skills and interactions. In one study (Paloutzian, Hasazi, Streifel, and Edgar, 1971) severely retarded children were trained in such tasks as passing a beanbag to another child or pulling another child on a wagon. Before these experiences the children had made no attempts to interact with others and simply played aimlessly by themselves. After training, the children began to observe the play of more advanced peers and in some cases began appropriate interactions themselves.

Unfortunately, behaviors developed by such special training do not always generalize. One retarded adolescent, trained to greet people, behaved this way so persistently that she had to be punished (Greenspan, 1979). In other cases, training disappears when reinforcement is no longer available. Following up a one-year training program in social competence skills, Lawrence and Kartye (1971) found that the severely and profoundly retarded girls who participated had lost most of their earlier social gains within four months, although they retained most of the self-help skills learned during the program. The results suggest that either long-term training or continued external reinforcement, or perhaps both, are needed to train severely retarded children to adapt socially. On the other hand, the findings also suggest that the task *can* be accomplished.

THE INTELLECTUALLY GIFTED AND CREATIVE

We now turn to the opposite end of the IQ spectrum, the exceptionally gifted. Because humans have always been fascinated by the unusual, many myths and attitudes have grown up around the exceptionally gifted and talented. Historically the gifted have been associated with either the supernatural or with madness (Albert, 1975). Goethe spoke of poets as "plain children of God," and the word "divine" is often applied to artists. For Aristotle, "there is no genius without madness."

These attitudes still exist today in stereotypes of the gifted as being strange, odd, socially inept, maladapted, and downright "crazy." But studies of the gifted paint a strikingly different picture. Several such studies began in the 1920s and 1930s. Among the most influential is the

Stanford study of the gifted, begun in 1922 by Lewis Terman. Terman attempted to identify factors that influenced life success among gifted men. The subjects were first rated on life success—the extent to which they made use of their abilities—and then the 150 who rated highest and the 150 who rated lowest were examined. The most spectacular difference, according to Terman, was the greater drive to achieve and the greater mental and social adjustment of the successful group. With regard to the notion that the gifted are strange, Terman said:

> Our data do not support the theory . . . that great achievement usually stems from emotional tensions that border on the abnormal. In our gifted group, success is associated with stability rather than instability, with absence rather than with presence of disturbing conflicts—in short with well-balanced temperament and with freedom from excessive frustrations.

What Is Creativity?

Most people recognize in others and in themselves something that seems to go beyond intelligence, something that might be labeled creativity. An exact definition of creativity, though, is hard to come by. Researchers have begun by asking whether creativity can, in fact, be distinguished from intelligence.

One strategy employed to test the validity of this distinction has been to compare "average" people with very successful people in various occupations, such as art, scientific research, mathematics, and writing. Are those who have made the most significant adult contributions the ones with higher intelligence? Did they have the better grades in school? In one study (Helson and Crutchfield, 1970) involving mathematicians, the index of creativity was nominations by other mathematicians for significant accomplishment. The highly creative scholars were compared with others, matched for age (they were all in their late 30s), who had doctorates from universities of equally high standing. The men in the two groups were approximately equal in terms of the amount of time they spent on their work, yet, by agreement of their peers, they differed markedly in terms of the quality of their products. It came as a surprise, then, that the two groups were entirely comparable in terms of IQ as usually measured. At this range of ability, intelligence was unrelated to creativity.

In fact, those who are creatively accomplished as adults are often not identifiable by school grades. "As students," writes researcher D. W. MacKinnon of one sample of creative individuals, "they were, in general, not distinguished for the grades they received, and in none of the samples did their high school grade-point average show any significant correlation with their subsequently achieved and recognized creativeness" (1968, p. 103).

Using a different strategy, Getzels and Jackson (1975) were able to distinguish two groups of adolescents attending a private school. One group was labeled "highly intelligent" and the other "highly creative." The groups were equally superior in academic achievement. But the highly intelligent students were in the top 20 percent on standard IQ measures but not in the top 20 percent on measures of creativity. The highly creative ones showed the reverse pattern. Several differences were apparent between the groups. Teachers expressed a clear preference for having the high IQ students in class compared to the highly creative. The high IQ students displayed the desire to possess qualities that would lead to later success. The creative students did not appear to select present goals on the basis of future success. Also, compared to the high IQ students, the creative students deemphasized the value of high marks, IQ, pep and energy, character, and goal directedness. They valued instead a wide range of interests, emotional stability, and a sense of humor. And finally, the relationship between students' personal aspirations and the qualities they believed teachers preferred differed for the two groups. The high IQ students held a self-ideal that was harmonious with the attributes they believed teachers approved of. The self-ideal of the highly creative was not only *not* harmonious, but was also negatively correlated with what they believed to be the teachers' ideal qualities.

From these studies, as well as a number of others, the conclusion is that, in general, creativity and intelligence refer to different aspects of human ability (Kogan, 1983). We may still ask, though, what kind of thinking is associated with creativity.

J. P. Guilford (1957, 1966) proposed that the distinction between convergent and divergent thinking is relevant for understanding creativity. *Convergent* thinking involves integration of established information to ar-

FIGURE 8–11
Creative products display appropriate yet novel use of elements and ideas. Bill Anderson, Monkmeyer.

rive at the standard, correct answer. *Divergent* thinking goes off in many directions to arrive at an answer in cases in which no one answer is necessarily correct. It is this divergent mode that indicates creativity, according to Guilford.

The most commonly used measures of divergent thinking involve *ideational fluency*—the ability to produce a large number of ideas when asked to be productive (Kogan, 1983). Ideational fluency can be tapped by asking children to name all the things they can think of that can be used for cooking, or all the things they can think of that are round. In more than seventy studies, ideational fluency tests of divergent thinking have been found to correlate positively with various indexes of real-life creative activity or accomplishment (Barron and Harrington, 1981).

What characteristics are associated with creativity in children? La Greca (1980) found that the most creative third and sixth graders, as measured by ideational fluency tests, were much better able than other children to verbalize strategies such as scanning the immediate environment for ideas. The less creative children tended to take a passive attitude toward the test. Usually they just waited for ideas to come to them.

Creativity in the Preschool Years

Researchers have been particularly interested in trying to understand signs of creativity in the preschool years, and in trying to foster creativity by cultivating it early in life. Creativity in young children shows itself as spontaneity, playfulness, and a tendency, even at a young age, to see the humorous side of things (Dansky, 1980). Singer and Rummo (1973), for example, measured creativity in a group of seventy-nine kindergarten children and then correlated the children's ideational fluency scores with teacher ratings of various aspects of the children's classroom behavior. They found, as did Dansky and Lieberman (1977), that the most creative children, as measured by the test, were generally more playful than other children; they also found the most creative children more erratic in their work and more likely to respond aggressively to frustration than other children.

Other researchers have sought to influence young children's creativity. Pepler and Ross (1981) presented 3- and 4-year-old children with convergent or divergent play materials to see if they could influence performance on a test of divergent thinking. The convergent play materials consisted of colored pieces that fit together into a form board. The divergent play materials consisted of unrelated play pieces such as an assortment of colored random shapes. The divergent play materials clearly helped subsequent performance on a test of ideational fluency. And the children's other play activities seemed to become more flexible and imaginative, which suggests that encouraging children to play in a creative fashion may produce general advances in tendencies to approach tasks creatively.

We may wonder, though, as we did with IQ, whether creativity in children this young is related to creativity as measured or expressed later in their lives. Harrington, Block, and Block (1983) reported the results of a longitudinal study of creativity spanning seven years, from preschool (age 4) to preadolescence (age 11). The preschool creativity test consisted of a question geared toward measuring a child's ability to come up with creative instances ("Tell me all the things you can think of that are round") and an alternative uses test ("Name all the different ways a newspaper, ceramic cup, table knife, and coat hanger can be used"). Answers to the instances test were considered high quality if they referred to objects that were truly round and not found in the testing room. Answers on the alternative uses test were considered high quality if they referred to possible but unintended uses, such as using a newspaper to start a fire.

Seven years later, when the children were in elementary school, they were all individually rated by their teachers for degree of creativity. As predicted, highly creative answers given by a child at age 4 significantly predicted high teacher ratings of creativity for that child at age 11. These results show the consistency of creativity in childhood and demonstrate that it is a characteristic which can be separated from general intelligence. They also demonstrate the importance of viewing creativity in terms of the quality as well as the sheer quantity of divergent thinking.

THEORIES OF INTELLIGENCE

Psychometric Theories

Thus far we have considered the "practical" side of intelligence—the use of mental tests to predict achievement in schools and to identify individuals whose intellectual skills are exceptional. We have also examined some of the factors associated with intelligence, such as home environment. In all these instances, we have been equating intelligence with performance on mental tests. In fact, psychologists who specialize in tests and measurement, *psychometricians*, have used test performance as the basis for elaborate *psychometric* theories of intelligence.

The great debate among psychometricians has been whether intelligence is best thought of as a series of independent, specific intellectual skills or whether it is more general and global, not divisible into components (Kail and Pellegrino, 1985). To test this idea, a group of individuals is given a large number of different tests, each of which is supposed to measure intelligence. It is assumed that success on some of the tests requires skill in one area, whereas success on other tests requires skill in other areas. For example, some tests might require skill in memory for verbal material; others might require the ability to work effectively with abstract mathematical concepts. The experimenter tries to discover different groups of tests, each of which requires a different skill. To achieve that objective, the experimenter uses a statistical technique called *factor analysis*. Cattell (1965) has suggested that the logic underlying this technique is similar to the logic a jungle hunter might use in deciding whether a set of dark blobs in a river is three separate rotting logs or a single alligator. To make this decision, the hunter watches for movement. If the blobs move together, it is assumed that they are part of the same structure, an alligator. If they do not move together, they are three different structures, three logs. Similarly, if changes in performance on one test are accompanied by changes in performance on a second test—that is, they move together—one could assume that the tests are measuring the same attribute or *factor*. It remains for the investigator to give a name to each factor.

Some research, beginning with the work of Charles Spearman (1904), supports the idea that a general factor, or *g*, is responsibile for performance on all mental tests. Other results are more consistent with the belief that intelligence consists of distinct abilities. For example, Thurstone and Thurstone (1941) concluded that there are seven primary abilities: perceptual speed, word comprehension, word fluency, space, number, memory, and induction. They also acknowledged a general factor that operated in all tasks, but emphasized that analysis of the several factors is more useful in assessing intellectual ability.

These conflicting findings have led many theorists to propose *hierarchical* theories of intelligence that include both general and specific components. Vernon (1965), for example, proposed the theory shown in Figure 8–12. At the top of the hierarchy is *g*. The first major distinction is between verbal-eductional ability (*v:ed*) and spatial-practical-mechanical ability (*k:m*). Each of these factors can be subdivided. The verbal-educational factor includes verbal and numerical skills; the spatial-practical-mechanical factor includes perceptual speed and spatial ability.

Another way to combine the general and specific approaches is to view intelligence as becoming more differentiated as a function of age and education. That is, intelligence may be global in young children and become more specific as they develop. Factor analytic studies provide results consistent with this view (Garrett, 1946). However, this research is complicated by the fact that tests administered at different age levels may not measure the same abilities. For example, tests of verbal ability contain different items at various ages, and the intellectual demands of those items may not be the same. So what appears to be differentiation due to age may reflect greater differences among test items for older individuals, *not* greater differences among older individuals. Because of this problem, the differentiation hypothesis remains reasonable but unproved.

FIGURE 8–12
Vernon's hierarchical theory of intelligence.
Adapted from Eysenck (1979). *The Structure and Measurement of Intelligence.* (New York: Springer-Verlag). By permission.

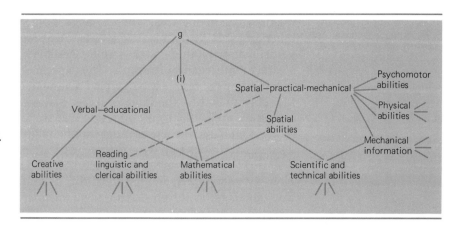

For most of the twentieth century, psychometric theories of intelligence evolved independently of the theories of intellectual development discussed in chapters 6 and 7. Only recently have developmental psychologists tried to integrate psychometric theories with developmental theories derived from Jean Piaget and information-processing psychology. These new theories draw on the assets of the traditional approaches to create a much broader theory of intelligence and its development. One ambitious theory of this sort is Howard Gardner's *theory of multiple intelligences* (1983). Instead of using test performance as the basis for his theory, Gardner proposes several "signs" that can be used to identify distinct intelligences:

1. *Isolation by brain damage.* Often injury to the brain impairs a specific intellectual skill, but leaves other skills intact.
2. *The existence of exceptional talent.* Some individuals are truly extraordinarily skilled in one intellectual domain, but ordinary—or even retarded—in most other domains.
3. *A distinct developmental history.* If an intelligence is independent, it should develop in a reliable sequence of initial, intermediate, and advanced levels of proficiency.
4. *An evolutionary history.* Intellectual skills have emerged as the human species has evolved. Hence, a well-defined evolutionary sequence helps to identify autonomous intelligences.
5. *A set of core operations.* If an intelligence is independent, associated with it should be a distinct set of mental operations.

Using these signs, Gardner identifies six distinct intelligences. Some are common to psychometric theories of intelligence: linguistic intelligence, logical-mathematical intelligence, and spatial intelligence. However, three intelligences are not: musical intelligence, bodily kinesthetic intelligence, and the personal intelligence. Gardner's view of musical intelligence gives a glimpse of this unique approach to characterizing intelligence. An impressive array of evidence supports Gardner's claim for a musical intelligence:

1. *Selective impairment.* Studies of individuals with brain damage demonstrate the independence of musical intelligence. The Russian composer Shebalin was afflicted with Wernicke's aphasia, in which speech remains fluent but comprehension is impaired. Nevertheless, Shebalin could understand and compose music as skillfully as ever. Another case of Wernicke's aphasia involved a pianist whose playing skill was unaffected by the damage to his brain. He remained able to recognize pieces and hear errors in a performance. Only when verbal skills were needed—for example, to identify a note by name—were his musical skills impaired by his aphasia (Gardner, 1982).

2. *Exceptional individuals.* Music is rich with legends of prodigies. The best known is Mozart, whose talent as a performer and composer was evident early in childhood. Less known are *idiot savants*, individuals who may suffer from extreme mental retardation, yet are musically quite talented. Gardner (1983) describes ". . . Harriet [who] was able to play 'Happy Birthday' in the style of various composers, including Mozart, Beethoven, Verdi, and Schubert. . . . At the age of three, her mother called her by playing incomplete melodies, which the child would then complete with the appropriate tone in the proper octave" (p. 121). Many idiot savants can play a tune correctly after a single hearing and do so without any formal musical training (Shuter-Dyson, 1982).

3. *The development of musical competence.* Children begin to sing as infants: By 2 or 3 months of age, babies often alternate between high- and low-pitched cooing. Also, when mothers coo along, infants often imitate the pitch and volume of the mothers' "songs."

This musical play continues in the preschool years. Children invent their own songs; they also experiment with different intervals between pitches. At the same time, some musical socialization is evident, as children learn phrases of familiar songs. However, by the end of the preschool years: ". . . the melodies of the dominant culture have won out, and the production of spontaneous songs and exploratory sound play generally wanes" (Gardner, 1983, p. 109).

For most children living in Western cultures, musical ability does not develop much after the preschool years. Individuals learn more songs, and sing them with greater precision and feeling, but there are no further qualitative changes. For musically talented children, however, skills continue to develop. In the early elementary school years,

> The child proceeds on the basis of sheer talent and energy: he learns pieces readily because of his sensitive musical ear and memory. . . . A period of more sustained skill building commences around the age of nine or so, when the child must begin to practice seriously, even to the extent that it may interfere with his school and his friendships. (Gardner, 1983, p. 111–112)

A second change occurs in adolescence, when young musicians must ". . . supplement their intuitive understanding with a more systematic knowledge of music lore and law" (Gardner, 1983, p. 111).

Musical development, then, has two tiers. One tier is for all individuals; the second, for the musically talented. Nevertheless, Gardner speculates that these tiers exist only because most Western cultures tolerate "musical illiteracy." Unlike reading, science, or math, instruction in music receives little emphasis in schools. Perhaps more individuals would progress to the second tier if systematic musical instruction were the rule.

As Gardner's work makes clear, the question "What is intelligence?" is still being debated. So it is obviously unwise and unfair to make important decisions about children (or adults) based solely on an intelligence test score. It is clear that people differ substantially from one another in how well they adapt to and deal with their environments. Much has been learned about these differences in the past 60 years; learning even more about the many facets of intelligence and how they develop remains an exciting task for psychologists.

SUMMARY

1. Intelligence testing has been common in schools for most of this century because it allows educators to predict school performance and place children according to their intellectual levels.

2. Test construction involves selecting a representative sample of test items and administering them to a *standardization* group. The test must also show consistency (*reliability*) and it must be related to school performance and other pertinent criteria (*validity*).

3. The original Stanford-Binet test became extremely popular because it introduced the concept of intelligence quotient, or IQ, which allowed individuals of different ages to be compared directly. The Stanford-Binet consists of many cognitive and motor tasks, ranging from easy to difficult.

4. The other widely used tests are the Wechsler tests, including the WAIS for adults, the WISC for school children, and the WPPSI for children 4 to 6.

5. None of these tests is appropriate for infants, for whom special tests have been developed. Most infant tests do not correlate very well with later test performance. In contrast, Wechsler and Stanford-Binet scores obtained at age 4 or 5 correlate quite well with IQ as an adolescent or adult.

6. IQ scores vary considerably for some individuals over the life span. Also, as people grow older certain aspects of their IQs, particularly those unrelated to experience (*fluid intelligence*), decline; verbal and other experience-related IQ items (*crystallized intelligence*) continue to rise into senior adulthood.

7. SES, race, and ethnicity are all related to IQ, in part because these variables are associated with the environments in which children are reared. The question of whether IQ tests are culturally fair has been a subject for debate and experiment.

8. Mental retardation is the condition that results from the combination of subaverage intellectual functioning and the presence of deficits in adaptive behavior. Some retardation occurs simply because a certain percentage of individuals is at the low end of the normal IQ distribution (*familial mental retardation*), but retardation can also be *biologically caused* by some particular damage or defect.

9. Mental retardation is usually scaled into three or four levels. *Mildly* retarded persons are rarely institutionalized and are quite

capable of filling many jobs. *Moderately* retarded individuals can work only in sheltered workshops and are often institutionalized. Those who are *severely* retarded may be trained to perform very simple tasks and are quite likely to be institutionalized. *Profoundly* retarded individuals are unable to communicate with others except on a primitive level and are almost always institutionalized.

10. The developmental model of retardation states that the development of intellectual skills follows the same course for normal and retarded individuals, so that a retarded child has the cognitive skills of a younger nonretarded child. The model has been useful in developing ways to teach retarded children memory strategies. With appropriate training and encouragement, many retarded individuals can also be taught relatively advanced social skills.

11. People with unusually high IQs were once thought to be peculiar or strange, but a classic study by Terman showed that, if anything, very bright individuals tend to be better adjusted and more stable than others. Terman also found that the degree of success actually achieved by the very bright depends on their drive to achieve and on the quality of their individual adjustment.

12. Creativity can be differentiated from IQ, and appears to involve *divergent* thinking—that is, the ability to let one's thought go off in many directions. Creativity has also been shown to be reasonably stable from the preschool years through adolescence to adulthood, provided appropriate tests are used.

13. *Psychometric theories of intelligence* have long been divided according to whether they conceive of intelligence as primarily a single factor (*g*) or a set of independent, specific factors. One solution is to view intelligence as *hierarchical*, with *g* at the top but with various specific skills (such as scientific ability, reading ability, and psychomotor ability) feeding into it.

14. Gardner's *theory of multiple intelligences* relies on signs rather than test scores to advance its claim that there are six different intelligences. These include three that parallel abilities found in psychometric theories (linguistic, logical-mathematical, and spatial intelligence) and three that are new (musical, bodily kinesthetic, and personal intelligence).

9 SOCIALIZATION

We all know the phrases and the routines of socialization: "Don't touch the stove—hot-hot." "Watch me." "This is the way to do it." "Say *please*." "Tell Mommy (or Daddy or Grandma) when you want to go to the bathroom." "Let Jackie play with your toys." and realize that these exchanges are a vital part of development—learning how to live as a member of our group. *Socialization* is the set of events and processes by which we acquire the beliefs and behaviors of the particular society and subgroup into which we are born (Maccoby, 1980). It depends in part on cognitive and language skills and in part on biological factors and the physical environment.

Many goals of socialization are common to all societies. At the same time, each society and subgroup evolves some more or less unique practices and goals in order to maintain itself in its particular ecological niche. As Lerner and Shea (1982) explain:

> As the settings within which humans lived changed and became more and more differentiated and complex, new adaptational demands were placed on people in order for them to maintain and perpetuate themselves. . . . Different units took on different roles, and role structure became more complex, more specialized, and more independent as society evolved.

> [Because] individuals needed the group for their survival at the same time that the group needed individuals (to populate and perpetuate it) children born into a society were always instructed in the rules and tasks of that society (i.e., they were socialized) in order to ensure their eventual contribution to society's maintenance. Society, the roles it evolves, and the process of socialization within society are all components of adaptive individual and social functioning. (p. 507)

Socialization depends on the contexts and settings in which it occurs (Bronfenbrenner, 1979). A child is associated with—and influenced by— many overlapping units: a national culture, one or more ethnic cultures, a local culture, a socioeconomic group, and a family, including parents, brothers and sisters, and other relatives. Each of these units plays a different role in the socialization process.

Parents are usually the first socializing agents to whom a child is exposed. In addition to representing the culture, they are also the bearers of their own individual characteristics, personal ideas, and values. But parents do not have sole influence for long. By the time the child is 2, siblings, relatives, and friends of the family interact with him or her to provide some modeling and perhaps even systematic reinforcement. Television viewing on a regular basis has also begun by this age. Next, playground, nursery school, and kindergarten experiences add the input of other children and other caretakers. Entry into grade school adds a wider assortment of peers. It also injects the routine of a formal and highly structured institution—the school and school authority. By adolescence, youngsters join peers in a distinctive subculture, and they begin to use the public news media. Adolescents also begin to affiliate with political and religious groups of their own choosing, and these institutions and people exert an influence that, like the others, will continue to operate indefinitely.

We will discuss how these influences combine and interact throughout the remainder of this book. We begin this chapter with a discussion of the family as the focal point of all socialization. We continue with an examination of the cultural aspects—the cross-cultural similarities and differences in socialization. We conclude with a closer look at the underlying mechanisms through which each of these forces exerts its influence. Not only do parents, peers, and teachers act as direct agents of socialization, and thereby influence the children with whom they come in contact, but they are, in turn, also influenced *by* them.

THE FAMILY

The family has many functions in societies: It serves as an economic unit, it helps satisfy adult sexual drives, and it assumes responsibility for a small number of people as they move through life. But perhaps its most widely recognized function is the care and socialization of new generations.

The exact form of the family may vary from society to society, and even within one society. In no society, however, is there a complete lack of family influence on the developing child, even when the responsibility for child rearing is more diffuse than it is in the United States. Parents are, in fact, usually considered the primary agents of socialization because their influence begins so early in life. Psychologists focus on the effects of parents and siblings living in the same household—that is, the so-called *nuclear family*.

Family Configuration

Family configuration is a term that refers to the number of adults and children in a nuclear family, and to the genders and relative ages of the children. A staggering number of different configurations is possible. Both parents can be present (an intact or two-parent family), or only a mother or father. In addition, each child may have no siblings, just one, or as many as three, four, five, or more. The siblings may be all boys, all girls, or an assortment; the siblings may also be separated by age differences as small as 11 months or as wide as 20 years. Each child's birth order also affects family configuration.

Not only do the number, configuration, and spacing of siblings have effects, but the different reactions of parents to these variables also influence socialization. Here is a personal description of one daughter's experience:

> I had the distinction of having one brother 6 years older than I—who reportedly greeted me with considerable pride and love. I was followed in 3½ years by two more brothers. This was our family until my sister arrived when I was almost 10 years old. My older brother was a model for me. I was able to follow my brother in important ways, primarily by doing well in school and being

active and agile physically. The entire family worked in the family business, which required fairly heavy outdoor physical activities. But as the only female besides my mother for many years, I also participated in household tasks and in caring for my younger brothers. In this respect I became a little mother, caring and bossy. This role was so strong that when I had two sons close in age many years later, I occasionally called them by the names of these brothers—in the correct age order. Despite the fact that I consider my childhood happy, I was lonely for a sister. Not another sibling, but a *sister*. One of the greatest joys of my life occurred early one Monday morning when my older brother returning on his bicycle from a telephone (as we had no home phone) announced, "It's a girl." Because my older brother was already 16 years of age he was able to visit our sister in the hospital; I had to wait several days. On the day she came home I pretended a stomach ache so that my father allowed me to skip school. I rushed to clean furiously so that all would be ready. For years I believed that my father thought that I had had a stomach ache. My sister has always been special to me. We talk sometimes of how different her family experiences were, as the last child with siblings so much older than she. In a real way, she grew up in a different family than I did.

In the discussion that follows we summarize a few of the major findings that have been reported about family configuration. As Bronfenbrenner (1979) points out, given the fact that the nuclear family is the central, dynamic system underlying our entire culture and society, it is surprising that there have been so few investigations of the family as a working unit.

First-Born Children. Possible differences between first-born and later born children have been among the most studied aspects of family configuration and socialization. A study of first- and second-born siblings, when each was 3 months old (Jacobs and Moss, 1976), found that mothers spent significantly less time in social, affectionate, or even caretaking activities with their second-born children. One reason for this appears to be that certain reactions from the first born when their mothers attended to the new babies were sufficient to get the mothers to shift their attention from the new babies to them.

Whether because of the additional attention they get or for other reasons, first-born children are generally more successful than later born children in a variety of ways: They speak at an earlier age, tend to perform better on tests of intellectual ability, are more likely to attend college, and are more likely to be recognized as scholars (Clausen, 1966). There is also evidence that they are achievement-oriented and somewhat conformist, and they adopt the standards and values of their parents (Altus, 1965).

Parents place great importance on their first children; they are tense about handling them; they hold high expectations for them; they give them attention and affection (Jacobs and Moss, 1976). First borns become the "little adults" in the family, garnering knowledge, power, authority, and responsibility (Sears, Maccoby, and Levin, 1957).

Younger Siblings.   Another consistent pattern for which there is substantial data involves children reared with the influence of older siblings (Sutton-Smith and Rosenberg, 1970). Boys of preschool age exhibit more feminine behavior when they have older sisters and more masculine behavior when they have older brothers. Girls who have older brothers, compared to those with older sisters, tend to be "tomboyish," and those who have brothers rather than sisters are more aggressive and ambitious and perform better on tests of intellectual capacity.

In an interesting study, Dunn and Kendrick (1981) observed 40 sibling pairs at home when the infant sibling was 8 and 14 months of age. The clearest finding was that the older siblings showed much more friendly behavior to their new brothers and sisters if both children were of the same sex than if they were of the opposite sex. Further, same-sex pairs became more friendly between 8 and 14 months, whereas opposite-sex pairs became more negative over the same period. One possible explanation of these findings is jealousy, since mothers interacted considerably more with their younger children if their sex differed from that of the older sibling.

Only Children.   One configuration that was long thought to produce special problems is the family with an only child. "Onlies" were viewed as selfish and egotistical, dependent, lonely, and unsociable—all presumably because they lacked the tempering influence of siblings and got too much parental atttention. But a major study comparing onlies both with first-born children who later had brothers and sisters and with later born children revealed that, if anything, onlies are better off than other children (Polit, Nuttall, and Nuttall, 1980). Only children were found to achieve higher educational levels and occupational status than other children, and to be more secure in their social adjustment.

Parenting Styles

If we were to observe parents as socializers, could we identify dimensions on which they differ? Investigators have attempted to answer this question through studies involving interviews, questionnaires, and ratings of parents and children: The overall results suggest that there are important differences in parenting styles, and that these differences are significantly related to children's social and personality development. Among the most important dimensions of parenting is the degree and type of control parents exercise over children's behavior. Diana Baumrind, of the University of California at Berkeley, has been studying parental-control patterns for more than twenty years. Baumrind distinguishes three broad patterns. Not all parents fall into one of the categories, but most do.

Baumrind calls the first type of parenting style *authoritarian*. Authoritarian parents are strict in the traditional, old-fashioned sense: They lay down the rules and expect them to be followed without argument. Infractions are punished and debate about the rules is firmly discouraged. Hard work, respect, and obedience are what authoritarian parents wish to cultivate in their children. The children are often expected to contribute their part to the family (for example, by performing household chores on a regular basis, as a matter of duty).

Authoritative parents take a more "modern" approach. They are reasonably firm, but favor giving explanations for rules and encouraging give-and-take and discussion.

Permissive parents adopt a laissez-faire attitude. They give their children a great deal of latitude and place few demands or restrictions on them. They are often not very involved with their children, though they are likely to be helpful or generous when called upon.

In many ways permissive parents seem to be the least successful. Their children tend to remain immature and display little self-control. Not having been taught responsibility and not having had leadership modeled for them, they also tend to lack these characteristics. Unconditional acceptance appears to be inconsistent with basic parental responsibility. Baumrind's (1975) observations led her to state: "The exalted value placed upon unconditional love has, in my view, deterred many parents from fulfilling important parental responsibilities" (p. 16).

Authoritarian parents do not do much better. Their children are poorly motivated and tend to lack independence. The boys especially tend to be somewhat hostile.

Authoritative parents, in contrast, tend to have children who are responsible, self-reliant, and friendly. They are the products of what Baumrind (1975) calls *unconditional commitment:*

> By this is meant that the parent continues to take care of the child because it is his or her child, and not because of the child's merits. . . . This abiding interest is expressed not by gratifying the child's whims, nor in being gentle and kind when the child is being obnoxious, nor in making few demands upon the child. . . . Unconditional commitment means that the child's interests are perceived as among the parent's most important interests. . . . (p. 21)

Mothers

Despite all that has been said about recent changes in the American family, and despite the enormous cultural variety that differentiates places, times, and peoples, mothers are still the primary caretakers of children, especially infants and young children. Mothers play so many vital roles that we often do not even stop to think about them—except perhaps on Mother's Day.

Mothers provide nourishment, warmth, and protection. They also provide important cognitive and social input, even when they seem to be only playing with their children. Consider the games mothers in all societies seem to play with their babies (Field and Widmayer, 1982). In addition to contributing to emotional attachment, these games teach cognitive motor skills ("peek-a-boo") and such rudimentary social skills as turn taking in social interaction ("pat-a-cake").

Working Mothers. In the past two decades there has been an enormous increase in the number of mothers working outside the home; in fact, a majority of mothers—and more than one-third of mothers of infants and young children—now work. Lois Hoffman (1979), who reports these facts, points out that this important social change raises a question: What are the effects of maternal employment upon children?

The answer is clearer for girls than for boys. Girls seem to benefit, especially from the independence training and modeling of achievement striving a working mother provides. Hoffman (1979) concludes:

> The daughters of working mothers are more outgoing, independent, active, highly motivated, score higher on a variety of indices of academic achievement, and appear better adjusted on social and personality measures (p. 864).

For boys the picture is a bit more complicated. They too receive independence training as a result of having a working mother, and this training contributes to their independence. A working mother helps to socialize a boy into the sort of domestic situation he will probably face as a father in the next generation, when more couples will be sharing the role of breadwinner. But sons of working mothers show slightly lower IQs than sons of nonworking mothers, which may be a reflection of somewhat reduced intellectual stimulation during the preschool and early elementary school years.

A fascinating additional effect of maternal employment is that mothers who work tend to encourage in their children those behaviors they perceive as adaptive in their own jobs (Piotrkowski and Katz, 1982). A mother who values using good grammar and being well-spoken for her job may be more likely to emphasize these skills to her children.

We do not want to paint an overly optimistic picture for children who have working mothers, however. If both parents work, or if the mother works and the father is absent, a great deal depends on the amount and quality of alternative care provided for the child. Some families are able to provide excellent alternative care. At the other extreme we find so-called latch-key children, who return from school daily to an empty home and who are left to their own devices or depend on their friends on the street for guidance during the afternoon and sometimes the evening as well. Our conclusion that children of working mothers can do as well as those of mothers who remain at home applies only to those children who have appropriate care. Those who are simply left by themselves, especially during the earlier years of childhood, may suffer considerably as a result of parent absence or neglect.

Fathers: Yesterday and Today

During the nineteenth century and the first half of the twentieth century, fathers in the United States rarely played more than a minor role in the care and socialization of infants and young children. In fact, most mammals divide responsibility so that the male provides for the protection and safety of the mother and offspring, but does not share the daily responsibilities of child rearing. But this system is not a biological imperative, for humans or for other animals. Primate males from species that ordinarily leave the child rearing to females will assume caretaking responsibilities when females are absent; the same is true of human fathers (Parke and Suomi, in press). Moreover, fathers in North America and elsewhere are doing more and more caretaking of their children, including quite young children and infants.

Michael Lamb (1979), a respected observer of changing parental roles in the past decade, has put the "rediscovery" of fatherhood this way:

> Not long ago in our own culture fathers neither sought nor assumed responsibility for the rearing of their children. This was especially true during the child's earlier years: Infant care was clearly perceived as the province of women. Today, however, increasing numbers of men appear eager to play an active and important role in childrearing, and a number of social scientists (both male and female) now recognize that for biological and social reasons most children have two parents—one of either sex. (p. 938)

Becoming a father can be an important source of personal growth and satisfaction. Recent longitudinal studies show that a father's relationship with his children can have a significant influence on his overall life satisfaction. And infants who develop strong attachments to their fathers as well as to their mothers tend to be better adjusted and find it easier to adjust to people (Biller, 1982). The characteristics of the father most clearly correlated to the child's development are paternal warmth, acceptance, and involvement (Weinraub, 1978).

In addition, boys' intellectual functioning and academic performance are related to the quality of their relationships with their fathers (Lamb, 1981). Girls' intellectual functioning is also related to their relationships with their fathers, but to a lesser extent.

Fathers also make significant contributions to their sons' self-esteem and personal adjustment. Fathers who are available and supportive, while at the same time setting appropriate limits for their sons, appear to have the best adjusted boys during the elementary school years (Biller, 1974). Boys who become the best adjusted and most interpersonally successful adults tend to grow up in families in which parents have compatible views and are both closely involved in the upbringing of their children. Boys who become juvenile delinquents in adolescence tend to come from father-absent homes or to have very poor relationships with their fathers (Block, 1971).

Fathers also play a critical role in their daughters' psychological development. Fathers who are themselves relatively masculine in their own behavior but who encourage femininity in their daughters tend to have girls who enjoy relatively smooth sex-role development. Like males, females who become the most well-adjusted adults tend to come from homes in which both parents are positively involved with their children (Block, von der Lippe, and Block, 1973).

As we noted in Chapter 4, mothers and fathers relate differently to their infants. Weinraub and Frankel (1977) found that mothers displayed more nurturance and vocalized more to their infants, whereas fathers were more active in roughhouse play with their children. Also, parents tended to play more with same-sex children. Clarke-Stewart (1978) observed fourteen infants from various economic levels at 15, 20, and 30 months of age with their mothers and fathers together, as well as with their mothers alone. Fathers engaged in more physical-social play; mothers concentrated on intellectual activities and interactions with objects. It appeared that the infants responded and cooperated more with the fathers; however, this may be more a reflection of the style of play than a parental preference on the part of the children. In the presence of the father the mother tended to take a low-key role, verbalizing less with the infant and generally not interfering in the father-infant interactions.

Interaction between parents and children is not a simple situation to analyze. All members of the family affect and are affected by each other. In this case, Clarke-Stewart hypothesized that the mother influences the behavior of the child, who in turn influences the father, who affects the behavior of the mother. Further studies are needed to make clear the similarities and differences in mother-infant and father-infant interactions.

About 10 percent of all families with children are "father only" households. How do these single fathers handle their nontraditional roles? We might suppose their relative lack of training and experience leaves them with an overwhelming disadvantage. But Lamb (1979) offers an interesting contrary view. He suggests:

> I believe that today's single fathers are more likely than single mothers to succeed in meeting the demands placed on them simply because they are a highly selected and self-motivated group. Societal and judicial prejudices ensure that mothers gain custody by default, whereas fathers who desire custody have to fight for it. (p. 942)

Father Absence.   When we think of the family in the United States, we tend to consider the intact nuclear family. Nevertheless, it is estimated

FIGURE 9-1
Developmental psychologists have come to appreciate the important role that fathers play in caring for their infants.   Sybil Shelton, Monkmeyer.

that 16 percent of all households are headed by a single parent (Sussman, 1978), and that about one in every six children under the age of 18 is living in a single-parent family (Bronfenbrenner, 1978). Although death obviously contributes to these statistics, divorce and separation are mostly responsible. And despite the recent trend of fathers' occasionally retaining custody of their children, most single-parent families are headed by women. So we have considerable interest in understanding the effects of *father absence* on children.

In her review of fifty-four studies of intellectual development, Shinn (1978) considered twenty-eight of them methodologically sound; of those twenty-eight, sixteen reported detrimental effects of father absence, nine found no significant effects, and three found positive or mixed effects. The measures used were performance in school and on achievement and IQ tests. There was some evidence that both absence caused by divorce and absence occurring during the preschool years are more strongly related to deficits. The data were inconclusive on the length of absence, but in homes where the father was absent children of all ages and both sexes showed poor intellectual performance.

Numerous studies have also demonstrated that father absence is related to depression, anxiety, aggression, and delinquency. The earlier the separation, the more strongly it is associated with poor social adjustment (Young and Parish, 1977). Many investigations have established a relationship between length of absence and maladjustment, and have also shown that divorce is a stronger correlate of social maladjustment than parental death (Lynn, 1974).

Father-absent girls have noticeably higher sex interest than girls from intact homes, and they are also more likely to act out and to become involved in delinquency. They also find it considerably more difficult to deal with men. Early father absence (before age 5) seems to have the greatest effect on producing these problems (Hetherington, 1972). Lack of opportunity to observe intimate male-female interactions might explain why both the boys and the girls who are most well-adjusted are those raised with the active involvement of both parents.

Despite the high interest in, concern about, and investigation into the effects of father absence, we still do not have a complete picture. Early research frequently lacked adequate controls and measures. Moderating variables, such as socioeconomic status, age and sex of the child, and length and kind of absence, have not been sufficiently studied. And once again it must be pointed out that the research is correlational, leaving open this question: Even if father absence is associated with certain developmental outcomes, is it the direct cause of the outcomes?

It is evident that families in which the father is absent may differ in many ways from two-parent families. On the whole, financial stress is higher and mothers may feel burdened by responsibility for the supervision and care of the family. On the other hand, the coping capacity of mothers varies, and some, particularly with the support of the women's movement, may enjoy the independence and challenges of being alone. The attitudes of mothers toward their dead or divorced husbands, or toward men in general, could influence children's development in certain areas. Finally, the loss of a father is tied to the previous dynamics of the family and the specific contributions the father made to them. As one researcher has put it:

> . . . we should not assume that all fathers, when present, give their children love, guidance, and security and their wives companionship and sexual satisfaction. If these attributes are absent in the first place, separation from such a father would naturally not represent much loss. In fact, the father is commonly absent precisely because he could not give these qualities to his family. Moreover, the idea that two parents are better than one is true only when the marriage and the parent-child relationships meet certain minimum standards. (Lynn, 1974, p.255)

Inadequate Fathering. It was established many years ago, before divorce and "father absence" were the issues they later became, that girls from mother-dominated homes (even if the father was "present") tended to have difficulty relating to males and to be disliked by boys. Subsequent research has helped to explain the underlying mechanism for these tendencies. Apparently parental discord can lead to *inadequate fathering*, if the father withdraws emotionally from the children and the family. Such withdrawal, like father absence, has repeatedly been shown to be associated with acting out among adolescent girls (Biller, 1982).

Divorce

We all know that family structure in the United States has changed in recent years. And we are all aware that the change is not always thought to be an improvement. It can be argued that the nuclear family as we know it is failing because it no longer meets the needs of many individuals in our society. But there is no assurance that the new structures will succeed, and at least during the transition some negative consequences are apparent.

The most striking change in marriage and family patterns in the past decade is the dramatic increase in the divorce rate. Hetherington (1979) points out that divorce is not a single event, but a sequence of events involving at least three and usually four steps:

- First is a breaking-up period when the equilibrium that previously existed in the family is replaced by separation and impending divorce.
- The second period is an experimental time when the family, now typically headed by the mother, tries a variety of arrangements to cope with the new situation.
- The third is achieving a new equilibrium as the family becomes firmly reorganized as a one-parent household.
- The fourth is a second reorganization; parents remarry and children must adjust to a stepparent and a new family configuration.

Child Abuse

Although the family is supposed to care for, socialize, and optimize the potential of children, it sometimes falls short of these goals. Children may be neglected, both physically and psychologically. And they may be abused—that is, physically or sexually harmed. This grave problem has not been solved, but we are learning more about it and how to deal with it.

The extent of physical abuse is difficult to estimate (Starr, 1979). One reason is that confrontations usually occur in the home. Also, some victims are afraid to mention the situation or are not in a position to do so. Preschoolers are often unable to report their troubles, or perhaps adults question the credibility of their stories. Abusers, too, are afraid or ashamed to tell the truth about their behavior.

Given these considerations, it is understandable that estimates of abuse vary widely. In a particularly interesting study, Gelles (1979) interviewed 1,146 parents from a national cross section of homes in which a couple and at least one child between the ages of 3 and 17 were living. One adult in each home was interviewed about his or her behavior with one particular child. Table 9–1 shows the percentage of parents who reported violently harming their children in various ways. Extrapolating these data to the child population at large, Gelles concluded that between 3.1 and 4 million children have been kicked, bitten, or punched at some time in their lives; that between 1.4 and 2.3 million have been beaten up; and that between 900,000 and 1.8 million have been attacked by their parents with a gun or knife. He also suggested that these estimates are low because of the many unreported cases.

Whether or not child abuse occurs de-

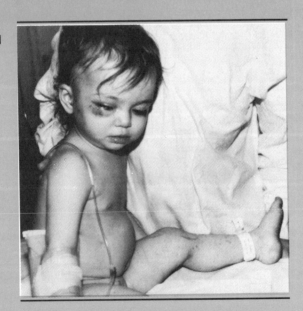

FIGURE 9–2
This 15-month-old girl is recovering in a hospital, after a court order finally removed her from the home in which she had been abused. UPI

TABLE 9–1
Percentage of Parents Who Reported Acting Violently Toward Their Children

Incident	Occurrence Once in Past Year	Occurrence More Than Twice in Past Year	Occurrence Ever
Slapped or spanked	5.2	43.6	71.0
Pushed/grabbed/shoved	4.3	27.2	46.4
Hit with something	1.0	9.8	20.0
Threw something	1.3	2.3	9.6
Kicked/bit/hit with fist	0.7	1.7	7.7
Beat up	0.4	0.6	4.2
Threatened with knife/gun	0.1	0.0	2.8
Used knife or gun	0.1	0.0	2.9

Source: Reprinted by permission of the publisher, from **Critical Perspectives on Child Abuse** edited by Richard Bourne and Eli Newberger (Lexington, Mass.: Lexington Books, D.C. Heath and Company, Copyright 1979, D.C. Heath and Company).

pends on many factors. Researchers have explored the question: What kind of parents are involved in child abuse? At least a small percentage of abusive parents were themselves abused as children (Parke and Collmer, 1975). And some abusive parents reverse roles with their children, perceiving the children as hostile adults. For example, the father of a nine-month-old boy, who had split his son's head, said, "He thinks he's boss—all the time trying to run things—but I showed him who is in charge around here!" (Gladston, 1965, p. 442). But some children are more likely to be abused than others. Children in the first three years of life seem most vulnerable (Fontana, 1973). Sons are somewhat more likely to be abused than daughters; moreover, a particular child in a family may be the only to be abused. Children who are born prematurely are at risk for abuse, as are the physically and mentally handicapped and perhaps those of particular dispositions (Vasta, 1982). Victims of child abuse tend to be babies and toddlers who whine or cry a lot (Vasta and Copitch, 1981).

A comprehensive account of child abuse must also consider broad social factors such as family stress and society's attitudes. Large family size, low income, low educational levels, and unemployment are related to abuse (Gil, 1979). Social isolation of the family and marital conflict are often present (Belsky, 1980; Friedman, Sandler, Hernandez, and Wolfe, 1981). The age-old belief that children are the property of the family, to be dealt with as the family wishes, also contributes to abusive care.

Treatment of child abuse typically focuses on parental counseling and parent-child interaction. Reported improvement rates range from 40 percent to 80 percent. One of the most comprehensive studies (Berkeley Planning Associates, 1977) concluded that even the best of treatments—a combination of parent aides or Parents Anonymous support groups and assignment of individual case workers—can be expected to produce the reduction or elimination of abuse in no more than about half of all cases. There is thus great need for prevention. This can come in the form of parental education in child development and management and in identification, support, and counseling of families at high risk for abuse.

Divorce produces serious disequilibrium for a time. For one thing, most children, understandably, strongly prefer to live in a two-parent family (Wallerstein and Kelly, 1980). Divorce also almost invariably confronts children with the problem of divided loyalties. They may be openly asked by one parent to join in criticizing the other, or they may deny some of the realities of the new situation in an attempt to reconcile their parents. One high school senior, for example, decided he wanted "only his mother and father" to attend his graduation:

> This meant, according to the son, his mother was to attend the ceremony with her ex-husband and not with her new husband. If she was unwilling to do this, then this young man was adamant that his mother was not to be present at all. The loyalty issues were made very clear, and decisions had to be made. In this case, the mother chose not to acquiesce to her son's demand, and for a number of years afterwards their relationship remained strained. The son's deep loyalty conflicts had produced a situation with no satisfactory solution. (Visher and Visher, 1979, p. 167)

In many divorce situations the children—both boys and girls—often feel guilty that they were somehow responsible for the divorce; they also commonly fantasize that some day their parents will be reunited. Sometimes these fantasies can persist for years (Visher and Visher, 1979). Divorce, however, does not always make life worse for a child. The evidence suggests that children may be better off in a single-parent family than in a two-parent family riddled with conflicts and fights between parents (Hetherington, Cox and Cox, 1978).

Children differ greatly in their reactions to divorce. Those who adjust well appear to come from homes in which there is relatively little change in financial situation (Hodges, Wechsler, and Ballantine, 1979), low parent conflict (Berg and Kelly, 1979), agreement between parents on discipline and child-rearing (Hetherington, Cox, and Cox, 1978), and a climate that encourages open discussion of the divorce (Jacobson, 1978). Children's adjustment to divorce is also related to their overall adjustment; the better adjusted a child is in general, the better he or she adjusts to divorce. Many of the adverse effects of divorce on children are only temporary. Within two years after divorce, most youngsters have overcome their hostility and readjusted to the new situation (Kurdek, Blisk and Siesky, 1981).

The increasing number of divorced fathers who are getting custody of their children has made possible a number of revealing comparisons. For example, children of divorce who live with same-sex parents (boys with their fathers and girls with their mothers) are better adjusted than those living with the opposite-sex parent (Santrock and Warshak, 1979). Children appear to do best after divorce when they can develop full relationships with both parents in their new situations (Visher and Visher, 1979).

It is increasingly common for people to divorce and marry for a second time, bringing with them (psychologically or literally) children from the previous marriage. Such families have been referred to as stepfamilies, but Wald (1981) points out that the term *remarried families* is less stigmatizing for what is inherently a very trying situation for all concerned. The first problem to be overcome is that people often remarry with the hope that their new marriage will be an idealized version of the previous, failed marriage. In reality, a remarriage is a far more complex arrangement to manage than a first marriage. It does not simply replace previous relationships, but instead it complicates them. "It has to be more complex," observes psychiatrist Leonard Friedman, "because there are many more relationships. The new ones are added on to the set of old ones, with many more possiblities for triangulation, conflicting loyalties, conflicts of interest, and guilt" (1983, p. 279). Friedman goes on to point out:

> People are set to see stepmothers and stepfathers as bad and stepchildren as neglected. . . . Overlaid on this is the common wish of the stepparent to prove the stereotype wrong by becoming a supermom or superdad. . . . There is never enough time to give all members of a remarried family the attention they need, and when the dream collapses, resentments mushroom. People are often unprepared to face the level of conflict and tension that is inevitable when children of prior family units are combined under one roof. (1983, p. 279)

The effects of remarriage are not necessarily bad, nor are they always the same. In one study, boys and girls in intact families were compared with children whose mothers were divorced and single, or divorced and remarried (Santrock, Warshak, Lindbergh, and Meadows, 1982). The most consistent findings were that boys in stepfather families displayed more competent social behavior than boys in intact families, whereas girls in stepfather families were more anxious than girls in intact families. Consistent with these results, boys in remarried families showed more warmth to their stepfathers than did girls. No important differences were observed between intact and divorced families. The authors concluded that the social behavior of children in remarried families is not necessarily less competent than the behavior of comparable children in intact or divorced families. Adjustment undoubtedly depends on a variety of factors, including cultural values and support.

CULTURAL INFLUENCES

Culture is the full set of specific attitudes, behaviors, and products that characterize an identifiable group of people. New members of a cultural group must be prepared to live in the culture into which they have been born. So, *enculturation*—teaching children cultural rules and habits is a major goal of all peoples. Nevertheless, the variation in socialization practices and expectations from one culture to another is enormous (Wagner and Stevenson, 1982).

People have probably always been fascinated by how others live. By the 1920s anthropologists were going into the field and bringing back detailed descriptions of cultures around the world. From Freud they borrowed a theoretical framework, and they began to direct their energies to the issues of child development and personality (Sears, 1975).

Two classic studies are Bronislaw Malinowski's test of Freudian theory conducted in the Trobriand Islands and Margaret Mead's examination of adolescence in Samoa. Malinowski reported that in a culture in which uncles played a dominant role in family life, boys did not appear to come into conflict with their fathers in the way Freud predicted. Mead (1928) concluded that the adolescent years in Samoa were more serene than those in the United States. Although these early studies had their methodological difficulties, they drew attention to the cultural context of development.

Of modern anthropological studies, Whiting and Child's (1953) survey of seventy-five cultures is still considered a classic. One of the main conclusions drawn from the study is that child training involves certain universals. All cultures must deal with eating behavior, evacuation of waste products, and the development of sexuality. Aggressive impulses and the growth of independent and responsible actions also must be shaped.

Another conclusion, however, pointed to the great variability in the specific goals of socialization and the ways in which they are attained. This can be seen dramatically in accounts of toilet-training practices found in two cultures. The Dahomeans of West Africa were rated as severe in their practices:

> A child is trained by the mother who, as she carries it about, senses when it is restless, so that every time it must perform its excretory functions, the mother puts it on the ground. Thus, in time, usually two years, the training process is completed. If a child does not respond to this training, and manifests enuresis (bedwetting) at the age of four or five, soiling the mat on which it sleeps, then, at first, it is beaten. If this does not correct the habit, ashes are put in water and the mixture is poured over the head of the offending boy or girl, who is driven into the street, where all the other children clap their hands and run after the child singing.
>
> Adida go ya ya ya
>
> "Urine everywhere."
>
> (Herskovitz, as cited by Whiting and Child, 1953, p. 75)

The practices of the Siriono show considerable overindulgence:

> Almost no effort is made by the mother to train an infant in the habits of cleanliness until he can walk, and then they are instilled very gradually. Children who are able to walk, however, soon learn by imitation, and with the assistance of their parents, not to defecate near the hammock.

286

When they are old enough to indicate their needs, the mother gradually leads them further and further away from the hammock to urinate and defecate, so that by the time they have reached the age of 3 they have learned not to pollute the house. Until the age of 4 or 5, however, children are still wiped by the mother, who also cleans up the excreta and throws them away. Not until a child has reached the age of 6 does he take care of his defecation needs alone. (Holmberg, as cited by Whiting and Child, 1953, pp. 75–76)

Similar differences are found for feeding and weaning practices. The Kwoma tribe, for example, is extremely indulgent:

Kwoma infants up to the time they are weaned are never far from their mothers. . . . Crying . . . constitutes an injunction to the mother to discover the source of trouble. Her first response is to present the breast. If this fails to quiet him, she tries something else. . . . Thus during infancy the response to discomfort which is most strongly established is that of seeking help by crying or asking for it. (Whiting as cited by Whiting and Child, 1953, pp. 91–92)

In contrast, Ainu children of Northern Japan have considerably different experiences:

Put into the hanging cradle . . . the poor little helpless creatures could not get out, and for the rest they were free to do whatever they were able. This usually meant a good deal of kicking and screaming until tired of it, followed by exhaustion, repose, and resignation. (Howard, as cited by Whiting and Child, 1953, p. 93)

Whiting and Child's examples are taken from descriptions of "non-industrialized" societies, but differences along many dimensions are also found in modern ones. In the Israeli kibbutz, children are tended to by many adults and actually live with peers in a building separate from the residence of their biological parents (Bettleheim, 1969). Infants in isolated communities in Guatemala spend their first year or so in small family huts with no windows. Seldom spoken to or played with, they are given simple toys of corn ears, wood, and clothing (Kagan and Klein, 1973). In contrast, children in middle-class New England are stimulated by parents and provided with pets and a large number of toys, including blocks, stuffed animals, dolls, and trucks (Fischer and Fischer, 1963).

Universal Goals of Parenting

From a cultural analysis of child-care customs, Robert LeVine (1974) has proposed a useful framework for relating child care to the overall setting and development of cultures. LeVine came to his ideas after he noted that a common hazard for African infants of the Gusii (Kenya) and Hausa (Nigeria) people is the cooking fire, especially when the fire is kept burning through the night for warmth. Perhaps, he speculated, this hazard had led to children's being carried on the backs of adults or otherwise restricted in mobility. Such a limitation might adversely affect the development of certain skills, but it would at least ensure survival, which must be the first priority.

LeVine proposed that many child-rearing customs might have been established to promote survival. Of course, other considerations also determine child-care practices. LeVine, in fact, suggests the following hierarchy of determinants:

1. The physical survival and health of the child including (implicitly) the normal development of his or her reproductive capacity during puberty.
2. The development of the child's behavioral capacity for economic self-maintenance during maturity.
3. The development of the child's behavioral capacities for maximizing other cultural values—e.g., morality, prestige, wealth, religious piety, intellectual achievement, personal satisfaction, self-realization—as formulated and symbolically elaborated in culturally distinctive beliefs, norms, and ideologies. (1974, p. 230)

These universal goals are arranged in a definite order. Sheer physical survival during childhood is required before any later capacities can develop and so it assumes paramount importance in environments that pose great danger to the young. In much the same way, economic self-maintenance must be considered before the relative luxury of maximizing one's status and prestige. Do things really work this way? The evidence suggests that they do.

LeVine's review of studies done in African, Latin American, and Indonesian communities with very high infant mortality rates shows that practices in these societies are highly responsive to environmental threats. The general pattern in these cultures is to keep the infant on or near the caretaker's body at all times, day or night, and to respond quickly to crying, usually by feeding. Development of self-maintenance skills receives little attention during this period. By Western standards these mothers rarely smile at their infants or even make eye contact with them.

In societies in which food and related materials for subsistence are scarce, we would expect that child-rearing customs would emphasize the development of behaviors that would ensure economic self-maintenance. The pattern that is found emphasized obedience, presumably because an obedient child can contribute to food and craft production, or at least babysit competently, thereby freeing parents to do productive labor. In the long run these children benefit from obedience training as much as or more than their parents. "The African parents with whom I have worked," writes LeVine, "want their children to become obedient in part because they believe it is the single most important quality involved in adult economic adaptation, and they are concerned that their children have the capacity to survive in a world of scarce and unstable resources" (1974, p. 237).

Following LeVine's hierarchy, it would not be surprising to find that societies like the United States would probably list as their first priority the maximizing of achievement, self-realization, and the like. As we see later, this appears to be true, at least for middle-class Americans.

Practices In
Communist
Countries

Most cultures follow child rearing practices that have evolved gradually over many generations. Communist countries are a striking exception. Following Marxist thinking, their child-rearing methods were purposely and consciously designed by experts to prepare children to live in a Communist society.

Child Rearing in the USSR.   From 1960 to 1967 Urie Bronfenbrenner, an American psychologist, visited the Soviet Union seven times as part of a research project on cross-cultural studies of child rearing. The insights he gained from his own observations and interviews were published in *Two Worlds of Childhood: U.S. and U.S.S.R.* (1970). According to Bronfenbrenner, Russian infants receive much more physical contact and affection—holding, kissing, hugging, cuddling—than American babies. However, they are given little freedom of movement and initiation, perhaps because there is considerable concern about environmental dangers. Maternal responsibility is diffused to relatives and even strangers. It is not unusual when riding public transportation to have a child placed in your lap by a parent or guardian. Strangers easily interact with children and are quickly called "tyotya" and "dyadya" (aunt or uncle).

Despite much affection and care, however, emphasis is placed on the development of obedience and self-discipline. In the preschools children learn early to care for themselves. By 18 months of age they are expected to have bladder and bowel control and are learning to dress themselves. They are exposed to programs designed for sensorimotor and language development. Socially their experiences are communal. Babies nap in rows and play in pens that provide close contact with the staff (see Figure 9–3). Even very young children are given communal chores, such as shoveling snow and caring for animals.

But parents still play a major role. Even though Soviet parents are likely to work long hours six days a week, they spend more time with their children than do U.S. parents. This is especially true of fathers. One study revealed that Soviet fathers spend an average of more than forty minutes a day with their children, compared with an average of about twelve minutes for U.S. fathers (Szalai, 1973).

Soviet "character education" illustrates the compelling force that can be generated when all the socializing agents to which a child is exposed make a joint, concerted effort to produce a particular kind of citizen. In the USSR the state assumes the leadership role in directing all aspects of

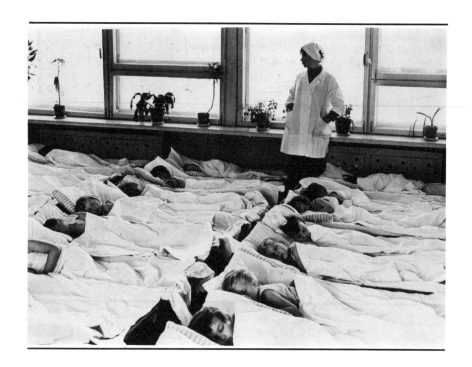

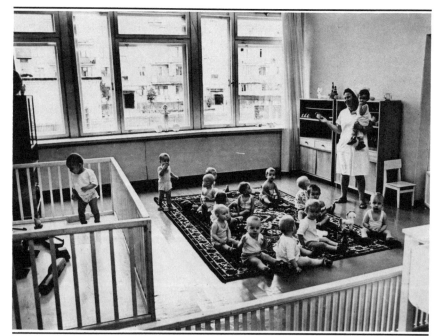

FIGURE 9–3
Russian babies napping in a dormitorylike setting. Bottom: A nursery in Volgograd, with raised playpens that facilitate face-to-face contact with the staff. Top photo; Novosti from Sovfoto; bottom photo, S. Golubev, Sovfoto.

TABLE 9–2
A Summary of Stated Objectives for Two Age Groups, Including the Explicit Goal of Character Training in the Soviet Union

Ages 7-11	Ages 16-18
Communist morality	
Sense of good and bad behavior Truthfulness, honesty, kindness Atheism: science vs. superstition Self-discipline Diligence in work and care of possessions Friendship with classmates Love of one's own locality and the Motherland	Collectivism, duty, honor, and conscience Development of will, patience, perseverance A Communist attitude toward work and public property Socialist humanism Soviet patriotism and proletarian internationalism
Responsible attitude toward learning	
Interest and striving for knowledge and skill Industry in study Organizing intellectual and physical work Striving to apply one's knowledge and ability in life and work	Understanding of the social significance of education Perseverance and initative in learning Increasing one's power of intellectual work (learning to plan one's work better, development of good work habits, self-criticism, etc.)
Cultured conduct	
Care, accuracy, and neatness Courtesy and cordiality Proper behavior on the street and in public places Cultured speech	Assimilation of norms of socialist community life Good manners and standards of behavior
Bases of esthetic culture	
Understanding of the beautiful in nature, in the conduct of people, and in creative art Artistic creativity	Esthetic appreciation of nature, social life, and works of art Artistic creativity
Physical culture and sport	
Concern for strengthening and conditioning one's body Sanitary-hygienic habits Preparation for sport and athletics	Maximizing the development of physical skills Mastering the rules of personal and social hygiene and sanitation Training and participation in sports Mastering hiking and camping skills

Source: From U. Bronfenbrenner. Two Worlds of Childhood: U.S. and U.S.S.R., © Russell Sage Foundation, Basic Books, Inc., Publishers, New York, 1970.

We wake, and get up from our beds,
And dress ourselves carefully.
"Let me comb your loosened plaits."
It is good to help each other.

FIGURE 9–4
Pages from *I Am on Duty Today.* Story by Yang Yi and Liang Ko. Illustrations by Ku Yin. Edited by Shanghai Juvenile Publishing House, Foreign Languages Press, Peking, 1966. Printed in the People's Republic of China. Distributed by Guozi Shudian (China Publications, Centre), P. O. Box 399, Peking.

We do not climb up trees or windows.
We take good care of the toys we share,
Rocking our wooden horses gently.
If anyone falls, I go to help them.

After our nap we have refreshments.
Tung-tung passes the sweets, I take
   round the biscuits.
The large and good ones I give to
   other children,
And keep the small ones for myself.

And now we tidy the tables and chairs,
And put away the books and toys.
All in order for tomorrow,
So our friends on duty will have no trouble.

socialization. Parents are provided with written materials, films, television programs, and the example of more experienced parents. Each of these sources emphasizes that parents are to openly express affection while at the same time setting down and enforcing clear standards of obedience and self-control. Parents are told it is their responsibility to provide their children with explanations and praise for obedience and punishment for disobedience.

The Soviet method relies heavily on psychological discipline rather than physical punishment, and parents are encouraged to withdraw affection for disobedience or misbehavior. Bronfenbrenner (1970) gives this example, from a Russian book on child rearing:

> For example, a mother says to her son: "Once again you disobeyed me by not coming home on time. Now I no longer wish to finish the chess match we began yesterday. It is even unpleasant for me to look at you." For the rest of the evening, she confines herself only to cold responses to her son's questions. (p. 13)

The same themes are also picked up at school. In fact, an official manual provides a socialization curriculum for each grade level (see Table 9–2). Within classrooms the children are organized into cells. Each child in a cell is told that he or she is personally responsible for the entire cell and every child in it; this is to foster peer responsibility. Social criticism is also strongly encouraged. Children are urged to point out each others' errors (of attitude as well as action) and to suggest ways of improvement.

Competition and striving for excellence is considered important in the Soviet system, but in the form of group competition rather than individual striving. Groups are formed for virtually all activities and they are scored on the performance of all members. A group is considered successful only if all members do well. The aim is to motivate group members to improve the performance of anyone who is not doing well. This is done by providing assistance when a member is having difficulty and by publicly chastizing a member who is disobedient, or uncooperative, or not trying hard enough.

Practices in China. As in the Soviet Union, socialization practices in Communist China are focused on creating citizens who will fit the political ideals of the state. This is illustrated in Figure 9–4, a facsimile of several pages of a "comic book" for Chinese children entitled *I Am on Duty Today*. As with the USSR, American observers have been impressed with the apparent effectiveness of these practices in producing dutiful, compliant children who are oriented toward group goals (Kessen, 1975).

So far in this chapter we have focused on who socializes children and on what their tasks and goals are in different cultural settings. Now we turn to how they do it—that is to the processes of socialization.

Socialization involves acquiring skills and knowledge. According to the prevailing cognitive-social learning view (Ladd and Mize, 1983), three broad processes can be distinguished: *direct instruction* (including coaching and exhortation), *shaping*, and observational learning or *modeling*—that is, the presentation of social models. All three teach children the social roles they and others can play in the culture. And all three are mediated by children's *social cognition*—their understanding of the social world. In real life the three processes typically operate together, as when a parent both shows and tells a child what to do in a particular social situation.

Direct Instruction

Direct instruction may include either specific or general information about what to do or say, and how or when to do or say it. The principal vehicle of direct instruction is language, and so direct instruction deals in concepts and ideas. As we saw in Chapter 5, instructions do not always convey what the communicator intends. In fact, a whole range of cognitive and social processes mediate what is understood, remembered, and believed.

Direct instruction provides both information on what to do and *behavioral instigation* or exhortation—that is, urging or persuading someone to adopt a particular goal or follow a particular course of action. Direct instruction can be broken down into parts, of which two seem especially important. First, direct instruction can provide the *intent* to learn or act differently, by explaining the importance of a particular practice, idea, or way of behaving. Second, direct instruction can provide *cognitive structure* by identifying relevant and irrelevant attributes of a situation or performance so children do not need to figure out underlying similarities on their own. For example, you might say to a child who has just made an unkind remark to a peer, "You weren't very nice to make fun of Johnnie. You wouldn't want someone to make fun of you."

Direct instruction is widely used by itself in training academic and occupational skills, but in transmitting social values and behavior it has typically been studied as a partner of modeling or shaping. Exhortations by themselves, such as an exhortation to share with others, are frequently effective in the presence of the authority figure who provides the exhortation, but are often ignored in the absence of such authority (Poulos and Liebert, 1972). On the other hand, providing reasons, explanations, and rationales may do much to facilitate children's adopting particular beliefs or practices, especially if incentives are given as well.

Shaping

We mention classical and operant conditioning in Chapters 2 and 7 as learning processes that allow an organism to benefit from experience. These basic conditioning processes continue to play a significant role throughout life. *Shaping* is the application of these processes to achieve social goals.

One of the first psychologists in the United States to think about shaping children was John Watson, the founder of modern behaviorism. Watson was convinced that given certain conditions and stimuli, responses are orderly and predictable. He enthusiastically advocated that conditioning principles be applied to shape and socialize children, and he was sure it could be done:

> Give me a dozen healthy infants, well-formed, and my own specified world to bring them up in and I'll guarantee to take any one at random and train him to become any type of specialist I might select—doctor, lawyer, merchant, chief and yes, even beggar-man and thief, regardless of his talents, penchants, tendencies, abilities, vocations, and race of his ancestors. (Watson, 1914; reprinted 1958, p. 104)

Watson, though, was more effective as an advocate than as an experimenter. His only remembered study, the case of little Albert (Watson and Rayner, 1920), stands as a curiosity as much as a milestone. Albert was an 11-month-old boy with no detectable fear except of loud sounds, such as that made by striking a steel bar behind him. Assuming that the sound was an unconditioned stimulus (UCS) that elicited fear, Watson and Rayner showed that they could induce or condition fear of a white rat (a CS) in Albert by systematically pairing exposure to the animal with the sound. After seven such presentations, the rat, which previously had not evoked any fear, elicited a sharp avoidance reaction that included crying and attempts to escape from the situation.

In a follow-up study, Mary Cover Jones (1924) was encouraged by Watson to show that fear responses can be partially extinguished by procedures similar to conditioning. Her subject, Peter, was a boy of 2 years and 10 months, who had previously developed a severe fear reaction to furry objects. Jones first arranged for Peter to play, in the presence of a rabbit, with three children who exhibited no fear of the animal. The treatment appeared to be working well when a setback occurred, due to Peter's illness and accidental exposure to a large dog. Jones then decided to treat the boy with a combination of exposure to fearless others and *counterconditioning*. The latter involved moving the animal progressively closer to Peter while he ate some of his favorite foods, thus pairing the feared stimuli with pleasantness. The boy's fear diminished with this treatment until he was even able to hold the rabbit by himself.

Watson's contribution was to pave the way for later generations of behavioral psychologists to study the question of the extent to which children can be shaped, purposely and accidentally. Central to this work were demonstrations of the effects of consequences on behavior.

The Importance of Consequences. The dictionary definition of *inconsequential*—without consequences—is, roughly, "devoid of meaning, significance, or importance." In fact, without actual or expected consequences, most socialization efforts would fail. Potential consequences provide motivation for learning new things and behaving in different ways.

Consequences can be positive or negative—pleasant or aversive. They can also be manifested as "something given or done" or as "something taken back or removed." The distinction is important. If you want to increase the likelihood that a child will act in a particular way, you can provide something (a smile or a spanking), or you can take something away (a previous restriction or a previous privilege). The effect of the consequence does not depend on whether it is given or taken, but only on whether the overall result is reinforcing or punishing. Thus, there are four different types of consequences: positive reinforcement, negative reinforcement, positive punishment, and negative punishment (cf. Whitehurst and Vasta, 1977). The four possibilities are shown in Table 9–3.

Positive *reinforcement* is the application of consequences that, when presented, tend to increase the likelihood of a response. Praise may positively reinforce a child's studying. *Negative reinforcement* also increases the likelihood of the response, but works in a different way. Negative reinforcement involves the ending of some experience or stimulation that is unpleasant, such as when a restriction is lifted for good performance.

The presentation of a stimulus that will discourage the reoccurrence of a particular response is *positive punishment*. Almost anyone will show a decline in responses that result in electric shock; shock is a punisher that is almost universally effective. Finally, *negative punishment* involves the reduction of a response by removing some stimulation or experience contingent on the occurrence of the response. Not allowing a child to watch televison in order to eliminate poor school grades is an example.

Consequences are judged by their effects and not by their intentions. For example, parents, teachers, and even peers may use frowns and various forms of verbal disapproval to discourage particular actions. Nevertheless, attention, even when it is tinged with criticism, often serves as a *positive reinforcer*. It increases the very behavior it is designed to discourage (e.g., Madsen, Becker, Thomas, Koser and Plager, 1968).

Consequences often combine to produce their influence. For example, learning tends to occur more quickly when mild punishment for unwanted responses is used to supplement reinforcement for desired responses (Whitehurst, 1969).

TABLE 9–3
Types of Consequences and Their Effects

Perceived Nature of the Consequence	Stimulus Presented (Positive)	Stimulus Taken Away (Negative)
"Good"	Example of Positive Reinforcement: Receiving a piece of candy as a reward for finishing one's vegetables.	Example of Negative Punishment: Having a curfew lifted for getting better grades.
"Bad"	Example of Positive Punishment: Receiving a spanking for coming home late.	Example of Negative Reinforcement: Losing television privileges for hitting another child.

Punishment. Spankings and other positive punishment (usually just called *punishment*) play an important role for many parents. According to one survey, virtually all parents (98 percent) use such punishment at least occasionally (Sears, Mccoby, and Levin, 1957). Whereas reinforcement is most effective in building new patterns of behavior, the effects of punishment are primarily *suppressive;* when punishment "works," it reduces the likelihood of certain noxious or potentially dangerous responses.

For ethical and philosophical reasons, many parents seek alternatives to positive punishment. One useful form of negative punishment is *time-out* which is an abbreviated way of saying "time-out from positive reinforcement" (Sherman and Bushell, 1975). For example, parents can reduce the oppositional behavior of their elementary school-age boys by isolating them in their bedrooms for five minutes (time-out) for each instance of such behavior they display (Wahler, 1969). (Oppositional responses might include refusing to do one's homework or fighting with parents about their selection of a television program chosen for family viewing.) Whereas time-out removes the opportunity to continue the oppositional behavior, *response cost* removes some tangible reinforcer already in the child's possession or one that would otherwise be due. Fines are the most obvious examples.

Response-cost and time-out techniques have been shown to be clearly effective when the loss to the individual being punished is substantial enough to outweigh the reinforcers associated with the response to be eliminated. Plainly, however, imposing a small fine on those who are caught engaging in some intrinsically rewarding activity (or, of course, in an activity that produces much extrinsic reinforcement) is hardly likely to be effective. The effectiveness of negative punishment also increases as the punishment becomes more severe (Burchard and Barrera, 1972).

Side Effects of Punishment. Punishing a child can have various possible side effects: avoidance of the punishing agent, emotional behavior, and an increased likelihood of aggression, especially the punishment of others, such as a younger brother or sister (Whitehurst and Vasta, 1977). For example, aggressive delinquent adolescents tend to be individuals who were themselves given physical punishment as children (Bandura and Walters, 1959). Such side effects need not occur if punishment is used carefully and in combination with positive reinforcement for alternative activities. Parents and other socializing agents who give a generous reward for one behavior but express a willingness to punish another are often seen as fair rather than cruel.

Observational
Learning
(Modeling)

Modeling involves observing and imitating the behavior of others, including parents and other adults, siblings and other children, and people in the electronic and print media. Modeling works by providing children with information which they can then use to guide their own actions in a range of situations. But the notion of the information value of modeling

FIGURE 9–5
Children learn both specific skills and more general role behaviors by observing adults. Nancy Hays, Monkmeyer.

cannot stand by itself, for it is the child's interpretation and understanding of what has been observed that is the real result of any modeling experience (Ladd and Mize, 1983).

Counterimitation. Exposure to a model can lead to relatively exact duplication of the model's behavior, either immediately or when the environmental conditions are right; this is *direct imitation*. Observing another's behavior also can *reduce* the probability of matching. The child who sees a peer burned by a hot stove, for example, typically will become *less* likely to touch the stove than previously: The model's action and its consequences are a guide for what should not be done. Such an outcome is known as *direct counterimitation*.

Inhibitory and Disinhibitory Effects. Modeling may also influence actions that fall into the same general class as those observed, but that are different in virtually all details. Youngsters who watch a movie filled with shooting and fighting, for example, may become more likely to yell at or push a younger sibling. In such a case aggressive responses in general have increased or have been *disinhibited*. Similarly, a child who, on the first day of class, sees that the teacher punishes a classmate for disrupting the lesson may be less likely to turn in homework assignments late. Failing to turn in homework and carrying on in class, though far from identical, fall into a common category of behavior—disobedience to the dictates of the teacher. The second child's general *inhibition* regarding breaking the rules may be traced to the first child's disruption of the class.

So far we have spoken of socialization as if it involved little thought on the child's part. This is not so. In fact, children almost never respond automatically or passively to efforts to socialize them. Rewards, punishments, instructions, and modeled examples are affected by children's interpretations of what they mean when they happen. The process of socialization is intertwined with the process of social cognition (Bandura, 1977; Mischel, 1979, Shantz, 1983).

Mischel's (1979) view of socialization, for example, focuses on social cognition, especially the content of children's thoughts. He has emphasized that all social behavior arises out of expectations, plans, encoding strategies, categorical ideas ("contructs"), and subjective values. Mischel claims that children as young as 8 are able to explain their plans to an adult, and to give examples of how they use plans to structure their own behavior. By age 10 or 11, many children have become sophisticated planners. Here is how one 11-year-old girl in Mischel's research explained how she would teach a plan to someone else, and contrasted it with how she would use a shorthand method to guide her own behavior:

> If I had to teach a plan to someone who grew up in the jungle—like a plan to work on a project at 10 a.m. tomorrow—I'd tell him what to say to himself to make it easier at the start for him. Like "if I do this *plan* on time I'll get a reward and the teacher will like me and I'll be proud." But for myself, I know all that already, so I don't have to say it to myself—Besides, it would take too long to say, and my mind doesn't have the time for all that, so I just remember that stuff about why I should do it real quick without saying it—It's like a method that I know already in math; once you have the method you don't have to say every little step. (Mischel, 1979, p. 749)

Similarly, children seem to pick up many ways of acting that no one tried to teach them. As Chandler and Boyes (1982) point out, even very young children think about their social worlds. Their cognitive understanding (which is itself continually changing) mediates and "subjectively deforms" all the social influences and lessons the world has prepared for them.

Psychologists interested in social cognition say we must look at the social world from the child's perspective. Children—and adults—respond not to environments or socializing agents themselves, but to their perception about what others know about them and expect. This means that children develop and maintain a coordinated and cross-referenced system of social understanding that underlies their specific actions and perceptions. One needs an informed knowledge base in order to navigate in the social world. The development of social cognition is the development of this knowledge base (Chandler and Boyes, 1982).

One important facet of social knowledge is understanding the causes of other people's behavior. Even preschool children know that certain experiences routinely lead to particular emotions. They know, for example, that compliments often make children feel happier and that aggression leads to sadness or anger (Barden, Zelko, Duncan, and Masters, 1980). Furthermore, young children can suggest appropriate experiences to change a person's emotional state. Asked how a child who is currently sad could be made to feel otherwise, 5-year-olds will mention activities such as inviting the child to play or asking the child to be a friend (McCoy and Masters, 1985).

However, young children's understanding of the causes of emotions is often limited to the typical response to a situation, which, of course, is not always appropriate. To illustrate, imagine it is a child's turn to feed the class hamster. Ordinarily children would be excited by this opportunity, and if 5-year-olds are asked to predict the hypothetical child's emotional state, they correctly say "happy" or "excited." Suppose, however, that on the previous day the child was bitten by the hamster. Ten-year-olds know that this prior experience means the typical emotion is no longer appropriate; the child would likely be afraid. However, 5-year-olds believe that the typical emotion—happiness—is still likely (Gnepp and Gould, 1985)

Age differences are particularly important when we consider children's perception and interpretation of their parents' behavior, especially behavior that reflects parents' efforts to socialize their children. William Damon (1980, 1983) has identified a gradual developmental progression in children's ideas about parental authority. In his research, children heard stories in which hypothetical children had been told by their parents to perform some chore (e.g., cleaning their rooms). Before the chore was finished, the opportunity arose for these hypothetical children to participate in some special event (e.g., going on a picnic), but the parent insisted that the children complete the chore. The subjects in Damon's research—4- to 11-year olds—were asked to decide whether the children in the story should obey their parents and also were asked to justify their choice.

At all ages children believed that parents should be obeyed, but the reasons for obedience differed for younger and older children. As shown in Table 9–4, preschoolers' close dependence upon parents is the basis for obedience. Slightly older children also consider the consequences of *failing* to obey. During the elementery school years, children believe parents should be obeyed because of parents' greater experience in human affairs and because they know that most parental requests stem from concern for their children.

This general developmental trend has been documented by other investigators. Consider a highly permissive mother who, for example, does not intervene when her child continues to play with a friend's toy, even though the friend wants the toy back. Typically 5- and 6-year-olds will judge this to be a "good mother," perhaps reflecting their own happiness at being allowed to continue to play with a special toy. However, 8- to 10-year-olds are likely to judge her to be a bad mother, reflecting their understanding that she is neglecting her parental responsibilities (Appel, 1977).

TABLE 9-4		
Children's Authority Conceptions		

Approximate age range	Authority legitimized by:	Basis for obedience
4 yrs. and under	Love; identification with self	Association between authority's commands and self's desires.
4–5 yrs.	Physical attributes of persons.	Obedience is a means for achieving self's desires.
5–8 yrs.	Social and physical power	Respect for authority figure's power.
7–9 yrs.	Attributes that reflect special ability, talent, or actions of authority figure.	Authority figure deserves obedience because of superior abilities or past favors.
8–10 yrs.	Prior training or experience with leadership.	Respect for authority figure's leadership abilities; awareness of authority figure's concern for subordinate's welfare.
10 yrs. and above	Situationally appropriate attributes of leadership.	Temporary and voluntary consent of subordinate; spirit of cooperation between leader and led.

Source: Based on W. Damon, Patterns of change in children's social reasoning: A two-year longitudinal study. *Child Development*, 1980, *51*, 1011.

It is not the case, however, that older children believe parents to be all-powerful—instead they have a surprisingly sophisticated understanding of parental rights and the reasons for them. To illustrate, we can return to our example involving the class hamster. Imagine two children, A and B, who are trying to decide whose turn it is to feed the hamster. Suppose a parent is visiting the class, as is a child from another school. Neither the parent nor the visiting child knows the two children nor the routine for selecting a child to feed the hamster. If the parent suggests that child A feed the hamster but the visiting child picks B, most 6- to 7-year-olds would believe that the adult should be obeyed. By age 10 or 11, children say that neither person has the authority to make a decision, because both lack the necessary expertise (Laupa and Turiel, 1986).

Thus, children gradually come to understand and evaluate why people—particularly parents—act as they do. This increased understanding means that as children develop they may respond differently to the same parental behavior. And these changing responses may modify parents' behavior, which we consider in the next section.

The tone of the discussion so far may suggest that socialization is the one-way, completely conscious influence of adults on the behavior of children. This, in fact, was the assumption many developmental psychologists made from the time of John Watson until as late as the 1960s. In the past few decades, however, developmental psychologists have realized that the process is never simple. Socialization is always complex and multidirectional, and it involves a set of dynamic reciprocal influences between the child and others in the environment.

From the moment of birth, children arrive with their own particular temperaments, and the way their temperamental characteristics fit with those of their mothers, fathers, and other family members immediately influences the way they are treated. The treatment they receive influences them, of course, and all of this happens not in the isolated context of two (or even three, four, or five) people, but in the context of the total social environment.

Keller and Bell (1979) designed an experiment to illustrate the power of a child's behavior to influence adults. They trained three 9-year-olds to be responsive or unresponsive to older people and then had college students (their subjects) work individually with one of the children to accomplish various tasks. When a child was told to be responsive he or she looked at the student's face, smiled frequently, and always answered quickly and appropriately when the students spoke to him or her. In the

FIGURE 9–6
A scheme for conceptualizing socialization as a complex set of interacting influences.

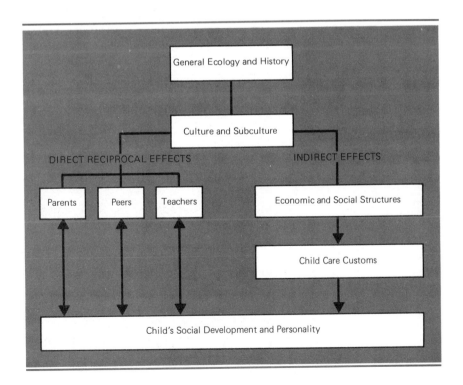

unresponsive condition, the child avoided looking at the student, rarely smiled, and responded to suggestions and questions either very slowly or not at all. The students whose children were told to be responsive were responsive themselves, generally using reasons and explanations in dealing with the children. When the very same children were unresponsive they provoked annoyance in the students, who typically responded by trying to assert their will or impose their power upon the children.

In fact, all socialization involves reciprocal influence. Figure 9–6 presents a schematic representation of how various forces interact with children and with each other to influence children's social development and personalities. We will have many opportunities to consider such interactions in the following chapters.

SUMMARY

1. Socialization is the entire set of events and processes by which children acquire the beliefs and behaviors of the particular society and subgroups into which they were born.

2. Socialization is a complex process, influenced indirectly by the general ecology and history of the group's culture and subculture, by economic and social structures, and child-care customs.

3. Parents, peers, and teachers act as direct agents of socialization. However, these people not only influence the children with whom they come into contact, but are also influenced by them. Thus, we say that all socialization involves *reciprocal influence*.

4. The family is the first major force responsible for socializing the child. Families differ in configuration. From the few combinations that have been studied extensively we know that first-born and only children tend to be more traditionally successful than other children and that later-born children in mixed families tend to take on some of the characteristics of their older opposite-sex siblings.

5. Marked differences in parenting styles have been noted. Along one dimension they have been cast as *authoritarian, authoritative,* or *permissive.*

6. Mothers are the single most important people in the lives of most infants and young children, and are thus primary socialization agents. Working mothers appear to have daughters who benefit from their mothers' dual roles. Sons of working mothers benefit in some ways, but they may be disadvantaged intellectually.

7. Young children often become quite attached to their fathers. Fathers also make an enormous contribution to children's social and intellectual development. Of course, not all fathers make positive contributions, and *inadequate fathering* has effects similar to *father absence.*

8. Almost half of all U.S. youngsters experience a divorce at some time during their childhood or adolescence. Guilt about

responsibility for the divorce, divided loyalties, and fantasies that the divorced parents will reunite are problems for children of both sexes. Being part of a *remarried family* complicates the picture further, especially for those who hope for magically improved relationships or quick adjustments.

9. Every culture appears to be concerned about *enculturation*— teaching children the culture's rules and habits.

10. Parents everywhere appear to have the same hierarchy of goals for their children, beginning with physical safety and survival, then the capacity for economic self-maintenance, and finally the ability to strive for higher forms of self-actualization.

11. The three principal modes of socialization are *direct instruction*, *shaping*, and *modeling*. All three are used to teach children about the social roles they and others can play in the culture, and all three are affected by children's cognitive understanding of social matters, by *social cognition*.

12. Direct instruction provides both information on what to do and *behavioral instigation*—urging or persuading someone to adopt a particular goal or follow a particular course of action. Direct instruction can provide *intent* to learn or act differently and *cognitive structure* by identifying the relevant and irrelevant attributes of a situation.

13. Shaping is the application of the basic conditioning processes to achieve social goals. It works by providing consequences which secure children's attention and motivate them. Consequences can involve either *reinforcement* or *punishment*, which in turn may be either *positive* (when the child receives something from a socializing agent) or *negative* (when the socializing agent takes something away from the child). *Time-out* and *response cost* are the two major forms of negative punishment.

14. Modeling involves observing and imitating the behavior of others, including an endless array of real people and media characters. Modeling involves more than simple imitation. A model's behavior, for example, can be accepted as a guide for what should not be done (*counterimitation*); it can also produce more general *inhibitory* and *disinhibitory* effects on whole classes of responses.

15. Children are not the passive recipients of efforts to socialize them. Rather, all socialization efforts are mediated by children's understanding the complex set of expectations, roles, and events that form the context for all their actions.

10 SELF-CONTROL, ACHIEVEMENT, AND MORAL VALUES

Young children's behavior is controlled to a large extent from outside influences: by the expectations of others, parental rewards and punishments, and peer pressures, to name a few. But as they grow older, children begin to behave "appropriately" without immediate, direct pressure from outside sources. They may continue to obey rules that were previously enforced by parents. They may decide, even when alone, to ignore immediate rewards in favor of long-range goals. They may impose relatively high standards on themselves. They may "do the right thing" when faced with a moral dilemma.

In this chapter we discuss three closely related aspects of the development of personal value systems: self-control, achievement standards and strivings, and moral values and behavior. Each of these areas entails developing a standard of some sort, and each is influenced strongly by cognitive and socialization processes.

Two broad theoretical approaches have guided most of the research we discuss: the *cognitive-behavioral* approach and the *cognitive-developmental* approach. There is no one specific theory behind either approach. Rather, they are general viewpoints or camps. And theorists and researchers within each camp differ among themselves.

The cognitive-behavioral approach draws heavily on the idea of socialization described in the previous chapter. It emphasizes the child's experiences (rewards, punishments, exposure to models, and so on) and the interpretations the child gives to these experiences. This view also assumes that children of any given age can be taught or trained to behave and react in many different ways if enough time, effort, and skill are put into the training (Bandura, 1977).

The cognitive-developmental view emphasizes the natural, built-in, age-related maturation of cognitive and biological processes as the driving force in personality development and social behavior. This view emphasizes stages or levels of cognitive development and assumes that everything a child thinks, says, and does is held together and partly generated by cognitive level. This view acknowledges that experience matters, just as the cognitive-behavioral view acknowledges the importance of cognitive ability in interpreting experience. But the difference in emphasis often leads to different kinds of experiments and different interpretations, observations, and data. These differences are clearly illustrated in the discussion that follows.

SELF-CONTROL

We say a person is showing *self-control* whenever he or she rises above the immediate pressures of the situation or avoids giving in to an immediate impulse. Much has been written about self-control—by philosophers and theologians as well as by research-oriented psychologists. Some psychologists have studied self-control as a global, unitary characteristic; but most break it down into two distinct types, *resistance to temptation* and *delay of gratification*.

Resistance to Temptation

Resistance to temptation means not taking an opportunity to engage in a socially prohibited but otherwise tempting act, such as cheating on a difficult exam or stealing someone else's property. Resistance to temptation differs from other forms of self-control because the emphasis is on whether or not the individual will follow an established rule. For this reason, the term *resistance to deviation* is preferred by some writers.

During the 1950s and 1960s, developmental psychologists devised laboratory tests that provided children with a temptation. The children were watched by hidden observers to see whether and how quickly they gave in. Several different types of questions were raised using these laboratory tests. Some researchers tried to determine the socialization practices that produce greatest and least resistance to temptation. Others were concerned with the situations that made resisting or giving in easier. Still others tried to show that behavior in the laboratory situation is a good predictor of other measures of self-control and personality functioning.

Physical versus Psychological Discipline. A classic study related 4-year-olds' resistance to temptation in the laboratory to the sort of discipline they received at home, as reported by their mothers (Burton, Maccoby, and Allinsmith, 1961). To determine the kinds of discipline used at home, the child's mother was interviewed intensively for about two hours. To assess tendencies to break or follow a stated rule, each child was introduced to a beanbag game, told the rules clearly, and left to play the game alone. The object of the game was to hit a wire stretched behind a board on which five lights were displayed in a row. Hitting the wire, it was explained, would turn one of the lights on. Each time this happened a bell would ring, signaling success. Players were to throw each of five bags over the board while standing behind a foot marker approximately five feet from the board; crossing the marker to be closer to the target would be a direct violation of the rules of the game. Before actually playing alone, each child was asked to select the toy he or she would like to win by getting "enough lights to win a prize."

Actually, the game was controlled by a hidden experimenter who not only made sure that everyone received the same score, but also monitored and recorded each child's behavior. (Controlling the scores in this way was necessary so that the temptation to cheat would not be related to possible differences in throwing ability.) Also built into the situation was a special incentive to cheat. Although only one light could be earned honestly, additional ones might be sought by stepping forward, moving the foot marker, retrieving bags, and hitting the wire with the hand. After three minutes, the experimenter returned to supervise another round for which a prize was awarded. This was done to check whether the children understood the rules, and to soothe feelings of failure among noncheaters and possible guilt among those who did cheat.

Burton and his associates were able to fit parental reports of disciplinary practices into two broad categories. Some mothers generally favored *physical* forms of discipline (slapping, spanking, shaking, and scolding). Others favored more *psychological* techniques (reasoning, with-

FIGURE 10–1
An important aspect of self-control is learning to resist temptation. Mimi Forsyth, Monkmeyer.

drawal of love, portrayal of suffering by the parent, and so on). The distinction proved to be quite valuable because of its relationship to actual resistance to temptation in the laboratory test. Children of mothers who preferred physical discipline were less likely to break the rules of the beanbag game and showed more self-control than children of mothers who preferred other methods.

The Burton findings suggest that direct physical discipline may be more effective than psychological discipline when a child is young. (Recall that these children were only 4 years old at the time of testing.) With the intellectual sophistication that comes as the child develops, psychological techniques become more effective. In fact, reasoning and explanation play a very important role in the development of self-control among older children (Hoffman, 1975).

Combining Reasoning and Punishment. Parents often provide rules for their children that are specific to the situation—for example, "Don't play with your father's sunglasses because if you drop them they might break." These directives, it is thought, help children evaluate their own behavior by explaining exactly *what* activity should be avoided and *why*. To see whether this is in fact the case, Cheyne (1969) explored the effects of a combination of verbal punishment with explicit verbal directives on kindergarten and third grade children. The children were assigned to one of three conditions:

1. Under the *punishment only* condition, children were told "That's bad." when they selected a certain toy to play with.

2. Under the *punishment plus simple rule* condition, children were told "That's bad. You should not play with that toy." when they selected a certain toy.

3. And under the *punishment plus elaborated rule* condition, children were told "That's bad. You should not play with that toy. That toy belongs to someone else."

When the children were left alone with the forbidden toy, those who had received the most information (those in the *punishment plus elaborated rule* condition) resisted touching and playing with it most often and for the longest periods of time. The amount of time that passed before children touched the toy is shown in Figure 10–2, which also indicates that the elaborated rule was more effective for the older children. Notice too that the older children deviated more quickly than the younger ones when rules were presented without any reason. Apparently, those old enough to benefit from a complete explanation resent not receiving one.

Reasoning versus Verbal Reproach.   In Cheyne's study, various levels of reasoning or explanation were added to the basic punishment experience. As expected, these additions increased the punishment's effectiveness. You might still wonder, though, whether resistance to temptation can be taught to older children through reasoning alone. One study at least has suggested that it can.

Leizer and Rogers (1974) taught a group of sixty first- and second-grade boys that they were not permitted to play with particular toys either through verbal punishment ("No! That's wrong. You must not pick that toy.") or through reasoning (by explaining that some of the toys

FIGURE 10–2
Amount of time (latency) before first deviation for kindergarten and third-grade boys and girls under various levels of rule structure in Cheyne's **experiment.** From J. A. Cheyne. "Punishment and Self-Control," paper presented at the R. H. Walters Memorial Symposium at the biennial meeting of the Society for Research in Child Development in 1969.

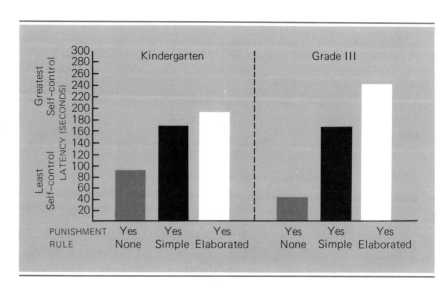

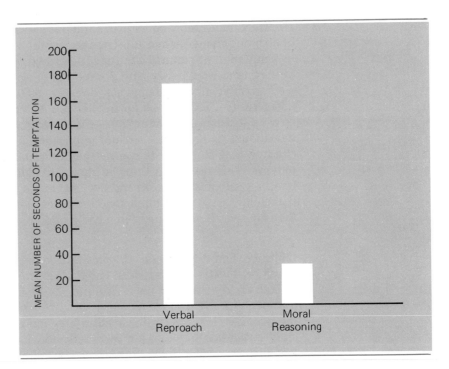

FIGURE 10–3
Mean number of seconds in which first- and second-grade boys in Leizer and Rogers's experiment played with a forbidden toy when alone, as a result of training through either verbal reproach or reasoning. (Reasoning was clearly the superior approach.) Data courtesy of Dr. Ronald W. Rogers.

were only for older boys). After this training, the experimenter left each child in a room with many toys, and through a one-way mirror observed how quickly the forbidden toy was touched (latency), how often it was touched (frequency), the length of time it was touched (duration), and whether the forbidden or the nonforbidden toy was touched first. On all four measures, resistance to temptation was stronger in the reasoning conditions. Figure 10–3 shows the results: Children in the reasoning condition spent significantly less time touching the forbidden toy than those in the verbal reproach condition. The overall effect was still evident fifteen days later. Numerous other studies also show that reasoning aids self-control by allowing children to attribute compliance to their own "goodness" rather than to some outside force of external constraints (Perry and Perry, 1983).

Emotional State. Most studies of resistance to temptation have focused on rewards and punishments and/or on various types of cognitive input. An additional factor has also been shown to influence resistance to temptation: the child's immediate emotional state. In a clear demonstration, Fry (1975) assigned 7- and 8-year-old boys and girls to one of three conditions, which varied in the mood they created. Children in the positive affect (or "think happy") group were induced to think about happy and pleasurable events; children in the negative affect ("think sad") group were induced to think about things that made them sad; and children in the neutral affect group were asked to assemble a very simple jigsaw puzzle. They thus interacted with an adult but presumably experienced little or no mood change as a result. Then each child was placed in a resistance-to-temptation situation like the ones described previously, and measures of the latency, frequency, and duration of deviations were obtained.

A positive mood state increased resistance to temptation on all three measures (see Figure 10–4 for frequency). A negative mood sharply decreased resistance to temptation—that is, increased the number of rule deviations. As Fry notes, a major implication of this experiment is that children may be taught to control their own mood states in various situations. This may help them to maintain self-control in a variety of tempting circumstances. In addition, of course, the results also suggest that children may be less able to follow rules or control themselves when they are sad, depressed, or "in a bad mood."

Objective Self-Awareness.   Increasing people's awareness of their own behavior, *objective self-awareness,* can increase many forms of self-control in both children and adults (Wicklund, 1975). Objective self-awareness may be indirectly fostered by many socialization practices—for example, punishing a child for a rule violation may have the effect of calling the child's attention to his or her own behavior. However, the most direct way to increase objective self-awareness is to hold a mirror up to the person's behavior. Investigators have found some intriguing ways to do just that.

One field experiment (Beaman, Klentz, Diener, and Svanum, 1980) illustrates how a simple tactic to increase self-awareness can increase resistance to temptation in a naturalistic situation. Beaman and his associates conducted their study on Halloween. The participants were children who came to trick or treat at thirteen homes. Each home had

FIGURE 10–4
Frequency of deviations exhibited in Fry's (1975) experiment as a function of whether a positive or negative mood had been induced.   From data in Fry (1975). Copyright © 1975 by the American Psychological Association. Reprinted by permission of the author.

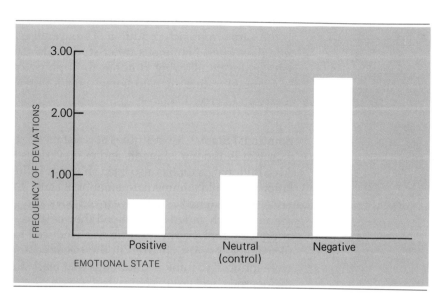

been selected and arranged so that inside a room near the front door was a large bowl filled with wrapped, bite-sized candy bars placed on a long, low table.

Whenever a child or a small group of children arrived at one of these homes, they were greeted by a female experimenter who praised their costumes, told each child he or she could take only *one* candy, asked each child his or her name and age, and excused herself "to go back to my work in another room." (However, unknown to the children, another observer remained hidden in the room and was able to observe how many candies each child actually took after the experimenter left.) In the self-awareness condition of the study, a large mirror was placed just behind the table with the candy bowl. The mirror was positioned so that the children would see themselves as they reached for the candy. In the control condition, the mirror was simply removed.

As predicted, boys who could not see themselves in the mirror were far more likely to take more than one candy than boys who could see themselves in the mirror. Equally interesting is the fact that the mirror had almost no effect on girls, who were quite likely to follow the rule even in the no-mirror condition.

The effects of inducing objective self-awareness through self-monitoring of one's own behavior is not limited to children. Guided self-observation has also been shown to play a significant role in helping adolescents and adults to resist temptation in such areas as smoking, overeating, and failing to complete homework assignments (Rimm and Masters, 1979). In one such study (Adesso, Vargas, and Siddall, 1979) adolescents who had been biting their nails for an average of almost twelve years showed a significant increase in nail length (the "hard" measure of whether nail biting has been reduced) at their four-month follow-up examination, merely as a result of self-awareness training. They were instructed to record every instance of their own nail biting (by keeping a tally on a 3×5 card) and chart the frequency of their nail biting. Once a week for four weeks their nails were measured. A comparable group of nail biters who just had their nails measured at the beginning and end of the study showed little change.

Delay of Gratification

In *Walden Two* (1948), B. F. Skinner's novel describing a utopia built on radical behavioral principles, preschool children are given lollipops every morning. The lollipops are not just a treat; they play an important role in teaching self-control. The lollipops are all dipped in powdered sugar so that a single touch of the tongue can be detected. The children are allowed to eat the lollipop in the afternoon only if they can keep from licking it at all in the meantime. In this situation, the child who takes a small immediate pleasure will have to forfeit a larger but delayed reward, the whole lollipop.

The child's problem is to learn *delay of gratification*, that form of self-control involved whenever children or adults postpone immediate reward for the sake of more valued outcomes that will come only with patience and effort. A college student who gives up a weekend movie today in order to study so that next week she can enjoy a movie *and* an A on her exam is displaying delay of gratification. So is the teenager who waits for a sale so that he can buy more (or better) clothes with the same money. How does delay of gratification emerge in childhood, and what are the psychological processes behind its development?

Importance of Modeling. There is a county in Nova Scotia, Canada, where conflicting subcultures have lived side by side for generations (Bandura and Walters, 1963). In the Acadian community of Lavallée, children are expected to control immediate impulses and work toward distant goals. Educational and vocational achievement is stressed. In this community parents spend large amounts of time with their children and transmit the adult patterns of their subculture with great efficiency. The children of Lavallée are unlikely to give in to the temptation to take an immediate small pleasure when it means forfeiting something worthwhile in the future.

In the same Nova Scotian county lives another group of people whose community is strikingly lacking in cohesion: fighting, drunkenness, theft, and other antisocial acts occur frequently. Adults in this subculture believe that "the best thing to do in life is to escape from one's problems as quickly as possible." Their children are exposed to models exhibiting an overwhelming preference for immediate gratification.

But what would happen if a child from this subculture was adopted by Acadian parents in Lavallée and an Acadian child from Lavallée was adopted by settlement parents? Would the behavior of either of these children be influenced by the new models with whom they would have contact?

Bandura and Mischel (1965) set up a laboratory experiment to test this question, and demonstrated the importance of modeling in the transmission of delay behavior. In the first part of the study, fourth- and fifth-grade children were given a delay-of-gratification test in which they were to make a series of fourteen choices between a small immediate reward and a larger delayed outcome. For instance, they were asked to choose between a small candy bar that would be given to them immediately or a larger one that would require a week of waiting. Children who displayed strong preferences for immediate reward or delayed reward were identified and then assigned to one of three conditions.

In the *live modeling condition* children observed an actual adult model make a series of choices between a less valuable item, which could be obtained immediately, and a more valuable item, which required delay.* The model consistently chose the immediate reward item in the presence of children who demonstrated a preference for the larger delayed re-

---

*The prizes between which the adult model chose were suitable for adults (chess sets, magazines, and so forth) and were different from the items between which the children subsequently chose. Thus, each child was able to imitate the "principle" underlying the model's behavior but was unable to copy the specific choices.

ward. The model observed by children who preferred smaller immediate rewards always selected the delayed reward item. In both cases, the model also briefly summarized a philosophy about the behavior he was displaying. For example, when the choice was between a plastic chess set to be given immediately and a more expensive wooden set to be given in two weeks, the model commented, "Chess figures are chess figures. I can get much use out of the plastic ones right away" (p. 701).

In the *symbolic modeling condition*, children were exposed to the same kind of sequence except that the model's choices and comments were presented in written form. In the *no model present condition*, children serving as controls for the possible effects of exposure to rewards were simply shown the series of paired objects. All children were then given a delay-of-reward test in the model's absence. To assess the stability of any changes in behavior, they also were given another test one month later.

The results of the experiment were clear: Children exposed to a model (live or symbolic) who delayed gratification shifted their own preferences so that on posttest about 50 percent of all their choices were for the larger outcomes that required waiting. Even after a month's time these effects were still present. On the other hand, in the majority of cases, children exposed to models who showed little self-control were easily swayed by the impulsive model and abandoned their own self-control. We might well expect, then, that a child from the settlement culture in Nova Scotia would be influenced by the self-restraint in the behavior of the Acadian citizens of Lavallée, and that the behavior of the Acadian child from Lavallée would be influenced toward less self-restraint through observation of role models in the settlement culture.

The Decision Process. Although Skinner's Walden Two community would certainly offer children a number of adult models of self-control, more direct efforts to teach delay of gratification are also prescribed. Here is the way Frazier, the storyteller of *Walden Two*, puts it:

> First of all, the children are urged to examine their own behavior while looking at the lollipops. This helps them to recognize the need for self-control. Then the lollipops are concealed and the children are asked to notice any gain in happiness or any reduction in tension. Then a strong distraction is arranged—say, an interesting game. Later the children are reminded of the candy and encouraged to examine their reaction. The value of the distraction is generally obvious. . . . When the experiment is repeated a day or so later, the children all run with the lollipops to their lockers . . . a sufficient indication of the success of our training. (1948, p. 108)

Skinner assumes that delaying gratification involves two steps: an initial decision that one wishes to wait and then an effort to maintain resolve and bridge the waiting time. Walter Mischel, who did much of the pioneering experimental work on delay of gratification, also views the underlying psychological process as involving these two steps. What is more, he has shown that the steps are influenced by different factors (Mischel, 1974).

In situations in which a child must choose between accepting or not accepting the frustration of delay for the sake of earning a superior outcome, he or she probably considers the subjective values of both immediate and delayed rewards and the probability of obtaining them (Mischel, 1958; Mischel and Metzner, 1962).

In the excerpt from *Walden Two*, for example, most youngsters would probably consider the delayed reward (a whole lollipop) superior to the immediate reward (a few licks of a lollipop). But the course of action also depends on the trustworthiness of the people giving the lollipops, which introduces an element of risk in waiting. And there is another consideration. In most life situations, attaining delayed rewards involves not only simply waiting, but also performing some required activity.

When the difference in value between the immediate and the delayed reward is slight and/or the risk of not being able to obtain the delayed reward is great, the rational choice (and the one children presumably make) is to take the immediate reward. When the difference in value is substantial and/or when obtaining the delayed reward is not too risky, the rational choice may be the delayed reward (Mischel and Staub, 1965).

Once the choice has been made to wait for the delayed but superior prize, another question arises. Will the child be able to go through with the plan? Although older children tend to show more self-control in this respect (Mischel and Metzner, 1962), delaying reward can be difficult at any age. Experimental work in this area is beginning to tell us how we tolerate a frustrating time span.

Maintaining Delay of Gratification. Freud (1959) suggested that delay of gratification could be maintained by creating mental images of the desired object, producing substitute satisfactions to ease the frustration of delay. Others have advanced similar notions. Using Freud's ideas as an initial framework, Mischel and his associates have conducted an exten-

FIGURE 10–5
A preschool child waiting for delayed gratification.
Courtesy of Dr. Walter Mischel.

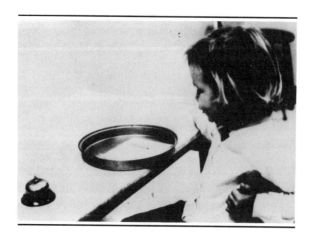

sive program of research aimed at understanding delay of gratification. Mischel and Ebbesen (1970), for example, predicted that children would find waiting for a delayed reward easiest when they could see the reward. Viewing rewards would serve as a vivid reminder that the reward was worth waiting for, and would also increase the child's trust that he or she would actually receive the reward. This prediction obviously contradicts the principle of distraction described in *Walden Two*.

To test their prediction, Mischel and Ebbesen set up the following situation. Three- to 5-year-old children first were asked which of two foods (cookies or pretzels) they preferred. Each youngster was then told he or she would wait alone in a room until the experimenter returned, when the preferred food would be provided. The child could call the experimenter back to the room at any time by a prearranged signal; but in this case only the nonpreferred food would be provided. The experimenter then left, leaving on the table both foods, the preferred food only, the nonpreferred food only, or neither food. He returned in fifteen minutes, or earlier if signaled by the child.

The length of time children in the different food conditions waited was the dependent measure of the study. Figure 10–6 shows that the results were the opposite of the investigators' expectations. That is, children who were exposed to neither of the foods delayed significantly more than those exposed to both or one of the foods. The children in this

FIGURE 10–6
Average amount of time children were able to wait for the delayed but preferred food in Mischel and Ebbesen's (1970) experiment. Note that children were able to wait longest when no foods were present in the room, and least able to control themselves when both foods were present. Which of the foods (delayed or immediate) was present did not seem to matter.   Adopted from Mischel and Ebbesen (1970). Copyright 1970 by the American Psychological Association. Reprinted by permission.

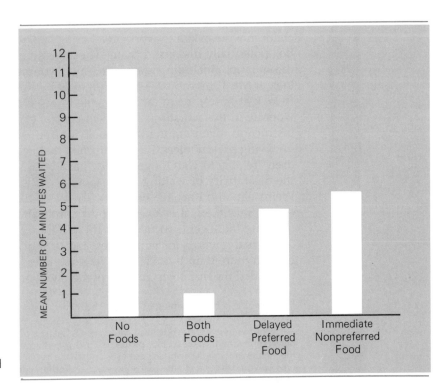

group were able to sit alone for an average of over eleven minutes—and 75 percent of them had to be interrupted at the fifteen-minute mark.

Observations of all the children's behavior through a one-way mirror provided a clue to how time was bridged. Elaborate distraction techniques were designed spontaneously: Some children sang, talked to themselves, and invented games. Among those children who successfully waited when food was present, many avoided looking at it by covering their eyes with their hands or resting their heads on their arms. Any activity that converted the situation into a less frustrating experience could increase delay time, so Mischel and his associates began to experiment directly with various techniques.

The focus of these later investigations has been cognitive in emphasis, in the sense that what the child *thinks* has been of central interest. One study showed that when children are asked to think about "fun things," their ability to bridge a wait period increases. If they think "sad thoughts," waiting is reduced; most children take the immediate reward and end the delay (Mischel, Ebbesen, and Raskoff, 1971). But what happens if the child thinks about the rewards themselves? Does such thought increase self-control? Or does it arouse appetites and decrease the ability to wait, just as the presence of the "real thing" did in Mischel and Ebbeson's (1970) original study? The answer to these questions suggests that some subtle and complex mental processes are involved in self-control.

One possibility, suggested by the work of Mischel and Patterson (1976), is that ability to delay gratification may be helped by clear plans or blueprints for action. In the Mischel and Patterson study, preschool children were asked to work on a boring task while an attractive Clown Box potentially distracted them. Those given a concrete way to handle the situation, including *what do do* (say to yourself, "I'm just not going to look at Mr. Clown Box!") and *when to do it* ("when Mr. Clown Box says to look at him"), were far better able to resist temptation and continue working in this situation. Thus, self-control can be gained through self-instruction, even among preschool children. More recent studies, also involving preschoolers, have confirmed that even these very young children are able to wait longer if they have been taught to verbalize about the desirability of waiting—for example, "It is good if I wait." (Miller, Weinstein, and Karniol, 1978).

Overall, then, it is *how* the child thinks about the desired object or outcome that seems to make all the difference. In one study, children facing real rewards for which they had to wait were able to delay gratification more than twice as long (eighteen versus eight minutes) if they pretended the real object in front of them was only a picture.* And think-

*This requires a bit of training of course. The following extract from the actual instruction used, illustrates the point:
. . . Close your eyes. In your head try to see the picture of the _____(immediate and delayed rewards). Make a color picture of (them); put a frame around them. You can see the picture of them. Now open your eyes and do the same thing. (more practice) . . . From now on you can see a picture that shows _____(immediate and delayed rewards) here in front of you. The _____aren't real; they're just a picture. . . . When I'm gone remember to see the picture in front of you. (Mischel, 1974, p. 285)

ing about an absent reward in a way that is concrete and arousing (for example, thinking about *eating* the pretzels or cookies for which one is waiting) robs the child of self-control almost as thoroughly as looking at the real thing.

Changes in Delay of Gratification.   One of the clearest findings regarding ability to delay gratification is that it increases with age. There is a substantial increase in delay behavior somewhere between the ages of 6 and 8 (Nisan, 1974).

Three broad explanations for this change have been offered. The classical psychoanalytic explanation focuses on the shift from the pleasure to the reality principle. Such a shift is said to result partly from experience and environmental pressures and partly from the internalization of parental standards. The cognitive-behavior explanation emphasizes experience, especially experience with the greater rewards that delay brings and with models who show delay of gratification. The cognitive-developmental explanation focuses on cognitive growth, including advances in the ability to understand the notion of time, to consider several dimensions of a problem simultaneously, and to structure information. The cognitive-developmental explanation differs from the other two in that changes in delay of gratification with age are assumed to be linked to overall cognitive growth.

Nisan and Koriat (1984) conducted an experiment in Israel with 5- and 6-year-old boys and girls to test several hypotheses derived from the cognitive-developmental perspective. Their basic procedure involved three phases. In the first phase, children were asked to recommend a choice between a small immediate reward and a large delayed reward to another child of their own sex, based on a story presented by the experimenter. To set the stage for phase one, children were told:

> Yesterday I was in another kindergarten and there was a nice boy/girl there called Yosi [Anat for girls]. Yosi/Anat likes to draw very much, and he/she made me a nice drawing. I told him/her that since he/she made such a nice drawing he/she could get a prize. The prize was either one chocolate bar today or two chocolate bars tomorrow. Yosi/Anat told me that he/she liked chocolate a lot and didn't know what to choose, so he/she asked me to ask other children what they suggested he/she should choose. Do you think it's better for him/her to choose one chocolate bar today or two chocolate bars tomorrow? (Nisan and Koriat, 1984, p. 494)

The experimenters assumed that, at this point in the procedure, the recommendation that a child made for Yosi or Anat was in fact the preference that child would have for him- or herself.

Everyone was presented the same cover story in phase one, but the experience of each child in phase two depended on the experimental condition to which the child had been randomly assigned.

In phase two, the *contradicting reasons and information* group was told about another child of the same sex as the subject who "also made a very

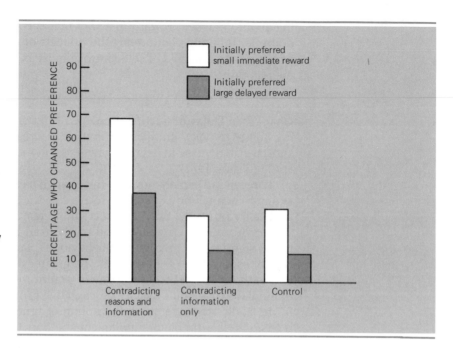

FIGURE 10–7
FIGURE 10–7
Percentage of children who changed their delay of gratification preferences in each group of Nisan and Koriat's (1984) experiment. From data in Nisan and Koriat (1984).

nice drawing" and also chose between the prize of one chocolate bar today and two chocolate bars tomorrow. Then the subject was told this other child's choice, which was always presented as the opposite of the one the subject had just chosen for Yosi or Anat (contradicting information), and was asked to explain why the other child might have made the choice he or she did. The subjects themselves generated the contradicting reasons—that is, reasons that might explain a preference opposite to their own. In the *contradicting information only* group, the subject was told of the other child's opposite choice but was not asked to supply reasons. Finally, the *control* group heard nothing of the other child's choice, but was instead told an irrelevant story about the other child's picture preferences.

During the third and final phase of the experiment, all children were asked to indicate their own preferences for one chocolate bar today or two chocolate bars tomorrow. The central measure in the experiment was the percentage of children in each group who changed the direction of their preferences between phase one and phase three. The results, displayed in Figure 10–7, show that information about another child's behavior, by itself, had almost no effect. Information coupled with self-generated reasons had a considerable effect, especially for children whose initial preferences had been immediate but who had been induced to think about and give reasons for delayed choices.

Significance of Laboratory Tests

In experimental research on delay of gratification, children are asked to wait briefly in unfamiliar settings or to imagine what other children might do. To what extent can we generalize these findings to children's ability to delay gratification in the home or at school? One of the most extensive investigations of resistance to temptation ever undertaken was recently reported by Funder, Block, and Block (1983). These investigators administered two laboratory tests of resistance to temptation to 116 children when they were 4 years old. They then followed the children for seven years to obtain follow-up data from teachers when the youngsters were 7 and 11. The purpose of the tests was to determine whether laboratory measures are really related to children's actual home and school behavior and personality characteristics.

In the first laboratory measure, the experimenter showed a child a gift-wrapped package, explained the package contained a present for the child, and then informed the child that he or she could actually have the gift after completing a complex and not-too-interesting puzzle. The child was given two minutes to work on the puzzle alone, and then was aided by the experimenter during the next two minutes to assure that the puzzle would be completed in four minutes. Then the experimenter busied herself for ninety seconds with some papers. She then told the child: "O.K., you can have your present now."

Throughout this entire sequence the children were carefully observed to determine how well they controlled impulses to look at, talk about, or take the presents before they completed the puzzles or before they were told to take them. Also recorded was whether a child opened the present immediately, on the way back to the nursery school, or waited until after school.

The second laboratory task involved bringing each child into a small room containing a set of attractive toys (including a doll and dollhouse and a toy marina with boats and a gas pump) and a set of unattractive "toys" (such as a comb and a "small, bent, green plastic tree"). Each child was told that he or she could play only with the unattractive objects because the attractive toys belonged to someone else. The experimenter then left the child alone in the room for six minutes, with the excuse that she had forgotten something in the next room. She then observed the child to see whether he or she attended to, moved toward, or attempted to reach toward, pick up, or play with any of the forbidden toys.

Remember that the major purpose of these tests was to determine whether laboratory measures such as these are really related to children's actual behavior and personalities. Among boys, ability to delay gratification at age 4, as measured by laboratory tests, was associated with ability to control impulses (in school at age 11) and ability to pay attention, concentrate, and behave dependably. In contrast, boys who showed least delay of gratification at age 4 tended as 11-year-olds to be restless and fidgety, emotional, irritable, and unstable, and to react immaturely under stress.

For girls, the ability to resist impulses at age 4 was *not* particularly related to later impulse control but was related to social competence. That is, 4-year-old girls who resisted temptation were judged in later years by teachers to be more socially resourceful and competent than other girls. The girls at age 4 who were unable to resist temptation appeared to have problems later. According to Funder and his associates, they "tended to go to pieces under stress, to be victimized by other children, and to be easily offended, sulky, and whiny." (Funder et al., 1983, p. 1212).

Thus, the Funder et al. study does document that brief laboratory measures of resistence to temptation do predict later development and do tap psychological processes that are relevant to life situations.

ACHIEVEMENT STANDARDS AND STRIVINGS

All people set achievement standards for themselves. People differ, though, in regard to the stringency of their self-imposed standards. Some schoolchildren, for example, will appear pleased and delighted to receive a B, while others will blame themselves for failing to get an A. Self-imposed standards of achievement are largely products of socialization. The question of how they are acquired has long intrigued developmental psychologists.

The Achieving Child

Achievement-oriented behavior may occur in the arts, in academic work, in sports, or any endeavor that involves level of competence. Competence, however, can be shown only in situations in which there is a "standard of excellence" for the performance that is agreed upon by those concerned.

Substantial differences in achievement striving among children of 5 years of age and older have been observed in a number of studies. Whereas some children show great persistence with tasks requiring skill and effort at this age, others do not. Similarly, whereas some children tend to seek recognition for achievement, others seem to care little for such reward. And it is not surprising that the emergence of achievement motivation is related to cognitive development, since children must recognize that their own abilities and efforts produce success or failure as a precondition for certain kinds of attainment striving (Weiner and Kun, 1976).

How, though, should we look at the differences that exist among children in their striving for success, even from the first school years? At one time psychologists thought that a clear line could be drawn between achievement and ability. Ability, it was claimed, referred to the child's inborn talents and aptitudes. Achievement referred to the child's accomplishments—that is, what he or she did with these talents. We now know that such a clear distinction is not possible and can, in fact, be quite misleading. All we can ever see is children's performance. This is the complex and inscrutable result of all that they are, all that they have experienced, and all that makes up their environment at the moment. For this reason, we use the terms *achievement*, *ability*, and *achievement/ability* interchangeably to refer to any of a child's achievement-related performances.

What Is Achievement Motivation?

Some theorists have focused on underlying differences in children's *achievement motivation* (also called *need achievement*), a concept used to try to predict and/or explain achievement behavior. In assessing the amount of achievement motivation possessed by a particular child, the examiner listens as the child tells a story about each of several ambiguous pictures. The child's replies are scored according to the frequency of achievement themes in the stories. This method, developed by David McClelland, is based on the assumption that achievement imagery in the youngster's storytelling reflects the degree of achievement motivation in the child's personality (McClelland, Atkinson, Clark, and Lowell, 1953).

In a work entitled *The Achieving Society,* McClelland (1961) took an unusual research tack. He attempted to predict the economic growth of twenty-three countries between 1929 and 1950 on the basis of the amount of achievement imagery appearing in their children's stories for the period 1920 to 1929. The achievement motive found in the children's stories correlated + .53 with an index of national economic growth. McClelland (1961) concludes from this and other similar studies that children's stories reflect ". . . the motivational level of the adults at the time they are published, perhaps particularly of the adults responsible for the education of children . . ." (p. 102). These findings dovetail with those of an experimental study in which preschool children's efforts to complete an achievement-related task increased after the children were read a story about the achievement-oriented behavior of a child of their own sex (McArthur and Eisen, 1975).

If there is an intrinsic motivation to perform well, accomplishing difficult tasks should be more satisfying than accomplishing easier tasks. To demonstrate this expected relationship, Harter (1977) gave first-grade boys and girls a series of puzzles representing four levels of difficulty. The children were observed secretly by trained recorders while they were absorbed in the task. The recorders scored each child's spontaneous smiling upon completion of each puzzle (e.g., no smile = 0; slight or half smile = 1; full smile or grin = 2). As expected, the children were more likely to smile, or to smile more broadly, when they solved difficult puzzles than when they solved easier ones (see Figure 10–8).

FIGURE 10–8
Average amount of smiling in Harter's (1977) study as first-grade boys and girls solved problems varying in difficulty. From data reported in Harter (1977).

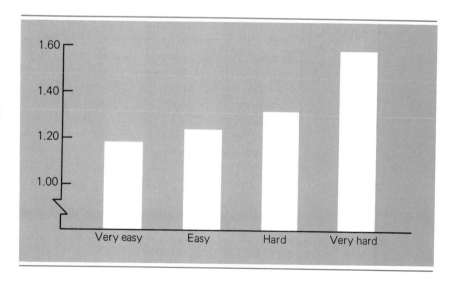

In a later study involving sixth-grade boys and girls, Harter (1980) found that problems labeled *very hard* by the youngsters brought less smiling and were rated as less enjoyable than those rated *hard*. When the children were questioned after the study, they explained that the very hard problems were simply too time-consuming and frustrating. It seems, then, that satisfaction comes from tasks that are neither too easy nor too difficult. Harter concludes that each of us seeks work that is challenging in relation to our abilities.

Understanding the Causes and Consequences of Achievement

Some children achieve easily; others reach the same level of achievement only after hard work. Many adults conclude that children in the first group are more able than those in the second, who compensate for their lack of ability by extra effort. Both ability and effort are ingredients of achievement in settings such as school or athletics.

The understanding that achievement has multiple causes develops gradually. Most children, prior to 7 or 8 years of age, attribute achievement entirely to effort, believing that a good deal of effort leads to achievement, while lack of effort results in failure. Not until the middle elementary school years do children understand the concept of ability, defined here as a limit on the extent to which effort translates directly into achievement (Nicholls, 1978).

Because older children have a more sophisticated understanding of the causes of achievement, they also are more likely to be influenced by the consequences of failing. For younger children, failure to achieve means that they did not try hard enough; consequently, the formula for greater success in the future is simple: Try harder. For older children, failure could mean that they did not apply enough effort, but if these children believe that they *did* try hard, then failure can only mean that they are untalented. Furthermore, if lack of talent is perceived as the cause of failure, there is no reason to expect added effort to improve the situation.

Rholes, Blackwell, Jordan, and Walters (1980) demonstrated this pattern of developmental change in a study in which they manipulated children's success or failure at finding pictures hidden in several puzzles. After either success on four puzzles or failure on four, children's performance was compared on a fifth puzzle. For 5- to 8-year-old children, success or failure on previous puzzles influenced neither the length of time they spent searching for pictures hidden in the fifth puzzle, nor their success or failure on the fifth puzzle. However, among 10-year-olds, children who experienced failure on the first four puzzles spent less time looking for pictures in the fifth puzzle and were less successful than children who had experienced success on the previous puzzles. Apparently the 10-year-olds, because they had worked hard to find the pictures hidden in the first four puzzles, interpreted their failure as reflecting lack of ability, and stopped trying.

The important message, then, is that children's greater understanding of achievement is not without cost. Among older children, failure to achieve—in the face of sufficient effort—may be interpreted as indicating lack of ability, resulting in less motivation to achieve (Covington and Omelich, 1979, 1981). Thus early patterns of achievement may lead to differences between individuals in their expectations for future achievement. We now examine these individual differences.

Locus of Control. Children differ in the extent to which they believe that their own actions can influence the outcome of events. Some tend to assume that they are responsible for their success and failures; others tend to attribute responsibility to outside agents, luck, fate, and other people.

The extent to which children believe that the locus of responsibility for achievement is internal rather than external can be measured by the "Intellectual Achievement Responsibility Questionnaire" (IAR), a thirty-four-item scale that measures responsibility for both pleasant and unpleasant consequences. Each item consists of a description of an achievement-related experience that might have occurred in the child's life, followed by one alternative stating that the event occurred because of the child's own actions and another stating that the event was caused by other forces. Exemplary items from the IAR Questionnaire are presented in Table 10–1. In answering the questionnaire, the child is asked to pick the answer for each item "that best describes what happens to you or how you feel."

Children who score high as "internalizers" on this scale tend to get better grades and to do better on achievement tests than do those who score high as "externalizers" (Gagne, 1975). In fact, in some situations the IAR scale is a better predictor of achievement than are measures of achievement motivation (Crandall, Katkovsky, and Preston, 1962). Internalizers may well show greater initiative and persistence in solving difficult problems and a willingness to modify their behavior to achieve desired goals. Externalizers may see little reason to initiate, persist, or

---

TABLE 10–1

Sample Items from the Intellectual Achievement Responsibility Questionnaire (IAR)

1. If a teacher passes you to the next grade, would it probably be
   _____ a. because she liked you, or
   _____ b. because of the work you did?
2. When you do well on a test at school, is it more likely to be
   _____ a. because you studied for it, or
   _____ b. because the test was especially easy?
3. When you read a story and can't remember much of it, is it usually
   _____ a. because the story wasn't well written, or
   _____ b. because you weren't interested in the story?
4. Suppose your parents say you are doing well in school. Is this likely to happen
   _____ a. because your school work is good, or
   _____ b. because they are in a good mood?

Source: Courtesy Virginia Crandall.

modify their behavior, since they believe the outcome is not under their control.

The relation between internal locus of control and academic achievement is significantly higher for males than for females, but does not seem to vary due to race or SES. The strength of the relation *does* vary depending on a student's grade in school: The relation is strongest for junior high school students and next strongest for those in grades four through six and in high school. Locus of control and achievement are only weakly related for college students, perhaps because they are already a group with an orientation toward academic achievement. The relation is weakest (and perhaps not present) for those in the first three grades of elementary school (Findley and Cooper, 1983).

What helps a child to develop internal control? The most important factor seems to be encouraging a child's self-reliance and independence in a nonauthoritarian environment (Crandall, 1973; Lifshiftz and Ramot, 1978; Wichern and Nowicki, 1976). For example, the earlier in life children are allowed to become independent (for instance, by staying overnight at a friend's house) the more internal is their locus of control orientation (Crandall, 1973).

Mastery versus Helplessness. Carol Dweck and her associates (e.g., Dweck, 1975; Dweck and Bush, 1976) view the locus of control scale as measuring the degree to which children have "mastery" versus "helpless" orientations. Dweck holds that orientation directly influences the responses of children of equal ability. Mastery-oriented children, who see deficiencies in performance as due to controllable factors such as the need to spend more time with a problem or put more effort into it, intensify their efforts in the face of initial confusion. Helpless children often reduce their efforts and may show deterioration in performance. In a way, the children's responses make good sense:

> To conclude that one does not have the ability to do well implies that an escalation of effort would be fruitless. . . . In contrast, the belief that one's failures are related to controllable factors such as effort, one's specific strategies, and the like, allows a child to maintain a high assessment of his or her ability, even in the face of obstacles. It also implies that an escalation of effort or an alteration of strategy in the face of failure is likely to pay off. (Licht and Dweck, 1984, pp. 628–629)

A recent experiment shows exactly how the process operates. Licht and Dweck (1984) gave fifth-grade boys and girls the Intellectual Achievement Responsibility Questionnaire and divided the youngsters into those with clear mastery or helplessness orientations. (Those whose scores fell in the middle of the scale were excluded from the remainder of the study.) Then the children were randomly assigned to groups. The legitimate material the experimental group was to learn was preceded by confusing, irrelevant, but apparently meaningful passages. The control

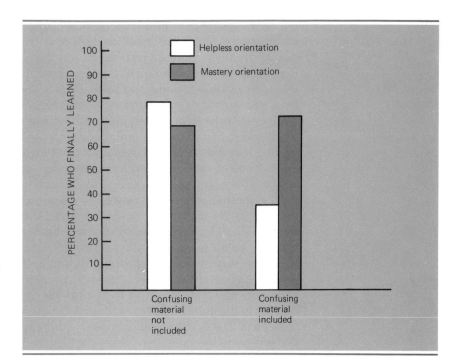

FIGURE 10–9
Percentage of elementary school children who finally learned the passages in Licht and Dweck's (1984) experiment. From data in Licht and Dweck (1984).

group had the same legitimate material to learn, but without the confusing passages.

Among those who received the legitimate material in a straightforward way, without irrelevant passages, no differences in learning were found between the mastery and helpless groups. When the material to be learned had been introduced with confusing passages, however, children with a helpless orientation were much less likely to learn than those with a mastery orientation. Moreover, the differences were even more pronounced after a review session, which was not confusing and was the same for everyone. Apparently, the helpless children were not easily able to overcome their confusion (see Figure 10–9).

SES and Achievement

One of the clearest facts about achievement is its association with socioeconomic status (SES). In general, the lower a child's SES background in terms of parents' income and employment status, the less the child achieves in school and later in life. Keep in mind, though, that this is a statement about population characteristics. There are *many* individual exceptions. We all know individuals from disadvantaged backgrounds who have made many outstanding achievements, as well as advantaged persons who have made disappointingly few.

A landmark study in explaining how social class differences might lead to differing levels of school achievement was done by Robert Hess and Virginia Shipman (1965, 1968). According to Hess and Shipman, lower-class families are status oriented—that is, they accept the status quo and view rules as unquestionable and appropriate. This orientation underlies the restrictive mode of dealing with the world that is taught through mother-child interaction. Middle-class families, in contrast, are thought to be person oriented. Because this approach emphasizes attention to individual feelings and roles, it leads to consideration of alternatives and variations rather than simple obedience.

To test these hypotheses, 163 mothers and their 4-year-old children were selected from four different social status levels, ranging from college-educated professional, executive, and managerial occupational levels to those from unskilled or semiskilled occupational levels, with fathers absent and families supported by public assistance.

The mothers were interviewed twice in their homes and were then brought to the university for testing and for interaction sessions with their children. During the sessions, each mother was taught three simple tasks by a staff member and was then asked to teach these tasks to her child.The tasks involved grouping plastic toys by color and function, grouping blocks by two characteristics simultaneously, and working together to copy patterns on an Etch-a-Sketch.

One of the more striking results was that person orientation increased with social class. The significance of the difference is captured in mothers' replies to the question: "Suppose your child was starting to school tomorrow for the first time. What would you tell him [her]? How would you prepare him [her] for school?" Table 10–2 contains the answers provided by two mothers, one person oriented and the other status oriented. Mother A has provided many reasons the child could use in deciding that school will probably be a pleasant and rewarding experience. While telling the child to obey the teacher, the mother has also given several reasons why this is a good idea. Mother B not only concentrates on a relatively minor aspect of the school experience, but also gives the child little reason to look forward to school. There is no basis to form any ex-

---

TABLE 10–2
What Mothers Tell their Children Prior to the First Day of School

A	B
"First of all, I would take him to see his new school, we would talk about the building, and after seeing the school I would tell him that he should meet new children who would be his friends; he would work and play with them. I would explain to him that the teacher would be his friend, and would help him and guide him in school, and that he should do as she tells him to." [P. 96]	"Well, I would tell him he going to school and he have to sit down and mind the teacher and be a good boy, and I show him how when they give him milk, you know, how he's supposed to take his straw and do, and not put nothing on the floor when he get through." [P. 96]

pectation, and the child can only carry out a set of instructions for which he or she has not been given a rationale. This finding serves as an example of the ways in which broad social context may be related to parent-child interaction and children's development.

Of course, the school plays its part too. Recently, Marsh and Parker (1984) reported a fascinating study in which they attempted to pull together and examine the relationships among SES, school achievement, and a variable that has been found to link the two—self-concept. The investigators obtained IQ scores, teacher ratings of academic ability, teacher ratings of students' self-concepts, and students' measures of their own self-concepts (via a self-description questionnaire), as well as family SES data for all sixth graders in several schools. An assessment of the relationships among SES, ability, achievement, and self-concept revealed the following pattern:

1. Children from higher SES homes had higher academic self-concepts.
2. Children with higher ability had higher academic self-concepts.
3. Children from higher SES schools, on the average, had *lower* academic self-concepts. Likewise, the higher the average ability of the children in a school, the lower the academic self-concept of any given child in that school was likely to be.
4. Teachers judged their students' academic self-concepts to be higher at higher SES schools. (In other words, the teachers' views of the students and the students' views of themselves appear to go in opposite directions.)

Marsh and Parker (1984) proposed a "frame of reference" hypothesis to explain the overall results:

(a) Children compare their own academic ability (more or less objectively perceived) with the abilities of other students within their school or reference group, and
(b) children use this relativistic impression of their academic ability as one basis for forming their academic self-concept. . . . (p. 217)

Let us see how the frame of reference helps us put this pattern of results together.

First, assume that a student's frame of reference for academic ability and academic self-concept is the other students at school. Second, assume that SES and academic ability/achievement are related, which we know they are. Therefore, a student at a low SES and/or low achievement/ability school will tend to look better to him- or herself, in comparison to others, than a student at a higher-level school. At a higher level school even a better student may not look that good to him- or herself, relative to the high-performing others who are his or her peers.

Meanwhile, students from higher SES backgrounds *are* doing better

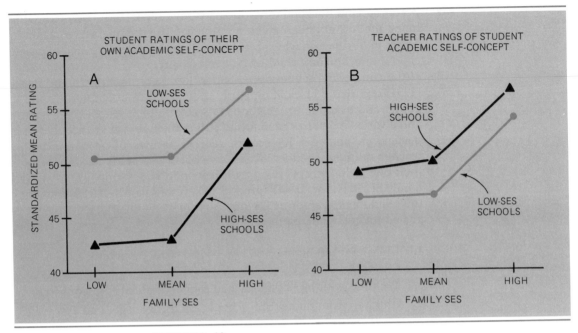

STUDENT RATINGS OF THEIR
OWN ACADEMIC SELF-CONCEPT

TEACHER RATINGS OF STUDENT
ACADEMIC SELF-CONCEPT

STANDARDIZED MEAN RATING

A

LOW-SES
SCHOOLS

HIGH-SES
SCHOOLS

B

HIGH-SES
SCHOOLS

LOW-SES
SCHOOLS

LOW   MEAN   HIGH
FAMILY SES

LOW   MEAN   HIGH
FAMILY SES

FIGURE 10–10

**The relations between the two SES variables and academic self-
concepts as judged by students themselves (Panel A) and by their
teachers (Panel B).**   From Marsh and Parker (1984). Copyright © 1984 by
the American Psychological Association. Reprinted by permission of the
author.

than those from lower SES backgrounds, and this is true regardless of
the schools they attend. Their higher academic self-concepts simply reflect this reality.

Finally, teachers' frames of reference are wider than students' because teachers compare students not just with other students at the same
school, but with other students at *other* schools. To the teachers, both
those from higher SES families and those from higher SES schools tend
to look better. This is, in fact, just the overall pattern obtained in the
Marsh and Parker study, as shown in Figure 10–10.

Other Factors
Related to
Achievement
Striving

Many factors influence achievement striving, including child-rearing
practices, consequences of all kinds, and one's beliefs about why some
people accomplish more than others.

Child-Rearing Practices.   Among the questions asked by parents and
educators, almost none is more frequent than, "What factors in child
rearing encourage and discourage achievement striving in youngsters?"
A complex answer is suggested by a number of different studies. Many
parental attitudes and child-rearing practices, including independent

Teachers' Emotional Reactions and Students' Self-Perceptions

When people act in a way that they could have avoided by effort—for example, if they fail a task at which they could have succeeded by trying harder—we become angry at them. When they fail in situations over which they have no control, we are more likely to be sympathetic (Weiner, 1982). This fact is widely known, even to children who have not taken psychology courses. It raises the interesting possibility that children may use the emotional reactions they receive from adults as cues. For example, one study presented children aged 5 to 11 and college students with stories in which a teacher responded with either sympathy or anger toward a failing student. When the subjects were asked why they thought the student in the story had failed, those who were told the teacher was angry almost always thought the student had failed because of lack of effort. When the teacher had reacted with sympathy, however, all but the youngest children tended to believe that the student failed because of lack of ability (Weiner, Graham, Stern, and Lawson, 1982).

The study by the Weiner group demonstrates how the emotions of a teacher can be used to infer the teacher's perceptions of a student. A more recent study set out to determine whether emotional reactions of an adult could also influence how children see their own failures.

Graham (1984) had sixth-grade boys and girls perform a series of puzzles selected to assure failure within the time period allowed, which was only one minute per puzzle. To make the failure experience more vivid,

. . . each child was first given a practice puzzle that the experimenter pretended to score. This puzzle was similar in complexity to those used during the failure induction, but pilot testing indicated that it was objectively easier and all subjects were able to solve the practice puzzle in approximately one minute [or less]. The ex-

FIGURE 10–11
Children's perceptions of why an adult thought they failed to solve the puzzles in Graham's (1984) experiment, as a function of the feelings expressed by the adult. From Graham (1984). Copyright © 1984 by the American Psychological Association. Reprinted by permission of the author.

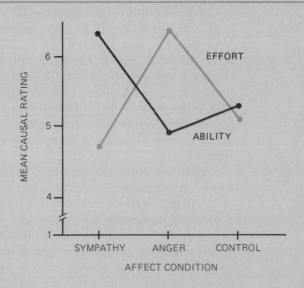

perimenter then asked subjects their birthdates and proceeded to look up their "scores." In an obvious manner, she consulted a bogus "Table of 6th Grade Norms" . . . and informed each subject that, "I have a pretty good idea of how you do on these puzzles compared to other kids your age." (p. 42)

All children were told at the end of every puzzle, "You didn't get that one right because you didn't solve it in time." Then the experimenter displayed either a sympathetic or an angry response, depending on the group to which the child had been assigned randomly. The *sympathy group* was always told, "I feel sorry for you because you haven't gotten any of these puzzles right so far." Children in the *anger group* were told instead: "I'm angry with you because you haven't gotten any of these puzzles right so far." The children in the *control group* were told only, "You didn't get that one right because you didn't solve it in time" (Graham, 1984, p. 43).

Then all children were asked, via a special scale, whether the adult considered their failures to be the result of insufficient ability or insufficient effort. As can be seen in Figure 10–11, angry adults led children to believe they were perceived as not trying hard enough, whereas sympathetic adults led children to believe the adult perceived them as low in ability.

But how about the children's perceptions of themselves? When these were measured, they revealed that children also tended to perceive themselves as having low ability if they had received sympathy from the adult. Children who received sympathy also had lower expectations than other children when asked if they thought they could solve another puzzle like the ones they had been trying. Teachers' reactions may thus be important in the shaping of children's beliefs about their abilities, which, in turn, can influence achievement striving.

training (Feld, 1959), reward for effort (Crandall, Preston, and Rabson, 1960), and encouragement of intellectual pursuits (Crandall, Katkovsky, and Preston, 1960b), are associated with achievement striving.

In a classic study, Winterbottom (1953) gave 8- to 10-year-old boys the beginnings of a story (e.g., "Brothers and sisters are playing. One is a little ahead.") and asked them to elaborate on it. The frequency of achievement themes in the boys' stories was then related to the child-rearing practices reported by their mothers. Winterbottom's principal finding was that mothers of high achievement-oriented boys differed from other mothers in (1) fostering early independence of thought and action—for example, encouraging the child to try things for himself; and (2) generously rewarding successful performance with affection and attention.

In another study (Rosen and D'Andrade, 1959), a team of investigators went into private homes to observe youngsters who were either high or low in achievement motivation. Each boy was given a demanding and potentially frustrating task: to build a tower out of irregularly shaped blocks with one hand—while blindfolded. The parents were asked to watch and were permitted to give any sort of rewards they wished as long as they did not touch the blocks or provide direct assistance. Confirming Winterbottom's report, mothers of high-achieving boys were warmer and more encouraging than other mothers. The fathers of low-

FIGURE 10–12
Achievement striving depends on the belief that accomplishment and success can be earned through one's own efforts. Mimi Forsyth, Monkmeyer.

achieving boys also differed from others in a noticeable way: They tried to make their sons' decisions for them and became quite irritated whenever the boys had any difficulty.

Overjustification Effect.　The idea of accomplishment being its own reward is an ancient one, and carries with it the warning that if children are always promised rewards for doing well in school (or in other areas), they may not learn the inherent satisfactions of the work itself. If an activity can be interesting in itself, then doing it for a reward spoils it.

The classic demonstration of this idea was reported by Lepper, Greene, and Nisbett (1973). In this experiment, preschool children who were offered a reward for engaging in an activity subsequently displayed *less* interest in the activity than children who were not offered a reward. Lepper and his colleagues called this result the *overjustification effect*. The implication is that children discount the interesting features of an activity (or are numbed to its pleasures) if the activity is overjustified by extrinsic rewards. One interesting sidelight: Overjustification effects do not seem to occur when the reward is verbal praise or encouragement; apparently only concrete, material rewards produce the effect (Lepper and Grene, 1978).

In addition to reducing interest, overjustification through external reward may reduce the quality of a child's achievement. In one study, a group of children made artworks in the belief that they were competing for a prize. Others were told that the same projects were to be done simply as one of a series of games they were playing. On measures of both creativity and flexibility in the use of materials, the work of the children who thought they were merely playing was superior (Amabile, 1983).

The presence of extrinsic reward has also been shown to influence selection of problems. Under reward or penalty conditions, elementary school children tend to choose easier problems (Pearlman, 1984). Pearlman also showed that the effects of an external contingency were greatest for youngsters with the highest IQs and the highest general motivation to achieve. Under no external reward conditions, these children have a strong inclination to choose more difficult problems than children with lower IQs or less motivation. So parents and teachers who pressure children to achieve by endless dangling of rewards (a gold star, a trip to the zoo, a VCR) may actually be teaching children to play safe rather than to shine.

An interesting extension of this work involves food preferences. Parents often worry that their children are not eating the right foods and may try to teach better eating habits through the use of rewards or threat of punishment: "You can go to the movies if you finish your peas." or "You can't watch TV tonight unless you finish your milk." Research shows that this strategy may backfire. Children who are induced by reward or punishment to eat certain foods end up liking those foods less (Birch, Marlin, and Rotter, 1984).

THE DEVELOPMENT OF MORAL VALUES

A major aspect of social development involves learning to deal with others. Part of what is considered appropriate depends on one's moral values. Broadly defined, the moral sphere encompasses the whole range of interpersonal reactions. Moral development involves attitudes, beliefs, and values, as well as actual behavior. Behaviors that are perceived as benefiting others—such as sharing, helping, and cooperating—fall into the moral sphere. These are often called "prosocial" behavior. Actions that threaten or harm others—hurting, killing, cheating, and lying—are also considered morally relevant and sometimes are referred to as "antisocial" behavior. Here we discuss theories of moral development and reasoning. In Chapter 11 we elaborate on what we know now about the development of morally relevant interpersonal reactions.

During their early years, most children develop a set of values or principles regarding correct, appropriate, or good behavior. But it is not clear how these values can be acquired and maintained without external pressures or constraints. The moral sphere is highly complex, involving what we say as well as what we do. Until recently *morality* has been an almost taboo word among psychologists because of its historical associations with religion and philosophy. But during the past decade, theory and research in this area have grown enormously.

The Psychoanalytic View

The traditional view of morality, favored in nineteenth-century Europe, presumed that values of the kind we call "moral" were provided by God. Then Freud suggested that the reverse is true: The newborn, he argued, is naturally without concern for the welfare of others. Moral values, if they are present at all, must be cultivated after birth. Psychoanalytic theory offers a view of moral development rooted in the emergence of the *superego*. The superego—a part of each individual's personality—is said to develop as the child "takes in" parental values, at about the fourth or fifth year of life.

The implications of Freud's theory, are straightforward. The child will either develop moral values like those of the parents or, if identification does not occur and the youngster has an inadequate superego, few moral values or none at all. In either case, though, the critical period is presumed to be the first few years of life.

An extensive review of the available evidence does *not* support this view of moral development (Hoffman, 1975). This does not mean that parents are not important models in the moral sphere, for they certainly are. But it is simply not plausible that early identification with parents is solely responsible for all our moral attitudes and actions in adulthood. Hoffman (1971), for example, points out that young children lack the cognitive skills needed to classify parental examples of moral behavior or infer their motivations, and that parents rarely express morally relevant feelings (e.g., guilt or self-criticism) in their children's presence. The importance of Freud's work was that it redirected our attention toward the social origins of moral values.

Kohlberg's Approach

Piaget was the first to suggest the possibility of a sequence of stages of moral growth, roughly paralleling his general theory of cognitive development. Another cognitive theorist, Lawrence Kohlberg, has explored the development of moral values within a cognitive stage theory framework. He has been concerned primarily with the development of moral judgments. The child, says Kohlberg, must be viewed as a "moral philosopher."

But what is the child's philosophy? To answer this question, Kohlberg analyzed free responses to hypothetical moral dilemmas such as the following:

> In Europe, a woman was near death from cancer. One drug might save her, a form of radium that a druggist in the same town had recently discovered. The druggist was charging $2,000, ten times what the drug cost him to make. The sick woman's husband, Heinz, went to everyone he knew to borrow the money, but he could only get together about half of what it cost. He told the druggist that his wife was dying and asked him to sell it cheaper or let him pay later: But the druggist said, "No." The husband got desperate and broke into the man's store to steal the drug for his wife. Should the husband have done that? Why? (Kohlberg, 1969, p. 379)

A child's responses to dilemmas such as this one are usually based on one or more general aspects of the problem, such as the motives or intentions of the people involved. After eliciting responses to a large number of dilemmas from many children, Kohlberg has been able to distinguish three levels of moral thinking: *preconventional, conventional,* and

TABLE 10–3
Kohlberg's Six Stages of Moral Development

Preconventional Level
Stage 1:
Punishment and obedience orientation. The physical consequences of an action
determine whether it is good or bad. Avoiding punishment and bowing to superior
power are valued positively.

Stage 2:
Instrumental relativist orientation. Right action consists of behavior that satisfies
one's own needs. Human relations are viewed in marketplace terms. Reciprocity
occurs, but is seen in a pragmatic way, i.e., "you scratch my back and I'll scratch
yours."

Conventional Level
Stage 3:
Interpersonal concordance (good boy—nice girl) orientation. Good behaviors are
those that please or are approved by others. There is much emphasis on conformity
and being "nice."

Stage 4:
Orientation toward authority ("law and order"). Focus is on authority or rules. It is
right to do one's duty, show respect for authority, and maintain the social order.

Postconventional Level
Stage 5:
Social-contract orientation. This stage has a utilitarian, legalistic tone. Correct
behavior is defined in terms of standards agreed upon by society. Awareness of the
relativism of personal values and the need for consensus is important.

Stage 6:
Universal ethical principle orientation. Morality is defined as a decision of
conscience. Ethical principles are self-chosen, based on abstract concepts (e.g.,
the Golden Rule) rather than concrete rules (e.g., the Ten Commandments).

postconventional. Within each of these three levels, Kohlberg (1963, 1967,
1976) suggests, are two discernible stages, producing the full complement of six stages shown in Table 10–3.

Concrete examples of the type of moral judgments made in response
to the dilemma described in the story of Heinz and his dying wife are
shown in Table 10–4. The stages are *not* differentiated by what decision
is made, but by the reasoning that underlies the decision.

According to Kohlberg, the preconventional child is often well behaved and sensitive to labels such as good and bad. But the latter are
interpreted simply in terms of their physical consequences (punishment,
reward, exchange of favors) or in terms of the power of those who make

TABLE 10–4
Moral Reasoning at Various Stages in Response to Heinz's Dilemma

Stage 1
Action is motivated by avoidance of punishment and "conscience" is irrational fear
of punishment.
Pro—If you let your wife die, you will get in trouble. You'll be blamed for not
spending the money to save her and there'll be an investigation of you and
the druggist for your wife's death.
Con—You shouldn't steal the drug because you'll be caught and sent to jail if you
do. If you do get away, your conscience would bother you thinking how the
police would catch up with you at any minute.

Stage 2

Action motivated by desire for reward or benefit. Possible guilt reactions are ignored and punishment viewed in a pragmatic manner. (Differentiates own fear, pleasure, or pain from punishment-consequences.)

Pro—If you do happen to get caught you could give the drug back and you wouldn't get much of a sentence. It wouldn't bother you much to serve a little jail term, if you have your wife when you get out.

Con—He may not get much of a jail term if he steals the drug, but his wife will probably die before he gets out so it won't do him much good. If his wife dies, he shouldn't blame himself; it wasn't his fault she has cancer.

Stage 3

Action motivated by anticipation of disapproval of others, actual or imagined hypothetical (e.g., guilt). (Differentiation of disapproval from punishment, fear, and pain.)

Pro—No one will think you're bad if you steal the drug but your family will think you're an inhuman husband if you don't. If you let your wife die, you'll never be able to look anybody in the face again.

Con—It isn't just the druggist who will think you're a criminal, everyone else will too. After you steal it, you'll feel bad thinking how you've brought dishonor on your family and yourself; you won't be able to face anyone again.

Stage 4

Action motivated by anticipation of dishonor, i.e., institutionalized blame for failure of duty, and by guilt over concrete harm done to others. (Differentiates formal dishonor from informal disapproval. Differentiates guilt for bad consequences from disapproval.)

Pro—If you have any sense of honor, you won't let your wife die because you're afraid to do the only thing that will save her. You'll always feel guilty that you caused her death if you don't do your duty to her.

Con—You're desperate and you may not know you're doing wrong when you steal the drug. But you'll know you did wrong after you're punished and sent to jail. You'll always feel guilt for your dishonesty and lawbreaking.

Stage 5

Concern about maintaining respect of equals and of the community (assuming their respect is based on reason rather than emotions). Concern about own self-respect, i.e., to avoid judging self as irrational, inconsistent, nonpurposive. (Discriminates between institutionalized blame and community disrespect or self-disrespect.)

Pro—You'd lose other people's respect, not gain it, if you don't steal. If you let your wife die, it would be out of fear, not out of reasoning it out. So you'd just lose self-respect and probably the respect of others too.

Con—You would lose your standing and respect in the community and violate the law. You'd lose respect for yourself if you're carried away by emotion and forget the long-range point of view.

Stage 6

Concern about self-condemnation for violating one's own principles. (Differentiates beween self-respect for general achieving rationality and self-respect for maintaining moral principles.)

Pro—If you don't steal the drug and let your wife die, you'd always condemn yourself for it afterward. You wouldn't be blamed and you would have lived up to the outside rule of the law but you wouldn't have lived up to your own standards of conscience.

Con—If you stole the drug, you wouldn't be blamed by other people but you'd condemn yourself because you wouldn't have lived up to your own conscience and standards of honesty.

Source: Rest. 1969. Unpublished doctoral dissertation, University of Chicago, 1969.

the rules. There is, then, no real standard of morality at the preconventional level. The conventional level is characterized by conformity to the existing social order and an implicit desire to maintain that order. Most American adults, according to Kohlberg, operate at the level of conventional morality. Finally, the postconventional level is said to be governed by moral principles that are universal, and therefore valid independent of the authority of the groups who support them.

Kohlberg reports that moral development may be either fast or slow, but that it does not skip stages. Evidence consistent with this claim comes from a major longitudinal study by Colby, Kohlberg, Gibbs, and Lieberman (1983) over a period of 20 years. As children and adolescents, and later as adults, subjects were tested with moral dilemmas like the one shown in Table 10–4. According to the theory, older individuals should have more advanced moral reasoning; in fact, the correlation between age and moral reasoning score was .78.

Two other aspects of the results provide even stronger evidence for Kohlberg's "stage" theory, which says that as a person's moral reasoning develops, it will progress through stages—that is, individuals should not "skip" stages as their reasoning develops. Consistent with this claim, in no instance did individuals skip stages. Another property of stage theory has to do with the direction of change. Individuals may either advance in their level of moral reasoning or stay at a particular level, but they should not regress (move to a lower stage). In the Colby sample, it was common for individuals to progress from one stage of reasoning to a more advanced stage, and when they did not progress, they usually remained at the same level. Only in 5% of the cases did subjects revert to a less advanced stage.

Another source of evidence for Kohlberg's theory is the relation between moral reasoning scores and moral action. The logic here is that individuals with more advanced moral reasoning would be compelled to moral action in situations where individuals with less mature reasoning might not act. Consider a situation in which a person must decide to help another. For children in the preconventional level of moral reasoning, action would be determined by the likelihood that they would be rewarded for helping (or punished for not helping), or the possibility that the person might return the favor in the future. These children would be unlikely to help in situations where there was little chance of reward, punishment, or help in return. Individuals in the conventional level know that helping is "good" behavior that is socially valued; these people would be more likely to help others in the absence of reward, punishment, or help in return.

A good deal of evidence supports this link between moral reasoning and moral action. For example, juvenile delinquents tend to have lower moral reasoning scores than non-delinquents (Blasi, 1980). Altruism is also related to moral reasoning: Individuals with higher moral reasoning scores are more likely to help than individuals with lower scores (Blasi, 1980). In another study, Gibbs, Clark, Joseph, Green, Goodrick, and Makowski (1986) asked high school teachers to rate students' moral courage. Teachers judged if pupils would defend their principles, even in difficult situations, or if they would act only when it was popular or convenient. Teachers' ratings of moral courage were significantly related to students' moral reasoning scores, but were unrelated to variables such as the students' IQ, empathy, and locus of control. Thus, moral thought appears to follow a universal pattern typical of all other kinds of thought; progress is characterized by increasing differentiation and integration.

Kohlberg's Critics. Kohlberg's conclusions have not gone unchallenged, and in fact his theory and the research on which it is based have been the subject of serious criticism on numerous logical and empirical grounds (Gibbs, 1977; Kurtines and Greif, 1974; Liebert, 1979; Simpson, 1974). We consider two interrelated examples, dealing with Kohlberg's claims that moral development is universal in its course and invariant in its sequence of development.

The most distinctive and controversial element in Kohlberg's theory is his claim that there are universal, absolute standards of right and wrong and that he has demonstrated their existence through scientific research. Kohlberg's claim to have discovered universally true moral principles, as the substance of postconventional morality is a radical departure from Piagetian and related cognitive-developmental theory. For example, at the empirical level there is some support for the sequence of development of moral justifications as proposed by Kohlberg, discovered cross-culturally for Stages 1 through 4 (Edwards, 1975; Kohlberg, 1969; Parikh, 1975; White, 1975). There appears to be almost no evidence to support the claim that Stages 5 and 6 are universal (Gibbs, 1977). To the contrary, they are not found in many cultures; and in the cultures in which they are found, they are found rarely.

The absence of Stages 5 and 6 in most cultures should not be surprising; postconventional moral reasoning as Kohlberg has defined it depends on a specific philosophical commitment. For example, in explaining Stage 6 moral reasoning Kohlberg states: "First of all, recognition of the moral duty to save a human life whenever possible must be assumed" (1971, p. 208). Kohlberg also defines Stage 6 partly in terms of accepting "the assumption that all other actors' claims (in a moral conflict) are also governed by the Golden Rule and accommodated accordingly" (1973, p. 643). Logical considerations alone simply do not give rise to these particular assumptions; rather, they reflect Kohlberg's own preferences and the beliefs of the particular culture of which he is a part.

Some critics have questioned Kohlberg's emphasis on justice as the sole basis for moral development. Carol Gilligan (1982, 1985) has proposed that moral reasoning—particularly for women—is also based on greater understanding of care and responsibility in interpersonal relationships. Gilligan (1982) writes:

> The moral imperative that emerges repeatedly in interviews with women is an injunction to care, a responsibility to discern and alleviate the "real and recognizable trouble" of this world. For men, the moral imperative appears rather as an injunction to respect the rights of others and thus to protect from interference the rights to life and self-fulfillment. (p. 100)

In interviews with women facing a real-life moral dilemma—whether to abort a pregnancy—Gilligan identified three developmental stages in reasoning, each characterized by greater understanding of caring and responsibility. In the first stage, individuals are concerned with the self and their own needs. This gives way in a second stage to caring for others and particularly to concern for dependent individuals. However, defining "care" only in terms of others creates tension, because the individual is excluding herself or himself. Hence, in the final stage, caring for others and for oneself become linked in a concern for caring in *all* human relationships and in denouncing exploitation and violence between people.

Thus, like Kohlberg, Gilligan believes that thinking about moral issues becomes progressively more sophisticated as individuals develop. And, also like Kohlberg, Gilligan has identified a number of distinct stages in this developmental sequence. But unlike Kohlberg, Gilligan believes these stages reflect progressively greater insights into caring, rather than justice.

Interactionist Perspectives

Freud's and Kohlberg's views of moral development are important in understanding how we have approached moral development up to now. Recently, however, a new look has emerged. Many developmentalists have begun to emphasize the interactions between content and structure, maturation and experience, and cognition and emotion. The new goal is to synthesize earlier work into an integrated view of morality and moral development (Nisan, 1984). James Rest has been an active thinker and researcher in this area for many years.

Rest has advanced a new theoretical model of morality, in which he tries to identify the processes that go into producing moral behavior. Rest (1984) says he was motivated to develop a new framework because existing theories "leave us dangling about how behavior, cognition and affect are related [and imply] the three elements have separate lives of their own" (p. 25). In his view, thought and emotion—thinking and feeling—are always interacting to produce action in the moral sphere. Rest concludes that morality involves four major components which interact to produce a child's (or adult's) reaction to any morally relevant situation.

In Rest's model the first component is *interpretation,* which involves both a cognitive and an emotional aspect. The cognitive aspect in interpretation involves identifying the moral dimensions of the problems, such as how the participants in the situation are, or would be, affected by various actions. The emotional component involves empathy for those who might suffer and disgust or revulsion for the behavior of those who might behave badly.

The second component is *formulating a plan of action* (figuring out what to do). This involves applying a moral standard or ideal, which entails both logic (the cognitive aspect) and attitudes and values (the emotional aspect).

The third component is *evaluation and decision:* evaluating the various possible courses of action and deciding what actually to do. Here a host of processes are said to interact, including calculating the relative utility of various goals and dealing with one's "nonmoral" impulses. As an illustration, Rest cites an experiment by Damon (1977) in which young children were asked how 10 candy bars should be distributed as rewards for making bracelets. The children described various schemes for a fair distribution and explained their reasons. But when children were actually given the 10 candy bars to distribute, they ignored the schemes and gave themselves more candy bars.

The fourth and final component is *executing and implementing a plan of action.* Moral action requires both "ego strength" and "self-regulation skills," in order to work around obstacles and unexpected difficulties, overcome fatigue, and keep the goal in view. Rest (1984) says: "In short, perseverance, resoluteness, and 'strong character' characterize Component 4 processes" (p. 33).

SUMMARY

1. Young children's behavior seems to be under the control of environmental constraints and biological urges. As children grow older, they begin to be controlled by their own internal values and standards. Psychologists have tried to understand this process through both the *cognitive-behavioral* and *cognitive-developmental* approaches.

2. Self-control is usually broken down into two components: *resistance to temptation* and *delay of gratification.*

3. A good deal of resistance to temptation involves rule adherence when alone. Older children are more likely to be rule obedient than younger children. For older children, reasoning appears to play an important role in developing resistance to temptation.

4. Children are more likely to break rules when they are in a bad mood. They are also more likely to resist temptation in laboratory situations if they provide self-guidance by verbalizing the rules to themselves. In addition, *objective self-awareness* appears to foster rule adherence.

5. Delay of gratification involves a superficially more evenhanded set of alternatives. No cheating is involved; a child just chooses between a little reward now or a bigger one later. But in reality, the ability to wait, in a free-choice situation, like the ability to follow rules even in a tempting situation, increases with age and is considered the more mature form of behavior.

6. People, even as children, have different tendencies to strive for achievement and excellence. The motivation to achieve appears to require exposure to numerous rewarded social models. Cognitive factors are also involved. These include expectations as to whether effort has more or less to do with success than luck or fate. Finally, emotional and cognitive factors intermingle—for example, when students interpret how their teachers perceive them.

7. Child-rearing factors are also associated with achievement striving. Parents of children with the strongest achievement

orientation seem to be warm and encouraging; they also continually praise accomplishment. Research is clear that when an otherwise interesting activity becomes *overjustified* by material incentives, much of the fun is taken out of it: It then becomes devalued and less likely to be pursued.

8. Measures of locus of control provide a concrete way of linking a cognitive orientation (a belief in internal controls as determinants of success or failure) to achievement. An internal orientation is associated with parental practices fostering self-reliance and independence.

9. Freud believed that character and conscience were the same thing. Freud also believed that each child has a *superego,* a part of individual personality that guides morality.

10. Kohlberg's approach is an elaborated version of the cognitive-developmental viewpoint. He concludes that moral development proceeds in a universal, invariant sequence through three levels— *preconventional, conventional, and postconventional.*

11. Several writers have recently taken interactionist perspectives, in which cognitive and emotional factors, as well as incentives and social models, are woven together in one overarching theory of moral development.

FRIENDSHIP, ALTRUISM, AND AGGRESSION

We begin learning how to get along with others from the moment we are born, and we never really stop. Very few of us will spend our lives in a mountain cave or a desert hut; we will be with other people most of the time. Humans need other humans—to survive and to function well. But how we express and fill these needs for others depends a great deal on the culture in which we are born or in which we live. In certain cultures behaviors that are appropriate and even required for boys are taboo for girls. Some types of social interactions expected of all members of one culture are prohibited for everyone in another. Among the Mundugumor, for instance, aggression and ruthlessness are virtually a way of life. The same behavior would be shocking to the Arapesh, an unusually passive people who make every effort to avoid conflict (Mead, 1935).

Or consider sharing, another important social behavior. As we saw in Chapter 9, sharing is an expected and valued norm for all Chinese children today. In contrast, sharing of possessions between certain social castes has traditionally been prohibited in India. Western cultures such as those of North America, Britain, and Western Europe show a mix of cultural values, and therefore wide variation in opinions and practices.

This chapter deals with three related aspects of getting along with and reacting to the needs and demands of others: friendship, altruism, and aggression. We begin with friendship, which encompasses a wide range of specific behaviors, as well as some very important skills and roles that make human intimacy possible and social life interesting and satisfying.

FRIENDSHIP

The ability to establish and maintain friendships lies at the very heart of human social existence. People everywhere seek friends with whom they can share thoughts, feelings, and the meaning of their lives. Over the course of a lifetime, having at least a few people as true friends is one of the great joys of having lived fully and well.

Only recently have psychologists begun to study friendship. A few began to do so in the 1940s, 1950s, and 1960s. From the seeds of their pioneering work we have today a substantial and important literature on the nature and development of friendship.

Sullivan's Stage Theory

Harry Stack Sullivan was a psychiatrist whose interpersonal theory of psychiatry has had a growing influence on psychologists and psychiatrists over the years. Sullivan (1953) suggested that the development of interpersonal relationships follows a stagelike sequence. Between the ages of 2 and 5, children's most important relationships are with adults, on whom they rely for their physical, social, and emotional needs. In the second stage, roughly between 4 and 8, children turn to peers as playmates and companions. But the relationships are typically short and the interactions superficial and self-serving.

The third stage, which occurs between 8 and 11, is the stage of *chumship*. In this stage children are able for the first time to form intense attachments to other children of the same sex. Chumships are character-ized by intimacy and reciprocity. They are reasonably stable over time, and involve a mutual give and take from which children learn to recog-nize and appreciate how the thoughts and feelings of others may be dif-ferent from their own. In general, research has supported the broad outline of Sullivan's position (Selman, 1981).

Boys' and Girls' Friendships

There is a strong tendency for young toddlers to prefer members of their own sex as friends, and this pattern continues throughout child-hood. At the same time, there is also a clear sex difference in patterns of friendships. Girls have a much stronger tendency than boys to develop exclusive friendships, and are also much less open than boys to admit-ting new members into their circle of friends (Lever, 1978). Perhaps boys are more accustomed than girls to group friendships because of their in-volvement in group sports. Perhaps girls prefer exclusive friendships precisely because they allow for more intimate relationships.

Friendship and Popularity

Masters and Furman (1981) have emphasized the importance of dis-tinguishing between friendship (in Sullivan's sense of chumship) and popularity. *Popularity* refers to being highly regarded, admired, and sought after by peers. *Friendship* refers to having a close, reciprocal re-lationship with at least one peer. Having a chum and being popular are independent of one another. A child may be very popular and not have a chum, or may have a chum and not be very popular. Then too, it ap-pears that some children have both—chums and popularity—and some have neither (McGuire and Weisz, 1982).

Who Is Popular? Popular children are perceived as being athletic, good looking, happy, and nice. (Friends are also perceived as being nice—and, of course, as friendly—but their most important characteristics are being kind and considerate).

Popularity in childhood is also related to developing a variety of social skills. Popular children are better able to learn how to initiate social in-teractions with other children. They are more skillful at communicating and better able to integrate themselves into an ongoing conversation or play session. In contrast, children who lack knowledge of what is con-sidered socially appropriate by their peers or who do not understand the values of the peer group are likely to be quite unpopular (Ladd and Oden, 1979).

Popular children also seem relatively gifted in assessing and moni-toring their own social impact in various situations and in tailoring their responses to the requirements of each new social situation (Kurdek and Krile, 1982). Given these facts, it is perhaps not surprising that relative popularity is quite stable. Popular youngsters are quite likely to remain popular, and unpopular youngsters are likely to remain unpopular (Bu-kowski and Newcomb, 1984).

Chumships and Popularity. Chumships are characterized by three features: reciprocity, stability, and behavioral involvement. To be chums, for instance, each of two children must name each other as best friends. This reciprocal liking must also be stable—that is, it must last for some period of time, at least several weeks and more typically several months. Here today/gone tomorrow relationships do not qualify as true chumships. Finally, chums must actually do things together and spend a fair amount of time with one another.

McGuire and Weisz's (1982) study of fifth- and sixth-grade children sheds light on chumship, and on the difference between chumship and popularity. It involved almost 300 boys and girls enrolled in North Carolina public schools, from whom they collected numerous observational, behavioral, and self-report records. They found, first of all, strong support for Masters and Furman's (1981) distinction between friendship and popularity. The two characteristics could both be reliably measured, but they were not related. Second, children with chums were more altruistic and better able to take other children's perspectives in various situations. Popular children, in contrast, were no better at perspective taking and no more likely to be altruistic than less popular children. Finally, and perhaps somewhat sadly given the other findings, it seemed that almost 60 percent of the children studied did not have chums, and were thus presumably losing out on the many social benefits such relationships can provide. As the investigators conclude: "Involvement with a chum is likely to be a significant asset in the child's social development. Unfortunately, our data indicate that many preadolescents may be deprived of chumship and its companion benefits"(p. 1483).

Origins of Friendship

Friendly relationships with peers can occur as early as the first year of life. Even infants as young as 6 months old show social recognition of one another by smiling, touching, or vocalizing (Hartup, 1983; Vandell, Wilson, and Buchanan, 1980).

Toddlerhood Friendships. Over the past decade there has been a tremendous increase in interest in young children's social interactions. During the toddler years, children begin to offer, accept, and share toys; they copy each other's motor acts in turn-taking fashion (reciprocal imitation); and they interact verbally in more varied and complex ways (Guralnick and Weinhouse, 1984).

Corsaro (1981) observed 3- and 4-year-olds in a nursery school for several months and noted that the children typically played with one another rather than by themselves. But their interactions tended to be rather short—usually less than ten minutes—and they often ended abruptly, with one of the children just walking off. By elementary school, though, friendships begin to become more stable.

Childhood Friendships: Beginnings of Intimacy and Self-Disclosure. One important function of friendship is the development of intimacy and *self-disclosure*, the process of communicating personal information about oneself to someone else (Chelune, 1979). Research with adults has established clearly that reciprocity has a strong influence on level of self-disclosure. We are more likely to tell someone our own intimate thoughts and feelings if they tell us about theirs. Many psychologists believe that intimate self-disclosure among children plays a central role in formulating and refining self-concept.

Sullivan (1953), for example, felt that mutual self-disclosure enables children to reduce distortions in their self-images. They learn to recognize how they are perceived by others and at the same time to appreciate the similarities and differences among people. Piaget (1962) offered an analysis of the importance of mutual self-disclosure among children along much the same lines. Moreover, research shows that children do reciprocate when intimate self-disclosures are offered by other children (Cohn and Strassberg, 1983).

Childhood Friendships and Later Development. Maas (1968) conducted a retrospective study of men's and women's friendships when they were children between 8 and 13 and found that those who were low in intimacy as adults had been lonely as children. The records also seemed to indicate that many of these individuals were isolated or rejected by peers during childhood. Results from other cross-sectional studies are consistent with this conclusion. Mannarino (1978), for example, found that young adolescent boys with close and stable friendships tended to have higher self-esteem than did other boys.

An interesting developmental shift occurs between childhood and adolescence in the way youngsters deal with friends compared to other classmates. Up to about the time children are in the fourth grade, they seem less likely to share with close friends than with other classmates with whom they are not particularly friendly, apparently because a degree of jealousy characterizes most of these friendships. Children at this age almost never like to feel they have less than others with whom they are in close contact (Rubin, 1980). By the time children are in the eighth grade, the picture changes. Friends are more likely to share with, and be helpful to, friends than other classmates. Berndt (1982) suggests that this development reflects increased preference for equality over competition and is part of passing from childhood to adolescence. "Adolescents," suggests Berndt, "have more mature conceptions of reciprocity and equality than young children [and] may also appreciate that competition between friends makes it difficult to maintain an intimate relationship" (1982, p. 1452).

Adolescent
Friendships

Friendships take on a special importance during early adolescence. Adolescents themselves report spending more time talking to peers than doing anything else; they also report that they are most happy when talking with peers (Csikszentmihalyi, Larson, and Prescott, 1977). Several factors make the increased importance of friendships during adolescence

Who Is Chosen As a Friend

Children tend to choose as friends those who are similar to them in age, sex, and race (Hallinan, 1979). They also tend to choose as friends those who are similar to them in attitudes toward school and in culture (Ball, 1981). There is even a tendency to pick friends who are similar in appearance. One team of researchers found that physically attractive children tended to have attractive friends, whereas homely children tended to have homely friends (Langlois and Downs, 1979).

In addition to the role similarity plays in selection, there is evidence that children and adolescents who do become quite friendly become more similar to one another over time as a result. Kandel (1978), for example, studied adolescent friendships and individual attitudes over a one-year period and found that friends gradually became more alike in

their attitudes toward marijuana use, delinquent activity, educational goals, and political identification.

Unsurprisingly, children prefer as friends those who they see as having desirable traits (Coie, Dodge, and Coppotelli, 1982) and those who treat them in a friendly and rewarding manner (Masters and Furman, 1981). Children are also quite willing to accept negative traits in their friends, provided that positive characteristics and behaviors balance out the less desirable ones (Bukowski and Newcomb, 1984).

No doubt there are many other reasons why children choose the friends they do, but one important reason appears to be that children choose friends who will help them maintain positive evaluations of themselves. According to recent work by Tesser and his

FIGURE 11–1
Student ratings of performance of (a) self; (b) most-preferred classmate; and (c) least-preferred classmate on activities the student has designated as relevant and irrelevant to his or her own self-definition. Adapted from Tesser, Campbell, and Smith (1984). Copyright © 1984 by the American Psychological Association. Reprinted by permission of the author.

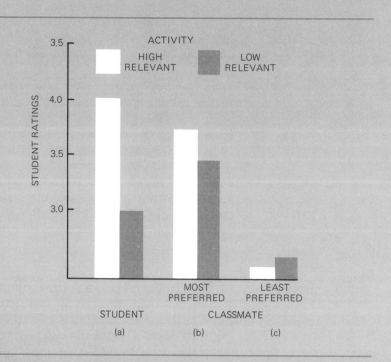

associates, maintenance of high self-esteem through friends is accomplished by two complementary processes: *reflection* and *comparison* (Tesser, Campbell, and Smith, 1984). Reflection involves taking pleasure in a friend's accomplishments and enhancing feelings about oneself by basking in the reflected glory of friends' reputations, abilities, or deeds. For reflection to be successful, a child must feel psychologically close to the other child and also believe that the other child possesses admirable characteristics. For example, an elementary school child may say such things as, "Sally and I walk to school together every day, and she's the best speller in the whole school." The other side of the coin to this process, however, is that having a highly successful friend can make a child look relatively less successful by comparison.

How do the two processes of reflection and comparison work together? According to Tesser and his associates, the answer lies in how they relate to a third variable, the *relevance of various activities* to the child. Specifically, Tesser and his associates proposed that children choose as close friends those who are better than they themselves are at activities they are not trying to excel at ("low relevance").

To test this hypothesis, Tesser and his associates asked 270 fifth- and sixth-grade children to each pick two classmates and four activities. One classmate was to be the child with whom each one most preferred to spend time; the other was to be the child with whom each least preferred to spend time. The activities were to be the two each student considered most important and the two each considered least important from a list provided by the investigators. A week later, students rated themselves and their most- and least-liked classmates on their performance of the chosen activities.

As shown in Figure 11–1, the overall theory received clear support. Students rated themselves as better than their most-preferred classmates on highly relevant activities, but they rated their most-preferred classmates as better than themselves on activities of low relevance. As Figure 11–1 also shows, least-preferred classmates were rated quite poorly on both types of activities.

both possible and desirable. One, of course, is that adolescents have increased cognitive abilities. They are better able than younger children to appreciate their friends' feelings, hopes, and uncertainties, and to appreciate differences between their friends' thoughts and their own (Selman, 1981).

Adolescents also have a heightened need for intimacy in friendship. One reason is that they are breaking away from the strong ties to home and parents that characterize childhood. Another is that they must come to grips with sexual feelings, impulses, and experiences; sharing these with friends is often helpful and reassuring. So it should not be surprising that adolescents are much more likely than children to mention sharing of intimate feelings in describing their close friendships. Nor should it be surprising that they actually do have more intimate knowledge of their close friends than children do (Berndt, 1982).

Sex differences in close friendships become even more pronounced. Girls are more likely to have very intimate relationships than boys, and they are more likely than boys to have one exclusive "best friend." They are also more likely to be concerned about the faithfulness of their friends and to worry about possible rejection by them (Berndt, 1981). Finally, by adolescence youngsters think of friendships more in terms of such abstract and enduring issues as acceptance, loyalty, intimacy, and sharing the same or similar views of the world (Furman and Bierman, 1984).

ALTRUISM

Most parents, most teachers, and most religions try to teach children to act in cooperative, helping, or giving ways—at least some of the time and in some situations. Such behavior is usually thought to be in the greater interest of others and society. Over the past twenty years or so, psychologists have come to call all these behaviors "prosocial." Most developmentalists use the term *prosocial behavior* to refer to any behavior that benefits another, regardless of its underlying motivation.

Altruism, on the other hand, tends to describe actions that are motivated by ideals of responsibility toward others or society, rather than to avoid punishment or serve selfish or personal needs (Eisenberg, 1982). As Perry (1983) points out, however, these distinctions are often easier to make in theory than in practice: when a prosocial behavior is also altruistic is not entirely clear in many situations. For this reason, the discussion here focuses on types of altruistic or prosocial behavior (cooperation, helping, and sharing) with a minimum number of assumptions about underlying motivations. Instead, we emphasize the role of various cognitive and social skills in the development, production, and maintenance of such behavior.

Cooperation

Generally speaking, *cooperation* refers to behavior in which two or more people work together for mutual benefit. Such action is considered prosocial because societies are to a great extent built on cooperative enterprise.

Stimulating Cooperative Behavior. What will stimulate the development of cooperation? First, verbally structuring situations in terms of mutual gain by creating a "we" rather than an "I" orientation seems to be important, so that children see themselves as working *with* rather than against each other (Kagan and Madsen, 1971). Second, and not surpris-

FIGURE 11–2
The willingness to cooperate for mutual enjoyment or benefit is evident at an early age.
© Peeter Vilms/
Jeroboam, Inc.

ingly, direct experience with the positive consequences of cooperation increases the likelihood that such behavior will occur. Guiding children into practical cooperative relationships and letting them directly experience the benefits markedly increases cooperation (Madsen, 1971).

Finally, modeled examples of cooperative behavior by other children can have a powerful influence. In one study (Liebert, Sprafkin, and Poulos, 1975) children were exposed to a 30-second television spot designed to teach cooperation through positive example. "The Swing," as this spot was called, opens with a boy and girl running across a field to reach the last remaining swing on a playground; they both reach the swing at the same time and immediately begin to struggle over it. After a moment during which battle seems inevitable, one of the youngsters produces the insight that they should take turns and suggests that the other child go first. Each of the children is finally shown taking her or his turn, joyfully swinging through the air with the help of the other while an announcer's voice says: "There are lots of things you can do when two people want the same thing. One is to take turns . . . and that's a good one." Children exposed to this example are considerably more likely to exhibit cooperative behavior in a test situation (see Figure 11–3).

The Importance of Situational Factors. A somewhat different perspective on the development of cooperative and competitive behavior is suggested by the recent work of Brady, Newcomb, and Hartup (1983). These

FIGURE 11–3
The effects of exposure to a cooperatively oriented television spot, "The Swing," on children's cooperative behavior. Control group children were shown commercial TV spots that did not have cooperative messages. In the test situations, children could cooperate by taking turns or they could compete unfruitfully. From Liebert, Sprafkin, and Poulos (1975). Copyright © by the Advertising Research Foundation.

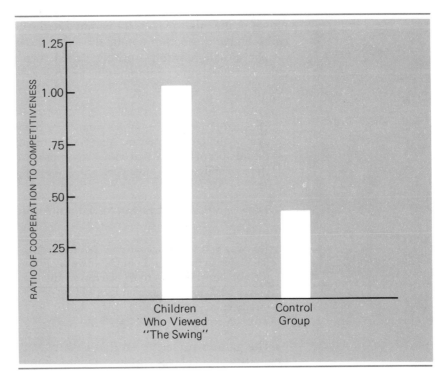

investigators point out that whether adults behave cooperatively or competitively is likely to be determined both by the structure of the situation and by the attitudes they bring with them. The question raised by Brady and her associates is this: "Are there important developmental changes in the ability to use and coordinate information from several sources when deciding whether to respond in a competitive or cooperative fashion?"

There are, as we know, many reasons to think there would be age differences in the ability to notice and use multiple and perhaps conflicting sources of information. Young children are likely to attend to the most obvious aspects of a complex situation, and to pay too little attention to, or even ignore, other aspects (Markman, 1977). They are also less likely to recognize the relative importance of various bits of information, even when they notice several kinds (Brown & Smiley, 1977). Finally, younger children are less likely to use systematic strategies to capitalize on several sources of information even when they notice the multiple cues and appreciate their possible significance (Flavell, 1977).

Brady and her associates decided to study the behavior of first-, third- and fifth-grade children during a game they could play cooperatively or competitively. Two experimental factors were systematically varied: the rules of the game and the behavior of the "other child." A special board game was devised in which a player's job was to land exactly on a series of "bridges" connecting ten colored sectors. Progress toward the finish line could only be made by landing exactly on the bridges. The other child, who was also to move a marker (taking turns with the subject), and who was said to be in an adjacent room, was actually nonexistent. The moves of the other player, transmitted to the child by an intercom, were controlled and programmed by the experimenters.

The situation was purposely varied through instructions favoring either cooperation or competition. For the *cooperative condition*, the rules were:

> The way you win prizes in this game is for you and the other player to cross as many bridges as you can. After we are through playing, we will count up the number of bridges that both of you crossed. Each of you will get as many chips as bridges both of you crossed. (Brady et. al., 1983, p. 401).

The *competitive condition* involved quite different instructions:

> The way you win prizes in this game is for you to cross more bridges than the player in the other room. After we are through playing, we will count up the number of bridges that you crossed and the number that he crossed. The player who crossed more bridges will get one chip for each bridge he crossed (Brady et. al., 1983, p. 401).

The game was set up so that each player's turn involved deciding where the other player's marker would be moved. A player could move so as to help or hinder the other player's movement. In other words, the

programmed responses of the cooperative companions were set up to facilitate the progress of the subject (to be cooperative), whereas the programmed responses of the competitive companions were set up to block
or impede the progress of the subject (to be competitive). The experimenters took great care to ensure that each child understood the nature
and rules of the game before beginning the actual play.

The pattern of results was quite clear-cut: For all three age groups, the
behavior of the companion had a strong effect on the subject's own behavior: Cooperative companions produced cooperative responses and
competitive companions produced competitive responses. But the situation (the "pay-off matrix") had virtually no effect on the first graders.
They willingly cooperated with a cooperative companion even in a competitive situation in which cooperation would assure that they would
lose the game. They were equally likely to impede the progress of a competitive companion even though they hurt themselves by doing so. The
third and fifth graders were decidedly more sophisticated. They took
both their companion's behavior and the rules of the game into account.
They made the most cooperative responses when dealing with a cooperative companion in a cooperative situation and the least cooperative
responses when facing a competitive companion in a competitive situation.

One interesting difference between the third and fifth graders also
emerged. If anything, the fifth graders bent over backwards to be cooperative, and were more likely to behave cooperatively even when they
faced uniformly competitive companions.

Brady and her associates did an additional experiment involving only
first graders to see whether children this young would become more
tuned to the importance of the rules of the game by making these features
more important to them. Additional training involved scorekeeping during the game, rehearsal of the game, and a combination of the two training procedures. Under these training conditions even first graders began
to appreciate the importance of taking their own interests into account
when facing competitive companions in competitive situations.

Helping

Like cooperating, helping is considered an important aspect of human social functioning; without it people could not get along. How does
the tendency to help others develop in children? Earlier we mentioned
Piaget's idea that cooperation and conflict are important factors in the
decline of egocentric thought. For Piaget, *egocentric* does not refer to selfishness, but rather to the inability to see things from another's point of
view. This ability to take another's perspective is called role-taking ability, and is closely related to the idea of empathy. Specifically, *role-taking
ability* is the ability to be aware of another person's feelings; *empathy* is
the ability to experience them yourself.

Empathy and Role-Taking Ability. Even newborns may cry when they
hear another baby cry. This happens so consistently that some psychologists believe the tendency to feel "empathic distress" is inborn.

Whether this is true or not, it is obvious that a baby's empathy is limited. Deeply felt empathy almost certainly depends on role-taking ability, and can occur in infants only when the other person's distress is open, intense, and obvious. As children grow older, both their role-taking abilities and their tendencies to behave altruistically increase (Hoffman, 1975b). Such behavior provides good support for the theory that role-taking ability, empathy, and altruism are closely related (Shaffer, 1979).

Hudson, Forman, and Brion-Meisels (1982) recently reported an experiment that clearly showed the link between empathy and role-taking ability in second graders. They began by giving every child a test of role-taking ability and then classifying the children as high, average, or low role takers on the basis of the test. Later, each child was given the job of teaching two younger children how to make paper caterpillars using scissors, glue, and crayons. The younger children could not do very well at this task on their own, so the second graders were in fact being tested in terms of how much help they would give. (Because IQ might influence ability to give help effectively, it was controlled in this experiment.)

The differences in the amount and quality of help offered by the two groups of role takers were quite striking. The high role takers not only answered questions willingly, but went out of their way to give helpful demonstrations, and to make numerous supportive comments. Low role takers either failed or refused to answer questions, or gave answers that were unhelpful or inadequate. Similar results have been obtained with older children (Barnett, Howard, Melton, and Dino, 1982) and adults (Toi and Batson, 1982).

Roots of Helping. Observational studies over the past ten years make it clear that the roots of empathy, helping, and caring begin very early in life. Rudimentary acts of helping and caring, as well as signs of emotional distress when others are hurt or uncomfortable, have been noted in toddlers as young as 18 months (Rheingold, Hay, and West, 1976). On the other hand, it is equally obvious that not all children react this way to the needs of others, either in toddlerhood or at later ages either.

What sort of early experience fosters altruism? To answer this question, Zahn-Waxler, Radke-Yarrow, and King (1979) systematically studied the behavior of sixteen parent-child pairs (seven boys and nine girls, all from intact families) for nine months while the children were between 15 and 30 months of age. Their summary description provides a vivid picture of the mothers whose children proved to be most empathic and altruistic:

> This mother brings the emotional stimulus events into focus. "Look what you did!" "Don't you hurt Amy—don't ever pull hair." She gives evidence of emotional investment in high expectations regarding the young child's behavior. "A very disturbing thing happened today, Judy bit me." "I expected a hug or statement that Jerry was sorry." . . . These mothers' effective "inductive" techniques are also "power-assertive" psychological techniques.

The effective induction is not calmly dispensed reasoning, carefully designed to enlighten the child; it is emotionally imposed, sometimes harshly or even forcefully. (Zahn-Waxler et al., 1979, p. 327)

Popularity and Helping. Popularity is related not only to the likelihood that children will help in any particular situation, but also to the type of help they will offer. Popular children tend to be somewhat more helpful than less popular children. They are also more likely to help in direct ways, and in ways that are obvious, visible to others, and conventional. Less popular children are likely to help behind the scenes and indirectly such as pointing out to a teacher that another child needs help. One reason for this difference appears to be that direct help is more acceptable from a popular peer. Unpopular children who attempt to help directly are perceived as intrusive; more popular peers who offer exactly the same help are likely to be greeted with appreciation and enthusiasm (Hartup, 1976).

Helping in Emergencies. What about helping other children when emergency situations occur? We know that adults are less likely to help when there are other bystanders than when they are alone. This has been explained as the "diffusion of responsibility" effect. When other bystanders are present, the responsibility experienced by any one of them is presumed to be diffused ("She could help, so I don't have to.") and thus helping becomes less likely (Latané & Nida, 1981). Does diffusion of responsibility in emergencies also occur with children?

Staub (1970) reported that it apparently did *not*, based on a study of first- and second-grade children who apparently were *more* rather than less likely to help if a peer was present. Recently, however, Peterson (1983) has reexamined the question.

In Peterson's study, first-, fourth-, and sixth-grade children were shown how to play a game involving wheels, cranks, handles, and other complex parts. Children in the so-called competence group were told the game sometimes got stuck and were given practice in getting it "unstuck" in case of difficulty; children in the control group were not given this training. After every child had played the game for a bit, all the children were moved to a waiting room and told that another child—the victim-to-be—was now playing the game. At this point half the children in each age and competence group were led to believe that there was a third child (the "other" bystander) in a room next to the game and waiting rooms; the remaining children heard no mention of another bystander. Then the "emergency" occurred: A young child's voice (actually prerecorded) came from the game room, crying:

"Oh, my finger!" "Oh, rats, it really hurts (sob)." "Oh, my hand is hurt, I can't get it out." "I can't get it out; I wish someone would help me." Between verbal cues, labored breathing and a struggle with the machine could be heard. (Peterson, 1983, pp. 875–876)

The results were quite straightforward. First, the likelihood of helping increased with age. Sixth graders were more likely to help than fourth graders and fourth graders were more likely to help than first graders. Second, the competence experience increased the likelihood of helping. Those who had had experience with fixing the complex and intricate-looking game were more likely to help than those who had not. Finally, contrary to Staub (1970) but consistent with numerous studies involving college students and older adults, being alone increased the likelihood of helping. This last finding was especially pronounced for girls.

Sharing

Through fate or circumstance, one person is often dependent on another's charity; indeed, charitable institutions in our society are very familiar. As James Bryan, a pioneer in the area, has written: "Most children in middle childhood will verbally, if not behaviorally, support the principle that one should aid the needy"(1970, p. 61). Further, the tendency to share increases with age throughout childhood (Rushton, 1982).

Mood and Emotional State. A child's willingness to share is influenced by her or his immediate emotional state. Children who are asked to think happy thoughts share more than those not given this positive set, whereas those asked to think sad thoughts tend to share a bit less than uninstructed control children also invited to share (Moore, Underwood, and Rosenhan, 1973). Similarly, the feeling or experience of being successful seems to produce a "warm glow of success" in children that makes them more generous. Failure and its associated feelings decrease

FIGURE 11—4
Average number of pennies donated by children after they were asked to think happy thoughts (right) or sad thoughts (left), or by those who were not asked to think about anything (center). Based on data from B. S. Moore, B. Underwood, & D. L. Rosenhan (1973) Affect and altruism. *Developmental Psychology.* Copyright © 1973 by the American Psychological Association. Reprinted by permission of the author.

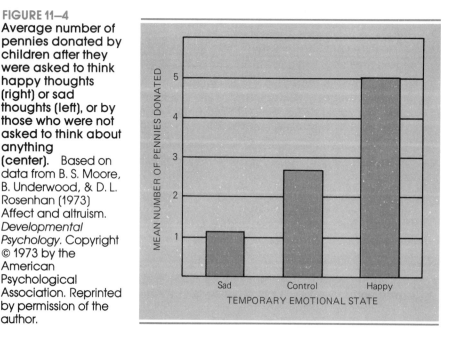

generosity in young and old alike (Isen, Horn, and Rosenhan, 1973). Finally, sharing seems to *produce* positive emotional feelings in donors, apparently because children and adults respond with empathy to the positive experiences of those with whom they share (Aronfreed, 1968).

Effects of Reward and Punishment. Perhaps the most obvious way to elicit sharing from children is to reward them directly for acts of generosity. After doing just this with 4-year-old children, Fischer (1963) found that youngsters became more likely to share marbles with unknown peers if such beneficence was directly rewarded with bubble gum. The brighter children in this study learned to share at a more rapid rate than the less intelligent ones, a result consistent with correlational data showing a significant relationship between intelligence and the development of a moral code in adolescence (Havighurst and Taba, 1949). However, the length of time these children shared after the experimenter and the promise of external reward were removed is unknown. This is an important question to answer, because parents and other adults are not always present to reward a child for sharing.

There is also the other side of the coin: We would expect that punishment for *not* sharing would also increase sharing in the future. Until recently developmental psychologists paid little attention to this possibility, but we now know that the threat of punishment for stinginess does increase immediate sharing. Such "help or else" training is extremely effective in transmitting a tendency to share, which often endures even after the threatening conditions are removed. Merely verbally pointing out the inequity between potential donors and recipients has little effect on subsequent sharing (Hartmann, Gelfand, Smith, Paul, Page, and Lebenta, 1976).

Why Children Share: A Developmental Analysis. Piaget (1932) suggested that the motives which cause children to share follow a developmental trend that parallels cognitive development. Piaget believed that the preoperational child's egocentrism made sharing unlikely. During the concrete operational period, children begin to appreciate the views of peers and thus are more likely to share with them. In one experiment designed to demonstrate this progression, Bar-Tal and his associates had pairs of kindergarten, second-grade, and fourth-grade children play a game and gave the winner seven pieces of candy as a prize, while the loser received none (Bar-Tal, Raviv, and Leiser, 1980). The question was: How much pressure would be required to cause the winner to share with the loser? It was answered by using a cleverly arranged set of events following the game.

Shortly after the candy distribution, the experimenter left the room for three minutes, so that the winner and loser were alone. When the experimenter returned she noted whether the winner had shared any candy with the loser. Children who shared under these circumstances were assumed to do so for altruistic reasons. If the winning child did not

share, the experimenter went on to the second condition. The following story was read to the children, with the sex referred to being the same sex as the children in the experiment:

> A child was invited to a birthday party and there received a bag filled with candy. On the way home the child met his/her friend who asked about the bag. The child said that he/she had received some candy and decided to share it with the friend. Both of them sat down and ate the candy. It is very nice to share candies with a friend. Good children share candy with other children who do not have any. (Bar-Tal, et al., 1980, p. 519)

After the story, the experimenter again left the room for three minutes and returned. Children who shared after hearing the story were assumed to have been motivated by the "norm of sharing"—sharing in situations in which it is generally considered a good thing to do. If the winner did not share after hearing the story, the experimenter went on to the next condition, in which she told the children that their teacher had promised to give an important role in an upcoming school play to one of the children who shared. The children were again left alone for three minutes. Winners who now shared were assumed to do so on their own initiative in the hope of receiving a specific external reward, the role in the play. If the winner still had not shared, the experimenter now told him/her to do so and went to the corner of the room for two minutes. Children who now shared were assumed to be motivated by compliance to authority. Finally, if the winners still had not shared, the experimenter again told her/him to do so, promising a "big prize" for compliance. This caused every winner who had not yet shared to now share with the loser.

The results of this experiment were quite clear. Only 7 percent of the kindergartners shared without promise of external reward, but 22.5 percent of the second graders and 38 percent of the fourth graders did so. Complementing this pattern, fully 24 percent of the kindergartners did not share until the last condition (when they were specifically told to share *and* offered a prize), whereas only 4 percent of the second graders and 1 percent of the fourth graders waited until the very end before sharing. Therefore, the data show that as children grow older (and, presumably, are better able to put themselves in the other child's shoes), their reasons for sharing become more altruistic and less dependent upon the motivation to comply with authority or to receive an external reward.

This tendency toward greater altruism seems to reflect changes in children's ideas about fairness (Damon, 1980; Hook and Cook, 1979). Preschool children often give little thought to fairness: Asked to divide rewards among a group of children, preschoolers typically want to keep all the rewards for themselves. Or they may allocate the rewards to a group of children to which they belong. A girl, for example, might say that only the girls should receive the reward. Older preschoolers and kindergarten children believe that rewards should be divided equally among all members in a class, regardless of their effort or need. Finally, beginning in the early elementary school years, there is growing awareness that fair distribution of rewards involves decisions about a number of factors, such as each child's efforts and needs, and the nature of the work leading to the reward. In short, as children's cognitive skills mature during the preschool and elementary school years, they begin to realize the complexities involved in deciding what is fair.

Effects of Behavioral Example. Behavioral examples are perhaps the most effective way to elicit and teach sharing (Rushton, 1975). Parents, of course, are the models to whom children are most continuously exposed, so it should come as no surprise that they too exert a powerful influence on sharing, as well as on cooperation and helpfulness.

In one recent field study, families with two girls (the older around 10 and the younger around 8) were observed at home, asked various questions, and given some games to work on together. The investigators were particularly interested in the example set by the mothers in these situations—that is, in how quickly and effectively they responded to each girl's request for help. They also noted the effect of the mothers' behavior on the girls. As might be expected, and quite consistent with modeling theory, the more responsive the mother was, the more likely the girls were to imitate her by being cooperative, helpful, sharing, and even less critical toward one another (Bryant and Crockenberg, 1980).

So far our discussion has focused on the prosocial side of social development. Now we turn to the other side of the coin and consider what is often thought of as the most serious form of antisocial behavior, aggression.

At some time or another virtually everyone aggresses—acts in a way that brings, or might bring, discomfort to someone else. We know that the type of aggression a person displays and the ability to control such action change in important ways with age and experience. The roots of these patterns and changes have long been of interest to developmental psychologists.

For our purposes, the determinants of aggression can be divided into two broad classes. Certain kinds of circumstances will draw out aggression more often than others and may therefore be thought of as *elicitors* of aggression. When people are attacked, they are likely to respond in kind, and so attack is an elicitor of aggression. Other determinants teach or encourage aggression; these are known as *cultivators* of a general pattern of responding.

We need to say something here about the difference between assertiveness and aggressiveness. In some contexts (for example, in business and politics) the words are used synonymously. We hear praise for an "aggressive business person" or an "aggressive program of affirmative action." Psychologists and other behavioral scientists, however, see an important difference between the ideas underlying the two terms. About two decades ago, Wolpe and Lazarus (1966) noted that, from a psychological perspective, *aggression* is "oppositional behavior which is socially reprehensible," whereas *assertiveness* is the "socially acceptable expression of personal rights and feelings" (p. 38). In a similar vein, Paul Mauger and his associates have pointed out that assertive behaviors are goal-directed actions to further the legitimate interests of individuals or the groups they represent, while respecting the rights of other persons. Aggressive behavior is intended to harm or injure, and is carried out without regard for the rights of others (Mauger, Adkinson, Hernandez, Firestone, and Hook, 1978). Aggression may be physical or verbal; it may be directed against people, animals, or things. Its aim is to hurt, damage, or destroy. Usually, aggression is accompanied by other outward or inward signs of anger, such as reddening of the face or increases in breathing and pulse rate.

Aggression Elicitors

Three major elicitors of aggression have been studied extensively: frustration, emotional arousal and catharsis, and competition.

Frustration. One view of how aggression is elicited is the famous frustration-aggression hypothesis, first spelled out by John Dollard and his associates at Yale in 1939. These theorists argued that *frustration,* defined as any blocking of goal-directed activity, naturally leads to aggression. According to the original statement, aggression was said to *always* be a consequence of frustration, and frustration was said to *always* lead to some form of aggression. Such a statement is too strong. In many cases most people, even if severely frustrated, will refrain from showing any direct acts of aggression; speeding drivers will not assault, or even raise their voices to, the police officer who has stopped them. And, other factors can often lead to acts of aggression.

Emotional Arousal and Catharsis.   Many parents feel their children are more likely to become aggressive (hitting a younger brother or sister, for example) when they are upset, agitated, or excited. Emotional arousal *does* influence a child's willingness to aggress but the process operates differently according to the youngster's sex. Boys' overall level of aggression increases when they are emotionally aroused, whereas in girls it decreases (Harris and Siebel, 1976). Socially learned anxiety about hostile impulses may well account for this pattern, since females are taught to feel guilty about their aggressive tendencies, while males are often led to believe that a willingness to aggress is brave or heroic.

At one time it was thought that people could reduce their levels of arousal by playing out their aggressive feelings verbally. But research has now shown that this type of *catharsis* does not occur.* Neither children nor adults seem able to "let off steam" by verbally expressing their hostilities (Mallick and McCandless, 1966). In fact, permitting both boys and girls to speak aggressive words has been shown to *increase* their willingness to punch other children (Slaby, 1975).

Competition.   Do highly competitive situations produce only sporting gamesmanship in children, or can they elicit outright hostility as well? This question was asked in a field experiment conducted by Rocha and Rogers (1976). In their study pairs of kindergarten and first-grade boys competed for a prize by building a tall tower out of blocks. In the high-competition group, few blocks were available; in the low-competition group, blocks were abundant. The results clearly showed that high competition elicited aggression as measured by interfering with one's partner and taking some of his blocks.

More distressing was the fact that boys in the high-competition group often abandoned the relatively practical tactics of interference (for example, toppling the other boy's blocks) in favor of out-and-out physical assaults. Figure 11–6 indicates that physical aggression was stimulated as much as interference by introducing the element of high competition into the game.

Some Cultivators of Aggressive Behavior   Although irritating or arousing events in the environment may provoke aggression, children's past learning experiences can also be responsible for their aggressive acts. Parents or other adults may reward

---

*The term *catharsis* can be traced to Aristotle, who believed that an audience could be drained of tragic emotions by watching a play. Freud later used the concept to refer to the release of pent-up or repressed feelings.

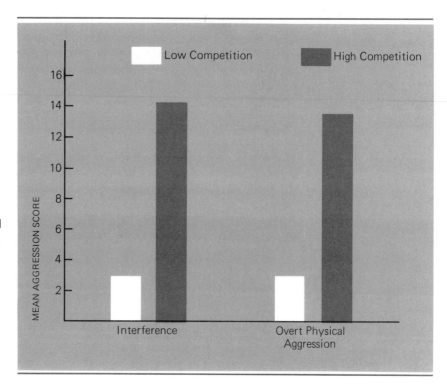

FIGURE 11–6
Results of Rocha and Rogers's experiment, showing that competitive situations may elicit overt physical aggression between children, as well as encourage interference with another child's efforts.

aggressive behavior and thus cultivate its occurrence. Slaby (1977), for example, reports that many teachers provide social reward (attention) to verbally aggressive children, thereby strengthening such behavior. In addition to a history of rewards and punishments, youngsters who have been given aggressive models will learn habits that can easily be activated whenever circumstances are right.

In a series of experiments done some years ago, Richard Walters and his associates demonstrated that even rewarding children for "make-believe" aggression in a play situation increases later aggressiveness against other children (Walters and Brown, 1963, 1964). In the 1963 experiment, for example, colored marbles were given as rewards to some children, on either a continuous or an intermittent schedule, for hitting a toy Bobo doll similar to the one in Figure 11–7. Children in a control group did not receive these rewards. Two days later each child was put in a potentially frustrating situation and left to play with another child who had not received any training in aggression. Children who had been rewarded intermittently for hitting the Bobo doll two days earlier showed significantly more aggression in this situation than did those in either of the remaining groups.

In a second experiment by these same investigators (Walters and Brown, 1964) some participants were rewarded only when they hit the Bobo sharply, while others were rewarded exclusively for weaker hits. Again, it was found that boys rewarded for the higher magnitude of

FIGURE 11–7
The "Bobo" doll used to study the influence of reward on aggressive behavior in the Walters experiments. From Bandura and Walters (1963). Copyright © 1963 by Holt, Rinehart, and Winston, Inc. Reprinted by permission of CBS College Publishing.

aggression were more aggressive in this new situation than those who had been rewarded for relatively mild play.

The Walters and Brown studies have several striking implications for socialization practices. Consider, for example, the father who encourages his son to roughneck with him in play and to smash away at punching bags, praising the lad for particularly forceful assaults. In addition to building a "real boy," such training may have the unintended effect of promoting aggression in other situations. And intermittent reinforcement (which had the greatest effect on children in the Walters experiments) will generally be provided simply because parents or other adults will not always be present to witness all the child's aggressive actions. The father who teaches his son to hit a punching bag, for instance, will not necessarily be on the playground when the child hits his friend.

Family Experiences. For years, pioneering researcher Gerald Patterson has pointed out that early family experiences are a prime training ground for learning patterns of aggression (Patterson, 1982; Patterson, Reid, Jones, and Conger, 1975).

Patterson's method is unique because his data and conclusions derive almost entirely from careful, systematic observations of aggressive children in their home environments. One fact that comes through clearly in this work is that parents and siblings play an enormous role in cultivating the behavior of aggressive children, and in ways that are subtle as well as obvious. Many parents and older siblings, for example, punish aggressive behavior. Although the immediate effect may be to suppress aggression, it also serves as a model and illustrates vividly that punishment "works" as a means of controlling others.

But it is not merely strong or aggressive parental responses that make for an aggressive child. Even low-key anger responses and unfair accusations by parents may pave the way for later aggressiveness. Finally, a vicious circle appears to develop in the families of many aggressive children. Compared to families with nonaggressive children, both aggressive children *and their parents* are more likely to respond to neutral behavior with aggression. Furthermore, once an aggressive exchange has begun, both parents and children are likely to escalate the exchange, rather than break it off (Patterson, 1984). And once a child has been labeled aggressive by parents and others, that child is more likely to be accused of aggression and to be singled out for punishment, even when the child has been behaving entirely appropriately on the occasion in question.

Dealing with Aggression

When a child behaves aggressively, many parents and teachers respond by punishing. Although this may seem quite a natural thing to do, the evidence is clear that the long-term effect is more likely to be an increase of aggressiveness rather than a decrease. There appear to be two reasons for this. One is the modeling effect. A parent who hits a child for aggression is saying, in effect, "You were right. The best way to get people to do what you want, or to stop them from doing what you don't want, is to hit them hard enough."

The second reason is that physical punishment often produces the very behavior it is intended to stop. Almost no one with any experience hits a child for crying. This tactic almost always fails because crying is a child's natural reaction to being hurt, so hitting for hurting will backfire and make the child cry more. Likewise, hitting a child for aggression does not usually inhibit aggression for very long, because aggression is often a natural response to being the target of aggression, regardless of the other person's motives. It is best to respond to young children's aggression by ignoring it, while at the same time reinforcing and encouraging various forms of nonaggressive social behavior.

The Influence of Television and Movies

Most children today are regular television watchers by the age of 3. By the time they are 15 they will have spent more time watching television than going to school. In fact, throughout childhood they will have spent more time watching television than in any other activity but sleep (Liebert, Sprafkin, and Davidson, 1982).

What do they see when watching all this television? The answer varies somewhat from child to child, but in the main the commercial entertainment shown on contemporary American television is of the "action-adventure" genre. This means that most of what they see contains a heavy dose of modeled aggression. Heroes and "good guys" on these shows almost invariably end up in a fist-, knife-, or gunfight with the "bad guys." The good guys always win, of course, and are typically rewarded with praise, admiration, and sometimes more tangible rewards (such as a vacation in the sun).

What are the effects of watching all these rewarded aggressive models for so long? This has not been an easy question to answer. Studies done in the 1960s by Bandura and his colleagues (Bandura and Walters, 1963) presented preschool children with aggressive modeling scenes on a simulated television set and demonstrated that children could learn new ways of behaving aggressively, which they demonstrated by assaulting a plastic "Bobo doll." But critics were quick to point out the limitations of these early "studies of TV violence" and doubted that such material could instigate aggressive behavior against real people (Hallaron, 1964; Klapper, 1968).

The next generation of studies attempted to answer Bandura's critics by replacing the Bobo doll with a human clown (Hanratty, Liebert, Morris, and Fernandez, 1969). To the surprise of many researchers and lay people, TV violence appeared to make children more aggressive toward other people, just as it did toward toy victims.

Numerous studies followed, most aimed at further mapping out and quantifying the relationship between TV violence and children's aggressive behavior. One such study, for example, showed that an eleven-day "diet" of aggressive cartoons led preschoolers to become more aggressive toward their peers (Steuer, Applefield, and Smith, 1971). In another study involving several individual experiments, some adolescent boys viewed aggressive movies for a week, while others were shown nonaggressive, control movies. The aggressive movies caused the boys to become more aggressive toward their peers, paralleling the earlier studies with young children. Still other investigators took a correlational tack, and related naturally occurring TV violence viewing (measured by questionnaires and diaries kept by young viewers) to various measures of aggressive behavior. Again, a clear link between TV violence viewing and aggression was regularly found (Liebert, Sprafkin, and Davidson, 1982).

One of the most methodologically sophisticated studies of TV violence and aggression ever done was reported recently by Huesmann, Lagarspetz, and Eron (1984). These investigators followed almost 1,000 elementary school boys and girls in both the United States and Finland for three years. Such an in-depth, cross-cultural study permitted an examination of both TV violence viewing and other factors as contributors to childhood aggression over time. It also provided an opportunity to consider the interaction among these factors. The results clearly supported the conclusion of earlier laboratory and field studies. The extent of TV violence viewing was again associated with—was, in fact, a predictor of—future levels of aggression for boys and girls in both cultures. In addition, the large sample size and the volume of detailed information available about the children and their families permitted Huesmann and his associates to identify some of the boundary conditions and moderating variables that increase and minimize the TV violence-aggression link.

One major finding from this study is that TV violence viewing and aggressive behavior are bidirectional in their effects. That is, watching TV violence stimulates a child to be more aggressive, while a child's becoming more aggressive stimulates additional TV violence viewing. Equally important is the demonstration that aggression is almost always multiply determined. In both Finland and the United States children who were most aggressive watched a lot of violent TV, believed that such shows portrayed life like it is, and identified strongly with the aggressive heroes in those shows. At the same time, these aggressive children also tended to have frequent aggressive fantasies, to have mothers who were quite aggressive themselves, to come from poorer than average homes, to do poorly in school, and to be unpopular with their peers.

What all this suggests, of course, is that TV violence is not *the* cause of aggression in children. Rather, it is *one* cause in a highly complex process. As we have already seen, similarly complex patterns have been found when we try to understand any other facet of children's social behavior.

Who Becomes Aggressive?

This question is often asked by parents, educators, and, of course, psychologists. The answer, unfortunately, it that there is no one answer. Some children tend to become aggressive more than others, partly because of what seem to be inborn dispositions. On the other hand, we have quite good evidence that the tendency to be more or less aggressive in various situations is learned.

Much is known about very aggressive children. They tend to be poor role takers; they have lower-than-average IQs; and they are often males. They are also likely to come from lower SES backgrounds. Many have parents who frequently resort to physical punishment.

Aggressive children are also low in empathy (Feshbach and Feshbach, 1969). This should not be surprising, since empathy involves the ability to experience other people's feelings as if they are our own—to become distressed when other people are hurt, for example. A child who experiences such "empathic distress" has a motivation to avoid hurting others. Highly aggressive children seem to lack this motivation. In fact, they actually appear to find other people's distress rewarding. A preschooler who attacks another child is likely to attack that child again if the victim cries or runs away (Patterson, Littman, and Bricker, 1967).

One experiment with preadolescent boys involved making each boy think he was punishing another boy for making mistakes in math problems. The punishment was to sound a noise in the other boy's earphones. The subjects could control the loudness of the sound by deciding which of ten buttons to press. The "other boy," supposedly in the next room, was to let the subject know how much he was hurt by responding with a "pain indicator" consisting of five lights, each with a label. The labels were arranged in order from (1) "Did not hurt my ears at all" to (10) "Hurt my ears so

much that my whole head hurts." (The lights were, in reality, controlled by the experimenter.)

Each boy in this experiment had been previously classified, on the basis of ratings by peers, as "high aggressive" or "low aggressive." The low-aggressive boys tended to punish the other boy with soft noises, even when the pain indicator suggested the other boy was not much bothered by the punishments. But the high-aggressive boys responded in quite a different way. They adjusted to the feedback from the other boy to maximize the amount of pain they gave him. For example, when the other boy said he was not hurt very much, the high-aggressive boys would up the level of punishment by choosing higher buttons and holding them down longer. In some cases, hurting the other boy even seemed to become the goal, and they were angry and annoyed if he was not being hurt enough. According to the investigators:

When the aggressive child is denied the satisfaction of knowing he has successfully injured his victim, he may in fact become extraordinarily hostile. That this may be the case was dramatically illustrated by the behavior of the high-aggressive boys in the low-pain-cues condition. Over the course of the test for aggression, as their victims continued to deny the experience of pain, many of these boys tried to evoke a pain response by simultaneously depressing noise buttons 8, 9, and 10 in an obvious attempt to maximize the noise level. (Perry and Perry, 1974, pp. 60–61)

The unfortunate fact about such children is that those who show high levels of antisocial aggression as youngsters are likely to become highly aggressive adolescents and adults. Chronic delinquents, for example, are much more likely than other children to have shown unusually high levels of aggressiveness when young (Loeber, 1982).

It is very important to note, however, that findings such as these do not necessarily mean that aggressiveness is inborn. Once a child starts being labeled aggressive, even when he or she is very young, environmental factors may lead him or her quite unwittingly along that path. For example, the attention a child gets may be quite reinforcing, even when it is intended to be disapproving or crit-

ical. The punishments parents and teachers dole out may increase the child's hostility and serve as further evidence that aggression "works." The companions and activities the child chooses may add to the problem. Even boys who are not very aggressive to begin with become more aggressive if they spend their time with other boys in rough and highly competitive physical activities (Bullock and Merrill, 1980).

Social Cognitive Processes in Aggression

It should come as no surprise, then, that aggression, like prosocial behavior, appears to have an important cognitive component (Shantz, 1983). For example, if a peer does something that is annoying, the response it brings usually depends on whether the action is seen as intentional or accidental. Dodge (1980) compared boys judged by their teachers as aggressive or nonagressive reacting to a situation in which their half-completed puzzle was dropped by another child. The other child stated he had a hostile intention, stated that dropping the puzzle was an accident, or made an ambiguous statement. Both aggressive and nonaggressive boys were most aggressive in the hostile-intent condition. Moreover, it was only in the ambiguous condition that the aggressive and nonaggressive boys differed. When the motives of the child who dropped the puzzle were ambiguous, aggressive boys typically assumed he had hostile intent, whereas nonaggressive boys did not.

At least some of this inappropriate responding occurs because these children are less skilled at interpreting behaviors and, *unable* to determine other children's intentions, often respond aggressively by default. For example, Dodge, Murphy, and Buchsbaum (1984) showed three brief videotapes to children. In two of the videotapes the same intention was shown in different settings; the third depicted a different intention. For example, one videotape might show a child deliberately erasing another child's writing from a blackboard; a second, one child deliberately knocking down another child's tower of blocks; a third, a child accidentally destroying another child's drawing. Compared to rejected and neglected children (who typically are aggressive as well), nonaggressive children were better able to select the episode in which the child's intention was different from the other two.

If aggressive children are unskilled at (a) recognizing the intentions of other people and (b) knowing an appropriate response for a given intention, would training these skills lead to improved social behavior? The answer seems to be "yes" (Asher and Renshaw, 1981). One approach is to teach aggressive children that aggression is painful and does not solve problems, and that there are more effective, prosocial ways to solve interpersonal disputes. This approach leads to reduced aggressive behavior and increased cooperation and constructive play (Zahavi and Asher, 1978).

SUMMARY

1. Learning how to get along with others includes making friends, developing prosocial and altruistic tendencies such as cooperating, helping, and sharing, and managing aggressive impulses and feelings.

2. Harry Stack Sullivan suggested that friendship patterns pass through a three-stage developmental sequence. The first stage involves mainly relationships with adults, to whom young children must turn for almost all their physical and emotional needs. During the second stage children turn to peers and playmates more for companionship, but not yet for much emotional support. During the third stage, *chumship*, children are able for the first time to form intense attachments with others, characterized by emotional intimacy and reciprocity.

3. There is a clear difference in the friendship patterns of boys and girls. Girls are much more likely to be exclusive— to have one or only a few close friends and to make it difficult or impossible for other girls to join their circle of friends. Perhaps because of their greater involvement in group activities, boys are not so exclusive and tend to be involved in larger and more flexible friendship groupings.

4. Masters and Furman draw an important distinction between friendship (or chumship) and popularity. Popularity involves being highly regarded, admired, and sought after by many peers. Friendships are characterized by reciprocity, stability, and behavioral involvement.

5. The developmental course of friendship has been examined in observational studies. Even infants under a year may show social recognition of one another by smiling, touching, or vocalizing. By toddlerhood sharing toys, turn taking, and playful interactions of five to ten minutes become common, but permanent and relatively stable friendship patterns have yet to appear.

6. During the kindergarten and early elementary school years the more enduring, chum-type friendships can first be seen. At this age (and later) children tend to choose as friends others who are like them in age, sex, race, and physical appearance. Friends also tend to become more similar to one another over time. This is particularly true in adolescence, when close friends become more and more alike in attitudes toward such matters as educational ambitions, drug use, and political affiliation and involvement.

7. Friendship also involves a complex social comparison process. In areas in which they are not too personally involved, children and adolescents like to take pleasure in their friends' accomplishments and most positive attributes, so they can bask in the reflected light

and glory. But youngsters are less likely to see their friends as better than they in matters of high personal relevance.

8. Friendship takes on new aspects and even greater importance during adolescence. Adolescents report spending more time talking to their friends than they do anything else. They are in the process of loosening many of the home ties of childhood, and turn increasingly to peers for support, acceptance, and sharing of feelings and experiences.

9. *Altruism* and *prosocial behavior* refer to cooperating, helping, and sharing, especially in circumstances and in ways that appear to be self-sacrificing rather than self-serving. Situational and cognitive factors appear to play a large role in whether children will cooperate or compete in various contexts.

10. Helping requires appropriate cognitive, emotional, and social skills. Among these are empathy and role-taking ability, and the kind of experience that leads children to believe they can successfully help in the situation.

11. Children are more likely to share when they are in a good mood, when they have been rewarded for sharing in the past, and when they have been exposed to sharing models. Cultural norms, as well as the examples of individual friends and family members, play major roles in the development of attitudes toward sharing.

12. *Aggression* is action designed to hurt others, and must be discriminated from assertiveness, "the socially acceptable expression of one's rights and feelings."

13. Frustration sometimes leads to aggression, but not always. Nor is all aggression the result of frustrated impulses. Neither is it true that aggression can ordinarily be "drained off" by engaging in aggressive fantasy or symbolic activities. In fact, many variables may elicit or cultivate aggression.

14. Three major *elicitors* of aggression are frustration, emotional arousal, and competition. Some *cultivators* are reward for aggression and exposure to aggressive models.

15. Years of research and hundreds of studies have been devoted to the question of whether exposure to TV violence leads to increased aggressive attitudes, impulses, and behavior. The overwhelming majority of research, including extensive and elaborate field studies as well as simpler laboratory demonstrations, suggests that an important link does exist.

16. The most aggressive youngsters appear to be those who have had aggressive models and inadequate home environments. They also tend to come from poorer than average homes, to do poorly in school, and to be unpopular with peers. Aggressive children are also low in empathy.

12 SEX ROLES AND GENDER IDENTITY

Of all the ways in which individuals are categorized, probably none is as influential as gender. Immediately after birth, family and well-wishers ask about the sex of a child. In one study, parents recorded telephone conversations in which they announced the births of their babies without mentioning whether the infants were girls or boys (Intons-Peterson and Reddel, 1984). In 80 percent of the conversations, the first question asked by well-wishers concerned the gender of the newborn (the health of the mother was most often the second question). Why should sex be of such overwhelming importance?

The reason is that the labels *female* and *male* do not refer simply to biological sex; they function as social categories that carry broad implications for development. Widely held assumptions, standards, and values are associated with sex. Individuals are perceived and treated differently according to sex. Even during the first weeks of life, gender influences whether babies are dressed in frilly pink gowns or simple blue suits, whether they are handled gently or less gently, and are considered sweet or strong.

Differences in the way females and males are perceived and treated influence the development of their knowledge, skills, behaviors, interests, and social roles. Biological differences between the sexes are also influential, of course, although the nature and extent of their effects are not firmly established. During the first few years of life, children develop *gender identity*—the sense of themselves as female or male. They also begin to acquire *sex roles*: that is, the behaviors, interests, and attitudes considered socially appropriate for females and males.

The acquisition of gender identity and sex role—which is called *sex typing* (Huston, 1983)—is our focus here. We examine the ways in which females and males are viewed by society, sex differences, developmental trends in early sex typing, influential theories that help explain sex typing, and important biological and social-psychological factors.

Because gender has such a central place in human interaction, it has been the subject of much research—and even more speculation. Today's heightened interest is due largely to concern about the negative impact of classification according to sex and especially to how females might be adversely affected. Such concern is reflected in various topics in this chapter, including the one we take first—that of sex stereotypes.

STEREOTYPES: HOW WE VIEW FEMALES AND MALES

Sex, or gender, stereotypes are the widespread, relatively stable beliefs and images that are held about the sexes (Tresemer and Pleck, 1974). They are abstractions or generalizations that may or may not be true. All societies hold stereotypes about the physical attributes, social roles, activities and interests, abilities, and social-psychological attributes of the sexes. These generalizations tend to be bipolar: what is feminine is not masculine, and what is masculine is not feminine (Deaux, 1985).

People often are unaware that they believe in stereotypes. As a simple demonstration, close your eyes and imagine the following scenes: a physician and a nurse caring for a child, a person chopping wood, a child setting the table for dinner. Chances are that you pictured a male physician and a female nurse in the first scene; a large, muscular man in the second scene; and a girl in the third scene. Such images would be consistent with gender stereotypes.

Females are typically viewed as physically small and weak; males as large and strong. The social role of females centers on the home and family relationships; the role of males emphasizes work outside the home and community leadership. Thus, cooking, sewing, and child care are considered feminine, whereas farming, fixing automobiles, and playing football are considered masculine.

Personality Stereotypes

Psychologists are particularly interested in sex stereotypes of social-psychological, or personality, attributes. In research about these stereo types, participants typically rate characteristics according to whether, or how strongly, they apply to males and females. As an example, consider the work of Broverman and her associates, who tested both college students and mental health professionals (Broverman, Broverman, Clarkson, Rosenkrantz, and Vogel, 1970; Broverman, Vogel, Broverman, Clarkson, and Rosenkrantz, 1972). Table 12–1 shows college students' judgments of certain attributes as masculine or feminine; mental health professionals largely agreed with this profile. In fact, the profile represents the traditional view of the sexes. More males than females are seen as rational, active, independent, competitive, and aggressive. More females than males are viewed as emotional, passive, dependent, sensitive, and gentle. The cluster of masculine traits is labeled *instrumentality*. When individuals engage in instrumental behaviors, they are acting on the world and influencing outcomes. The cluster of feminine traits is labeled *expressiveness*. It refers to behaviors concerned with interpersonal relationships and emotional functioning.

So-called masculine attributes are typically favored over so-called feminine traits. But some feminine attributes are seen positively (see Table 12-1). Evaluation depends on what dimension of functioning is examined. For example, Stoppard and Kalin (1983) asked college students to evaluate competence, adjustment, and interpersonal functioning based on written descriptions of persons. Each student was presented with personality descriptions that varied in terms of masculine/feminine attributes and social desirability/undesirability. Each of the descriptions was applied to both a male and a female.

The overall results of the study showed that persons with masculine traits were rated more highly on *both* adjustment and competence. Those with feminine traits were rated more highly on interpersonal functioning. (This pattern existed regardless of whether the attributes were socially desirable or undesirable, although the desirable attributes were more highly evaluated.) Thus, expressiveness was valued, but it seemed to fall short of the value placed on masculine traits.

The traditional stereotypes have changed somewhat in the last few decades. Most notable is a change in the perception of women's social

TABLE 12–1
Stereotypes of Masculinity and Femininity. The shaded items are more highly valued than their counterparts.

Masculine	Feminine
Very aggressive	Not at all aggressive
Very independent	Not at all independent
Not at all emotional	Very emotional
Almost always hides emotions	Does not hide emotions at all
Very objective	Very subjective
Not at all easily influenced	Very easily influenced
Very dominant	Very submissive
Likes math and science very much	Dislikes math and science very much
Not at all excitable in a minor crisis	Very excitable in a minor crisis
Very active	Very passive
Very competitive	Not at all competitive
Very logical	Very illogical
Very worldly	Very home-oriented
Very skilled in business	Not at all skilled in business
Very direct	Very sneaky
Knows the way of the world	Does not know the way of the world
Feelings not easily hurt	Feelings easily hurt
Very adventurous	Not at all adventurous
Can make decisions easily	Has difficulty making decisions
Never cries	Cries very easily
Almost always acts as a leader	Almost never acts as a leader
Very self-confident	Not at all self-confident
Not at all uncomfortable about being aggressive	Very uncomfortable about being aggressive
Very ambitious	Not at all ambitious
Easily able to separate feelings from ideas	Unable to separate feelings from ideas
Not at all dependent	Very dependent
Never conceited about appearance	Very conceited about appearance
Thinks men are always superior to women	Thinks women are always superior to men
Talks freely about sex, with men	Does not talk freely about sex, with men
Uses very harsh language	Doesn't use harsh language at all
Not at all talkative	Very talkative
Very blunt	Very tactful
Very rough	Very gentle
Not at all aware of feelings of others	Very aware of feelings of others
Not at all religious	Very religious
Not at all interested in own appearance	Very interested in own appearance
Very sloppy in habits	Very neat in habits
Very loud	Very quiet
Very little need for security	Very strong need for security
Does not enjoy art and literature at all	Enjoys art and literature
Does not express tender feelings at all easily	Easily expresses tender feelings

Source: From Broverman, Vogel, Broverman, Clarkson, and Rosenkrantz (1972).

role. During the 1970s and into the 1980s, attitudes became more favorable toward the participation of women in the work force and in family decision making (Thornton, Alwin, and Camburn, 1983). Once seen as maladjusted and less feminine than homemakers, today career-oriented women are viewed as psychologically adjusted and satisfied (Yogev, 1983). Such change is important, because stereotypes operate in complex ways that powerfully influence the development of sex roles and gender identity.

Stereotypes are not simply neutral descriptions of the sexes; rather, they act as differential prescriptions, norms, or standards for males and females. Socialization is generally aimed at developing members of society to fit these standards. Boys are encouraged to be active, competitive, and logical; girls are encouraged to be dependent, emotional, and passive. Furthermore, the boundaries between the sexes are kept relatively rigid and clear so that individuals know when they are stepping out of their prescribed sex roles (Tresemer and Pleck, 1974). Individuals also apply these standards to themselves. This process may begin quite early in life, because virtually all preschoolers have some knowledge of their culture's assumptions and views of the sexes (Weinraub et al., 1984).

Stereotypes set up expectations that according to gender, individuals will appear, act, and feel in particular ways. These expectations, in turn, affect how we perceive and treat others. In one fascinating demonstration of sex-biased perceptions, college students watched a videotape of a 9-month-old child labeled as a girl, Dana, or a boy, David (Condry and Condry, 1976). The infant was shown responding to a teddy bear, a jack-in-the-box, a doll, and a buzzer. The students were asked to rate whether the infant reacted with pleasure, anger, or fear, and the degree of intensity with which the infant responded. At the end of the videotape they were also asked to describe the infant on several attributes, such as quiet/loud and aggressive/passive.

The results generally showed that perceptions of the infant varied depending on whether the child had been labeled a girl or a boy. When labeled Dana, the infant was viewed as displaying less aggressiveness, pleasure, and anger, and more fear. For instance, Dana's reaction to the jack-in-the-box was seen more as fear; the same reaction in David was seen more as anger.

Another investigation shows that adults may also be judged according to sex stereotypes. Adult participants were asked to judge the persuasiveness of a hypothetical communicator, labeled female or male, on an opposite-sex colleague (Eagly, 1983). When labeled male, the communicator was judged more successful. The effect of gender labeling was weakened when the participants were given other information about the situation (for example, that the female communicator was the boss). But without such information, gender was used to form the perception of another person.

Explanations of others' behaviors, which are called *attributions* for behavior, have also been linked to general beliefs about gender. One study, for example, measured attitudes toward women as managers and then related them to attributes for women's success (Garland and Price, cited by Deaux, 1984). People who held positive views of women were more likely to attribute success to effort and ability; people who held the most

375

negative views were more likely to attribute success to luck or to the ease of the task.

Given the many ways in which stereotypes function, it is not surprising that they are woven into most accounts of sex typing. However, since stereotypes may or may not accurately describe the sexes, it is important to ask if and how the sexes actually differ.

SEX DIFFERENCES: FACT AND FICTION

We all recognize that the sexes differ in interesting ways. Primary differences in the reproductive system are obvious, as are secondary characteristics such as voice pitch, beard growth, and breast development. Males are typically larger and stronger than females throughout most of the life span. They display a more developed musculature, whereas females have a greater proportion of fat tissue. Females also have a lower mortality rate from the moment of conception, and they are less susceptible to many diseases and dysfunctions (Hetherington, 1970). Subtle brain differences based on sex are also thought to exist—for example, in the hypothalamus. The physical differences just described are largely attributed to biological programming. To be sure, females would show greater strength in gymnastic feats were they encouraged to do so, but the female body plan might still set limits on such strength, just as it sets the foundation for gymnastic flexibility.

The picture is less clear when intellectual and psychosocial attributes are examined. In 1974 Maccoby and Jacklin wrote an extremely influential book in which they summarized results from approximately 1,500 research studies relevant to sex differences, for the most part in the young. They concluded that gender differences had been established in only four areas—verbal ability, mathematical ability, visual-spatial ability, and aggression. They also suggested that the findings were too ambiguous or inadequate to draw conclusions about many behaviors, such as activity level, anxiety, compliance, dominance, and nurturance. Other presumed sex differences were labeled cultural myths because, according to Maccoby and Jacklin, research evidence did not support them. These included the beliefs that girls are more social and suggestible than boys, have lower self-esteem, are less analytic in thinking, and lack achievement motivation.

Maccoby and Jacklin's conclusions did not go unquestioned. Block (1976) noted that Maccoby and Jacklin had included some weak studies and had defined behaviors in ways in which other researchers might not. Block argued, in fact, that the conclusions might have been different had other procedures and definitions been used. Several other investigators questioned findings about specific behaviors. More recent reviewers have used statistical techniques that allow them to detect small but significant differences that previously went undetected (Eagly, 1983). Overall, the Maccoby and Jacklin review stimulated much research on sex differences in both children and adults. It now appears that gender differences may be somewhat more extensive than Maccoby and Jacklin had suggested—but, as we will see, the issue is not easily settled. Table 12-2 presents some of the research findings.

TABLE 12–2
Some Areas In Which Female and Male Performances Have Been Compared

Intellectual

Mathematics	No differences in early childhood. From adolescence through adulthood, males generally score higher.
Verbal Ability	No or small differences in childhood. From adolescence through adulthood, females generally score higher.
Visual-spatial Ability	At least from adolescence, through adulthood, males score higher.

Social-Psychological

Motive to Achieve	No overall differences in achievement-relevant situations. Males may be more motivated in challenging, competitive situations; females by work and the presence of others.
Activity Level	Differences are often not found. When they are, boys usually score higher.
Aggression	Males are more aggressive from the preschool years into adulthood. Differences may be greater early in life.
Altruism/Empathy	Differences in altruism are often not found. When they are, females are slightly more altruistic. Females are more empathic as measured by self-reports, but this difference is not found by other measures.
Anxiety	Females may be more susceptible from childhood through adulthood, but much of the data are self-reports.
Impulsivity	Young males appear to show less delay of gratification and more risk taking, temper tantrums, and disruptive behavior. Systematic study of adults is lacking.
Social Compliance	Girls comply more to adults, although not to peers. At all ages females appear to be more influenced in social situations, especially under group pressure.
Social Orientation	Girls play in smaller groups and maintain greater proximity to others. Women are superior to men in interpreting nonverbal behavior of others. Females are more interpersonally involved and their friendships are intimate, supportive networks. Male friendships are more oriented to collective activities and loyalties. In middle adulthood, intimacy may decrease for females and increase for males.

Based primarily on Bee and Mitchell (1984), Block (1983), Deaux (1985), Eagly and Carli (1981), Eisenberg and Lennon (1983), Hyde (1981, 1984b), Maccoby and Jacklin (1974, 1980), Shigetomi, Hartmann, and Gelfand (1981), and Wylie (1979).

Intellectual Abilities

Based on a long fascination with intellectual ability, researchers continue to investigate gender differences in verbal, mathematical, and visual-spatial abilities.

Females have typically been given the edge in verbal ability. However, such sex differences exist primarily after adolescence (Maccoby and Jacklin, 1974). One extensive study, in fact, found no differences at all in verbal ability among very talented seventh and eighth graders (Benbow and Stanley, 1980). Sex differences favoring males have been found in mathematical ability by early adolescence (Benbow and Stanley, 1983). But here too, differences are not inevitable: Paulsen and Johnson (1983) found no sex differences in fourth, eighth, and eleventh graders from middle- and upper-class families. By the time they complete high school girls have enrolled in fewer math courses than boys, and it has been suggested that this accounts for the differences found. For the most part, however, male superiority persists, although to a lesser extent, when math background is taken into account.

A relatively consistent gender difference favoring males is also evident for visual-spatial ability, at least by adolescence (Meece, Parsons, Kaczala, Goff, and Futterman, 1982). Interest in visual-spatial ability rests in part on its association with mathematical achievement. Scores on visual-spatial and mathematics tests are moderately correlated. When visual-spatial ability is taken into consideration, sex differences in mathematics are reduced or eliminated. And verbal ability also correlates with math performance, indicating the multiple facets of mathematics.

The many analyses of gender differences in intellectual abilities hardly present a clear picture. First, it is not simply the case that girls or boys are superior in verbal, mathematical, and visual-spatial abilities. Rather, each of these abilities consists of numerous skills in which the sexes may or may not differ. For example, there is some evidence that boys are superior in mathematical reasoning but that girls do as well and sometimes better than boys in computation (Deaux, 1985). Second, gender differences may be moderated by many factors. Visual-spatial performance, for example, may vary with physical maturation, body type, personality traits associated with masculinity and femininity, experience with spatial activities, family and social class, and specific task. Third, according to recent analyses, intellectual gender differences appear to be quite small.

Meta-analysis is a technique for combining the results of many different studies and drawing a "weighted" conclusion about group differences. Some of the findings from Hyde's (1981) meta-analyses of intellectual abilities are shown in Figure 12–1. Assuming normal distributions of performance scores, there is a large overlap in male and female scores, indicating that the sexes are more alike than different in intellectual performance. However, more females excel in verbal tasks and show inadequacies in mathematics and visual-spatial tasks, whereas the re-

FIGURE 12–1
The normal distributions in A approximate male and female performance on verbal tasks; the distributions in B approximate male and female performance on mathematical and visual-spatial tasks. From Hyde (1981).

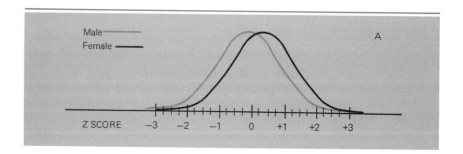

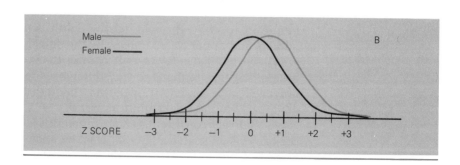

verse is true for males. At the same time, remember that the curves reflect sex differences on the average, and that the patterns do not apply to all females and all males.

Social Behavior

Among the numerous social behaviors that have been examined for gender differences are altruism, social compliance and conformity, and aggression.

As we saw in Chapter 11, research on altruism evaluates willingness to help others in a variety of ways, including sharing personal resources. The stereotype that females are more altruistic than males is well established, but research does not consistently support this general belief (Shigetomi, Hartmann, and Gelfand, 1981). Most studies show no gender differences, and when differences do occur, females have only a slight edge over males.

Situational factors undoubtedly play a role in determining altruism, so it would not be surprising for males to be more altruistic than females in some situations. Nevertheless, females apparently receive credit for altruism that exceeds their actual deeds, whereas males may not be credited when credit is due. Why is this so? Shigetomi (1981) and her colleagues offer one possible explanation: Girls behave in ways that are not in themselves altruistic but that lead others to perceive altruism. Research on gender differences in empathy provides some support for this hypothesis (e.g., Hoffman, 1977). Empathy is reported by girls more than by boys (Eisenberg and Lennon, 1983). Because empathy is believed to be a forerunner of altruism, such reports may lead to the perception that girls are more altruistic than boys.

Experiments on social compliance and conformity examine compliance to anothers' directions, influence from the verbal messages of a communicator, and conformity to the opinions and perceptions of the group in which one finds oneself. It is widely held that females are less independent than males and are thus more open to social influence. Does research support this view? Considerable evidence indicates that very young girls are more likely than young boys to comply with the directions of adults (Maccoby and Jacklin, 1974). Girls and women are also influenced more than their male counterparts in a variety of situations, especially when group pressure is operating (Eagly, 1978; Eagly and Carli, 1981). The gender differences are, however, small. Moreover, male researchers are more likely to find female conformity than are female researchers (Eagly and Carli, 1981).

Assuming that a small gender difference does exist, however, we may ask why females are more easily influenced than males. One hypothesis is that females are socialized in accordance with the gender stereotype. Eagly (1983) speculates that sex differences in *social role status* are an important factor. Social roles are arranged in a hierarchy of power, and individuals who occupy roles of power are believed to have the right to influence others. Because males typically hold higher positions in work and marriage, they are more often given the power to influence. Maleness is then linked to status, competence, and high value. According to

FIGURE 12–2
Although males are often more aggressive than females, females are certainly capable of displaying aggression and do so in a variety of situations.   David S. Strickler, Monkmeyer.

this interpretation, when females are in roles associated with power (for example, when they are managers at work), they become the influencers. In fact, evidence exists to support this proposition.

Perhaps the most firmly established difference between the sexes is greater aggressiveness in males. This pattern, found in most cultures, may appear as early as the preschool years and continue into adulthood (Hyde, 1984). Despite the consistency of the research results, the gender differences may be quite small, certainly not nearly as large as one would gather from all that has been written about them (Hyde, 1984b; Maccoby and Jacklin, 1974). In fact, such sex differences tend to be larger among preschool children than among older children, adolescents, and adults.

Display of aggression also depends on situational factors. Males are surely not aggressive in most situations, and females can be aggressive (Figure 12–2). For example, when confronted with male partners who became increasingly aggressive, women's levels of aggression escalated in turn, wiping out the initial gender difference (Taylor and Epstein, cited by Frodi et al., 1977).

How Important Are Sex Differences?

What conclusions can we reach about the importance of gender differences? There is no easy answer to this question, because it is difficult to judge the impact of any differences between the sexes. Nevertheless, it is helpful to review the following points:

1. Differences do exist in several physical, intellectual, and psychosocial attributes. Some differences appear during childhood; some are apparent in adolescence; some begin at or persist into adulthood. Many

other characteristics are being investigated. However, the more extensive the research, the more complex the results. Gender differences can vary with a host of factors, including past experience, social class, attitudes, and specific tasks and situations. Situational factors may be especially important in determining social behaviors. And in any event, gender differences may wax and wane with the sociopolitical and economic spirit of the times, making them particularly difficult to track down.

To complicate matters even more, some of the variations found in research studies of sex differences can be attributed to bias. Furthermore, differences between the sexes have broad social implications that may prejudice researchers or others who report the findings. Both male and female investigators may be more likely to report results favorable to their own sex (Deaux, 1985).

2. Laboratory results indicate that when gender differences are found, they are quite small. There is much overlap between the sexes, and the stereotypes may often be exaggerated compared to actual differences. This can limit life choices for both sexes. At the same time, sex differences are not unimportant. Even with small average differences, such as those shown in Figure 12–1, inequality exists at the ends of the distributions. Thus, for example, females do not reach the high level of performance attained by a small percentage of males in mathematics, which can limit their career choices and successes.

3. We must also consider that the research setting itself, although certainly helpful in describing sex-related behaviors, gives an incomplete picture. Indeed, the absence or smallness of gender differences reported in laboratory studies is often viewed suspiciously by those who observe people in everyday life. This is partly because the sexes vary in ways not emphasized by laboratory research: in occupations, interests, and activities, to name a few. Were we to observe males and females as they go about their everyday lives, we would be struck by many differences, even today. Few females would be playing football or fishing, and even fewer males would be taking ballet lessons.

4. Finally, the establishment of sex differences is often taken as proof that either biological or environmental variables are responsible for certain attributes and roles of the sexes. But descriptions of behaviors can tell us little about what determines or maintains those behaviors.

THEORIES OF SEX TYPING

Theories of gender-identity and sex-role development emphasize various aspects of sex typing. Historically, Freud's psychoanalytic view led the way, and it still has influence. However, social learning and cognitive approaches now vie for leadership in explaining sex typing.

The Psychoanalytic View

Freud first presented his perspective of gender development in the 1905 edition of *Three Essays on the Theory of Sexuality*. As we saw in Chapter 4, Freud hypothesized that during the phallic stage of development, from approximately 3 to 6 years of age, children experience a conflict that plays a central role in gender development. The male child, desirous of his mother, fears castration at the hands of his father. He resolves this Oedipal conflict by identifying with his father, thereby vicariously possessing his mother. According to Freud, identification is a special emotional tie based on the need to be loved or on the fear of one's parents. Identification results in the young boy's becoming like his father in ways that are relevant to gender.

Freud faced a theoretical dilemma in accounting for female development. He believed that girls experienced something like the Oedipal conflict, but that they formed a sexual attachment to their fathers. Assuming as he did that *both* sexes became attached to the mother very early in life during the oral and anal stages, how could Freud explain the female's attachment to her father? Freud dealt with this dilemma by proposing *penis envy* in females (Stewart, 1976). Of females, he said:

> They notice the penis of a brother or playmate, strikingly visible and of large proportions, at once recognize it as the superior counterpart of their own small and inconspicuous organ [the clitoris], and from that time forward fall a victim to envy for the penis. . . . [The young girl] makes her judgment and her decision in a flash. She has seen it and knows that she is without it and wants to have it. (Freud, 1925, in Stewart, 1976, pp. 49–50.)

According to Freud, the girl holds her mother responsible for her physical shortcomings, and maternal attachment weakens. One more step completes the development of the girl into a woman: In some unknown way the wish for a penis is substituted by the wish for a child. This leads to identifying the father as a love object and to feeling jealousy toward the mother. The child now must deal with this *Electra* conflict, which she does by internalizing her mother's behavior.

One important side effect of Freud's explanations relates to the growth of the superego. Recall that according to psychoanalytic theory the superego is born when the Oedipal or Electra conflict is resolved. Freud believed this process to be powerful and dramatic in boys because it is motivated by fear of castration. Because the castration complex is lacking in girls, motivation to resolve the conflict is weaker and it may not be well resolved. This, in turn, presumably results in a relatively weaker superego in women.

Social Learning Theory

According to social learning theorists like Albert Bandura (1969, 1977) and Walter Mischel (1966, 1970), learning processes determine children's adoption of gender-related behaviors. Both believe the same learning principles involved in the socialization of other behaviors can be applied to sex role development. And typical of this view, the process is seen as a cumulative one, even though the early years may be more important. Bandura has described the early and on-going socialization process in this way:

Sex-role differentiation usually commences immediately after birth when the baby is named and both the infant and the nursery are given the blue or pink treatment depending upon the sex of the child. Thereafter, indoctrination into masculinity and femininity is diligently promulgated by adorning children with distinctive clothes and hair styles, selecting sex-appropriate play materials and recreational activities, promoting associations with same-sex playmates, and through nonpermissive parental reactions to deviant sex-role behavior. (1969, p. 215)

The social learning view emphasizes reinforcement and punishment in the acquisition of sex roles. It is assumed that parents and others deliberately or inadvertently shape appropriate gender roles in children. In short, girls are taught to be submissive, emotional, and neat, to play with dolls, and to prefer reading to mathematics. Boys are encouraged to be independent, aggressive, and achievement-oriented, to play with trucks and hammers, and to excel in mathematics. Even more weight is assigned to observational learning. Opportunities for such learning are seen in children's exposure to models—to parents, other adults, peers, and models in literature and on television. In fact, although parents are considered potent models, the stage on which sex roles develop throughout life goes far beyond the nuclear family.

Mischel and Bandura emphasize the impact of the environment on the adoption of gender-related behaviors, but mental processes are incorporated into their theories. They recognize that people come to categorize themselves as either male or female, and that such categorization affects how individuals perceive and respond to experiences. Reinforcement and punishment may set up expectations about the future consequences of gender-related behaviors; these cognitions, in turn, affect future behaviors. And, as with all observational learning, what is learned from gender models, and what is imitated or not, depend on many cognitive variables.

Cognitive Theories

Based on Piaget's formulations, cognitive-developmental theory was set forth by Kohlberg (1966; Kohlberg and Ullian, 1974). Its main focus is on the construction of the concept of gender. Kohlberg stressed that children gradually develop a basic understanding that they are of either the female or the male sex. Gender then serves to organize many perceptions, attitudes, values, and behaviors. Full understanding of gender is said to develop gradually in three steps.

First, children recognize that they are either boys or girls, and label themselves accordingly. Such self-recognition is presumed to be based on physical differences between the sexes, particularly size and strength. Next, children come to recognize gender *stability*; that is, that gender does not change over time, and that boys invariably become men and girls invariably become women. Finally, children understand gender *consistency*, that maleness and femaleness do not change over situations or according to personal wishes. The achievement of stability and consistency together provide gender *constancy*, and with it the completion of a basic gender identity. The entire process is said to occur by 6 or 7 years of age.

It is at this time that gender identity is thought to become a powerful organizer of children's social perceptions and actions (Kohlberg and Ullian, 1974). Based on what they already know about femaleness and maleness, children actively seek to shape their behavior to fit gender stereotypes. They are motivated by the need for self-consistency and self-esteem. Children who identify themselves as males, for example, are interested in and value males and the activities and attributes of males. Thus, children become active self-socializers.

Of course, as cognitive development proceeds, changes occur in the understanding of gender identity and sex roles. At first based on physical differences between the sexes, understanding next rests on social functions typically prescribed for the sexes. In providing reasons why they thought that males are smarter than females, a 6-year-old boy thought it was due to males having "bigger brains," but a fifth-grade boy thought it was due to males having jobs that required them to think and "figure things out" (Kohlberg and Ullian, 1974, p. 215, 217). Fifth-graders are also likely to believe that although people are not compelled to carry out gender-related functions and roles, it is better if they do. By adolescence it is understood that individuals have some choices and are able to break sex stereotypes. Such changing ideas about sex roles are viewed as relatively independent of cultural training and reinforcement.

In recent years, other cognitive theories have been described. Martin and Halverson (1981; 1983) and Bem (1981) propose that sex typing derives, at least in part, from children's processing information from the environment on the basis of *gender schemas*. Schemas are cognitive con-

FIGURE 12-3
Once basic gender identity has been established, the child actively seeks to shape his or her behavior to match sex identity. Rita Freed, Nancy Palmer Photo Agency.

structs—networks of associations—that influence perception, regulate behavior, and provide a basis for interpreting information.

Martin and Halverson propose that sex stereotypes are the basis for two schemas involved in sex typing. One schema is an *in-group-out-group* schema that consists of all the general information used to categorize behaviors, activities, and objects as female or male. This schema guides behavior by informing the child what is sex appropriate. For example, if a girl is presented with a doll, she will decide that dolls are for girls, and since she is a girl, dolls *are for her*. She will avoid a truck as a thing *not for her*. The second, more specific schema is an *own-sex* schema, which consists of information about the behavior, activities, and objects that characterize one's own gender. This schema contains detailed plans of action required to conduct sex-appropriate behaviors. Having selected the doll, a girl will learn how to interact with the doll. These actions then become part of her own-sex schema. As a child grows older, his or her own-sex schema is elaborated.

Martin and Halverson's theory predicts that schemas affect attention, memory, and the interpretation of information. For example, Martin and Halverson (1983) suggest that stereotypes are almost self-perpetuating, because information consistent with a particular stereotype is remembered and inconsistent information is distorted to make it conform to the stereotype. They tested this hypothesis by showing 5- and 6-year-old children pictures of males and females performing sex-consistent or sex-inconsistent activities (a boy playing with trains, a girl sawing wood). One week later, memory was evaluated. When the performers were females, sex-consistent pictures were remembered better; when the performers were males, sex-inconsistent pictures were remembered better. Moreover, children tended to distort sex-inconsistent pictures; that is, they changed the sex of the performer to conform to gender stereotypes. Other investigations have found that memory for sex-consistent pictures is better than that for sex-inconsistent pictures (Cann and Newbern, 1984).

Bem's (1981) discussion of sex typing emphasizes that society teaches the young child two basic things about gender. It teaches the wide network of sex-related associations that serves as a cognitive schema. And it teaches that the difference between the sexes is relevant to virtually all aspects of functioning. Thus, society makes the gender schema extremely important. Children choose from among the many dimensions of human personality only those that apply to their own genders. Their self-concepts become sex typed. Moreover, they learn to evaluate themselves in terms of gender schema. Bem also suggests that the gender schema is not equally important to all individuals, but is most important to those who are strongly sex typed. These individuals rely heavily on gender to organize their behavior and self-concepts. For example, Signorella and Liben (1984) found that children with highly stereotyped views of the sexes had better memory of pictures that were consistent with gender stereotypes. As we see later, Bem questions society's emphasis on gender distinctions.

Of all the theories described here, the views of Freud are probably least influential today. Many developmentalists reject the idea of penis envy. There is also no evidence that one sex is morally superior to the other (Walker, 1984). In addition, the concept of identification has been seriously questioned. Social learning theorists have challenged this idea, arguing that identification can be viewed more simply as imitation of the same-sex parent (Bandura, 1969). Overall, the questions raised certainly cast serious doubt on many of Freud's claims.

Social learning and cognitive theories all recognize both social and cognitive factors in sex typing, but each makes specific contributions to knowledge about the formation of gender identity and sex roles. By emphasizing the influence of agents of socialization, social learning theory has generated much research into whether and how parents and other agents actually shape gender roles. The cognitive approach draws special attention to the growth of individuals' conceptions of themselves and others as males and females, and predicts change in these conceptions. It also emphasizes that children act as self-socializers by processing information and shaping their behaviors and interests according to gender standards.

Although no one theory of sex typing provides a complete framework for explaining all the psychological and social facets of sex typing, in combination the theories just described go a long way in addressing the major issues.

EARLY SEX TYPING

A considerable amount of work during the last few decades provides a view of the development of gender identity and sex roles. Although developmental changes occur throughout adulthood, much of the research highlights childhood and adolescence, when growth is most dramatic. Based on Huston's (1983) review of this work and specific research studies, we examine major aspects of sex typing.

Gender Identity

The newborn probably has no knowledge of itself as an identity separate and distinct from others, much less an understanding of itself as a male or female. Many investigators have asked when self-identity first develops. Information has been obtained by ingenious studies of infants' abilities to recognize themselves visually and distinguish themselves from others. As early as 1877 Darwin noted that his infant son would look at a mirror image of himself and exclaim "Ah!" when his name was spoken (Damon and Hart, 1982). Darwin took this as a sign of self-recognition. Perhaps the most extensive recent work on early self-knowledge is the series of studies conducted by Lewis and Brooks-Gunn (1979) with children 9 to 24 months of age. These researchers observed infants looking into mirrors, with and without rouge on their noses. Many of the infants looked at, smiled at, and touched the mirror images as well as their own bodies, and made faces. Lewis and Brooks-Gunn were especially interested in the infants' touching their own rouge-dabbed noses, because this behavior required that infants recognize the mirror images as not just people, but as themselves. Such self-recognition began at 15 to 18 months of age and increased after that.

The researchers also studied the reactions of babies when they were exposed to pictures of themselves, their parents, an unfamiliar 8-month-old, and unfamiliar peers, children, and adults of both sexes. Overall, by 21 to 24 months (and probably earlier) infants distinguished their pictures from others. And by 15 to 18 months of age some babies responded differentially to pictures of males and females. It thus appears that the construction of the social category of gender begins remarkably early in life.

By the time they are 2 to 3 years of age, children accurately label themselves and others as females or males (Slaby and Frey, 1975). However, limitations in their knowledge are seen in their answers to questions such as these:

When you grow up, will you be a mommy or a daddy? (This question addresses gender stability.)

If you played (opposite sex of subject) games, would you be a girl or a boy? (This question addresses gender consistency.)

Could you be a (opposite sex of subject) if you wanted to be? (This question also addresses gender consistency.) (Slaby and Frey, 1975, p. 851)

Two-year-olds are unable to answer these questions correctly, but virtually all 7-year-olds can do so. Here is the conversation between Johnny, a 4½-year-old who understands gender stability, with Jimmy, a 4-year-old who does not.

Johnny: I'm going to be an airplane builder when I grow up.

Jimmy: When I grow up, I'll be a mommy.

Johnny: No, you can't be a mommy, you have to be a daddy.

Jimmy: No. I'm going to be a mommy.

Johnny: No, you're not a girl; you can't be a mommy. (Kohlberg and Ullian, 1974, p. 211)

Cognitive-developmentalists correctly noted that constancy of gender typically develops in a particular progression. Gender stability is achieved before gender consistency. This pattern has been found in the United States, Nepal, Samoa, and Kenya (Munroe, Shimmin, and Munroe, 1984). Because gender is initially based on superficial physical characteristics—such as size, hair length, and clothing—the acquisition of gender constancy requires the child to come to understand that gender is based on a more fundamental quality that does not change. Perhaps it is not surprising, then, that gender constancy is related to children's mastery of the concept of conservation (DeVries, 1974), and to intellectual ability as measured by vocabulary (Gouze and Nadelman, 1980).

Toy Stereotypes and Preferences. Parents quite accurately report that their daughters and sons prefer particular toys over others. Children as young as 18 months of age begin to display a preference for toys that are considered sex-appropriate. This preference, demonstrated by actual play or by children's choosing pictures of toys, is firmly established by 3 years of age. It is displayed in the home, preschool, and laboratory (Connor and Serbin, 1977). Between 2 and 3 years of age, children also learn that a wide array of toys and play activities are considered masculine or feminine (Kuhn, Nash, and Brucken, 1978). But toy preferences precede both knowledge of stereotypes and gender constancy. In this instance, the cognitive-developmental hypothesis that sex-related behaviors *follow* gender constancy is not supported (Perry, White, and Perry, 1984). Early toy preferences are probably strongly shaped by reinforcement and encouragement from parents and others. Biological predisposition cannot be completely ruled out, however. For example, if females are biologically prone to be less active than males, they may respond more positively to toys that require little activity.

Peer Preferences. A preference for same-sex peers is evident by the end of the preschool period (LaFreniere, Strayer, and Gauthier, 1984). This tendency may begin very early. LaFreniere and his colleagues directly observed the interactions of children 1 to 6 years of age who were at-

FIGURE 12–4
**Throughout
childhood most
youngsters prefer to
interact with peers of
their own sex.** Mike
L. Wannemacher,
Taurus Photos.

tending a day-care center in Montreal. The youngest children observed (16.8 month olds) showed no sex preference; however, 27-month-olds began to display same-sex preferences. In general, preference to affiliate with children of one's own sex increased with age, so that 6-year-olds chose same-sex partners 20 percent more often than would be expected by chance, or 70 percent of the time.

The authors of this study speculated about the reasons for their findings. Adults may reinforce same-sex peer affiliation. And perhaps children seek the company of same-sex peers to learn more about gender schemas. However, LaFreniere and his colleagues emphasize the roles of compatibility and reinforcement within gender. For example, girls share with girls a preference for certain toys, engage in relatively less rough play, and are more responsive than boys to the requests and verbal prohibitions of other girls. Such compatibility may arise from socialization and/or biological sex differences. But in any event, children's preference for same-sex peers increases during childhood, reaching a peak in preadolescence (Hartup, 1983). It subsequently decreases, due at least in part to romantic and sexual attraction (Sagar, Schofield, and Synder, 1983).

Stereotypes and Expectations about Occupations and Activities. By 4 or 5 years of age children hold stereotypic views of adult occupations and activities. They know that females become teachers, nurses, and secretaries, and that boys become doctors, pilots, and carpenters. Young children typically state aspirations for sex-appropriate work (Huston, 1983). In a recent study, 120 preschoolers, second graders, and fifth graders were asked, "What do you want to be when you grow up?" As shown in Table 12–3, boys overwhelmingly selected occupations that are traditionally viewed as male. In contrast, 50 percent of the girls chose traditionally female occupations and 38 percent traditionally male occupations or jobs considered neutral with regard to sex (Franken, 1983).

Sex typing was thus clearly evident for the boys, but much less so for the girls. The children were also asked to indicate whether thirty particular occupations could be assumed by men, women, or both; ten of the occupations were traditionally male (carpenter, doctor), ten were tradi-

TABLE 12–3
Percent of Boys and Girls Naming Traditionally Male, Traditionally Female, and Neutral Occupations as Vocational Aspirations

	Boys	Girls
Traditionally male	88	23
Traditionally female	2	50
Neutral	5	15
(Don't know)	5	12

Data from Franken (1983).

tionally female (librarian, teacher), and ten were gender-neutral (salesperson, travel agent). Fifty-three percent of the children's responses indicated that they believed both sexes could do the job. This belief increased with grade level.

In general, children's *knowledge* of stereotypes increases with experience. However, *acceptance* of stereotypes declines during this time. That is, children begin to view stereotypes as rules or generalizations that can be violated, at least to some extent in some situations. Interestingly, this developmental trend toward flexibility may parallel the growth of understanding of social conventions (Turiel, 1978). Carter and Patterson (1982) evaluated children's flexibility toward toy and occupational stereotypes, a social convention (the convention of using utensils for eating), and a scientific rule (concerning the specific gravity of rocks). As Figure 12–5 indicates, flexibility concerning both gender stereotypes and the rule of etiquette increased with age in kindergarten to eighth-grade children. Flexibility concerning the scientific law decreased.

FIGURE 12–5
Children's thinking about sex stereotypes for toys and occupations paralleled their thinking about a social convention. With increased cognitive maturity, they considered the stereotypes and rule of etiquette as flexible. They increasingly considered the scientific law as inflexible.   From Carter and Patterson (1982).

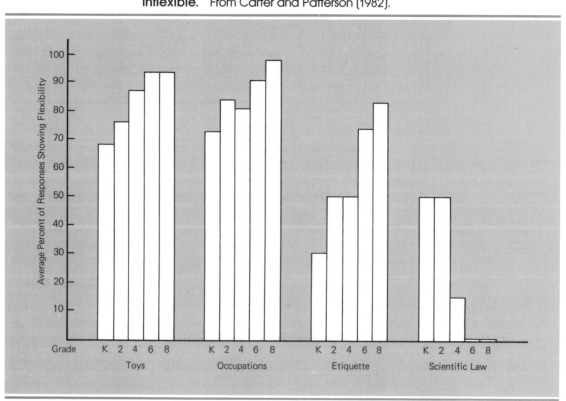

Another interesting finding has emerged from the research. Girls' preferences for feminine activities and interests appear to increase until age 5 or 6, but then decline during childhood, perhaps into adolescence. In fact, girls show increased preferences for things considered masculine, whereas boys' preferences continue to increase for sex-appropriate activities and interests. This pattern can be interpreted in several ways. Perhaps some qualities—such as high activity or intellectual challenge—are inherent in stereotypic masculine pursuits, and these qualities become increasingly attractive to females. Or perhaps both sexes realize early that society places greater value on maleness over femaleness. In this case, females might adopt male preferences, while males would continue on the same course. But there is also evidence that males are more stringently socialized according to gender than females. (It's much worse to be a "sissy" than a "tomboy.") To the extent that socialization is effective, males have fewer choices to deviate from gender-role prescriptions.

Stereotypes of Social-Psychological Attributes. Gender stereotyping of social-psychological attributes appears to lag behind that of activities and interests (Huston, 1983). Understanding social-psychological characteristics undoubtedly requires greater ability to abstract than does understanding activities and interests. Nevertheless, investigations indicate that some 5-year-olds do begin to accumulate knowledge of the more abstract characteristics of individuals. Williams, Bennett, and Best (1975), for example, translated the items of a previously used checklist into stories such as:

> One of these people is emotional. They cry when something good happens as well as when everything goes wrong. Which is the emotional person? (p.637)

Children were asked to select the person from a picture of two adults, one clearly a female and the other a male. The sex-stereotype scores of kindergarteners correlated significantly with their scores on a vocabulary IQ test—that is, the brighter children held stronger stereotypes. Second graders selected more stereotypic responses than did the younger children, and fourth graders performed at about the same level as the second graders. There was also some indication that male stereotypes were learned earlier than female stereotypes.

In a similar study, Best and her colleagues found that 61 percent of the items were stereotyped by American 5-year-olds, that stereotyping increased progressively in 8- and 11-year-olds, and that 11-year-olds approached the level shown earlier by college students (Best, Williams, Cloud, Davis, Robertson, Edwards, Giles, and Fowles, 1977). Similar data were obtained for children in England and Ireland.

Does this mean that stereotypes for social-psychological characteristics do not change as children develop? There is not enough evidence to answer this question (Huston, 1983). Participants in the studies just described were requested to select one or the other sex to match a certain stereotype—and flexibility did not increase with age. When the research task allows participants to assign characteristics to *both* sexes, the results are mixed. Because it is relatively difficult to learn social-psychological stereotypes, considerable cognitive capacity may be required before these stereotypes can be dealt with in a flexible way. Be that as it may, social-psychological stereotypes are similar to other stereotypes in that females may often reject attributes prescribed for their own sex in favor of those prescribed for males.

It is obvious from our discussion that sex typing involves many social and cognitive factors. Less obvious is the role of biological factors. Biological influences clearly interact with social and cognitive variables to produce gender development. But the extent and nature of such interaction are often debated.

BIOLOGICAL INFLUENCES

Interest in biological effects on sex typing revolves around two related questions. One of these concerns the manner in which biology helps determine biological sex, gender identity, and sex roles in all individuals. The other question concerns the role biology might play in determining sex differences. Most individuals today who believe that biology is important in creating sex differences do not claim a direct and rigid path from biology to gender-related behavior. Their more moderate position is described by this statement:

> . . . if these [sex] differences exist, do they seem to be inborn or related in some way to physiology? That is, are there any physiological tendencies that would lead cultures toward a sexual division of some roles? Are there gender differences that result in different response preferences or thresholds or tendencies?
>
> . . . This is not to say that individuals of either sex could not learn the sensitivities and behavior more typical of the other. Rather, it means that in the normal course of events more individuals of one sex would, with greater ease, tend to develop characteristics thought to be typical of that sex. (Bardwick, 1979, pp. 162, 165)

That the sexes find it easier to develop in one way rather than in another is at least consistent with the fact that similar sex differences are found around the world. In his review of hundreds of anthropological descriptions D'Andrade (1966) pointed to the well-known physical differences and to the common patterns in the division of labor. Male activities involve action that is strenuous, cooperative, and may require travel. Female activities are physically easier, more solitary, and less mobile. Of special interest to our discussion, D'Andrade reported that males were found to be more sexually active, more deferred to, more dominant and aggressive, less nurturant, less responsible, and less emotionally expressive than females. It is possible, of course, that the data—collected by anthropologists of different peoples in strange cultures—are biased by the investigators' stereotypes. But the hypothesis that biological sex differences underlie at least some gender differences in behavior is not unreasonable.

What role do biological factors play? A model proposed by Money and Ehrhardt provides a broad picture of how biological, social, and cognitive variables interact in gender development.

Money and Ehrhardt's Model

Money and Ehrhardt (1972) drew on extensive research and clinical work. They view their model as similar to a relay race in which gender is initiated by the sex chromosomes and then carried along by various biological and psychosocial variables. As shown in Figure 12–6, the XY or XX chromosome pair acts on the fetal gonads (sex organs) so that either the testes or the ovaries develop. If the gonads are to be testes, differentiation begins after the sixth week of gestation; differentiation of the ovaries would begin several weeks later. Direct chromosomal influence ends at this point. If the gonads differentiate into testes, the testes secrete male hormones that bring about the growth of the male reproductive system. Otherwise the gonads become ovaries, which secrete female hormones that cause the growth of the female reproductive organs. The sex hormones also cause differences in the nervous system, includ-

FIGURE 12–6
The major steps in the relay model of gender development proposed by Money and Ehrhardt.
Adapted from J. Money and A. Erhardt, © 1972, The Johns Hopkins University Press.

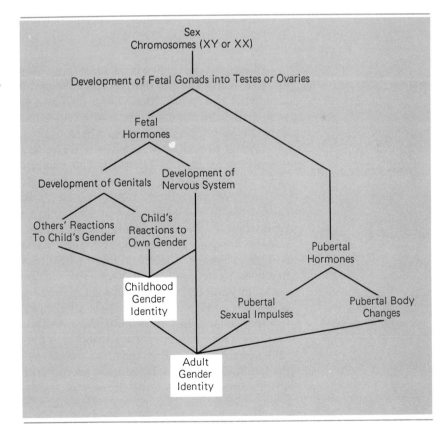

ing different nerve pathways from the reproductive system to the central nervous system and different functioning of the hypothalamus.

According to Money and Ehrhardt, the major turning points in prenatal development are now complete, and the burden of growth rests with both genital and nervous system differences. Genital differences are crucial because they are the basis for children being assigned as males or females, and thus being treated differently by others. But children also respond to their own gender, shaping themselves to fit the stereotypes of masculinity or femininity.

The final step occurs at puberty, when changes in hormonal functioning result in further growth of the reproductive system, increased sexual impulses, and the growth of secondary sexual characteristics. Adult gender identity is forged from these events, continuing differences in nervous system functioning, and the childhood gender identity.

As this model makes clear, differences in the sex chromosomes, sex hormones, reproductive system, and nervous system are the critical biological determinants of gender. Their influences on sexual functioning are well recognized. But researchers are especially interested in their possible effects on behavior not directly related to sexual functioning. Many research studies involve animals because ethical considerations do not permit such experimentation with humans. However, observational studies of humans have been conducted. We will look at some of the research findings by focusing on specific behaviors.

"Tomboyishness"
in Girls

Although most of us would agree that "tomboys" usually grow up to more or less fit the standards for femaleness, by definition tomboys are somewhat masculine. Money and Ehrhardt (1972) studied an unusual sample of girls who displayed tomboyish behavior. The investigation involved twenty-five girls who had been born with masculinized external sex organs (the clitoris was extremely enlarged or penis-like and an "empty" scrotum was obvious). The malformations had occurred because of a genetic dysfunction of the adrenal glands or because the mothers had been given hormones to prevent miscarriages. Both conditions caused the girls to be exposed to masculine hormonal substances at the time when the external sex organs were developing prenatally. The internal sex organs were not affected. The girls had received surgery to correct the external genitals, and those with adrenal gland dysfunction also had been treated with hormones.

Money and Ehrhardt compared the behavioral characteristics and anticipations of these girls with those of normal matched control groups, using questionnaires and conducting interviews with the girls and their mothers. The girls were generally tomboys of high energy who preferred athletic activities, male playmates, and slacks instead of dresses. While the tomboyishness was considered a long-term style, these girls were not strictly opposed to wearing dresses for special occasions. Nor did they engage in fighting. They placed less value on both motherhood and marriage, expressing interest in establishing careers. Typically, they preferred masculine toys and lacked interest in infant caretaking. The findings indicated, though, that childhood sexuality and romantic fantasy and anticipations did not differ from those of the controls.

Money and Ehrhardt attributed the differences they discovered in the masculinized girls to hormonal influences on the fetal brain. Studies of animals have shown that such masculinization can affect social as well as sexual behavior. Money and Ehrhardt suggested that specific pathways in the brains of their experimental subjects had been affected—pathways involved in dominance, energy expenditure, and maternal behavior. Brain pathways related to love and eroticism, they suggested, had not been influenced, indicating perhaps that in humans this area of functioning is decided by postnatal factors.

The Money and Ehrhardt hypothesis is intriguing and it warrants serious consideration. But as the investigators themselves have noted, it is extremely difficult to draw conclusions about prenatal influences on particular brain pathways. Moreover, it is quite possible that the girls had been treated in subtle ways that might account for the results. Finally, the data consisted only of reports by the girls and their parents, which raises questions about the accuracy of such information.

Are Sex Differences in Aggression and Visual-Spatial Ability Inborn?

Because interest in biological influences is deeply rooted in the age-old question of whether sex differences are inborn, specific behaviors for which sex difference are strongly suspected have become a particular focus of study; examples are aggression and visual-spatial performance.

Aggression. Several reasons exist for suspecting that aggression is determined at least in part by biological variables (Maccoby and Jacklin, 1974, 1980). As we have already seen, sex differences in human aggression are not only widespread, but evident a few years after birth. It is unlikely that socialization accounts for early aggression, because parents do not appear to shape aggression differentially in their very young children. In addition, similar gender differences are found in nonhuman species, and male sex hormones have been associated with such aggression (Huston, 1983).

Hormones may regulate aggression and other behaviors in two ways (Parke and Slaby, 1983). First, the presence or absence of certain hormones during sensitive periods of prenatal growth may permanently organize parts of the biological systems that control the behaviors. In nonhuman species, such an influence has been demonstrated in regard to aggression. That is, the presence of male hormones at sensitive times in developing females can lead to unusually high levels of aggression in later life, and the presence of female hormones at sensitive times in developing males can reduce later fighting in these males (Tieger, 1980). The second way in which hormones may regulate aggression is that, depending on blood levels, hormones may *activate* aggression at any one time. Evidence exists for an association between levels of the male hormone, testosterone, and fighting in rodents and primates. Also, injections of testosterone in female primates have resulted in increased aggression (Joslyn, 1973). Nevertheless, the testosterone/aggression link is not always found, which suggests that other factors are involved. It is also often difficult to interpret the relationship between hormonal levels and aggression, because hormones not only influence environmental events but are affected by them. And generalizations from nonhuman species to humans cannot automatically be made.

What is the evidence for hormonal influence in human aggression? There seems to be little or no evidence for an organizing effect on human aggression (Tieger, 1980). The Money and Ehrhardt (1972) study of prenatally masculinized girls found several behavioral differences between these girls and a control group, but no differences in aggression. Later variations on this investigation support the finding. The picture is somewhat different for the activating influence of testosterone. Olweus, Mattsson, Schalling, and Lowe (1980) found a positive relationship between testosterone levels in male adolescents and their self-reports of aggression, frustration level, and aggressive attitudes. Hormone level was related more strongly to aggressive responses to provocation than to unprovoked aggression. Limited evidence also exists for an association between testosterone levels and criminal behavior in males, and testosterone levels and aggression in females (Parke and Slaby, 1983). But this relationship may be quite indirect. For example, testosterone is related to muscularity and strength, which may well affect aggression.

Visual-spatial ability. Investigations into biological influences on suspected gender differences in visual-spatial ability have focused on the sex chromosomes and brain functioning. As with aggression, these studies attempt to explain why males outperform females.

One suggestion is that a recessive gene on the X chromosome facilitates visual-spatial ability. In this case, males would have an advantage because they would inherit high ability when their mothers transmit the recessive gene on the X chromosome. Females would inherit high ability only when both parents pass on a recessive gene on the X chromosomes. Despite some early positive evidence, this hypothesis has not been supported, although it requires further evaluation (Boles, 1980; Thomas, 1983; Vandenburg and Kuse, 1979).

Speculation that sex differences in visual-spatial ability are due to differential brain functioning rests on the fact that in most adults the right hemisphere of the cortex is specialized for the processing of visual-spatial information and the left hemisphere for the processing of verbal information. In adult males the cortex seems to be more specialized than in adult females, which suggests that the right hemisphere in males can process visual-spatial information more efficiently (Huston, 1983).

An interesting aspect of visual-spatial ability is an association with the timing of puberty: Both females and males who experience late maturation have sometimes been found to perform better on tests of visual-spatial ability than those who mature earlier (Newcombe and Bandura,

1983). Since boys typically mature two years later than girls, this relationship might help account for the gender difference. But how? Waber (1977) proposed that brain specialization in childhood ceases around the time of puberty. Late maturers thus have more time for specialization and become more specialized—hence, more skillful in processing visual-spatial information. Whether this proposal will hold up to testing remains to be seen. At least one important study found that specialization in girls was unrelated to both visual-spatial ability and the timing of puberty (Newcombe and Bandura, 1983). In fact, high visual-spatial ability was associated with girls' interests in masculine pursuits, masculine personality, and the desire to be a boy.

Overview. Overall, evidence for biological influences appears moderate for aggression and even weaker for visual-spatial ability. This does not mean that biological influences are not operating. It does strongly suggest that much is yet to be discovered about these influences, and that they do not play an overwhelming role in gender development. As Money and Ehrhardt (1972) note, in no event can social-psychological events be ignored.

Money and Ehrhardt provide dramatic support for this position in studies of children who come into the world with external sex organs that do not match their chromosomes and/or internal sex organs. These children are sometimes mislabeled *boy* or *girl* and are subsequently reared as such. They develop healthy gender identities consistent with their *labeling*, providing that they are treated consistently like one sex or the other from early in life. If a chromosomal girl born with male organs is labeled and reared as a boy, the child will identify as a boy. Even more intriguing, if gender must be reassigned—due, for example, to late discovery of the condition or late decisions about surgical treatment of the sex organs—the child seems to be able to accept the reassignment if it occurs during the first few years of life. As time passes, the child's chance of adjusting normally lessens. Psychosocial variables are critical in these cases. Gender identity is not predestined by the sex chromosomes, nor by hormones. In the same way, it is unlikely that behavioral sex differences are biologically predetermined.

SOCIALIZING AGENTS

Anthropological studies have been used as evidence for biological factors in gender development, but they have also been used to argue for socialization effects. Despite the similarities described by D'Andrade (1966), cross-cultural variability also exists. Consider, for example, a report of three tribes that differed on the expression of aggression by the sexes. The study, reported years ago by Margaret Mead (1935), revealed that all combinations of sex-role aggression are possible.

The Arapesh, one of the tribes studied by Mead, expect both males and females to behave in ways that would be considered passive and feminine in Western cultures. Both sexes are taught to be cooperative and responsive to the needs of others. Among the Mundugumor, in contrast, members of both sexes are expected to act in a way that would be considered almost a stereotype of masculinity by our standards. Both men and women are expected to be ruthless and aggressive, and to be unresponsive in relationships with others. The third tribe described by Mead, the Tchambuli, shows a pattern of sex-role expectations directly opposite to that familiar in Western European and Anglo-Saxon countries. The women are expected to be aggressive and dominant, while the males are passive and emotionally dependent. Although this kind of variability may be determined by differences in genes among the three cultures, it is likely that different socialization practices at least partly account for them.

Socialization obviously requires time, so the very early appearance of sex differences would lend support to the influence of biological factors. In fact, few studies of neonates and infants have demonstrated any gender differences (Birns, 1976). There are exceptions. In a well-controlled investigation, Phillips, King, and DuBois (1978) observed the activity of neonates during the first two days of life and found higher levels of wakefulness, facial grimacing, and low-intensity motor activity for males. Moss (1967) showed that at 3 weeks and again at 3 months, boys cried more and slept less than girls. But neither early presence or early absence of gender differences is firmly established; rather, the differences emerge clearly during the years from 2 to 5. By then, there is time for a good deal of socialization to have occurred.

We have already seen that two socialization processes are emphasized by social learning theorists and recognized by virtually all other major theorists: learning that occurs through direct interaction, often with reinforcement and punishment, and learning that occurs through the observation of gender models.

Differential Treatment of the Sexes

Parents, teachers, and other socializing agents influence the young by the ways in which they interact and provide consequences for children's behavior. If sex roles are taught in this manner, we would expect to see boys and girls being treated differently with regard to sex-typed behaviors. However, a problem of interpretation exists: Differential treatment might be a response to sex differences in children's behavior as well as a cause (Huston, 1983). A way to at least partly solve this problem is to determine whether socializing agents respond to children differently based only on gender. In the Condry and Condry (1976) study, college students rated an infant's behavior differently depending on the perceived gender of the child. Are actual parents influenced by knowing just the gender of children? It appears so.

In one study, parents of newborns rated newborn daughters as smaller, softer, and more finely featured than newborn sons, even though the infants did not differ physically in these ways. The fathers also perceived the daughters as less strong (Rubin, Provenzano, and Luria, 1974). Parents of older children perceive girls as more fragile and worry more about them (Maccoby and Jacklin, 1974). They also hold stereotypic expectations and values.

Teachers too have conventional attitudes toward the sexes (Minuchin and Shapiro, 1983). They expect boys to be more unruly and to have more learning problems; they tend to anticipate that boys and girls will display different abilities and interests.

Considerable evidence has accumulated that, in fact, parents treat their daughters and sons differently. Boys are encouraged to engage in gross motor activity, whereas girls are encouraged to show dependency, affection, and tenderness. Girls are also subjected to more restriction of their freedom (Block, 1983). Parents encourage stereotypic activities by presenting sex-typed toys and assigning sex-typed household jobs to older children. Social behavior seems to be less stereotyped by parents. But despite parental aspirations for intellectual achievement for both sons and daughters, long-range expectations are higher for sons. Moreover, when they interact with their preschool children in teaching situations, parents demand independence from sons and are more likely to respond quickly to daughters' requests for aid (Block, 1979).

As important as mothers are in the socialization of children, fathers may be the major socializers of sex role. More than mothers, they view boys and girls as different and treat them according to stereotypes. They have repeatedly been found to encourage gender-related play, to use physical and verbal prohibitions more with boys, and to accept dependency more in girls (Snow, Jacklin, and Maccoby, 1983). Even with children as young as 1 year of age, fathers interact differently with sons and daughters: They punish boys more, initiate physical contact and proximity more with girls, and are less likely to give dolls to boys.

It is interesting to speculate on the reasons for such paternal interaction. Boys are more stringently socialized than girls; they are more rigidly reinforced for appropriate behaviors and punished for inappropriate behaviors. When they become parents they may therefore be doing nothing more than acting on their own relatively rigid gender identities. On the other hand, the more flexible maternal socialization style may reflect the fact that girls are less stringently socialized. The maternal role may also demand more sensitivity to the individual needs of children, so that mothers place such needs ahead of society's stereotypes.

Research into the direct influence of teachers on sex typing presents a more ambiguous picture than that for parents (Fagot, 1977). Inexperienced teachers, both male and female, respond positively when children act in stereotypic ways. However, experienced teachers of both sexes tend to want children to behave in ways that are considered feminine—that are task-oriented, quiet, nonaggressive, nondisruptive, and perhaps dependent (Minuchin and Shapiro, 1983). It appears that appropriate classroom behavior is of first importance. In fact, there is concern that boys suffer in the feminine atmosphere of the classroom.

This may or may not be the case. Teachers do have more negative interactions with boys: they scold them more, with louder reprimands, and often treat disruptive behavior with disapproval. However, boys'

FIGURE 12–7
Sex-role learning is reinforced and encouraged both directly and in subtle ways. © Alice Kandell, Photo Researchers; Christa Armstrong, Photo Researchers (for mother and daughter sewing).

communications dominate the classroom, teachers give boys more attention overall, and the quality of instruction given to boys may be superior to that given to girls (Sadker and Sadker, 1985). When boys ask questions, they receive lengthier and more precise answers than do girls; boys are also encouraged to solve problems on their own. Dweck and her colleagues have shown that teachers' criticism of girls may refer more to the intellectual aspects of tasks, whereas their criticism of boys may refer more to motivational failings (Dweck, Davidson, Nelson, and Enna, 1978). Differences in criticism appeared related to girls' attributing their failure to lack of ability and boys attributing their failure to lack of effort. Many teacher-student interactions would seem to work against females as far as instruction, passivity, and self-confidence are concerned. Teacher attention and reinforcement can influence many behaviors, including sex-typed behaviors, but the effects appear complex (Serbin, Connor, and Citron, 1981).

Earlier we mentioned that children's preference to interact with same-sex peers is observed during the second year of life, reaches a peak in preadolescence, and then declines. It is quite striking that by age 3 children reinforce each other for sex-appropriate behaviors and punish each other for inappropriate behaviors (Huston, 1983). Children, especially boys, who engage in cross-sex activities are criticized and often socially isolated. In fact, at preschool age, peers may be more demanding as socializers of sex role than parents or nursery school teachers. Given that acceptance of gender stereotypes decreases with age, we could speculate that tolerance of inappropriate behavior in peers would increase. Of course tolerance might grow more rapidly for some behaviors (occupational choice and activities) than for others (personality traits such as assertiveness). But changes across the life span are still to be charted.

Exposure to Stereotypic Gender Models

Children are continually exposed to gender models. Some changes have occurred in sex roles during the last few years; many more women now have careers, and some men are assuming more responsibility for child care. But most adults still show traditional work and activity patterns, as well as social norms. Moreover, television continues to portray the sexes in stereotypic ways (Liebert, Sprafkin, and Davidson, 1982). Consistent with earlier studies, the U.S. Commission on Civil Rights reported that during the time period from 1969 to 1977, females occupied only 27 percent of all TV roles. Over half of the females portrayed had no occupations, even though TV females fall into the younger age groups that are well represented in the real working world. Because females comprise slightly over half of the U.S. population, this distorted underrepresentation conveys a lack of value, power, and status. With regard to social behavior, females are shown as more attractive, altruistic, sociable, sympathetic, rule abiding, and peaceful than males. Males are portrayed as the more aggressive, dominant, powerful, persistent, rational, and intelligent (Donagher, Poulos, Liebert, and Davidson, 1975).

Given the availability of gender models, observational learning must play an important role in the formation and modification of gender schemas. Children form concepts by abstracting common threads from many sources; one source of information about gender is provided by gender models. The popularity of same-sex affiliation suggests that children expose themselves to same-sex models. When they are presented models of both sexes, children do not typically attend more to models of their own sex (Huston; 1983). However, regardless of the sex of the model, behavior that matches gender stereotypes is recalled better. This may be especially true for those who apply stereotypes to a wide range of events. In any case, children also tend to transform inappropriate behaviors into appropriate behaviors when they recall modeled acts.

Thus, children learn by observation about both sexes, not just their own, and they particularly learn about stereotypic behaviors. When it actually comes to imitating behaviors, children tend to imitate same-sex models. Overall, it seems that once children begin to acquire gender schemas, modeling effects depend heavily on already-existing concepts of gender.

SEX ROLES IN TRANSITION

We hear much today about important changes in sex roles. One of the most obvious is the continued movement of women into paid employment outside the home. The U.S. Department of Labor projects that 57 percent of all women will be in the workforce by 1990, compared to 76 percent of all men (Best, 1981). For the most part, women's occupations still remain limited by stereotyping, lack of early training, or attitudes that keep women from entering certain fields. However, the number of females in medicine, law, and engineering has increased during the last decade. And prejudice against women's occupational competence seems to be lessening, especially when women have high professional status (Isaacs, 1981). Pressure for change in other gender prescriptions and in the values placed on femininity and masculinity is also obvious.

Masculinity and femininity have traditionally been seen as opposite poles on one dimension of behavior. Individuals possessing many of the attributes at the male pole were considered highly masculine; individuals possessing many of the attributes at the female pole were considered highly feminine. Individuals were *either* masculine *or* feminine. But new efforts to study and measure masculinity and femininity (Bem, 1974; Spence, Helmreich, and Stapp, 1975) produced a new view of masculinity and femininity as two independent dimensions of behavior. Individuals may be rated high on instrumentality/low on expressiveness, low on instrumentality/high on expressiveness, high on both dimensions, or low on both dimensions. When so rated, individuals are respectively labeled masculine, feminine, androgynous, and undifferentiated. These terms refer to the orientation of the individuals' sex typing.

Androgyny is of great interest to both psychological theorists and feminists. The term, which originated from the Greek *andro* (male) and *gyn* (female) nicely captures the idea that androgynous individuals display both instrumental and expressive behaviors. They may be passive in some situations and aggressive in others; cold in one instance and warm in another; dependent in one relationship and independent in another. Bem (1974) and others have argued that the ability to react with such a broad range of behaviors is psychologically healthier than being restricted to instrumental or expressive behaviors. The traditional belief that masculine sex typing is healthy for males and feminine sex typing is healthy for females is rejected. Research does show that androgyny is adaptive: Androgynous college students were found to have high self-esteem (Spence, Helmreich, and Stapp, 1975); androgynous females showed less social conformity than stereotypic females (Brehony and Geller, 1981); and androgynous college students were more comfortable participating in opposite-gender activities (Bem and Lenney, 1976).

Still, the picture is not as clear as it might seem. Because androgyny encompasses both feminine and masculine attributes and behaviors, researchers have asked whether one or the other of these dimensions is actually responsible for the adaptive, healthy characteristics of androgynous persons. They found that the masculine dimension largely accounts for them; for example, for positive mental health and self-esteem (Taylor and Hall, 1982; Whitley, 1983). Other researchers, measuring masculinity alone, insist on its adaptive qualities. For example, Hansson and his colleagues concluded that masculine women seem to adjust better to divorce than feminine women (Hansson et al., 1984).

Sexist Language and Gender Development

Individuals advocating changes in sex roles draw attention to stereotypic models and differential treatment of males and females in the home, school, and workplace. They also often speak out against the use of sexist language—that is, language forms that are biased in some way. It is argued that sexist language sets up biased expectations of the sexes that, in turn, affect the development of gender roles. The function of language in gender development has not been extensively studied by professionals, although language would seem to be of theoretical importance. A crucial step in the construction of gender identity is the use of gender labels, and language could also be expected to shape stereotypes and gender schemas. Investigation of the effects of sexist language has implications for both social and theoretical concerns (Hyde, 1984a).

A few researchers have begun to examine the influence of the use of male pronouns to refer to both sexes. According to the rules of grammar *he* and *his* are neutral with regard to gender when they do not specifically reference a male individual. Thus, the sentence "The child must work hard if he is to graduate." grammatically refers to a child of either sex. But does such language carry psychological meaning different from its intended grammatical meaning?

Moulton, Robinson, and Elias (1978) explored just this question in a study involving college students. Each student was asked to make up a story about a fictional character in response to a short theme. One of the themes, for example, was:

"In a large coeducational institution the average student will feel isolated in _____ introductory courses." (p. 1034).

The blank was variously filled in with either *his, their,* or *his or her,* and each student received only one of these forms. The gender of the fictional characters was the dependent variable. The results showed that when the pronoun *his* was used, 35 percent of the fictional characters were female; when *their* was used, 46 percent were female; when *his or her* was used, 56 percent were female. This pattern held for participants of both sexes, although females were more likely than males to write about female characters. In discussing this finding, the researchers pointed out that the use of *his,* led participants to think of males. In this situation, *his* was not psychologically neutral.

More recently, Hyde (1984a) extended the Moulton et al. work to children. In an initial study, she asked first, third, and fifth graders, as well as college students, to make up a story about a child referred to as *he, they,* or *he or she.* Children's understanding of the use of gender-neutral masculine pronouns was assessed by questioning them in various ways. For example, they were directly asked:

"When you use 'he' in a sentence, does it always mean it's a boy? For example, when I say 'When a kid goes to school, he often feels excited on the first day,' does that mean the kid is a boy?" (p. 699).

In a second study with third and fifth graders, Hyde again used the story task, but now the pronoun *she* was included in the description for some of the children. Understanding of gender-neutral pronouns was again assessed, and a new task was also added: the Wudgemaker task. Wudgemakers were described as factory workers who assemble

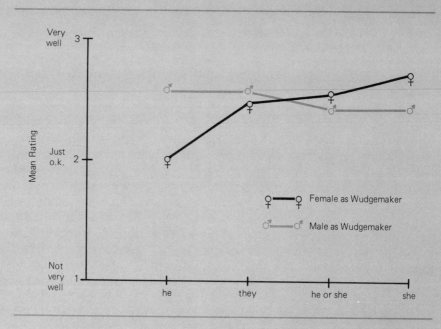

FIGURE 12–8

Average ratings of how well women and men would do as Wudgemakers, according to pronouns used in the description. From Hyde (1984).

plastic parts; they were variously referred to as *he, they, he or she,* or *she.* The job description itself was neutral with regard to sex. Children were asked to rate how well women and men could do the job.

In general, the college students performed like those in the Moulton et al. study. *His* produced the lowest percentage of female stories and *his or her* produced the highest. Females wrote about female characters more than males did. Among the children, *he* again elicited the lowest percentage of female characters in both studies—only 7 percent overall. In contrast, 77 percent of the stories had a female character when *she* was used in the second experiment. The majority of the children did not know the grammatical rule, and apparently believed that *he* always means a male. On the Wudgemaker task, rat-

ings of men as Wudgemakers were not affected by use of the pronouns. Ratings of women in the job were affected: They were lowest when *he* was used in the description and highest when *she* was used.

These findings strongly suggest that masculine pronouns employed as gender-neutral words in gender-neutral situations are not always psychologically neutral. The short-term effect, in many instances, may be disadvantageous for females. Long-term effects might also be anticipated through influences on gender schemas. For example, the use of *he* to refer to physicians and engineers may indeed influence stereotypes and evaluations of females in these positions. Further research into the impact of sexist language would certainly seem to be worthwhile.

Feminine traits are seen as valuable for interpersonal functioning and masculine traits are seen as valuable for adjustment and competence. In the final analysis, adjustment and competence may be broader areas of functioning or may themselves be more highly valued. For example, Orlofsky and Stake (1981) showed that femininity in both sexes is related to

FIGURE 12–9
Recent advocacy for changes in sex roles focuses on increased opportunity for females—whether to practice law, work in coal mines, or have paper routes. Bettye Lane, Photo Researchers.

the interpersonal domain—sensitivity to feelings and a capacity for caring—and that masculinity is related to the achievement domain.

The fact that some masculine behaviors and activities are so highly valued is also reflected in the ways in which changes are occurring in sex roles. When we speak of transcending sex roles, we frequently mean that women should be given the opportunity to be more like men. However, the traditional masculine role has serious disadvantages, as described by one concerned male:

> It is not just the traditional female role which has disadvantages. Sociologists remind us that, according to statistics, men have a higher criminal record, more stress and illness due to strenuous work, higher suicide rates, and, as a rule, die at an earlier age than women. In school it is the boys who have the greater adaption problems. Men who are divorced and living alone have greater difficulties managing than do divorced women. The interpretation is that the social pressures on the man to assert himself, to fight his way in life, to be aggressive, and not to show any feelings create contact difficulties and adaption difficulties. Sociologists consider that one should not speak of "the problems of woman's role in society" but of "the sex-role problem," in order to emphasize that the problem also concerns the traditional male role. (Palme, 1972, p. 241)

Thus it can be argued that a balance of positive instrumentality and expressiveness is most adaptive across life's many tasks. This can occur only if sex roles are relatively flexible. However, resistance to flexible gender roles is strong. Social change is stressful because the fabric of social life comes undone, often with few or no alternative frameworks. And sex roles are strongly tied to identity, so that change can be threatening to the concept of the self. Perhaps the most extreme concern is that a loosening of sex roles will foster changes in sexual behavior itself. It is highly unlikely that allowing greater overlap between the sexes with regard to occupation and social behavior will bring about such consequences. Money and Ehrhardt (1972) have made the distinction between "procreative imperatives"—those tied to impregnation, menstruation, gestation—and the many options for behavior that are peripheral to these functions. They note that children develop a secure sex identity when there are clear cultural signals about procreative imperatives, no matter what the signals concerning peripheral options.

Bem (1981) argues that the distinction between the sexes is subtly woven into perception, behavior, and values to an unwarranted degree:

> In elementary schools, for example, boys and girls line up separately or alternately; they learn songs in which the fingers are 'ladies' and thumbs are 'men'; they see boy and girl paper doll silhouettes alternately placed on the days of the month in order to learn about the calendar. (p. 363)

According to Bem, such experiences overemphasize gender. Gender schemas come to include not only aspects directly related to sex (reproductive function, sexual attractiveness, and the like), but an enormous number of elements not central to sex. Bem suggests that we think seriously about limiting the scope of gender schemas to aspects relevant to sexual functioning. Gender schemas would then cease to have the overwhelming power to organize and thereby control so many individual interests, activities, aspirations, and behaviors.

SUMMARY

1. Categorization according to gender has a powerful influence on development throughout the life span. *Male* and *female* function as social categories that have broad implications for many aspects of individuals' lives—for assumptions and expectations concerning activities, roles, preferences, attitudes, and behaviors.

2. Gender *stereotypes* are widely held beliefs about gender that may or may not be true. They are applied to diverse aspects of existence. Females are viewed as physically weak, quiet, and *expressive*; males are seen as strong and *instrumental*. These generalized views of the sexes set up expectations, attributions, and standards for others' and one's own behavior, based on gender.

3. There is a great deal of interest in actual differences between the sexes. Several physical differences are agreed upon, but less agreement has been reached for social-psychological attributes. Overall, gender differences appear small, at least in laboratory studies, and depend on many other factors, such as social class, situations, specific tasks, and sex-role orientation. All these factors, plus the fact that gender-related behavior may change over time, make the task of understanding gender differences difficult.

4. Theories about the development of *gender identity* (awareness of one's self as either male or female) and *sex roles* (acquisition of behaviors and attitudes associated with gender) emphasize various biological and psychological variables.

5. Psychoanalytic theory stresses resolution of the *Oedipal* and *Electra* conflicts. Social learning theory emphasizes operant learning and observational learning. Cognitive-developmental theory hypothesizes that after children acquire a constant gender identity, they attempt to match their behavior to this identity. Other cognitive theories emphasize that children aquire gender schemas—networks of associations—and use these schemas in processing information.

6. Empirical investigation tells us much about the developmental course of gender identity and sex roles. By about 18 months of age children are already constructing gender as a social category, and by 2 to 3 years of age they label themselves as boys or girls. By 6 or 7 years of age they have recognized gender *stability*—that is, that gender does not change over time—and gender *consistency*—that maleness and femaleness do not change over situations or according to personal wishes—which together provide gender *constancy*.

7. Much before gender constancy is achieved, children show gender-related stereotypes, preferences, and behavior. Toy preferences may begin as early as 18 months of age; peer preferences are evident early in the third year and increase into preadolescence; by 4 or 5 years of age children hold stereotypic views of adult occupations.

8. Gender stereotyping of social-psychological attributes begins during the preschool years but probably lags behind stereotyping of activities and occupations. Knowledge of stereotypes generally increases throughout childhood, but acceptance of them, at least in some domains, declines. Another general trend is for girls, but not boys, to begin to prefer some opposite-sex standards for themselves.

9. Interest in biological effects on gender development focuses on biology's role in producing biological sex, sex typing, and sex differences. It is argued that innate factors make it more likely

that persons of one sex would develop certain characteristics compared to persons of the other sex. The evidence for biological influence is relatively weak, and much is yet to be learned.

10. It is clear that cultural and social variables affect the development of gender. Cross-cultural variability and lack of sex differences very early in life are consistent with the socialization hypothesis. Parents perceive their daughters and sons differently from birth onward and treat them in different ways. Fathers may be especially important in the socialization of gender role. The school environment also plays a role, but the influence of teacher-child interaction appears complex. Peers strongly reinforce sex stereotypic behaviors, at least in early and middle childhood.

11. The observation of stereotypic models in the home, school, other environments, and in the media is thought to have a strong influence on gender development. Despite recent changes in sex roles, stereotypic modeling is pervasive, providing opportunities for reinforced modeling and for the construction of stereotypic gender schemas. Children learn from models of both sexes, and imitate same-sex models.

12. Sex roles are changing, as is obvious by the increased number of women in paid employment and in occupations previously considered masculine. Advocates of sex role change point to differential experiences of the sexes and to adverse effects of sexist language.

13. Masculinity and femininity had once been conceived as one dimension of behavior with two opposite poles; it is now more often considered two dimensions, instrumentality and expressiveness.

14. Although high value is placed on masculinity, the masculine sex role is related to negative outcomes as well. In the final analysis, limiting gender schemas and sex roles to behaviors that are connected to reproduction could increase individual freedom.

13 BEHAVIOR PROBLEMS: DEVELOPMENT GONE AWRY

We have come far in describing and discussing the basic processes of development. With few exceptions—notably mental retardation and genetic disorders—our focus has been on normal processes that lead to typical behaviors and attitudes. This chapter is devoted to a fuller discussion of childhood and adolescent behavior problems.

Enormous attention is now being paid to the behavior difficulties of the young. This was not always so. Not until the middle 1800s were efforts made to classify and understand childhood and adolescent behavior disorders (Rie, 1971). Mental retardation was most studied; also noted were hyperactivity, aggression, and psychosis, as well as "masturbatory insanity." Heredity and biological causes were emphasized; psychological causes, if mentioned at all, were seen as acting directly on the nervous system by irritating the brain and exhausting the nerves. Young people who displayed behavior problems were often considered possessed, wicked, insubordinate, and incorrigible.

The 1900s brought notable positive change. The problems of youth were distinguished from adult behavioral disorders, and more serious attention was given to psychological and social causes. Today the study of behavior problems has entered a new phase in which increased knowledge of normal development is being used to explain the development of disordered behaviors.

We begin by examining some connections between normal and unusual development, then sample some of the problems that may arise. Next, we look at treatment issues and approaches, including the treatment of specific disorders. Finally, we discuss the prevalence and persistence of various disorders.

DEFINITION AND CAUSES

Disordered behaviors, whether displayed by the young or the old, attract attention because they are often strange or disruptive. People react to them with curiosity, confusion, fear, anger, or embarrassment. Society is motivated to understand and treat behavioral dysfunctions partly in response to these negative reactions, but also out of concern for the individuals themselves.

The study and treatment of behavior disorders have historically been left to clinical psychologists, researchers specializing in abnormal psychology, psychiatrists, and social workers. These professionals have grappled with identifying and describing behavior problems and have searched for causes and workable treatments. Developmental psychologists, more interested in normal growth, have only recently begun to apply their knowledge to understanding behavior disorders. Nevertheless, a developmental perspective is tied to major questions about problem behaviors. One of these questions concerns the definition and identification of problem behaviors; another concerns causation.

What Is Problem Behavior?

There is no simple way to define disordered functioning. However, all behavior disorders are "abnormal" in that they are unfavorable deviations from average or standard behaviors. ("Abnormal" means away from the norm.) Obviously, then, standards must exist against which to judge behaviors. These standards derive from what happens in normal development.

Development may deviate from the normal in many ways. The rate of growth of skills and knowledge may be retarded. Three-year-olds typically speak in short sentences; most 10-year-olds still prefer same-sex to other-sex friendships; most 19-year-olds use formal operational thinking to some extent. Not meeting these basic growth norms can signal that "something is wrong." Behaviors can also be disturbed in degree; that is, they may occur too frequently or infrequently, be too intense or too weak, endure over too long or too short a period of time. For example, it is not unusual for a child to exhibit fear, but the child may be judged to have a problem if he or she is fearful in many situations, has extremely intense reactions, and does not "grow out of" the fears. Finally, behaviors may emerge in odd forms, such as stuttering (Garber, 1984).

Information about the processes underlying normal development can be of enormous help in defining and understanding behavior disorders. For example, Piaget's theory of cognitive development describes normal thought processes, but it has been productively applied to defining the cognitive functioning of mentally retarded persons. To take another example, a recent study shows that aggressive boys display a deviant attributional process; that is, when confronted with an ambiguous provocation, they attribute hostility to the provoker (Bobbitt and Keating, in press, cited by Sroufe and Rutter, 1984). Knowing about this process may help us understand aggression.

The Causes of Behavior Disorders

Individuals interested in behavioral disorders are, in some sense, all developmentalists, because they seek the roots, or origins, of behavior. Both normal and abnormal behaviors arise from interactions among a common set of variables: genetic disposition, bodily structure and function, cognition, and socioemotional factors.

Consider, for example, the well-established fact that boys exhibit more behavioral deviance than girls in many disorders, including learning difficulties, hyperactivity, bed wetting, and antisocial behavior. Why should this be so? Explanations for this sex difference rest on broad developmental hypotheses, which fall into two general types: those that focus on the biological endowment of the sexes and those that focus on social variables (Eme, 1979). The lack of genes on the Y chromosome is suspect because it is clearly related to dysfunctions such as color blindness and hemophilia; perhaps it is also related to behavior problems through subtle biochemical pathways. Certain male vulnerabilities are well recognized: males appear to suffer more from major diseases, malnutrition, and poverty. These facts all suggest some biological basis for the sex differences in disturbance.

But we also know that boys and girls are differentially socialized. This may produce more antisocial behavior in males. Male deviance may be reported more frequently. Mothers tend to believe that difficulties with girls are temporary (Shepherd, Oppenheim, and Mitchell, 1966), and parents and teachers are less tolerant of male hyperactivity, lack of persistence, distractibility, and disruption (Serbin and O'Leary, 1975). Perhaps adult tolerance is lower for males because adults have generally experienced greater difficulty in handling males. In effect, then, biological endowment may interact with socialization and social expectation to create a vicious cycle for the male child.

Most major developmental theories have been used to explain behavior dysfunctions. Psychoanalytic theory has played a central role in offering hypotheses, but social and cognitive learning theories are now given more weight. Not surprisingly, various biological influences have also been hypothesized. But despite the wealth of hypotheses, the causes of many behavioral disorders are still not clear.

Childhood and adolescent behavior disorders are extremely diverse in severity, type, and course of development. Problems can arise in all areas of functioning—social, emotional, intellectual, perceptual, and motor—and these areas overlap and affect each other.

PROBLEMS IN ELIMINATION AND EATING HABITS

The development of appropriate control over the basic physiological functions of elimination and eating is a socialization goal in all societies. Children's physical health may be directly influenced by the habits they form. Just as important, the development of proper habits is related to psychosocial growth, particularly with regard to the child-parent relationship. When socialization proceeds smoothly, both child and parents feel satisfaction and a sense of competence. In the face of difficulties, interpersonal conflict and other negative consequences can occur. In some cases the handling of these tasks may set the stage for the child's future style of interaction with parents and even with others. Lack of control of elimination can also result in poor peer relationships and ostracism in school (Parker and Whitehead, 1982).

It is common for children to have some problems in acquiring elimination and eating behaviors. Although the difficulties may be solved by parents themselves, professional assistance is often sought when developmental or cultural norms are not being met (Routh, Schroeder, and Koocher, 1983).

Toilet Training

The concern of parents about toilet training is reflected in a survey showing that of twenty-two categories of possible preschool problems, parents rated difficulties in toilet training as second in importance (Mesibov, Schroeder, and Wesson, 1977).

Attitudes toward toilet training have changed markedly over the years (Walker, 1978). Early and strict training was once advocated. Children who trained easily were considered intellectually superior, and their parents were viewed as exceptional. More permissive attitudes eventually prevailed, and many parents simply believed that no effort was necessary—or sufficient—to train the child. The more reasonable middle-of-the-road approach recognizes that toilet control depends upon maturation, but is aided by parental encouragement of practices accepted by society.

Enuresis.   The decision to label a child enuretic very much depends on normative data about bladder control. In the United States about 50 percent of 2-year-olds achieve daytime bladder control; this figure rises to 85 percent for 3-year-olds and 90 percent for 4-year-olds (Erickson, 1978; Walker, 1978). Night control is achieved more slowly; one investigator reported that it is established by 67 percent of 3-year-olds, 75 percent of 4-year-olds, 80 percent of 5-year-olds, and 90 percent of 8½-year-olds (Harper, cited by Walker, 1978). Figure 13–1 shows this comparison. *Nocturnal enuresis,* or night-time bedwetting, the most frequent clinical complaint regarding elimination, is rarely considered a problem before 3 years of age, may not be reported until school age, and decreases markedly by adolescence. It occurs more frequently in males than in females and in children from families that have a history of enuresis, and that fall into the lower socioeconomic classes (O'Leary and Wilson, 1975).

The suspected causes of enuresis can be classified as emotional, organic, and learning defects. The psychodynamic view emphasizes emotional factors. Freud suggested that enuresis is the result of repression of the basic sexual desires and is a form of direct sexual gratification. The view that bedwetting is a symptom of such deep intrapsychic conflict is reflected in descriptions of enuresis as suppressed masturbation or ejaculation (Walker, 1978). But enuretic children do not appear to be emotionally disturbed, aside from having slightly more than usual anxiety related to family disruption and situational stress. Organic factors such as chronic disease, structural abnormalities, and small capacity of the bladder play a role in a small percentage of cases. Immaturity of the nervous system and/or deficits in learning to awake before urination occurs

FIGURE 13–1
Percentage of children at various ages achieving daytime and nighttime bladder control.

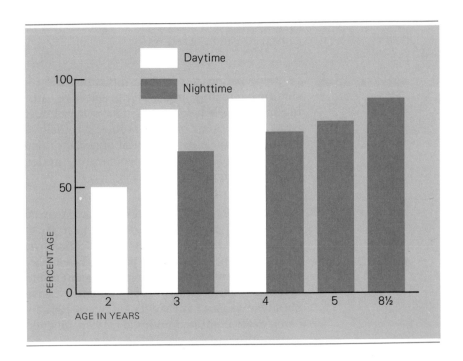

are probably responsible for most of the cases. The condition is subject to treatment from a learning point of view.

Encopresis. *Encopresis*, a much rarer problem, refers to inappropriate defecation, usually when the child is awake. Estimates of the frequency of the disorder range from 1.5 to 5.6 percent (Walker, 1978). Although most studies of encopresis have simply been case reports, several organic conditions are known to result in the disorder, including allergies to food, infections of the large intestine, and abnormalities of the intestinal tract. Encopresis is frequently associated with constipation, which, in turn, may be caused by diet, reaction to stress, and the like. Defecation occurs alternately with constipation or the seeping out of fecal material. A much smaller number of children suffer from diarrhea, seemingly as a reaction to stressful situations.

As with enuresis, emotional disturbance has been suggested as a cause. Both erotic gratification and hostile, aggressive emotions are implicated by Freudian theorists. The data do not support either these notions or the idea of family disturbance as a cause (Walker, 1978). One of the most extensive investigations, however, found that encopretic children fall into two general classes: those for whom original bowel training had been successful but then deteriorated, and those who had never been successfully trained (Anthony, 1957).

The youngsters in the two groups differed in an interesting way. The former typically had been subjected to coercive toilet-training practices from which they were now apparently rebelling. The latter had experienced a generally neglectful upbringing. In both instances, it appears that teaching parents to train (or retrain) their children can solve the problem (Conger, 1970). When untreated, encopresis tends to disappear by adolescence (Parker and Whitehead, 1982), but by then it may have caused considerable stress.

Eating Habits

Many eating and feeding difficulties are reported in the young, including overeating, undereating, selective eating, bizarre habits, annoying mealtime behavior, and delays in self-feeding (Wicks-Nelson and Israel, 1984). Some of these problems actually threaten the health of the child; most cause psychological or social difficulties. Our discussion focuses on two eating problems currently under extensive investigation: obesity and anorexia nervosa.

Obesity. Obesity is defined in terms of excessive body weight (15 to 20 percent overweight) or excessive body fat. An estimated 20 to 30 percent of the U.S. population is obese. Great concern is expressed about obesity: Weight loss programs, diet pills, and diet books are almost a fad. The trim body that is put forth as ideal is undoubtedly extreme and unrealistic, but overweight can have negative consequences. And although obesity increases with age, being overweight in youth is associated with being overweight in adulthood (Miller, Billewicz, Thomson, 1972).

Childhood obesity may contribute to medical problems, such as later cardiovascular disease. Obese children also may be viewed unfavorably by their peers. Children consider obese children as less liked than those with recognizable physical handicaps (Maddox, Back, and Liederman, 1968). Even kindergarten children appear to dislike fat figures (Lerner and Schroeder, 1971). Nevertheless, research findings on the psychological effects of obesity are contradictory.

Some indicate no differences in psychological adjustment between obese and normal-weight persons; others show that obese children have poorer self-concepts and more psychological problems (Wadden, Foster, Brownell, and Finley, 1984). Perhaps obesity adversely affects only some, such as those who seek treatment. In studying obese children enrolled in a weight-loss program, Israel and Shapiro (in press) requested the parents of the children to rate their offspring on a variety of problems. Compared to children in the general population, the ratings were higher for obese children of both sexes, but they were not as high as ratings of problem behaviors for children being seen in psychological clinics (Figure 13–2). We must be cautious in interpreting these results, because the behavioral problems reported in obese children may be the result of being overweight. However, it seems likely that the negative way in which obesity is viewed influences development and that some psychological difficulty is probable.

What causes obesity? Despite the ease with which many of us might answer this question, obesity is not completely understood. Weight gain is directly due to excessive calorie intake and/or inadequate calorie expenditure, which suggests that it may result from certain eating or activ-

FIGURE 13–2
Average behavior problem scores for children in the general population, overweight children enrolled in a weight-loss program, and children seen in psychological clinics. Adapted from Israel and Shapiro (in press).

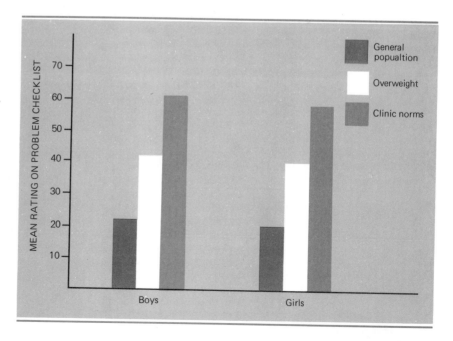

ity patterns. In fact, obese children, even as young as 1½ years of age, appear to eat faster than nonobese children (Drabman, Cordua, Hammer, Jarvie, and Horton, 1979; Marston, London, and Cooper, 1976). This eating pattern may be related to lack of self-control. Children rated low on self-control have been found to interrupt their eating less than children rated higher (Israel, Stolmaker, and Prince, 1984).

Lewittes and Israel (1978) found a relationship between children's delay of gratification and how overweight they were. In this study children could earn a desired food for themselves, or for themselves and others, by waiting alone in a room until the experimenter returned. If they did not wait the entire time, they could earn a less desired food. Overweight children showed less delay than normal-weight children when they were earning the reward for only themselves.

Other research suggests that obese children may be less physically active. However, since the findings are inconsistent, the role of activity level in obesity is unclear (Wicks-Nelson and Israel, 1984). Even if eating and activity patterns of obese children differ from those of normal children, the causes of these patterns remain unknown. They may be biological, psychological, or some combination.

There are many biological theories concerning body weight. *Set point theory* suggests that each person has a point at which body weight is set and maintained, and that the hypothalamus plays a central role in this process (Powley, 1977). Obese individuals are presumed to have a high

FIGURE 13–3
Obesity can have adverse physical and psychological effects. Esaias Baitel, Rapho/Photo Researchers.

set point. *Fat cell theory* focuses on the importance of fat tissue in determining body weight. It is assumed that increases in the number of fat cells or in their size can result in obesity, and that obese persons have a large number of fat cells. Dieting is thought to reduce the size of the cells but not the number, so that dieting goes only so far in reducing obesity. Another biological proposal suggests that obese persons, due to the *lack of an enzyme,* use less energy in cellular functioning, which results in fewer calories being expended and more fat storage (DeLuise, Blackburn, and Flier, 1980). But the evidence for these theories is limited.

On the other hand, the effects of psychosocial factors are widely noted. Overweight parents are more likely to have overweight children (Charney, Goodman, McBride, Lyon, and Pratt, 1976). Because this relationship exists in adoptive families, some psychosocial variables are involved—probably diet or learning (Garn, Cole, and Bailey, (1976). Not surprisingly, social learning theorists emphasize that inappropriate food intake and activity level are learned behaviors. Children undoubtedly imitate the eating habits of others. And eating often results in immediate pleasure, whereas the negative effects of obesity are delayed. Eating may also be so closely connected to social events that it is almost automatic in many situations. Furthermore, individuals may learn to reduce boredom and anxiety by consuming food. The mass media, especially television, appear to encourage children to consume foods that are generally high in fat, sugar, and salt (Liebert, Sprafkin, and Davidson, 1982). Any or all of these variables may well play a role in determining obesity, either alone or in combination with biological predispositions.

Anorexia Nervosa.   Anorexia nervosa refers to a persistent refusal to eat that seems motivated by fear of excessive body weight. Unlike obesity, which often begins quite early in life, this condition typically begins in adolescence. Found primarily in females, anorexia is either increasing in the population or being diagnosed more frequently (Swift, 1982). The characteristic change from normal body size to skeleton-like proportions is quite dramatic in many cases. The seriousness of this disorder is reflected in the following description:

> . . . she looked like a walking skeleton, with her legs sticking out like broomsticks, every rib showing, her shoulder blades standing up like little wings. Her mother mentioned, "When I put my arms around her I feel nothing but bones, like a frightened little bird." Alma's arms and legs were covered with soft hair, her complexion had a yellowish tint, and her dry hair hung down in strings. Most striking was the face—hollow like that of a shriveled-up old woman with a wasting disease, . . . Alma insisted that she looked fine and that there was nothing wrong with her being so skinny. "I enjoy having this disease and I want it." (Bruch, 1979, pp. 2–3)

The word *anorexia* means loss of appetite, but adolescents diagnosed as suffering from anorexia nervosa may actually have to fight the impulse to eat. They are often preoccupied with food, hoard food, and follow monotonous diets. Some eat in uncontrolled binges and then deliberately vomit or use laxatives (Neuman and Halvorson, 1983). (Bingeing followed by voluntary vomiting and laxative use is central in a disorder known as *bulimia*. Anorexics and bulimics share some of the same concerns about being obese, but bulimics usually maintain normal body weight while experiencing bouts of bingeing/vomiting). Amenorrhea, the absence or suppression of menstruation, frequently occurs in anorexic females, as do biological disturbances such as low blood pressure and chemical imbalances. As in the case just described, anorexic adolescents have a distorted body image: They insist they are overweight even when they are painfully thin.

What are the causes of such strange self-starvation? Because anorexia has such dramatic effects on the body, it is not surprising that biological causes have been sought. Malfunctioning of the hypothalamus is suspect, but definitive evidence is lacking (Russell, 1970). Should hypothalamic abnormality be found, we would be left with the question of the direction of causality. Starvation or psychological stress could cause hypothalamus dysfunction, rather than the other way around.

The typical profile of the anorexic adolescent is that of a well-behaved, conscientious, somewhat introverted and perfectionistic individual who is usually a good student. In some cases self-starvation is traceable to a realistic fear of obesity, but there is no clear explanation of why an adolescent persists in extreme dieting. Perhaps the behavior is a response to the stress of puberty itself, for which the girl has no adequate coping skills (Katz, 1975). The families of anorexics are typically of middle or upper social classes; they are often affluent and well-educated. However, mothers are described as dominant and intrusive, while fathers are viewed as passive and ineffectual (Sours, 1974). Such clinical description may or may not stand up to controlled studies. Moreover, families are usually observed *after* the adolescents have displayed life-threatening behaviors, so that the direction of cause and effect is difficult to establish.

Various psychological explanations have been suggested. The psychodynamic model focuses on disturbed sexuality, guilt, aggression, or the mother-child relationship. Minuchin and his colleagues (1978) take a family systems approach, suggesting that the families of anorexics are highly involved and enmeshed in each other. The child learns to be subordinate to the family and is protected in return. At adolescence the child is unable to achieve the individual identity necessary at this time of life, but begins to rebel by refusal to eat. The social learning model conceptualizes self-starvation in anorexics as learned and maintained largely by reduction of anxiety about weight gain or by positive reinforcement through attention (Leitenberg, Agras, and Thomson, 1968).

The cause (or causes) of anorexia nervosa is unclear at the present, and much of the research so far has been based on uncontrolled clinical studies. What is clear is that the condition has serious consequences. About one-third of anorexics remain chronically ill or die (Bemis, 1978).

Fortunately, controlled research into the cause and treatment of the disorder is going forward.

<table>
<tr><td>

EMOTIONAL DISORDERS: FEARS AND DEPRESSION

</td><td>

The study of emotional disorders in children has focused on fears, anxiety, worry, and depression. Our discussion is limited to childhood fears and to depression.

</td></tr>
</table>

Fears and Phobias

Anyone observing children—or looking back on his or her own childhood—knows that fearful situations are encountered almost daily. The Moro reflex, in which the newborn throws back its head and extends its arms outward in response to sudden noise or loss of support, is often considered to be an innate fear reaction. Other fearlike behaviors are exhibited during the first year. Infants placed on the visual cliff at about 6 months of age appear frightened of the apparent depth, and fear of strangers occurs by about 7 months of age.

In a classic study, Jersild and Holmes (1935) disclosed a number of fears common in infancy and early childhood, including fear of noise, strange objects, imaginary creatures, the dark, animals, being alone, dreams, and threats of harm from fire, traffic, and the like. Bauer (1976) interviewed kindergarteners and second and sixth graders about the things they most feared, what they were afraid of when they went to bed, and whether and what kinds of dreams scared them. As Table 13–1 shows, fears of bodily and physical danger increased with age, whereas fear of monsters/ghosts and animals decreased.

Fears of boys and girls from ages 6 to 16 have also been assessed by requesting their parents to complete a lengthy rating scale (Miller, Barrett, Hampe, and Noble, 1972). Three primary dimensions emerged from this study: fear of physical injury and personal loss, fear of natural events such as storms and the dark, and fear reflecting psychic stress (such as fears of exams, social events, making mistakes, and being criticized). The investigators suggested that fear of physical injury and fear involving

TABLE 13–1
Percentage of School Children Reporting Various Kinds of Fears

	Bodily Injury and Physical Danger	Monsters and Ghosts	Animals
Kindergarten	11	74	42
Second grade	53	53	40
Sixth grade	55	5	10

Source: Reprinted with permission from the Journal of Child Psychology and Psychiatry, Vol. 17, Bauer "Percentage of Kinds of Fears." Copyright 1976, Pergamon Press, Ltd.

psychic stress emerge early and continue throughout the life span. On the other hand, fear of natural events tends to disappear with age or to focus on the dark and loneliness. Sexual and moral fears emerge more clearly during adulthood.

In a recent review, Rutter and Garmezy (1983) noted that at least four different groups of fears can be identified on the basis of developmental patterns. The first group is characteristic of infancy; it includes fear of noises, of falling, and of strange persons and objects. These fears peak before the age of 2 and decrease rapidly during the preschool years. Another group of fears arises during the preschool years, only to decrease during middle childhood. It includes fear of animals, the dark, and imaginary creatures. A third group shows a less consistent age trend. It includes specific fears, such as fears of snakes and storms, that often arise in childhood and remain relatively common in adulthood. Also included are more generalized fears that may be associated with timid and anxious temperament, such as fear of meeting strangers. Finally, some unusual fears tend to appear in late childhood and adolescence, or even in adulthood. These include fear of closed (claustrophobia) and open (agoraphobia) spaces.

Rutter and Garmezy consider the first three groups part of normal development. However, these fears can become "abnormal" if they become excessive and incapacitating. The fears in the fourth group are considered abnormal; they occur with low frequency and may persist even with treatment.

Of course, individual children vary a great deal in the fears they exhibit and in the intensity with which they display fearfulness. In addition, a gender difference appears from about the time children enter school. From that time onward females exhibit more specific fears and more phobias—that is, severe and unrealistic fears of specific events, people, and circumstances. During middle childhood girls also display more general fearfulness. The explanation for these gender differences remains uncertain, although differential expectations for the sexes probably is at least partly involved.

Excessive Fears. Although fears are common and can be useful in signaling potentially dangerous situations, in excess they create considerable discomfort and social drawbacks.

Why are some people too fearful? Perhaps some biological factor predisposes individuals toward excessive fears. Parents and professionals describe some children as generally timid, cautious, and inhibited (Kagen, Reznick, Clarke, Snidman, and Garcia-Coll, 1984). This temperamental tendency, which shows some stability over time, is associated with a specific pattern of heart functioning when children are confronted with unfamiliar events. Nevertheless, learning is always involved in the development of phobias. Watson and Rayner conditioned fear in the young child, Albert, by pairing a neutral stimulus with noise that already

FIGURE 13—4

Fears can be useful, but excessive fears can cause discomfort and social drawbacks for a child. © Frostie 1978, Woodfin Camp & Associates.

elicited fear. Such classical conditioning may play a role in creating apparently irrational phobias.

In one study, over half of the fearful undergraduates recalled a specific learning experience that could have accounted for their fears (Rimm, Janda, Lancaster, Nahl, and Dittmar, 1977). Children may also be reinforced for behaving fearfully and may learn fears by observing others react in that fashion. Freudian views of phobias hold that such simple learning experiences are not enough. According to psychoanalytic theory, psychic conflict must also be present and somehow related to the phobic situation. For a specific application of these psychological explanations we turn to school phobia, which has been studied extensively.

School Phobia. The term *school phobia* seems simple enough to define: It should refer to an irrational, strong fear of the school situation that would lead to resistance to going to or remaining in school. In fact, although the avoidance of school is very much a part of the disorder, the motivation for avoidance is complicated.

It is helpful, to begin with, to distinguish school phobic children from truants, both of whom refuse to attend school (Galloway, 1983). Truant children tend to be intermittently absent, wander from their homes, get into trouble by lying and stealing, and experience inconsistent home discipline. Phobic children display fear of school, worry about academic performance, suffer nausea and abdominal pain, and worry about their parents. They remain mostly at home when they are not in school, sometimes for long periods of time.

Fear of leaving the parent has been given as much weight, if not more, than fear of school itself as a cause of school phobia. Eisenberg (1958), for example, argued that school phobic children and their mothers have developed a mutually dependent relationship in which separation is difficult or disturbing. School merely represents an occasion that demands separation. Eisenberg studied eleven preschool children (six boys and five girls) with separation problems. Observation of the mothers and their offspring at the beginning of nursery school attendance showed that the mother contributed at least as much as the child to the separation problem.

> During the first days a typical child would remain close to mother and then begin to oscillate toward and away from the attractions of the play area. As the child began to look less at mother and move away from her, she would take a seat closer to the child and occasionally use a pretext of wiping his nose or checking his toilet needs for intruding into the child's activity. Separation was as difficult for mother as for the child. Similar resistance to separation was shown by the mother when she was required to move to an adjacent room as part of the program for reducing the mutual separation anxiety. (Hetherington and Martin, 1972, p. 59)

Such separation anxiety on the part of both parent and child is viewed as fulfilling basic needs. The child may fear being left alone in the world, and may worry about death of the parent (Kennedy, 1965). The parent may have ambivalent feelings toward the child, but is often overprotective and overindulgent (Gordon and Young, 1976). Psychodynamic theorists emphasize that both child and parent suffer from conflict about dependency.

Social learning theorists also acknowledge that fear of losing the mother may be involved in many cases of school phobia. However, they are less likely to focus on psychic conflict. Garvey and Hegrenes (1966), for example, suggest that school becomes a conditioned stimulus for fear by being paired with fear-eliciting statements such as, "One of these days when you come home from school, I won't be here." Staying at home reduces fear, and is therefore reinforced. Social learning theorists also take into account that the school situation may elicit specific and quite understandable fear reactions. One investigation found that 50 percent of the children expressed fear of academic failure and of particular teachers (Hersov, 1960b). Avoidance of school would certainly seem to be profitable in those situations. Moreover, secondary reinforcers such as toys, television, and attention in the home may strengthen the child's desire to remain there.

It appears that various factors are involved in different cases of school phobias. The child who has strong dependency habits that are encouraged by the parent, who is unhappy in school, and who receives reinforcement for staying at home would seem to be the most vulnerable to this dysfunction.

Depressive Disorders and Feelings

Depressive disorders in the young have only recently received widespread attention. In part, this is because depression is defined in terms of adult depressive disorders. Depression, as such, is characterized by mood disturbances (feelings of sadness, being "blue," irritability), bodily disturbances (sleeplessness, poor appetite, slowed or agitated movements), and certain cognitions (guilt, low self-esteem, self-reproach). Because young children were considered too immature for the cognitions involved in depression, and because the reported frequency of childhood depression was low, depression in children was largely ignored. Then the idea of *masked depression* was introduced (Malmquist, 1977). Children were said actually to experience depression, but the depression was masked by other maladjustments such as hyperactivity, bodily complaints, and low academic performance. In fact, it was argued that childhood depression was very common (Rutter and Garmezy, 1983). Today, neither of these extreme views is popular, but controversy still surrounds childhood depression.

One reason is that depression in the young is particularly difficult to assess. The most common techniques are self-reports and clinical interviews (Kazdin and Petti, 1982). Assessment requires the individual to describe how she or he feels and to connect these feelings with personal meanings (Rutter and Garmezy, 1983). Some success is now being achieved with children older than 6 years of age. However, self-report and clinical evaluations only moderately agree with each other, and self-reports tend to disagree with the reports of parents. In fact, parents and teachers may fail to report depression in children who say they are depressed (Moretti, Fine, Haley, and Marriage, 1985).

The potential of parents to miss depression in their offspring may be especially important in very young children. Prior to school age, children lack the capacity to describe their emotional states in detail—leaving adults the difficult task of deciding whether children are experiencing the sadness, low self-esteem, rejection, guilt, and hopelessness that are often a part of depression in older individuals. Fortunately, recent research confirms that specific nonverbal reactions, such as lack of smiling, frowning, and slowness to respond, are associated with depression in children. Judgments of these reactions may prove helpful in identifying depression in very young children (Kazdin, Sherick, Esveldt-Dawson, and Rancurello, 1985).

Nevertheless, we must consider another complicating factor: If depression occurs in very young children, it is likely to manifest itself in different ways than it does in older children and adolescents. Identification of depression thus depends on the age of those being assessed.

Suicide in the Young

Suicide is especially tragic when it occurs in the young. It is the tragedy of suicide among children and adolescents, not its frequency, that compels attention. Table 13–2 shows the 1970 and 1980 suicide rates for different age groups of white males, who are more vulnerable to suicide than black males and females of both races. (Females *attempt* suicide more than males, however.) Suicide in children is rare, but its occurrence increases sharply in adolescence—by one estimate a hundredfold from under age 10 to 10 to 14 years of age, and another tenfold from 10 to 14 to 15 to 19 years of age (Rutter and Garmezy, 1983). Moreover, suicide in adolescents and young adults is on the rise, and is now the second leading cause of death among adolescents (accidents are the first).

Suicidal behavior in children has been studied primarily in psychiatric hospital units to which children had been admitted for suicidal thinking, threats, or actual attempts. Serious threats and attempts have been linked to being male, significant psychological loss, poor school achievement, marital disintegration, and family violence (Kosky, 1983). Many of the children appeared depressed before and after the suicidal behavior. Nevertheless, not all were depressed, and not all depressed hospitalized children were suicidal. Anxiety and hostility were evident. Cohen-Sandler (1982) and her colleagues interpreted the behavior of the children in their study as a last-ditch strategy to change intolerable situations and to gain love and attention.

Most theoretical accounts of suicide focus on adults and emphasize individual psychological states or broader social conditions (Davison and Neale, 1982). The psychoanalytic view suggests that the death instinct is at the root of suicide. Freud emphasized the complex role that loss of a love object can play. He suggested that to compensate for the loss of a loved one, the individual incorporates the dead love object into the psychic structures. When the love has been ambivalent, hate as well as love are felt toward the incorporated object, leading to depression. Anger may be experienced due to feelings of abandonment. When hate, depression, and anger are strong, they may lead to suicide.

Durkheim's theory focuses on societal causes of suicide (Davison and Neale, 1982). This sociologist proposed three fundamental

TABLE 13–2
U.S. Suicide Rates Per 100,000 Population In White Males, According To Age

	1970	1980
5–14 years	.5	.7
15–24	13.9	21.4
25–34	19.9	25.6
35–44	23.3	23.5
45–54	29.5	24.2
55–64	35.0	25.8
64 and over	41.1	37.5

U.S. Bureau of the Census, *Statistical Abstract of the United States: 1984* (104th ed.). Washington, D.C.; U.S. Government Printing Office, 1983.

kinds of self-destruction. *Altruistic* suicide involves a predetermined sacrifice for society, such as the self-immolations that occurred during the Vietnam war. *Anomic* suicide is due to a sense of disorientation that may be caused by a dramatic change in a person's life. *Egoistic* suicide is due to a lack of supportive ties to society and a sense of alienation.

Following a sociological analysis, McAnarney (1979) proposed that the United States is becoming less socially cohesive and that adolescents are strongly and adversely affected. Surveying reports from several nations, this investigator found that suicide is correlated with weak family ties, weak formal religion, and high mobility and transition—all of which are apparent in the United States today.

Empirical studies implicate the following factors in adolescent suicide: loss of a love object, low self-esteem, depression, suggestibility, impulsiveness, aggression turned inward, and environmental stresses including family disorganization and social isolation (Wenz, 1979). In short, many adolescent suicide attempters suffer some psychiatric disturbance and/or environmental deprivation. Among college students, who have a relatively high rate of suicide, self-destruction was correlated with depression and other emotional disturbance, loss of a significant other, low grades, and academic and social pressure (Miller, 1975).

Many factors linked to adolescent suicide behavior appear to be related to children's suicidal behavior as well. What then protects young children but not adolescents from suicide? There are several possibilities (Shaffer and Fisher, 1981). Depression is associated with suicide in older people, and depression is less frequent in childhood. A second possibility is that the family usually provides more protection for young children than for adolescents. Third, immaturity may protect children from being preoccupied with the abstract idea of death and from being able to plan a suicide—protections that are lost at adolescence. The increased frequency of suicide in adolescence makes it important that research focus not only on the causes of suicide, but also on factors that can protect young people from self-inflicted harm.

Developmental Trends. Although assessment problems are serious, some conclusions about developmental trends may be drawn from surveys of the general population and clinical samples of children.

Depression has been reported in the very young. Spitz (1946) noted that infants in orphanages frequently displayed crying, apathy, withdrawal, and sleep disturbance. He attributed these behaviors, to separation and loss of the mother or a primary mother figure. However, it is doubtful that maternal loss is exclusively related to this condition—and at any rate, the condition appears to be rare (Rutter and Garmezy, 1983). Unhappiness and misery upon separation from the primary caretaker is not uncommon for children 6 months to 4 years of age. On the other hand, it is doubtful that low self-esteem, guilt, or self-blame is common at this age.

Unhappiness and distress are reported quite frequently, among both preadolescent boys and girls, perhaps in 10 to 12 percent of the population. Even in clinic populations, though, depression is only rarely considered the central problem. With the onset of adolescence, major changes occur. Reports of depressed feelings increase and so does the diagnosis of a depressive disorder, with prevalence in girls becoming greater than in boys. Suicide attempts and completions also increase; at least some of the cases are associated with depression (Hawton, 1982). In adulthood, depression is even more common.

Although these developmental trends appear clear, there are still questions. Can we assume, for example, that depression in the young is a specific, primary disorder, independent of other maladjustments? This is an important question: If depression is a specific disorder, it is appropriate to search for specific causes and treatments. A few studies of children and adolescents referred for treatment have shown that some can be identified on the basis of self-reports as being primarily depressed (Puig-Antich, 1982). But depressive symptoms often overlap with other problems. For example, children in grades 3 to 6 who were reported by their parents as depressed also showed conduct problems, anxiety, hyperactivity, learning problems, perfectionism, psychosomatic complaints, and muscular tension (Leon, Kendall, and Garber, 1980).

Perhaps some depressed children have general difficulties rather than a specific depressive disorder. Or perhaps depression in youth may be normal, transitory behavior (Lefkowitz, and Burton, 1978). Depressive feelings and other signs of depression (such as sleeplessness and appetite loss) are reported often in children, but relatively little is known about the intensity of these behaviors and their stability over time. It appears that a complex relationship exists between childhood and adulthood depression. We will look at this relationship later in the chapter.

Causes of Depression.   A common theme in psychological theories is that depressed individuals suffered early separation or loss or otherwise experienced a poor parent-child relationship. In fact, early parental rejection and loss has been associated with depression in children and adolescents (Lefkowitz and Tesiny, 1984). Bowlby (1980) proposed that the child who experiences an insecure attachment to the parent, lack of love, or parental death may interpret a later loss in terms of personal inability which, in turn, leads to depression. Some learning explanations also involve the effects of loss and separation (Lewinsohn, 1974). Here the child is viewed as suffering from a lack of a primary source of reinforcement, which leads to depression. Behavioral explanations also propose that inadequate reinforcement results from other factors. For example, lack of social skills would reduce the chance of children's receiving reinforcement from peers.

The role of cognitions is increasingly emphasized as a factor in depression. Beck (1967, 1976) assumes that depression results from the way individuals interpret life events. He hypothesizes that errors in thinking about the world distort even mildly adverse events into thoughts of self-blame and failure. Seligman and his colleagues offer a *learned helplessness* explanation of depression (Seligman, 1974; Seligman and Peterson, in press). They suggest that some individuals come to view themselves as having little control over the environment. Such learned helplessness is associated with depressed mood. Parental separation may be a specific case in which the child's inability to bring the parent back leads to learned helplessness.

Many theorists look to biological variables in explaining negative mood. Hormonal changes at puberty, for example, might play a role in the rise in depression with adolescence (Sroufe and Rutter, 1984). Antidepressive medication aimed at altering the biochemistry of the nervous system appears to alleviate symptoms of depression in some adults, which suggests a biochemical basis. Some attention is being given to genetic influence, based on evidence of heredity in certain depressive disorders in adults, as well as histories of depression in relatives of depressed children (Brumback, Jackoway, and Weinberg, 1980).

Research into the role of biological factors requires further efforts, as does the entire question of the causes of depression. In the final analysis, we might anticipate that different explanations will be required for subsets of depression—for example, for infants versus adolescents and transitory versus chronic symptoms. It is also likely that interactions among learning histories, current life events, and perhaps biological predispositions will ultimately explain the negative feelings and thoughts that are central in depression.

HYPERACTIVITY

Unlike the emotional disorders just discussed, hyperactivity seems to be directed at others. This may be quite unintentional, because hyperactive children lack control of their behavior in many situations and, indeed, often appear to be driven by some internal force.

First described in 1845 by a German physician, Henrich Hoffmann (Cantwell, 1975), hyperactivity was not really studied until the late 1950s. At that time concern was growing for children with learning and behavior problems, both of which are frequently displayed by hyperactive children (Safer and Allen, 1976). Then, in the late 1960s, drug treatment for the disorder began, further increasing interest and concern. Today hyperactivity is one of the most commonly recognized childhood problems; it occurs in 5 to 10 percent of all elementary school children, with a sex ratio of three to four boys to one girl (Ross and Pelham, 1981).

What Is Hyperactivity?

There is a strong tendency to view hyperactivity as a *syndrome*—that is, a cluster of maladaptive behaviors, often referred to as the hyperkinetic syndrome, hyperkinetic impulse disorder, or hyperkinesis.

Hyperactive children are active beyond what is typical for their age, especially in structured situations that require motor control. One investigative team described such children in this way:

Hyperactive children seem to be constantly searching for something interesting. In an office they often act as though they are "turning over rocks" to see what interesting things may lie below. Unfortunately, this applies to dismantling the dictaphone, turning over the ashtray, and uprooting the rubber plant. (Klein and Gittelman-Klein, 1975, p. 53)

In the classroom hyperactive children leave their seats frequently and fidget restlessly. Parents of such children report that their children always seemed unusually energetic, fidgety, and unable to keep their hands still. This overactivity often begins early in childhood and is a serious problem when the child begins school.

Another major feature is deficiency in attention. Hyperactive children skip from activity to activity; they rarely watch an entire television program or complete a school assignment. Teachers complain that they do not pay attention to directions and cannot concentrate. Attention deficits are so widely noted that they are now considered central in hyperactivity (Douglas, 1980, 1983). The problem may be distractibility—that is, an inability to ignore disruptions from the environment. Distraction is likely when an activity is boring or difficult and the distractors are new or interesting. However, the more basic problem appears to be difficulty in *sustaining* attention, or in Douglas's words in "the investment, organization, and maintenance of attention and effort" (1983, p. 291).

The third major sign of hyperactivity is impulsivity which, simply put, is acting without thinking. The child may run across a street without looking for oncoming traffic, or jump into a swimming pool without being able to swim (Cantwell, 1975). Impulsivity in the classroom includes interrupting others' speech, calling out, or clowning (Routh, 1980). In the laboratory it is displayed when the child is asked to select from a set of slightly varying pictures the one that matches a standard picture. Relatively rapid selection along with numerous errors on the Matching Familiar Figures Test are interpreted as indications of impulsivity (Rutter and Garmezy, 1983).

Two other problem areas—conduct disturbance and academic deficits—are so common that they may be considered secondary manifestations of hyperactivity. Misconduct is noted in perhaps as many as 80 percent of the cases (Safer and Allen, 1976). Parents and teachers complain of aggression, quarreling, disobedience, temper tantrums, negativism, bullying, bossiness, and low frustration tolerance. It is not surprising, then, that these children are not liked by their peers and are rejected.

Hyperactive children perform poorly on tests of reading, spelling, arithmetic, and other academic subjects (Silver, 1981). By the time they reach adolescence 50 to 60 percent of hyperactive children have failed more than one grade (Milich and Loney, 1979). Keogh (1971) has speculated on the relationship between hyperactivity and poor academic performance. She suggests three possibilities: that some neurological impairment causes both conditions, that hyperactivity interferes with attention so that learning is inadequate, or that impulsivity interferes with learning. There is growing evidence that the child's failure to "stop, look, and listen'' is more strongly associated with poor task performance and academic achievement than is high activity level (Edelbrock, Costello, and Kessler, 1984).

In the United States the concept of hyperactivity as a syndrome is based on the belief that overactivity, attention deficits, and impulsivity frequently occur together. However, several studies show that these behaviors are not significantly related in either hyperactive or nonhyperactive populations (Barkley, 1981; Kenny, 1980; Langhorne, Loney, Paternite, and Bechtholdt, 1976). Children labeled hyperactive may well be a mixed group: some overactive, some inattentive, some impulsive, and some a combination of these behaviors (Barkley, 1981). Moreover, children may appear hyperactive in many situations or be hyperactive in one situation but not another (Luk, 1985). For example, Henker and Whalen (1980) exposed boys to four study situations that varied in difficulty of task and in whether the child had to work according to his own or a teacher's pace. When the situation was least challenging the hyper-

FIGURE 13–5
Hyperactivity is associated with conduct disturbance and low school achievement.   Suzanne Szasz, Photo Researchers.

active boys attended to the task, as did the nonhyperactive children, but they attended less when the task was most challenging. There is also evidence that ratings of hyperactivity vary from school to home situations.

The Causes of
Hyperactivity

Hyperactivity has long been associated with the idea that some kind of nervous system dysfunction exists, although it may be minimal (Ferguson and Pappas, 1979). The search for biological causes has taken many paths. There is tentative evidence that heredity may play a role (Heffron, Martin, and Welsh, 1984). Minor physical abnormalities in neonates, prenatal and birth complications, abnormal biochemistry, and abnormal EEGs and other signs of neurological dysfunction have been reported (Zametkin, Karoum, Rapoport, Brown, and Wyatt, 1984). In addition, hyperactive children may have a less than normally unresponsive nervous system (Ross and Pelham, 1981). These signs are not absolutely associated with hyperactivity, however; they also appear in children with other kinds of disorders. Nevertheless, a biological cause for at least some cases of hyperactivity is likely.

One environmental influence that has been investigated is lead poisoning from air pollution or eating flakes of leaded paints. Children exposed to high levels of lead during early development display unusual motor behavior, learning difficulties, irritability, and the like (Henker and Whalen, 1980). In a fascinating study, Needleman and others (1979) measured lead in the teeth of 5- to 7-year-old children. The children were classified as high or low exposure subjects. They were then extensively examined through social histories, parent and teacher reports, medical examinations, and neurophysiological tests. Those who had higher levels of lead performed less well on tests of attention, language, and intelligence. They were also judged by teachers as more distractible and impulsive.

Diet is also implicated in hyperactivity. It was once proposed that increased intake of various vitamins could have a calming and organizing effect on children. Based on inconsistent research findings and evidence for some risk of negative side effects, the American Academy of Pediatrics does not support vitamin supplementation (Varley, 1984). Some professionals and many parents suspect that simple sugar can cause behavior disturbances. Although a few studies show a relationship between sugar intake and behavior problems, other data do not.

The diet hypothesis that has received the most attention is Feingold's (1975) claim that foods containing artificial dyes and flavors, certain preservatives, and naturally occurring salicylates (for example, apricots, tomatoes, and cucumbers) cause hyperactivity. Feingold claimed that 25 to 50 percent of hyperactive–learning disabled children could benefit from a special diet that eliminated these substances (Harley and Matthews, 1980). His proposition received a great deal of media coverage and was adopted by many parents. Research evidence indicates that the diet may help a small number of children, particularly preschoolers (Weiss, 1982).

This finding does not match the popularity of the approach among parents, who are exposed to considerable media hype and who perhaps are attracted by a "natural" approach to solving their children's problems (Varley, 1984).

Finally, although learning theorists do not specifically suggest that hyperactivity is caused through learning, behaviors relevant to hyperactivity may be shaped and maintained by the environment (O'Leary, 1978). For example, learning to remain in one's seat in school and to attend to relevant tasks can be modified by numerous behavioral procedures (Ayllon and Rosenbaum, 1977). Exposure to filmed models or to a particular teacher's style has been shown to change children's behavior (Ridberg, Parke, and Hetherington, 1971). Perhaps some cases of hyperactivity can be attributed to a predisposition for the disorder that is made worse by certain environmental circumstances.

Whatever the causes of hyperactivity, the disorder persists over several years, although problems decrease as children mature. More will be said about hyperactivity when we discuss treatment later in this chapter. First, however, we turn to two childhood dysfunctions characterized by extreme deviations from the normal course of development.

INFANTILE AUTISM AND CHILDHOOD SCHIZOPHRENIA

Although all the disorders we have discussed can seriously affect development, none affect children quite as much as infantile autism and childhood schizophrenia. Both disorders involve severe distortions in basic psychological processes. Infantile autism and childhood schizophrenia had once been referred to as psychoses and schizophrenia—terms also applied to severe thinking, emotional, and social disturbances in adults. It had been assumed that both disorders were like adult schizophrenic processes, with somewhat different symptoms than those found in adults. Childhood schizophrenia is still viewed in this light, but autism is now seen as a pervasive developmental disorder unrelated to schizophrenia. Autistic children may display some of the same behaviors as schizophrenic children, but many symptoms do not overlap, and the two groups differ in other ways as well.

Infantile Autism

In 1943, Leo Kanner described eleven severely disturbed children whose behavioral patterns, he claimed, could be differentiated from those of other seriously disturbed children. He later (1944) coined a new label for the syndrome—early *infantile autism*—and noted that it included about 10 percent of all severely disturbed children, and affected more boys than girls.

On the basis of case studies Kanner described many characteristics of autistic children that have stood the test of time. He noted an inability to relate to people from almost the beginning of life. Parents described their children to Kanner as "self-sufficient," "happiest when left alone," and "like in a shell," (1973, p. 33). Kanner referred to this extreme aloneness as *autism,* absorption in the self or one's own mental activity. He pointed to several other features. Often, the children displayed unusual speech patterns, were delayed in speech, or developed virtually no speech. They were obsessed by sameness in the environment. For example, one child was upset by changes in routine and placement of furniture. Finally, Kanner noted that the children were strongly attracted to inanimate objects and repetitious action.

Kanner proposed that the basic defect in autism is a profound disturbance in socioemotional functioning, which leads to language and other deficits. There is much evidence that abnormal social interaction begins early in life and endures into adulthood (Hobson, 1984). But the more accepted view today is that some cognitive dysfunction underlies abnormal social and emotional behavior.

Although autism is associated with all degrees of intellectual ability, about 75 percent of the children show some impairment in general intelligence (Rutter and Garmezy, 1983). Many of them engage in behaviors that suggest deficits in sensory-motor processing. For example, they fail to respond to sounds, flap their hands and arms, show a bizarre preoccupation with moving objects, whirl, and rock (Table 13–3). Some researchers believe that a basic perceptual disturbance prevents the autistic child from constructing a stable world. This in turn prevents the development of normal language and social interaction (Ornitz, 1978). Others give primary importance to language/communication deficits.

The pervasiveness of language dysfunction is evident in one study

TABLE 13–3
Percentages of Autistic Children with Disturbances of
Sensory-Motor Processing

Disturbance	Percentage
Ignored or failed to respond to sounds	71
Excessively watched the motion of own hands or fingers	71
Stared into space as if seeing something that was not there	64
Preoccupied with things that spin	57
Preoccupied with minor visual details	57
Preoccupied with the feel of things	53
Let objects fall out of hands as if they did not exist	53
Preoccupied with scratching surfaces and listening to the sound	50
Agitated at being taken to new places	48
Agitated by loud noises	42
Flapped arms or hands in repetitive way	76
Whirled around without apparent reason	59
Rocked head or body	51
Ran or walked on toes	40

From Ornitz, 1978.

showing that half of the autistic children were without speech at 5 years of age, and that 75 percent of those with speech displayed unusual language (Rutter, 1978). *Echolalia*—the echoing back of the speech of others—and *pronoun reversals*—referring to the self as "you" or "he" or "she"—are common patterns. Autistic children do relatively poorly on tasks that need verbal abstraction, even when no actual speech is required. They also have particular difficulty with the meanings and social context of language (Tager-Flusberg, 1981).

Despite considerable research, we do not yet know much about the psychological processes of autism. The absence of social interaction is striking, but it has received little observation and experimentation (Rutter and Garmezy, 1983). For example, in reporting that some autistic children become attached to their mothers, Sigman and Ungerer (1984) noted the absence of this basic finding in the research literature. At the present time we can conclude that some kind of cognitive deficit probably underlies social and emotional disturbance. But the relationship between the two remains clouded.

What Causes Autism? Kanner described the parents of his autistic sample as upper class, highly intelligent, professionally accomplished, and preoccupied with scientific, literary, and artistic abstractions. He later said that the children had been exposed to mechanical, cold attention to material needs (Kanner, 1949). But Kanner did not believe that "refrigerator parents" were enough to explain autism (Kanner, 1943; Kanner and Eisenberg, 1956). However, others put forth the idea that certain parental behaviors could explain the condition. Bettelheim (1967a, 1967b), for example, hypothesized that normal development depends on the child's acting successfully in the environment to fulfill needs and on communicating with others. If all goes well, the child continues to act in the world and develops a sense of the self. If parents are unresponsive during the first few years of life, the child perceives the environment as threatening and destructive and withdraws into an autistic "empty fortress." Ferster (1961, 1966) also emphasized the role of parental interaction in autism. Drawing on learning theory, he noted that parents are crucial in shaping the behavior of their offspring through reinforcement and punishment. Parents of autistic children, he hypothesized, failed in this function, due to their preoccupation with other activities, rejection of their children, depression, and the like.

As fascinating as these psychological theories are, they are not really accepted today. Although many parents of autistic children are highly intelligent and fall into the upper social classes, the entire spectrum of intelligence levels and social classes is represented (Tsai, Stewart, Faust, and Shook, 1982). These parents display no tendency toward thought disorders, schizophrenia, obsession, deviant personality, or lack of empathy (McAdoo and DeMyer, 1978). When they occasionally appear different from parents of normal children, it is likely that the difference stems from having an autistic child rather than the other way around

(Cantwell, Baker, and Rutter, 1978). This is not to say that the family environment plays no role in shaping or maintaining autistic behavior, but the family environment does not seem to explain the severity and bizarre quality of autism.

On the other hand, evidence for biological causes is accumulating. Hereditary factors are suggested by the Folstein and Rutter (1978) study in which autistic identical and fraternal twins were compared. Thirty-six percent of the identical, but none of the fraternal, pairs were concordant for the condition. Family studies also provide some evidence for genetic influence (Rutter and Garmézy, 1983). Although only about 2 percent of the siblings of autistic children display the condition, this figure is fifty times the expectation for the general population. In 25 percent of families a history of speech delay is found, raising the possiblity of the inheritance of a broad cognitive/linguistic disability.

Autism is also associated with such medical disorders as rubella and syphilis in neonates (Rutter and Garmezy, 1983). It is not unusual for autistic children to have seizures and to develop epilepsy on reaching adolescence. Autistic children also suffer a greater incidence of adverse prenatal and perinatal complications (Campbell, Geller, and Cohen, 1977). Abnormalities have been found in EEG recordings as well as in the biochemistry of the nervous system. But efforts to find specific brain dysfunctioning have not been successful. All the evidence taken together points to the likelihood that autism may result from nervous system damage that occurs from conception to the first few years of life (Hagamen, 1980). The environment may play a role by interacting with biological factors to produce the condition or to maintain it in some way.

Childhood Schizophrenia

Of all the professionals associated with the study of childhood schizophrenia, Lauretta Bender stands out as a pioneer. Working at New York City's Bellevue hospital for many years, she described, treated, and followed the development of a group of severely disturbed children. Bender believed that no matter what their age, her patients suffered from schizophrenia that manifested itself in different ways depending on the developmental status of the children. Bender (1972) noted disturbances in every aspect of nervous system functioning: vegetative, motor, perceptual, intellectual, emotional, and social. Sleeping and eating were disturbed, as well as growth patterns and the timing of puberty. The children's movements were awkward, and they displayed intellectual retardation, language problems, distorted thinking, and disturbed social relationships. Bender viewed the primary psychological problem as difficulty in identifying one's self and thus difficulty in relating to the rest of the world.

More recently, Eggers (1978) has decribed a sample of children, aged 7 to 13, whom he considers schizophrenic. Those under 10 showed sudden personality changes including reduced activity, narrowing of interests, speech disturbance, disturbed movement and posture, negativism, and loss of contact with reality. Some grew cold toward loved ones, and even brutal to their pets. Some were anxious, distrustful, and injurious to objects as well as to themselves. Delusions and hallucinations appeared. In one form of delusion the children seemed to lose identity, and to see themselves as animals, other people, or inanimate objects.

According to Eggers, the older children in the sample showed symptoms that are even more similar to adult schizophrenia. They reported auditory and visual hallucinations, and their delusions were more systematized and abstract. Green and others (1984) also noted these behaviors in children labeled schizophrenic; they found that 79 percent of the sample had auditory hallucinations, 46 percent had visual hallucinations, and 54 percent had delusions. These children thus had some loss of contact with reality.

Causes of Childhood Schizophrenia.   Evidence exists for biological causes of the condition. Childhood schizophrenia has been associated with medical conditions, pregnancy complications (such as bleeding and toxemia), and severe maternal illness (Rieder, Broman, and Rosenthal, 1977). Nervous system dysfunction has been inferred from abnormal posture, gait, motor coordination and muscle tone, sensory functioning, and EEG recordings, as well as reports of convulsions. Kallmann and Roth's (1956) study of preadolescent twins revealed 70.6 percent concordance in identical twins, compared to 17.1 percent in fraternal pairs. Other studies suggest that schizophrenia appears in the parents of disturbed children with a greater frequency than would be expected for the general population (Fish and Ritvo, 1979).

This last fact implicates the environment as well as hereditary factors, of course. As with autism, family environment and interaction have been extensively studied, and no specific patterns have been uncovered. Unlike autism, however, childhood schizophrenia is associated with parental psychopathology and low social class. The meaning of this difference is unclear. Overall we may probably conclude that biological factors are important and that inheritance is likely in some cases. It is also likely that childhood schizophrenia actually represents different conditions that arise from different causes.

What Happens to
Severely Disturbed
Children?

The prognosis for infantile autism is disheartening. Kanner (1973) reported that of ninety-six autistic children, only eleven were maintaining themselves when they were in their second and third decades of life. In a later comparison, Lotter (1974) indicated that in three independent investigations conducted in England and the United States, 62 percent, 61 percent, and 74 percent of the disturbed children were judged as having poor or very poor status several years after initial contact. Figure 13–6 shows the consistency in judgments in these investigations. The children rated as having poor and very poor status were severely handicapped and unable to lead independent existences, compared with the minority

FIGURE 13–6
Percent of children
judged good, fair, or
poor/very poor
several years after
initial contact.
Adapted from
Lotter, 1974.

Outcome Status	Middlesex Study	Maudsley Study	Illinois Study
Good	14	14	10
Fair	24	25	16
Poor	14	13	24
Very poor	48	48	50

who were leading normal social lives, functioning in school, or making progress in these areas despite significant behavioral abnormalities. This finding has been confirmed by more extensive reviews that followed the children into early adulthood (Lotter, 1978; Rutter and Garmezy, 1983).

Do certain variables predict outcome? In trying to account for his "emergers," Kanner was able to point to only two facts: All eleven had been able to speak before the age of 5 years, and none had been committed to a state institution. Several studies have linked speech capacity, IQ performance, and original severity of the disorder to outcome. Lotter (1978) found that the 50 percent or so most severely affected youngsters in his study remained severely handicapped, whereas the others' outcomes were more varied. Adolescence appears to be a time of important transition: Some children deteriorate, but others improve, particularly in terms of social behavior.

In his study of childhood schizophrenia, Eggers (1978) reported that about half of the children showed good improvement, and that some of these recovered. About one-third showed very poor status, and the remainder were rated as fair to poor. All the children who had become disturbed before the age of 10 years had poor outcomes. Above-average intelligence was related to positive outcome. Children also had a better chance of recovery if they had once been kind, warm-hearted, and capable of making friends, and if they had once had outside interests. Less favorable outcome was related to children's being inhibited, insecure, shy, and introverted. Eggers' report is somewhat more favorable than usual, but it too presents a rather bleak picture. Such tragedy underscores the need for continuing research into causes and treatment.

TREATMENT

So far in this chapter we have focused on descriptions and causes of several behavioral disorders: habit disturbances, fears and depression, hyperactivity, and infantile autism/childhood schizophrenia. We now look at various efforts to treat behavior disorders in the young. In the United States, vigorous intervention efforts began in the 1930s, largely inspired by the writings of Freud. A number of clinics opened to provide treatment based on traditional psychoanalytic and counseling therapy. Then, in the 1950s, came an explosion of new therapeutic techniques, due in part to Hans J. Eysenck's (1952) and E. E. Levitt's (1957) reports of the failure of the then-current approaches to treatment. Whereas the traditional approaches had emphasized relatively lengthy "talking" techniques, the new methods focused on behavioral techniques, the use of medication, and participation of the child's family and school (McDermott and Char, 1984). Along with changes in treatment methods came sensitivity to certain issues concerning treatment of the young.

Working with Child and Adolescent Clients

The professional care of the young frequently involves several disciplines: psychologists, teachers in regular and special classrooms; psychiatrists, other physicians, nurses; social workers; and representatives of the legal system. It is usual for a psychologist working with young clients to have contact with other professionals.

Treating young people is fundamentally different from treating adults. The young have relatively little control over whether or not they participate in treatment or who they will see. Children, and to a lesser extent adolescents, enter treatment at the suggestion or coercion of adults. Professionals must therefore be especially sensitive to the child's perspective and motivation.

Dealing with youthful clients typically demands working closely with parents, who vary greatly in their sensitivities and capacities to bring about productive change. Differences in parental attitudes and expectations were described in a study of the way two groups of families reported child problems (Thomas, Chess, Sillen, and Mendez, 1974). One group consisted of working-class families, the other of middle- and upper middle-class families. Both groups exhibited high family stability and showed no differences in the prenatal and perinatal complications surrounding the development of their children. They differed strikingly, though, in both the number and kinds of problems they reported in their children.

By the time the children were 9 years old, 31 percent of the middle-class as opposed to 10 percent of the working-class children were diagnosed as having behavior disorders. The middle-class parents were child-problem-oriented and aware of theories of child development that emphasized early problems as causes of later functioning. The working-class parents were concerned about the well-being of their offspring but not with psychological functioning. Their attitude was shown by the remark, "He's a baby—he'll outgrow it" (Thomas et al., 1974, p. 56). Working-class parents also appeared to place fewer demands on their children to feed and dress themselves and follow through on verbal task directions. Finally, they were less optimistic about obtaining help for their children. They reported fewer disturbances, but the kinds of problems they reported were relatively severe. These parental differences are bound to influence intervention efforts.

For the most part, it is safe to assume that parents have their children's welfare at heart. Nevertheless, parental needs and judgments can work against youthful clients. Take the case of authoritarian parents who bring their son to a clinic for conduct problems. It is questionable that the child will be "helped" by being encouraged to bring his behavior into line with the parents' expectations for excessive obedience. In this case, the

Close-up

All treatment efforts are based on the assumption that human beings are capable of change. Kendall, Lerner, and Craighead (1984) argue, however, that change is influenced by developmental processes. Interventions must be planned according to what is known about these processes. Based on research in child development, these writers suggest that it is helpful to look at three aspects of the child: the child as stimulus, the child as processor, and the child as agent.

The Child as Stimulus. First consideration is given to the well-established fact that socialization is reciprocal, that children influence parents (and other agents of socialization) and are influenced by them. The child influences parents and receives feedback as a result of these effects, and feedback may further influence development. Children with "difficult" temperament may influence their caretakers in ways such that they are treated, in turn, in certain ways, which then increase the risk of behavioral dysfunctions (Thomas and Chess, 1976). So it is necessary to evaluate the stimulus quality of the child, the reactions of the caretakers, feedback to the child, and the resulting effects on the child. Moreover, interventions should focus not on the child or parents, but on the interactive system.

The Child as Processor. Individuals undergo developmental change that makes it more or less likely that a specific therapy technique will be successful. Children are all too often seen as alike when, in fact, they show enormous variability. Developmental data offer guidelines for evaluating children and for selecting intervention techniques that might best fit the child's developmental status.

One example concerns the use of self-instruction techniques to facilitate self-control. These techniques assume that some children can benefit from being trained to guide their own behavior by verbal self-directions or instructions (Kendall and Braswell, 1982). The children are taught self-directions and how to use them. For example, impulsive children are taught steps for problem solving, and are encouraged to say the steps to themselves at the appropriate moments. Developmental status influences the success of this treatment: children under 6 years do not readily respond.

The Child as Agent. Children generally benefit by being able to meet the demands of the social environments in which they find themselves; that is, by attaining a "good fit." Of course, good matches do not always occur, so it is helpful for children to be able to change situations and/or modify themselves. By having this flexibility, children become their own agents for change.

If flexibility is to be a goal of intervention, what guidelines for therapy might be productive? Certainly it would be important to assess the child's ability to size up situations, judge his or her own characteristics, and evaluate the match between the two. Assessments must also be made of the child's ability to select situations in which a good fit is easily achieved. When selection is impossible and the fit is not good (when a child is assigned to a teacher with whom conflict is inevitable), assessment must be made of the child's ability to modify the situation or him- or herself. These assessments would guide further intervention goals, but in one way or another efforts would be made to enhance the child's self-regulation.

Suppose, for example, a 10-year-old girl was performing poorly in mathematics and believed that she could do little to improve this situation. In other words, she felt powerless. How could this child be helped? Bandura and Schunk (1981) showed that children doing poorly in mathematics, who also perceived themselves as ineffective in bringing about change, withdrew from the situation. Withdrawal resulted in missed opportunities for practice and improvement. Bandura and Schunk increased the children's belief in themselves as having the power to effect change, and improvement in mathematics followed. Flexibility for change in this case rested on the therapists' modifying the children's cognitions about themselves.

therapist's primary task might be to modify parental expectations because the child's behavior is not disturbed by most standards. There are obvious ethical considerations in a situation like this. In fact, balancing the interests of young clients and their parents can be the most challenging part of treating youth.

An Overview of
Psychological
Treatment
Approaches

The ways in which behavior disorders are evaluated and treated depend in part on the age of the clients and the nature of the disorder. The theoretical assumptions of therapists also determine what happens to children and adolescents once they enter treatment.

Traditional Psychoanalytic Therapy. Traditional Freudian theory holds that behavior problems are symptoms of underlying conflict among instinctual demands (id), conscious thoughtful regulation (ego), and self-evaluative thoughts (superego). The conflict is said to be unconscious, and treatment is designed to bring it into consciousness, resulting in resolution of the conflict and relief of the symptoms. Therapy focuses on the patient's free verbal associations, dream interpretation, the patient-therapist relationship, and "working through" the conflict.

The application of Freudian theory to the treatment of childhood disorders can be traced to the therapy of Little Hans, which was conducted by Hans's father under Freud's supervision. Five-year-old Hans was reported to have an unexplainable and irrational fear of horses, severe enough to prevent his going into the streets. Freud explained that Hans unconsciously desired his mother and felt simultaneous hate, love, and fear toward his father. The fear, however, was projected onto horses, the animals' muzzles and blinders seeming to represent the father's mustache and eyeglasses. Treatment consisted of the father's interpreting Hans's remarks so as to gradually bring the underlying conflict into consciousness:

On April 25, 1908, Hans, who had just reached the age of five, was answering some of his father's questions. In a climate of confidence and acceptance, he admitted that he would like to see him dead and marry his mother. This was the culminating point of the therapeutic process, and from that time on, the remnants of the phobia gradually receded: the Oedipus complex had been overcome. (Cited by Ellenberger, 1970, p. 509)

439

FIGURE 13–7
Despite variations, all family therapy approaches consider the family critical for therapeutic change.   Linda Ferrer, Woodfin Camp & Associates.

Treatment of children by analytic methods was carried on by Freud's daughter Anna, who explored inner conflicts, particularly those that are unconscious. But Anna Freud emphasized that treating children is different from treating adults (A. Freud, 1946). One difference is that children do not easily enter into free association about their inner lives. Other ways must be found to uncover conflict, such as observing the child at play, examining the child-parent relationship, and studying the child-therapist relationship. Finally, the therapist must educate the parents as to the child's problems while directly guiding the child in conducting his or her instinctual life.

Axline's Nondirective Play Therapy.   Nondirective therapy is based on the humanistic view of development. Virginia Axline's work represents the nondirective approach as it is applied to children. Axline reflects the optimism of the humanistic view with these words:

There seems to be a powerful force within each individual which strives continuously for complete self-realization. This force may be characterized as a drive toward maturity, independence, and self-direction. It goes on relentlessly to achieve consummation, but it needs good "growing ground" to develop a well-balanced structure. Just as a plant needs sun and rain and good rich earth in order to attain its maximum growth, so the individual needs the permissiveness to be himself, the complete acceptance of himself—by himself, as well as by others—and the right to be an individual. . . . (1947, p. 10)

Axline points out that when the individual is prevented from achieving complete realization of the self, tension, friction, and resistance occur. Drive for self-realization continues, however, resulting in an outward fight to establish a self-concept or an inner struggle. The person may show withdrawal, daydreaming, repression, and regression, that is maladjusted behavior. The aim of nondirective therapy is to permit the individual to be him- or herself and to begin to realize the power to think, decide, and mature.

This goal is reached within the context of free play, the child's most natural form of expression. Play is used for expressing insecurity, fear, confusion, aggression, and tension. Axline provides eight guidelines for conducting therapy. As Table 13–4 shows, the therapist is indeed nondirective, as well as accepting. Children's responses to this therapeutic experience, according to Axline, are captured by one 7-year-old boy's spontaneously crying out, "Oh, every child just once in his life should have a chance to spill out all over without a 'Don't you dare! Don't you dare! Don't you dare!' " and an 8-year-old girl's exclaiming, "In here I turn myself inside out and give myself a shake, shake, shake, and finally I get glad all over that I am me."

Family Therapy.   All family therapy approaches view the family as a critical component of therapeutic change. However, they are quite varied in specific assumptions and techniques. Parents may be seen by a separate therapist or with the child. In some cases the child's problems are the only issue; in others more emphasis is given to broad family issues. In most cases, however, the family's role is to assist the child.

The family systems approach identifies the entire family as the focus

---

TABLE 13–4
Guidelines For Nondirective Play Therapy

1. The therapist must develop a warm, friendly relationship with the child.
2. The therapist accepts the child exactly as he or she is.
3. The therapist establishes a feeling of permissiveness in the relationship so that the child feels freedom of expression.
4. The therapist is alert to recognize the feelings of the child and reflect them back, thereby fostering the child's self-insight.
5. The therapist maintains a deep respect for the child's ability to solve problems.
6. The child leads the way; the therapist follows.
7. The therapist does not attempt to hurry the therapy along.
8. The therapist establishes only those limitations that are necessary to anchor the therapy to the world of reality and to make the child aware of his or her responsibility in the relationship.

From Axline, 1947, pp. 73–74.

of treatment (Bowen, 1980). Here, the family is considered to be a complex unit that may instigate and maintain the child's disordered behavior. An example of this approach is Minuchin's conceptualization of anorexia nervosa, in which the adolescent is unable to achieve an individual identity within an enmeshed family. The family systems approach views interaction of the family as the problem, not the adolescent him- or herself. Treatment aims to uncover and modify maladaptive family structures and interactions.

Behavior Modification. Of all of the innovative treatment approaches that have appeared, perhaps none is as popular today as behavior modification. Within this model, maladaptive behaviors are considered learned ways of dealing with the world that are in themselves the problems. The child's behaviors are not viewed as symptoms of underlying conflicts. Rather, the behaviors themselves are the direct focus of therapy. Critics of behavior modification argue that an approach that ignores deep inner causes will not be effective in the long run because new symptoms of the underlying problem will appear. Investigations into this possibility show that new symptoms do *not* occur (Lazarus, 1963; Weitzman, 1967; Wolpe, 1958).

Many types of therapy rely on tests of personality or adjustment to assess difficulties. Behavior modification relies more on direct observation and assessment of the actual behavior of each youngster. Obviously a child's behavior can be altered successfully only if something is done with him or her. In this sense, manipulation is involved in all types of therapy. Behavior modification is characterized by a very specific, detailed, and systematic plan for intervention, generally with an eye to altering particular consequences for behaving in certain ways. When a manipulation is tried, an immediate effort is made to determine whether the desired changes are occurring. If not, a different manipulation is introduced, and then it is evaluated. Repeated assessment, based on regular direct evaluation, is typical of the approach.

The behavioral approach reflects recent interest in the internal processes of thinking and imagining. Cognition is considered to influence which environmental events are attended to, how the events are interpreted, and how the events might affect behavior. With regard to behavior change, this cognitive-behavioral view focuses particularly on the development of self-control. For example, hyperactive children are taught to direct their own behavior by using self-statements.

Some Examples of
Treatments

Let us now look at a few specific examples of treatment of very different kinds of childhood behavioral problems. These examples emphasize the behavioral approach, but they also reflect interest in family and teacher involvement and demonstrate the use of medications.

Enuresis. Earlier we pointed out that the difficulty of enuretic children, viewed in learning terms, is that they have not learned to awaken before bedwetting occurs. Presumably this is because internal stimulation (bladder tension) does not arouse them from sleep. Many years ago Mowrer and Mowrer (1938) related the problem to classical conditioning. They reasoned that the desired response could be produced by pairing the ringing of a fairly loud bell (a UCS, or unconditioned stimulus, which would inevitably awaken the child) with bladder stimulation (the CS, or conditioned stimulus). Waking up—an unconditioned response (UCR) to the bell—should then become a conditioned response to the bladder tension alone, permitting the child to reach the toilet in time.

The Mowrers attempted to treat enuretic youngsters accordingly. The children slept on a specially prepared pad made of two pieces of bronze screening separated by a heavy layer of cotton. When urination occurred it would seep through the fabric, close an electrical circuit, and cause the bell to ring. After repeated pairings, bladder tension alone would be expected to waken the child. Thirty children were treated by the Mowrers in this way, for a maximum period of two months, and bedwetting was successfully eliminated in every case. The bell and pad apparatus devised by the Mowrers has been successfully used ever since. Approximately 75 percent of the children treated with it have been helped initially; relapses are quite common but many respond to retraining (Doleys, 1977).

An alternate method, dry-bed training, is also currently being researched. Based more on operant conditioning, this method incorporates several procedures (Azrin, Sneed, and Foxx, 1974). The urine alarm is placed in the parents' bedroom to awaken them in the event of the child's wetting. The first step is an intensive night of training. Therapists come into the home and explain the procedures. Before going to bed the child practices appropriate toileting behaviors, and then he or she is awakened each hour, praised for dryness, and given liquids. Wetting episodes are followed by the child's changing the bed and nightclothes and by practicing appropriate toileting. On subsequent nights parents direct these procedures, as well as positively reinforce the child on the day following any dry night. After seven consecutive dry nights the alarm is removed, but cleanliness training and toileting practice are provided if morning bed inspection reveals a wet bed. To date, evaluations of the method indicate that it can help a great majority of children, with a short period of training (Griffiths, Meldrum, and McWilliam, 1982).

Hyperactivity. Behavior modification and medication are the most common treatments of hyperactivity. Various kinds of behavior modification strategies are used, but positive reinforcement by teachers and parents is the predominant approach. Families are trained in observation and management techniques aimed at reducing aggression, irritability, and noncompliance in the home (O'Leary and Pelham, 1978). For example, in one study both teachers and parents were extensively involved in observing the child's behavior. Positive reinforcers and punishment for inappropriate behavior were controlled by the parents, who had ongoing contact with the therapists during the eight-week treatment (Git-telman, Abikoff, Pollack, Klein, Katz, and Mattes, 1980).

The use of medication to alleviate hyperactivity is based on the assumption that some nervous system dysfunction underlies the condition. Stimulant drugs such as Ritalin, Dexedrine, Benzedrine, and Cylert are most commonly used. On the surface, stimulant drugs would seem to be inappropriate for hyperactive children. As it turns out, they generally have a paradoxical effect in that they calm behavior rather than excite it. No satisfactory explanation exists for this strange effect.

Stimulants provide at least short-term help to many children (Abikoff and Gittelman, 1985). The following improvements have been recorded: reduced aggression and impulsivity, increased sustained attention, improved short-term memory, improved performance of rote-learning and fine motor tasks, and increased goal-directed behavior (Weiss, 1979). Stimulants apparently increase attention and decrease impulsivity, which in turn improve learning, perception, and motor ability. However, there is little evidence that stimulants improve academic performance (Hechtman, Weiss, and Perlman, 1984). Moreover, research points to other failures of medication and to possible disadvantages.

Perhaps as many as 35 percent of hyperactive children do not respond to stimulant medication. Negative side effects, such as short-term anorexia, nausea, insomnia, and headaches, sometimes occur. There is also a need to monitor possible retardation of physical growth and increases in heart rate and blood pressure (Hechtman et al., 1984). Finally, the long-term effects are disappointing. Follow-up research tends to show that hyperactive children, both treated and untreated, continue to display educational, work, and social difficulties into adolescence and young adulthood.

Infantile Autism.   Although autism is extremely difficult to treat, some success has been achieved with learning procedures and a programmatic approach.

Notable in this area is the work of O. Ivar Lovaas and his associates (Lovaas, 1968; Stevens-Long and Lovaas, 1974). These researchers found that self-destructive action is reduced by isolating the children, echolalic speech is decreased by nonattention, and normal speech is gradually shaped by food rewards for imitation of the experimenter's verbalizations (Figure 13–8). Realizing that social reinforcement is the cornerstone for building and modifying behavior in the natural environment and that autistic children appear unresponsive to such reinforcement, Lovaas and his associates try to establish the importance of social rewards by pairing them with tangible ones (Lovaas, 1968). For example, when food reinforcement is presented for a particular act, it is paired with the word "good." Later, praise alone may become a reinforcer.

The use of highly structured behavioral tasks is embedded in TEACCH, a statewide program that began as a research project at the University of North Carolina (Schopler, Mesibov, and Barker, 1982).

FIGURE 13–8
The use of positive
reinforcement—food
and praise—is
helpful in the
shaping of
appropriate
behavior in autistic
children.
Photograph by Allan
Grant, by permission.

(TEACCH stands for Treatment and Education of Autistic and related Communications Handicapped Children.) TEACCH operates five regional centers and thirty-five classrooms located in the public schools. The program encourages and organizes cooperative efforts among parents, teachers, and therapists.

At the regional centers children receive individualized assessment that provides a basis for treatment. Classroom teaching is tailored to meet the child's needs. Teachers also instruct parents on home teaching programs. Parents are given training as co-therapists for their children, as well as counseling. Help is given to strengthen family adjustment and community support.

The effectiveness of TEACCH is evaluated in various ways. For example, autistic children who received highly structured operant conditioning sessions were compared to those who received nondirective and psychoanalytic play therapy. The structured approach was more effective in bringing about change in attention, affect, language, and bizarre behavior. Parental teaching skills have also been evaluated by rating mother-child interaction before treatment and two months later. Improvement was noted on all measures including organization of material, teaching pace, language use, behavior control, and atmosphere of enjoyment. When asked to evaluate TEACCH, parents rated it as extremely helpful in improving their children's behavior and in increasing their own understanding and feelings of competence. Thus, although autism continues to have negative consequences of varying degrees on youth and their families, TEACCH helps reduce the consequences.

Concern about behavioral disorders is reflected in two fundamental questions frequently asked of mental health professionals: How many young people show behavior disturbances? How likely is it that problem behaviors continue in later life?

Both questions are of enormous importance; they have implications for all youth and their families and thus for social policy regarding treatment and behavioral research. But they are not easy questions to answer.

One way to study prevalence is to survey cases that arise in clinics, hospitals, schools, and in the offices of various professional workers. This method is not without its weaknesses. Disorders are defined differently by various workers, and they may be based on differential expectations according to the socioeconomic class and sex of the children being surveyed. In addition, many go unreported altogether.

Another way to evaluate prevalence is to survey all children in a geographic area or a representative sample of the area. Although this procedure, known as an *epidemiological study*, also suffers from the just-described weaknesses, it does provide a rough estimate of what might be considered normal childhood problems that are judged tolerable or temporary.

Some general conclusions can be drawn from the different investigations (e.g., Anthony, 1970; Gould, Wunsch-Hitzig and Dohrenwend, 1981; Jenkins, Owen and Hart, 1984). First, severe disorders are relatively infrequent. For instance, mental retardation occurs in about 3 percent of the overall population, whereas infantile autism occurs in about .04 percent. Second, the prevalence of less severe problems in the general population is quite high. For example, 5 to 10 percent of all school-age children are diagnosed as hyperactive. Mothers typically report high frequencies of behavior disturbances in their children. In one study, mothers of a representative sample of all 6- to 12-year-olds in Buffalo, New York, reported that 49 percent of their youngsters were overactive, 48 percent lost their tempers twice weekly, 28 percent experienced nightmares, and 10 percent wet the bed (Lapouse and Monk, 1958). Third, age is associated with prevalence; the tendency is for problems to decline in school-age children and to increase somewhat in adolescence. As we have seen, the prevalence of specific disorders often varies with age. Some disorders appear more frequently in young children than in older children (e.g., bed wetting); some appear more frequently in adolescents than in young children (e.g. depression); some change with age (e.g., lying); and others vary little with age (e.g. autism).

Research has also provided detailed information about the likelihood of dysfunctions in the young persisting into the later years. Severe disorders, such as mental retardation and autism, often persist into adulthood, with or without treatment. Antisocial behaviors (aggression, truancy, vandalism) also show relatively high continuity (Robins, 1966, 1974), and some individuals diagnosed as hyperactive in childhood have educational, work, and social problems as adults. Nevertheless, a good deal of instability also has been noted. Many adolescents who commit acts of aggression and theft become well-adjusted adults. And children judged to be shy, withdrawn, or inhibited are typically no more likely to display maladapted behavior in later life than are children judged "normal" (Kohlberg, LaCrosse, and Ricks, 1972).

Still, the link between earlier occurring and later occurring behavioral dysfunctions is probably extremely complex. To take the example of depression: children diagnosed as depressives are not likely to be so diagnosed in adulthood, and when adult depressives had psychiatric disturbances as children, the disturbances generally had not been depressions. However, the *combination* of poor peer relationships, conduct disorders, and emotional disturbance in childhood does predict adult depression. Sroufe and Rutter (1984) suggest that the link between early and later behavior in this case depends on childrens' displaying general age-related malfunctioning (as shown by poor peer relationships and conduct problems) along with emotional problems. They argue that only by better understanding the general signs of maladjustment *at specific ages* can we hope to predict later disorders from earlier disorders. This task would be sizable, but the reward enormous. By pinpointing the predictors of later disturbances, we would have early indicators for interventions.

SUMMARY

1. Behavioral disorders of the young are receiving much attention today, but only in this century have they been extensively studied. Developmental psychologists have only recently joined this effort, although the concept of development has been important in defining behavioral disorders.

2. All behavioral dysfunctions are abnormal or atypical in that they are deviations from normal development. Deviation may be apparent in the rate of growth or in the frequency, intensity, duration, quality, or underlying processes of behaviors. Boys are at greater risk for behavioral dysfunction than girls. However, the causes of most behavioral disorders are still to be clarified.

3. Children commonly have some difficulties surrounding habits of elimination and eating, which can affect their health and social relationships. *Enuresis* and *encopresis* (inappropriate bladder and bowel elimination) are defined in terms of developmental norms.

4. The obese child probably suffers from social adversity, although psychological maladjustment is not inevitable. Obese children appear to eat faster than nonobese children, and a lack of self-control may be involved in eating patterns. Obese children may also be less physically active. Among the several biological theories are those that focus on set point, the importance of fat cells, and cell metabolism. Learning of poor eating habits is also widely recognized as a possible cause of obesity.

5. Anorexia nervosa is seen primarily in adolescent girls and is characterized by a refusal to eat, by excessive thinness, disturbed body image, amenorrhea and other medical disturbance, and

perhaps bizarre eating habits. The anorexic girl is often well behaved, conscientious, somewhat introverted, and perfectionistic. The psychodynamic view focuses on disturbed sexuality, guilt, aggression, or the mother-child relationship. Family theories hypothesize that disturbance in family relationships underlies anorexia. Social learning theory emphasizes fear of overweight and family relationships.

6. Excessive fears and depression are among the emotional disturbances found in children and adolescents. Parental and self-reports reveal many specific fears that change in content with age and often disappear spontaneously.

7. *Phobias* are excessive and unrealistic fears that require treatment. Temperament and learning experiences may be the basis of phobias. In *school phobia*, worries about school, an excessively dependent parent-child relationship, and reinforcement for school refusal are viewed as likely causes.

8. Mood and bodily disturbances and depressive cognitions are the hallmarks of *depression*, which is difficult to assess in the young. Disagreement exists over the concept of masked depression and whether depression is possible in young children.

9. *Suicidal behavior* is related to depression, but not inevitably so. Suicide is rare in children but increases with age. Studies of suicidal children and adolescents reveal depression, anger, low self-esteem, problems in the family, and social isolation. Suicidal behavior is often considered to be a cry for help.

10. About 5 to 10 percent of elementary school children are diagnosed as *hyperactive*. Overactivity, impulsiveness, and attention deficits are the primary manifestations of this disorder. Many hyperactive children also exhibit disturbance in conduct and academic deficiencies. Nervous system dysfunctions has long been suspected as a cause of hyperactivity, and some support exists for this proposition. Environmental hypotheses are also being explored: lead exposure, diet, and the role of learning.

11. *Infantile autism* is characterized by social isolation, language disturbance, a desire for sameness in the environment, and stereotypic, bizarre behaviors. *Childhood schizophrenia* is characterized by disturbances in speech, motor functioning, posture, personality, and contact with reality. Biological causes seem central in both these disorders.

12. Treatment of youth is approached in various ways, but it always requires special sensitivities. Interventions can be enhanced or limited by developmental status and processes. *Psychoanalytic therapy* emphasizes intrapsychic conflicts; *nondirective play therapy* focuses on the child's capacity for psychological health; *family therapy* assumes that the family is a critical component of the child's behavior and treatment; *behavior modification* views the opportunity for new learning as central to therapy.

Summary

13. An issue that has implications for treatment and social policy is the prevalence of behavioral problems, which can be studied in clinic populations or in the population at large (epidemiological studies). Severe disorders are uncommon; less severe disorders appear much more frequently.

14. Specific disorders are age related, and a general tendency exists for problems to decrease in childhood and increase in adolescence. Research shows that some dysfunctions persist into adulthood, but many do not.

14 THE ROAD TO MATURITY

Until quite recently, most theory and research in developmental psychology focused on infancy and childhood. Now developmentalists agree that the end of childhood is only one milestone in human development.

Here we will consider four overlapping issues that are encountered repeatedly throughout life: (1) identity formation; (2) occupational choice and change; (3) romance, marriage, and family life; and (4) biological aging and mortality. Our discussion begins with the central issue of any individual's life—personal identity formation.

IDENTITY FORMATION

If asked "Who are you?" or "Will you tell us about yourself?" most of us would be able to provide descriptions of ourselves. We would surely identify our sex, probably our age, and perhaps some physical attributes such as height and eye color. We would describe our relationships, the kind of work we do, our beliefs and expectations, and our social and psychological characteristics. One way or the other we would have little difficulty in answering the question, because we long ago began to acquire a sense of self—that is, an identity or self-concept.

Identity formation has long interested philosophers, but Erik Erikson has been foremost among psychologists in focusing on it. The word *identity* means sameness, oneness, or the distinguishing attribute of an individual's personality (Webster's New Collegiate Dictionary, 1973). According to Erikson, identity is characterized by the "actually attained but forever to-be-revised sense of the reality of the self within social reality" (1968, p. 211). It is a subjective sense of continuity and sameness. A lifelong process, identity formation begins in childhood and is considered a vital step during adolescence.

The Self in Childhood

The most consistent finding about identity formation in childhood is a shift in the basis of sense of self—from concrete physical attributes, material possessions, and activities to more abstract social characteristics, thoughts, and emotions (Harter, 1983). Four-year-olds tend to distinguish themselves from others according to their curly hair, the bike they own, or the games they play. Activities are especially important for preschoolers. By the time children are 8 or 9 years of age, they distinguish the physical self from the mental self. Now one is different from others not just because one looks different, but because one has distinct feelings and thoughts. The basic nature of the self becomes more internal—more psychological. One account of this transformation is offered by Selman (1980, cited in Damon and Hart, 1982).

According to Selman, the young child initially is unaware of psychological experience as separate from physical action and attributes. Desires, preferences, and choices are based on physical functioning. As one child put it: "If I say that I don't want to see a puppy ever again, then I really won't ever want to" (1982, p. 852). The volitional self for this child is connected to the physical action of speech. By about age 6, children understand that inner experience is not the same as outer experience, but they believe that inner and outer experience are consistent. By approximately age 8, children realize that inner experience may not be consistent with external action. This is a significant change. Children now can consciously determine when and to what extent inner experience will match outer behavior. They are able consciously to deceive or put on facades. More important, they come to a fuller appreciation of the private, subjective part of the self.

Guardo and Bohan (1971) studied the subjective "I" in 6- to 9-year-olds. They proposed that a subjective sense of self involves the person being aware that he or she is "one being with a unique identity who has been, is, and will be a male (or female) human separate from and entirely like no other" (p. 1911). Such awareness was expected to change as cognitive ability developed. Guardo and Bohan interviewed children about four dimensions of identity. Table 14–1 defines the dimensions and the primary interview questions. In addition, children were asked why they thought as they did. The results showed that 6- and 7-year-olds viewed themselves as distinct sexual, human individuals—mostly on the basis of physical appearance and behavioral abilities. Continuity with the future was based mainly on their continuing to have the same name. Continuity with the past was confusing for the 6-year-olds but better recognized by 7-year-olds.

Children of 8 and 9 based their identity on personalized attitudes and feelings, as well as on physical appearance and behavior. Their comments reflected the abstract idea of being a singular and unique human connected to past and future. And these older children perceived that given certain unlikely conditions, one's identity had other possibilities. For example, in responding to the question about individuality, one boy said that change " . . . is not possible. . . . I don't know. . . . Well if there was a machine that you could do it with, it would be possible (p. 1971)." As the researchers note, this kind of thinking is consistent with Piaget's conceptualization of the child at the concrete operational level. At this level, children are able to consider possibilities that are tied to the con-

---

TABLE 14–1
Dimensions of the Self and Interview Procedure in the Guardo and Bohan Study

Dimension	Procedure
Humanity: awareness of distinctly human potential and experience.	Children were asked whether they could assume the identity of a pet animal.
Sexuality: sense of one's own maleness or femaleness.	Children were asked whether they could assume the identity of an opposite-sex sibling or peer they had named.
Individuality: awareness of being singular and unique.	Children were asked whether they could assume the identity of a same-sex sibling or peer they had named.
Continuity: experience of being continuous with what one was in the past and will be in the future.	Children were asked how long they had been the boy or girl they now were, whether they would be the same when they grow up, and the like.

crete world. The Guardo and Bohan investigation not only confirms the developmental shift to psychological attributes as an important basis for the sense of self, but also links the change to cognitive growth.

Another development occurring during childhood is particularly noteworthy—children's increasing perception of themselves as social beings. Even very young children identify themselves in terms of social group membership; that is, they are Boy Scouts or members of the gymnastic team or the like. The idea of social being grows in complexity. A central element is increased awareness of self in relation to other individuals. Children judge themselves according to what they observe or otherwise know about others, and these judgments become part of the self. Moreover, the self is shaped by what children believe others think of their abilities, appearance, and character. How they are perceived by others takes on new importance with the coming of adolescence.

Identity Formation in Adolescence

Identity formation is usually viewed as central in adolescent development (Marcia, 1979). In describing themselves, adolescents increasingly use abstract psychological and social terms. Perhaps even more striking, adolescents come to have a new respect for their ability to monitor, manipulate, and judge their thinking and actions (Harter, 1983). They now can think about the process of thought itself. Self-reflection and self-awareness may become acute, with rejection of previous concepts about the self and a search for a new identity that integrates elements from the past and the present.

Erikson's View. According to Erikson's stage theory, the crisis of adolescence is *identity versus role confusion*. The basis of the crisis lies not only in societal demands regarding impending adulthood, but also in the physical changes taking place. Previous trust in one's physical being and bodily functions can be reestablished only by a reevaluation of the self. Adolescents seek to discover who they will become.

How does the adolescent achieve this vital identity? Erikson suggests that our culture allows a moratorium during which the rapidly developing child has the opportunity to become integrated into society. A certain amount of experimentation is expected. The adolescent may indeed "try on" various commitments and identities much as one tries on new clothes before selecting the best fit. This "trying on" is manifested in many ways: endless examination with others of the self, vocations, ideologies; a rich fantasy life involving the taking of a variety of roles; identification with particular individuals, frequently involving hero worship. Choosing a vocation is particularly important. "Falling in love" can be a means to arrive at a definition of self by seeing oneself reflected in and gradually clarified through another (Erikson, 1963).

Most psychologists, whether or not they agree with Erikson's stage theory, agree on the importance of identity formation in adolescence. Erikson's formulations have generated considerable research during the last three decades.

The dominant approach was initiated by Marcia's conceptualization of *identity status* (Bourne, 1978a, 1978b; Marcia, 1980). Identity statuses are means of resolution for the identity crisis in late adolescence. They are examined by semistructured interviews about occupation and ideology (politics and religion). The presence or absence of a decision-making process (crisis) and degree of commitment to a position are determined. Marcia proposed that adolescents can be classified into four major statuses: achievement, moratorium, foreclosure, and diffusion. Table 14–2 defines the statuses and also provides a sketch of each. In general, achievement and moratorium have been considered the more advanced statuses.

If identity formation as Erikson views it is a developmental task, age changes in status would be anticipated. Studies with late adolescents have shown that over the college years those who initially experience identity diffusion in Erikson's sense gradually move toward more advanced levels of identity status (Adams and Fitch, 1982). Further identity development among college students is associated with the ability to enter into, and succeed in, intimate relationships. As personal identity development advances, so does the ability to enter into intimate relationships (Fitch and Adams, 1983). Meilman's (1979) cross-sectional study of males 12 to 24 years of age also showed a clear pattern reflecting an increase in achievement status and a decrease in foreclosure and moratorium statuses. Nevertheless, females often do not show this developmental pattern (Bourne, 1980). Moreover, two investigations that followed the same individuals for more than three years revealed that no identity status is necessarily stable (Bourne, 1978a). This, of course, fits

TABLE 14–2
Four Identity Statuses and Their Attributes

Achievement	Moratorium	Foreclosure	Diffusion
CRISIS HAS BEEN EXPERIENCED AND COMMITMENT MADE	ONGOING CRISIS: INDECISION AND STRUGGLE ABOUT ALTERNATIVES	STATIC POSITION WITH MAINTENANCE OF CHILDHOOD VALUES WITHOUT CRISIS	COMMITMENT LACKING: CRISIS MAY OR MAY NOT HAVE OCCURRED
Achievement oriented	High anxiety	High authoritarianism	Withdrawn; lack of intimate relationships
Socially adaptive	High conflict with authority	Close to parents	Somewhat conforming
High levels of intimacy in relationships	Low authoritarianism	High need for social approval	
High levels of moral reasoning, need for complexity, cultural sophistication.	Relate to parents with guilt and ambivalence	Low autonomy	
		Low anxiety	

Adapted from Bourne, 1978b.

with the idea that identity, at least for some people, is continually re-worked as new circumstances are met. Dissolution and reconstitution may indeed be crucial in adolescence, but they occur throughout life.

The Storm of Adolescence: Fact or Fiction?

Because adolescence involves a search for individual identity, and an implicit breaking away from the childhood notion of simply being a part of the family, many theorists have viewed it as a stormy time.

G. Stanley Hall, the founder of child study in the United States, was

455

among the first psychologists to investigate and speculate about adolescence in this way. He was particularly influential in popularizing the storm and stress view. Hall's ideas, presented in *Adolescence* (1904, 1905), depended heavily on evolutionary theory. Hall viewed development as occurring in stages that parallel the development of the human species. He speculated that from infancy to adolescence the child reflects human history—from its apelike ancestry through primitive cave dwelling, hunting, and fishing. Hall believed that adolescence represents the most recent stage of human development. And he also noted that enormous storm and stress occurred because of conflict between impulses such as sensitivity versus cruelty, selfishness versus altruism, and radicalism versus conservatism. Hall's idea of storm and stress is still followed by many contemporary theorists and by the general public as well (Grinder, 1978).

The Psychoanalytic View. Psychoanalytic theorists believe that upheaval is a necessary and even positive aspect of adolescent development (A. Freud, 1972). According to Freud, puberty is bound to bring disturbances. In fact, a lack of disturbance may actually be a sign that normal growth is off its course. Anna Freud spoke directly to this issue with these words:

> We know that the character structure of a child at the end of the latency period represents the outcome of long drawn-out conflicts between id and ego forces. The inner balance achieved . . . is preliminary only and precarious . . . [I]t has to be abandoned to allow adult sexuality to be integrated into the individual personality. The so-called adolescent upheavals are no more than the external indications that such internal adjustments are in progress. (1972, pp. 317–318)

The Social Learning View. Not all investigators are convinced that storm and stress must be a part of adolescence. Bandura (1964) has argued that the disturbance is greatly exaggerated and suggested that the following tendencies have led to overemphasizing the role of "storm and stress" in the lives of young people:

1. *Overinterpretation of adolescent nonconformity and fads.* Faddish group behavior does occur, but Bandura argues that adult behavior reflects it as well. In this respect, adolescents are not all that different.

2. *Mass-media sensationalism.* The adolescent of the media is portrayed as passing through a semidelinquent or neurotic phase, because that character seems so much more fascinating than the run-of-the-mill, relatively undisturbed adolescent.

3. *Overgeneralization from deviant youth.* Descriptions of adolescents often come from mental health professionals who actually come into contact with a biased sample.

4. *Overemphasis on biological determinants of sexual behavior.* This view paints the adolescent as in the throes of sudden erotic conflict, rather than under the more moderate influence of social learning variables that largely govern human sexuality.

Bandura also proposed that society's expectation that adolescents be rebellious, wild, and unpredictable increases the chance of just such outcomes. Although adolescence might not be completely problem free in any event, the cultural commitment to the storm and stress hypothesis becomes a self-fulfilling prophecy.

Development and Change in Adulthood

While adolescence is often considered the most important time of life for identity formation, the process of discovering and defining oneself continues through the entire life span. Erikson divided the adult years into three stages that describe issues crucial to identity during various periods of life. Table 14–3 shows these stages and also shows the four preceding stages, which were discussed in Chapter 4.

According to Erikson (1968), the young adult faces the crisis of trying to establish intimate, sharing relationships with others that involve personal commitment. Although these relationships include friendships of various sorts, establishing a special sexual bond is paramount. Such *intimacy* goes beyond an obsessive reduction of sexual tensions to mutual sexual experiences that regulate the differences between the sexes and between individuals. True intimacy means that one is willing to be at least partly defined by one's mate. Erikson notes that intimacy is not possible until the psychosocial conflict of the adolescent stage is resolved—that is, until a sense of identity is achieved. Only when a person is secure in the self can he or she risk fusion with another. Failure to develop intimacy results in what Erikson labels *isolation*, which is characterized by settling for stereotyped interpersonal relations.

In middle adulthood, it is necessary to extend the commitment to a wider range of people. The guidance and nurturance of the younger generation is the most obvious example of this extended commitment. Such

TABLE 14–3
Erik Erikson's Stages of Life

Chronological Age	Stage
Infancy	Basic trust vs. mistrust
1½-3 years (approximately)	Autonomy vs. shame, doubt
3-5½ years (approximately)	Initiative vs. guilt
5½-12 years (approximately)	Industry vs. inferiority
Adolescence	Identity vs. role confusion
Young adulthood	Intimacy vs. isolation
Adulthood	Generativity vs. stagnation
Maturity	Ego integrity vs. despair

generativity results in an enrichment of the individual through an expansion of interests and investment in others. When generativity is not achieved, a sense of *stagnation*, boredom, and impoverishment develops. Individuals who are stagnant may begin to indulge themselves as if they were children, and such self-concern may lead to their becoming physical or psychological invalids. Another very unfortunate result is that the next generation will not receive the guidance required for proper development.

Finally, in the later years, development focuses on the integration of life's experiences—on embracing these experiences as inevitable aspects of oneself—and on accepting an orderliness in life and death. In Erikson's words, *ego integrity* is:

> . . . the acceptance of one's one and only life cycle and of the people who have become significant to it as something that had to be and that, by necessity, permitted of no substitutions. It thus means a new and different love of one's parents, free of the wish that they should have been different, and an acceptance of the fact that one's life is one's own responsibility. It is a sense of comradeship with men and women of distant times and of different pursuits who have created orders and objects and sayings conveying human dignity and love. (1968, p. 139)

A meaningful old age, according to Erikson, encompasses an interest in what survives the self and in how the limitations of the self might be transcended. It tends to involve a detached but active concern with traditions and philosophy, bringing to life an accumulated knowledge and mature judgment. The lack of ego integrity in the later years is characterized by *despair* and disgust. There is despair that time is too short to try out alternative paths to integrity, that another life cannot be started. Despair often manifests itself in a chronic displeasure with institutions and with people.

Whereas Erikson's classic analysis is mainly theoretical, other psychologists have taken an empirical approach to identity development and change in adulthood. The contributions of Daniel J. Levinson and his colleagues are particularly enlightening.

Levinson and his coworkers (Levinson, Darrow, Klein, Levinson, and Braxton, 1974; Levinson, Darrow, Klein, Levinson, and McKee, 1978) conducted in-depth interviews with men of four occupational groups: blue- and white-collar workers in industry, business executives, academic biologists, and novelists. The researchers met with each man initially from ten to twenty hours and then interviewed the men again two years later. Central to the thinking of the investigators was the concept of the life structure: the ways in which the individual is plugged into society (roles, memberships, interests, styles of living, goals), as well as the personal meanings, fantasies, and values experienced by the individual.

From the interviews, Levinson and his colleagues were able to describe several developmental periods and transitions from early to mid-

TABLE 14—4
Male Development Periods during Early and Middle Adulthood, from Levinson et al.

Periods of Development	Ages
Leaving the Family Transition	16–18 to 20–24
effort to establish oneself independent of the family	
Getting Into the Adult World	early 20s to 28
a new home base	
exploration and commitment to adult roles	
fashioning an initial life structure	
Age Thirty Transition	28 to 30
reassessment of life structure	
Settling Down	early 30s to 38
establishing a stable niche	
making it: upward strivings	
becoming one's own man: giving up mentors	
emphasizing parts of the self and repressing others	
The Mid-Life Transition	38 to early 40s
reassessment of life structure	
Restabilization to Middle Adulthood	middle 40s

From Levinson, Darrow, Klein, Levinson, and Braxton, 1974.

dle adulthood (see Table 14–4). The life course they described consists of relatively stable periods interrupted by transitions that can be calm or chaotic. In either case, the transitions involve a crisis of reassessment of one's life and new commitments to the current structure or to a new structure. If a new life structure is chosen, dramatic shifts in occupation, life style, and marital status may occur.

The Midlife Transition. Of the five transitions found by Levinson and his colleagues, the midlife transition can be the most dramatic. This is how the investigators described it:

> The Mid-Life Transition occurs whether the individual succeeds or fails in his search for affirmation by society. At 38 he thinks that if he gains the deserved success, he'll be set. The answer is, he will not. . . . The central issue is not whether he succeeds or fails in achieving his goals. The issue, rather, is what to do with the *experience of disparity* between what he has gained in an inner sense from living within a particular structure and what he wants for himself. . . . To put it differently, it is not a matter of how many rewards one has obtained; it is a matter of the *goodness of fit between the life structure and the self*. (Levinson et al., 1974, p. 254)

Other theorists believe that the midlife transition consists of distinct phases. Cytrynbaum, Blum, Patrick, Stein, Wadner, and Wilk (1980) propose at least three phases in the midlife period. The first is *destructuring*, brought about by biological decline and recognition of the inevitability of

TABLE 14–5

Stages of the Midlife Transition

Precipitators of the Destructuring Process	Reassessment	Reintegration and Restructuring	Behavioral and Role Change
1. Biological change and decline	1. Reassessment of primary relationships and current identity and life structure	1. Testing in reality, and/or rehearsing in fantasy different visions of primary relations to men, women and children	1. Recommit, modify, or dramatically change behavior and/or relationship to primary family and/or work systems
2. Life-threatening illness	2. Emergence of real or fantasized transitional partners	2. Integration of the more creative forces in personality	2. Act on creating legacy, sense of community, mentoring, or other expression of generativity
3. Death and illness of significant others	3. Mourning and grieving losses; Oscillate between depression and elation	3. Realignment of defenses and consolidation of primary polarities, such as male-female and detructiveness-creativeness	
4. "Time left to live"			
5. Cultural and social structural transitions such as "empty nest," early retirement, status loss	4. Internal distress, reappearance of suppressed components of personality		
6. Confrontation with death, mortality, death anxiety	5. Reactivation of mother-son, mother-daughter separation/ individuation struggle		

Adapted from Cytrynbaum et al. (1980), 469. Copyright © 1980 by the American Psychological Association. Reprinted by permission of publisher and author.

personal death. The second is *reassessment*, which involves a shift in perspective and priorities. The third is *reintegration* and *restructuring* to produce a commitment to generativity in Erikson's sense (see Table 14–5).

Many factors may trigger movement into the midlife period, but there is a consensus that one of them is coming to grips with the fact of human mortality. Like it or not, somewhere between the ages of 35 and 50 each individual comes to the profound personal realization that he or she will grow old and die. A feeling of midlife transition is often triggered by the onset of a life-threatening illness (Blum, 1979). In addition to recognizing one's personal mortality, the midlife transition also involves recognition of biological limitations and health risks; restructuring of sexual identity and self-concept; reorientation to work, career, creativity, and achievement; and reassessment of primary relationships (Levinson et al. 1978).

OCCUPATIONAL CHOICE AND CHANGE

Few aspects of our lives are as important to us as our work careers. Beginning with early childhood, children are asked what they "want to be when they grow up." Until recently, most people chose an occupation somewhere between childhood and adolescence and then pursued that occupation for their entire working lives. And until recently, almost all men but only a minority of women had occupations outside the home. Today women are almost as likely as men to have some kind of career. For both sexes, occupational change is a serious possibility at least once during adulthood.

Vocational Choice

Ideally, each of us should have the opportunity to follow a vocation that suits our talents, interests, and personality. It is not a simple matter, even for an adult, to assess oneself adequately, to be aware of the wide range of vocations and how to prepare for them, and then to make a realistic "best" choice. For the adolescent, the task is even more difficult, and unfortunately the ideal is seldom achieved.

What factors determine vocational choice? It is possible to place them into several broad categories.

Society's Needs and Rewards. Society sets the limits within which any young person can realistically choose a vocation. Today there is considerably less opportunity for agricultural and unskilled workers because our society has become highly technical. Many recent Ph.D.s also are having trouble finding positions because society's needs in certain areas have shrunk or because too many people have prepared for them. On the other hand, an increasing need is anticipated for social service workers. Young people try to direct themselves toward areas in which they think the best job opportunities exist. Although this may be a reasonable

FIGURE 14–2
Important career decisions are typically made during adolescence. Mimi Forsyth, Monkmeyer.

approach, it is doubtful that employment opportunities can be projected accurately and completely for more than a few decades.

Aside from changing demands, other social determinants come into play. Individuals must meet the requirements of any job—that is, they must be trained for any one particular opening. Also, the amount of reward given by society—in terms of financial return, prestige, or freedom—determines which adolescents will enter certain vocations. In one study, involving 384 high school students who were college applicants, occupational preference was most heavily influenced by money and status (Pachter, 1978). Interestingly, these students were uncertain about future opportunities; many planned on preparing for two different lines of work at the same time.

Social Class and Attitudes. Vocational aspirations of adolescents have always been clearly related to their socioeconomic backgrounds, with youth from the higher classes selecting the more prestigious vocations (Conger and Petersea, 1984). This pattern is demonstrated by the results of a classic study in which adolescents from a small midwestern city listed their preferred future occupations. Of those categorized in Classes I and II, the higher social strata, 77 percent chose business and professional vocations, whereas only 7 percent of those in the lower social strata did so (Figure 14–3). Many of these adolescents were also undecided about their futures.

Although adolescents of various social classes may hold different values in regard to occupations, other reasons probably exist for this finding. Children often follow in their parents' footsteps simply because they are rewarded for doing so. Some lower-class youths may be discouraged from upward job mobility because it is threatening to the older generation. But for the most part, parents of *all* classes, including the poor, have high aspirations for their offspring. So the problem may be more that lower SES adolescents simply lack information about how to enter certain vocations, or they may consider certain choices unrealistic.

Sex Differences. There are sex differences in vocational selection. In fact, selection itself is considered far more important for males than for females. Occupational choice not only potentially defines the social status of the male and his family, but is considered part of his identity as a male and as a person. For many adolescent girls, choosing occupations means merely picking jobs that will serve as stopgaps until they settle down to homemaking. The high percentage of women in the workforce contradicts this notion—but many working women still do not view their occupations as central to their identities, despite the influence of the women's movement. For other women, occupational choice is very important. And in contrast to earlier times, many women today no longer prefer traditionally female occupations (Clemson, 1981).

Females also get less family support than males in financing professional educations. In a recent study of 183 families, 80 percent indicated

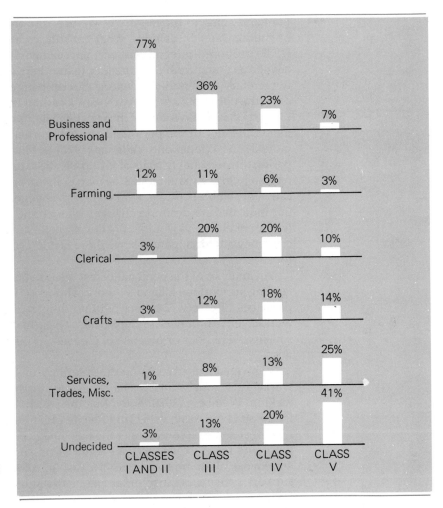

FIGURE 14–3
Percentage of adolescents of different socioeconomic classes selecting various occupational aspirations.
Adapted from K.C. Garrison (1956). *Psychology of Adolescence,* 5th ed., p. 418. Reprinted by permission of Prentice-Hall, Inc., Englewood Cliffs, New Jersey. Data of Garrison's text were taken from A. B. Hollingshead (1949) *Elmtown's Youth.* New York: John Wiley & Sons, Inc. Reproduced by permission of John Wiley & Sons, Inc.

they would give the career goals of their sons priority over the career goals of their daughters if finances were tight (Peterson, Rollins, Thomas, and Heaps, 1982).

Later Occupational Decisions

Occupation serves to define individuals in important ways: in social status, economic well-being, life style, and values. Psychologists and sociologists have studied occupational choice and adjustment, stages of occupational development, and social influences on occupational patterns. We will focus on three topics of special interest: midcareer changes, retirement, and multiple roles.

Midcareer Changes. Midcareer changes are becoming more common in our society. Some are due to a reassessment of life's purpose; some to an involuntary change of employment that is often caused by automation; and some to the reentry of women into the job market after years of childrearing. In defining what constitutes a career change, Holland (1973) proposed categories of occupational environments and described change as going from one category to another. The typist who advances to secretary does not experience a career change, but the executive who quits the corporate structure to open a restaurant certainly does.

Part of Holland's career theory suggests that when the job environment does not fit the personality of the worker, midcareer changes are more likely. Wiener and Vaitenas (1977) tested this hypothesis by comparing the personality traits of forty-five midcareer changers, all involved originally in occupations such as management and law, with sixty-six vocationally stable controls, who were also engaged in similar occupations but indicated no desire to change. Wiener and Vaitenas predicted that the career changers would score lower on personality tests measuring ascendancy and dominance, since these factors were considered necessary for success in such occupations.

An analysis of the personality test results confirmed their hypothesis, lending support to Holland's theory. Thomas (1977) described similar experiences of career changers who no longer felt compatible with their working environments, either because the initial matches of job and personality were poor or because of changes in their values and personalities.

We have focused so far on the voluntary midlife career changers, but workers also must adjust to change due to circumstances not of their own making. Weinberg (1970) noted that the psychological adjustment to automation is not easy, especially for the older worker. When the worker no longer senses a control over the machine because of its sophistication, he or she often experiences a feeling of personal worthlessness. Also, employees often are faced with the task of relocation without adequate support systems because of layoffs or the shutdown of industries. Retraining programs have been shown to offer some relief for displaced workers. Warr and Lovatt (1977) interviewed 1,655 ex-employees of a steel factory in Great Britain where a retraining program was offered. They found that the younger employees were more likely to make use of the retraining programs although the older workers had priority. Those who took the job retraining were more likely to find new employment, but the new jobs tended to pay less, particularly to the older workers.

Perhaps the most significant career change currently is that of women reentering the job market in midlife. In recent years the number of women in the paid labor force has increased dramatically. Often these women suffer from "job overload," which is the addition of the employee role to the homemaking role without benefit of good support systems. Such innovations as flexible work schedules, maternity leaves, and day care centers improve the situation of the working woman, but they are slow in coming. Furthermore, job choices for the reentering woman are often not adequately thought out and therefore lead to a sense of frustration.

Retirement. Retirement designates the period in life when one's role as a paid worker ceases. It is becoming an increasingly common role adjustment in our society. Retirement originated as a voluntary act or as a way for society to care for people unable to work, but it has become mandatory in many occupations. But this policy was never implemented at some of the highest occupational levels, such as those of Supreme Court justice and senator. The capable performance of individuals in their 70s and 80s holding these positions suggests that mandatory retirement policies are based more on the lack of enough jobs than on older people's ability to perform the work.

Retirement can be viewed from three perspectives: as a life event, as a process, or as the adopting of a new role. As an *event* retirement is momentary and usually not celebrated the way we celebrate noteworthy milestones such as marriage. Even when formally acknowledged, the ritual is likely to involve looking back rather than looking forward. From the *process* perspective, retirement begins with the first acknowledgment that one's employment will someday cease. Atchley (1972) reported that all but 10 percent of adults expect to retire, the majority before the age of 60. This is not to say that ending paid employment is considered the end of a fulfilling and productive life. As younger workers develop a realistic attitude toward retirement and are able to plan for it, the adjustment to "forced" leisure will probably be seen as a more positive experience (Glamser, 1976). Finally, retirement can be viewed as a *social role*. The retiree is expected to cease engaging in work and work-related roles while increasing time spent with family and friends in leisure and nonwork activities.

Peppers (1976) found that both the quality and quantity of leisure activity of the retired correlated positively with life satisfaction. Increases in social and physical activities had the strongest positive effect. The retired persons who preferred solitary or sedentary life styles had established those patterns well before the age of retirement, which suggests that retirement is a continuation of a life style, rather than an abrupt change.

Fillenbaum (1971) proposed that degree of job satisfaction would be inversely related to attitudes toward retirement. She found little to support this idea, however. It appeared instead that the acceptance of retirement as an integral part of the life cycle was a determinant of attitudes toward retirement. Interests beyond the work role also influenced retirement satisfaction. Fillenbaum commented: "Only when the job is of prime importance as the central organizing factor in a person's life should it affect . . . retirement attitude" (1971, p. 247).

Financial security is also a determinant of satisfaction. For example, Kutner, Fanshel, Togo, and Langner (1970) reported that one-half of those rated well-to-do, compared with less than one-fourth of those rated low in socioeconomic status, expressed a high degree of contentment. Kutner and his associates also found that, independent of income, elderly citizens who worked indicated higher morale than those who did not. Even though poor health and other factors may have contributed to the lower morale of those who were not employed, the evidence still suggests that, for those over 65, continuing to work in some capacity may entail rewards above and beyond financial gains.

Older women, a group that constitutes an expanding proportion of retirees, have been largely ignored by researchers (Jaslow, 1976). It has been assumed that the work role has less psychological significance for women. However, in sampling 2,398 women over the age of 65, Jaslow found that with the exception of the highest economic group, morale was highest for those currently employed, next highest for retirees, and lowest for women never having had paid employment. This study suggests the need for including women in research on work and retirement.

Multiple Roles and Job Satisfaction.   Until recently it was believed that being involved in more than one role caused strain and perhaps suffering (Goode, 1960). It has become clear, however, that multiple life roles are more likely to be a source of satisfaction than a source of stress. Barnett (1982), for example, has reported that working mothers of preschool children have a heightened sense of well-being compared to those who do not work outside the home. Both women and men who are married experience higher job satisfaction than those who are single or divorced (Crosby, 1982), regardless of the quality of the marriages (Bersoff and Crosby, 1984). Work life and personal life are closely related.

ROMANCE, MARRIAGE, AND FAMILY LIFE

Marriage, parenting, and family life are the most important aspects of most adults' lives. As they entered their senior years, the men in Terman's study of gifted men (Chapter 8) said a happy family life was the most important goal they had set for themselves. And in a survey of the quality of American life, U.S. adults rated marriage as the most important life domain, even ahead of health and income (Doherty and Jacobson, 1982). There is little doubt that sexuality plays a fundamental role in the formation and maintenance of these intimate relationships. So we begin our discussion with the awakening of sexual interests during adolescence.

Awakening of Sexual Interests

Sexual interest awakens about the time of puberty for both sexes, but the form it takes is quite different for boys and girls. For boys, adolescent sexuality begins between ages 14 and 16 with erotic dreams, often accompanied by the release of semen during sleep. During the day, the adolescent boy may find himself suddenly displaying an erection and fantasizing about sexual activities. For girls, adolescence is more likely to bring romantic fantasies. As one report puts it, "The sexual desire in males is centered clearly in the genitals, a factor which pushes them in an almost irresistible fashion. Although the physiological maturity of the girls is clearly evidenced by menarche, there is no corresponding immediate increase in sexual desire" (Turner and Helms, 1979, p. 264). For

FIGURE 14–4
Development of intimate relationships and sexuality are important in the process of achieving identity. David S. Strickler, Monkmeyer.

this reason, Turner and Helms conclude that whereas a boy's interest in girls is *erotic*, a girl's interest in boys is *romantic*. By later adolescence, boys too begin to experience romantic feelings. And for both sexes, the feeling of being in love is often the motivation and justification for sexual activities.

The first expressions of romantic and sexual interests usually take place at parties and involve experimentation with kissing, hugging, and light petting. By midadolescence a majority of youngsters have also gone on their first individual dates.

Imperfect though it may be, dating serves at least six functions:

1. Recreation, entertainment, social participation
2. Status seeking
3. Sexual gratification
4. Courtship and mate selection
5. Socialization of heterosexual interaction
6. Independence from adult norms (e.g., crossing social class lines)

Exactly how the dating process is functioning depends on age and individual needs and desires. But one thing is certain: Adolescent steps toward intimate relationships and sexuality are important in the process of achieving an identity.

Marriage and Family

Earlier in the text we discussed family influences on the child. Here we view the family from the vantage point of adulthood. Although adult life styles appear more variable now than they did in the past, most individuals still experience the "traditional" nuclear or extended family. In

467

fact, over 90 percent of all adults marry at some time in their lives, and most do so by age 25. Further, the great majority of these people have children, usually two as opposed to the three or four previous generations had (Glick, 1979).

In our culture we say that we marry for love; indeed, being in love appears to be a strong motivating force for marrying. But many other factors are involved in the selection of a spouse. As unromantic as it may be, proximity plays a role: We marry those who live nearby. In general, *homogamy* (the mating of like with like) is the rule with regard to age, social class, family background, religion, values, and perhaps even personality. Families undoubtedly encourage homogamy, feeling more comfortable with such potential family members and perhaps believing that "like with like" stands a better chance of survival. Finally, readiness for marriage is important. Such a feeling may be based on the age the individual thinks society prescribes for marriage; economic, educational, and occupational circumstances; and psychological needs. Historically women have had less power over marital selection than men (Troll, 1975). Some of the reasons are that women usually cannot directly initiate contact, are in greater supply, and have a shorter age range during which they are considered good candidates.

Marital Satisfaction.   Do adults like their marital experiences? The divorce rate in the United States certainly would lead us to answer a resounding "no" to this question. But the majority of divorced people remarry; one study estimated that 80 percent remarry and that 30 percent of all marriages are remarriages (Dean and Gurak, 1978). If Americans are disappointed in marriage, they apparently have not given up trying to find happiness in this relationship. Moreover, married people report

FIGURE 14–5
Learning to plan activities with one's mate is important as one develops the basis for family life.   Freda Leinwand, Monkmeyer.

being happier than divorced, widowed, or single people throughout their lives, and they also enjoy better physical and mental health than any of the other groups (Vernbrugge, 1979).

But the success and benefits of marriage depend on many factors. For example, early marriage is a hindrance to later development for most young people. Marrying in one's teens appears to lead to having more children, achieving less educationally and occupationally, and being more likely to divorce (Otto, 1979). Elder and Rockwell (1976) found that women who married under age 19 tended to experience "relative deprivation" throughout their lives, including inadequate material resources and an overwhelming child-care burden. Those who married after 22 tended to advance in social class, and this was true regardless of whether they had gone to college or ended their educations with high school. According to Hogan (1978), there is a typical sequence for young men: First finish school, then get a job, and then get married. Those who follow this sequence are more likely to have successful marriages and are less likely to divorce than those who follow another sequence (e.g., marrying before finishing school or getting a job).

Marital satisfaction also fluctuates over time. Several studies show a modest relationship between the family cycle and satisfaction (Lee, 1978). The example shown in Figure 14–6 indicates that the high satisfaction of the beginning years of marriage decreases as offspring grow older, and reaches the lowest point as the children approach adulthood and move out. As a couple is once again without children in the home,

FIGURE 14–6
Percentage of adults reporting that they are very satisfied according to stage of marriage.
Adapted from B. C. Rollins and H. Feldman (1970). Marital satisfaction over the family life cycle. *Journal of Marriage and the Family, 32,* 20–28. Copyrighted © 1970 by the National Council on Family Relations. Reprinted by permission.

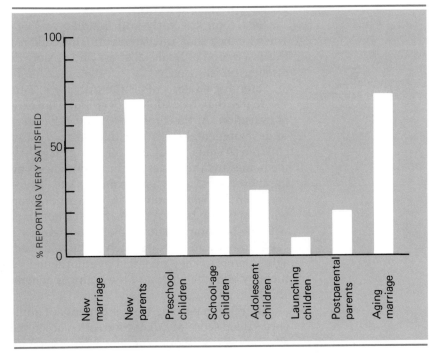

satisfaction gradually increases into the retirement years. This pattern is particularly interesting because, due to smaller family size, earlier departure of the last child from the home, and longer average life span, the length of the postparental years of marriage is increasing. Nevertheless, a word of caution is in order: Since virtually all the studies of marital satisfaction are cross-sectional, generational (cohort) effects cannot be ruled out. Furthermore, the results may be biased by the obvious fact that only couples who are still together are included in the study samples.

Stages of Parenting. Throughout early and middle adulthood the parental role usually dominates much of the activity and efforts of adults. Alpert and Richardson (1980), who explored parenting as a major task of adulthood, describe five stages. The first stage is the period before becoming parents. For couples today, this is a time of decision making. Young adults today are much more likely than those in previous generations to plan on combining parenting and occupational/career roles. It appears, however, that the decision to have children is often made without a clear notion of what being a parent involves.

The next stage, for those who do choose to be parents, is pregnancy. Pregnancy can be a time of stress for couples. The third stage is childbirth and the postpartum period. Some women experience a degree of depression shortly after childbirth. New fathers may often show signs of depression as they experience loss of attention from their wives and difficulty developing father/husband roles for themselves. What all this suggests is that having a new baby requires considerable adaptation by both parents (Weinberg, 1979), even though couples may indeed experience great joy in their newborns.

Next come the early and middle years of parenting, which begin when infancy ends and extend until the child reaches adolescence. Often this is a period of financial stress and anxiety (Rapoport, Rapoport, and Strelitz, 1977).

Parenting adolescents is the fifth stage. Parents experience stress to the degree that their adolescent children are experiencing stormy periods of transition. At this time there is what has been called an "interlocking of developmental tasks" for middle-aged parents and their adolescent children (Aldous, 1978). The offspring may show uncertainty about leaving home, and their quest for independence may cause friction. And during these years, anywhere from the late 30s to the middle 50s, couples are often heavily involved in occupational and civic responsibilities, which may also burden the marital relationship. Both parents must deal with the beginning signs of biological aging. At the same time, middle-aged women and men are often in the role of adult children to their own aging parents. They may feel overburdened by the demands made on them by both the older and the younger generations (Hess and Waring, 1978).

As children become truly independent adults, many parents experience a deep sense of satisfaction, often accompanied by relief. Occasionally, though, mothers experience depression in the form of the "empty nest syndrome'' as their children leave home after many years of dependence (Haskins, 1978).

Postparental Years. During the postparental years a couple must adjust to being a couple again. If large differences in interests and styles of functioning have occurred, the task may be difficult. Nevertheless, many advantages exist: freedom from constant concern about children, previously impossible privacy, increased leisure time, and lessening of financial strain. With health and wealth usually stable, the early postparental years hold the opportunity for new enjoyments. For some, these enjoyments include grandparenting. Neugarten (1978) has labeled retired postparental couples who are grandparents the *young-old*. Retirement itself, however, may be stressful, due in part to a growing concern for aging parents.

FIGURE 14–7
During the postparental years parents must come to view and deal with their children as adults. © Christa Armstrong. Rapho/Photo Researchers.

Marital and family ties are considered the primary source of happiness, fulfillment, companionship, and social involvement for the elderly. Lee (1978) examined the association between marital satisfaction and general morale in couples in their late 60s who had been married once. He found a significant correlation between the measures for both sexes, though the association was somewhat stronger for women. Given this association, it is fortunate that older couples assess their marriages positively and report improvement in them.

If a couple has children, it is probable that the family has become extended: Among those over 65, 94 percent are grandparents and 46 percent are great-grandparents (Shanas, 1980). Still, most elderly people live alone, and, in fact, this trend has been increasing. In 1975, only 18 percent of all elderly people who had children lived in the same household as one of their children. Thirty-four percent, however, lived apart from their children but very close to at least one of them. But whether or not the elderly live alone, they are still members of a family, they are generally engaged in its reciprocal helping and support patterns, and they play significant roles in the more subtle interactions involving affection and transmission of values (Troll, 1971).

Sexual Activity and Attitudes in Adulthood

The early adult years are a time of increasing sexual activity, but this pattern reverses itself in the middle 30s, and decline is gradual throughout the remainder of life (Martin, 1977). Table 14–6 indicates the frequency of sexual intercourse as reported by almost 500 men and women. Frequency does decrease with age, but men report more activity than women.

TABLE 14–6
Frequency of Sexual Intercourse Reported by Participants in a Cross-Sectional Study

Group	None	Once a Month	Once a Week	2–3 Times a Week	More Than 3 Times a Week
Men					
46–50	0	5	62	26	7
51–55	5	29	49	17	0
56–60	7	38	44	11	0
61–65	20	43	30	7	0
66–71	24	48	26	2	0
Total	12	34	41	12	1
Women					
46–50	14	26	39	21	0
51–55	20	41	32	5	2
56–60	42	27	25	4	2
61–65	61	29	5	5	0
66–71	73	16	11	0	0
Total	44	27	22	6	1

Source: "Sexual Behavior in Middle Life," by E. Pfeiffer, A Verwoerdt, and G. Davis, American Journal of Psychiatry, 1972, **128**, 84.

The Climacteric. The *climacteric* refers to the biological and psychic changes that accompany the termination of the reproductive period in the female and the normal lessening of sexual activity in the male (Rogers, 1979).

In males, the climacteric is not associated with dramatic change. Aging males do show some sexual performance changes: Erections are not attained as quickly and ejaculations are of less duration and force (Masters and Johnson, 1966). There have been reports of complaints of nervousness, irritability, depression, lack of concentration, and the like (Elias, Elias, and Elias, 1977). But for the most part males do not seem stressed by such symptoms in relation to a specific climacteric. Furthermore, the differential effects of lowered levels of sex hormones and psychosocial factors are not at all clear. Masters and Johnson (1966) include the following psychosocial factors in lessening male responsiveness:

1. Monotony associated with a long-standing sexual relationship that may involve lack of interest on the part of the female, loss of attractiveness of the female, and failure of the relationship to develop
2. Preoccupation with career
3. Physical or mental fatigue
4. Excessive alcohol consumption
5. Physical and mental dysfunction of either partner
6. Fear of failure to perform

In females the climacteric is commonly known as *menopause*. It is characterized by cessation of the menses, atrophy of the reproductive organs, thinning of the vaginal wall, and decreased vaginal lubrication during sexual stimulation. Hot flashes, insomnia, depression, and crying may occur. Many women do not report these symptoms, however. In one study of the objective records from a general health screening of 329 menopausal women, only 25 percent of the participants had experienced these traditional symptoms (Goodman, Stewart, and Gilbert, 1977). Menopause usually does not influence sexual activities; in one study, for example, 65 percent of the women said that menopause had no effect on their sexual relations (Neugarten, 1967).

The Later Years. Investigations of the elderly indicate that even though there may be a lessening of interest and activity in sexual relations, for many this period of life cannot be described as sexless. One investigation showed, for example, that of 149 men and women between the ages of 60 and 93 who were living with their spouses, 54 percent still engaged in sexual relations (Newman and Nichols, 1960). Studying individuals from the time they were 67 until they reached age 77, another team of researchers reported that their subjects showed no decline in interest in sex (Pfeiffer, Verwoerdt, and Wang, 1969). It is obvious that sexual relations can be important and pleasurable over most of the life span. Moreover, there is agreement that interest in sex during the later years, as well as the capacity to perform, depends on regularity of sexual activity and is correlated with sexual activity during the earlier years (Brecher, 1984).

One advantage for males is that generally the control of ejaculation is better in the 50- to 70-year-old age group than in the 20- to 40-year-old age group (Masters and Johnson, 1970). Often an older man does not have the specific drive to ejaculate more than every second or third time he has intercourse. With both partners accepting the fact that ejaculation on each occasion is not necessary, a more satisfactory sexual relationship may be maintained. Further, the delay in erection coincides with a delay in the lubrication of the vaginal area of an older female partner. Masters and Johnson (1970) suggest that if the male is encouraged to ejaculate on his own demand schedule and to have intercourse as it fits both partners' interests, the average married couple is capable of functioning sexually into their 80s, providing they both enjoy good health.

The fact that men report greater interest and participation in sexual activity (Pfeiffer, Verwoerdt and Davis, 1972) must be interpreted within the context of our times. Since women traditionally marry men older than themselves, they face periods of being without available sexual partners. In one study (Verwoerdt, Pfeiffer and Wang, 1969), 92 percent of unmarried women reported that sexual activity was continually absent and 45 percent reported that sexual interest was absent as well. Unmarried men did not respond in a similar fashion. Only 18 percent were sexually abstinent and only 15 percent reported no interest in sex. It is possible that future generations of older women will not experience the same sexual deprivation. Young women today are beginning to be more concerned with sexual fulfillment, and it is likely that this concern will continue throughout their lifetimes. Future studies of sexual behavior and attitudes in older adults may thus present a changing picture.

BIOLOGICAL AGING AND MORTALITY

Rhodes (1983) defines biological aging as all the "anatomical and physiological changes that occur with age" (p. 329). There is a general biological decline in all humans beginning at about age 30, but it is gradual and its rate and degree vary for the different organ systems. As shown in Figure 14–8, the speed of nerve conduction, for example, declines little; metabolic rate diminishes less than 20 percent between the ages of 30 and 90; but maximum breathing capacity is reduced to less than one-half of its full level. Markedly different patterns are also found for the various sensory systems. Hearing begins to decline relatively early, and the decline may be pronounced by age 60. On the other hand, taste and visual acuity remain quite constant until age 50 and then begin to decline (Corso, 1971). By this time the eyes frequently require more light, and the lenses have lost elasticity so that focusing on near objects is more difficult. Smell may show very little change across the life span (Rovee, Cohen, and Shlapack, 1975).

Individual differences are apparent in the decline of the biological systems. Most of us have probably observed that some elderly people biologically resemble those many years younger. Research substantiates this

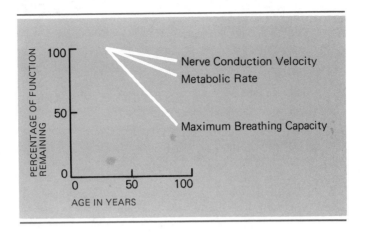

FIGURE 14–8
Loss of biological capacity with age varies across different functions. From D. Hershey (1974). *Lifespan and Factors Affecting It.* Courtesy Charles C. Thomas, Publisher, Springfield, Ill.

picture. For example, one investigation compared 71-year-old men with younger men and found few differences between a subgroup of very healthy old men and the younger men (Birren, Butler, Greenhouse, Sokoloff, and Yarrow, 1963).

In general, age brings an increasing number of long-term chronic illnesses: arteriosclerosis is a common example. In addition, by age 65 more than half of all Americans have some form of heart disease and an almost equal number are afflicted with arthritis. In contrast, the rate of short-term diseases decreases and is lower for those over 65 than for members of any other age group. In the course of living, individuals build up a large number of immunities that heighten their resistance to many acute diseases (Estes, 1969).

Throughout adulthood people become aware of and concerned about physical decline and increased health risks. From middle age onward, both sexes regret losing the beauty of youth and begin to focus on health. Here too, however, individual reactions differ to both the prospects and the reality of poor health. Moreover, older people are relatively optimistic.

When Shanas (1968) interviewed 2,500 senior citizens concerning their own estimates of their health, 52 percent stated that they were in good health, 30 percent said their health was fair, and only 18 percent indicated that they were in poor health. Fully 75 percent considered their own health better than that of their contemporaries. It is interesting, too, that no direct relationship exists between age and how the elderly evaluate their health—that is, as many 80-year-olds as 65-year-olds rate their health as good or fair. Apparently they take age norms into consideration, because infirmities that might lead individuals of 65 to declare their health poor result in very different conclusions in those over 80.

Theories of
Biological Aging

Ponce de Leon's pursuit of the fountain of youth, which resulted in the discovery of Florida in 1512, is just one reminder of a centuries-old attempt to "cheat death." Once people turned to magic; now they turn to science.

One approach to the study of aging is to examine the lives of people who have unusually long life spans. Alexander Leaf (1973) observed remote villages in Ecuador, West Pakistan, and the Soviet Union in which the population lived to older ages than people in the surrounding areas. Life in these villages was not identical, of course, but Leaf noted the strong possibility that genetic factors, a diet low in calories and fats, and physical activity are correlated with longevity. He also suggested the importance of psychological factors. People in these remote places were untouched by the stress and concern common in industrial societies. And the aged themselves had high social status and were expected to be active, contributing members of society.

Even though psychological variables are recognized as determinants of aging, there is enormous interest in biological factors. That different species have different life spans argues for the importance of biological factors. Individual cells multiply only to a finite number. In general, the longer the life span of the species, the greater the number of times its cells multiply (Marx, 1974). The role of genetic control is widely accepted: The offspring of parents with long life spans live longer than others (Leaf, 1973), and identical twins have more similar life spans than fraternal twins (Kallmann and Sander, 1949).

The exact processes of biological aging are now being investigated. One general proposal is that cells of the body that can multiply throughout the life span (e.g., white blood cells) increasingly undergo mutation or make errors in copying that cause them to be defective. Another idea is that cells that cannot multiply (e.g., neurons) wear out or become inefficient. Connective tissue undergoes change over time that may be important to aging. Other investigators suggest that the immune system comes to reject or attack parts of the body as well as foreign substances (Busse, 1977).

Whatever the mechanisms of aging, it does not seem likely that a fountain of youth will be discovered soon. Humans must contend with the fact that aging and decline in health have implications for virtually all areas of functioning, from motor ability to how they think about themselves.

Psychomotor
Slowing

There is little argument that with middle age comes a slowing of behavior. Psychomotor slowing has been studied with many tasks, but reaction time has been particularly popular. In a simple reaction time test some kind of stimulus is presented, such as a flash of light or a noise, and the individual is expected to respond as quickly as possible. Figure 14–10, which shows that reaction time to an auditory stimulus decreases during childhood and then gradually increases after age 30, represents the general psychomotor slowing that occurs during adulthood.

Slowing is one of the most general and significant changes in the behavior of older humans (and of older organisms in other species as well). It involves all aspects of perceptual, motor, and cognitive functioning (Salthouse and Kail, 1983). Slowing is noticeable by the early 30s and continues throughout adulthood into old age. Older adults who are free of illness, physically fit, and get regular exercise display less slowing than those who are less fit (Birren et al., 1980).

Muscular functions themselves seem to slow with age, but the speed

FIGURE 14–10
Reaction time to auditory stimuli in relation to age. From J. E. Birren (1964). *The Psychology of Aging.* Englewood Cliffs, N.J.: Prentice-Hall, Inc. Originally from Y. Koga and G. M. Morant, On the degree of association between reaction times in the case of different senses. *Biometrika*, 1923, **15**, 355–359.

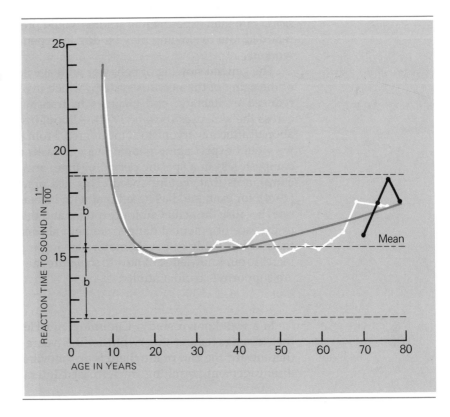

of the decisions that guide these movements and the time needed to monitor them are the principal causes for the slowing of reaction time. When movements are simple and can be prepared in advance, changes with age are relatively small. If preparation is not possible, or the movements are to be made rapidly, or are complex, there is a greater change with age, often at the points of decision making. The more complex the signals and responses, the more age change is apparent (Welford, 1977).

Decrements in reaction time are also sometimes associated with hypertension and poor cardiovascular functioning. Poor reaction time can, in fact, predict cardiovascular impairments (Abrahams and Birren, 1973). This suggests that older individuals who are physically fit should perform better on reaction time tasks than those less physically fit. Spirduso (1975) has confirmed that physical fitness is associated with faster responding among older people. Performance on four tasks was studied in sixty men classified as older or younger athletes or nonathletes. The older athletes were not only superior to the older nonathletes, but they also surpassed the young nonathletes on some of the tasks.

There is evidence too that practice can lead to improved response speed (Hoyer, Labouvie, and Baltes, 1973; Salthouse and Somberg, 1982). Hoyer and his associates, for example, demonstrated that response speed in elderly females 70 years old could be modified with reinforced or unreinforced practice. On-the-job practice and experience seem to make a difference too. Studies of on-the-job performance indicate that speed and accuracy improve in workers until ages 35 to 45, after which accuracy remains high and speed maintains itself or decreases, but at a *slower* rate than experimental studies would predict (Welford, 1977). This retarded rate of slowing may be due to experience on the part of older workers.

The general slowing of behavior with age is viewed as an expression of the aging of the nervous system, which involves the loss of neurons, reduced excitability, and changes in transmission of nerve impulses across the synapses (Birren, 1974). Although subject to individual variation, it affects everyone to some degree. From a functional point of view, we would expect aging people to avoid tasks that require speed, to accomplish less in a specific period of time, and to be less efficient in circumstances that require speed. This has practical implications. Birren (1974), for example, has noted that with increasing age the accident rate rises because the actual motor response and the ability to make decisions in the face of potential danger are both slowed. He has also suggested that further study of psychomotor slowing is necessary so that we can increase our knowledge of how to structure the environment in ways that are supportive to older adults.

The Final Years: Disengagement or Activity?

In a well-known study, Cumming and Henry (1961) set out to test their disengagement theory of the final years of life. The theory states that toward the end of life there is an "inevitable mutual withdrawal or disengagement, resulting in decreased interaction between the aging person and others in the social system . . ." (1961, p. 14). The investigators studied a sample of healthy, financially secure 50- to 90-year-olds over a period of several years and were able to trace a decline in interaction by examining such aspects as the number of social roles they held, the amount of time they spent with various other people, and their reactions to their own lives.

Several of the Cumming and Henry hypotheses or assumptions are interesting in what they suggest. They propose, for example, that disengagement involves not only the withdrawal from others (except for intimate kin), but also a preoccupation with the self. An important factor in this shift is a change in perception of time. The individual begins to measure life in terms of time from death, instead of time from birth. Many activities once considered important are put aside as having only *previous* value. The disengaged, according to Cumming and Henry, are tranquil as they gradually loosen or sever their ties. This withdrawal is a universal event that probably helps ease tensions between generations, because it means the "moving over" of the older generation out of the way of the younger.

Although there is little disagreement that people are involved in less social interaction as they become old, disengagement theory has not been well received. Some argue that the source of withdrawal is not the individuals' desires, but a society that pushes the elderly out of the mainstream. Furthermore, many behavioral scientists disagree with the notion that the disengaged person is content and tranquil. In short, it is not at all clear that inactivity and focus on the self is the ideal condition for the aged.

Several investigators have addressed these issues, and many have proposed that *activity* (interpersonal or otherwise), and not disengagement, is positively correlated with high morale. In general, the weight of the evidence seems to support this notion. Successful aging (as determined by self-report scales and ratings of old people in general) is associated with active daily pursuits (Schonfield, 1973). Health, however, remains an important variable, regardless of activity or nonactivity. Personality may also be important. Havighurst, Neugarten, and Tobin (1968) described several "types" of people, some of whom seem to be successful with disengagement. They have high self-concepts, are self-directed, and are interested in the world, although not particularly in its interpersonal aspects. Disengagement may also be satisfying to dependent and passive people. Clearly, it is a mistake to stereotype the elderly, to ignore individual needs and desires and force them into particular life patterns.

For example, there is considerable discussion about the living conditions of the aged in terms of the impact of living with peers versus living with younger people. Frequently, emphasis is placed on the value of contact with those of the younger generation. However, Rosow (1967) examined the relation between living circumstances and friendship patterns among 1,200 aged residents of Cleveland; he was especially interested in the effects on those over 65 of having few or many age peers

FIGURE 14–11
Conditions of life for elderly people vary remarkably in the United States today. Photos by Elizabeth Crews and Karen R. Preuss, Jeroboam and Paul S. Conklin, Monkmeyer.

living nearby. The question is an important one because loneliness is a significant problem among the elderly today. It is a product of loss of spouses and friends, together with feelings of isolation and social inactivity, and leads to anxiety and depression (Schultz and Moore, 1984).

Rosow's basic finding was that the greater the concentration of old people, the more friends each resident made. This result was in direct opposition to theories of social integration that stress the importance of older individuals living among younger ones. The density of senior citizens residing in the immediate area was particularly important to working-class individuals. Those of higher socioeconomic status were likely to have friends outside the neighborhood, but former blue-collar workers depended almost exclusively on those who lived nearby for companionship. The same tendency applied to those older than 75; they too drew very heavily on their age peers in the immediate neighborhood for friendship.

Nevertheless, individuals exhibited a wide range of attitudes concerning their social lives. Rosow identified four basic themes that seemed common to fairly large groups within the population. He labeled "cosmopolitan" the approximately 30 percent who had little contact with their neighbors and appeared content with the arrangement. The 20 percent who visited infrequently and desired more interpersonal stimulation were termed "isolated." The label "sociable" was applied to the 23 percent who indicated a high degree of social contact and who were satisfied with their social lives. The term "insatiable" was used for the 10 percent having a high level of contact and desiring more. It would seem, then, that a relatively active life with interpersonal relationships is best, but that some people enjoy a less active existence and that optimal conditions vary a good deal among individuals.

Facing the End of Life

A central fact of adulthood is that with each year after 30, it becomes increasingly likely that death will occur. Not only does death become more probable between ages 30 and 90, but the rate of increase of its probability also accelerates.

Causes of death can be categorized as *extrinsic* and *intrinsic*. Extrinsic causes are the most common and immediate ones. Heart disease, other vascular ailments, cancer, and accidents accounted for almost 75 percent of all deaths in 1980 (U.S. Bureau of the Census, 1983). Intrinsic causes are those involving certain general factors: Cells wear out and many do not reproduce themselves; the strength of bones and the elasticity of blood vessels decrease; overall resilience declines; injuries take longer to heal; and illnesses are more difficult to shake off. Evidence for the importance of these intrinsic factors has led some experts to conclude that further progress in increasing the life span may depend on finding a way to slow down the overall cycle.

Old age and death have not been favorite topics in our society, which values youth and activity. It is frequently pointed out that we have pushed the aged into lonely nursing homes and the dying into isolated hospital rooms. Recently the taboos and negative attitudes have weakened. In the mid-1950s psychology and other disciplines came to view death as an area for investigation (Kastenbaum and Costa, 1977). Perhaps our aging population, threats of wars, and a need to reexamine basic values have each played a part in encouraging this trend.

The Dying Process: Kübler-Ross's Work

Elisabeth Kübler-Ross (1969) has conducted interviews with terminally ill patients for many years. She has suggested that dying consists of five stages:

1. At first the patient *denies* impending death, perhaps thinking a mistake has been made in the diagnosis. The reality of death is isolated psychologically, and the individual may not want to talk about the seriousness of his or her condition.

2. *Anger and resentment* set in, however, when death as a real event is recognized. Patients may direct these reactions toward anyone

available—family, friends, or medical personnel—presumably because their own situation seems unfair in the face of others' well-being.

3. Some acceptance does occur, however, and the patient begins to *bargain,* to ask, as it were, for time off in the procession toward death. Thus, he or she may try to take up life's tasks or to plan to live long enough to attend a special event or complete a special task.

4. The next step involves *depression,* which occurs when illness intrudes upon bargaining. Depression may be a reactive type stemming from shame or guilt at being disfigured by illness, or a preparatory type. The latter has its basis in feelings of loss of the meaningful aspects of one's life—of loved ones, of the natural beauty of the world, of the ability to be independent.

5. Finally, though, death is *accepted* as inevitable. The person frequently is tired, unemotional, and seemingly just waiting for the last event of life.

Kübler-Ross believes that many terminally ill patients progress through all the stages. Some do not; a few, for example, may simply continue to deny that they will die.

Although Kübler-Ross has made an important contribution by calling attention to the dying process and to the need for compassionate support, how general her findings are will require further investigation. For example, she studied a particular group of people, those who were dying from terminal cancer. It may be that those who are not afflicted with terminal illnesses do not progress through these proposed stages.

Adjusting to Death

The tasks of facing old age and death probably begin relatively early, although they grow more central over time. Preschool children do not understand death as complete and final, but between the ages of 5 and 7 most achieve a basic understanding of what it means to die (Speece and Brent, 1984).

Adults pay increasing attention to death with advancing age (Cameron, Stewart, and Biber, 1973). But it is not clear, at least for the healthy aged, that such thoughts in any way reduce life's enjoyment or that they can be equated with *concern* about dying. Only 10 to 30 percent of the elderly express fear of death (Jeffers and Verwoerdt, 1969). Those expressing fear tend to lack a religious orientation and experience rejection and depression. More than death, older people fear prolonged illness; pain; loss of social role, self-determination, and dignity; and dependency. They worry about being a burden to others. Some view death in positive terms—as the time of meeting dead loved ones, of going home or back to God, or as a reward for living life well.

Death of a Spouse. Those whose spouses have just died are at a greater risk than their peers for both depression and physical illness and also have shortened life expectancies. There are, however, considerable individual differences that are not yet well understood. Reviewing the literature in this area, Stroebe and Stroebe (1983) observe: "Whereas some people recover from grief on the death of a partner relatively unscathed, for others bereavement is associated with extremely debilitating mental and physical effects that may persist for years" (p. 279).

Impending Death. How do the elderly adapt to death when it is near? Kastenbaum (1979) has observed that they draw upon the past in several ways:

1. *Validation* involves searching past experiences for successes. Recalling earlier success can reassure individuals that they are capable of being successful in the present. Such personal validation is of special importance when people in the immediate environment lack knowlege of an older person's past.

2. *Boundary setting* refers to determining the aspects of the past that might better be set aside as belonging only to the past. The house in which children were reared, the shops that were visited, the coworker of many years ago, and memories of a dead spouse must all be dealt with. Is it better to retain them in active memory and meaning—or to set them aside? Kastenbaum believes that whatever the decision, much of the coping effort of old people who are in transition or crisis concerns finding out the answer to this question. Moreover, it is an intellectually and emotionally demanding task.

3. *Replaying* refers to the retelling of highly selective, emotionally laden anecdotes and experiences. Young people too appear to replay favorite stories, but perhaps replaying increases with age partly because the wellspring of experience is deeper. Kastenbaum has noted that replaying seems dissociated from time:

   . . . we might compare replaying to a person reaching into a sort of personal juke-box where a few precious records or endless-reel tapes have been chosen from all the music heard over a lifetime. The date the recording was pressed hardly matters any more; it has some other quality that makes it important to the individual. (1979, p. 617)

   Replaying may enable the person to bear the lack of gratifications in the immediate environment. And it may serve as an alternative to being oriented to the future, where little except death exists.

Along these same lines, Butler (1964) has described the process of the *life review*, which consists of reminiscence of the past, particularly of unresolved conflicts. The life review is not an attempt to live in the past, but an effort to integrate experience and bring it into perspective. Butler has suggested that although reviewing life may not always be positive, it often facilitates an integration of personality and experience. It is perhaps partly through this process that individuals may, to recall Erikson's

"I Want to Go Home": A Very Old Lady Dies in Style* by Nancy Williams

Anna Grace Pequignot died in 1976, age ninety-six. Nancy Williams wrote this account of her mother's brief final illness and death in a letter to her daughter Christina, who was living overseas.

Dearest Chris,

What I want you to know surely about Grandma is that her death was a triumph of spirit. We wished so much that you had been there so that you could have seen that for yourself. The boys didn't stay at the hospital to be dutiful, they really wanted to be there; nor were any of us depressed at watching her die. She did it exactly the way she had lived, with style and humor and incredible courage. I want to describe those hours to you because you belonged there. If it's too much, darling, just read it in bits.

Mother had the sense to phone me at twelve-thirty on Sunday afternoon, saying in a rather burbly voice that she hadn't been able to dial my number but had had to ask the operator, and that she was the most confused person in Ann Arbor. So we went right over. She was sitting in her chair in the living room and did seem confused and uncomfortable. Her first Grandma-like act was to refuse to let me feed her soup and toast or to have a tray on her lap. After she had eaten she said she needed to go to the bathroom and, thank you, she did not need us to help her with that either.

When she was through she allowed us to help her to bed. Daddy and I have the feeling that from that moment she turned things over to God and to other people; she'd done all she could and now it was up to others. During the last month or so she had gradually and oh so reluctantly let go of the last of the duties that made life bearable to her: ironing for me, bringing over to Daddy her business matters, watering her plants. On the other hand, the preceding Friday night she had come over to supper all decked out in her shocking-pink sweater and skirt and matching hair ribbon, to help celebrate Rhys's being accepted into graduate school, and enjoyed her dry martini and shrimp salad and mince pie.

We phoned Dr. Payne to see if there was anything we could do to make Mother more comfortable; neither of us was particularly alarmed, feeling she was just fading a little more. We discussed asking her to come to our house but agreed to hang on as long as possible to everyone's desire to have her be in her own house, since Mother's independence was all-important to her. After Daddy had gone home to do some work, Mother said I should turn off the lights when I left, a typical energy-conserving remark. When I said I was staying, she protested.

I felt uneasy in the living room, so I sat beside her bed. She was able to talk, though with increasing difficulty, and her eyes were mostly closed. She said this prayer: "Dear Jesus, sweet Jesus, forgive me all my sins. Not my will, but thine be done. I'm not afraid to die. Dear God, let me go." Then she thanked Him for her children "and all the kind people who have helped me all my life." Later she seemed to think I'd said something about a "cardinal" when we'd talked of calling a priest. I said if we were going to try for a cardinal, we might as well shoot for the Pope. At which a nice smile went over her face.

Soon Dr. Payne arrived. After checking Mother he told me in his kind, plain way that she was very seriously ill, that she had congestive heart failure, probably renal failure as

---

*From N. Williams, " 'I Want to Go Home': A Very Old Lady Dies in Style," in R. Gross, B. Gross, and S. Seidman (eds.), *The New Old: Struggling for Decent Aging* (Garden City, N.Y.: Anchor Press/Doubleday, 1978).

well; quite possibly pneumonia. He added, "You know, she will be very mad at us if we bring her back." So I told him that we all wanted Mother to do what she most wanted now, to die as soon as possible, and that we wanted her to be comfortable. We decided that it wasn't feasible for me to try to care for her at home (her home), that nurses at the hospital would be able to move her, change her (renal failure), administer oxygen. After Dr. Payne had called an ambulance and left, I sat by Mother and she roused herself to say another prayer; "If I were to make my last statement, it would go like this. This is what it would be like. 'Dear Jesus, not my will but thine be done. Forgive me for my sins. And please, *please*, don't let me be too much trouble.'" At which, needless to say, I nearly dissolved, and kissed her and said she had never been a trouble. She looked at me and said, "Is this it?" I wish now I'd said that perhaps it was. I think I told her that I didn't know but I thought everything was going to be all right.

Rhys and young Lloyd arrived just before the ambulance. The five or six young men who came with the ambulance were just darling with Mother. They called her "Anna," which she might not have appreciated if she'd been her old self, one of them, "Anna dear," and they each described to her what they were about to do. I thought Mother by then did not hear or care much. I was wrong. She told the ambulance squad not to make too much commotion and alarm the other apartment dwellers, and not to use the siren, because there was enough noise pollution around already.

Then began the final eight hours. We got to the hospital at 6:25 P.M. Sunday, and Mother died at about one-fifty the next morning. As the four of us sat by Mother's bed, nurses administered oxygen and tried to make her a little more comfortable. She kept the plastic gizmo around her head and in her nostrils for an hour, maybe, then decided that was enough; every time any of us or a nurse would try to reinsert it, she would firmly, very firmly, remove it. About eight or so, Dr. Payne

came and said to forget it if she felt so strongly. Rhys holds that it wasn't just the discomfort, that she didn't want any delaying tactics.

One of the most wondrous moments was when the boys returned from making phone calls and I said, "Mother, Lloyd and Rhys are here now." She opened her eyes and said, "Thank you for coming to help me die." At which point Lloyd knelt down by her bed and kissed her hand and said, "I love you, Granny," and Rhys stood on the other side and held her other hand. And Mother smiled, quite fleetingly, but she smiled.

During Dr. Payne's visit, he sat by her bed and she tried to talk to him. What finally came out after laborious minutes was, "I'll give up smoking if. . . . " Dr. Payne just sat there quietly, his chin on the bedrail, waiting, not trying to interpret, just waiting. Mother never did finish her sentence, but Dr. Payne told me the next thing that he knew beyond a doubt was that what she was trying to say was, "I'll stop smoking if you don't stop me from dying." A long and fond admirer of my mother in all her stubborn independence, he observed that he didn't consider her offer a very good bargain under the circumstances.

Then there was the time when Mother opened her eyes and said, "Am I dead?" And I said, "Not yet, Mom." At which point she said, with fierce intensity, "Oh, God." The boys both thought she looked beautiful. I think they hadn't seen her hair down in a long time; it was indeed very long. They said she looked like an American Indian and were especially moved when she asked whether she was dead, because an old Indian man in the movie *Little Big Man* had said just those words and looked just like her when he was dying and the rain had fallen on his face and roused him. Rhys told Mother how pretty she looked. Again that fleeting smile went across her face, and she blew him two kisses, that familiar ironic gesture of hers when somebody paid her a compliment.

When we made these little jokes we were pleased when Mother understood and smiled. But after a while I think we all sensed that perhaps we were pulling her back to life in the same way as the oxygen and that we needed to let her go. Afterward Lloyd quoted Ram Dass to the effect that when a person is dying its important for him to know it's all right to let go, that he doesn't have to hang on.

A splendid episode: Mother had had the bedpan, but almost immediately afterward needed it again. She tried to tell us she wanted it by making the letter "p" with her index finger and thumb and the index finger of her other hand (either for "pot" or "pee"). When we didn't get it, she pointed to her crotch, and when we still didn't understand, she finally managed to really spit out, "P, as in Piss!" And when the nurses were putting the bedpan under her, she pulled down her hospital gown and whispered, "Modesty, you know." The boys loved that.

I guess the last little joke we had was when a nurse wiped Mother's lips with a cool cloth. She grimaced and drew back and my husband said quickly, "That's a dry martini, Bobby." The little smile appeared.

There isn't much more to tell. From time to time Mother would say, "Oh, God," as though pleading with him. At one point she said, "I want to go home." When I made some feeble explanation about the hospital's greater comforts, she shook her head impatiently. And I belatedly knew what home she was talking about. Hallelujah! We all held her hands and stroked her hair and said, "Hi, Granny." About midnight the nurses moved her to a private room. About one o'clock Daddy and the boys left, to get some sleep before work the next day. I lay down on some put-together chairs, relieved that Mother seemed to be really resting for the first time. I could hear a little breath once in a while. After a few minutes a nurse came in, checked Mother's pulse, and said, "I think she's gone."

I just stayed there a bit, saying good-by. When a very brisk young night nurse appeared, I said, "What will you do with my mother's body tonight?" She replied, "The eye man will be here in fifteen minutes to remove her cornea and then we'll put her in the cooler till morning." Can you imagine? She should be held for a witness, as my mother used to say. I just packed up my things, pulled the sheet up around Mother (saying to myself that it was so damn hot in that hospital she'd probably enjoy being in the cooler), and went out.

words, come to affirm their lives as the one and only life they could have had. Perhaps this leads to acceptance of and serenity toward what is yet to come—whether one believes it will be a true afterlife or a spiritual or physical union with the universe.

We think it is fitting to end this book with the story of one woman's death. In the eyes of her daughter, she "did it exactly the way she had lived, with style and humor and incredible courage" (Williams, 1978, p. 161).

SUMMARY

1. Four separable but overlapping issues are encountered repeatedly on the road to maturity: (1) identity formation; (2) occupational choice and change; (3) romance, marriage, and family life; and (4) biological aging and mortality.

2. According to Erikson, the major psychological crisis of adolescence is *identity verses role confusion.* To achieve identity adolescents enjoy a moratorium during which they can "try on"

various identities before selecting the one that best fits themselves.

3. At any particular time an adolescent may have any of four identity statuses: achievement, moratorium, foreclosure, or diffusion.

4. There is controversy about whether adolescents in search of identity invariably experience stormy periods. There is no doubt, though, that adolescence entails breaking away from some of the family ties of childhood and establishing closer involvement with the attitudes, values, and goals of peers.

5. Identity development does not end with the beginning of adulthood. Rather, it is a lifelong process. Erikson notes that the identity issues of adulthood are intimacy, generativity, and ego integrity. Levinson and his associates have found support for the belief that identity continues to develop and change in adulthood, and have called particular attention to the midlife transition, during which many individuals reassess and partially restructure their personal and vocational lives.

6. The first important occupational decisions are made during adolescence, shaped by such factors as society's needs and rewards, social class and attitudes, and gender. Important occupational decisions are also made later in life—midcareer changes. The final event in the occupational sphere is retirement, which proves more satisfactory when the individual enjoys good health, financial security, and gratifying leisure and recreational activities.

7. A happy family existence is for many the most important goal in life. Beginning with the sexual and romantic impulses of adolescence, most individuals choose to marry and have children. Marital happiness depends on many factors, but timing seems to be especially important.

8. Parenting is a central aspect of family life, and appears to go through five stages: (1) the decision to become parents; (2) pregnancy; (3) childbirth and the immediately ensuing period; (4) the early and middle years of childhood; and (5) parenting of adolescents. Thereafter, parents must adjust to the "empty nest" of the postparental years, learn to deal with their children as adults, and become "simply a couple again."

9. Sexual activity and interest gradually decline in later life. The decline is associated with the *climacteric*—the biological and psychic changes that accompany the termination of the reproductive period in the female and the normal middle-age lessening of sexual activity in the male.

10. Biological aging is a process that begins while one is still a young adult. Though debates continue as to the precise mechanisms of biological aging, all agree that there is a general slowing of psychomotor functions that extends to all aspects of perceptual, motor, and cognitive functioning.

11. Death, too, must be faced by all of us. According to Elisabeth Kübler-Ross, the dying process consists of five stages: denial, anger and resentment, bargaining, depression, and, finally, acceptance. In adjusting to death people often try retrospectively to validate their lives and to review and replay significant moments and experiences. How well a person adjusts to death depends very much on how well they have adjusted to life.

GLOSSARY

A

acceptance-rejection A dimension of parental behavior that refers to the respect and love, or lack of both of them, that parents feel for their children.

accommodation Piaget's term for the act of improving one's cognitive model of the world by adjusting it to external reality.

achievement Any action directed at gaining approval or avoiding disapproval from oneself or from others for competence in performance where public standards of excellence are applicable.

adaptation One of two functional invariants in Piaget's theory, which refers to the constant adjustments that occur between stimuli that are perceived and the mental structures used to interpret these stimuli.

afterbirth The placental membranes, which are discharged after the fetus has emerged from the uterus.

aggression Action that brings, or has the potential to cause, discomfort to someone else. The type of aggression a person displays and his or her ability to control such action change in important ways with age and experience.

allele Each member of a gene pair is called an allele.

altruism Unselfish action that is not motivated by self-interest.

amnion A thin membrane that forms a sac around the embryo.

androgyny Exhibiting both stereotypic masculine and feminine behaviors.

anoxia A lack of oxygen, occurring at birth if the umbilical cord fails to provide oxygen until the newborn begins to use his or her lungs.

assimilation Piaget's term for the interpretation of reality in terms of one's internal model of the world constructed from previous knowledge.

attachment The affectionate, reciprocal relationship that is formed between one individual and another, especially between a child and primary caretakers.

autosomes All of the chromosomes in humans except the sex chromosomes.

B

babbling Infant speech, common from 4 to 12 months of age, that consists of alternating vowel and consonant sounds.

behavioral instigation The process of urging or persuading someone to adopt a particular goal or follow a particular course of action.

behavior genetics The study of genetic influence on behavior.

breech position An abnormal birth position, with the fetus's buttocks emerging first instead of the normal head first delivery.

bulimia A behavioral disturbance characterized by binge eating, concern about not being able to stop eating voluntarily, self-induced vomiting and laxative use, depressed mood, and self-deprecating thoughts.

C

Caesarean section The surgical removal of the fetus through the uterine and abdominal walls.

canalization A genetic predisposition for the development of certain characteristics thought to be adaptive for a species. Such development is not easily interfered with by environmental factors.

case study The systematic description of the behavior of a single individual.

chorion The outer embryonic membrane that is associated with the formation of the placenta.

chromosome A threadlike structure in the cell nucleus that contains the genetic code in the form of DNA. Twenty-three pairs of chromosomes are found in all body cells except the gametes, which contain twenty-three single chromosomes.

circular reaction An event that occurs by chance and pleases an infant, who tries to repeat it.

classical conditioning A learning process whereby an individual begins to respond to a stimulus (CS) that had not previously elicited a response, as a result of repeated pairing with a stimulus (UCS) that does produce the response.

climacteric The biological and psychic changes that accompany the termination of the reproductive period in the female and the normal diminution of sexual activity in the male.

cohort effects Differences between age groups (cohorts) that result from chance environmental events rather than from significant developmental processes.

conception The union of ovum and sperm resulting in the creation of the zygote.

concordance In genetic research, similarity of individuals; for example, in hair color, intelligence, and schizophrenia.

configuration A map-like organization of the landmarks and routes in an environment.

continuum of caretaking casualty The relationship between the quality of the caretaking environment and the quality of the child's development.

continuum of reproductive casualty The relationship between degree of pregnancy and birth complications and degree of adverse developmental outcomes. Greater complications are associated with greater adversity.

correlation Pertains to the relationship between two or more factors or variables.

correlational method A method used to investigate the existing relationship between two or more events or variables. This method does not permit causal inferences to be drawn directly, and events or experiences are not manipulated.

critical period A very short span of time in the early life of an organism during which the organism may be especially sensitive to specific influence.

cross-sectional study A study of a group of individuals of various ages at a specific point in time to determine developmental changes.

cross-sequential designs Research designs that employ several different age groups at one time, but follow them longitudinally rather than relying on "one-shot" observations.

crystallized intelligence The ability to understand relationships, make judgments, and solve problems based on cultural information and skills.

cultural norms Standards of a culture by which behaviors are judged.

culture The full set of specific attitudes, behaviors, and products that characterize an identifiable group of people.

D

debriefing The entire postexperimental explanation given subjects about the nature and purpose of the study in which they have participated.

dependent variable A measurable aspect of the subject's behavior that may change as the independent variable is altered.

developmental norms The standards by which the development of skills, knowledge, and social behavior among children is judged.

differential attrition Differences in the number or characteristics of subjects who drop out of a study that are relevant to the treatment they received.

differentiation The progressive refinement of motor development, usually in reference to infants or young children.

discrimination The process by which a person learns to respond to a specific stimulus and not to other, similar ones.

dishabituation The recovery of a habituated response when a new stimulus is presented.

DNA (deoxyribonucleic acid) DNA carries genetic information in chromosomes from generation to generation.

dominant gene The dominant gene will display itself in an offspring when paired with a dissimilar form for a particular characteristic.

Down's syndrome A chromosomal aberration resulting in moderate to severe retardation. It occurs in about one in every 500–600 births. Most Down syndrome victims have an extra, free-floating #21 chromosome.

E

echolalia Abnormal repetition of the speech of others, commonly found in infantile autism and sometimes in childhood schizophrenia.

ego One of Freud's three structures of personality, the ego appears during the first year of life in response to the infant not being able to have everything he or she wants, and is the practical, rational component of personality.

egocentrism The preoperational child does not appreciate the fact that, literally and figuratively, others have different views of the world.

electra conflict In Freudian theory, the conflict experienced by girls during the phallic stage of development, when the child desires her father and fears her mother.

electroencephalogram A record of the electrical activity of the brain, obtained from electrodes placed on the scalp.

embryo In prenatal development, the name assigned to the developing organism from about the second to eighth week after conception.

empathy The ability to experience another person's feelings yourself.

encopresis Inappropriate defecation.

enculturation The process of teaching children all the rules and habits of the culture into which they were born.

enuresis An inability to control one's bladder functions; bedwetting.

epidemiological study The study of the frequency of a behavior (disorder) within a specific population; for example, of the frequency of hyperactivity in children.

epistemology Branch of philosophy that deals with the origin and nature of knowledge.

erythroblastosis A condition occurring when there is Rh incompatibility between a mother and her offspring. It is the actual destruction of the offspring's red blood cells by antibodies produced in the mother's system in reaction to the foreign protein (Rh factor) that is threatening her system.

ethology The study of animal behavior, often aimed at developing an understanding of social behavior. Its basic premise is that all animals, including humans, possess species-wide characteristics that are the foundation for the development of social behaviors.

experimental method A method of developmental research, it involves the manipulation of various treatments, circumstances, or events to which a person is exposed, allowing inferences as to causal relationships between such manipulations and subsequent behavior.

expressive language learning A style of learning language in the preschool years in which children's language consists of some names of objects and many phrases.

expressiveness A term referring to stereotypic feminine characteristics such as emotional, passive, dependent, and sensitive.

extinction The gradual diminution of a conditioned response, resulting in the eventual elimination of the response.

F

fetal alcohol syndrome The pattern of congenital malformation of the fetus due to daily consumption of three or more drinks by the mother during pregnancy. The greatest risk occurs during the twelfth to the eighteenth weeks of pregnancy and also during the last trimester.

fetus The name assigned to the organism created by the union of a sperm and an ovum from about the eighth week after conception until birth.

fixation Freud used this term to describe a child's inability to move from one stage of development to the next. He posited that frustration, overindulgence, or a combination of the two result in fixation.

fluid intelligence The capacity to perceive relationships and strategies; to have the capacity to deal with any problem.

fraternal (dizygotic) twins Twins resulting from two independent unions of ova and sperm that occur at about the same time. Fraternal twins are genetically no more alike than are nontwin siblings.

functional invariant A part of the intellect that, according to Piaget, is constant throughout development and consists of the twin processes of organization and adaptation.

G

gametes The reproductive cells; the ova in the female, the sperm in the male.

gender consistency The understanding that gender does not change over situations or according to personal wishes.

gender constancy Understanding of the concept of gender that consists of gender stability and gender consistency. When gender constancy is achieved, usually by six or seven years of age, gender identity is complete.

gender schemas Cognitive constructs or associations about femaleness and maleness that influence perception aand regulate behavior.

gender stability The understanding that gender does not change over time and that boys become men, and girls become women.

gene Genes, composed of DNA, are centrally involved in protein synthesis and act as blueprints for development.

generalization A situation in which one stimulus can be substituted for another and still produce the same response.

genotype The entire genetic endowment of an individual.

geriatrics The field of study that focuses on understanding and treating problems of the elderly.

gerontology The study of all facets of aging.

grammar The study of the rules followed in producing "permissible language constructions."

groupings The structures of thought in the concrete operational period of Piaget's theory.

H

habituation After repeated presentation of the same stimulus the initial reflexive response will diminish and eventually disappear. This adjustment to a stimulus is known as habituation.

handedness Also known as laterality, this term refers to the preference for using one hand over the other.

heterozygous   This term is used to describe gene pairs whose alleles are different.

hierarchic integration   As a result of differentiation, an infant is able to integrate individual actions into more complex and sophisticated patterns of behavior; this process is known as hierarchic integration.

homozygous   A term used to describe gene pairs whose alleles are the same.

hypothetical-deductive reasoning   Reasoning that starts with a fact or premise and leads to conclusions.

I

id   One of three structures of personality as set forth by Freud. He defined the id as a reservoir of primitive instincts and drives that is present at birth. It is the force that presses for immediate gratification of bodily needs and wants.

identical (monozygotic) twins   Twins resulting from one union of an ovum and sperm. The single zygote divides into two, with the new zygotes having identical genes.

identity   Sameness, oneness, or the distinguishing attribute of personality of an individual. A subjective sense of continuity and sameness.

imprinting   An innate, instinctual form of learning that takes place during a critical period in the individual's life. It often refers to the following response in animals.

inbreeding   Used in animal studies, it refers to the mating of related animals with the intent, over generations, of producing a "pure" strain in which the animals are genetically alike.

independent variable   In an experimental situation the independent variable is a condition created by the experimenter or a manipulation of the subject by the experimenter.

inductive reasoning   Reasoning that involves determining facts from different experiences.

information processing   An approach to cognitive development that emphasizes the similarities between human thinking and the processes of a modern computer.

informed consent   The ethical requirement that subjects have sufficient information about a research project to make an informed decision as to whether they choose to participate.

instrumentality   A term referring to stereotypic masculine characteristics such as aggressiveness, rationality, high activity, and independence.

intelligence quotient   (IQ) A number representing intellectual ability. The ratio of an individual's mental age to his or her chronological age, multiplied by 100. It is often calculated by statistical computation.

intersensory behavior   The interaction of two or more sensory systems.

introversion   Introversion and extroversion are directly opposite approaches to the social environment. An introvert is extremely shy and anxious in novel social situations and is always ready to withdraw from people. An extrovert is friendly, at ease among people, and is ready to seek out others in social situations.

J

juvenile delinquency   Acts committed by youth, under sixteen or eighteen years of age, that are not in keeping with the law.

K

Kleinfelter's syndrome   A chromosomal aberration found exclusively in phenotypic males. Such males generally have an additional X chromosome (although some have more than one additional X chromosome), and suffer from atypical sexual development and skeletomuscular abnormalities. Some are of below normal intelligence.

L

labor   The process by which the fetus is expelled from its mother's uterus, occurring within a few hours to a few weeks after lightening.

landmarks   Salient, distinctive objects in an environment.

learned helplessness   A sense of lack of control over one's environment that is learned through experiences in which one's behavior was ineffective.

learning   This term refers to all those processes by which an activity originates or is changed through reacting to an encountered situation.

lightening   The beginning of the biological preparation for birth. Toward the end of gestation the head of the fetus turns down, relieving the pressure against the mother's diaphragm.

longitudinal study   The process of observing or testing an individual or individuals at different points in their lives, noting stability and change in their behavior and characteristics over time.

long-term store   A permanent memory that contains a person's knowledge.

M

masked depression   Term referring to the idea that depression may be hidden by other behavioral disturbances, such as hyperactivity or antisocial actions.

maturation The changes that take place more or less inevitably in all normal members of a species so long as they are provided with an environment suitable to the species.

mediator Any mental event that intervenes between a stimulus and a response.

meiosis The specialized cell division of the reproductive cells that occurs during cell maturation resulting in the gametes having half of the number of chromosomes as other cells.

mental age (MA) An individual's mental age is equivalent to the chronological age of those whose performance he or she equals.

mental retardation Significantly subaverage general intellectual functioning existing concurrently with deficits in adaptive behavior.

meta-analysis A mathematical technique for combining the results of many research studies and drawing a weighted conclusion about group differences.

metamemory People's informal knowledge or intuitions about memory and themselves as memorizers.

mitosis Typical cell division in which chromosomes in each cell duplicate before the cell divides into two identical daughter cells.

mnemonics Memory strategies that are used to aid retention.

monitoring Checking one's ongoing intellectual acts to see if they are effective.

morphology The study of the formation of words.

motor program A mental representation of a motor sequence.

M space Information-processing capacity in Pascual-Leone's theory.

myelination Growth of the fatty tissue that surrounds nerves.

N

neonate The name given to a newborn from birth to about one month of age.

nuclear family The group of parents and siblings living in the same household.

O

observational learning Learning that results from viewing the behavior of others, presented both live and symbolically.

oedipal conflict In Freudian theory, the conflict experienced by boys during the phallic stage of development, when the child desires his mother and fears his father.

operant conditioning This type of learning focuses on the consequences (rewards or punishments) that follow behavior.

optimal level In Fischer's skill theory, a limit on information-processing capacity.

ordinality Knowledge of which of two numbers is larger.

ova Egg cells produced in the ovaries that combine with sperm to produce the zygote.

overextension An incorrect use of a word that indicates that the child's meaning of the word is broader than an adult's meaning.

P

penis envy In Freudian theory, the girl's desire to have a penis and the female tendency to be envious of males.

perception The integration of impulses from the different sense organs and the comparison of these impulses with previous input; the selection, organization, and modification of specific input by the brain.

period of concrete operations The third of Piaget's four stages of intellectual development.

period of formal operations The fourth of Piaget's four stages of intellectual development.

permissiveness-restrictiveness A dimension of parental behavior that describes the degree to which parents permit their offspring autonomy and freedom in their actions.

phenotype The outward manifestation of one's genetic makeup.

phobia Anxiety or fear of an object or situation, which is judged excessive and inappropriate.

phonemes Single sounds grouped together; the raw materials of speech.

placenta A structure that develops in the uterus following conception through which nutrients and wastes are exchanged between mother and fetus.

polygene inheritance Inheritance of a characteristic that is influenced by many genes.

postterm birth A birth is considered postterm when it occurs forty-two or more weeks into gestation.

preferential looking The preference an infant might exhibit for one object over another when two or more objects are presented. Preference is displayed by looking at one object and not the other, or by looking for a longer period of time at one than the other.

preformation An archaic theory that assumed the adult was preformed in the gametes.

premature A birth is considered premature when it occurs before thirty-eight weeks of gestation.

preoperational period The second of Piaget's four stages of intellectual development.

preparedness Refers to the idea that members of a species are genetically influenced to learn certain responses more readily than other responses.

pronoun reversal Abnormal speech pattern in which speakers refer to themselves as "you" or "she" or "he" and refer to others as "I" or "me." Found often in infantile autism.

psychosis Severely disturbed behavior in which distortions in the rate, timing, and sequence of many basic psychological processes are evident.

R

range of reaction The broadest possible expression of a genotype. The range of reaction may be broad or narrow, depending on the particular genotype and the environment.

recapitulation The belief that each individual's development (ontogeny) repeats the development of its species (phylogeny).

recast When adults repeat a young child's remark, but elaborate and make it grammatically correct.

recessive gene When dissimilar genes for a characteristic have been transmitted to an offspring, the recessive form will not be displayed. A recessive trait will only appear in an offspring if both parents have transmitted it.

referential language learning A style of learning language in the preschool years in which children's language consists almost entirely of names of objects.

reflex action Unlearned and automatic specific responses to specific stimulation.

reliability This term refers to the consistency of a test.

representative sample A group that accurately and proportionately displays the characteristics to which generalizations are to be made.

Rh factor This protein, named after the Rhesus monkey in which it was first discovered, is found in the blood and is inherited by 85 percent of the general population. If a mother and offspring display Rh incompatibility, complications can develop.

rhoGAM A substance that can prevent erythroblastosis formation in the mother.

role-taking ability The ability to be aware of another person's feelings and perspective.

routes Course leading from one landmark to another.

S

scheme For Piaget, a scheme is the mental structure underlying a sequence of behaviors.

schizophrenia A psychosis that is characterized by disturbances in reality relationships and concept formations, as well as affective, behavioral, and intellectual deficits. Schizophrenics may experience delusions and hallucinations, communicate in a disorganized way, and display inappropriate emotions.

secular growth trend Refers to the trend for people to be larger and to mature earlier than they did in former eras.

self-control Self-control has been characterized as one's ability to rise above the immediate pressures of a situation and to be able to avoid succumbing to an immediate impulse.

self-disclosure The process of communicating personal information about oneself to someone else.

semantic feature theory A theory of the acquisition of meaning in which children gradually acquire distinct features of a word's meaning.

semantics The study of the relationship of language to meaning.

sensation Sensation involves stimulation of the sensory receptors by physical energies from the internal and external environment.

sensory memory A memory store where information from the senses is held very briefly.

sensory-motor period The first of Piaget's four stages of intellectual development.

sex chromosomes The X and Y chromosomes. Human females have only X chromosomes; males have X and Y chromosomes.

sex (gender) role The behaviors and roles that society prescribes for the sexes.

sex (gender) typing The acquisition of gender identity and sex role.

sex-linked inheritance Inheritance of a characteristic that is influenced by genes on the sex chromosomes.

shaping The application of basic conditioning processes to achieve socialization goals.

short-term store A temporary, working memory of limited capacity.

social cognition Individuals' cognitive understanding of their own and others' social behavior, including its motives, meaning, and consequences.

socialization The processes by which individuals acquire the knowledge, skills, attitudes, and values of the society or subgroups of the society to which they belong.

social referencing Searching another's face or behavior for information about ambiguous environmental events.

society A group of people who live together and share common institutions, traditions, activities, behaviors, interests, beliefs, and values.

socioeconomic status (SES) This is indicated by occupation, income, and education; such characteristics define our stratified society.

standardized test A test in which the apparatus, procedure, and scoring have been fixed so that exactly the same test is given at different times and places.

stereotype Widely-held, agreed-on images and beliefs about certain groups of individuals; for example, about females and males.

superego The personality component, posited by Freud, emerging during the third or fourth year of life. It is the "moral agent," which develops as the child identifies with its same-sex parent and begins to absorb society's standards of right and wrong.

syntax The aspect of grammar that concerns itself with how words are combined into phrases and sentences.

T

temperament Behaviors such as activity level and introversion-extroversion that are viewed as relatively stable characteristics of a person. Temperament is considered by many to have biological roots.

teratology The name given to the study of malformations and other deviations from normal prenatal development.

Turner's syndrome Sex chromosome aberration occurring in phenotypic females. Most frequently the female has a single X chromosome (XO). Mental deficiencies occur in about 20 percent of the cases. Other abnormalities include a lack of ovarian tissue, failure to develop secondary sex characteristics, short stature, and deformity of the neck and forearm.

U

umbilical cord The "lifeline" comprised of arteries and veins that serves as a transport system between the developing child and his or her mother.

underextension An incorrect use of a word that indicates that the child's meaning of the word is more narrow than an adult's meaning.

V

validity The degree to which a test actually measures what it purports to measure.

visual acuity The relative ability of individuals to detect both small stimuli and small details of large visual patterns.

visual fixation Visual fixation is determined by whether or not an infant will look at an object presented to him or her, and has been used to measure whether or not the infant sees the stimulus.

Z

zygote The cell mass that is the result of the union of an ovum and a sperm.

REFERENCES

Abel, E. L. (1980). Fetal Alcohol Syndrome: Behavioral teratology. *Psychological Bulletin, 87,* 29–50.

Abikoff, H., & Gittelman, R. (1985). The normalizing effects of methylphenidate on the classroom behavior of ADDH children. *Journal of Abnormal Child Psychology, 13,* 33–44.

Abravanel, E. (1967). Developmental changes in the inter-sensory patterning of space. *Proceedings of the 75th Annual Convention of the American Psychological Association, 2,* 161–162.

Abravanel, E., & Sigafoos, A. D. (1984). Exploring the presence of imitation during early infancy. *Child Development, 55,* 381–392.

Acredolo, L. P. (1978). Development of spatial orientation in infancy. *Developmental Psychology, 14,* 224–234.

Acredolo, L. P. (1979). Laboratory versus home: The effect of environment on the 9-month-old infant's choice of spatial reference system. *Developmental Psychology, 15,* 666–667.

Acredolo, L., & Hake, J. L. (1982). Infant perception. In B. B. Wolman (Ed.), *Handbook of developmental psychology.* Englewood Cliffs, N.J.: Prentice-Hall.

Adams, G. R., & Fitch, S. A. (1982). Ego state and identity status development: A cross-sequential analysis. *Journal of Personality and Social Psychology, 43,* 574–583.

Adams, J. A. (1984). Learning of movement sequences. *Psychological Bulletin, 96,* 3–28.

Aiken, L. (1978). *Later life.* Philadelphia: W. B. Saunders.

Ainsworth, M. D. S. (1967). *Infancy in Uganda,* Baltimore: Johns Hopkins Press.

Ainsworth, M. D. S. (1973). The development of infant-mother attachment. In B. M. Caldwell and H. N. Riccinti (Eds.), *Review of child development research, Vol. 3.* Chicago: University of Chicago Press.

Ainsworth, M. D. S. (1977). Infant development and mother-infant interaction among Ganda and American families. In P. H. Leiderman, S. R. Tulkin, and A. Rosenfeld (Eds.), *Culture and infancy: Variations in the human experience.* New York: Academic Press.

Ainsworth, M. D. S., & Bell, S. M. (1974). Mother-infant interaction and the development of competence. In K. Connolly and J. Bruner (Eds.), *The growth of competence.* London: Academic Press.

Ainsworth, M. D. S., & Wittig, B. A. (1969). Attachment and exploratory behavior of one-year-olds in a strange situation. In B. M. Foss (Ed.), *Determinants of infant behavior.* London: Methuen.

Alberman, E. (1982). The epidemiology of congenital defects: A pragmatic approach. In M. Adinolfi, P. Benson, F. Giannelli, and M. Seller (Eds.), *Clinics in developmental medicine, No. 83. Paediatric research: A genetic approach.* Philadelphia: J. B. Lippincott.

Alberts, E., Kalverboer, A. F., & Hopkins, B. (1983). Mother-infant dialogue in the first days of life: an observational study during breast-feeding. *Journal of Child Psychology and Psychiatry, 24,* 145–161.

Aldous, J. (1978). *Family careers: Developmental change in families.* New York: Wiley.

Aleksandrowicz, M. K., & Aleksandrowicz, D. R. (1974). Obstetrical pain-relieving drugs as predictors of infant behavior variability. *Child Development, 45,* 935–945.

Allen, G. L. (1981). A developmental perspective on the effects of "subdividing" macrospatial experience. *Journal of Experimental Psychology: Human Learning and Memory, 7,* 120–132.

Allen, G. L., Kirasic, K. C., Siegel, A. W., & Herman, J. F. (1979). Developmental issues in cognitive mapping: The selection and utilization of environmental landmarks. *Child Development, 50,* 1062–1070.

Alley, T. R. (1983). Growth-produced changes in body shape and size as determinants of perceived age and adult caregiving. *Child Development, 54,* 241–248.

Alpert, J. L., & Richardson, M. S. (1980). Parenting. In L. Poon (Ed.), *Aging in the 1980s*. Washington, D.C.: American Psychological Association.

Amabile, T. M. (1983). *The social psychology of creativity*. New York: Springer-Verlag.

Anastasi, A. (1958). Heredity, environment, and the question of "How?" *Psychological Review, 65*, 197–208.

Anastasi, A. (1982). *Psychological testing* (5th ed.). New York: Macmillan.

Anders, T. F., Carskadon, M. A., & Dement, W. C. (1980). Sleep and sleepiness in children and adolescents. In I. Litt (Ed.), *Pediatric clinics of North America*, Vol. 27, No. 1.

Anooshian, L. J., Pascal, V. U., & McCreath, H. (1984). Problem mapping before problem solving: Young children's cognitive maps and search strategies in large-scale environments. *Child Development, 55*, 1820–1834.

Anooshian, L. J., & Siegel, A. W. (1985). From cognitive to procedural mapping. In C. J. Brainerd & M. Pressley (Eds.), *Basic processes in memory development*. New York: Springer-Verlag.

Anooshian, L. J., & Young, D. (1981). Developmental changes in cognitive maps of a familiar neighborhood. *Child Development, 52*, 341–348.

Anthony, E. J. (1957). An experimental approach to the psychopathology of childhood: Encopresis. *British Journal of Medical Psychology, 30*, 146–175.

Anthony, E. J. (1970). The behavior disorders of childhood. In P. H. Mussen (Ed.), *Carmichael's manual of child psychology*. Vol. 2. New York: John Wiley.

Appel, Y. H. (1977). Developmental differences in children's perception of maternal socialization behavior. *Child Development, 48*, 1689–1693.

Appleman, P. (Ed.). (1970). *Darwin, a Norton critical edition*. New York: W. W. Norton.

Arlin, P. K. (1975). Cognitive development in adulthood: A fifth stage? *Developmental Psychology, 11*, 602–606.

Aronson, E., & Rosenbloom, S. (1971). Space perception in early infancy: Perception within a common auditory-visual space. *Science, 172*, 1161–1163.

Ashcraft, M. H. (1982). The development of mental arithmetic: A chronometric approach. *Developmental Review, 2*, 212–236.

Asher, S. R., & Renshaw, P. D. (1981). Children without friends: Social knowledge and social-skill training. In S. R. Asher and J. M. Gottman (Eds.), *The development of children's friendships*. Cambridge: Cambridge University Press.

Ashton, B. G. (1967). *Genes, chromosomes and evolution*. London: Longsman, Green, & Co.

Aslin, R. N., Pisoni, D. B., & Jusczyk, P. (1983). Auditory development and speech perception in infancy. In M. M. Haith and J. J. Campos (Eds.), *Handbook of child psychology (Vol. 3)*. New York: Wiley.

Axline, V. M. (1947). *Play therapy*. Boston: Houghton Mifflin.

Ayllon, T., & Rosenbaum, M. S. (1977). The behavioral treatment of disruption and hyperactivity in school settings. In B. B. Lahey & A. E. Kazdin (Eds.), *Advances in clinical child psychology, Vol. 1*. New York: Plenum.

Azrin, N. H., Sneed, T. J., & Foxx, R. M. (1974). Dry Bed Training: Rapid elimination of childhood enuresis. *Behaviour Research and Therapy, 12*, 147–156.

Azrin, N. H., & Thienes, P. M. (1978). Rapid elimination of enuresis by intensive learning without a conditioning apparatus. *Behavior Therapy, 9*, 342–354.

Baldwin, A. L. (1967). *Theories of child development*. New York: John Wiley.

Ball, S. J. (1981). *Beachside comprehensive*. Cambridge, Eng.: Cambridge University Press.

Balla, D., & Zigler, E. (1979). Personality development in retarded persons. In N. R. Ellis (Ed.), *Handbook of mental deficiency*. Hillsdale, N.J.: Lawrence Erlbaum.

Bancroft, J., Axworthy, D., & Ratcliffe, S. (1982). The personality and psycho-sexual development of boys with 47XXY chromosome constitution. *Journal of Child Psychology and Psychiatry, 23*, 169–180.

Bandura, A. (1969). Social-learning theory of identificatory processes. In D. A. Goslin (Ed.). *Handbook of socialization theory and research*. Chicago: Rand McNally.

Bandura, A. (1977). *Social learning theory*. Englewood Cliffs, N.J.: Prentice-Hall.

Bandura, A. (1965). Influence of models' reinforcement contingencies on the acquisition of imitative responses. *Journal of Personality and Social Psychology, 1*, 589–595.

Bandura, A., & Schunk. D. H. (1981). Cultivating competence, self-efficacy, and intrinsic interest through proximal self-motivation. *Journal of Personality and Social Psychology, 41*, 586–598.

Banks, M. S., & Salapatek, P. (1983). Infant visual perception. In P. H. Mussen (Ed.), *Handbook of child psychology, Vol. 2*. New York: John Wiley.

Barden, R. C., Zelko, F. A., Duncan, S. W., & Masters, J. C. (1980). Children's consensual knowledge about the experimental determinants of emotion. *Journal of Personality and Social Psychology, 39*, 968–976.

Bardwick, J. M. (1979). *In transition*. New York: Holt, Rinehart and Winston.

Barenboim, C. (1977). Developmental changes in the interpersonal cognitive system from middle childhood to adolescence. *Child Development, 48,* 1467–1474.

Barkley, R. A. (1981). Hyperactivity. In E. J. Mash & L. G. Terdal (Eds.), *Behavioral assessment of childhood disorders.* New York: Guilford Press.

Barnett, M. A., Howard, J. A., Melton, E. M., & Dino, G. A. (1982). Effect of inducing sadness about self or other on helping behavior in high- and low-empathic children. *Child Development, 53,* 920–923.

Barnett, R. C. (1982). Multiple roles and well-being: A study of mothers of pre-school age children. *Psychology of Women Quarterly, 1,* 175–178.

Barron, F., & Harrington, D. M. (1981). Creativity, intelligence, and personality. *Annual Review of Psychology, 32,* 439–476.

Bates, E., Benigni, L., Bretherton, I., Camaioni, L., & Volterra, L. (1979). Cognition and communication from nine to thirteen months: Correlational findings. In E. Bates (Ed.), *The emergence of symbols: Cognition and communication in infancy.* New York: Academic Press.

Baumrind, D. (1975). *Early socialization and the discipline controversy.* Morristown, N.J.: General Learning Press.

Bauer, D. H. (1976). An exploratory study of developmental changes in children's fears. *Journal of Child Psychology and Psychiatry, 17,* 69–74.

Beck, A. T. (1967). *Depression: Clinical, experimental, and theoretical aspects.* New York: Harper & Row.

Beck, A. T. (1976). *Cognitive therapy and the emotional disorders.* New York: International Universities Press.

Bee, H. L., & Mitchell, S. K. (1984). *The developing person: a life-span approach.* New York: Harper & Row.

Beilin, H. (1965). Learning and operational convergence in logical thought development. *Journal of Experimental Child Psychology, 2,* 317–339.

Belmont, J. M., Butterfield, E. C., & Borkowski, J. G. (1978). Training retarded people to generalize memory methods across memory tasks. In M. M. Gruneberg, P. E. Morris, & R. N. Sykes (Eds.), *Practical aspects of memory.* New York: Academic Press.

Belsky, H. (1980). Child maltreatment: An ecological integration. *American Psychologist, 35,* 320–335.

Bem, S. L. (1974). The measurement of psychological androgyny. *Journal of Consulting and Clinical Psychology, 42,* 155–162.

Bem, S. L. (1981). Gender schema theory: a cognitive account of sex typing. *Psychological Review, 88,* 354–364.

Bem, S. L. & Lenney, E. (1976). Sex typing and the avoidance of cross-sex behavior. *Journal of Personality and Social Psychology, 33,* 48–54.

Bemis, K. M. (1978). Current approaches to the etiology and treatment of anorexia nervosa. *Psychological Bulletin, 85,* 593–617.

Benbow, C. P., & Stanley, J. C. (1980). Sex differences in mathematical ability; fact or artifact? *Science, 210,* 1262–1264.

Benbow, C. P., & Stanley, J. C. (1983). Sex differences in mathematical reasoning ability: more facts. *Science, 222,* 1029–1031.

Bender, L. Childhood schizophrenia. (1972). In S. I. Harrison & J. F. McDermott (Eds.), *Childhood psychopathology.* New York: International Universities Press.

Berg, B., and Kelly, R. (1979). The measured self-esteem of children from broken, rejected, and accepted families. *Journal of Divorce, 2,* 363–370.

Berkeley Planning Associates. (1977). *Evaluation of child abuse and neglect demonstration projects 1974–1977* (Vol. 2): *Final Report.* Berkeley: Author, December (NTIS No. PB–278 439).

Berko, J. (1958). The child's learning of English morphology. *Word, 14,* 150–177.

Berndt, T. J. (1982). The features and effects of friendship in early adolescence. *Child Development, 53,* 1447–1460.

Berndt, T. J. (1981). Relations between social cognition, nonsocial cognition, and social behavior: The case of friendship. In J. H. Flavell & L. D. Ross (Eds.), *Social cognitive development: Frontiers and possible futures.* Cambridge, Eng.: Cambridge University Press.

Berry, A. C. (1982). Changes in genetic counselling during the last 25 years. In M. Adinolfi, P. Benson, F. Giannelli, and M. Seller (Eds.), *Clinics in developmental medicine, No. 83. Paediatric research: A genetic approach.* Philadelphia: J. B. Lippincott.

Bersoff, D., & Crosby, F. (1984). Job satisfaction and family status. *Personality and Social Psychology Bulletin, 10,* 79–83.

Best, C. T., Hoffman, H., & Glanville, B. B. (1982). Development of infant ear asymmetries for speech and music. *Perception and Psychophysics, 31,* 75–85.

Best, D. L., Williams, J. E., Cloud, J. M., Davis, S. W., Robertson, L. S., Edwards, J. R., Giles, H., & Fowles, J. (1977). Development of sex-trait stereotypes among young children in the United States, England, and Ireland. *Child Development, 48,* 1375–1384.

Best, F. (1981). Changing sex roles and worklife flexibility. *Psychology of Women Quarterly, 6,* 55–71.

Bettelheim, B. (1967a). *The empty fortress.* New York: Free Press.

Bettelheim, B. (1967b, February 12). Where self begins. *New York Times.*

Biller, H. B. (1974). *Paternal deprivation.* Lexington, Mass.: Lexington Books, Heath.

Biller, H. B. (1982). Fatherhood: Implications for child and adult development. In B. Wolman (Ed.), *Handbook of developmental psychology.* Englewood Cliffs, N.J.: Prentice-Hall.

Birch, H. G., & Lefford, A. (1963). Intersensory development in children. *Monographs of the Society for Research in Child Development, 28,* Whole No. 89.

Birch, H. G., & Lefford, A. (1967). Visual differentiation, intersensory integration and voluntary motor control. *Monographs of the Society for Research in Child Development, 32,* Serial No. 110.

Birch, L. L., Marlin, D. W., & Rotter, J. (1984). Eating as the "means" activity in a contingency: Effects on young children's food preference. *Child Development, 55,* 431–439.

Birns, B. (1965). Individual differences in human neonates' responses to stimulation. *Child Development, 36,* 249–256.

Birns, B. (1976). The emergence and socialization of sex differences in the earliest years. *Merrill-Palmer Quarterly, 22,* 229–254.

Birren, J. E., Woods, A. M., & Williams, M. V. (1980). Behavioral slowing with age: Causes, organization, and consequences. In L. Poon (Ed.), *Aging in the 1980s.* Washington, D.C.: American Psychological Association.

Blasi, A. (1980). Bridging moral cognition and moral action: A critical review of the literature. *Psychological Bulletin, 88,* 1–45.

Blau, T. H. Torque and schizophrenic vulnerability. (1971). *American Psychologist, 32,* 997–1005.

Blehar, M. C., Lieberman, A. F., & Ainsworth, M. D. S. (1977). Early face-to-face interaction and its relation to later infant-mother attachment. *Child Development, 48,* 182–194.

Block, E. M., & Kessell, F. S. (1980). Determinants of the acquisition order of grammatical morphemes: A re-analysis and re-interpretation. *Journal of Child Language, 7,* 181–188.

Block, J. (1976). Debatable conclusions about sex differences. *Contemporary Psychology, 21,* 517–522.

Block, J. (1971). *Lives through time.* Berkeley: Bancroft Books.

Block, J., von der Lippe, A., & Block, J. H. (1973). Sex-role and socialization: Some personality concomitants and environmental antecedents. *Journal of Consulting and Clinical Psychology, 41,* 321–341.

Block, J. H. (1983). Differential premises arising from differential socialization of the sexes: Some conjectures. *Child Development, 54,* 1335–1354.

Bloom, L. M. (1970). *Language development: Form and function in emerging grammar.* Cambridge, Mass.: M.I.T. Press.

Bloom, L. M. (1973). *One word at a time: The use of single word utterances before syntax.* The Hague: Mouton.

Bloom, L. M., Lifter, K., & Hafitz, J. (1980). Semantics of verbs and the development of verb inflections in child language. *Language, 56,* 386–412.

Bloom, L., Rocissano, L., & Hood, L. (1976). Adult-child discourse: Developmental interaction between information processing and linguistic knowledge. *Cognitive Psychology, 8,* 521–552.

Blum, L. S. (1979). Implications of life-threatening illness for midlife development. In S. Cytrynbaum (Chair), *Midlife development: Influences of gender, personality, and social system.* Symposium presented at the meeting of the American Psychological Association, New York, September.

Boles, D. B. (1980). X-linkage of spatial ability: A critical review. *Child Development, 51,* 625–635.

Borkowski, J. G., & Cavanaugh, J. C. (1979). Maintenance and generalization of skills and strategies by the retarded. In N. R. Ellis (Ed.), *Handbook of mental deficiency* (2nd ed.). Hillsdale, N.J.: Lawrence Erlbaum Associates.

Bornstein, M. H., Kessen, W., & Weiskopf, S. (1975). Color vision and hue categorization in young human infants. *Science, 191,* 201–202.

Botwinick, J. (1977). Intellectual abilities. In J. E. Birren & K. W. Schaie (Eds.), *Handbook of the psychology of aging.* New York: Van Nostrand Reinhold.

Bouchard, T. J. (1983). Do environmental similarities explain the similarity in intelligence of identical twins reared apart? *Intelligence, 7,* 175–184.

Bowen, M. Introduction: Family systems theory. In S. I. Harrison & J. F. McDermott, Jr. (Eds.), *New directions in child psychopathology, Vol. 1,* New York: International Universities Press.

Bower, T. G. R. (1974). *Development in infancy.* San Francisco: W. H. Freeman.

Bower, T. G. R. (1977). *The perceptual world of the child.* Cambridge, Mass.: Harvard University Press.

Bowerman, M. (1976). Semantic factors in the acquisition of rules for word use and sentence construction. In D. M. Morehead & A. E. Morehead (Eds.), *Normal and deficient child language.* Baltimore: University Park Press.

Bowerman, M. (1978). The acquisition of word meaning: An investigation into some current conflicts. In N. Waterson & C. Snow (Eds.), *The development of communication.* Chichester, Eng.: Wiley.

Bowerman, M. (1982). Reorganizational processes in lexical and syntactic development. In E. Wanner & L. R. Gleitman (Eds.), *Language acquisition: The state of the art.* Cambridge, Eng.: Cambridge University Press.

Bowlby, J. (1969). *Attachment and loss. Vol. 1.* New York: Basic Books.

Bowlby, J. (1980). *Attachment and loss. Vol. 3.* New York: Basic Books.

Brackbill, Y. (1958). Extinction of the smiling response in infants as a function of reinforcement schedule. *Child Development, 29,* 115–124.

Brady, J. E., Newcomb, A. F., & Hartup, W. W. (1983). Context and companion's behavior as determinants of cooperation and competition in school-age children. *Journal of Experimental Child Psychology, 36,* 396–412.

Bradley, R. H., & Tedesco, L. A. (1982). Environmental correlates of mental retardation. In J. R. Lachenmeyer & M. S. Gibbs (Eds.), *Psychopathology in children.* New York: Gardner Press.

Braine, M. D. S. (1963). The ontogeny of English phrase structure: The first phrase. *Language, 39,* 1–13.

Braine, M. D. S. (1976). Children's first word combinations. *Monographs of the Society for Research in Child Development, 41,* (Serial No. 164).

Brainerd, C. J. (1977). Cognitive development and cognitive learning: An interpretative review. *Psychological Bulletin, 84,* 919–939.

Brainerd, C. J. (1978). *Piaget's theory of intelligence.* Englewood Cliffs, N.J.: Prentice-Hall.

Brainerd, C. J. (1981). Working memory and the developmental analysis of probability judgment. *Psychological Review, 88,* 463–502.

Brazelton, T. B. (1970). Effect of prenatal drugs on the behavior of the neonate. *American Journal of Psychiatry, 126,* 1261–1266.

Brazelton, T. B. (1973). Neonatal behavioral assessment scale. *Clinics in developmental medicine, No. 50.* Spastics International Medical Publications in association with William Heinemann Medical Ltd., London.

Brecher, E. M. (1984). *Love, sex, and aging.* Mount Vernon, N.Y.: Consumers Union.

Brehony, K. A., & Geller, E. S. (1981). Relationships between psychological androgyny, social conformity, and perceived locus of control. *Pscyhology of Women Quarterly, 6,* 204–217.

Bretherton, I. (1985). Attachment theory: Retrospect and prospect. In I. Bretherton & Waters, E.

(Eds.), Growing points of attachment theory and research. *Monographs of the Society for Research in Child Development, 50* (1–2, Serial No. 209).

Broadhurst, P. L. (1958). Studies in psychogenetics: The quantitative inheritance of behavior in rats investigated by selective and cross-breeding. *Bulletin of the British Psychological Society, 34,* 2A (Abstract).

Brodzinsky, D. M., & Rightmyer, J. (1980). Individual differences in children's humor development. In P. McGhee & A. Chapman (Eds.), *Children's humour.* Chichester, Eng.: Wiley.

Bronfenbrenner, U. (1979). Contexts of child rearing: Problems and prospects. *American Psychologist, 34,* 844–850.

Bronheim, S. P. (1978). Pulmonary disorders: Asthma and cystic fibrosis. In P. R. Magrab (Ed.), *Psychological management of pediatric problems, Vol. 1.* Baltimore, Md.: University Park Press.

Bronson, G. (1974). The postnatal growth of visual capacity. *Child Development, 45,* 873–890.

Brooksbanks, B. W. L., & Balázs, R. (1981). Aspects of the biochemical development of the brain. In K. J. Connolly & H. F. R. Prechtl (Eds.), *Clinics in developmental medicine No. 77/78. Maturation and development: Biological and psychological perspectives.* Philadelphia: J. B. Lippincott.

Broverman, I. K., Broverman, D. M., Clarkson, F., Rosenkrantz, P. S., & Vogel, S. R. (1970). Sex-role stereotypes and clinical judgments of mental health. *Journal of Consulting and Clinical Psychology, 34,* 1–7.

Broverman, I. K., Vogel, S. R., Broverman, D. M., Clarkson, F. E., & Rosenkrantz, P. S. (1972). Sex-role stereotypes: A current appraisal. *Journal of Social Issues, 28,* 59–78.

Brown, A. L., Campione, J. C., & Murphy, M. D. (1974). Keeping track of changing variables: Long-term retention of a trained rehearsal strategy by retarded adolescents. *American Journal of Mental Deficiency, 78,* 446–453.

Brown, A. L., Campione, J. C., & Murphy, M. D. (1977). Maintenance and generalization of trained metamnemonic awareness by educable retarded children. *Journal of Experimental Child Psychology, 24,* 191–211.

Brown, A. L., & Scott, M. S. (1971). Recognition memory for pictures in preschool children. *Journal of Experimental Child Psychology, 11,* 401–412.

Brown, A. L., & Smiley, S. S. (1978). The development of strategies for studying texts. *Child Development, 49,* 1076–1088.

Brown, A. L., & Smiley, S. S. (1977). Rating the importance of structural units of prose passages: A

500

problem of metacognitive development. *Child Development, 48,* 1–8.

Brown, J. L. (1964). States in newborn infants. *Merrill-Palmer Quarterly, 10,* 313–327.

Brown, M. (1978, Sept. 18). Why genetic defects may be a thing of the past. *New York Magazine.*

Brown, R. (1965). *Social psychology.* New York: Free Press.

Brown, R. (1973). *A first language: The early stages.* Cambridge, Mass.: Harvard University Press.

Brown, W. T., Mezzacappa, P. M., & Jenkins, E. C. (1981, November 7). Screening for fragile X syndrome by testicular size measurement. *Lancet,* 1088.

Bruch, H. (1979). *The golden cage: The enigma of anorexia nervosa.* New York: Vintage Books.

Brumback, R. A., Jackoway, M. K., & Weinberg, W. A. (1980). Relations of intelligence to childhood depression in children referred to an educational diagnosis center. *Perceptual and Motor Skills, 50,* 11–17.

Bruner, J. S., & Koslowski, B. (1972). Visual preadapted constituents of manipulatory action. *Perception, 1,* 3–14.

Bryant, B. K., & Crockenberg, S. B. (1980). Correlates and dimensions of prosocial behavior: A study of female siblings with their mothers. *Child Development, 51,* 529–554.

Bryant, P. E., Jones, P., Claxton, V., & Perkins, G. M. (1972). Recognition of shapes across modalities by infants. *Nature, 240,* 303–304.

Bukowski, W. M., & Newcomb, A. F. (1984). Stability and determinants of sociometric status and friendship choice: A longitudinal perspective. *Developmental Psychology, 20,* 941–952.

Bullock, D., & Merrill, L. (1980). The impact of personal preference on consistency through time: The case of childhood aggression. *Child Development, 51,* 808–814.

Burleson, B. R. (1982). The development of comforting communication skills in childhood and adolescence. *Child Development, 53,* 1578–1588.

Burns, K. A., Deddish, R. B., Burns, W. J., & Hatcher, R. P. (1983). Use of oscillating waterbeds and rhythmic sounds for premature infant stimulation. *Developmental Psychology, 19,* 746–751.

Burton, R. (1984). A paradox in theories and research in moral development. In W. Kurtines & J. Gewirtz (Eds.). *Morality, moral behavior, and moral development.* New York: Wiley-Interscience.

Butterworth, G., & Castillo, M. (1976). Coordination of auditory and visual space in newborn infants. *Perception, 5,* 155–161.

Caldwell, B. (1964). The effects of infant care. In M. Hoffman & L. Hoffman (Eds)., *Review of child development research. Vol. 1.* New York: Russell Sage Foundation.

Caldwell, B. M., & Richmond, J. B. (1962). The impact of theories of child development. *Children, 1962, 9,* 73–78.

Caldwell, B. M., Wright, C. M., Honig, A. S., & Tannenbaum, J. (1970). Infant day care and attachment. *American Journal of Orthopsychiatry, 40,* 397–412.

Campbell, M., Geller, B., & Cohen, I. L. (1977). Current status of drug research and treatment with autistic children. *Journal of Pediatric Psychology, 2,* 153–161.

Campione, J. C., & Brown, A. L. (1977). Memory and metamemory development in educable retarded children. In R. V. Kail & J. W. Hagen (Eds.), *Perspectives on the development of memory and cognition.* Hillsdale, N.J.: Lawrence Erlbaum Associates.

Campos, J. J., Barrett, K. C., Lamb, M. E., Goldsmith, H. H., & Stenberg, C. (1983). Socioemotional development. In P. H. Mussen (Ed.), *Handbook of child development, Vol. 2.* New York: John Wiley.

Campos, J. J., Langer, A., & Krowitz, A. (1970). Cardiac response on the visual cliff in prelocomotor human infants. *Science, 170,* 196–197.

Cann, A., & Newbern, S. R. (1984). Sex stereotype effects in children's picture recognition. *Child Development, 55,* 1085–1090.

Cantwell, D. P. (1975). *The hyperactive child.* New York: Spectrum.

Cantwell, D. P., Baker, L., & Rutter, M. (1978). Family factors. In M. Rutter and E. Schopler. (Eds.), *Autism: A reappraisal of concepts and treatment.* New York: Plenum.

Capute, A. J., Accardo, P. J., Vining, E. P. G., Rubenstein, J. E., & Harryman, S. (1978). *Primitive reflex profile.* Baltimore: University Park Press.

Caputo, D. V., & Mandell, W. (1970). Consequences of low birth weight. *Developmental Psychology, 3,* 363–383.

Carmichael, L. (1970). Onset and early development of behavior. In P. H. Mussen. (Ed.), *Carmichael's manual of child psychology* (3rd ed.). New York: John Wiley.

Carter, C. O. (1964). The genetics of common malformation. In *Congenital malformations: Papers and discussions presented at the second international conference on genetic malformations.* New York: The International Medical Congress.

Carter, D. B., & Patterson, C. J. (1982). Sex roles as social conventions: The development of children's conceptions of sex-role stereotypes. *Developmental Psychology, 18,* 812–824.

Case, R. (1978). Intellectual development from birth to adolescence: A neo-Piagetian interpretation. In R. Siegler (Ed.), *Children's thinking: What develops?* Hillsdale, N.J.: Lawrence Erlbaum Associates.

Cazden, C. B. (1968). The acquisition of noun with verb inflections. *Child Development, 39,* 433–448.

Chandler, M., & Boyes, M. (1982). Social-cognitive development. In B. Wolman (Editor). *Handbook of developmental psychology.* Englewood Cliffs, New Jersey: Prentice-Hall.

Chapman, R. H. (1975). The development of children's understanding of proportions. *Child Development, 46,* 141–148.

Charney, E., Goodman, H. C., McBride, M., Lyon, B., & Pratt, R. (1976). Childhood antecedents of adult obesity: Do chubby infants become obese adults? *The New England Journal of Medicine, 295,* 6–9.

Chelune, G. J. (1979). Measuring openness in interpersonal communication. In G. J. Chelune & Associates (Eds.), *Self-disclosure.* San Francisco: Jossey-Bass.

Chess S. (1974). The influence of defect on development in children with congenital rubella. *Merrill-Palmer Quarterly, 20,* 255–274.

Chess, S., & Thomas, A. (1972). Differences in outcome with early intervention in children with behavior disorders. In M. Roff, L. Robins, and M. Pollack (Eds.), *Life history in psychopathology, Vol. 2.* Minneapolis: University of Minnesota Press.

Chess, S., & Thomas, A. (1977). Temperamental individuality from childhood to adolescence. *Journal of the American Academy of Child Psychiatry, 16,* 218–226.

Clark, E. V. (1973). What's in a word? On the child's acquisition of semantics in his first language. In T. E. Moore (Ed.), *Cognitive development and the acquisition of language.* New York: Academic Press.

Clark, H. H., & Clark, E. V. (1977). *Psychology and language.* New York: Harcourt Brace Jovanovich.

Clarke-Stewart, K. A., & Fein, G. G. (1983). Early childhood programs. In P. H. Mussen (Ed.), *Handbook of child psychology, Vol. 2.* New York: John Wiley.

Cleary, T. A., Humphreys, L. G., Kendrick, S. A., & Wesman, A. (1975). Educational uses of tests with disadvantaged students. *American Psychologist, 30,* 15–41.

Clemson, E. (1981). Disadvantaged youth: A study of sex differences in occupational stereotypes and vocational aspirations. *Youth and Society, 13,* 39–56.

Cochrane, M. M. (1977). A comparison of group day and family child-rearing patterns in Sweden. *Child Development, 48,* 702–707.

Cohen, L. B. (1979). Our developing knowledge of infant perception and cognition. *American Psychologist, 34,* 894–899.

Cohen, R., & Schuepfer, T. (1980). The representation of landmarks and routes. *Child Development, 51,* 1065–1071.

Cohen, R., & Weatherford, D. L. (1980). Effect of route travelled on the distance estimates of children and adults. *Journal of Experimental Child Psychology, 29,* 403–412.

Cohen-Sandler, R., Berman, A. L., & King, R. A. (1982). A follow-up study of hospitalized suicidal children. *Journal of the American Academy of Child Psychiatry, 21,* 398–403.

Cohn, N. B., & Strassberg, D. S. (1983). Self-disclosure reciprocity among preadolescents. *Personality and Social Psychology Bulletin, 9,* 97–102.

Coie, J., Dodge, K., & Coppotelli, H. (1982). Dimensions and types of social status: A cross age perspective. *Developmental Psychology, 18,* 557–571.

Collis, G. M. (1977). Visual co-orientation and maternal speech. In H. R. Schaffer (Ed.), *Studies in mother-infant interaction.* London: Academic Press.

Condon, W. S., & Sander, L. W. (1974). Neonate movement is synchronized with adult speech. *Science, 183,* 99–100.

Condry, J., & Condry, S. (1976). Sex differences: A study of the eye of the beholder. *Child Development, 47,* 812–819.

Conger, J. C. (1970). The treatment of encopresis by the management of social consequences. *Behavior Therapy, 1,* 389–390.

Conger, J. J., & Petersen, A. C. (1984). *Adolescence and youth: Psychological development in a changing world.* New York: Harper & Row.

Connor, J. M., & Serbin, L. A. (1977). Behaviorally based masculine- and feminine-activity-preference scales for preschoolers: Correlates with other classroom behaviors and cognitive tests. *Child Development, 48,* 1411–1416.

Copans, S. A. (1974). Human prenatal effects: Methodological problems and some suggested solutions. *Merrill-Palmer Quarterly, 20,* 43–52.

Cornell, E. H., & Hay, D. H. (1984). Children's acquisition of a route via different media. *Environment and Behavior, 16,* 627–641.

Corsaro, W. A. (1981). Friendship in the nursery school: Social organization in a peer environment. In S. R. Asher & J. M. Gottman (Eds.), *The development of children's friendships.* Cambridge, Eng.: Cambridge University Press.

Cousins, J. H., Siegel, A. W., & Maxwell, S. E. (1983). Way finding and cognitive mapping in large scale environments: A test of a developmental model. *Journal of Experimental Child Psychology, 35*, 1–20.

Crawley, S. B., Rogers, P. P., Friedman, S., Iacobbo, M., Criticos, A., Richardson, L., & Thompson, M. (1978). Developmental changes in structure of mother-infant play. *Developmental Psychology, 14*, 30–36.

Crnic, K. A., Ragozin, A. S., Greenberg, M. T., Robinson, N. M., & Basham, R. B. (1983). Social interaction and developmental competence of preterm and full-term infants during the first year of life. *Child Development, 54*, 1199–1210.

Crosby, F. (1982). *Relative deprivation and working women.* New York: Oxford University Press.

Csikszentmihalyi, M., Larson, R., & Prescott, S. (1977). The ecology of adolescent activity and experience. *Journal of Youth and Adolescence, 6*, 281–294.

Cultice, J. C., Somerville, S. C., & Wellman, H. M. (1983). Preschoolers' memory monitoring: Feeling of knowing judgments. *Child Development, 54*, 1480–1486.

Curtis, L. E. & Strauss, M. S. (1983). *Infant numerosity abilities: Discrimination and relative numerosity.* Paper presented at the biennial meeting of the Society for Research in Child Development, Detroit.

Cytryn, L., & Lourie, R. S. (1980). Mental retardation. In H. I. Kaplan, A. M. Freedman, & B. J. Sadock (Eds.), *Comprehensive textbook of psychiatry/ III,* Vol. 3. Baltimore, MD.: Williams & Wilkins.

Cytrynbaum, S., Blum, L., Patrick, R., Stein, J., Wadner, D., & Wilk, C. (1980). Midlife development: A personality and social systems perspective. In L. Poon (Ed.), *Aging in the 1980s.* Washington, D.C.: American Psychological Association.

Daker, M., & Mutton, D. (1982). Recent advances in clinical cytogenetics. In M. Adinolfi, P. Benson, F. Giannelli, and M. Seller (Eds.), *Clinics in developmental medicine No. 83. Paediatric research: A genetic approach.* Philadelphia: J. B. Lippincott.

Damon, W. (1977). *The social world of the child.* San Francisco: Jossey-Bass.

Damon, W. (1980). Patterns of change in children's social reasoning: A two-year longitudinal study. *Child Development, 51*, 1010–1017.

Damon, W. (1983). *Social and personality development: Infancy through adolescence.* New York: W. W. Norton.

Damon, W., & Hart, D. (1982). The development of self-understanding from infancy through adolescence. *Child Development, 53*, 841–864.

D'Andrade, R. G. (1966). Sex differences and cultural institutions. In E. E. Maccoby (Ed.), *The development of sex differences.* Stanford, CA: Stanford University Press.

Darwin, C. (1871). *The descent of man and selection in relation to sex.* London: John Murray.

Davison, G. C., & Neale, J. M. (1978, 1982). *Abnormal psychology.* New York: John Wiley.

Deaux, K. (1984). From individual differences to social categories. *American Psychologist, 39*, 105–116.

Deaux, K. (1985). Sex and gender. *Annual Review of Psychology, 36*, 49–81.

DeFries, J. C. & Plomin, R. (1978). Behavioral genetics. *Annual review of psychology, 29*, 473–515.

DeHirsch, K., Jansky, J., & Langford, W. S. (1976). Comparisons between prematurely and maturely born children at three age levels. *American Journal of Orthopsychiatry, 36*, 616–628.

DeLoache, J. S. (1984). Oh where, oh where: Memory-based searching by very young children. In C. Sophian (Ed.), *Origins of cognitive skills.* Hillsdale, N.J.: Lawrence Erlbaum Associates.

DeLuise, M., Blackburn, G. L., & Flier, J. S. (1980). Reduced activity of the red-cell sodium-potassium pump in human obesity. *New England Journal of Medicine, 303*, 1017–1022.

Denney, N. W. (1982). Aging and cognitive changes. In B. B. Wolman (Ed.), *Handbook of developmental psychology.* Englewood Cliffs, N.J.: Prentice-Hall.

Dennis, W., & Dennis, M. G. (1940). The effects of cradling practices upon the onset of walking in Hopi children. *Journal of Genetic Psychology, 56*, 77–86.

deVilliers, J. G., & deVilliers, P. A. (in press). The acquisition of English. In D. I. Slobin (Ed.), *The cross-linguistic study of language acquisition.* Hillsdale, N.J.: Lawrence Erlbaum Associates.

DeVries, R. (1974). Relationship among Piagetian, IQ and achievement assessments. *Child Development, 45*, 746–756.

Dickerson, J. W. T. Nutrition, brain growth, and development. (1981). In K. J. Connolly and H. F. R. Prechtl (Eds.), *Clinics in developmental medicine No. 77/78. Maturation and development: Biological and psychological perspectives.* Philadelphia: J. B. Lippincott.

Dion, K. K. (1974). Children's physical attractiveness and sex as determinants of adult punitiveness. *Developmental Psychology, 10*, 772–778.

Dion, K. K., & Stein, S. (1978). Physical attractiveness and interpersonal influence. *Journal of Experimental Social Psychology, 14*, 97–108.

Dodge, K. A. (1980). Social cognition and children's aggressive behavior. *Child Development, 51*, 162–170.

Dodge, K. A., Murphy, R. R., & Buchsbaum, K. (1984). The assessment of intention-cue detection skills in children: Implications for developmental psychopathology. *Child Development, 55,* 163–173.

Doherty, W. J., & Jacobson, N. S. (1982). Marriage and the family. In B. Wolman (Ed.), *Handbook of developmental psychology*. Englewood Cliffs, N.J.: Prentice-Hall.

Doleys, D. M. (1977). Behavioral treatments for nocturnal enuresis in children: A review of the recent literature. *Psychological Bulletin, 84,* 30–54.

Donagher, P. C., Poulos, R. W., Liebert, R. M., & Davidson, E. E. (1975). Race, sex, and social example: An analysis of character portrayals on interracial television entertainment. *Psychological Reports, 38,* 3–14.

Douglas, V. I. (1980). Higher mental processes in hyperactive children. In R. M. Knights & D. J. Bakker (Eds.), *Treatment of hyperactive and learning disordered children*. Baltimore, Md.: University Park Press.

Douglas, V. I. (1983). Attentional and cognitive problems. In M. Rutter (Ed.), *Developmental neuropsychiatry*. New York: Guilford Press.

Downs, R. M., & Stea, D. (1973). Cognitive maps and spatial behavior: Processes and products. In. R. M. Downs & D. Stea (Eds.), *Image and environment: Cognitive mapping and spatial behavior*. Chicago: Aldine.

Drabman, R. S., Cordua, G. D., Hammer, D., Jarvie, G. J., & Horton, W. (1979). Developmental trends in eating rates of normal and overweight preschool children. *Child Development, 50,* 211–216.

Dreyer, P. H. (1982). Sexuality during adolescence. In B. B. Wolman (Ed.), *Handbook of developmental psychology*. Englewood Cliffs, N. J.: Prentice-Hall.

Dunn, J., and Kendrick, C. (1981). Social behavior of young siblings in the family context: Differences between same-sex and different-sex dyads. *Child Development, 52,* 1265–1273.

Dweck, C. S. (1975). The role of expectations and attributions in the alleviation of learned helplessness. *Journal of Personality and Social Psychology, 31,* 674–685.

Dweck, C. S., & Bush, E. S. (1976). Sex differences in learned helplessness: I. Differential debilitation with peer and adult evaluators. *Developmental Psychology, 12,* 147–156.

Dweck, C. S., Davidson, W., Nelson, S., & Enna, B. (1978). Sex differences in learned helplessness: II. The contingencies of evaluative feedback in the classroom; and III. An experimental analysis. *Developmental Psychology, 14,* 268–276.

Eagly, A. H. (1978). Sex differences in influence ability. *Psychological Bulletin, 85,* 86–116.

Eagly, A. H. (1983). Gender and social influence. *American Psychologist, 38,* 971–981.

Eagly, A. H., & Carli, L. L. (1981). Sex of researchers and sex-typed communications as determinants of sex differences in influenceability: A meta-analysis of social influence studies. *Psychological Bulletin, 90,* 1–20.

Eckert, H. M. (1973). Age changes in motor skills. In G. L. Rarick (Ed.), *Physical activity*. New York: Academic Press.

Edelbrock, C., Costello, A. J., & Kessler, M. D. (1984). Empirical corroboration of attention deficit disorder. *Journal of the American Academy of Child Psychiatry, 23,* 285–290.

Eggers, C. (1978). Course and prognosis of childhood schizophrenia, *Journal of Autism and Childhood Schizophrenia, 8,* 21–36.

Eichorn, D. H. (1963). Biological correlates of behavior. In H. W. Stevenson (Ed.), *Child psychology*. Chicago: The University of Chicago Press.

Eilers, R. E., Gavin, W. J., & Oller, D. K. (1982). Crosslinguistic perception in infancy: Early effects of linguistic experience. *Journal of Child Language, 9,* 289–302.

Eimas, P. D. (1975). Speech perception in early infancy. In L. B. Cohen and P. Salapatek (Eds.), *Infant perception: From sensation to cognition, Vol. 2*. New York: Academic Press.

Eisenberg, L. (1958). School phobia: A study in the communication of anxiety. *American Journal of Psychiatry, 114,* 712–718.

Eisenberg, N. (Ed.). (1982). *The development of prosocial behavior*. New York: Academic Press.

Eisenberg, N., & Lennon, R. (1983). Sex differences in empathy and related capacities. *Psychological Bulletin, 94,* 100–131.

Eisenberg, R. B. (1976). *Auditory competence in early life*. Baltimore: University Park Press.

Elder, G. H., & Rockwell, R. C. (1976). Marital timing in women's life patterns. *Journal of Family History, 1,* 34–53.

Ellenberger, H. F. (1970). *The discovery of the unconscious*. New York: Basic Books.

Eme, R. F. (1979). Sex differences in childhood psychopathology: A review. *Psychological Bulletin, 86,* 574–595.

Engen, T., Lipsitt, L. P., & Kaye, H. (1963). Olfactory responses and adaptation in the human neonate. *Journal of Comparative and Physiological Psychology, 56,* 73–77.

Erikson, E. H. (1963). *Childhood and society*. New York: W. W. Norton.

Erickson, M. (1978). *Child psychopathology*. Englewood Cliffs, N.J.: Prentice-Hall.

Ervin, S. (1964). Imitation and structural change in children's language. In E. H. Lenneberg (Ed.), *New directions in the study of language*. Cambridge, MA: MIT Press.

Ervin-Tripp, S. (1970). Discourse agreement: How children answer questions. In J. R. Hayes (Ed.), *Cognition and the development of language*. New York: Wiley.

Evans, P. (1982). 'Paul Polani'. In M. Adinolfi, P. Benson, F. Giannelli, and M. Seller (Eds.) *Clinics in developmental medicine, No. 83. Pediatric research: A genetic approach*. Philadelphia: J. B. Lippincott.

Eysenck, H. J. (1952). The effects of psychotherapy: An evaluation. *Journal of Consulting Psychology, 16*, 319–324.

Fagot, B. I. (1977). Teachers' reinforcement of sex-preferred behavior in Dutch preschools. *Psychological Reports, 48*, 902–907.

Fantz, R. L. (1958). Pattern vision in young infants. *Psychological Record, 8*, 43–47.

Fantz, R. L. (1961). The origin of form perception. *Scientific American, 204*, 66–72.

Fantz, R. L. (1969). Studying visual perception and the effects of visual exposure in early infancy. In D. Gelfand (Ed.), *Social learning in childhood*. Belmont, CA: Brooks/Cole.

Fantz, R. L., Fagan, J. F., & Miranda, S. (1975). Early vision selectivity. In L. B. Cohen and P. Salapatek (Eds.), *Infant perception: From sensation to cognition: Basic visual processes. Vol. 1*. New York: Academic Press.

Fantz, R. L., Ordy, J. M., & Udelf, M. S. (1962). Maturation of pattern vision in infants during the first 6 months. *Journal of Comparative & Physiological Psychology, 55*, 907–917.

Farber, S. (1981). Telltale behavior of twins. *Psychology Today, 15*, 58–80.

Farran, D. C., & Ramey, C. T. (1980). Social class differences in dyadic involvement during infancy. *Child Development, 51*, 254–257.

Feingold, B. F. (1975). *Why your child is hyperactive*. New York: Random House.

Ferguson, C. A., & Macken, M. A. (1983). The role of play in phonological development. In K. E. Nelson (Ed.), *Children's language* (Vol. 4). Hillsdale, N.J.: Lawrence Erlbaum Associates.

Ferguson, H. B., & Pappas, B. A. (1979). Evaluation of psychophysiological, neurochemical, and animal models of hyperactivity. In R. L. Trites (Ed.), *Hyperactivity in children*. Baltimore, Md.: University Park Press.

Ferreira, A. J. (1969). *Prenatal environment*. Springfield, Ill.: Charles C Thomas.

Ferster, C. B. (1961). Positive reinforcement and behavioral deficits of autistic children. *Child Development, 32*, 437–456.

Ferster, C. B. (1966). The repertoire of the autistic child in relation to principles of reinforcement. In L. Gottschalk & A. H. Averback (Eds.), *Methods of research of psychotherapy*. New York: Appleton-Century-Crofts.

Feshbach, N. D., & Feshbach, S. (1969). The relationship between empathy and aggression in two age groups. *Developmental Psychology, 1*, 102–107.

Field, T. (1978). Interaction behaviors of primary versus secondary caretaker fathers. *Developmental Psychology, 14*, 183–184.

Field, T. (1980). Interactions of pre-term and term infants with their lower-and middle-class teenage and adult mothers. In T. Field (Ed.), *High-risk infants and children*. New York: Academic Press.

Field, T. M., and Widmayer, S. M. (1982). Motherhood. In B. J. Wolman (Ed.), *Handbook of developmental psychology*. Englewood Cliffs, N.J.: Prentice-Hall.

Field, T., Woodson, R., Greenberg, R., & Cohen, D. (1982). Discrimination and initiation of facial expressions by neonates. *Science, 218*, 179–181.

Findley, M. J., & Cooper, H. M. (1983). Locus of control and academic achievement: A literature review. *Journal of Personality and Social Psychology, 44*, 419–427.

Fischer, K. W. (1980). A theory of cognitive development: The control and construction of hierarchies of skills. *Psychological Review, 87*, 477–531.

Fischer, K. W., & Pipp, S. L. (1984). Processes of cognitive development: Optimal level and skill acquisition. In R. J. Sternberg (Ed.), *Mechanisms of cognitive development*. New York: W. H. Freeman.

Fish, B., & Ritvo, E. R. Psychoses of childhood. (1979). In J. D. Noshpitz (Ed.), *Basic handbook of child psychiatry, Vol. 2*, New York: Basic Books.

Fitch, S. A., & Adams, G. R. (1983). Ego identity and intimacy status: Replication and extension. *Developmental Psychology, 19*, 839–845.

Flavell, J. H. (1963). *The developmental psychology of Jean Piaget*. New York: Van Nostrand.

Flavell, J. H. (1974). The development of inferences about others. In T. Mischel (Ed.), *Understanding about other persons*. Oxford: Blackwell, Basil & Mott.

Flavell, J. H. (1985). *Cognitive development*. (2nd edition) Englewood Cliffs, N.J.: Prentice-Hall.

Flavell, J. H., Beach, D. R., & Chinsky, J. M. (1966). Spontaneous verbal rehearsal in a memory task as a function of age. *Child Development, 37*, 283–299.

Flavell, J. H., Friedrichs, A. G., & Hoyt,

J. D. (1970). Developmental changes in memorization processes. *Cognitive Psychology, 1,* 324–340.

Flavell, J. H., & Wellman, H. M. (1977). Metamemory. In R. V. Kail & J. W. Hagen (Eds.), *Perspectives on the development of memory and cognition.* Hillsdale, N.J.: Lawrence Erlbaum Associates.

Folstein, S., & Rutter, M. (1978). A twin study of individuals with infantile autism. In M. Rutter & E. Schopler (Eds.). *Autism: A reappraisal of concepts and treatment.* New York: Plenum.

Forssman, H. (1976). Epilepsy in an XXY man. *Lancet, 1,* 1389.

Fozard, J. L. (1980). The time for remembering. In L. W. Poon, J. L. Fozard, L. S. Cermak, D. Arenberg, and L. W. Thompson (Eds.), *New Directions in Memory and Aging.* Hillsdale, N.J.: Lawrence Erlbaum Associates.

Franken, M. W. (1983). Sex role expectations in children's vocational aspirations and perceptions of occupations. *Psychology of Women Quarterly, 8,* 59–68.

Frankenburg, W. K., & Dobbs, J. B. (1969). *Manual, Denver Developmental Screening Test.* Mead Johnson Laboratories.

Freedman, D. G. (1968). Personality development in infancy: A biological approach. In S. L. Washburn and P. C. Jay (Eds.), *Perspectives on human evolution.* New York: Holt, Rinehart & Winston.

Freedman, D. G. (1971). Behavioral assessment in infancy. In G. B. A. Stoelinga and J. J. Van Der Werff Ten Bosch (Eds.), *Normal and abnormal development of brain and behavior.* Leiden: Leiden University Press.

Freedman, D. G., & Keller, B. (1963). Inheritance of behavior in infants. *Science, 10,* 196–198.

Freud, A. (1946). *The psycho-analytical treatment of children.* New York: International Universities Press.

Freud, S. (1949). *An outline of psycho-analysis.* Translated and newly edited by J. Strachey. New York: W. W. Norton.

Friedman, L. J. (1983). Understanding stepfamilies (Review of E. Wald's The remarried family). *Contemporary Psychology, 28,* 279.

Friedman, R. M., Sandler, J., Hernandez, M., & Wolfe, D. A. (1981). Child abuse. In E. J. Mash & L. G. Terdal (Eds.), *Behavioral assessment of childhood disorders.* New York: Guilford Press.

Frodi, A., Lamb, M., Leavitt, L., & Donovan, W. (1981). Father's and mother's responses to infant smiles and cries. *Infant Behavior and Development, 1,* 187–198.

Frodi, A., Macaulay, J., & Thome, P. R. (1977). Are women always less aggressive than men? A review of the experimental literature. *Psychological Bulletin, 84,* 634–660.

Funder, D. C., Block, J. H., & Block, J. (1983). Delay of gratification: Some longitudinal personality correlates. *Journal of Personality and Social Psychology, 44,* 1198–1213.

Furman, W., & Bierman, K. L. (1984). Children's conceptions of friendship: A multimethod study of developmental changes. *Developmental Psychology, 20,* 925–931.

Furrow, D., Nelson, K., & Benedict, H. (1979). Mothers' speech to children and syntactic development: Some simple relationships. *Journal of Child Language, 6,* 423–442.

Fuson, K. C., Richards, J., & Briars, D. (1982). The acquisition and elaboration of the number word sequence. In C. J. Brainerd (Ed.), *Children's logical and mathematical cognition.* New York: Springer-Verlag.

Galloway, D. (1983). Research note: Truants and other absentees. *Journal of Psychology and Psychiatry, 24,* 607–611.

Garber, J. (1984). Classification of childhood psychopathology: A developmental perspective. *Child Development, 55,* 30–48.

Garcia, J., & Koelling, R. A. (1966). Relation of cue to consequence in avoidance learning. *Psychonomic Science, 4,* 123–124.

Gardner, H. (1982). Artistry following damage to the human brain. In A. W. Ellis (Ed.), *Normality and pathology in cognitive functions.* New York: Academic Press.

Gardner, H. (1983). *Frames of mind: The theory of multiple intelligences.* New York: Basic Books.

Gardner, R. A., & Gardner, B. T. (1969). Teaching sign language to a chimpanzee. *Science, 165,* 664–672.

Garn, S., Cole, P. E., & Bailey, S. M. (1976). Effect of parental fatness levels on the fatness of biological and adoptive children. *Ecology of Food and Nutrition, 6,* 1–34.

Garrett, H. E. (1946). A developmental theory of intelligence. *American Psychologist, 1,* 372–378.

Garvey, C., & Berninger, G. (1981). Timing and turn taking in children's conversations. *Discourse Processes, 4,* 27–59.

Garvey, C., & Hogan, R. (1973). Social speech and social interaction: Egocentrism revisited. *Child Development, 44,* 562–568.

Garvey, W. P., & Hegrenes, J. P. (1966). Desensitization techniques in the treatment of school phobia. *American Journal of Orthopsychiatry, 36,* 147–152.

Gelman, R. (1980). What young children know about numbers. *Educational Psychologist, 15,* 54–68.

Gelman, R. (1982). Basic numerical abilities. In R. J. Sternberg (Ed.), *Advances in the psychology of hu-*

man intelligence (Vol. 1). Hillsdale, N.J.: Lawrence Erlbaum Associates.

Gelman, R., & Gallistel, C. R. (1978). *The child's understanding of number*. Cambridge, Mass.: Harvard University Press.

Gesell, A. (1940). The stability of mental-growth careers. *39th Yearbook of the National Society for the Study of Education*, Part II, 149–159.

Gesell, A., & Ames, L. B. (1947). The development of handedness. *Journal of Genetic Psychology, 70,* 155–175.

Gewirtz, J. L. (1968). The role of stimulation in models for child development. In L. L. Dittmann, (Ed.), *Early child care: The new perspective*. New York: Atherton Press.

Gewirtz, J. L. (1972). Attachment, dependence, and a distinction in terms of stimulus control. In J. L. Gewirtz (Ed.), *Attachment and dependency*. Washington, D.C.: V. H. Winston & Sons.

Gholson, B., & Beilin, H. (1979). A developmental model of human learning. In H. W. Reese and L. P. Lipsitt (Eds.), *Advances in child development and behavior*, Vol. 13. New York: Academic Press.

Gibbs, J. C., Clark, P. M., Joseph, J. A., Green, J. L., Goodrick, T. S., & Makowski, D. (1986). Relations between moral judgment, moral courage, and field independence. *Child Development, 57,* in press.

Gibson, E. J., & Walk, R. D. (1960). The "visual cliff." *Scientific American, 202,* 64–71.

Gibson, E. J., & Walker, A. S. (1984). Development of knowledge of visual-tactual affordance of substance. *Child Development, 55,* 453–460.

Gil, D. G. (1979). Unraveling child abuse. In R. Bourne & E. H. Newberger (Eds.), *Critical perspectives on child abuse*. Lexington, MA.: Lexington Books, Heath.

Gillberg, C., Carlström, G., & Rasmussen, P. (1983). Hyperkinetic disorders in seven-year-old children with perceptual, motor, and attentional deficits. *Journal of Child Psychology and Psychiatry, 24,* 233–246.

Gillberg, C., Waldenström, E., & Rasmussen, P. (1984). Handedness in Swedish 10-year-olds. Some background and associated factors. *Journal of Child Psychology and Psychiatry, 25,* 421–432.

Gilligan, C. (1982). *In a different voice: Psychological theory and women's development*. Cambridge, MA.: Harvard University Press.

Gilligan, C. (1985). Remapping development. Paper presented at the biennial meeting of the Society for Research in Child Development, Toronto, Canada.

Ginsburg, H. (1975). *The psychology of arithmetic thinking*. Unpublished manuscript.

Ginsburg, H. (1977). *Children's arithmetic: The learning process*. New York: D. Van Nostrand.

Gittelman, R., Abikoff, H., Pollack, E., Klein, D. F., Katz, S., & Mattes, J. (1980). A controlled trial of behavior modification and methylphenidate in hyperactive children. In C. K. Whalen & B. Henker (Eds.), *Hyperactive children*. New York: Academic Press.

Gladston, R. (1965). Observations on children who have been physically abused and their parents. *American Journal of Psychiatry, 122,* 440–443.

Glick, P. C. (1979). The future of the American family. *Current Population Reports (Special Studies Series P–23, No. 78)*. Washington, D.C.: U.S. Government Printing Office.

Gliner, C. R. (1967). Tactual discrimination thresholds for shape and texture in young children. *Journal of Experimental Child Psychology, 5,* 536–547.

Glucksberg, S., & Krauss, R. M. (1967). What do people say after they have learned to talk? Studies of the development of referential communication. *Merrill-Palmer Quarterly, 13,* 309–316.

Glucksberg, S., Krauss, R. M., & Weisberg, R. (1966). Referential communication in nursery school children: Method and some preliminary findings. *Journal of Experimental Child Psychology, 3,* 333–342.

Gnepp, J., & Gould, M. E. (1985). The development of personalized inferences: Understanding other people's emotional reactions in light of their previous experiences. *Child Development, 56,* in press.

Goldberg, S. (1978). Prematurity: Effects on parent-infant interaction. *Journal of Pediatric Psychology, 3,* 137–144.

Goldberg, S. (1983). Parent-infant bonding: Another look. *Child Development, 54,* 1355–1382.

Goode, W. J. (1960). A theory of role strain. *American Sociological Review, 25,* 483–496.

Gordon, A. M. (1984). Adequacy of responses given by low-income and middle-income kindergarten children in structured adult-child conversation. *Developmental Psychology, 20,* 881–892.

Gordon, D. A., & Young, R. D. (1976). School phobia: A discussion of etiology, treatment, and evaluation. *Psychological Reports, 39,* 783–804.

Gottlieb, G. (1983). The psychobiological approaches to developmental issues. In P. H. Mussen (Ed.), *Handbook of child psychology, Vol. 2*. New York: John Wiley.

Gould, M. S., Wunsch-Hitzig, R., & Dohrenwend, B. (1981). Estimating the prevalence of childhood psychopathology. *Journal of the American Academy of Child Psychiatry, 20,* 462–476.

Gould, S. J. (1981). *The mismeasure of man.* New York: Norton.

Gouze, K. R., & Nadelman, L. (1980). Constancy of gender identity for self and others in children between the ages of three and seven. *Child Development, 51,* 275–278.

Gottesman, I. I., & Shields, J. A. (1972). *Schizophrenia and genetics: A twin study vantage point.* New York: Academic Press.

Gottesman, I. I., & Shields, J. A. (1973). Genetic theorizing and schizophrenia. *British Journal of Psychiatry, 122,* 15–30.

Graham, S. (1984). Communicating sympathy and anger to black and white children: The cognitive (attributional) consequences of affective cues. *Journal of Personality and Social Psychology, 47,* 40–54.

Green, W. H., Campbell, M., Hardesty, A. S., Grega, D. M., Padron-Gayol, M., Shell, J., & Erlenmeyer-Kimling, L. (1984). A comparison of schizophrenic and autistic children. *Journal of the American Academy of Child Psychiatry, 23,* 399–409.

Greenberg, J., & Kuczaj, S. A. (1982). Toward a theory of substantive word-meaning acquisition. In S. A. Kuczaj (Ed.), *Language development* (Vol. 1.). Hillsdale, N.J.: Lawrence Erlbaum Associates.

Greenfield, P. M., & Smith, J. H. (1976). *The structure of communication in early language development.* New York: Academic Press.

Greeno, J. G. (1980). Psychology of learning, 1960–1980: One participant's observations. *American Psychologist, 35,* 713–728.

Greenspan, S. (1979). Social intelligence in the retarded. In N. R. Ellis (Ed.), *Handbook of mental deficiency: Psychological theory and research.* Hillsdale, N.J.: Lawrence Erlbaum Associates.

Griffiths, P., Meldrum, C., & McWilliam, R. (1982). Dry-bed training in the treatment of nocturnal enuresis in childhood: A research report. *Journal of Child Psychology and Psychiatry, 23,* 485–495.

Grimm, H. (1975). *Analysis of short-term dialogues in 5–7 year olds: Encoding of intentions and modifications of speech acts as a function of negative feedback.* Paper presented at the Third International Child Language Symposium, London.

Grinder, R. E. (1967). *A history of genetic psychology.* New York: John Wiley.

Groen, G. J., & Resnick, L. B. (1977). Can preschool children invent addition algorithms? *Journal of Educational Psychology, 69,* 645–652.

Grossman, H. J. (Ed.). (1977). *Manual on terminology and classification in mental retardation: 1977 revision.* Washington, D.C.: American Association on Mental Deficiency.

Grossman, H. J. (Ed.). (1983). *Classification in mental retardation.* Washington, D.C.: American Association on Mental Deficiency.

Gruen, G. E., & Vore, D. A. (1972). Development of conservation in normal and retarded children. *Developmental Psychology, 6,* 146–157.

Guardo, C. J., & Bohan, J. B. (1971). Development of a sense of self-identity in children. *Child Development, 42,* 1909–1921.

Guralnick, M. J., & Weinhouse, E. (1984). Peer-related social interactions of developmentally delayed young children: Development and characteristics. *Developmental Psychology, 20,* 815–827.

Hagamen, M. B. (1980). Autism and childhood schizophrenia. In J. E. Bemporad (Ed.), *Child development in normality and psychopathology.* New York: Brunner/Mazel.

Hallinan, M. T. (1979). Structural effects on children's friendships and cliques. *Social Psychology Quarterly, 42,* 43–54.

Hamerton, J. L. (1982). Population cytogenetics: A perspective. In M. Adinolfi, P. Benson, F. Giannelli, and M. Seller (Eds.), *Clinics in developmental medicine, No. 83. Paediatric research: A genetic approach.* Philadelphia: J. B. Lippincott.

Hansson, R. O., Knopf, M. F., Downs, E. A., Monroe, P. R., Stegman, S. E., & Wadley, D. S. (1984). Femininity, masculinity, and adjustment to divorce among women. *Psychology of Women Quarterly, 8,* 248–260.

Hardwick, D. A., McIntyre, C. W., & Pick, H. L. (1976). The content and manipulation of cognitive maps in children and adults. *Monographs of the Society for Research in Child Development, 41,* Serial #166.

Hardyck, C., & Petrinovich, L. F. (1977). Left-handedness. *Psychological Bulletin, 84,* 385–404.

Haring, N. G., & Bricker, D. (1976). Overview of comprehensive services for the severely/profoundly handicapped. In N. G. Haring & L. J. Brown (Eds.), *Teaching the severely handicapped.* New York: Grune & Stratton.

Harley, J. P., & Matthews, C. G. (1980). Food additives and hyperactivity in children: Experimental investigations. In R. M. Knights and D. J. Bakker (Eds.), *Treatment of hyperactive and learning disordered children.* Baltimore, Md.: University Park Press.

Harlow, H. (1971). *Learning to Love.* New York: Ballantine.

Harlow, H. F., & Harlow, M. K. (1970). The young monkeys. In P. Cramer (Ed.), *Readings in developmental psychology today.* Del Mar, CA: CRM Books.

Harlow, H. F., & Zimmerman, R. R. (1959). Affectional responses in the infant monkey. *Science, 130,* 431–432.

Harrington, D. M., Block, J., & Block, J. H. (1983). Predicting creativity in preadolescence from divergent thinking in early childhood. *Journal of Personality and Social Psychology, 45,* 609–623.

Harter, S. (1983). Developmental perspectives on the self-system. In P. H. Mussen (Ed.), *Handbook of child psychology, Vol. 4.* New York: John Wiley.

Hartup, W. W. (1976). Peer interaction and the behavioral development of the individual child. In E. Schopler & R. J. Reichler (Eds.), *Psychopathy and child development: Research and treatment.* New York: Plenum Press.

Hartup, W. (1983). Peer relations. In P. H. Mussen (Ed.), *Handbook of child psychology, Vol. 4.* New York: John Wiley.

Harvey, P. G. (1984). Lead and children's health–recent research and future questions. *Journal of Child Psychology and Psychiatry, 25,* 517–522.

Haskins, E. B. (1978). Effects of empty nest transition on self-report of psychological and physical well-being. *Journal of Marriage and the Family, 40,* 549–558.

Hawton, K. (1982). Attempted suicide in children and adolescents. *Journal of Child Psychology and Psychiatry, 23,* 497–503.

Hay, D. F., Nash, A., & Pedersen, J. (1983). Interaction between six-month-old peers. *Child Development, 54,* 557–562.

Hayes, C. (1951). *The ape in our house.* New York: Harper & Row.

Hazen, N. L., Lockman, J. J., & Pick, H. L. (1978). The development of children's representations of large-scale environments. *Child Development, 49,* 623–636.

Hechtman, L., Weiss, G., & Perlman, T. (1984). Young adult outcome of hyperactive children who received long-term stimulant treatment. *Journal of the American Academy of Child Psychiatry, 23,* 261–269.

Hecox, K. (1975). Electrophysiological correlates of human auditory development. In L. B. Cohen & P. Salapatek (Eds.), *Infant perception: From sensation to cognition* (Vol. 2). New York: Academic Press.

Heffron, W. A., Martin, C. A., & Welsh, R. J. (1984). Attention deficit disorder in three pairs of monozygotic twins: A case report. *Journal of the American Academy of Child Psychiatry, 23,* 299–301.

Henker, B., & Whalen, C. K. (1980). The changing faces of hyperactivity: Retrospect and prospect. In C. K. Whalen & B. Henker (Eds.), *Hyperactive children.* New York: Academic Press.

Herman, J. F., Roth, S. F., & Norton, L. M. (1984). Time and distance in spatial cognition development. *International Journal of Behavioral Development, 7,* 35–51.

Hersov, L. A. (1960). Refusal to go to school. *Journal of Child Psychology and Psychiatry, 1,* 137–145.

Hess, B. B., & Waring, J. M. (1978). Parent and child in later life. In R. M. Lerner & G. B. Spanier (Eds.), *Child influences on marital and family interaction: A life-span perspective.* New York: Academic Press.

Heston, L. L. (1966). Psychiatric disorders in foster home reared children of schizophrenic mothers. *British Journal of Psychiatry, 112,* 819–825.

Hetherington, E. M. (1970). Sex typing, dependency, and aggression. In T. D. Spencer and N. Kass (Eds.), *Perspectives in child psychology: Research and review.* New York: McGraw-Hill.

Hetherington, E. M. (1972). Effects of father absence on personality development in adolescent daughters. *Developmental Psychology, 7,* 313–326.

Hetherington, E. M. (1979). Divorce: A child's perspective. *American Psychologist, 31,* 851–858.

Hetherington, E. M., Cox, M., & Cox, R. (1978). The aftermath of divorce. In J. H. Sevens, Jr., and M. Mathews (Eds.), *Mother-child, father-child relations.* Washington, D.C.: National Association for the Education of Young Children.

Hetherington, E. M., & Martin, B. (1972). Family interaction and psychopathology in children. In H. C. Quay and J. S. Werry, (Eds.), *Psychopathological disorders of childhood.* New York: John Wiley.

Hobson, R. P. (1984). Early childhood autism and the question of egocentrism. *Journal of Autism and Developmental Disorders, 14,* 85–103.

Hodapp, R. M., & Mueller, E. (1982). Early social development. In B. B. Wolman (Ed.), *Handbook of developmental psychology.* Englewood Cliffs, N.J.: Prentice-Hall.

Hodges, W. F., Wechsler, R. C., & Ballantine, C. (1979). Divorce and the preschool child: Cumulative stress. *Journal of Divorce, 3,* 55–68.

Hoff-Ginsberg, E., & Shatz, M. (1982). Linguistic input and the child's acquisition of language. *Psychological Bulletin, 92,* 3–26.

Hoffman, L. W. (1961). The father's role in the family and the child's peer group adjustment. *Merrill-Palmer Quarterly, 7,* 97–105.

Hoffman, L. W. (1979). Maternal employment: 1979. *American Psychologist, 34,* 859–865.

Hoffman, M. L. (1975b). Developmental synthesis and cognition and its implications for altruistic motivation. *Developmental Psychology, 11,* 607–622.

Hoffman, M. L. (1977). Sex differences in empathy and related behaviors. *Psychological Bulletin, 84,* 712–722.

Hogan, D. P. (1978). The variable order of events in the life course. *American Sociological Review, 43,* 573–586.

Holmes, D. L., Nagy, J. N., Slaymaker, F., Sosnowski, R., Prinz, S. M., & Pasternak, J. F. (1982). Early influences of prematurity, illness, and prolonged hospitalization on infant behavior. *Developmental Psychology, 18,* 744–750.

Holmes, L. B. (1978). Genetic counseling for the older pregnant woman: New data and questions. *The New England Journal of Medicine, 298,* 1419–1421.

Hook, J. G., & Cook, T. D. (1979). Equity theory and cognitive ability of children. *Psychological Bulletin, 86,* 429–445.

Horn, J. M., Loehlin, J. C., & Willerman, L. (1979). Intellectual resemblance among adoptive and biological relatives: The Texas Adoption Project. *Behavior Genetics, 9,* 177–207.

Horn, J. M. (1983). The Texas Adoption Project: Adopted children and their intellectual resemblance to biological and adoptive parents. *Child Development, 54,* 268–275.

Householder, J., Hatcher, R., Burns, W., & Chasnoff, I. (1982). Infants born to narcotic-addicted mothers. *Psychological Bulletin, 92,* 453–468.

Hudson, L. M., Forman, E. A., & Brion-Meisels, S. (1982). Role-taking as a predictor of prosocial behavior in cross-age tutors. *Child Development, 53,* 1320–1329.

Huesman, L. R., Lagarspetz, K., & Eron, L. (1984). Invervening variables in the TV violence-aggression relation: Evidence from two countries. *Developmental Psychology, 20,* 746–775.

Hunt, J. McV. (1979). Psychological development: Early experience. *Annual Review of Psychology, 30,* 103–43.

Huston, A. C. (1983). Sex typing. In P. H. Mussen (Ed.), *Handbook of child psychology,* Vol. 4. New York: John Wiley.

Huttenlocher, J., Smiley, P., & Charney, R. (1983). Emergence of action categories in the child: Evidence from verb meanings. *Psychological Review, 90,* 72–93.

Hyde, J. S. (1981). How large are cognitive gender differences? *American Psychologist, 36,* 892–901.

Hyde, J. S. (1984a). Children's understanding of sexist language. *Developmental Psychology, 20,* 697–706.

Hyde, J. S. (1984b). How large are gender differences in aggression? A developmental meta-analysis. *Developmental Psychology, 20,* 722–736.

Ingram, D., Christensen, L., Veach, S., & Webster, B. (1980). The acquisition of word-initial fricatives and affricates in English by children between 2 and 6 years. In G. Yeni-Komshian, J. F. Kavanagh, & C. A. Ferguson (Eds.), *Child phonology* (Vol. 1). New York: Academic Press.

Inhelder, B., & Piaget, J. (1958). *The growth of logical thinking from childhood to adolescence.* New York: Basic Books.

Intons-Peterson, M. J., & Reddel, M. (1984). What do people ask about a neonate? *Developmental Psychology, 20,* 358–359.

Ironsmith, M., & Whitehurst, G. J. (1978). How children learn to listen: The effects of modeling feedback styles on children's performance in referential communication. *Developmental Psychology, 14,* 546–554.

Isaacs, M. B. (1981). Sex role stereotyping and the evaluation of the performance of women: changing trends. *Psychology of Women Quarterly, 6,* 187–195.

Israel, A. C., & Shapiro, L. G. (In press). Behavior problems of obese children in a weight reduction program. *Journal of Pediatric Psychology.*

Israel, A. C., Stolmaker, L. S., & Prince, B. (1984). The relationship between impulsivity and eating behavior in children. *Child and Family Behavior Therapy, 5,* 71–75.

Jacobs, B. S., & Moss, H. A. (1976). Birth order and sex of sibling as determinants of mother-infant interaction. *Child Development, 47,* 315–322.

Jacobs, P. A., Brunton, M., & Melville, M. M. (1965). Aggressive behavior, mental subnormality and the XYY male. *Nature, 208,* 1351–1352.

Jacobson, D. S. (1978). The impact of marital separation/divorce on children: III. Parent-child communication and child adjustment, and regression analysis of findings from overall study. *Journal of Divorce, 2,* 175–194.

Jacobson, J. L., Jacobson, S. W., Fein, G. G., Schwartz, P. M., & Dowler, J. K. (1984). Prenatal exposure to an environmental toxin: A test of the multiple effects model. *Developmental Psychology, 20,* 523–532.

Jagiello, G. (1982). Meiosis and the aetiology of chromosomal aberrations in man. In M. Adinolfi, P. Benson, F. Giannelli, and M. Seller (Eds.), *Clinics in developmental medicine, No. 83. Paediatric research: A genetic approach.* Philadelphia: J. B. Lippincott.

Jakobson, R. (1962). Why "mama and papa"? In *Selected writings of Roman Jakobson.* The Hague: Mouton.

Jenkins, S., Owen, C., & Hart, H. (1984). Continuities of common behaviour problems in preschool children. *Journal of Child Psychology and Psychiatry, 25,* 75–98.

Jensen, G. D. (1965). Mother-infant relationship in the monkey *Macaca nemestrina:* Development of specificity of maternal response to own infant. *Journal of Comparative and Physiological Psychology, 59,* 305–308.

Jensen, M. D., Benson, R. C., & Bobak, I. M. (1981). *Maternity care.* St. Louis, Missouri: C. V. Mosby.

Jersild, A. T. (1968). *Child psychology.* Englewood Cliffs, N.J.: Prentice-Hall.

Jersild, A. T., & Holmes, F. B. (1935). *Children's fears.* New York: Bureau of Publications, Teacher's College, Columbia University.

Joffe, L. S., & Vaughn, B. E. (1982). Infant-mother attachment: Theory, assessment, and implications for development. In B. B. Wolman (Ed.), *Handbook of developmental psychology.* Englewood Cliffs, N.J.: Prentice-Hall.

Johnson, J. E., & Hooper, F. H. (1982). Piagetian structuralism and learning: Reflections on two decades of educational applications. *Contemporary Educational Psychology, 7,* 217–237.

Jones, M. C. (1965). Psychological correlates of somatic development. *Child Development, 36,* 899–911.

Jones, M. C., & Mussen, P. H. (1958). Self-conceptions, motivations, and interpersonal attitudes of early and late maturing girls. *Child Development, 29,* 491–501.

Joslyn, W. D. (1973). Androgen-induced social dominance in infant female rhesus monkeys. *Journal of Child Psychology and Psychiatry, 14,* 137–145.

Jusczyk, P. W. (1981). The processing of speech and nonspeech sounds by infants: Some implications. In R. N. Aslin, J. R. Alberts, & M. R. Peterson (Eds.), *Development of perception* (Vol. 1). New York: Academic Press.

Kagan, J., Kearsley, R. B., & Zelazo, P. R. (1975, February). The effects of infant day care on psychological development. Paper presented at the American Association for the Advancement of Science meeting, Boston. (ERIC Document Reproduction Service No. ED 122 946.)

Kagan, J., Reznick, S., Clarke, C., Snidman, N., & Garcia-Coll, C. (1984). Behavioral inhibition to the unfamiliar. *Child Development, 55,* 2212–2225.

Kail, R. (1984). *The development of memory in children* (2nd. ed.). New York: W. H. Freeman.

Kail, R., & Bisanz, J. (1982). Information processing and cognitive development. In H. W. Reese (Ed.), *Advances in child development and behavior* (Vol. 17). New York: Academic Press.

Kail, R., & Pellegrino, J. W. (1985). *Human intelligence: Perspectives and prospects.* New York: W. H. Freeman.

Kail, R. V., & Siegel, A. W. (1977). The development of mnemonic encoding in children: From perception to abstraction. In R. V. Kail & J. W. Hagen (Eds.), *Perspectives on the development of memory and cognition.* Hillsdale, N.J.: Lawrence Erlbaum Associates.

Kallmann, F., & Roth, B. (1956). Genetic aspects of preadolescent schizophrenia. *American Journal of Psychiatry, 112,* 599–606.

Kamii, C., & DeVries, R. (1977). Piaget for early education. In M. C Day & R. K. Parker (Eds.), *The preschool in action.* Boston: Allyn & Bacon.

Kamii, C., & DeVries, R. (1978). *Physical knowledge in preschool education: Implications of Piaget's theory.* Englewood Cliffs, N.J.: Prentice-Hall.

Kandel, B. B. (1978). Homophily, selection, and socialization in adolescent friendships. *American Journal of Sociology, 84,* 427–436.

Kanner, L. (1944). Early infantile autism. *Journal of Pediatrics, 25,* 211–217.

Kanner, L. (1949). Problems of nosology and psychodynamics of early infantile autism. *American Journal of Orthopsychiatry, 19,* 416–426.

Kanner, L. (1973). *Childhood psychoses: Initial studies and new insights.* Washington, D.C.: V. H. Winston & Sons.

Kanner, L., & Eisenberg, L. (1956). Early infantile autism, 1943–1955. *American Journal of Orthopsychiatry, 26,* 55–65.

Karp, L. E. (1976). *Genetic engineering: Threat or promise?* Chicago: Nelson-Hall.

Katz, J. (1975). Hormonal abnormality found in patients with anorexia nervosa. *Journal of the American Medical Association, 232,* 9–11.

Kazdin, A. E., & Petti, T. A. (1982). Self-report and interview measures of childhood and adolescent depression. *Journal of Child Psychology and Psychiatry, 23,* 437–457.

Kazdin, A. E., Sherick, R. B., Esveldt-Dawson, K., & Rancurello, M. D. (1985). Nonverbal behavior and childhood depression. *Journal of the American Academy of Child Psychiatry, 24,* 303–309.

Keil, F. C., & Batterman, N. (1984). A characteristic-to-defining shift in the development of word meaning. *Journal of Verbal Learning and Verbal Behavior, 23,* 221–236.

Keller, B. B., & Bell, R. Q. (1979). Child effects on adult's method of eliciting altruistic behavior. *Child Development, 50,* 1004–1009.

Kendall, P. C., & Braswell, L. (1982). Cognitive-behavioral self-control therapy for children: A components analysis. *Journal of Consulting and Clinical Psychology, 50,* 672–689.

Kendall, P. C., Lerner, R. M., Craighead, W. E. (1984). Human development and intervention in childhood psychopathology. *Child Development, 55,* 71–82.

Kendler, H. H., & Kendler, T. S. (1975). From discrimination learning to cognitive development: A neobehavioristic odyssey. In W. K. Estes (Ed.), *Handbook of learning and cognitive processes* (Vol. 1). Hillsdale, N.J.: Lawrence Erlbaum Associates.

Kendler, T. S. (1963). Development of mediating responses in children. In J. C. Wright & J. Kagan (Eds.), *Basic cognitive processes in children. Monographs of the Society for Research in Child Development, 28,* 33–51.

Kendler, T. S. (1979). The development of discrimination learning: A levels-of-functioning explanation. In H. W. Reese & L. P. Lipsitt (Eds.), *Advances in child development and behavior* (Vol. 13). New York: Academic Press.

Kennedy, W. A. (1965). School phobia: Rapid treatment of fifty cases. *Journal of Abnormal Psychology, 70,* 285–289.

Kenny, T. J. (1980). Hyperactivity. In H. E. Rie & E. D. Rie (Eds.), *Handbook of minimal brain dysfunctions.* New York: John Wiley.

Keogh, B. K. (1971). Hyperactivity and learning disorders: Review and speculation. *Exceptional Child, 38,* 101–109.

Kessen W. *The child.* New York: John Wiley, 1965.

Kessen, W., Haith, M. M., & Salapatek, P. H. (1970). Infancy. In P. H. Mussen (Ed.), *Carmichael's manual of child psychology,* New York: John Wiley.

Kessen, W. (1975). *Children in China.* New Haven: Yale University Press.

Kety, S. S., Rosenthal, D., Wender, P. H., and Schulsinger, F. (1976). Studies based on a total sample of adopted individuals and their relatives: Why they were necessary, what they demonstrated and failed to demonstrate. *Schizophrenia Bulletin, 2,* 413–428.

Klahr, D. (1982). Nonmonotone assessment of monotone development: An information processing analysis. In S. Strauss and R. Stavy (Eds.), *U-shaped behavior growth.* New York: Academic Press.

Klaus, M. H., & Kennell, J. H. (1978). Parent-to-infant attachment. In J. H. Stevens, Jr. and M. Mathews (Eds.), *Mother/child and father/child relationships.* Washington, D.C.: The National Association for the Education of Young Children.

Klein, D. F., & Gittelman-Klein, R. (1975). Problems in the diagnosis of minimal brain dysfunction and the hyperkinetic syndrome. In R. Gittelman-Klein (Ed.), *Recent advances in child psychopharmacology.* New York: Human Sciences Press.

Klinnert, M., Campos, J. J., Sorce, J., Emde, R. N., & Svejda, M. (1983). Emotions as behavior regulators: Social referencing in infancy. In R. Plutchik and H. Kellerman (Eds.), *Emotions in early development, Vol. 2, The emotions.* New York: Academic Press.

Knobloch, H., & Pasamanick, B. (1974). *Gesell and Amatruda's developmental diagnosis.* New York: Harper & Row.

Kogan, N. (1983). Stylistic variation in childhood and adolescence: Creativity, metaphor, and cognitive style. In P. H. Mussen (Ed.), *Handbook of child psychology* (Vol. 3). New York: Wiley.

Kohlberg, L. (1966). A cognitive-developmental analysis of children's sex-role concepts and attitudes. In. E. E. Maccoby (Ed.), *The development of sex differences.* Stanford: Stanford University Press.

Kohlberg, L., LaCrosse, J., & Ricks, D. (1972). The predictability of adult mental health from childhood behavior. In B. Wolman (Ed.), *Manual of child psychopathology.* New York: McGraw-Hill.

Kohlberg, L., & Ullian, D. Z. (1974). Stages in the development of psychosexual concepts and attitudes. In R. C. Friedman, R. M. Richart, & R. L. Van Wiele (Eds.), *Sex differences in behavior.* New York: John Wiley.

Kolata, G. B. (1978). Behavioral teratology: Birth defects of the mind. *Science, 202,* 732–734.

Konner, M. (1982). Biological aspects of the mother-infant bond. In R. N. Emde and R. J. Harmon (Eds.), *Development of attachment and affiliative systems.* New York: Plenum Press.

Kopp, C. B., & Krakow, J. B. (1983). The developmentalist and the study of biological risk: A view of the past with an eye toward the future. *Child Development, 54,* 1086–1108.

Kopp, C. B., & McCall, R. B. (1982). Predicting later mental performance for normal, at-risk, and handicapped infants. In P. B. Bates & O. G. Brim (Eds.), *Life-span development and behavior* (Vol. 4). New York: Academic Press.

Kosky, R. (1983). Childhood suicidal behavior. *Journal of Child Psychology and Psychiatry, 24,* 457–468.

Kotelchuck, M. (1972). The nature of a child's tie to his father. Unpublished doctoral dissertation, Harvard University.

Kotelchuck, M., Zelazo, P., Kagan, J., and Spelke, E. (1975). Infant reaction to parental separations when left with familiar and unfamiliar adults. *Journal of Genetic Psychology, 126,* 255–262.

Krauss, R. M., & Weinheimer, S. (1964). Changes in reference phrases as a function of frequency of usage in social interaction: A preliminary study. *Psychonomic Science, 1,* 343–346.

Kreutzer, M. A., Leonard, C., & Flavell, J. H. (1975). An interview study of children's knowledge about memory. *Monographs of the Society for Research in Child Development, 40* (1, Serial No. 159), 1–58.

Kuczaj, S. A. (1981). More on children's failure to relate specific acquisitions. *Journal of Child Language, 8,* 485–487.

Kuczaj, S. A. (1983). "I mell a kunk!"—Evidence that children have more complex representations of word pronunciations which they simplify. *Journal of Psycholinguistic Research, 12,* 69–73.

Kuhn, D., Nash, S. C., & Brucken, L. (1978). Sex-role concepts of two- and three-year-olds. *Child Development, 49,* 445–451.

Kurdek, L. A., Blisk, D., and Siesky, A. E. (1981). Correlates of children's long-term adjustment to their parents' divorce. *Developmental Psychology, 17,* 565–579.

Kurdek, L. A., & Krile, D. (1982). A developmental analysis of the relation between peer acceptance and both interpersonal understanding and perceived self-competence. *Child Development, 53,* 1485–1491.

Labov, M., & Labov, T. (1978). The phonetics of cat and mama. *Language, 54,* 816–852.

Labov, W. (1970). The logic of nonstandard English. In F. Williams (Ed.), *Language and poverty: Perspectives on a theme.* Chicago: Markham.

Ladd, G. W., & Mize, J. A. (1983). A cognitive-social learning model of social-skill training. *Psychological Review, 90,* 127–157.

Ladd, G. W., & Oden, S. (1979). The relationship between peer acceptance and children's ideas about helpfulness. *Child Development, 50,* 402–408.

LaFreniere, P., Strayer, F. F., & Gauthier, R. (1984). The emergence of same-sex affiliative preferences among preschool peers: A developmental/ethnological perspective. *Child Development, 55,* 1958–1965.

Lagerspetz, K. (1961). Genetics and social causes of aggressive behavior in mice. *Scandinavian Journal of Psychology, 2,* 167–173.

La Greca, A. M. (1980). Can children remember to be creative? An interview study of children's thinking processes. *Child Development, 51,* 572–575.

Lamaze, F. (1970). *Painless childbirth.* Chicago: Henry Regnery Co.

Lamb, M. E. (1975). The relationships between infants and their mothers and fathers. Doctoral dissertation, Yale University.

Lamb, M. E. (1976). Interactions between eight-month-old children and their fathers and mothers. In M. E. Lamb, (Ed.), *The role of the father in child development.* New York: John Wiley.

Lamb, M. E. (1977). Father-infant interaction in the first year of life. *Child Development, 48,* 167–181.

Lamb, M. E. (1978). Social interaction in infancy and the development of personality. In M. E. Lamb (Ed.), *Social and Personality Development.* New York: Holt, Rinehart, & Winston, 1978.

Lamb, M. E. (1979). Parental influences and the father's role: A personal perspective. *American Psychologist, 34,* 938–943.

Lamb, M. E. (Ed.). (1981). *The role of the father in child development* (2nd ed.). New York: J. Wiley.

Lamb, M. E. (1982). Parent—infant interaction, attachment, and socioemotional development in infancy. In R. N. Emde and R. J. Harmon (Eds.), *The development of attachment and affiliative systems.* New York: Plenum Press.

Lamb, M. E., Frodi, A. M., Hwang, C-P., Frodi, M., & Steinberg, J. (1982). Effect of gender and caretaking role on parent-child interaction. In R. N. Emde and R. J. Harmon (Eds.), *The development of attachment and affiliative systems.* New York: Plenum Press.

Lamb, M. E., & Hwang, C-P. (1982). Maternal attachment and mother-neonate bonding: A critical review. In M. E. Lamb and A. L. Brown (Eds.), *Advances in developmental psychology,* Vol. 2. Hillsdale, N. J.: Lawrence Erlbaum Associates.

Landau, B. (1982). Will the real grandmother please stand up? The psychological reality of dual meaning of representations. *Journal of Psycholinguistic Research, 11,* 47–62.

Landau, B., Gleitman, H., & Spelke, E. (1981). Spatial knowledge and geometric representation in a child blind from birth. *Science, 213,* 1275–1278.

Langhorne, J., Loney, J., Paternite, C., & Bechtholdt, H. (1976). Childhood hyperkinesis: A return to the source. *Journal of Consulting and Clinical Psychology, 85,* 201–209.

Langlois, J. H., & Downs, A. C. (1979). Peer relations as a funciton of physical attractiveness: The eye of the beholder or behavioral reality? *Child Development, 50,* 409–418.

Langlois, J. H., & Stephan, C. (1977). The effects of physical attractiveness and ethnicity on children's behavioral attributions and peer preferences. *Child Development, 48,* 1694–1698.

Lapouse, R., & Monk, M. (1958). An epidemiologic study of behavior characteristics in children. *American Journal of Public Health, 48,* 1134–1144.

Lappé, M., & Morison, R. S. (Eds.). (1976). Ethical and scientific issues posed by human uses of molecular genetics. *Annals of the New York Academy of Science, 265.*

Latané, B., & Nida, S. (1981). Ten years of research on group size and helping. *Psychological Bulletin, 89,* 308–324.

Laupa, M. & Turiel, E. (1986). Children's conceptions of adult and peer authority. *Child Development, 57*, in press.

Lazarus, A. (1963). The result of behavior therapy in 126 cases of severe neuroses. *Behavior Research and Therapy, 1*, 69–79.

Lefkowitz, M. (1981). Smoking during pregnancy: long-term effects on offspring. *Developmental Psychology, 17*, 192–194.

Lefkowitz, M., & Burton, N. (1978). Childhood depression: A critique of the concept. *Psychological Bulletin, 85*, 716–726.

Lefkowitz, M., & Tesiny, E. P. (1984). Rejection and depression: Prospective and contemporaneous analyses. *Developmental Psychology, 20*, 776–785.

Leitenberg, H., Agras, W. S., & Thomson, L. E. (1968). A sequential analysis of the effect of selective positive reinforcement in modifying anorexia nervosa. *Behaviour Research and Therapy, 6*, 211–218.

Lenneberg, E. H. (1967). *Biological foundations of language.* New York: Wiley.

Leon, G. R., Kendall, P. C., & Garber, J. (1980). Depression in children: Parent, teacher and child perspectives. *Journal of Abnormal Child Psychology, 8*, 221–235.

Leonard, L. B. (1975). The role of nonlinguistic stimuli and semantic relations in children's acquisition of grammatical utterances. *Journal of Experimental Child Psychology, 19*, 346–367.

Leonard, L. B. (1976). *Meaning in child language.* New York: Grune & Stratton.

Lepper, M. R., & Greene, D. (1978). Overjustification research and beyond: Toward a means-ends analysis of intrinsic and extrinsic motivation. In M. R. Lepper & D. Greene (Eds.), *The hidden costs of reward.* Hillsdale, N.J.: Lawrence Erlbaum Associates.

Lepper, M. R., Greene, D., & Nisbett, R. E. (1973). Undermining children's intrinsic interest with extrinsic rewards: A test of the overjustification hypothesis. *Journal of Personality and Social Psychology, 28*, 129–137.

Lerner, R. M., & Shea, J. A. (1982). Social behavior in adolescence. In B. Wolman (Ed.), *Handbook of developmental psychology.* Englewood Cliffs, N.J.: Prentice-Hall.

Lerner, R. M., & Schroeder, C. (1971). Physique identification preference, and aversion in kindergarten children. *Developmental Psychology, 5*, 538.

Lester, B. M. (1975). Cardiac habituation of the orienting response to an auditory signal in infants of varying nutritional status. *Developmental Psychology, 11*, 432–442.

Lester, B., & Brazelton, T. B. (1980). Cross-cultural assessment of neonatal behavior. In H. Stevenson and D. Wagner (Eds.), *Cultural perspectives on child development.* San Francisco: W. H. Freeman and Co.

Lever, J. (1978). Sex differences in the complexity of children's play and games. *American Sociological Review, 43*, 471–483.

Levitt, E. E. (1957). The results of psychotherapy with children: An evaluation. *Journal of Consulting Psychology, 21*, 189–196.

Lewinsohn, P. (1974). A behavioral approach to depression. In R. J. Friedman & M. M. Katz (Eds.), *The psychology of depression: Contemporary theory and research.* Washington, D. C.: Winston.

Lewis, M., & Brooks-Gunn, J. (1979). *Social cognition and the acquisition of self.* New York: Plenum Press.

Lewis, M., & Wilson, C. D. (1972). Infant development in lower-class American families. *Human Development, 15*, 112–127.

Lewittes D. J., & Israel, A. C. (1978). The effects of other-oriented consequences for ongoing delay of gratification in children. *Developmental Psychology, 14*, 181–182.

Lewkowicz, D. J., & Turkewitz, G. (1982). Influence of hemispheric specialization in sensory processing on reaching in infants. *Developmental Psychology, 18*, 301–308.

Liben, L. S., & Belknap, B. (1981). Intellectual realism: Implications for investigations of perceptual perspective taking in young children. *Child Development, 52*, 921–924.

Licht, B. G., & Dweck, C. S. (1984). Determinants of academic achievement: The interaction of children's achievement orientations with skill area. *Developmental Psychology, 20*, 628–636.

Liebert, R. M., & Poulos, R. W. (1975). Television and personality development: Socializing effects of an entertainment medium. In A. Davids (Ed.), *Personality development and psychopathology: Current topics* (Vol. 2). New York: Wiley.

Liebert, R. M. (1979). Moral development: A theoretical and empirical analysis. In G. J. Whitehurst, and B. Zimmerman (Eds.), *The functions of language and cognition.* New York: Academic Press.

Liebert, R. M., Sprafkin, J. N., & Davidson, E. S. (1982). *The early window: effects of television on children and youth.* Elmsford, N.Y.: Pergamon Press.

Liederman, P. H. (1983). Social ecology and childbirth: The newborn. In N. Garmezy and M. Rutter (Eds.), *Stress, coping, and development in children.* New York: McGraw-Hill.

Light, L. L., & Anderson, P. A. (1983). Memory for scripts in young and older adults. *Memory & Cognition, 11*, 435–444.

Lind, J. 1973: personal communication, as cited by Klaus, M. H., and Kennell, J. H. Parent-to-infant attachment, in J. H. Stevens, Jr. & M. Matthews (Eds.), *Mother/child, father/child relationships*. Washington, D. C., The National Association for the Education of Young Children, 1978.

Lipsitt, L. P. (1983). Stress in infancy: Toward understanding the origins of coping behavior. In N. Garmezy and M. Rutter (Eds.), *Stress, coping, and development in children*. New York: McGraw-Hill.

Lipsitt, L. P., Engen, T., & Kaye, H. (1963). Developmental changes in the olfactory threshold of the neonate. *Child Development, 34*, 371–376.

Lipsitt, L. P., & Levy, N. (1959). Electrotactual threshold in the neonate. *Child Development, 30*, 547–554.

Lockman, J. J., & Pick, H. L. (1984). Problems of scale in spatial development. In C. Sophian (Ed.), *Origins of cognitive skills*. Hillsdale, N.J.: Lawrence Erlbaum Associates.

Lodico, M. G., Ghatala, E. S., Levin, J. R., Pressley, M., & Bell, J. A. (1983). The effects of strategy-monitoring training on children's selection of memory strategies. *Journal of Experimental Child Psychology, 35*, 263–277.

Loeber, R. (1982). The stability of antisocial and delinquent child behavior: A review. *Child Development, 53*, 1431–1446.

Loehlin, J. C., & Nichols, R. C. (1976). *Heredity, environment and personality*. Austin: University of Texas Press.

Lotter, V. (1974). Social adjustment and placement of autistic children in Middlesex: A follow-up study. *Journal of Autism and Childhood Schizophrenia, 4*, 11–32.

Lotter, V. (1978). Follow-up studies. In M. Rutter and E. Schopler, (Eds.), *Autism: A reappraisal of concepts and treatment*. New York: Plenum.

Lovaas, O. I. (1968). Some studies in the treatment of childhood schizophrenia. In J. M. Schlien (Ed.), *Research in psychotherapy: Proceedings of the third conference*. Washington, D. C.: American Psychological Association.

Luk, S. (1985). Direct observation studies of hyperactive behaviors. *Journal of the American Academy of Child Psychiatry, 24*, 338–344.

Luparello, T., Lyons, H. A., Bleecker, E. R., & McFadden, E. R. (1968). Influence of suggestion on airways reactivity in asthmatic subjects. *Psychosomatic medicine, 30*, 819–825.

Maas, H. S. (1968). Preadolescent peer relations and adult intimacy. *Psychiatry, 31*, 161–172.

Macken, M. A., & Ferguson, C. A. (1983). Cognitive aspects of phonological development: Model, evidence, and issues. In K. E. Nelson (Ed.), *Children's language* (Vol. 4). Hillsdale, N.J.: Lawrence Erlbaum Associates.

Maccoby, E. E. (1980). *Social development*. New York: Harcourt Brace Jovanovich.

Maccoby, E., & Feldman, S. (1972). Mother-attachment and stranger-reactions in the third year of life. *Monographs of the Society for Research in Child Development, 37*, (no. 1, serial no. 146).

Maccoby, E. E., & Jacklin, C. N. (1974). *The psychology of sex differences*. Stanford, Ca: Stanford University Press.

Maccoby, E. E., & Jacklin, C. N. (1980). Sex differences in aggression: A rejoinder and reprise. *Child Development, 51*, 964–980.

MacFarland, A. (1975). Olfaction in the development of social preferences in the human neonate. In M. A. Hofer (Ed.), *Parent-infant interaction*. Amsterdam: CIBA Foundation Symposium.

Maddox, G. L., Back, K. W., & Liederman, V. R. (1968). Overweight as social deviance and disability. *Journal of Health and Social Behavior, 9*, 287–298.

Maier, H. W. (1969). *Three theories of child development*. New York: Harper & Row.

Malmquist, C. P. (1977). Childhood depression: A clinical and behavioral perspective. In J. G. Schulterbrandt & A. Raskin (Eds.), *Depression in childhood: Diagnosis, treatment, and conceptual models*. New York: Raven Press.

Mannarino, A. P. (1978). Friendship patterns and self-concept development in preadolescent males. *Journal of Genetic Psychology, 133*, 105–110.

Maratsos, M. (1983). Some current issues in the study of the acquisition of grammar. In J. H. Flavell & E. M. Markman (Eds.), *Handbook of child psychology* (Vol. 3). New York: Wiley.

Marcia, J. E. (1980). Identity in adolescence. In J. Adelson (Ed.), *Handbook of adolescent psychology*. New York: John Wiley.

Marg, E., Freeman, D. N., Peltzman, P., & Goldstein, P. (1976). Visual acuity development in human infants: Evoked potential measurements. *Investigative Opthamology, 15*, 150–153.

Markman, E. (1977). Realizing that you don't understand: A preliminary investigation. *Child Development, 48*, 986–992.

Marsh, H. W., & Parker, J. W. (1984). Determinants of student self-concept: Is it better to be a relatively large fish in a small pond even if you don't learn how to swim as well? *Journal of Personality and Social Psychology, 47*, 213–231.

Marston, A. R., London, P., & Cooper, L. M. (1976). Note on the eating behaviour of children varying in weight. *Journal of Child Psychology and Psychiatry and Allied Disciplines, 17*, 221–224.

Martin, C. L., & Halverson, C. F., Jr. (1981). A schematic processing model of sex typing and stereotyping in children. *Child Development, 52*, 1119–1134.

Martin, C. L., & Halverson, C. F., Jr. (1983). The effects of sex-typing schemas on young children's memory. *Child Development, 54*, 563–574.

Masters, J. C., & Furman, W. (1981). Popularity, individual friendship selection, and specific peer interaction among children. *Developmental Psychology, 17*, 344–350.

Matheny, A. P., Wilson, R. S., & Dolan, A. B. (1976). Relations between twins' similarity of appearance and behavioral similarity: Testing an assumption. *Behavior Genetics, 6*, 343–351.

Mauger, P., Adkinson, D. R., Hernandez, S. R., Firestone, G., & Hook, J. D. (1978). *Can assertiveness be distinguished from aggressiveness using self-report data?* Paper presented at the meeting of the American Psychological Association, Toronto, Canada, August.

Maurer, D., & Salapatek, P. (1976). Developmental changes in the scanning of faces by young infants. *Child Development, 47*, 523–527.

McAdoo, W. G., & DeMyer, M. K. (1978). Personality characteristics of parents. In M. Rutter & E. Schopler (Eds.), *Autism: A reappraisal of concepts and treatment.* New York: Plenum.

McAnarney, E. (1979). Adolescent and young adult suicide in the U.S.—A reflection of societal unrest? *Adolescence, 14*, 765–774.

McCall, R. B., Parke, R. D., & Kavanaugh, R. D. (1977). Imitation of live and televised models by children one to three years of age. *Monographs of the Society for Research in Child Development, 42*, Whole No. 173.

McCarthy, D. (1954). Language development in children. In L. Carmichael (Ed.), *Manual of child psychology.* New York: Wiley.

McCartney, K. (1984). Effect of quality of day care environment on children's language development. *Developmental Psychology, 20*, 24–260.

McCartney, W. (1968). *Olfaction and odours.* New York: Springer-Verlag.

McClearn, G. E. (1970). Genetic influences on behavior and development. In P. H. Mussen (Ed.), *Carmichael's manual of child psychology.* 3rd. ed. New York: John Wiley.

McCoy, C. L. & Masters, J. C. (1985). The development of children's strategies for the social control of emotion. *Child Development, 56*, 1214–1222.

McCrea, J., & Herbert-Jackson, E. (1976). Are behavioral effects of infant day care programs specific? *Developmental Psychology, 12*, 269–270.

McDermott, J. F., & Char, W. F. (1984). Stage-related models of psychotherapy with children. *Journal of the American Academy of Psychiatry, 23*, 537–543.

McGhee, P. E. (1976). Children's appreciation of humor: A test of the cognitive congruency principle. *Child Development, 47*, 420–426.

McGhee, P. E. (1979). *Humor: Its origin and development.* San Francisco: W. H. Freeman.

McGuire, K. D., & Weisz, J. R. (1982). Social cognition and behavior correlates of preadolescent chumship. *Child Development, 53*, 1478–1484.

McKusick, V. A. (1975). *Mendelian inheritance in man.* Baltimore, Md.: John Hopkins Press.

McNeill, D. (1970). *The acquisition of language.* New York: Harper & Row.

Mead, M. (1935). *Sex and temperament in three primitive societies.* New York: Morrow.

Meece, J. L., Parsons, J. E., Kaczala, C. M., Goff, S. B. & Futterman, R. (1982). Sex differences in math achievement: Towards a model of academic choice. *Psychological Bulletin, 91*, 324–348.

Meltzoff, A. N., & Moore, M. K. (1971). Imitation of facial and manual gestures by human neonates. *Science, 198*, 75–78.

Meltzoff, A. N., & Moore, M. K. (1983). Newborn infants imitate adult facial gestures. *Child Development, 54*, 702–709.

Mendelsohn, E., Robinson, S., Gardner, H., & Winner, E. (1984). Are preschoolers' renamings intentional category violations? *Developmental Psychology, 20*, 187–192.

Mercer, J. R. (1971). Sociocultural factors in labeling mental retardates. *The Peabody Journal of Education, 48*, 188–203.

Mervis, C. B., & Pani, J. (1980). Acquisition of object categories. *Cognitive Psychology, 12*, 496–522.

Mesibov, G. B., Schroeder, C. S., & Wesson, L. (1977). Parental concerns about their children. *Journal of Pediatric Psychology, 2*, 13–17.

Milewski, A. E. (1979). Visual discrimination and detection of configurational and invariance in 3-month-old infants. *Developmental Psychology, 15*, 357–363.

Milich, R., & Loney, J. (1979). The role of hyperactivity and aggressive symptomatology in predicting adolescent outcome among hyperactive children. *Journal of Pediatric Psychology, 4*, 93–112.

Miller, F. J., Billewicz, W. Z., & Thomson, A. M. (1972). Growth from birth to adult life of 442 Newcastle-Upon-Tyne children. *British Journal of Preventative and Social Medicine, 26*, 224–230.

Miller, J. P. (1975). Suicide and adolescence. *Adolescence, 10*, 11–24.

Miller, R. W. (1974). Susceptibility of the fetus and child to chemical pollutants. *Science, 184,* 812–813.

Miller, L. C., Barrett, C. L., Hampe E., & Noble, H. (1972). Factor structure of childhood fears. *Journal of Consulting and Clinical Psychology, 39,* 264–268.

Minuchin, P. P., & Shapiro, E. K. (1983). The school as a context for social development. In P. H. Mussen (Ed.), *Handbook of child psychology, Vol. 4.* New York: John Wiley.

Minuchin, S., Rosman, B. L., & Baker, L. (1978). *Psychosomatic families: Anorexia nervosa in context.* Cambridge, Mass.: Harvard University Press.

Mischel, W. (1966). A social-learning view of sex differences in behavior. In E. E. Maccoby (Ed.), *The development of sex differences.* Stanford, CA: Stanford University Press.

Mischel, W. (1970) Sex-typing and socialization. In P. H. Mussen, (Ed.) *Carmichaels' Manual of child psychology, Vol. 2.* New York: John Wiley.

Mischel, W. (1979). On the interface of cognition and personality: Beyond the person-situation debate. *American Psychologist, 34,* 740–754.

Molfese, D. L., Freeman, R. B., & Palermo, D. S. (1975). The ontogeny of brain lateralization for speech and nonspeech stimuli. *Brain and Language, 2,* 356–368.

Molfese, D. L., & Molfese, V. J. (1979). Hemispheric and stimulus differences as reflected in the cortical responses of newborn infants to speech stimuli. *Developmental Psychology, 15,* 505–511.

Money, J., & Ehrhardt, A. (1972). *Man and woman; boy and girl.* Baltimore: Johns Hopkins University Press.

Moore, M. L. (1983). *Realities in childbearing.* Philadelphia: W. B. Saunders.

Moretti, M. M., Fine, S., Haley, G., & Marriage, K. (1985). Childhood and adolescent depression: Child-report versus parent-report information. *Journal of the American Academy of Child Psychiatry, 24,* 298–302.

Moss, H. A. (1967). Sex, age and state as determinants of mother-infant interaction. *Merrill-Palmer Quarterly, 13,* 19–36.

Moss, H. A., Robson, K. S., & Pedersen, F. (1969). Determinants of maternal stimulation of infants and consequences of treatment for later reactions to strangers. *Developmental Psychology, 1,* 239–246.

Moulton, J., Robinson, G. M., & Elias, C. (1978). Sex bias in language. "Neutral" pronouns that aren't. *American Psychologist, 33,* 1032–1036.

Mowrer, O. H., & Mowrer, W. M. (1938). Enuresis: A method for its study and treatment. *American Journal of Orthopsychiatry, 8,* 436–447.

Moynahan, E. D. (1978). Assessment and selection of paired associate strategies: A developmental study. *Journal of Experimental Child Psychology, 26,* 257–266.

Mueller, E., & Lucas, T. A. (1975). A developmental analysis of peer interactions among toddlers. In M. Lewis & L. A. Rosenblum (Eds.), *Friendship and peer relations.* New York: John Wiley.

Munroe, R. H., Shimmin, H. S., & Munroe, R. L. (1984). Gender understanding and sex role preference in four cultures. *Developmental Psychology, 20,* 673–82.

Munn, N. L. *Psychology: The fundamentals of human adjustment.* Boston: Houghton Mifflin, 1946.

Murray, F. B. (1982). Teaching through social conflict. *Contemporary Educational Psychology, 7,* 257–271.

Muuss, R. E. (1972). Adolescent development and the secular trend. In D. Rogers (Ed.), *Issues in adolescent development.* New York: Appleton-Century-Crofts.

Myers, M. & Paris, S. G. (1978). Children's metacognitive knowledge about reading. *Journal of Educational Psychology, 70,* 680–690.

Neale, J. N., & Oltmanns, T. F. (1980). *Schizophrenia.* New York: John Wiley.

Needleman, H. L., Gunnoe, G., Leviton, A., Reed, R., Peresie, H., Maher, C., & Barrett, P. (1979). Deficits in psychological and classroom performance of children with elevated dentine lead levels. *New England Journal of Medicine, 300,* 689–695.

Nelson K. (1973). Structure and strategy in learning to talk. *Monograph of the Society for Research in Child Development, 38,* No. 149.

Nelson, K. (1974). Concept, word, and sentence: Interrelations in acquisition and development. *Psychological Review, 81,* 267–285.

Nelson, K. (1975). The nominal shift in semantic-syntactic development. *Cognitive Psychology, 7,* 461–479.

Nelson, K. (1981). Individual differences in language development: Implications for development and language. *Developmental Psychology, 17,* 170–187.

Nelson, K. E. (1982). Experimental gambits in the service of language acquisition: From the Fifffin Project to Operation Input Swap. In S. A. Kuczaj (Ed.), *Language development* (Vol. 1). Hillsdale, N.J.: Lawrence Erlbaum Associates.

Neuman, P. A., & Halvorson, P. A. (1983). *Anorexia nervosa and bulimia.* New York: Van Nostrand Reinhold Company.

Newcombe, N., & Bandura, M. (1983). Effect of age at puberty on spatial ability in girls: A question of mechanism. *Developmental Psychology, 19,* 215–224.

Newcombe, N., & Zaslow, M. (1981). Do $2^1/2$-year-olds hint? A study of directive forms in the speech of $2^1/2$-year-old children to adults. *Discourse Processes, 4,* 239–252.

Newell, K. M. & Kennedy, J. A. (1978). Knowledge of results and children's motor learning. *Developmental Psychology, 14,* 531–536.

Newman, H. H., Freeman, F., & Holzinger, K. J. (1937). *Twins: A study of heredity and environment.* Chicago: University of Chicago Press.

Newport, E. L., Gleitman, L. R., & Gleitman, H. (1977). Mother, I'd rather do it myself: Some effects and non-effects of maternal speech style. In C. E. Snow and C. A. Ferguson (Eds.), *Talking to children: Language input and acquisition.* Cambridge, Eng.: Cambridge University Press.

New York Times (1975, Sept. 30). Family ponders its rare, fatal hereditary disease.

Nichols, R. C. (1978). Heredity and environment: Major findings from twins tudies of ability, personality, and interests. *Homo, 29,* 158–173.

Nisan, M. (1974). Exposure to rewards and the delay of gratification. *Developmental Psychology, 10,* 376–380.

Nisan, M. (1984). Content and structure in moral judgment: An integrative view. In W. Kurtines & J. Gewirtz (Ed.), *Mortality, moral behavior, and moral development.* New York: Wiley-Interscience.

Nisan, M., & Koriat, A. (1984). The effect of cognitive restructuring on delay of gratification. *Child Development, 55,* 492–503.

O'Connor, M. J., Cohen, S., & Parmelee, A. H. (1984). Infant auditory discrimination in preterm and full-term infants as a predictor of 5-year intelligence. *Developmental Psychology, 20,* 159–165.

Offenbach, S. I., Gruen, G. E., & Caskey, B. J. (1984). Development of proportional response strategies. *Child Development, 55,* 963–972.

O'Leary, K. D. & Wilson, G. T. (1975). *Behavior therapy: Application and outcome.* Englewood Cliffs, N.J.: Prentice Hall.

O'Leary, K. D. (1978, August). Pills or skills for hyperactive children. Manuscript based on Presidential address, Clinical Division, Section III, Experimental-Behavioral Science, American Psychological Association, Toronto, Canada.

O'Leary, S. G., & Pelham, W. E. (1978). Behavioral therapy and withdrawal of stimulant medication with hyperactive children. *Pediatrics, 61,* 211–217.

Olweus, D., Mattsson, A., Schalling, D., & Low, H. (1980). Testosterone, aggression, physical and personality dimensions on normal adolescent males. *Psychosomatic Medicine, 42,* 253–269.

Orlofsky, J. L., & Stake, J. E. (1981). Psychological masculinity and femininity: Relationship to striving and self-concept in the achievement and interpersonal domains. *Psychology of Women Quarterly, 6,* 218–233.

Ornitz, E. M. (1978). Neurophysiologic studies. In M. Rutter & E. Schopler (Eds.), *Autism: A reappraisal of concepts and treatment.* New York: Plenum.

Ornstein, P. A. (1977). Memory development in children. In R. M. Liebert, R. W. Poulos, and G. S. Marmor, *Developmental psychology* (2nd ed.). Englewood Cliffs, NJ: Prentice-Hall.

Ornstein, P. A., Naus, M. J., & Liberty, C. (1975). Rehearsal and organizational processes in children's memory. *Child Development, 46,* 818–830.

Otto, L. B. (1979). Antecedents and consequences of marital timing. In W. R. Bun, R. Hill, F. I. Nye, & I. L. Reiss (Eds.), *Contemporary theories about the family* (Vol. 1). New York: Free Press.

Oviatt, S. L. (1980). The emerging ability to comprehend language: An experimental approach. *Child Development, 51,* 97–106.

Oviatt, S. L. (1982). Inferring what words mean: Early development in infants' comprehension of common object names. *Child Development, 53,* 274–277.

Pachter, E. F. (1978). The pre-professionals: A self-portrait by late adolescents. *The Andover Review, 5,* 62–75.

Palme, O. (1972). The emancipation of man. In M. S. Mednick and S. S. Tangri (Eds.), New perspectives on women. *Journal of Social Issues, 28,* 237–246.

Papoušek, H., & Papoušek, M. (1983). Biological basis of social interactions: Implications of research for an understanding of behavioural deviance. *Journal of Child Psychology and Psychiatry, 24,* 117–129.

Parke, R. D. & Collmer, C. W. (1975). Child abuse: An interdisciplinary analysis. In E. M. Hetherington (Ed.), *Review of child development research.* Chicago: University of Chicago Press.

Parke, R. D., & Slaby, R. G. (1983). The development of aggression. In P. H. Mussen (Ed.), *Handbook of child psychology, Vol. 4.* New York: John Wiley.

Parke, R. D., & Sawin, D. B. (1976). The father's role in infancy: A reevaluation. *The Family Coordinator, 25,* 365–371.

Parke, R. D., & Sawin, D. B. (1980). The family in early infancy: Social interactional and attitudinal analysis. In F. A. Pedersen (Ed.), *The father-infant relationship: Observational studies in a family context.* New York: Praeger.

Parke, R. D., & Suomi, S. (in press). Adult male-infant relationships: Human and nonhuman primate evidence. In K. Immelmann, G. Barlow, M. Main, & L. Petrinovitch (Eds.), *Behavioral development: The Bielefeld interdisciplinary project*. New York: Cambridge University Press.

Parker, L., & Whitehead, W. (1982). Treatment of urinary and fecal incontinence in children. In D. C. Russo & J. W. Varni (Eds.), *Behavioral pediatrics*. New York: Plenum Press.

Pascual-Leone, J. (1970). A mathematical model for the transition rule in Piaget's developmental stages. *Acta psychologica, 32*, 301–345.

Pascual-Leone, J. (1980). Constructive problem for constructive theories: The current relevance of Piaget's work and a critique of information processing psychology. In H. Spada and R. Kluwe (Eds.), *Developmental models of thinking*. New York: Academic Press.

Patterson, G. R. (1982) *A social learning approach to family intervention* (Vol. 3): *Coercive family processes*. Eugene, Or.: Castalia.

Patterson, G. R. (1984). Microsocial process: A view from the boundary. In J. C. Masters and K. Yarkin-Levin (Eds.), *Boundary areas in social and developmental psychology*. New York: Academic Press.

Patterson, G. R., Littman, R. A., & Bricker, W. (1967). Assertive behavior in children: A step toward a theory of aggression. *Monographs of the Society for Research in Child Development, 32* (5, Serial No. 113).

Patterson, G. R., Reid, J. B., Jones, R. R., & Conger, R. E. (1975). *A social learning approach to family intervention* (Vol. 1): *Families with aggressive children*. Eugene, Or.: Castalia.

Paulsen, K., & Johnson, M. (1983). Sex role attitudes and mathematical ability in 4th-, 8th-, and 11th-grade students from a high socioeconomic area. *Developmental Psychology, 19*, 210–214.

Pearlman, C. (1984). The effects of level of effectance motivation, IQ, and penalty/reward contingency on the choice of problem difficulty. *Child Development, 55*, 537–542.

Peiper, A., & Eibl-Eibesfeldt, I. (1967). *Grundrib der vergleichenden Verhaltensforschung, Ethologie*. Piper & Co. Verlag Munchen.

Pepler, D. J., and Ross, H. J. (1981). The effects of play on convergent and divergent problem solving. *Child Development, 52*, 1202–1210.

Perlmutter, M. (1980). *New directions for child development* (Vol. 10): *Children's memory*. San Francisco: Jossey-Bass.

Perry, D. G. (1983). Some dangers in defining altruism too narrowly. Review of N. Eisenberg's The development of prosocial behavior. *Contemporary Psychology, 28*, 590–591.

Perry, D. G., & Perry, L. C. (1974). Denial of suffering in the victim as a stimulus to violence in aggressive boys. *Child Development, 45*, 55–62.

Perry, D. G., & Perry, L. C. (1983). Social learning, causal attribution, and moral internalization. In J. Bisanz, G. Bisanz, & R. Kail (Eds.), *Learning in children*. New York: Springer-Verlag.

Perry, D. G., White, A. L., & Perry, L. C. (1984). Does early sex typing result from children's attempts to match their behavior to sex role stereotypes? *Child Development, 55*, 2114–2121.

Peterson, G. W., Rollins, B. C., Thomas, D. L., & Heaps, L. K. (1982). Social placement of adolescents: Sex-role influences on family decisions regarding the careers of youth. *Journal of Marriage and the Family, 44*, 647–658.

Peterson, L. (1983). Role of donor competence, donor age, and peer presence on helping in an emergency. *Developmental Psychology, 19*, 873–880.

Phillips, S., King, S., & DuBois L. (1978). Spontaneous activities of female versus male newborns. *Child Development, 49*, 590–597.

Piaget, J. (1932). *The moral judgment of the child*. New York: Free Press. (reprinted 1965)

Piaget, J. (1952). *The origins of intelligence in children*. New York: International Universities Press.

Piaget, J. (1962). *The language and thought of the child*. New York: World.

Piaget, J., & Inhelder, B. (1956). *The child's conception of space*. Boston: Routledge & Kegan Paul.

Piaget, J., & Inhelder, B. (1967). *The child's conception of space*. New York: Norton.

Piaget, J., & Inhelder, B. (1969). *The psychology of the child*. New York: Basic Books.

Piaget, J., Inhelder, B., & Szeminska, A. (1960). *The child's conception of geometry*. New York: Basic.

Piotrkowski, C. S., & Katz, M. H. (1982). Indirect socialization: The effect of mother's jobs on academic behaviors. *Child Development, 53*, 1520–1529.

Plomin, R. (1984). Childhood temperament. In B. Lahey and A. Kazdin (Eds.), *Advances in clinical child psychology*, Vol. 6. New York: Plenum Press.

Plomin, R., & DeFries, J. C. (1983). The Colorado Adoption Project. *Child Development, 54*, 276–289.

Plomin, R., DeFries, J. D., & Loehlin, J. C. (1977). Genotype-environment interaction and correlation in the analysis of human behavior. *Psychological Bulletin, 84*, 309–322.

Plomin, R., DeFries, J. C., & McClearn, G. E. (1980). *Behavioral genetics: A primer*. San Francisco: W. H. Freeman and Co.

Polit, D. F., Nuttall, R. L., & Nuttall, E. V. (1980). The only child grows up: A look at some characteristics of adult only children. *Family Relations, 29,* 99–106.

Poon, L. W. (1985). Differences in human memory with aging: Nature, causes, and clinical implications. In J. E. Birren and K. Warner Schaie (Eds.), *Handbook of the Psychology of Aging* (2nd ed.). New York: Van Nostrand Reinhold.

Poon, L. W., Walsh-Sweeney, L., & Fozard, J. L. (1980). Memory skill training for the elderly: Salient issues on the use of imagery mnemonics. In L. W. Poon, J. L. Fozard, L. S. Cermak, D. Arenberg, and L. W. Thompson (Eds.), *New Directions in Memory and Aging.* Hillsdale, N.J.: Erlbaum Associates.

Poulos, R. W., & Liebert, R. M. (1972). Influence of modeling, exhortative verbalization, and surveillance on children's sharing. *Developmental Psychology, 6,* 402–408.

Powley, T. L. (1977). The ventromedial hypothalamic syndrome, satiety, and a cephalic phase hypothesis. *Psychological Review, 84,* 89–126.

Pratt, M. W., McLaren, J., & Wickens, G. (1984). Rules as tools: Effective generalization of verbal self-regulative communication training by first-graders. *Developmental Psychology, 20,* 893–902.

Pratt, M. W., Scribner, S., & Cole, M. (1977). Children as teachers: Developmental studies of instructional communication. *Child Development, 48,* 1475–1481.

Prechtl, H. F. R. (1977). *The neurological study of newborn infants.* London: SIMP/Heinemann Medical; Philadelphia: Lippincott.

Prechtl, H. F. R. (1981). The study of neural development as a perspective of clinical problems. In K. J. Connolly and H. F. R. Prechtl (Eds.), *Clinics in developmental medicine No. 77/78. Maturation and development: Biological and psychological perspectives.* Philadelphia: J. B. Lippincott.

Premack, D. (1976). *Intelligence in ape and man.* Hillsdale, NJ: Lawrence Erlbaum Associates.

Pressley, M., Levin, J. R., & Ghatala, E. S. (1984). Memory-strategy monitoring in adults and children. *Journal of Verbal Learning and Verbal Behavior, 23,* 270–288.

Price, W. H., & Whatmore, P. B. (1967). Criminal behavior and the XYY male. *Nature, 213,* 815.

Puig-Antich, J. (1982). The use of RDC for major depressive disorders in children and adolescents. *Journal of the American Academy of Child Psychiatry, 21,* 291–293.

Ramsey, D. S. (1980). Onset of unimanual handedness in infants. *Infant Behavior and Development, 3,* 377–385.

Rapoport, R. Rapoport, R. N., & Strelitz, Z. (1977). *Fathers, mothers, and society.* New York: Basic Books.

Ratcliffe, S. G., & Field, M. A. S. (1982). Emotional disorder in XYY children: Four case reports. *Journal of Child Psychology and Psychiatry, 23,* 401–406.

Reed, E. W. (1975). Genetic abnormalities in development. In F. D. Horowitz (Ed.), *Review of child development research.* Chicago: University of Chicago Press.

Rees, L. (1964). The importance of psychological, allergic and infective factors in childhood asthma. *Journal of Psychosomatic Research, 7,* 253–262.

Rest, J. (1984). The major components of morality. In W. Kurtines & J. Gewirtz (Eds.), *Morality, moral behavior, and moral development.* New York: Wiley-Interscience.

Rheingold, H. R., Hay, D. F., & West, M. J. (1976). Sharing in the second year of life. *Child Development, 47,* 1148–1158.

Rhodes, S. R. (1983). Age-related differences in work attitudes and behavior: A review of conceptual analysis. *Psychological Bulletin, 93,* 328–367.

Ridberg, E. H., Parke, R. D., & Hetherington, E. M. (1971). Modification of impulsive and reflective cognitive styles through observation of film mediated models. *Developmental Psychology, 5,* 369–377.

Rie, H. E. (1971). Historical perspectives of concepts of child psychopathology. In H. E. Rie (Ed.), *Perspectives in child psychopathology.* New York: Aldine-Atherton.

Rieder, R. O., Broman, S. H., & Rosenthal, D. (1977). The offspring of schizophrenics. *Archives of General Psychiatry, 34,* 789–799.

Rimm, D., Janda, L. H., Lancaster, D. W., Nahl, M., & Dittmar, K. (1977). An exploratory investigation of the origin and maintenance of phobias. *Behavior Research and Therapy, 15,* 231–238.

Robins, L. (1966). *Deviant children grown up: A sociological and psychiatric study of sociopathic personality.* Baltimore: Williams & Wilkins.

Robins, L. N. (1974). Antisocial behavior disturbances of childhood: Prevalence, prognosis, and prospects. In E. J. Anthony (Ed.), *The child in his family.* New York: John Wiley.

Robinson, M. N., & Robinson H. B. (1976). *The mentally retarded child.* New York: McGraw-Hill.

Robson, K. S., & Moss, H. A. (1971). Bethesda, Maryland: Child Research branch, NIMH. Unpublished findings as cited in H. F. Harlow.

Robson, K. S., Pedersen, F. A., and Moss, H. A. (1969). Developmental observations of dyadic gazing in relation to the fear of strangers and social approach behavior. *Child Development, 40,* 619–627.

Rogoff, B., Ellis, S., & Gardner, W. (1984). Adjustment of adult-child instruction according to child's age and task. *Developmental Psychology, 20,* 193–199.

Rose, S. A. (1983). Differential rates of visual information processing in full-term and preterm infants. *Child Development, 54,* 1189–1198.

Rosenthal, D. (1970). *Genetic theory and abnormal behavior.* New York: McGraw-Hill.

Ross, A. O., & Pelham, W. E. (1981). Child psychopathology. *Annual review of psychology, 32,* 243–278.

Ross, G., Kagan, J., Zelazo, P., & Kotelchuck, M. (1975). Separation protest in infants in home and laboratory. *Developmental Psychology, 11,* 256–257.

Routh, D. K. (1980). Developmental and social aspects of hyperactivity. In C. K. Whalen and B. Henker (Eds.), *Hyperactive children,* New York: Academic Press.

Routh, D. K., Schroeder, C. S., & Koocher, G. P. (1983). Psychology and primary health care for children. *American Psychologist, 38,* 95–98.

Rovee, C. K., Cohen, R. Y., & Shlapack, W. (1975). Life-span stability in olfactory sensitivity. *Developmental Psychology, 11,* 311–318.

Rovet, J., & Netley, C. (1982). Processing deficits in Turner's Syndrome. *Developmental Psychology, 18,* 77–94.

Rubin, J. Z., Provenzano, F. L., & Luria, Z. (1974). The eye of the beholder: Parents' views on sex of newborns. *American Journal of Orthopsychiatry, 44,* 512–519.

Rubin, Z. (1980). *Children's friendships.* Cambridge, Mass.: Harvard University Press.

Ruff, H. A. (1980). The development of perception and recognition objects. *Child Development, 51,* 981–992.

Ruff, H. A. (1984). Infants' manipulative exploration of objects: Effects of age and object characteristics. *Developmental Psychology, 20,* 9–20.

Rugh, R., & Shettles, L. B. (1971). *From conception to birth.* New York: Harper & Row.

Rushton, J. P. (1982). Social learning theory and the development of prosocial behavior. In N. Eisenberg (Ed.), *The development of prosocial behavior.* New York: Academic Press.

Russell, G. (1983). *The changing role of fathers?* St. Lucia, Australia: University of Queensland Press.

Russell, G. F. M. (1970). Anorexia nervosa: Its identity as an illness and its treatment. In J. H. Price (Ed.), *Modern trends in psychological medicine: II.* New York: Appleton-Century-Crofts.

Rutter, M. (1978). Diagnosis and definition. In M. Rutter and E. Schopler, (Eds.), *Autism: A reappraisal of concepts and treatment.* New York: Plenum.

Rutter, M., & Garmezy, N. Developmental psychopathology. (1983). In P. H. Mussen (Ed.), *Handbook of child psychology, Vol. IV.* New York: John Wiley.

Sachs, J., & Devin, J. (1976). Young children's use of age-appropriate speech styles in social interaction and role-playing. *Journal of Child Language, 3,* 81–98.

Sachs, J. S., Brown, R., & Salerno, R. A. (1976). Adults' speech to children. In W. van Raffler Engel & Y. LeBrun (Eds.), *Baby talk and infant speech (Neurolinguistics 5).* Amsterdam: Swets & Zeitlinger.

Sadker, M., & Sadker, D. (1985, March). Sexism in the schoolroom of the '80s. *Psychology Today,* pp. 54–57.

Safer, D. J., & Allen, R. P. (1976). *Hyperactive children. Diagnosis and management.* Baltimore: University Park Press.

Sager, H. A., Schofield, J. W., & Synder, H. N. (1983). Race and gender barriers: preadolescent peer behavior in academic classrooms. *Child Development, 54,* 1032–1040.

Saint-Anne Dargassies, S. (1966). Part V: Neurological maturation of the premature infant of 28 to 41 weeks gestational age. In F. Falkner (Ed.), *Human development.* Philadelphia: W. B. Saunders.

Salapatek, P., & Kessen, W. (1966). Visual scanning of triangles by the human newborn. *Journal of Experimental Child Psychology, 3,* 155–167.

Salguero, C. (1980). Adolescent pregnancy: A report on ACYF-funded research and demonstration projects. *Children Today, 9,* 10–11.

Salthouse, T. A., & Kail, R. (1983). Memory development throughout the lifespan: The role of processing rate. *Life-span development and behavior, 5,* 90–116.

Salthouse, T. A. & Somberg, B. L. (1982). Skilled performance: The effects of adult age and experiences on elementary processes. *Journal of Experimental Psychology, 111,* 176–207.

Sameroff, A. J., & Cavanaugh, P. J. (1979). Learning in infancy: A developmental perspective. In J. D. Osofsky (Ed.), *Handbook of infant development.* New York: Wiley.

Sameroff, A. J., & Chandler, M. J. (1975). Reproductive risk and the continuum of caretaking casualty. In F. D. Horowitz (Ed.), *Review of child development research.* Chicago: University of Chicago Press.

Santrock, J. W., & Warshak, R. A. (1979). Father

custody and social development in boys and girls. *Journal of Social Issues, 35,* 112–125.

Santrock, J. W., Warshak, R., Lindbergh, V., & Meadows, L. (1982) Children's and parent's observed social behavior in stepfather families. *Child Development, 53,* 472–480.

Sarnat, H. B. (1978). Olfactory reflexes in the newborn infant. *Journal of Pediatrics, 92,* 624–626.

Scarr, S.. (1984). What's a parent to do? *Psychology Today, 18,* 58–63.

Scarr, S. (1969). Social introversion-extroversion as a heritable response. *Child Development, 40,* 823–832.

Scarr, S. (1981). *Race, social class, and individual differences in IQ.* Hillsdale, N.J.: Lawrence Erlbaum Associates.

Scarr, S., & Kidd, K. K. (1983). Developmental behavior genetics. In M. M. Haith and J. J. Campos (Eds.), *Handbook of child psychology. Vol 2, Infancy and developmental psychobiology.* New York: John Wiley.

Scarr, S., & McCartney, K. (1983). How people make their own environments: A theory of genotype environment effects. *Child Development, 54,* 424–435.

Scarr, S., & Weinberg, R. A. (1983). The Minnesota Adoption Studies: Genetic differences and malleability. *Child Development, 54,* 260–267.

Scarr, S., & Weinberg, R. A. (1976). The IQ performance of black children adopted by white families. *American Psychologist, 31,* 726–739.

Scarr-Salapatek, S. (1975). Genetics and the development of intelligence. In F. D. Horowitz (Ed.), *Review of child development research.* Chicago: University of Chicago Press.

Scarr-Salapatek, S., & Williams, M. L. (1973). The effects of early stimulation on low-birth-weight infants. *Child Development, 44,* 94–101.

Schaefer, W. S., & Bayley, N. (1963). Maternal behavior, child behavior and their intercorrelations from infancy through adolescence. *Monographs of the Society for Research in Child Development, 28,* 1–27.

Schaffer, H. R. (1973). The multivariate approach to early learning. In R. A. Hinde & J. Stevenson-Hinde, (Eds.), *Contraints in learning.* Englewood Cliffs, N. J.: Prentice-Hall, Inc.

Schaffer, H. R., & Emerson, P. E. (1964). The development of social attachments in infancy. *Monographs of the Society for Research in Child Development, 29,* No. 3.

Schafe, K. W., & Parham, I. A. (1977). Cohort-sequential analysis of adult intellectual development. *Developmental Psychology, 13,* 649–653.

Scheinfeld, A. (1973). *Twins and supertwins.* Baltimore: Penguin Books.

Schmidt, C. R., & Paris, S. G. (1984). The development of verbal communication skills in children. In H. W. Reese (Ed.), *Advances in child development and behavior* (Vol. 18). New York: Academic Press.

Schopler, E., Mesibov, G., & Baker, A. (1982). Evaluation of treatment for autistic children and their families. *Journal of the American Academy of Child Psychiatry, 21,* 262–267.

Schultz, N. R., & Moore, D. (1984). Loneliness: Correlates, attributions, and coping among older adults. *Personality and Social Psychology Bulletin, 10,* 67–77.

Schwartz, R. G., & Leonard, L. B. (1982). Do children pick and choose? An examination of phonological selection and avoidance in early lexical acquisition. *Journal of Child Language, 9,* 319–336.

Seligman, M. E. (1970). On the generality of the laws of learning. *Psychological Review, 77,* 406–418.

Seligman, M. E. P. (1974). Depression and learned helplessness. In R. J. Friedman & M. M. Katz (Eds.), *The psychology of depression: Contemporary theory and research.* Washington, D. C.: Winston.

Seligman, M. E. P., & Peterson, C. A. (In press). A learned helplessness perspective on childhood depression: Theory and research. In M. Rutter, C. E. Izard, & P. Read (Eds.), *Depression in childhood: Developmental perspectives.* New York: Guilford Press.

Selman, R. L. (1981). The child as a friendship philosopher: A case study in the growth of interpersonal understanding. In S. R. Asher & J. M. Gottman (Eds.), *The development of children's friendships.* Cambridge, Eng.: Cambridge University Press.

Serbin, L. A., Connor, J. M., & Citron, C. C. (1981). Sex-differentiated free play behavior: Effects of teacher modeling, location, and gender. *Developmental Psychology, 17,* 640–646.

Serbin, L., & O'Leary, K. D. (1975, December). How nursery schools teach girls to shut up. *Psychology Today,* 57–58.

Shaffer, D., & Fisher, P. (1981). The epidemiology of suicide in children and young adolescents. *Journal of the American Academy of Child Psychiatry, 20,* 545–565.

Shaffer, D. R. (1979). *Social and personality development.* Monterey, Calif.: Brooks/Cole.

Shah, F., Zelnik, M., & Kantner, J. (1975). Unexpected intercourse among teenage unwed mothers. *Family Planning Perspectives, 7,* 39–44.

Shantz, C. U. (1975). The development of social cognition. In E. M. Hetherington (Ed.), *Review of child development research* (Vol. 5). Chicago: University of Chicago Press.

Shantz. C. U. (1983). Social cognition. In J. Flavell and E. Markman (Editors). *Handbook of Child Psychology, Vol. 3.* New York: Wiley.

Shatz, M., & Gelman, R. (1973). The development of communication skills: Modifications in the speech of young children as a function of the listener. *Monographs of the Society for Research in Child Development, 38* (5, Serial No. 152).

Shatz, M., & Gelman, R. (1977). Beyond syntax: The influence of conversational constraints on speech modifications. In C. E. Snow & C. A. Ferguson (Eds.), *Talking to children: Language input and acquisition.* Cambridge, Eng.: Cambridge University Press.

Shepherd, M., Oppenheim. A. N., & Mitchell, S. (1966). Childhood behavior disorders and the child guidance clinic: An epidemiological study. *Journal of Psychology and Psychiatry, 7,* 39–52.

Shigetomi, C. C., Hartmann, D. P., & Gelfand, D. M. (1981). Sex differences in children's altruistic behavior and reputations for helpfulness. *Developmental Psychology, 17,* 434–437.

Shirley, M. M. (1933). The first two years: A study of twenty-five babies. *Intellectual development (Institute of Child Welfare Monograph Series,* No. 7). Minneapolis: University of Minnesota Press.

Shore, C., O'Connell, B., & Bates, E. (1984). First sentences in language and symbolic play. *Developmental Psychology, 20,* 872–880.

Shuter-Dyson, R. (1982). Musical ability. In D. Deutsch (Ed.), *The psychology of music.* New York: Academic Press.

Siegel, A. W., Allen, G. W., & Kirasic, K. C. (1979). Children's ability to make bidirectional distance comparisons: The advantage of thinking ahead. *Developmental Psychology, 15,* 656–657.

Siegel, A. W., Kirasic, K. C., & Kail, R. V. (1978). Stalking the elusive cognitive map: The development of children's representations of geographic space. In I. Altman & J. Wohlwill (Eds.), *Human behavior and environment: Advances in theory and research* (Vol. 3). New York: Plenum.

Siegel, A. W., & White, S. H. (1975). The development of spatial representations of large-scale environments. In H. W. Reese (Ed.), *Advances in child development and behavior* (Vol. 10). New York: Academic Press.

Siegel, O. (1982). Personality development in adolescence. In B. B. Wolman (Ed.), *Handbook of developmental psychology.* Englewood Cliffs, N.J.: Prentice-Hall.

Siegler, R. S. (1975). *Stages as decision rules.* Paper presented at the annual meeting of the Jean Piaget Society, Philadelphia.

Siegler, R. S. (1976). Three aspects of cognitive development. *Cognitive Psychology, 8,* 481–520.

Siegler, R. S. (1981). Developmental sequences within and between concepts. *Monographs of the Society for Research in Child Development, 46,* Serial #189, 1–74.

Siegler, R. S., & Atlas, M. (1976). Acquisition of formal scientific reasoning by 10- and 13-year-olds: Detecting interactive patterns in data. *Journal of Educational Psychology, 68,* 360–370.

Siegler, R. S., Liebert, D. E., & Liebert, R. M. (1973). Inhelder and Piaget's pendulum problem: Teaching preadolescents to act as scientists. *Developmental Psychology, 9,* 97–101.

Siegler, R. S. & Liebert, R. M. (1972). Effects of presenting relevant rules and complete feedback on the conservation of liquid quantity task. *Developmental Psychology, 7,* 133–138. (a)

Siegler, R. S. & Liebert, R. M. (1972). Learning of liquid quantity relationships as a function of rules and feedback, number of training problems, and age of subject. *Proceedings of the 80th Annual Convention of the American Psychological Association, 7,* 117–118. (b)

Siegler, R. S. & Liebert, R. M. (1975). Acquisition of formal scientific reasoning by 10- and 13-year-olds: Designing a factorial experiment. *Developmental Psychology, 11,* 401–402.

Siegler, R. S., & Robinson, M. (1982). The development of numerical understandings. In H. W. Reese & L. P. Lipsitt (Eds.), *Advances in child development and behavior* (Vol. 16). New York: Academic Press.

Siegler, R. S., & Shrager, J. (1984). Strategy choices in addition: How do children know what to do? In C. Sophian (Ed.), *Origins of cognitive skills.* Hillsdale, N.J.: Lawrence Erlbaum Associates.

Sigman, M., & Ungerer, J. A. (1984). Attachment behaviors in autistic children. *Journal of Autism and Developmental Disorders, 14,* 231–244.

Signorella, M. L., & Liben, L. S. (1984). Recall and reconstruction of gender-related pictures: Effects of attitude, task difficulty, and age. *Child Development, 55,* 393–405.

Silver, L. B. (1981). The relationship between disabilities, hyperactivity, distractibility, and behavioral problems. *Journal of Child Psychiatry, 20,* 385–397.

Silverman, I. W., & Rose, A. P. (1982). Compensation and conservation. *Psychological Bulletin, 91,* 80–101.

Simon, H. A. (1981). *The sciences of the artificial* (2nd ed.). Cambridge: MIT Press.

Simpson, G. G., Pittendrigh, C. S., & Tiffany,

L. H. (1957). *An introduction to biology.* New York: Harcourt Brace Jovanovich Inc.

Singer, D. L., & Rummo, J. (1973). Ideational creativity and behavioral style in kindergarten-age children. *Developmental Psychology, 8,* 154–161.

Singer, J. B., & Flavell, J. H. (1981). Development of knowledge about communication: Evaluations of explicitly ambiguous messages. *Child Development, 52,* 1211–1215.

Singer, J. L., & Singer, D. (1981). *Television, imagination, and aggression: A study of preschoolers.* Hillsdale, N.J.: Lawrence Erlbaum Associates.

Siqueland, E. R., & Lipsitt, L. P. (1966). Conditioned head-turning in human newborns. *Journal of Experimental Child Psychology, 3,* 356–376.

Skuse, D. (1984a). Extreme deprivation in early childhood-I. Diverse outcomes for three siblings from an extraordinary family. *Journal of Child Psychology and Psychiatry, 25,* 523–541.

Skuse, D. (1984b). Extreme deprivation in early childhood-II. Theoretical issues and a comparative review. *Journal of Child Psychology and Psychiatry, 25,* 543–572.

Slaby, R. G., & Frey, K. S. (1975). Development of gender constancy and selective attention to same-sex models. *Child Development, 46,* 849–856.

Slobin, D. I. (1970). Universals of grammatical development in children. In G. B. Flores d'Arcais & W. J. M. Levelt (Eds.), *Advances in psycholinguistics.* Amsterdam: North-Holland.

Smith, M. C. (1975). Children's use of the multiple sufficient cause schema in social perception. *Journal of Personality and Social Psychology, 32,* 737–747.

Snow, M. E., Jacklin, C. N., & Maccoby, E. E. (1983). Sex-of-child differences in father-child interaction at one year of age. *Child Development, 54,* 227–232.

Sonnerschein, S. (1984). How feedback from a listener affects children's referential communication skills. *Developmental Psychology, 20,* 287–292.

Sontag, L. W. (1944). Differences in modifiability of fetal behavior and psychology. *Psychosomatic Medicine, 6,* 151–154.

Sours, J. A. (1974). The anorexia nervosa syndrome. *International Journal of Psycho-Analysis, 55,* 567–576.

Spearman, C. (1904). "General intelligence" objectively determined and measured. *American Journal of Psychology, 15,* 201–293.

Spears, W. C., & Hohle, R. H. (1967). Sensory and perceptual processes in infants. In Y. Brackbill (Ed.), *Infancy and early childhood. A handbook and guide to human development.* New York: Free Press.

Speece, M. W., & Brent, S. B. (1984). Children's understanding of death: A review of three components of the death concept. *Child Development, 55,* 1671–1686.

Speer, J. R., & Flavell, J. H. (1979). Young children's knowledge of the relative difficulty of recognition and recall memory tasks. *Developmental Psychology, 15,* 214–217.

Spelke, E. (1979). Perceiving bimodally specified events in infancy. *Developmental Psychology, 15,* 626–636.

Spence, J. T., Helmreich, R. L., & Stapp, J. (1975). Ratings of self and peers on sex-role attributes and their relation to self-esteem and conception of masculinity and femininity. *Journal of Personality and Social Psychology, 32,* 29–39.

Spitz, R. A. (1946). Anaclitic depression. *Psychoanalytic study of the child, 2,* 313–342.

Spitz, R. A. (1965). *The first year of life.* New York: International Universities Press.

Sroufe, L. A. (1979). The coherence of individual development: Early care, attachment, and subsequent developmental issues. *American Psychologist, 34,* 834–841.

Sroufe, L. A., Fox, N. E., & Pancake, V. R. (1983). Attachment and dependency in developmental perspective. *Child Development, 54,* 1615–1627.

Sroufe, L. A., & Rutter, M. (1984). The domain of developmental psychopathology. *Child Development, 55,* 17–29.

Standley, K., Soule, D., & Copans, S. A. (1979). Dimensions of prenatal anxiety and their influence on pregnancy outcome. *American Journal of Obstetrics and Gynecology, 135,* 22–26.

Stark, R. E. (1980). Stages of speech development in the first year of life. In G. Yeni-Komshian, J. F. Kavanagh, & C. A. Ferguson (Eds.), *Child phonology* (Vol. 1). New York: Academic Press.

Starkey, P., & Cooper, R. G. (1980). Perception of number by human infants. *Science, 210,* 1033–1035.

Starr, R. H. (1979). Child abuse. *American Psychologist, 34,* 872–878.

Staub, E. (1970). A child in distress: The influence of age and number of witnesses on children's attempts to help. *Journal of Personality and Social Psychology, 14,* 130–140.

Stechler, G., & Halton, A. (1982). Prenatal influences on human development. In B. B. Wolman (Ed.), *Handbook of developmental psychology.* Englewood Cliffs, N.J.: Prentice-Hall.

Steiner, J. E. (1979). Human facial expressions in response to taste and smell stimulation. In H. Reese

& L. Lipsitt (Eds.), *Advances in child development and behavior*, Vol. 13. New York: Academic Press.

Stephan, C. W., & Langlois, J. H. (1984). Baby beautiful: Adult attributions of infant competence as a function of infant attractiveness. *Child Development, 55,* 576–585.

Stern, C. (1973). *Principles of human genetics.* San Francisco: W.H. Freeman.

Stern, M., & Hildebrandt, K. A. (1984). Prematurity stereotypes: Effects of labeling on adults' perceptions of infants. *Developmental Psychology, 20,* 360–362.

Sternberg, R. J., & Powell, J. S. (1983). The development of intelligence. In P. H. Mussen (Ed.), *Handbook of child psychology,* Vol. 3. New York: John Wiley.

Steuer, F. B., Applefield, J. M., & Smith, R. (1971). Televised aggression and the interpersonal aggression of preschool children. *Journal of Experimental Child Psychology, 11,* 442–447.

Stevens-Long & Lovaas, I. O. (1974). Research and treatment with autistic children in a program of behavior therapy. In A. Davids, (Ed.), *Child personality and psychopathology: Current topics,* Vol. 1. New York: Wiley Interscience.

Stevenson, H. W. (1972). *Children's learning.* New York: Appleton-Century-Crofts.

Stewart, R. S. (1976). Psychoanalysis and sex differences: Freud and beyond Freud. In P. C. Lee & R. S. Stewart (Eds.), *Sex differences: Cultural and developmental dimensions.* New York: Urz.

Stone, L. J., Smith, H. T., & Murphy, L. B. (1973). *The competent infant.* New York: Basic Books.

Stoppard, J. M., & Kalin, R. (1983). Gender typing and social desirability of personality in person evaluation. *Psychology of Women Quarterly, 7,* 209–218.

Strauss, M. S., & Curtis, L. E. (1981). Infant perception of numerosity. *Child Development, 52,* 1146–1152.

Strauss, M. S., & Curtis, L. E. (1984). Development of numerical concepts in infancy. In C. Sophian (Ed.), *Origins of cognitive skills.* Hillsdale, N.J.: Lawrence Erlbaum Associates.

Streissguth, A. P., Martin, D. C., Barr, H. M., Sandman, B. M., Kirchner, G. L., & Darby, D. L. (1984). Intrauterine alcohol and nicotine exposure: Attention and reaction time in 4-year-old children. *Developmental Psychology, 20,* 533–541.

Stroebe, M. S., & Stroebe, W. (1983). Who suffers more? Differences in health risks of the widowed. *Psychological Bulletin, 93,* 279–301.

Strupp, H. H. (1967). *An introduction to Freud and psychoanalysis.* Woodbury, New York: Barron's Educational Series.

Sullivan, H. S. (1953). *The interpersonal theory of psychiatry.* New York: Norton.

Suomi, S. J., & Harlow, H. F. (1972). Social rehabilitation of isolate-reared monkeys. *Developmental Psychology, 6,* 487–496.

Svejda, M. J., Pannabecker, B. J., & Emde, R. N. (1982). Parent-to-infant attachment. In R. N. Emde and R. J. Harmon (Eds.), *The development of attachment and affiliative systems.* New York: Plenum Press.

Swift, W. J. (1982). The long-term outcome of early onset anorexia nervosa: A critical review. *American Journal of the American Academy of Child Psychiatry, 21,* 38–46.

Switzky, H., Rotatori, A. F., Miller, T., & Freagon, S. (1979). The developmental model and its implications for assessment and instruction for the severely/profoundly handicapped. *Mental Retardation, 17,* 167–170.

Szalai, A. (Ed.). (1973). *The use of time: Daily activities of urban and suburban populations in twelve countries.* The Hague: Mouton.

Tager-Flusberg, H. (1981). On the nature of linguistic functioning in early infantile autism. *Journal of Autism and Developmental Disorders, 11,* 45–65.

Tanner, J. M. (1970). Physical growth. In P. H. Mussen (Ed.), *Carmichael's manual of child psychology* (3rd. ed.). New York: John Wiley.

Tanner, J. M. (1978). *Foetus into man.* Cambridge, MA.: Harvard University Press.

Taylor, M. C., & Hall, J. A. (1982). Psychological androgyny: Theories, methods, and conclusions. *Psychological Bulletin, 92,* 347–366.

Taylor, S. P., & Langer, E. J. (1977). Pregnancy: A social stigma? *Sex Roles, 3,* 27–35.

Tesser, A., Campbell, J., & Smith, M. (1984). Friendship choice and performance: Self-evaluation maintenance in children. *Journal of Personality and Social Psychology, 46,* 561–574.

Thelen, E., & Fisher, D. M. (1982). Newborn stepping: An explanation for a "disappearing" reflex. *Developmental Psychology, 18,* 760–775.

Thelen, E., & Fisher, D. M. (1983). From spontaneous to instrumental behavior: Kinematic analysis of movement changes during very early learning. *Child Development, 54,* 129–140.

Thomas, A., & Chess, S. (1976). Evolution of behavior disorders into adolescence. *American Journal of Psychiatry, 133,* 539–542.

Thomas, A., Chess, S., & Birch, H. G. (1970). The origin of personality. *Scientific American, 223,* 102–109.

Thomas, A., Chess, S., Sillen, J., & Mendez, O. (1974). Cross-cultural study of behavior in children with special vulnerabilities to stress. In D. F. Ricks, A. Thomas, & M. Roff (Eds.), *Life history research in psychopathology.* Minneapolis: University of Minnesota Press.

Thomas, H. (1983). Familial correlation analyses, sex differences, and the X-linked gene hypothesis. *Psychological Bulletin, 93,* 427–440.

Thompson, R. A., Lamb, M. E., & Estes, D. (1982). Stability of infant-mother attachment and its relationship to changing life circumstances in an unselected middle class sample. *Child Development, 53,* 144–148.

Thompson, W. R. (1954). The inheritance and development of intelligence. *Research Publications of the Association for Research in Nervous and Mental Diseases, 33,* 209–331.

Thompson, W. R., & Grusec, J. E. (1970). Studies of early experience. In P. H. Mussen (Ed.), *Carmichael's manual of child psychology.* New York: John Wiley.

Thorndike, E. L. (1898). Animal intelligence: An experimental study of the associative process in animals. *Psychological Review Monograph Supplement, 2* (4, Whole No. 8).

Thorndike, E. L. (1905). *The elements of psychology.* New York: Seiler.

Thornton, A., Alwin, D. F., & Camburn, D. (1983). Causes and consequences of sex-role attitudes and attitude change. *American Sociological Review, 48,* 211–227.

Tieger, T. (1980). On the biological basis of sex differences in aggression. *Child Development, 51,* 943–963.

Till, R. E. (1985). Verbatim and inferential memory in young and elderly adults. *Journal of Gerontology, 40,* 316–323.

Tizard, B., & Hodges, J. (1978). The effect of early institutional rearing on the development of eight year old children. *Journal of Child Psychology and Psychiatry, 19,* 99–118.

Tizard, B., & Rees, J. (1974). A comparison of the effects of adoption, restoration to the natural mother, and continued institutionalization on the cognitive development of four-year-olds. *Child Development, 45,* 92–99.

Toi, M., & Batson, C. D. (1982). More evidence that empathy is a source of altruistic motivation. *Journal of Personality and Social Psychology, 43,* 281–292.

Trabasso, T., Isen, A. M., Dolecki, P., McLanahan, A. G., Riley, C. A., & Tucker, T. (1978). How do children solve class-inclusion problems? In R. Siegler (Ed.), *Children's thinking: What develops?* Hillsdale, N.J.: Lawrence Erlbaum Associates.

Trehub, S. E. (1976). The discrimination of foreign speech contrasts by infants and adults. *Child Development, 47,* 466–472.

Tresemer, D., & Pleck, J. (1974). Sex-role boundaries and resistance to sex-role change. *Women's Studies, 2,* 61–78.

Tsai, L., Stewart, M. A., Faust, M., & Shook, S. (1982). Social class distribution of fathers of children enrolled in the Iowa Autism Program. *Journal of Autism and Developmental Disorders, 12,* 211–221.

Tulving, E., & Pearlstone, Z. (1966). Availability versus accessibility of information in memory for words. *Journal of Verbal Learning and Verbal Behavior, 5,* 381–391.

Turiel, E. (1978). Distinct conceptual and developmental domains: Social conventions and morality. In C. B. Keasey (Ed.), *Nebraska Symposium on Motivation, Vol. 25.* Lincoln: University of Nebraska Press.

Turner, J. S., & Helms, D. B. (1979). *Lifespan development.* Philadelphia: W. B. Saunders.

U.S. Bureau of the Census. (1979). Marital status and living arrangements. *Current Population Reports (Series P-20, No. 388).* Washington, D.C.: U.S. Government Printing Office.

Updegraff, R. (1930). The visual perception of distance in young children and adults: A comparative study. *University of Iowa Studies of Child Welfare, 4,* (No. 40).

Vandell, D. L., Wilson, K. S., & Buchanan, N. R. (1980). Peer interaction during the first year of life: An examination of its structure, content, and sensitivity to toys. *Child Development, 51,* 481–488.

Vandenberg, S. G., & Kuse, A. R. (1979). Spatial ability: A critical review of the sex-linked major gene hypothesis. In M. A. Wittig and A. C. Petersen (Eds.), Sex-related differences in cognitive functioning. New York: Academic Press.

Varley, C. K. (1984). Diet and the behavior of children with attention deficit disorder. *Journal of the American Academy of Child Psychiatry, 23,* 182–185.

Vasta, R. (1982). Physical child abuse: A dual-component analysis. *Developmental Review, 2,* 125–149.

Vasta, R., & Copitch, P. (1981). Simulating conditions of child abuse in the laboratory. *Child Development, 52,* 164–170.

Ventura, S. J. (1977). Teenage childbearing: United States, 1966–1975. *Monthly Vital Statistics Re-*

ports. Washington, D.C.: National Center for Health Statistics, 26 No. 5 (Supp.).

Vernbrugge, L. M. (1979). Marital status and health. *Journal of Marriage and the Family, 41,* 267–285.

Vernon, P. E. (1965). Ability factors and environmental influences. *American Psychologist, 20,* 723–733.

Vernon, P. E. (1979). *Intelligence: Heredity and environment.* San Francisco: W. H. Freeman.

Visher, E. P., & Visher, J. S. (1979). *Stepfamilies: A guide to working with stepparents and stepchildren.* New York: Bruner/Mazel.

Vital and Health Statistics. (1972). Infant Mortality Rates: Socioeconomic Factors. Series 22, No. 14. Rockville, MD.: U.S. Department of Health, Education, and Welfare.

Volterra, V., Bates, E., Benigni, L., Bretherton, I., & Camaioni, L. (1979). First words in language and action: A qualitative look. In E. Bates (Ed.), *The emergence of symbols: Cognition and communication in infancy.* New York: Academic Press.

Waber, D. P. (1977). Sex differences in mental abilities, hemispheric lateralization, and rate of physical growth at adolescence. *Developmental Psychology, 13,* 29–38.

Wachs, T. D. (1983). The use and abuse of environment in behavior-genetic research. *Child Development, 54,* 396–407.

Wachs, T. G., & Gruen, G. E. (1982). *Early experience and human development.* New York: Plenum.

Wadden, T. A., Foster, G. D., Brownell, K. D., & Finley, E. (1984). Self-concept in obese and normal-weight children. *Journal of Consulting and Clinical Psychology, 52,* 1104–1105.

Waddington, C. H. (1957). *The strategy of the genes.* London: Allen and Unwin.

Wagner, S., Winner, E., Cicchetti, D., & Gardner, H. (1981). "Metaphorical" mapping in human infants. *Child Development, 52,* 728–731.

Wagner, D. A., & Stevenson, H. W. (Eds.). (1982). *Cultural perspectives on child development.* San Francisco: W. H. Freeman.

Wald, E. (1981). *The remarried family: Challenge and promise.* New York: Family Service Association.

Walk, R. D., & Gibson, E. J. (1961). A comparative and analytical study of visual depth perception. *Psychological Monographs, 75,* (15, Whole No. 519).

Walker, C. E. (1978). Toilet training, enuresis, and encopresis. In P. R. Magrab, (Ed.), *Psychological management of pediatric problems.* Baltimore: University Park Press.

Walker, L. J. (1984). Sex differences in the development of moral reasoning: A critical review. *Child Development, 55,* 677–691.

Wallerstein, J. S., & Kelly, J. B. (1980). *Surviving the break-up: How children and parents cope with divorce.* New York: Basic Books.

Walters, J., Connor, R., & Zunich, M. (1964). Interaction of mothers and children from lower-class families. *Child Development, 35,* 433–440.

Warden, D. A. (1976). The influence of context on children's use of identifying expressions and references. *British Journal of Psychology, 67,* 101–112.

Waterman, A. S., & Gold, J. (1975). A longitudinal study of ego development at a liberal arts college. *Journal of Youth and Adolescence, 5,* 361–369.

Waters, E., Matas, L., & Sroufe, L. A. (1975). Infants' reactions to an approaching stranger: Description, validation, and functional significance of wariness. *Child Development, 46,* 348–356.

Weatherley, D. (1964). Self-perceived rate of physical maturation and personality in late adolescence. *Child Development, 35,* 1197–1210.

Weiner, B. (1982). The emotional consequences of causal attributions. In M. S. Clark & T. Fiske (Eds.), *Affect and cognition: The 17th annual Carnegie symposium on affect.* Hillsdale, N.J.: Lawrence Erlbaum Associates.

Weiner, B., Graham, S., Stern, P., & Lawson, M. (1982). Using affective cues to infer causal thoughts. *Developmental Psychology, 18,* 278–286.

Weiner, B., & Handel, S. J. (in press). Anticipated emotional consequences of causal communications and reported communication strategy. *Developmental Psychology.*

Weiner, G. (1968). Scholastic achievement at age 12–13 of prematurely born infants. *Journal of Special Education, 2,* 237–250.

Weinraub, M., Clemens, L. P., Sockloff, A., Ethridge, T., Gracely, E., & Myers, B. (1984). The development of sex role stereotypes in the third year: Relationships to gender labeling, gender identity, sex-typed toy preference, and family characteristics. *Child Development, 55,* 1493–1503.

Weisz, J. R. (1980). Developmental change in perceived control: Recognizing noncontingency in the laboratory and perceiving it in the world. *Developmental Psychology, 16,* 385–390.

Weisz, J. R. (1981). Illusory contingency in children at the state fair. *Developmental Psychology, 17,* 481–489.

Weinberg, S. (1979). *Measurement of stressful life events associated with transition to parenthood.* Paper presented at meeting of the American Psychological Association, New York, September.

Weiss, B. (1982). Food additives and environmental chemicals as sources of childhood deficit disorder. *Journal of the American Academy of Child Psychiatry, 21,* 144–152.

Weiss, G. (1979). Controlled studies of efficacy of long-term treatment with stimulants of hyperactive children. In E. Denhoff & L. Stern (Eds.), *Minimal brain dysfunction.* New York: Masson Publishing.

Weitzman, B. (1967). Behavior therapy and psychotherapy. *Psychological Review, 74,* 300–317.

Wellman, H. M. (1977). Preschoolers' understanding of memory-relevant variables. *Child Development, 48,* 1720–1723.

Wellman, H. M., Ritter, K., & Flavell, J. H. (1975). Deliberate memory behavior in the delayed reactions of very young children. *Developmental Psychology, 11,* 780–787.

Wender, P. H., Rosenthal, D., Rainer, J. D., Greenhill, L., & Sarbin, B. (1977). Schizophrenics' adopting parents. *Archives of General Psychiatry, 34,* 777–784.

Wenz, F. V. (1979). Sociological correlates of alienation among adolescent suicide attempts. *Adolescence, 14,* 19–30.

Werner, E. E. (1980). Environmental interaction. In H. E. Rie and E. D. Rie, (Eds.), *Handbook of minimal brain dysfunctions.* New York: John Wiley.

Werner, E. E., & Smith, R. S. (1977). *Kauii's children come of age.* Honolulu: University of Hawaii Press.

Werner, H. (1948). *Comparative psychology of mental development.* Chicago: Follet.

Werner, H., & Kaplan, B. (1963). *Symbol formation.* New York: Wiley.

Werry, J. S. (1972). Psychosomatic disorders (with a note on anesthesia, surgery, and hospitalization). In H. C. Quay, & J. S. Werry (Eds.), *Psychopathological disorders in children.* New York: John Wiley.

Whitehurst, G. J., & Sonnenschein, S. (1981). The development of informative messages in referential communication: Knowing when versus knowing how. In W. P. Dickson (Ed.), *Children's oral communication skills.* New York: Academic Press.

Whitehurst, G. J., & Vasta, R. (1977). *Child behavior.* Boston: Houghton Mifflin.

Whitley, B. E., Jr. (1983). Sex-role orientation and self-esteem: A critical meta-analytic review. *Journal of Personality and Social Psychology, 44,* 765–778.

Wicks-Nelson, R., & Israel, A. (1984). *Behavior disorders of childhood.* Englewood Cliffs, N.J.: Prentice-Hall.

Wilkinson, A. (1976). Counting strategies and semantic analysis as applied to class inclusion. *Cognitive Psychology, 8,* 64–85.

Wilkinson, L. C., Wilkinson, A. C., Spinelli, F., & Chiang, C. P. (1984). Metalinguistic knowledge of pragmatic rules in school-age children. *Child Development, 55,* 2130–2140.

Williams, J. E., Bennett, S. M., & Best, D. L. (1975). Awareness and expression of sex stereotypes in young children. *Developmental Psychology, 11,* 635–642.

Williams, R. J. (1946). *The human frontier.* New York: Harcourt Brace Jovanovich.

Wilson, R. S. (1978). Synchronies in mental development: An epigenetic perspective. *Science, 202,* 939–948.

Wilson, R. S. (1983). The Louisville Twin Study: Developmental synchronies in behavior. *Child Development, 54,* 298–316.

Wishart, J. G., & Bower, T. G. R. (1982). The development of spatial understanding in infancy. *Journal of Experimental Child Psychology, 33,* 363–385.

Witkin, H. A., Mednick, S. A., Schulsinger, F., Bakkestrøm, E., Christiansen, K. O., Goodenough, D. R., Hirshhorn, K., Lundsteen, C., Owen, D. R., Philip, J., Rubin, D. B., & Stocking, M. (1976). Criminality in XYY and XXY men. *Science, 193,* 547–555.

Wolff, P. H. (1969). The natural history of crying and other vocalizations in early infancy. In B. M. Foss (Ed.), *The determinants of human behavior.* London: Methuen.

Wolff, P. H. (1981). Normal variations in human maturation. In K. J. Connolly and H. F. R. Prechtl (Eds.), *Clinics in developmental medicine No. 77/78. Maturation and development: Biological and psychological perspectives.* Philadelphia: J. B. Lippincott.

Wolpe, J. (1958). *Psychotherapy by reciprocal inhibition.* Stanford: Stanford University Press.

Wolpe, J., & Lazarus, A. A. (1966). *Behavior therapy techniques: A guide to the treatment of the neuroses.* New York: Pergamon Press.

Wood-Gush, D. G. M. (1960). A study of sex drive of two strains of cockerels through three generations. *Animal Behavior, 8,* 43–53.

Wootten, J., Merkin, S., Hood, L., & Bloom, L. (1979). Wh-questions: Linguistic evidence to explain the sequence of acquisition. Presented at the biennial meeting of the Society for Research in Child Development.

Wylie, R. C. (1979) *The self-concept. Vol. 2.* Lincoln, Nebraska: University of Nebraska Press.

Yang, R. K., Zweig, A. R., Douthitt, T. C., & Federman, E. J. (1976). Successive relationships between maternal attitudes during pregnancy, analgesic medication during labor and delivery, and newborn behavior. *Developmental Psychology, 12,* 6–14.

Yarrow, L. J. (1972). Attachment and dependency. In J. L. Gewirtz (Ed.), *Attachment and dependency*. New York: V. H. Winston & Sons.

Yarrow, L. J., Goodwin, M. S., Manheimer, H., & Milowe, I. D. (1978, March). Infant experiences and cognitive and personality development at ten years. Paper presented at the annual meeting of the American Orthopsychiatric Association, Washington, D.C.

Yarrow, L. J., & Pedersen, F. A. (1972). Attachment: Its origins and course. In *The Young Child: Reviews of Research*, Vol. I. Washington, D.C.: National Association for the Education of Young Children.

Yesavage, J. A., Rose, T. L., & Bower, G. H. (1983). Interactive imagery and affective judgments improve face-name learning in the elderly. *Journal of Gerontology, 38*, 197–203.

Yogev, S. (1983). Judging the professional woman: Changing research, changing values. *Psychology of Women Quarterly, 7*, 219–234.

Youniss, J. (1980). *Parents and peers in social development: A Sullivan-Piaget perspective*. Chicago: University of Chicago Press.

Yurcheno, H. (1970). *A mighty hard road: The Woody Guthrie Story*. New York: McGraw-Hill.

Yussen, S. R., & Bird, J. E. (1979). The development of metacognitive awareness in memory, communication, and attention. *Journal of Experimental Child Psychology, 28*, 300–313.

Zahavi, S. L., & Asher, S. R. (1978). The effect of verbal instructions on preschool children's aggressive behavior. *Journal of School Psychology, 16*, 146–153.

Zahn-Waxler, C., Radke-Yarrow, M., & King, R. A. (1979). Child rearing and children's prosocial initiations toward victims of distress. *Child Development, 50*, 319–300.

Zametkin, A. J., Karoum, F., Rapoport, J. L., Brown, G. L., & Wyatt, R. J. (1984). Phenylethylamine excretion in attention deficit disorder. *Journal of the American Academy of Child Psychiatry, 23*, 310–314.

Zelazo, P. R. (1976). From reflexive to instrumental behavior. In L. P. Lipsitt (Ed.), *Developmental psychobiology*. Hillsdale, N.J.: Lawrence Erlbaum Associates.

Zelazo, P. R., Zelazo, N., & Kolb, S. (1972). "Walking" in the newborn. *Science, 176*, 314–315.

Zelnik, M., & Cantnor, J. F. (1980). Sexual activity, contraceptive use and pregnancy among the metropolitan area teenagers. 1971–1979. *Family Planning Perspectives, 12*, 355–357.

Zimmerman, B. (1982). Piaget's theory and instruction: How compatible are they? *Contemporary Educational Psychology, 7*, 204–216.

Zimmerman, B. J., & Rosenthal, T. L. (1974). Observational learning of rule-governed behavior by children. *Psychological Bulletin, 81*, 29–42.

NAME INDEX

534

SUBJECT INDEX

Idiot savants, 268
Imitation
  deferred, 183
  direct, 299
  grammar acquisition through, 164–65
Imitative aggression, 207
Impairment, selective, 267
Imperatives, "procreative", 406
Imprinting, 125–26
Impulsivity, 428
Inadequate fathering, 281
Inbreeding experiments, 40–41
Inductive reasoning, 189
Industry vs. inferiority stage, 121, 122
Infant Behavior Record, 240
Infantile autism, 431–34, 444–45
Infant-parent relationship. See Mother-
  infant relation; Parent-infant
  relationship
Infants. See also Early behavior and
  experience
  at-risk, 75–76
  Hopi, 94
  intelligence tests for, 240–43
  landmark knowledge acquisition in,
    224–25
  large-for-date, 74
  perception of numerosity of, 217–19
  selective orientation to mother, 128
  sex typing and, 386–87
Inference, 18, 19, 188
Inferiority vs. industry stage, 121, 122
Inflection, 158
Influenza A, 68
Information gathering, 105
Information processing approach to
  cognitive development. See
  Cognitive development
Informed consent, 22
In-group-out-group schema, 385
Inheritance, genetic, 36–40
Inhibitory effects of modeling, 299
Initiative vs. guilt stage, 121, 122
Insecurely attached (classification), 131
Instigation, behavioral, 295
Instinct, death, 424
Institutionalization, separation and,
  136–40
Instruction
  direct, 295
  timing of, 190
Instrumental behaviors, 373
Integration, hierarchic, 90
Integrity, ego, 458
Intellectual ability, sex differences and,
  377–79. See also Intelligence
"Intellectual Achievement Responsibility
  Questionnaire" (IAR), 325
Intelligence, 234–70
  adoption studies of, 48–49
  autism and, 432
  contents of, 179–80
  crystallized, 245–46
  definition of, 46–50, 235
  fluid, 245–46
  genetics and, 46–50
  gifted and creative individuals, 261–65
  intellectual functioning and, 261
  mental retardation, 253–61
    causes of, 254–55

cognitive deficits and, 257
  familial, 254
  levels and measurement of, 255–57
  memory strategies and, 258–59
  social and emotional factors in, 257–
    60
  social skills and, 261
musical, 267–69
PKU and, 32
polygene inheritance and, 39
tests, 235–53
  aging and, 245–47
  for children and adults, 237–40,
    243–45
  construction principles for, 235–37
  for infants, 240–43
  IQ scores, 240–45
  parental interaction and, 247–48
  SES, race, ethnicity and, 248–53
  types of, 237
theories of, 265–69
  multiple intelligences, 267–69
  psychometric, 265–66
twin studies of, 46–48
Intelligence quotient (IQ). See IQ
Interactionist perspectives on moral
  development, 340–41
"Interlocking of developmental tasks",
  470
Internal causes, 208
"Internalizers", 325–26
Interpersonal relationships. See
  Aggression; Altruism; Friendship
Interpretation in observational learning,
  207–8
Intersensory perception, 115–16
Intimacy, 346–47, 457
Intonation, 147–48
Intrinsic causes of death, 481
Introversion, 50–52
"Intuitions", 199
Invariants, functional, 179–80
IQ, 238–39. See also Intelligence
  constancy in, 244–45
  race and, 249–50
  SES and, 248–51
Iron deficiency, 68
Irreversible thinking, 184
Isolation, 457
Israeli children, kibbutz-reared, 138
Item selection in test construction, 235–36

"Job overload", 464
Joseph's disease, 54
"Jumping genes", 30

Kibbutz-reared Israeli children, 138
Knowledge. See also Cognitive
  development; Learning; Skills
  of configurations, 228–30
  of landmarks, 223–27
  of listener, speaking effectively and,
    170–71
  quantitative, 217–23
  of routes, 227–28
  social, 300–302
  spatial. See Way-finding skills of
    stereotypes, 390
Kwoma tribe, 287

Labor, 71, 72
Laboratory tests of self-control, 320–22
Lamaze programs, 72
Landmark knowledge, 223–27
Language
  autism and, 432–33
  sexist, 403–4
Language acquisition, 144–65. See also
  Communication
  combining words, 157–65
    grammar acquisition, 162–65
    grammatical morphemes, 158–62
    two-word sentence, 157–58
  learning words and meanings, 150–56
    cognitive development and, 152–53
    semantic development, 153–56
    styles of, 150–52
  preverbal behavior and, 145–50
    speech perception, 145–46
    speech production, 146–50
  SES and, 166–67
Large-for-date infants, 74
Latency stage, 120, 121
Laterality, 94
Lavallée, 314–15
Law of effect, 102
Lead poisoning, 69, 430
Learned helplessness explanation of
  depression, 426–27
Learning. See also Cognitive development
  conditioning and, 205–6
  defined, 205
  development of phobias and, 420–21
  discovery, 190
  hyperactivity and, 431
  infantile autism and, 444–45
  instrumental (operant conditioning),
    102–3
  mediated, 208–9
  neonatal, 80
  observational, 103–5, 206–8, 298–99
  route, 227–28
  social. See Social learning theory
Left-handedness, 94
Libido, 118
Life review, 483–86
Life structure, 458–59
Lightening, 71
Listening, effective, 174
Little Hans, therapy of, 439
Live modeling condition, 314–15
Locomotion, development of, 91
Locus of control, 325
Logical structures, 191–92
Loneliness, 480
Longitudinal research, 15–16
Long-term memory, 210
Looking, preferential, 105–6
Louisville Twin Study, 47–48

MA, 238
Magnitude of correlation, 13
Manual skills, 91–92
Mappings, abstract, 201
Maps, cognitive, 228–30
Marriage, 467–72
Masculinity. See Sex roles and gender
  identity
Masked depression, 423

Sociological interpretation of suicide, 424–25
Sound spectrograph, 147
Spatial knowledge. *See* Way-finding skills
Speaking, effective, 168–74
Speech
  parental, 163–64
  perception of, 145–46
  production of, 146–50
  telegraphic, 158–59
Spouse, death of, 482–83
Stability, gender, 383–84, 387
Stage, psychosexual and psychosocial, 120–21
Stage theories, 6, 338. *See also* Cognitive development; Psychoanalytic approach
Stagnation, 458
Standardization procedures, 236
Stanford-Binet tests, 238–39
Statistical correlation, 13–14
Status
  identity, 454–55
  social role, 379–80
Stepping reflex, 78, 79, 95
Stereotypes
  about work, 389–92
  gender, 372–76
    of behavior, 388–92
    exposure to, 401
    knowledge of, 390
    modeling and, 401
    operation of, 375–76
    of personality, 373–75
Stimulants for hyperactivity, 444
Stimulus, child as, 438
Stop consonants, 147
Story task, 403
Stranger anxiety, 129
Strange Situation instrument, 131
Strategies
  elaboration, 214–15
  memory, 211–17
    metamemory and, 213–17
    for study, 212–13
    of young children, 213
  repetition, 214–15
  for task completion, 196–200
Strength, ego, 341
Stress, maternal, 66–67
Structural genes, 30
Structures(s)
  cognitive, 295
  life, 458–59
  logical, 191–92
  mental, 179–80
Struggle for existence, 26
Students' self-perceptions, 331–32
Study strategies, 212–13
Style(s)
  of language learning, 150–52
  parenting, 275–76
Subtraction skills, 222–23
Sucking reflex, 78
Suicide, 424–25
Superego, 117, 335, 382, 439
Survival of the fittest, 26
"Swing, The", 351
Symbolic modeling condition, 315
Symbols, vocal and gestural, 152–53

Syndrome, defined, 427
Syntactic development, 162–63
Syphilis, 68

Tabula rasa perspective, 2
Task(s)
  balance scale, 193–94
  interlocking of developmental, 470
  story, 403
  Wudgemaker, 403–4
Taste, 106–7
TEACCH, 444–45
Teachers
  sex-role socialization and, 399–400
  student self-perceptions and, 331–32
Television, aggression and, 364–66
Telegraphic speech, 158–59
Temperamental, resistance to, 307–13
  discipline and, 308–9
  emotional state and, 311–12
  objective self-awareness and, 312–13
  reasoning-punishment combination and, 309–10
  reasoning vs. verbal reproach and, 310–11
Teratology, 64
Tertiary circular reaction, 182–83
Testability of theory, 7
Testosterone, 396
Tests, intelligence, 235–53
  aging and, 245–47
  for children and adults, 237–40, 243–45
  construction principles for, 235–37
  for infants, 240–43
  IQ scores, 240–45
  parental interaction and, 247–48
  SES, race, ethnicity and, 248–53
  types of, 237
Tests of self-control, 320–22
Texas Adoption Project, 48–49
Thalidomide, 68–69
Theory, role of, 7–10
Third variable problem, 19
Thought
  action-based, 184
  centered, 184–85
  convergent vs. divergent, 263–64
  egocentric, 185–86, 353
  -emotion interaction in moral action, 340–41
  irreversible, 184
Three Essays on the Theory of Sexuality (Freud), 381
Tiers in Fischer's theory, 201
Time, perception of, 479
Time-out techniques, 298
Timing of instruction, 190
Tobacco, 69
Toddlerhood friendships, 346
Toilet training, 119, 122, 412–14
"Tomboyishness", 394–95
Touch, 107–8, 115–16
Toxoplasmosis, 68
Toy stereotypes and preferences, 388
Training
  dry-bed, 443
  in solving Piagetain operations, 194–95
  toilet, 119, 122, 412–14
Transition, midlife, 459–60

Treatment and Education of Autistic and related Communications Handicapped Children (TEACCH), 444–45
Treatment for behavior problems, 436–46
  of child and adolescent clients, 437–39
  developmental guidelines for, 438–39
  examples of, 442–47
  psychological, 439–42
Trobriand Islands, 286
Trust vs. mistrust stage, 121
Tuberculosis, 68
Turner's syndrome, 56
Twin births, 61
Twin studies
  of extreme deprivation, 140–41
  genetics and, 42–45
  of intelligence, 46–48
  of schizophrenia, 52–53
  of social behavioral and personality variations, 50–52
Two-word sentence, 157–58
Two Worlds of Childhood: U.S. and U.S.S.R. (Bronfenbrenner), 289

Ultrasound, 54
Unconditional commitment, 276
Unconditional stimulus (UCS), 101
Unconditioned response (UCR), 101
Underextension of meanings, 155
Underlining, as study strategy, 212
U.S. Commission on Civil Rights, 401
U.S. National Commission for Protection of Human Subjects of Biomedical and Behavioral Research, 20
Universal goals of parenting, 287–89
Urine alarm, 443
USSR, child rearing in, 289–94

Validation, impending death and, 483
Validity, test construction and, 237
Variables
  independent and dependent, 18
  separation of, 189
Verbal ability, female advantage in, 377, 378
Verbal mediation, 208–9
Verbal rehearsal, 211
Verbal reproach, reasoning vs., 310–11
Vineland Social Maturity Scale, 255
Vision, 108–17
Visual acuity, 109
Visual cliff, 113, 114
Visual-spatial ability, sex differences in, 377–78, 396–97
Vitamin supplementation, 430
Vocal symbols, 152–53
Voluntary grasp, 95

Walden Two (Skinner), 313, 315
Walking, development of, 95
Way-finding skills, 178, 223–32
  of blind children, 231
  cognitive maps, 228–30
  route learning, 227–28
  sequence of acquisition of, 231–32
Wechsler scales, 239–40
"Wired-in" behaviors, 123